THE EROSION OF A RELATIONSHIP

THE EROSION OF
A RELATIONSHIP

INDIA AND BRITAIN SINCE 1960

MICHAEL LIPTON

AND

JOHN FIRN

Published for

THE ROYAL INSTITUTE OF
INTERNATIONAL AFFAIRS

by

OXFORD UNIVERSITY PRESS
London   New York   Delhi

1975

*Oxford University Press, Ely House, London W.*1

GLASGOW NEW YORK TORONTO MELBOURNE WELLINGTON
CAPE TOWN IBADAN NAIROBI DAR ES SALAAM LUSAKA ADDIS ABABA
DELHI BOMBAY CALCUTTA MADRAS KARACHI LAHORE DACCA
KUALA LUMPUR SINGAPORE HONG KONG TOKYO

ISBN 019 218310 9

© Royal Institute of International Affairs 1975

Text set in 10/12 pt. Monotype Times Roman, printed by letterpress,
and bound in Great Britain at The Pitman Press, Bath

CONTENTS

5. INVISIBLES

6. PRIVATE INVESTMENT

7. AID TO INDIA

8. TECHNICAL ASSISTANCE

STATISTICAL APPENDIX

CONTENTS

PREFACE

The idea for this book came to the authors early in 1970. We felt that it would be rewarding to trace a single, deeply-rooted relationship between a rich country —Britain—and a poor country—India—through the UN's 'Development Decade' of the 1960s; and to do so with as much as possible of the relevant quantitative detail. What was planned as a short essay became a mammoth task, for three main reasons. First, much more relevant material was available than we had expected. Second, the facts kept changing; not in the trivial (though time-consuming) sense that tables had to be updated, but in deeper ways: events confirmed what in 1970 was our 'prediction' that the Indo-British relationship had reached the bottom of a (possibly overdue) decline; and interpretations of the rich-poor relationship, by journalists as well as academics, polarized into 'dominance' and 'inter-dependence' viewpoints that needed to be tested with the Indo-British material. Third, and relevant to both these points, the facts pointed to certain hypotheses about the post-colonial link between Britain and India—that initial (and largely inertial) 'neo-colonial' links gave way to diversification by *both* countries, which in turn imposed disadvantages on each; that this sequence was conditioned by some special circumstances, notably India's size, diversity, and degree of self-rule in advance of formal decolonization; that trade adjustments preceded others—which could be examined only in the light of a much greater amount of work than we had at first envisaged.

Both books and tables, however, must have a cut-off point. Our last revision took place in February 1974. Events since then should be used to test the ideas of this book, not to judge its accuracy. Even in spring 1974, much has happened. In the subcontinent, the apparent rapprochement between India, Pakistan, and Bangladesh over the aftermath of the 1971 hostilities has been carried further, with the agreement to release the remaining Pakistani detainees in India and Bangladesh; once Pakistan recognizes Bangladesh, we shall see how the underlying subcontinental issues (notably the unsettled conflicts over Kashmir, and the long-fallow possibilities of trade) reassert themselves. In Britain, a new Labour government has once again increased aid to India and is committed to attempt 'renegotiation' with EEC (and to recommend to the voters that Britain leave EEC if these fail); but there is still no long-term commitment to Indo-British trade liberalization or indeed aid expansion, and even in the unlikely event that Britain withdraws from the EEC, it is hard to see how complementaries between India and 'the West', on a scale to match the possibilities we later discuss, could be achieved by trade expansion involving India and Britain alone. On the world stage, the Indo-Soviet discussions of 1973 have led to further plans for massive trade expansion; if the new British government abides by its predecessor's commitment to rent Diego Garcia to the USA for naval use, Soviet pressures for countervailing bases in the area will become stronger. Since India is faced by rises in import prices over 1973 (due to oil price increases) amounting in 1974 to some 15–20 per cent of its total home-financed investment, the blandishments that a relatively wealthy country in need of naval facilities can offer are considerable. We may be sure that India will try hard and subtly to avoid undue pressures (and that its foreign minister played the Soviet card when he persuaded Iran to advance cheap credit for some oil); but the options, fort his desperately poor country, are not many and a bad harvest could reduce them to just one. Britain might help—the colonial aftermath and the subsequent exaggerated disengagement are over now—but not alone. Somehow Western Europe and India must provide each other with options, and benefits.

But readers must assess for themselves whether subsequent events confirm the theses of this book. We, the authors, would like to thank Bill Morris-Jones, Hugh Tinker, and Paul Streeten for valuable criticisms; many, inevitably anonymous, Indian and British officials for their patience; the librarians of the Indian High Commission in London, the Institute of Development Studies at Sussex University, the Royal Institute of International Affairs at Chatham House, and the Statistical Reference Library at Edinburgh University for their guidance; and Hermia Oliver for her scholarly and creative editorial help.

M.L. and J.F.

June 1974

Postscript (*August 1975*)

It is too soon to assess the duration, or long-term effects, of Mrs Gandhi's measures under the State of Emergency imposed on India on 26 June 1975. As regards the impact on Indo-British relations, it is relevant to recall the EEC's attitude towards trade agreements with Greece and, more recently, with Portugal: that, while other people's countries are fully independent, the state of their internal democratic freedoms is relevant to the perceived self-interest of the EEC in developing links with them. Such pressures would be more convincing if Britain – and the EEC – had, in the past, accorded India attention, trade priority, or aid in accordance with its 'liberal' freedoms, its poverty, or even its size.

1 RELATIONS BETWEEN BRITAIN AND INDIA 1960-70

1. The purpose of this book

We are trying to explain the delayed but rapid erosion of what less then twenty years ago seemed a strong, stable, and peacefully decolonized relationship. For about two centuries India and Britain were locked in the most important colonial connection in the history of mankind.[1] Britain's withdrawal from India in 1947 was perhaps the world's first decolonization that can be seen as planned, gradual, voluntary, and—as regards the ending of the colonial relationship itself—peaceful.

In 1947 there seemed excellent prospects for a lasting and powerful if informal alliance, political and economic. In the heyday of Nehru and neutralism, before Suez and the Russo-American détente, while India's foreign-exchange position depended on strong sterling balances rather than on US aid and Soviet barter-trade—from 1948 to mid-1956—the mutual influence of Britain and India remained almost as strong as in the colonial era, though more voluntary and equal. Yet today the relationship has been worn away beyond recognition. Whether in trade flows, capital movements, military relationships, educational links, or diplomatic influence, India attaches much more importance to the USSR and the USA than to Britain; and Britain to France and West Germany than to India. In time of peace and without overt mutual hostility, no pair of major nations has let slip, so quickly, links of such size and weight. We hope to explain and evaluate this process.

The book has two secondary aims, one explicit and methodological, the other implicit and theoretical. Explicitly, we shall be testing the power of measurement to assess a relationship between two nations.[2] Implicitly, we suggest hypotheses about relations between an ex-colonial and a decolonized country. In general: are our findings for Indo-British relations, that apparent robustness for 10–15 years was followed by the accelerated and subtly connected attenuation of numerous apparently separate links, relevant to (say) Franco-African relations in the 1970s? In the main, however, we seek to explain the particular rather than to imply the general; the analysis of waning Indo-British relations throughout the UN's 'Development Decade' is more than enough in itself.

2. The Indian and British situations: effects on the relationship

A platitude of international theory, often neglected in applied discussions both scholarly and journalistic, is that the relationship between two countries will depend substantially on the characteristics (and hence problems and require-ments) of each of them. Britain and India have in common liberal parliamentary democracy; old and rigid but pluralist and absorbent cultures; unity maintained despite serious centrifugal forces; mixed but sluggish economies; and middle rank as 'world powers'. Britain is wholly unlike India in being a declining power; in having (by world standards) a medium-sized and slowly growing population; in being rich; in enjoying relations with neighbours that are in general better than her relations with distant powers, especially superpowers; in her commitment to a military bloc; in her heavy dependence on trade in goods and services to produce a surplus in support of net export of capital; and in having been a major colonial power for 200 years, and virtually without colonies only since the mid-1960s. The effects of these similarities and differences recur through this book; one or two implications for Indo-British relations are considered below.

(i) EFFECTS OF COMMON FEATURES

(a) *Parliamentary democracy*. The Indian constitution is eclectic. Its federalism and Supreme Court remind one of the USA; the *nominal* status of its Planning Commission, of the USSR; the presidency, of the French Fourth Republic; and the provisions for local government, of the work of Jean-Jacques Rousseau. The basic provisions, however, owe much to the Westminster model: bicameral legislatures, quinquennial elections subject to the prime minister's right to dissolve parliament, and guaranteed liberal freedoms. Overall, India is one of the few poor countries to have retained multi-party liberal democracy. Parliament is sovereign; federal units (states) are often run by coalitions opposed to the party of central government; the judiciary is embarrassingly independent;[3] the press is genuinely free. There are blemishes—President's Rule as a political weapon against recalcitrant states, the denial of free debate in Nagaland and Kashmir—but Britain's convenient lack of constitutional limits on parliament scarcely veils comparable blemishes.[4] In their tolerance for free expression, even for racist or anti-democratic parties, Britain and India are exceptionally close to liberal-democratic ideals—arguably closer than, say, the USA or West Germany. Does this help Britain and India to establish close relations with each other?

In two ways it might help. First, liberal democracies share a major interest in limiting the power of other countries to spread totalitarian influence by force. Second, each should be able to understand and tolerate the free expression in the other hostile views. These two potential aids to a good relationship between liberal democracies have, in the case of India and Britain, often been warped into hindrances.

Britain and India have interpreted constraint of totalitarian powers in different and, as regards the USSR, increasingly conflicting ways. Britain has identified herself with the western military alliance, and more recently moved to enter the EEC;[5] her choice of allies, military and to some extent economic, has been determined not by 'democracy' but, at least in part, by their adherence to anti-communism, or even, more especially, to capitalism. India approached the problem first by non-alignment, later by links with both the USA and the USSR aimed at security against China and Pakistan, and most recently by increasingly close relations with the USSR (see pp. 34 and 181).

Tolerance of free mutual criticism has also become soured. In Britain, many people increasingly see India as just one of a group of non-white states to whom 'we gave freedom' and who reward us with obloquy; that Britain had first taken the freedom away, and deserves some of the obloquy, merely adds guilt to the bad effect on the relationship. In India, irritation at free, half-informed, and hostile British comment increasingly verges on censorship (pp. 196f.). The reason for India's growing hostility to British criticism is that the power to criticize effectively is not equal between Britain and India. *In principle* Indian television is as free to criticize Britain as the reverse. In practice, could it afford the time, personnel, and risk of giving offence; get through to a similarly big or inter-national audience; or adopt the ever-so-slightly paternal and knowing tone of so much western, and especially British, comment? On these resentful asym-metries, the clichés of free reciprocal criticism have foundered.

With the undermining of their special strenths as democracies in building a relationship, the Indo-British link has suffered badly from their special weakness: the need for makers of foreign policy to attend to pressures, not so much from the masses (whose voting behaviour owes little to events abroad), but from sub-elites speaking for interest groups. For example, India has a huge minority of Moslems; Congress wants their leaders to mobilize Moslem support for the party; a few of those leaders detest Israel; partly for that reason, since 1967 India has adopted an anti-Israeli policy extreme enough to damage relations even with Britain.[6] Conversely Britain has a small, though vocal, minority of racists.[7] The success of their spokesmen in persuading governments of both parties to adopt real or apparent 'racial' legislation has severely and progressively damaged relations with India (pp. 171f.), though the firmness of Mr Heath's government in resisting such pressures and discharging its obligations to admit British Asians expelled from Uganda in September 1972 did something to mend matters. For democracies to build good relations in the face of their own atavists is especially difficult.

(b) *Cultural similarities.* For Britain and (to a lesser extent) India, foreign conquests are now remote. Each civil service is dominated by a pluralist elite, narrowly based socially but highly competent and therefore sometimes com-placent and resistant to change. The inevitable effect is to slow down the administrative response to foreign political inputs, and sometimes even to the decisions of the home government. Efficient pursuit of old policies, plus com-placent resistance to new ones, can mean a series of missed opportunites— witness Britain's astonishing failure for twenty years after 1947 to make much of either the Commonwealth or the European option—but it also discourages instant foreign-policy-making. Thus British foreign policy did not 'go Pakistani' after Wilson's off-the-cuff remarks about the 1965 war (p. 203); and India has not implemented her half-decision to compel British visitors to have visas, a policy widely supported as retaliation for the brusque treatment of Indian visitors to Britain (p. 170). British partisanship over Kashmir would win enemies without encouraging a settlement; Indian official retaliation against immigration officers at Heathrow would merely discourage both tourism and business. The buffers of adminstrative inertia are sometimes welcome.

The danger is that in both countries they create first illusion, later unduly deepening despair. For instance, some fall after 1947 in India's and Britain's share in each other's trade was natural. However, hardly any of the fall happened in the 1950s (partly due to slow commercial and administrative responses). This lag fostered the illusion of a 'natural' trading relationship unchanged save for decolonization. Hence the decline of the 1960s was faster because pent-up, and more surprising because preceded by stability (pp. 22–5).

(c) *Controlled separatism.* Until the spate of separatisms of the late 1960s— the Basques, Biafra, Brittany, 'East Pakistan', Quebec—Britain and India seemed threatened by *unusually* severe centrifugal forces. Britain in Northern Ireland, like India in Kashmir and Upper Assam, has experienced fissiparous tendencies acute by comparison with countries of a similar level of development. Indian and British foreign policies are likely to be affected by their politicians' wish to preserve national cohesion.

While India's and Britain's problems are similar, the effects on foreign policy are different. The Eire government has made some attempt to suppress violent organizations seeking to 'unite' Northern Ireland by force; Pakistan and China, with a stronger sense of grievance (and a better case), have encouraged and perhaps fomented separatism within India's borderlands. If Eire were to support Northern Ireland's separatists with propaganda and arms, conflict with Eire over the North might well become a central theme for Britain's foreign policy, just as conflict with Pakistan over Kashmir became for India's. A less moderate government in Eire, or a government in Pakistan ready to settle with India over Kashmir, might reverse the positions and priorities of both India and Britain; the wish to hold one's 'own' land and people, and the helpful or hostile attitude of neighbours towards that wish, can easily become the dominant force in a country's foreign policy.

(d) *Mixed economies.* Indian society contains important, though slowly declining, relationships 'feudal' in the sense of resting on an implicit, involuntary, and unequal treaty under which people are assigned mutual social and economic obligations by birth. Caste allocation of jobs is still dominant in villages; the widespread *jajmani* system compels barbers, carpenters, etc. to give specialized services, as required, to landowners for a traditionally-determined share of the crop; many of India's 8mn families of 'attached' landless labourers are working for the 'attaching' farmer in a futile attempt to pay off mounting debts; and in each case the father's rights and duties bind his sons. Both capitalism and state intervention are eroding Indian feudalism. 'Indian socialism' is often overrated by politicians, Indian or American: India features a public-sector share in investment close to Britain and below "free-enterprise" Pakistan; in the 1960s the proportion of people in India without subsidized health or education was far higher than in Mr Dudley Senanayake's 'Conservative' Ceylon. However, after nationalization of the domestic banks in 1960 and increasing state control of exports and imports in 1970, India is clearly a mixed economy. So, of course, is Britain, with half her investment and a quarter of her workforce in the public sector and with small but significant feudal elements in a landed aristocracy, a mainly hereditary second chamber, and an established church that is the country's biggest property-owner.

Like liberal democracy, 'economic mixedness', while shared by Britain and India, has asymmetric effects on their relationship. Once more, the reason lies in its rich-poor, investor-host aspects. Britons own a good deal of capital in India (pp. 85–6), and British companies and shareholders feel hampered by Indian feudalism and threatened by Indian socialism—or its rhetoric. Indians own much less capital in Britain, and their interest in our socio-economic system is therefore less inevitably commercial. British businessmen, and (to the extent that it represents them) the British diplomatic service, are thus regularly affronted by (and make disparaging comments on) decisions about caste or nationalization that are the responsibility of Indians. Indian businessmen, since they do not invest significantly in Britain, are not correspondingly irritated or irritating.

The asymmetry of irritation is part of any relationship between a rich economy with a capitalist sector investing abroad, and a poor economy with a capitalist sector not investing abroad. Neo-colonial exploitation, 'underdeveloped' suspicion, and mutual intolerance all seem to have been surprisingly small—not significantly to blame for the weakening of Indo-British relations. Thus Mrs Gandhi's stance of 1969–72, combining a marked leftward move with the reassertion of 'strong government', was generally welcomed in British newspapers, even those closest to business interests.

Indo-British relations have suffered less from clashes of economic ideology than because mixed economies encourage foreign misunderstanding of domestic political rhetoric regarding the mixture. British businessmen, especially in small firms lacking time or resources to follow the Indian scene, are often over-concerned about attacks on private foreign investment intended by Indian government spokesmen for domestic consumption (p. 84). Indian politicians sometimes accept at face value the gestures towards international equalization made by Mr Wilson at party conferences, or by Mr Heath at the UN, and are duly shocked by subsequent British actions.

(ii) EFFECTS OF DIFFERENCES

(a) *Changing power status.* Britain and India are 'middle powers', but their status has been diverging. Admittedly both have experienced slow growth in living standards since 1947, compared with most of the world. In India, however, rapid population increase (in so many ways a curse) has converted this to a fairly rapid growth in *total* output and hence in most of the determinants of international power: size of imports, size of exports, diversity, and reserve capacity to pursue conflicts by force. India, moreover, has been 'emergent'—discovering her role and hence turning away from ad hoc pressures to recognition and pursuit of self-interest (pp. 210f.). Hence India, despite slow growth in income *per head*, has (even before her success in the war of 1971) been a rising power—compare her responses to China in 1962 and 1965—while Britain has declined. Dean Acheson's celebrated remark that 'Britain has lost an empire but had not found a role' was just, though not quite accurate. Britain was obsessed with finding a role, with *acting as* a leader of the Commonwealth or the EEC. That role was and is quite unacceptable to the rest of the cast. Britain's chronic balance-of-payments problem, slow growth, and lack of imagination, and not mainly objective or external factors, have so far prevented her from developing, and concentrating on, attainable foreign-policy objectives, rather than a quest for 'leadership' to no clear purpose.

There are distinct limits to possible relations between (1) two superpowers, (2) a superpower and a middle power, and (3) two middle powers; and, in the last category, the relationship between a rising and a declining power is subject to special strains. As the rising power's needs and horizons expand, her markets, diplomacy, and defence policy all feature the replacement of powers in decline, both by her own growing capacities and by other relatively stronger powers, notably superpowers. For example, in the 1960s British sales of military equipment to India lost ground, both to Indian arms producers and to the USSR (ch. 11).

Many Britons, on the left as well as the right, view the ex-colonies with a somewhat possessive paternalism, and react with hurt hostility when India diversifies away from Britain; especially, perhaps, as they are choking back a (justified) suspicion that Britain is partly responsible. The 1930s liberal who fought with Laski (but not with Gandhi) for Indian independence feels let down by a son, the Blimp feels betrayed by an upstart, when India and Pakistan turn for the alleviation of disputes to Russia instead of Britain; neither liberal nor Blimp seems to realize that relations between nations depend on present power and policy, not on past loyalty. If Britain, now a declining middle power, seeks a special relationship with any other countries, her increasingly scarce external energies must be summoned, led, and *concentrated* on those countries; turning them into scapegoats is no substitute. Only after the examination of Indo-British relations in detail can we turn in the final chapter to the question of what advantages (if any) both parties could gain from their reconstruction.

(b) *Emigrants, immigrants, and populations.* With buoyant demand and near-full employment, Britain—with slow growth of labour force and few workers left on the land—has suffered chronic (though not uninterrupted) shortages of most categories of workers for a third of a century. Despite intermittent unemployment, this formed a natural attraction to immigrants from low-wage countries—especially as British policy, very liberal towards Commonwealth immigrants until 1962, became progressively less so, and thereby advertised to potential migrants that they had better come soon if they wanted to get in at all. India's rapid population growth, small capital stock, and crucial land shortage, in a nation where seven people in ten live off the land, make her a natural source of emigrants. The problems created by the consequent flows (and barriers erected against them) for Indo-British relations are discussed in Chapter 10.

Migration is the most striking issue, but India's population problem colours many of her relations with other nations. In particular, western donors recognize that aid for population control promises a very high increase in Indian welfare per £ spent.[8] However, for the rich and prosperous west, whose own population growth suffices to cause ever-worsening pollution of the *world* biosphere, to lecture poor nations on the need for birth-control would risk suspicion and resentment. India's elite[9] has been mature enough, and sufficiently secure in India's size and power, to express these feelings much less than many other poor nations; but the wish to avoid difficulties has induced Britain to tread much more warily in offering India aid for birth-control than donors like Sweden. Short-run sweetness has counted for more than light.

(c) *Rich and poor*. The above comparisons have touched upon the 'rich-poor' aspects of Indo-British relations. India is one of the world's poorest countries, with income-per-person below African and far below Latin American levels. However, India's size, industrialization, strategic importance, developed administrative and business elite, and old and complex culture enable her to treat with rich countries (except superpowers) at least equally, especially since she depends on economic links with rich nations—aid, trade, skilled personnel, private foreign investment—less than most poor countries. Further, British aid has been a small part of India's total, given on relatively easy terms (pp. 108f.), and seldom if ever abused to corrupt the elite; while British private capital in India has been managed for satisfactory rather than extortionate returns, subjected to liberal rules on profit repatriation, and controlled by companies not disposed to sudden repatriations of capital. Hence the mutual suspicions of a rich-poor relationship have been softened.

Thus, especially given the mood during and after decolonization, Britain's and India's failure to develop a strengthening relationship cannot be blamed mainly on income differences, and even with hindsight remains odd. It is truistic, but nevertheless true, that rich as well as poor risk economic sluggishness, political turmoil, and moral decay if in the year 2000 the slums and cholera of Calcutta still coexist with computers and space-travel. India and Britain provided almost ideal conditions in the 1960s for realizing that decade's 'conventional wisdom', a rich-poor developmental partnership. They enjoyed a historical link gradually, and at last happily, made free; little reason for big-power arrogance or poor-country inferiority complex; and big potential joint economic gains, in trade complementarity and perhaps in the usefulness of Britain's private investment in India to Indians and Britons. Yet India and Britain drifted apart: Britain claiming to seek entry to a European Economic Community to make it less inward-looking; India as she diversified, turning first towards a determined non-alignment, but subsequently redefining this to cover closer links with both superpowers, and more recently with the USSR alone. Since this process of drifting apart was in no sense historically necessary, we regard it—*given an act of will*—as reversible. Not until the final chapter of the book can we judge whether it is *worth* reversing for Britain or India, given the alternative uses of their scarce energies and resources.

(d) *Blocs and neighbours.* Britain has attempted to retrieve her waning power by embodying it in blocs: first in Nato (and subsequently in Cento and Seato), military and inevitably US-dominated responses to a Soviet aggressiveness partly real, partly imagined, and partly potential; more recently in Efta and EEC, partly solidifying devices to prepare for a possible US withdrawal from Europe, mainly trade-freeing devices to assist accurate specialization during European growth, but (despite current illusions) no likelier to pay special attention to the interests of a sluggish Britain than were the earlier and more openly military alliances.

Both Britain's military-ideological commitment to the West and her later links with Europe have made Indo-British relations difficult. India's bad relations with her main neighbours, China and Pakistan, impelled her to turn for defence support—certainly arms sales, possibly some form of tacit guarantee against China—to the superpowers; she could not afford to antagonize either, after the Chinese invasion of 1962, and her condemnations of Soviet policy in Czechoslovakia and of US policy in Vietnam were equally muted where in the 1950s they would have been equally outspoken. India's transition, from the moral curator of neutralism to a self-interested middle power with threatened borders, has compelled discretion. India has preserved her self-respect by redirecting her moral outspokenness towards non-superpowers, notably Britain, which on several issues in the 1960s was indeed vulnerable. But this has not improved Indo-British relations. More important, in military matters, Britain's perception of her interests, and location of troops and outlays, has concentrated less and less on areas of interest to India (pp. 187–8)—and India has increasingly wanted it that way. By 1970 she was outspokenly hostile to British naval involvement in Indian Ocean defence (even apart from issues involving South Africa). In economic matters, British trade and investment patterns echoed and anticipated formal treaties concentrating them on Europe.

(e) *Different trade-capital positions.* Britain, being small, must spend about a quarter of her income on imports; India, bigger in area and population, spends under a tenth. Britain's great dependence on trade increases both the threat potential of foreign countries against her, and the effort (and cost) it is worth her while to incur abroad, both to win friends and to protect trade routes. Britain's position as a major foreign investor reinforces this. India's small trade-dependence reduces her reliance on good overseas relations, especially as her emphasis on capital-goods industries during the Second and Third Plans (1956–66) reduced the role of imports even for future industrial expansion.

India, like other poor countries, has relied on foreigners for a substantial part of her investment—about 13 per cent in the late 1960s, all through aid, since finance for new private investment is well below profit repatriations (pp. 81–3, 74–5). Britain since 1965 has given only about 7 per cent of India's aid (though for various reasons—see p. 105—its true value is closer to 13 per cent) and does not *in effect* tie it to British exports, so that it plays little role in raising British influence in India.

In foreign trade rich countries usually seek surpluses, to strengthen their currencies and their influence. Hence trading partners allowing them to run such surpluses constitue a threat potential to and a source of influence on them. A poor country seeks trading partners who will permit her to run bilateral deficits, helping her to finance her development; such trading partners have threat potential, and hence influence, in the poor country. But Britain has been selling India much less than India has been selling Britain (p. 23; see however, p. 69). Thus neither partner has the full influence that trade might normally confer, because neither is, through its bilateral dealings, offering the other those changes in payments positions that are most urgently required.

(f) *Ex-colonizer and ex-colony*. This distinction is still a major influence on Indo-British relations. Many of the features considered above—rich-poor, investor-recipient, declining-emergent—rest upon the former colonial relationship to some extent.

The 'mature relationship' which Michael Stewart called for (p. 16) cannot be built on blurred memories of a colonial relationship that did so little to solve India's key problems of this century—population, cereal farming, urban slums, industrial development. Of course colonization did much for Indian transport, law, administration, and even unity. But the post-colonial link has to rest on joint interests, not ex-colonial sentiment. The metropolis naturally builds up exploitative relations with the colony; the story of the 'Home Charges' between the wars (pp. 22, 68–9) reveals the historical obstacles in the way of expanded and mutually useful economic links. By definition, however, such obstacles recede into the past; so, unfortunately, do even the currently and mutually useful patterns of trade and investment associated with them. Independent India had to be convinced that these patterns could be made developmental where they had once been exploitative; decolonizing Britain had to be convinced that they could remain profitable even when stripped of the colonial bias in her favour. A major effort of reconstruction would have been required. In the 1960s it was not forthcoming.

The specific historical relationship between India and Britain, then, presented opportunities which were not grasped because the underlying common economic interests, and the corresponding trade and capital flows, were not sufficiently fostered. The *general* situations of Britain and India have created further opportunities and problems: Britain as ex-colonizer and now nominal 'head' of the Commonwealth; and India as the archetypal and largest excolony, and hence the respected and resented 'head' of the Third World. From the British end, bilateral relations with India have been increasingly mediated through

Commonwealth organizations and discussions: not only the meetings of prime ministers and finance ministers, but also since 1964 the Commonwealth Secretariat, whose spokesmen semi-publicly resented the fact that Britain in 1970 discussed joining the European Community bilaterally with each Commonwealth state, not multilaterally through the Secretariat. There is much to be said for a genuinely multilateral Commonwealth, so that bilateral complaints about British conduct—over Kenyan Asians or South African arms—do not threaten the organization itself; but the present uneasy multilateral façade, whose resources, institutions, and initiatives stay centred on London, is irritating for many members. India as a sovereign power needs no mediator in her dealings with *Britain;* yet a multilateral Commonwealth would suggest, promisingly, Ottawa or Lusaka for an attempt to help India and Pakistan over any dispute where outside help might be useful. (The Kashmir dispute was exacerbated in the 1960s by schoolmasterly treatment from London.)

From the Indian end, her position as biggest and earliest of the Third World's independent Commonwealth countries creates a natural mediating role between the rich 'white' Commonwealth and the more recently independent poor members. This role has not been adopted, partly for fear of arousing resentment in Africa, but mainly because the general weakening of links with Britain in the 1960s has left India with little to lose from complete identification with any challenges to London that might come from African Commonwealth members. Indian government spokesmen have told their questioning MPs that India would stay in the Commonwealth as long as it was useful to India—but by 1970 heavy hints were being dropped that a renewal of British arms sales to South Africa would cast doubt on that usefulness. Indeed, East African proposals of a defence agreement with Britain, as an 'insurance policy' against Russia, were badly set back by India's insistence that she wanted no major British (or other) naval presence in the Indian Ocean, and that as far as Indian facilities went there *was* no Soviet presence. This may have been for Indian or even Soviet consumption; but in 1960, even in 1965, would not India have been leading any initiative for joint Commonwealth action in this field, if the alternative might be the break-up of the Commonwealth itself? If, as we shall argue, these changes can largely be traced to the rapid erosion of Indo-British economic links in the 1960s, that alone has much to answer for.

3. A declining relationship?

Several of the British and Indian characteristics discussed above—rich-poor, metropolis-excolony, capital exporter-capital importer—render many indicators of the relationship asymmetric. There are many British and Indian nationals in each other's countries (pp. 155, 162) but Britons in India are mostly businessmen, with a sprinkling of experts, volunteers, and diplomats; Indians in Britain— apart from migrants—are mostly students and visitors. Indian press coverage, but not research, about Britain is excellent. British press coverage, but not research, about India is poor.

In asking whether the relationship has declined we are thus bound to ask asymmetric questions: about British investment and arms sales and aid to India; about Indian emigration and study in Britain. Only in trade is there some symmetry.

It is a symmetry in asymmetric decline. British exports to India fell, in real terms, by over two-thirds in the 1960s; Britain bought a falling *share* of her total imports from India (p. 44) but the real value increased. Trade held up fairly well until the late 1950s, then declined sharply, a pattern later repeated by other indicators. The rapid decline of the 1960s is explained in Chapters 2–4; but whatever its causes, economic interest has to be the basis of any strong relationship between two distant and independent nations, and if that basis is eroded, a cultural or sentimental residue cannot help much.

Before 1947 much Indo-British trade was artificial. British exports to India were boosted by restrictions against competitors; Indian exports to Britain tended to come from British-owned factories and plantations, and to offer rather small benefits to Indian wage-earners or tax-gatherers. It was natural for such trade to decline somewhat after independence. However, the major *complementarities* between British output, skill-intensive and capital-using, and India's labour-intensive output have not been fully used in the trading patterns that have developed since 1960. Britain erected 'voluntary' quota barriers against Indian textile exports, and through Efta eroded the advantages enjoyed in British markets by Indian manufactured exports as a whole. India has turned increasingly to aid-financed trade with the USA and barter trade with Eastern Europe and the USSR,[10] the latter less complementary to India (in the sense of having less radically different labour and capital endowments) than Britain as a trading partner. British entry to EEC will, even more, turn her trade into exchanges of similar products with neighbours.

There is less of a decline in capital movements (chs. 6 & 7). Almost half India's foreign-owned capital—over 3 per cent of *all* her fixed non-farm capital—is British-owned, though the proportion (but not the absolute amount) fell during the 1960s. The erosion of British exports to India helps British capital in India— less bought from ICI or Unilever should mean more bought from ICI (India) or Hindustan Lever—so it is surprising that the British share in India's total foreign-owned capital has fallen. Still, if foreign-owned capital earning fair rates of post-tax profit remains acceptable, the British stake is big enough to be important in a revived relationship. Is this also true of aid (ch. 7)? The real value of *all* British aid declined by one-fifth from 1964 to 1970,[11] as inflation and devaluation raised export prices, while balance-of-payments problems were seen as preventing the expansion of aid rather than as requiring other re-adjustments. By 1970 Britain was supplying less aid to India than was West Germany. There has been a real recovery since, but the European Development Fund will compete with India for limited UK aid.

Other measurable aspects of the relationship—military, diplomatic, educational, journalistic—seem to have turned downwards around the early 1960s, despite surprising resilience from 1947 to about 1959. General political factors are testing this weakened relationship. The period 1968–71 saw increasing overt mutual annoyance. Britain annoyed India about migration (see pp. 67–71); by her policy on Southern Africa; and by her treatment of Commonwealth interests in negotiations with EEC (placing the butter exports of 3mn wealthy New Zealanders above the manufacturing exports of 540mn poor Indians). India annoyed Britain by apparently not recognizing genuine British defence worries about the Indian Ocean shipping routes and by what seemed—for a potential mediator—an extreme attitude on the Middle East. British policy on Bangladesh in 1971 may have only papered over the cracks. There is a limit to the capacity of an economically eroded relationship to tolerate recurring political stress.

4. Tension: the unimportance of neo-colonialism

A relationship between two countries may decline or break down for three sorts of reason: tension, intention, or inattention. We have indicated some recent tension in Indo-British relations, but their post-independence history does not suggest *inevitable* tension between a rich ex-colonizer and a poor ex-colony. It arose from specific events, not from the inner logic of the relationship. If since 1960 that relationship had remained healthy—if its basis in trade and capital flows (and perhaps its background in diplomacy and education) had not been weakened by rational or irrational action and inaction from both London and Delhi—strains in the 1970s over migration or even Indian Ocean defence would not threaten it. If there were a basis in mutual economic gain, it would pay both sides to resolve particular strains, in order not to disrupt the relationship.

Yet it is often argued that rich, ex-colonial, white countries are *inevitably* locked in a tense, neo-colonial relationship with poor, non-white ex-colonies. The Indo-British link is so huge an exception as to invalidate any such rule. It arises because India, though poor, is strong and sophisticated enough not to be long or grossly exploited. No businessmen, British or other, could corrupt India's Administrative Service to serve foreign commercial interests, as Ghana's, under Nkrumah, was corrupted. No foreign power could use aid to 'buy' India's political and administrative elite and persuade her, say to adopt approved policies towards South Africa. It is relevant that, unlike most poor countries, India from 1947 to 1972 enjoyed on the whole improving terms of trade, and relations with overseas investors based on liberal inflows of capital and outflows of profits—the latter not extortionate, negligible or secret.[12]

There *are* problems in any relationship between India and a big western nation. In India, voices as unambiguously favourable to democracy as K. N. Raj (when vice-chancellor of Delhi University) have expressed deep misgivings about the persons, examples, and life-styles that accompany not only private foreign investment but also aid. Britain, by taking doctors trained at India's expense, is a *net* receiver of almost £6 mn of technical assistance each year (p. 135). And a trading relationship with a partner that negotiates to join a major new economic grouping (with a common external tariff), without the consultation or consideration automatically accorded wealthier countries, obviously presents problems. But it would be far-fetched to interpret as neo-colonialism a British link with India involving effectively untied aid loans, since 1965 at negligible interest; a growing Indian bilateral export surplus; and post-tax profits on British private foreign capital of about $8\frac{1}{2}$ per cent per year in manufacturing, probably less elsewhere (pp. 111, 23, 91). The tensions of the relationship have been extrinsic, imposed upon a weakened and neglected bond, not part of the nature of that bond.

5. Intention: geographic realignments

The weakening of Indo-British relations owes something to the intended acts of businessmen, and to a lesser extent of politicians and others. Such acts hardly ever aimed at weaker relations; but they were the easily foreseeable result. In international affairs as in law, men, must be held to will the natural consequences of their acts, at least when such consequences are not too difficult to foresee.

Basic was the weakening of trade relations. Both India and Britain increased export prices faster than major competitors (p. 25); hence in each country customers redirected orders to cheaper suppliers. Both India and Britain grew more slowly than most world markets; each country's producers found one another a decreasingly promising market compared with more dynamic alternatives. Hence there was intentional substitution, by British and Indian buyers and sellers, of trade with third parties for trade with each other. A determined effort would have been required to prevent the trade basis of Indo-British relations from being undermined. Instead, both governments hastened the trend by their new geographical commitments (p. 24).

Realignments of trade, investment, and military links towards nearby countries *as such* seem odd. Transport costs have risen more slowly than prices of traded goods[13], so that the gains from electing to trade over short distances have dwindled. Moreover, while British growth has fallen behind her neighbours, the latter in 'catching up' have developed a structure of output increasingly like Britain's own; the rapidly expanding trade within Efta and EEC is an exchange of more and more similar cars, machine tools, and foodstuffs. Hence the 'gains from trade' within Western Europe have declined; a car made in Dagenham is increasingly likely, if sold to West Germany, to be replaced by a similar imported car. At the same time workers in Western Europe (including Britain) have become increasingly leisure-oriented, scarce, and costly, while machinery has become more plentiful. This has increased the advantages of importing such items as jute and cotton textiles (made with much labour and little machinery) from countries like India, in return for 'capital-intensive' and sophisticated exports. This does not invalidate the case for free intra-European trade, but it does suggest that replacing £100 each of Indo-British and Franco-Algerian trade by £100 each of Franco-British and Indo-Algerian trade will damage all four nations. Trade in dissimilar goods, which can be made at home only at great cost, is replaced by trade in goods very like those a country makes for herself.

Thus the growing moves towards geographic trading blocs, in South America and Africa as well as Europe, damage all parties unless they create *very much* more trade among bloc members than they divert away from non-bloc members. Hence trade blocs such as Efta and EEC, and perhaps Indo-Soviet links, must be designed with special care. Indo-British relations, not only in trade, have suffered from the failure, in designing the new regionalism, to consider adequately more distant links.

It is, of course, true that both countries have been deliberately replacing their artificial colonial relationship by new links with third parties. While Britain still owns almost half the foreign private capital in India, *new* overseas support for Indian capital development (over 10 per cent of *total* Indian investment in 1955–70) has come mainly from US aid, recently mediated and co-ordinated with other donors (as well as supplemented) by the World Bank in the aid consortium. India has remained the largest single recipient of UK aid, but a major effort of concentration by Britain would have been needed to fill a substantial part of Indian needs; and Britain has been one of the most diffuse of major donors (p. 101). The effort could well have been made; the economic and political yield of extra UK aid for India, to both donor and recipient, was and is probably higher than for Africa (p. 117). But the alignment of British aid in the early 1960s towards newly-independent African Commonwealth countries was certainly intentional. So were British measures since the early 1960s to limit the outflows of private foreign capital (p. 81).

India too has, in part, consciously realigned her position away from Britain. The very high level of Indo-British trade at Independence was partly the result of unequal arrangements imposed in the colonial era (p. 43); India was bound to seek diversification, through the lag was surprisingly long. In fields as remote as education and defence, institutions linked to Britain (or even following British patterns) did not obviously serve Indian interests after independence, and the shift towards other countries, again mostly the superpowers, was a sensible decision (pp. 141, 184).

Furthermore, in retreat as in advance, trade and 'the flag' have seemed to march in each other's footsteps. The closer economic alignment of Britain with Europe was matched by her military withdrawal from 'east of Suez', and her growing fears of US military withdrawal from Europe. The closer economic alignment of India with the USSR has had, as its parallel, the efforts of each nation to find in the other an ally against China. Yet the age of ICBMs seems a strange time for regional military huddles; just as the falling cost of freight, relative to traded products, sits oddly with the regionalization of trade.

Reasons are not justifications. Both India and Britain have 'disengaged' the baby with the bathwater. The baby is not drowned yet, but both parents seem at times to be doing their worst. Resuscitation is still possible; it need not be artificial; but, if it is worth doing, it had better be quick.

6. Inattention: the victory of the short run

We have argued that India wanted closer links with Russia, Britain with EEC, and that the weakening of Indo-British relations was an unsought but natural result, since too little was done to prevent it. Inattention, not tension or intention, explains the failure of both countries to take such action. The very depth, age, and apparent ease of relations between Britain and India—old cultures, democratic, slow-moving, similar in so many ways—has lulled both countries' leaders into a complacent belief that nothing particular need to be done to keep that relationship healthy: except that 'belief' is too strong a word for the torpid, half-conscious ideology of neglect.

The decline of diplomatic, cultural, and military relations is a natural concomitant of weakening trade links. In trade promotion, in trade relations with third parties, in tariff and quota structures—nowhere has either country done much to secure these links (pp. 47, 56–9).

This inattention to fundamentals has been pointed up by occasional, unplanned emphasis on minor issues. As if by an invisible hand, the concessions that one nation can, without threats, obtain from another are rationed; goodwill cashed on one issue is not available for another. For example, by pressing Britain on BBC policy (p. 196), India draws upon the stock of potential concessions on matters relating to Britain's entry into EEC. Conversely, if Britain compels Indian visitors to wait for hours at her High Commission in New Delhi for de facto visas (and subjects them to harassment at Heathrow), then her prospects for Indian agreement on oceanic defence dwindle. If concessions are rationed by goodwill, their unplanned use on minor issues means that they (and their donors) are exhausted when major issues arise. The ration can be surprisingly small if the basic relationship is weakening.

Systematic attention to the relationship, by both countries, would have been required to stop it weakening. India's independence, Britain's European realignments, both nations' diversification away from colonial patterns—all these created pulls on India and Britain away from their former links. Yet these links, modified to help both countries take full advantage of their changing trade complementarities, could have joined a rich and a poor country to their common advantage. Why was this not done?

Sir Edward (later Viscount) Grey, as foreign secretary in 1914, was asked how far ahead the Foreign Office ought to look; 'about a week', he replied. Mr Harold Macmillan, asked to identify the main problem he had faced between 1957 and 1964, unhesitatingly replied, 'Events'. Despite the efforts of a small Planning Staff, the British Foreign Service has always stressed the smooth management of day-to-day requirements of an accepted policy rather than the analysis of benefits and costs of alternative policies. Indeed, some forms of expertise required to make such assessments were viewed with scepticism in the Foreign and Commonwealth Office (FCO), except in the Overseas Development Administration (ODA) itself; and its responsibilities were in general limited to aid issues. (Even in ODA there were doubts about such assessments, as witness the shortage of economists to evaluate aid at the recipient end; there was one in Delhi in 1966–7, but he had no predecessor or successor, despite his recognized major contribution to aid rationalization.) The European debate dominated such time as FCO could allocate to long-term thinking from 1957 to 1971. On issues like Kashmir and the Sino-Indian border, there does not seem to have been much advance planning. Even where European and Indian problems met, they received little attention; neither Board of Trade nor FCO seems to have given prolonged thought in 1970–1 to the import of Indian and Pakistani manufactures into Britain after her entry into EEC, while incomparably less important issues like New Zealand lamb and Mauritius sugar received constant attention.

A sophisticated, experienced, and 'established' Foreign Service, even across such discontinuities as the Chinese hostilities of 1962 and the Brussels negotiations of 1971 managing a smoothly continuous foreign policy: this was the story in India as well Britain. But is not the justified complacency of able diplomats slow death to an *apparently* healthy relationship under subtle but increasing stress? It has precluded long-term measures to reverse the steady erosion of the relationship's economic base; it has permitted short-term ad hoc responses to a whole series of minor crises that have exhausted goodwill without repairing relations. The fact that the sickness is largely economic, but is treated (or ignored) by doctors skilled almost exclusively in traditional political diplomacy, has made inattention to fundamentals certain.

Neither nation's elite has given the relationship the priority required to rethink it. Michael Stewart, in a celebrated speech in 1968, called for a 'mature relationship'; this was during the only visit by either country's foreign secretary to the other country between 1947 and 1971. Maturity cannot be posthumous. No Indian or British prime minister officially visited the other's country in the 1960s. In 1969 Mr Wilson withdrew his acceptance of an invitation to India, diverted by some domestic crisis more important than our relationship with one-sixth of the world. Mr Heath found time for a Delhi stop-over on his way to the Singapore Commonwealth Prime Ministers' Meeting in January 1971, and Mrs Gandhi for a return stop-over in London (between Vienna and Washington) in October 1971: valuable contacts that did something to improve relations, but were much briefer than the more frequent contacts at this level from British visits to Holland, or Indian visits to Nepal. In the 1960s the trade ministers visited each other's countries only once (Mr Douglas Jay in 1965, Mr Manubhai Shah in 1966). Perhaps the delay in diversification during the 1950s, and its amazing speed in the 1960s caught the makers of foreign policy unawares. Certainly the low priority each national élite accorded to Indo-British relations has produced an inattention to their decline, a refusal to rethink and reactivate them, that is largely responsible for their present enfeeblement.

7. The prospects of measurement

This book attempts a numerical analysis of the state of relations during the 1960s. We have not tried to construct any single overall index of Indo-British relations. Such an index would involve assigning arbitrary measures of relative importance to trade, aid, defence, cultural and other contacts, and the relations among movements in these particular contacts is one of the main themes.

Yet, if 'international relations' is to become a predictive science (however partially), its practitioners must ultimately develop some such index of the total bilateral link, construct it for many countries, and see what caused it to change. This will involve a process of comparative analysis, probably involving correlation methods. In this extremely early stage of quantification and prediction in the study of international relations, we felt that we could contribute more by a modest attempt to measure, analyse, and interrelate the changes in *particular* areas of the Indo-British relationship, rather than by constructing a single but highly tentative overall measure. We have consistently tried to break down the measurable aggregates into their component parts: to ask in *which* traded goods, arms, forms of education, Britain and India have replaced each other by domestic (or new foreign) suppliers—and when. If the 'leading indicators' in several changing bilateral links can be identified, we shall be well on the way towards an overall indicator.

The quality of data available to us is in general good, partly because each country's estimates serve as a check on the other's; but three caveats are needed. First, data on bilateral 'invisible' trade—banking, shipping, insurance, tourism, and other services—are not available in nearly as much detail, or as readily, as for visibles. Inferences about Indo-British payments, and hence about the location and strength of political pressures, from trade data alone could be invalidated by bilateral flows on invisibles account. Second, for data collected regularly at ports and by central banks, disaggregated economic information is often out of date. Until recently the analysis of British capital and investment in India had to rely on very outdated (1966) estimates.[14] Third, British defence support of India is irritatingly *semi*-secret: official trade figures amalgamate and conceal information about bilateral military shipments; civil servants from both countries are reluctant to give figures that are, in fact, published, but in unlikely (because inappropriate) ways. Data concealed in UK publications could once be found in UN and OECD sources, but must now be laboriously inferred.[15] It would help if the military authorities decided just what *was* secret and published the remainder clearly and accessibly. In general, however, data on Indo-British bilateral relations—diplomatic, educational, and even journalistic, as well as economic—are good enough for 'measurement' of these relations to be a sensible target, at least over a decade or more; annual fluctuations can be very misleading.

This book contains little sophisticated statistical analysis. In this new field, we have tried to avoid doubtful inferences, and to emphasize the questions of real interest for international relations. For example, we have not distributed the blame for falling British exports to India numerically among such major causes as slow Indian growth, British uncompetitiveness, etc.; such sorting-out is full of uncertainties (especially since prices and incomes in third countries are relevant too), and anyway the techniques involved answer the wrong questions. They tell us how much of the variation, among years or commodity groups, in the rate of export decline could be attributed to interannual or inter-group *differences* in prices, in consumer incomes, etc. The type of question of interest to students of Indo-British relations is rather why Indian purchases from Britain fell so fast and so far in the 1960s in response to *a particular set* of price and income relations and variations. After all, such purchases had risen, despite similar price and income considerations, in the 1950s; other countries, similarly placed to India, expanded purchases from Britain in the 1960s; and India substantially raised her imports in the 1960s from the USA, which also became less competitive over the decade.

All this is not to say that numerical analysis is useless; only that it is most useful when most simple, and confined to central issues, at this early stage of measurement in international relations. For example, simple arithmetic shows that in the 1960s *at most* 3 per cent of the fall in Britain's share of Indian imports, and *at most* 7 per cent of the fall in India's share of British exports, can be blamed on a structure of British sales to India in 1960 ill placed to meet, respectively, changing Indian needs or changing British supply capacities (pp. 33, 32). This puts the onus not on initial trade structures but on events, and on policies ill suited to exploit (or to compensate for) the effect of such events on British exports to India. As we shall now see, a similar analysis applies to most, but not all, of the relationships considered in this book.

2 BRITISH-INDIAN TRADING RELATIONS:

THE CONTEXT

> I am sure everyone would wish to make it plain to countries abroad that, great as may be our desire to give them, as far as is compatible with fairness to our own manufacturers, access to this great consuming market, to a large extent the amount of that access must depend not only on us but on them. Unless they are willing to give us access to their market, as we give them access to ours, eventually ours must disappear.
> OLIVER STANLEY, *president of the Board of Trade, in the House of Commons on 24 May 1938, before the 1939 Indo-British trade agreement.*

> We cannot serve our own interests and those of our traditional friends in the way we would like unless we secure a substantial increase in our trade and a stimulus to growth and investment. This was what the Government sought from the EEC.
> MICHAEL NOBLE, *minister of trade, in speech to Commonwealth Chambers of Commerce in London, 8 June 1972 after the ending of the 1939 Indo-British trade agreement.*

1. Introduction

There are some dramatic facts to explain; for example, in 1970, British exports to India were worth half as much as in 1960, and one-third of the real 1956 level. A proper explanation requires a setting, both historical and geographical. The first deliberate and systematic contact between Britain and India came through trade. Ever since James Lancaster's visit to India in 1591,[1] trade has remained the most important of the many bilateral links.

Much of the decline in Indo-British trading relations since 1947, indeed, represents a natural acceleration of a fairly prolonged period of cultural and economic decolonization. In the eighteenth century, some mercenaries of the East India Company were cutting off the hands of Bengali weavers caught competing with British goods. Alongside such methods of economic colonialism, other internal restrictions actually prevented the flow of Indian goods within India, while British goods had free entry.[2] Yet between 1918 and 1939 senior British civil servants in India repeatedly and to some extent successfully pressed Whitehall to rearrange preferences to stimulate Indian industry and trade. Since 1947, independent India has naturally sought to speed up the removal of those trading links with Britain that were merely colonial survivals; the excessive protection of Indian domestic production diagnosed by some writers[3] may be explained partly by the felt need to give an especially hard push in favour of domestic industries which had earlier been penalized by reverse protection in favour of imports from the UK.

Apart from this semi-political factor, the decline in trade has been accelerated by changes in three economic factors: prices, incomes, and preference patterns of producers and buyers ('technology and tastes'). Prices of British goods sold to India have outpaced those of their competitors: the same applies to Indian goods exported to Britain. Real income has grown more slowly in Britain than in most of India's other customers, so that a further downward pressure has operated upon the share of trade that India can do with Britain; similarly real income has been growing more slowly in India than in most of Britain's other trading partners. As for tastes, the rapid rise in incomes in developed countries since 1945 has been accompanied by growing consumer awareness of, and hence preference for, just those products made in other developed countries—cars, refrigerators, and the like; while changes in production technology have led producers in the west to shift away from many of the raw materials produced in poor countries.

Thus we have four 'natural' factors tending to reduce the share of trade that Britain and India do with one another: retreat from an artificially expanded colonial level; falling competitiveness in the exports of both countries; relatively slow real growth in both countries; and shifts in tastes, by both suppliers and buyers, in rich countries in general away from exports by poor countries.[4]

After an initial historical survey of Indo-British trading relations, we shall examine the importance of these four explanations in the trade decline. They do not explain everything; policy by both governments and both private sectors—unconcern rather than hostility—played its part; so did the fact that British aid to India (p. 111) was more liberal, less rigidly tied to the donor's exports, than aid from other major donors. However, the major conclusion from the commodity analysis of Indo-British trade since 1947, and especially after 1957, is that quite substantial shifts in policy emphasis by both Britain and India would have been necessary to stem the decline. With the causes of decline isolated, we shall consider the likely prospects and the policy options.

2. The historical background

The Indo-British trade relationship might be dated from the granting of the East India Company's Royal Charter on 31 December 1600. Trade between Britain (or more accurately England) and the East Indies grew rapidly under the control and direction of the East India Company. During the eighteenth century the value of average annual imports from the East Indies into England and Wales increased from a little over £500,000 to nearly £5 mn, while exports rose from a mere £100,000 to £2·2mn. 'Much of the difference between inward and outward shipments was made up by the export from England of silver bullion'.[5] By the end of the century, both the size of the apparent deficit on the British trade account with the East Indies and the bullion shipments had been reduced by the East India Company's practice of using a proportion of the revenues of Bengal for the purchase of goods in India for exportation to England, and thus the use of statistics of the *value* of imports from the East Indies over-states the actual visibles deficit.

Modern trade relations began with the opening of the Suez Canal in 1869. Indeed, the demand for a fast, cheap Indo-British route made the Canal worth building. Once it was opened, Britain was well placed to dominate Indian trade until independence, although against an increasingly articulate (if ultimately sub-servient) voice from the Indian Civil Service as well as the independence movement.

We are trying to *measure* Indo-British relations. But how can we measure recent trade in its historical perspective? Separate data for India exist only since 1947, so we must aggregate figures for Indian and Pakistani trade since 1947 in order to permit comparisons with earlier years. This is fraught with problems.[6] Table 2.1 shows that, even before the opening of the Suez Canal, India was a major trading partner for Britain: the fourth largest user of British produce and the third biggest source of Britain's imports. Britain, of course, loomed much larger in India's trade picture than India did in Britain's. Around 1870[7] Britain supplied almost 80 per cent of Indian imports, while only 10 per cent of Britain's imports came from India. Similarly, while 8 per cent of Britain's exports went to India, half of India's exports were sent to Britain. Over the following century this British dominance has been increasingly eroded (table 2.3).

In the century after 1870, the value of each country's exports to the other rose greatly, although the absolute figures conceal price inflation and changes in the content of the trade figures. The decline of mutual trade *shares* has varied. India's share in Britain's foreign trade held up until the 1940s, since when it has fallen, drastically in the 1960s. Britain's share of 'Indian' imports has declined steadily since the 1880s, but the proportion of 'Indian' exports destined for the UK fluctuated around 25–30 per cent for much of the period, and again the decline has come largely in the 1960s. The mutual trade disengagement is dramatically illustrated in Figures 1 and 2. Two features stand out. First, if we ignore the depression of the 1930s, the 1960s are the earliest period when the value of British trade with India-plus-Pakistan has declined. Secondly, in all cases these historical declines accelerated sharply, not as we might expect shortly after independence, but around 1958–60.

From 1869 to 1921 British exports to India increased much faster than British imports from India. Therefore a £14·7 mn trade deficit (1869) had by 1921 been turned to an annual surplus of £64·5 mn for the UK. A growing British presence in India, especially during the First World War, an increasing market in India for industrial goods, and the cheapening of transport by the Suez Canal produced an enormous increase in British sales to India. Much of this increase was in machinery and transport equipment; these were in demand in the expanding Indian economy, where domestic manufacture was often suppressed to preserve the market for British manufacturers. By 1941 the position had been reversed; an enormous fall in British exports to British India, and a substantial rise in British imports from British India, had turned a bilateral British trade surplus of £64·5mn into a deficit of £31·4mn. It is controversial how much of this was due to the preferences negotiated in the 1932 Ottawa Agreement, which is still much resented in India. Much of the change in India's position was surely due to the fact that, while her exports with low income-elasticities such as tea and cloth were bought by Britain even during the slump, British manufacturers' exports were seriously retarded by the decline in Indian customers' real income.

In any event, the citizens of British India (unlike those of independent India) had scant cause to welcome a growing trade surplus with Britain, because it was the colonial power that decided how the accumulated reserves were to be used. The notorious Home Charges[8] amounted to a fine imposed upon India for her favourable bilateral balance with Britain. Although India's total export earnings fell sharply during the 1930s with the decline in commodity prices, Britain refused to consider any reduction in Home Charges. According to one unofficial source, India shipped an estimated £240mn. of gold to Britain over 1931–37—an amount greater than the total British gold reserves before 1930.[9] This enormous outflow of specie, despite India's huge and growing visible surplus with Britain, had much to do with the invisibles account proper, apart from the Home Charges; but even India's invisibles deficit reflected neither the market nor British generosity, but returns on enormous British investments in India, together with artificial restrictions on indigenous Indian banking, shipping, and insurance.[10]

The Second World War strengthened both India's visible trade surplus and Britain's need to keep control over the corresponding accumulated Indian reserves of foreign exchange. Total British exports fell sharply because of the needs of war production; British exports to India were disproportionately affected because their shipping requirements (including convoy protection) conflicted especially sharply with war needs. Although Britain's bilateral deficit with British India was barely 5 per cent of her total deficit on trade account, it sufficed to accumulate a British trading debit with India of £243mn. during the war. At least the British government, having brought colonial India into both world wars without a semblance of consent, agreed to compensate India for part of her war expenditure with sterling securities. Hence by 1945/6 Indian sterling balances stood at £1,300mn.[11] In the hands of the independent governments of India and Pakistan, and freed from the arbitrary Home Charges, these reserves constituted until the late 1950s a pool of foreign exchange from which traditional levels of imports from Britain could be either financed or (if that was not necessary) made to seem safe. Once the balances were exhausted in the crisis of 1957–8, the stage was set for an accelerated—because delayed—'decolonization' of Indian import patterns.

Indeed, most aspects of Indo-British trade relations changed very slowly between 1947 and the late 1950s (tables 2.4–2.7). However, by 1968 UK exports to India and Pakistan had fallen well below their 1957 peak. Indeed, at current prices the 1970 level of British exports to India-plus-Pakistan was not far above the level of £108·8mn achieved in 1921; at 1921 prices it would have been much less. The share of British exports going to India and Pakistan tumbled from a postwar peak of 9·2 per cent in 1956 to only 1·3 per cent in 1970.[12] The share of Britain's imports originating in India and Pakistan declined rather sooner than did the share of British exports to those countries, mainly because the latter were protected by the existence of the sterling balances to pay for them; once again there is some evidence of a sharpening of the trend around the early 1960s.

So far the view has been mainly British; what of the Indian perspective? Britain dominated the trade accounts of British India much more than vice versa from 1869 to 1947 (table 2.3). Until 1900 roughly 70 per cent of British India's imports came from Britain, and another 20 per cent from other British Empire countries, where British interests predominated. These two markets in turn absorbed over half of the subcontinent's exports. The Ottawa Pact of 1932 at least safeguarded part of this market for India's traditional exports at higher prices than would otherwise have prevailed. Nevertheless, trade dependence fell off steadily for India. During the Second World War British control of Indian foreign trade was revived with a ban on Indian trade with the Axis powers, which had accounted for about 20 per cent of Indian imports (and of exports) in the immediate prewar period. This trade was, for the most part, diverted to the rest of the Empire.

For at least ten years after independence and partition, Indo-British trade relations changed slowly; but by the end of the 1960s Britain's long dominance in the 'Indian' market had ended. It was replaced in effect by an aid-financed diarchy: in 1969–70 the USA bought 15·4 per cent of subcontinental exports and supplied in turn 30·0 per cent of imports, largely because US grants and loans were conditonal upon the purchase of US products; the USSR, a relative latecomer to the area, had by 1969–70 picked up 9·8 per cent of subcontinental exports and 5·9 per cent of imports,[13] partly because her aid agreements accompanied bilateral trade contracts involving a substantial expansion of barter trade.[14]

3. Post-independence trade relations

The first twenty years of British trade with independent India have permitted India to build up a growing visible surplus which could be[15] used (as it could not in the days of the Home Charges) to finance other import needs at a time of general balance-of-payments restriction upon India's development path.

British exports to India reached a record £176·5mn in 1957, but declined to £72·9mn in 1970,[16] although there has been a substantial recovery from that trough since then (with the dollar value doubling from 1970 to 1972), partly related to increased arms shipments, and partly to a renewed growth of tied aid. As the sterling price of British exports rose by 23·6 per cent over 1957–70, the 1970 volume was just one-third of its 1957 level.[17] Total Indian exports to Britain have done better, and though the current level is below that of the early 1950s, the decline seems to have been checked since 1965. However, because of the 71 per cent rise in the rupee price of Indian exports between 1957–8 and 1969–70,[18] the volume of trade was barely 60 per cent of its 1957–8 level.[19] Between 1960 and 1970 India's total visible surplus with Britain (as measured from the British side) came to some £228·5mn,[20] certainly greater than the transfer of UK aid net of repayments of capital and interest (pp. 108–9).

Figures 3 and 4 illustrate the effect on trade *shares*. After 1957, Britain and India began to play progressively less important parts in one another's trade structures. The decline was much faster than would have been suggested by extrapolation of historical trends (table 2.5).

We shall assess this sharp decline in the context of world trade generally, and investigate the responsibility of price changes, income changes, tastes, and policies. First, however, it might pay to inquire whether Indo-British trade relations were typical of a post-colonial disengagement (table 2.6). Of course, the exercise is fraught with difficulties; in general, if the imperial power and the former colony are large and near one another, one would expect a large 'natural' level of trade between them even after the post-colonial readjustment, so that a comparison of, say, Franco-Algerian and Indo-British trade trends might not be appropriate. As yet, little econometric work has been done on the factors influencing the trade links between countries, probably because such factors include political variables.[21]

Before examining table 2.6, we should briefly consider just what decolonization implies in economic terms for the trade relationship between an imperial and a colonial country. Principally, it increases the decolonized country's freedom to act in its own interests: to pursue a trade policy best suited to its development potential and requirements. Such a country can alter its import pattern to take advantage of cheaper sources than previously, enter into aid-trade agreements without hindrance, and change its exports should this be desirable. This theoretical freedom is often circumscribed by political or military constraints—and by the degree of economic neo-colonialism exerted by the former colonial power. At the extreme, several 'independent' states of Africa have public investment wholly, and current government budgets largely, financed by the ex-colonial power. In so far as the Yaoundé Conventions made it harder for 'francophone' Africa to sell manufactures and processed foods to the EEC, the fact that its civil servants are often effectively paid by Paris is a compensation as well as an explanation. On the other hand India and Indonesia, being large and strong-willed, were never bound as tightly—or as generously—as Gabon or Malawi.

Did the British-Indian exports link then weaken more than one should expect? In the 1950s Britain and India retained their importance, as mutual trade partners, better than did many pairs of countries still in a colonial relationship, largely because India's sterling balances gave her special freedom in importing from the UK and thus less incentive to look for alternative sources of supply (pp. 35–6). In the 1960s, however, Indo-British trade links declined faster than the average of 'ex-colonial' links in table 2.6. In 1960–70 the share of India in total UK exports fell 78 per cent, as against a 52 per cent average fall for ex-colonies in the former metropolis; for shares in the ex-colony's imports, the corresponding falls are 66 and 29 per cent. With the end of the sterling balances, India turned more to aid finance, often linked to trade (chs 3 & 7), and began to license imports with more regard to cost and other factors (financing, export credit availability, etc.). With Britain's relatively fast inflation over the 1960s, her sales to India were worse eroded than those in several other metropolis–ex-colony relationships. It will be interesting to see how far 'francophone' Africa follows, in the 1970s, India's path of trade diversification.

The other trade link, British imports from India, also declined less in the 1950s, but more in the 1960s, than most comparable colonial or ex-colonial links. Indeed, India actually raised the share of exports sent to Britain in the 1950s. Again, however, a decline set in and accelerated in the 1960s.

Although the figures in table 2.6 require caution, the decline in Indo-British trade—especially in the 1960s—does seem larger than has occurred in the case of other decolonizations, especially since Britain and India, being big and diversified as well as partially complementary traders, might be expected to have a large amount of natural and quite non-colonial trade to cushion any decline.[22] The influence of prices, incomes, and tastes will be examined in detail later; but first, to the historical context, we should add a geographical one.

4. The relationship in the world trade context

Countries export and import different goods, adopt different policies, and devalue at different times. International comparisons are therefore difficult. Nevertheless, since 1953 British export performance has been persistently inferior to that of most other developed countries, as has India's relative to most other less developed countries (table 2.7). India and Britain have exported poorly to each other partly because both have been poor exporters overall.

By 1970, in dollar terms, India had lost 64 per cent of her 1950 share of world exports, and Britain 38 per cent of her share (table 2.7), while both had lost around 20 per cent of their 1960 share. Export earnings have lagged behind those of similar economies, for whereas the rise in export earnings by developed countries was 493·2 per cent over 1950–70 Britain's rose by only 204·4 per cent, and India's growth of 76·8 per cent compares very unfavourably with the 192·3 per cent achieved by all less developed countries (l.d.c.s).[23] Matters are even worse than they seem, for both British and Indian growth in earnings owed more to inflation than did growth in their respective country groups. Hence an even poorer performance of Britain and India can be seen in their slow growth rates in export *volume:* Britain's rising by 97 per cent whilst the index of all developed countries rose by 341 per cent, and India's rising by 29 per cent against 167 per cent for all l.d.c.s (including petroleum producers) in 1950–70.

The situation as regards export prices is more complex. Britain's and India's export prices outpaced their respective groups (table 2.7). Now if these rises represented a growing world demand for their exports compared with the exports of respective trading rivals, Britain and India could congratulate themselves. Had this been so, however, they would hardly have suffered declining shares of world trade. These suggest inflation of export prices, relative to competitors, for reasons unconnected with demands peculiar to British or Indian exports; purchasers have switched to countries whose export prices have risen more slowly. In aggregate, both Britain's and India's internal inflations have outpaced their respective groups,[24] and in particular those of direct competitors. Both Britain and India have been prone to transmit domestic inflation to export prices, and the market power of each country (as a major participant in the world output of some goods) has been weakened in the long term as more competitive countries began to produce those goods or substitutes for them. Cost inflation can boost export proceeds only in the short term, for both consumer demand and alternative producers soon react to uncompetitive prices. Both India and Britain have painfully learned this lesson in basic economic theory during the 1960s, and the commodity analysis in the following two chapters demonstrates that the process selectively reduced British and Indian competitiveness in *each other's* markets, thereby contributing to the erosion of mutual influence, to the benefit of more successful trading partners.

The trading weaknesses of Britain and India have been remarkably similar. Both raised their exports, but neither quickly enough to finance growing imports. Both found themselves confronted in the mid-1960s with similar arguments for devaluation—to improve export competitiveness—and both resisted these arguments for too long. Indeed, the rate of growth of both countries' income terms of trade—i.e. the purchasing power of their exports, allowing for the rate of change of import prices—was remarkably similar: for 1957–65, it was 4·4 per cent for the UK and 4·3 per cent for India. These rates contrast unfavourably with those for developed countries (8·1 per cent) and less developed countries (5·1 per cent).[25]

Some of the explanations frequently given for Britain's poor export performance in 1958–66 are plainly wrong. It is not true that the geographical composition or commodity structure of British exports was biased towards slowly-growing markets or commodities, or was particularly sluggish. It is impossible to prove, and sometimes hard to understand, statements that British outlays on overseas sales, after-sales service, etc., were inadequate;[26] it has never been shown that additional outlays of this sort would have earned an adequate return in foreign exchange, or that they were 'insufficient' compared with the outlays of Britain's competitors in third markets.[27] Indeed the Brookings Institution's study of the UK economy, carried out in 1968, shows that about 60 per cent of the UK's loss of her share of world trade can be explained by a decline in British price competitiveness alone.[28] Price factors are also partly to blame for Britain's loss of market share in India.

What of India's declining market share in Britain? Again, there is no shortage of trade structuralists to suggest that India's stagnant export earnings reflect a commodity structure, in particular of traditional exports, giving little room for expansion as customers' incomes grow. However, just like the British structuralists, they leave open the question of why (and whether) exports have not moved away from such an allegedly unfavourable structure. Some of the attempts to absolve India from price uncompetitiveness seem contradictory: da Costa, for instance, argues that 'the demand for our exports in the period [1953–62] was . . . moderately inelastic with respect to export prices', but later states that his calculations also reveal that 'the elasticities of substitution seem to be fairly high for our key exports'.[29] Certainly most Indian exports have had to face worsening restrictions by developed customers, more usually via quotas than tariffs. The 'voluntary' quotas on jute and cotton-textile imports into Britain since 1957 and India's growing relative disadvantages in the EEC spring to mind. However, other l.d.c.s—South Korea, Hong Kong, even to some extent Pakistan—have overcome similar handicaps.

Much of the blame certainly lies on the supply side, in India as in Britain. There has been a rise in Indian export prices relative to competitors, and buyers have naturally responded by switching purchases elsewhere.[30] Measures to improve the supply side have often been introduced too late to benefit exports (p. 47), and domestic markets have been expanding so rapidly that the export incentive of producers has been correspondingly weakened; when population grows by 2½ per cent per year, Indian textiles are diverted from exports accordingly. India, as a major exporter in most of the export markets where she competes, can for a while make as well as take world prices, but when new suppliers undercut such prices, then India's export revenues ultimately suffer.[31] Thus India's market shares have been eroded by Ceylonese and recently East African teas, and by Pakistani, Hong Kong, and South Korean textiles. Until recently, Indian export duties on jute manufactures and tea have worsened the situation, by being oriented towards internal revenue-raising at the expense of export promotion.

A great deal of quantitative analysis of the causes of poor export performance has been done, both for Britain and for India.[32] It is clear in retrospect that most of the blame for Britain's poor export performance lay with her inadequate and worsening price competitiveness, at least until the 1967 devaluation. Probably this is also a large part of the explanation for India, though lagging world demand for major exports, government policy, and the special problem of semi-monopoly pricing have played their part here too. At this stage, we need do no more than recognize that both Britain and India have performed worse, in aggregate, than the rich and poor worlds to which they respectively belong; that they cannot shift much of the blame for this on to their trading partners; but that the special decline of their bilateral trade links requires some special explanation over and above these general trends. It is to these bilateral flows that we now turn.

3 BRITISH EXPORTS TO INDIA

> We have the right to expect from India an open market for our goods as a compensation for the very serious liabilities which her possession and defence have laid upon our foreign policy.
>
> SIR HENRY JAMES SUMNER MAINE, quoted in Charles P. Kindleberger, *Power and Money* (1970), p. 75.

What happened between 1957 and 1970 to turn the previous relative stability of British exports to India into an accelerating decline (table 2.4)? One factor is that India ran out of freely-usable foreign exchange (notably the sterling balances) during the 1957–8 crisis; she became increasingly dependent for imports on aid, and on barter deals tied to purchases from particular countries. British aid, especially in 1965–70, was less tightly 'tied'. Moreover, Indian priorities among *types* of imports did not help Britain, especially as India industrialized.

However, this is not the whole story. The decline in British exports to India has four main causes: British policy affecting supplies to India; Indian policy affecting demand for British goods; the structure, competitiveness, and sales effort associated with British exports; and the shift in income, distribution, and tastes affecting the demand of Indians for British goods.

1. British policy

In 1958 the Commonwealth took 37 per cent of British exports; EEC, Efta, and the USA took 32 per cent. By 1970 the proportions had changed radically, to 20 per cent and 48 per cent respectively. There was also a shift towards the developed Commonwealth, whose share of British exports to the Commonwealth rose from 45 per cent in 1958 to 49 per cent in 1968 (Fig. 3a).[1] The UK's membership of Efta since 1958, and her repeated and ultimately successful attempts to enter EEC, indicated an increasing orientation towards Western Europe. The British balance-of-payments position necessitated policy measures seeking to control British imports and, now that rising oil prices cancel out many of the gains from exchange-rate flexibility, will again do so; hence selective efforts to reduce tariff and quota restrictions within Western Europe are bound to imply a reduction in British trade with other parties. The effective exclusion of exports from l.d.c.s from the tariff reductions in the Dillon and Kennedy rounds, and the assumption of Board of Trade officials that any implementation of Unctad resolutions on generalized preferences is 'of course excluding textiles', were further indications of the trend of British policy.

With such guidance as to what would prove profitable, major British companies concentrated their sales-promotion efforts in Europe. The British National Export Council laid special stress on the activities of the Export Council for Europe, and the new British Overseas Trade Board (BOTB), set up as a successor to the BNEC by the Conservative government in March 1971, has in effect endorsed the earlier recommendations of the Duncan Report on Overseas Representation (see p. 41) and decided to concentrate its efforts on Western Europe, North America, and Japan. This naturally implies poorer personnel, less advertising funds, and less top-flight managerial effort for British sales in poor countries in general, and in India in particular, although the potential of the Indian market was later recognized—in principle—by the British Overseas Trade Board.

Since India is more industrialized than most poor countries (and it is on industrial products that inter-European trade concentrates), her trade with Britain suffers a bigger proportionate reduction, because of redirection of British efforts towards Europe, than does the trade of l.d.c.s as a whole; her spare industrial capacity, moreover, eases the task of replacing diverted British goods. But this is not the whole story. 'It is perhaps a reflection of the interest, or more properly the lack of interest, that the successive Presidents of the Board of Trade have shown towards [India and Pakistan] . . . that Mr Jay is the first President to have visited either of them since their independence.'[2] He is still the only one to have done so.

British *import* policy, too, has provided India with neither the goodwill nor the opportunities for earning sterling likely to help British *exports* to India. When Anthony Crosland, who succeeded Douglas Jay at the Board of Trade, accepted the tariff on Commonwealth textiles proposed in the 1969 report of the Textile Council,[3] it marked the culmination of a series of measures that appeared protectionist and hostile to Indian textile interests; this nearly led to the collapse of the Indo-British trade treaty, even before its inevitable supersession when Britain entered EEC. (Ironically, the treaty was briefly salvaged in December 1971, by measures which temporarily *increased* British protectionism (p. 58.) Nor are Indian feelings about British goods improved when British textile manufacturers express their fears that wicked foreign governments will use 'devious and unscrupulous methods to overcome the tariff'.[4]

Surprisingly the Duncan Report, while recommending a larger role for British diplomats in trade promotion, nevertheless suggests, by its relegation of India to the 'Outer Area', that our commercial and diplomatic representation there should decline[5]—although India, unlike Western Europe, is an area where British exports have done extremely badly, and where new exporters in particular are likely to need the linguistic skills and political savoir-faire of an experienced commercial diplomat. As recently as 1964 a British chancellor of the exchequer recognized that 'by the end of the century India could be the most important market in the world for British goods'.[6] By the end of the decade it seemed that for 'British' one should substitute 'somebody's'. At least the BNEC in August

1970 set up a special subcommittee to investigate the steep decline in British exports to India over the 1960s and to make recommendations to improve the situation.[7] Although neither the BNEC nor its successor (BOTB) released the findings of this committee, it seems as though the blame was pinned on India: for the import controls introduced to save essential foreign exchange; for the success in its import substitution attempts; and for the active efforts to diversify trade away from Britain. British companies were seemingly exonerated, and anyway, it didn't really matter , as 'the prospects in this area were not of sufficient immediate promise' to justify 'any concerted British attack on the markets of the Indian sub-continent'![8] Economics apart, one wonders who at FCO is concerned with offering India options in a trade scene (p. 34) increasingly dominated by the USSR.

2. Indian policy

This has aimed at establishing a domestic industrial base rather than at increasing the gains from trade by specialization. The central government, which itself plays a dominant role in foreign trade through the import needs of the public sector, in 1970 enlarged that role by taking over much of the private import trade, especially in essential metals and raw cotton.

Normally the Indian government refuses to allow import of major items that can be manufactured internally. 'Can be' allows numerous interpretations, but this rule ought generally to favour those countries, such as Britain, exporting more complex and sophisticated goods to India. Much depends on how import controls are interpreted; although they have existed since 1951, it was not until the foreign-exchange crisis of 1957–8 that they were rigidly applied and strengthened. The rupee devaluation led to the slight relaxation of some import controls,[9] but the subsequent changes have been concerned mainly with expanding the number of sectors and commodities where import control is practised. Currently, within the limits permitted by foreign-exchange availability, priority goes to imports of raw materials, components, and spare parts needed for a number of key industries.

By 1970 the position had become rather complicated. Some items were imported only through state agencies; others were linked to the importer's promise to export 10 per cent of total output, failing which he lost his import licence, and also his licence to expand production capacity.[10] Some goods bore heavy new import duties; for instance, as from the Union Budget of February 1969, completely assembled motor vehicles imported into India faced a 100 per cent ad valorem import duty levy. Other goods were simply banned. In April 1968 imports of 260 items were banned because of their (supposed) indigenous availability,[11] and many other goods have been added since. By 1971 state control of foreign trade was almost complete with the government receiving power to control and regulate imports and exports for indefinite periods. Further, 70 per cent of total Indian imports were being made by state agencies and the government had announced plans to take over the entire import trade 'as soon as possible'.[12]

There is no reason why all this should cause the British share in Indian imports to decline, unless British exports are of such a commodity composition as to be peculiarly affected. However, most donors of aid to India have, by double-tying and other such devices (pp. 110–12), compelled the Indian government to use that aid for their own exports—in two major cases, Soviet barter exports and US food aid, for their own exports of named commodities—while British aid has always been fairly liberal, and in 1965–70 was effectively, though not nominally, untied from British exports.[13]

From the viewpoint of British exports to India, the connection between aid and trade is important. Indian import policy is to use tied aid for all capital goods, and to allocate all other foreign exchange giving priority to raw materials and components. Such a policy must—without any Indian wickedness—imply diversion of UK aid to lower the UK's share of Indian imports, given the commodity structure of British trade with India. The very large impending growth in the claims of oil upon Indian import outlays—estimates of the share by 1980 range from 40 to 70 per cent, as against about 15 per cent in the early 1970s—strengthen such pressures.

India's own increasing manufacturing capacity has added more and more items to the list of goods which are forbidden or restricted for import to India. An example of the procedure for linking import substitution to the development of indigenous industry can be seen in engineering. Any applicant for an import licence for engineering plant worth over £42,000 must advertise to domestic manufacturers in the *Indian Trade Journal*. If there is any response, the Directorate of Technical Development will refuse the import licence.[14] This sort of thing 'certainly helps to develop India's industry [but] without regard to cost'.[15] There is defiance here of efficient economic specialization, but the construction of a diversified industrial base is seen by Indian planners as an end in itself. It means, for instance, that the import content of Indian-built buses, trucks, and cars is only 10–15 per cent (even the British figure has not fallen below 6 per cent).[16] Import substitution, expecially in capital-goods industries—in accordance with the Mahalanobis strategy of 1955–60 to build up a heavy industrial base first—has certainly reduced British sales to India; but it is not at all clear why these should have been damaged so much more than, say, sales from Japan or Germany or the USA.

3. Structural factors of decline

(i) BRITISH EXPORT STRUCTURE

Was the structure of British exports to India in 1960 to blame for their falling share in total British exports in the 1960s? Did we sell India things whose supplies we were expanding more slowly than our total export supplies? We believe this is only a minor factor. 4·2 per cent of all British exports were sent to India in 1960, but only 0·9 per cent in 1970 (table 3.2). If in 1970 Britain had sent India the same share of her exports in *each commodity group* as she sent in

1960, we can calculate from table 3.2 that 4.1 per cent of British exports in 1970 would have gone to India. Therefore, at most, only 2·8 per cent (i.e. 4·23–4·14 as a percentage of 4·23–0·90) of the decline in Britain's export share sent to India in the 1960s can be blamed on a commodity group structure of British exports to India, ill equipped in 1960 to follow the 'growth sectors' in *total* British export supplies.

British exports to India have always been primarily of manufactured goods: even in 1872–3, when detailed figures are first available, 78 per cent of British exports to India were of manufactured goods, mainly of cotton, woollen, and silk piecegoods, machinery, and railway materials.[17] The proportion rose between the 1870s and 1911 (when 94 per cent of British exports to India were in manufactures) and changed relatively little over the next fifty years; by 1970 85·5 per cent of British exports were of manufactured goods in categories 5–8 of the Standard International Trade Classification (SITC).[18] Throughout the 1960s there was no great difference between the composition of British exports to India and to the rest of the world (table 3.2) in broad aggregate terms, although if individual commodity groups—especially group 7, machinery and transport equipment—were disaggregated, this similarity would be less marked.[19] The table suggests prima facie that the decline in the share of British exports sent to India throughout the 1960s cannot be due to the *changing* commodity structure of such exports; for it changed very little over the 1960s.

Britain's exports to India are somewhat more concentrated in four major commodity groups (chemicals, manufactured goods, machinery and transport equipment, and miscellaneous manufactures) than exports to the world as a whole, as one would expect with exports to a single country, which would have more specific needs than the total market for British sales. When India is compared with other countries buying similar values of British commodities in the period, there is no great difference in the concentration of their imports from Britain by commodity groups. There have been some changes in the commodity composition of British exports to India over the 1960–70 period in the distribution of manufactures between the four major manufacturing groups, chiefly the declining share of machinery and transport equipment (mainly because of the effect of Indian import-substitution policies) and the rise in chemicals and miscellaneous manufactures.[20] Yet even these changes have been small.

The relative structural stability of British exports to India is partly due to the slow structural change of the Indian economy; the composition of Indian GNP by main commodity groups has not changed greatly over the period.[21] Moreover, the nature of traditional Indo-British trading links, and the small degree of change over the period in major British firms and managing agencies in India, rendered Indian demands for British exports less flexible among commodities than the demand of many other customers for these exports, and indeed than the demand of India for exports from other countries. But it is also true that the rapid expansion of Indian imports from non-British sources enabled Indian markets to be much more flexible in the commodity composition of non-British purchases than in that of British purchases. In any event, if we are seeking to explain the decline in the share of British exports going to India from 4·1 per cent in 1960 to 0·9 per cent in 1970, not much weight—at the very most 5 per cent, and we should guess about half that—can be attached to their commodity structure, at least in the sense that the *supply* of British exports to India did not (in 1960) show a structure much less prone to expansion than that of British export supply as a whole.[22]

(ii) INDIAN IMPORT STRUCTURE

Can the blame for Britain's export performance be substantially placed on a 1960 export structure heavy on items featuring sluggish growth in Indian *demand*? We believe not. Britain's share in total Indian imports fell from 17·9 per cent in 1960 to 6·4 per cent in 1969, but recovered to 8·1 per cent in 1970, the latest year for which information is available at time of writing. From tables 3.3 and 3.4 we can calculate that if Britain had supplied India with the same share of her imports *in each commodity group* in 1970 (strictly 1970–1) as she did in 1960 her share of total Indian imports would have been 17·2 per cent. Therefore *at most* 6·8 per cent (i.e. 17·88–17·22, as a percentage of 17·88–8·10) of the decline in Britain's share of Indian imports, 1960–8, can be blamed on a structure of British exports to India, ill equipped in 1960 to follow the 'growth sectors' in total Indian demand.

British exports to India are indeed very different in commodity structure from total Indian imports (table 3.4). However, Indian import structure in the 1960s by major commodity groups was fairly stable. Britain was, of course, ill placed to share in India's growing demand for imported food (SITC 0); conversely, the enormously expanded role of Indian chemicals imports would have boosted Britain's performance, had not her share of the Indian market plummeted from 22 per cent in 1960 to 6 per cent in 1968 and 8 per cent in 1970 (table 3.4).

So far we have looked at the structure of Indian imports by *value*, and found the changes hindered Britain rather little. An aspect of relative *price*-structure helped Britain; her share of Indian imports would have fallen even faster but for the sharp rise in the prices of the sorts of imports where Britain is best represented in India—general manufactures and machinery—compared with other Indian imports.[23] In 1960–70 these two groups of exports comprised over 75 per cent of British exports to India, but under half total Indian imports (table 3.3); their volume actually fell between 1960/1 and 1968/9, by almost 40 per cent in general manufactures and almost 20 per cent in machinery and transport.

Hence, even if Britain were 'stuck' during the 1960s with the initial (1960) structure by commodity-groups, in value terms, of her sales to India, it explains at most 7 per cent of the fall in Britain's share of the Indian market; in volume terms, even less. However, in smaller commodity sub-groups the case may be a little stronger. Some traditional British exports have been harshly affected by specific Indian import substitution. Indian imports of iron and steel and of metal manufactures fell by almost two-thirds in these eight years, while transport equipment and electrical machinery fell by almost 40 per cent, all in volume terms. Table 3.4[24] shows that the blame for Britain's declining exports cannot be much to do with the changes in the structure of Indian imports, for between 1960 and 1968 Britain's share of Indian imports fell substantially within every important commodity category.[25]

How should we account for the decline of Britain's trade with India, if there is not a great deal attributable to the changing structure of either British exports or Indian imports? There are really three relevant questions. To whom has the UK lost? Why? Finally, could the loss have been avoided?

4. The geographical composition of Indian imports

The most striking change (table 3.6) has been the incursion of East European countries into the Indian market, more than quadrupling their share between 1960 and 1970 (the share fell back in 1971–72 but must have grown). This expansion was largely due to the conclusion of a number of barter agreements in 1963, 1966, and 1968 between India and the Soviet Union in commodities such as machine tools, rolled steel products, and medical instruments, which had previously figured large in British exports to India. [26] Such barter deals or trade agreements were linked to Soviet loans, a policy at once more liberal and less liberal than that of most western lenders; more because India could repay loans in kind, less because the loans are fully double-tied.

The USA has enjoyed the largest share of the Indian import market since before 1960. In the mid-1960s the share was inflated by food aid imported under US Public Laws 480 and 665 to fill gaps created by inadequate Indian harvests. By the end of the decade agricultural production within India was moving towards self-sufficiency and the resultant decline in food aid meant that the artificially high share of the USA in Indian imports had begun to shrink.

The redirection of India's import requirements towards the Soviet bloc seems likely to continue, unless challenged by a more liberal trade agreement with EEC than the precedent of the December, 1973, agreement suggests is probable. Both US and World Bank aid are likely to be directed proportionately away from India; US aid because of the eventual decline in India's need for regular food aid[27] and the progressive withdrawal of the USA from Asian involvements (pp. 188f.), and World Bank aid because of conscious regional diversification. Aid and trade are closely related, so that the trends of table 3.6 are likely to continue and intensify, especially if the growing mood of protectionism results in aid being even more tightly tied to trade. The growing share of India's imports 'pre-empted' by oil must further cut the west's share. If the west regards the political implications as unpalatable, then a conscious policy of trade generation will be needed; if poor countries too are to be asked to liberalize, they must be tided over (as were Taiwan, South Korea, and Pakistan) by aid-financed foreign exchange.

5. The reasons for decline

If we leave aside public and private policy decisions in both countries, there are three major reasons for the decline of the British share in Indian imports over the 1960s: the decline in the late 1950s and early 1960s of the large sterling balances India had built up during the Second World War; the relatively small *size* (for all its *real value*—p. 105) of *net* British official aid in recent Indian economic development; and the relative worsening of British export competitiveness in the Indian market. The first cause was, given the circumstances, largely unavoidable. The other two imply that the decline was, at least with hindsight, avoidable had Britain taken her trade with India more seriously.

(i) THE STERLING BALANCES

Before 1939 India maintained sterling balances in the form of securities with the Bank of England as part of her currency reserve. In 1939 they totalled Rs640mn (£48mn). During the war internal military purchases by India for the Allies, made in exchange for sterling securities, together with Britain's agreement to shoulder part of India's 'own' war expenditure, supplemented the favourable Indian trade balances with Britain, with the result that by 1945–6 India had over Rs17,330mn (£1,300mn) of sterling to her credit. Immediately after the war the British government showed its gratitude for India's wartime contributions to the Allied cause by scaling down the balances because the purchases made by Britain had allegedly been made at inflated prices, and thus India was only 'really' entitled to balances that would have resulted from purchases made at normal market prices. It was also suggested that the balances should not be released in toto immediately as the British national income would fall by 1 per cent for every Rs1,330mn released (the fact that much of the balances would be spent on British goods does not seem to have been recognized). The situation was resolved after the election of the Labour government in 1945, and an agreement was quickly reached—to release the sterling balances in instalments.[28]

At partition, independent India was credited with Rs15,160mn of balances (£1,130mn), and the first instalment was released by Britain in August 1947. Between 1951 and 1961 the first two Five-Year Plans relied heavily for their imports on these holdings of sterling, which were consequently drawn down by around Rs7,360mn, mostly during 1956–8, when a substantial gap opened up between Indian import needs and her foreign-exchange earnings. The liquidation of these balances continued during the Third Plan period, though at a slower rate. By 1965 they had fallen to Rs880mn, causing great concern, as the Indian government had, and still has, by law to maintain Rs850mn of sterling reserves as backing for the rupee currency of India.

The rapid liquidation of the sterling balances and its effects on Indian imports from Britain can be seen in Figure 3.1. When the largest falls in foreign-exchange holdings occurred[29]—1950–1, 1955–6, 1956–7, and 1959–60[30]—British exports to India achieved record levels, both in value and as a share of independent India's total imports. India during the 1950s was in some degree tied to purchasing from Britain, because of the restricted convertibility of her sterling and the dollar shortage. Further, the major role played in the Indian import sector by the British-dominated managing agencies, together with the heavy British involvement in some of the Indian industrial sectors, meant that Britain was still regarded as the principal and traditional supplier of the industrial goods needed for the industrialization strategy of the first two development plans. British exports therefore remained an important proportion of Indian imports throughout the 1950s.

The 'crisis of ambition' in 1956–8 meant a rapid run-down of India's foreign-exchange reserves, and although the 'core' Second Five-Year Plan was able to continue because of this, the near-exhaustion of the reserves by 1960 forced the Indian government 'to turn around from pillar to post in search of foreign aid'[31] for the Third Plan. The sterling balances held by India had in fact fulfilled the function of aid, thus holding the British share of Indian imports at a higher level than would otherwise have been expected. With the change in emphasis towards aid during the 1960s, British exports to India have fallen off, as Britain has been only a relatively minor aid donor.[32] The role of India's holdings of sterling balances in the context of the decline of British exports to India is that their existence in the 1950s delayed the weakening of trade links between Britain and India until the 1960s, when the direction of Indian foreign trade came under the influence of the rapid development of aid agreements following the establishment of the Aid India Consortium (AIC) in 1958.

(ii) AID TO INDIA AND BRITISH EXPORTS

The relationship of British official aid and British exports to India is treated on pp. 115–17, but some indications of the importance of that link will be briefly examined here, as part of the fall-off in British exports is undoubtedly due to the replacement of the sterling balances by official aid as the major external source of development finance. Since the start of the Second Plan in April 1956, official government aid has played a steadily increasing role in financing Indian economic development. The share of Indian imports covered by aid had risen sharply, until by the annual plans of the late 1960s utilized aid represented some 53 per cent of India's import bill (table 3.7), though this, of course, is a very small part of her investment needs, let alone of her GNP.

If we assume that trade is related to aid, then the British share of official aid utilized by India, the effectiveness of tying of British aid, and the commodity composition of British exports and Indian imports will all affect the British share of Indian aid-financed imports. During the 1960s Britain was only a minor donor of official aid to India. Between April 1961 and March 1970, she contributed only 7·0 per cent of total utilized official grants and loans made available to India by donor countries.[33] It is of interest that whereas in 1960 the British share of total Indian imports was 17·9 per cent, by 1969 it was down to 6·4 per cent, slightly less than the British share of utilized aid to India during 1969–71 (7·4 per cent, see pp. 104–5). If partially tied aid covered an ever-larger proportion of Indian imports then, given the small British aid contribution, the British share of Indian imports was bound to fall.

Almost all British aid to India in 1965–70 was single-tied,[34] whereas most other major aid donors double-tied their commitments. In such a situation it was only to be expected that India would get the most out of her foreign-exchange resources by diverting British aid towards those capital goods and components that would have been bought from Britain anyway, thus leaving the sterling earned from trade with Britain free to switch towards priority raw materials and components purchased outside the bounds imposed by aid agreements. Some of this switched aid was still spent in Britain,[35] but as the commodity structure of British exports to India differed considerably from the structure of total Indian imports, much of this switching was away from potential British exports.[36]

Official Indian policy reinforced this structural dissimilarity, in that tied aid was and is used for all capital goods, and all remaining foreign exchange is allocated to give priority to raw materials and components. These are not in the main trade sectors of importance to Britain, although 'Kipping aid' (p. 108) has undoubtedly helped keep up the level of British exports of industrial components.

All this is undeniably pessimistic (the logic implies that the only lower limit on UK exports to India is UK gross single-tied aid), but ignores the fact that Britain does much better from her contribution to multilateral aid to India, which seemingly brings back 50 per cent more in export earnings than the British multilateral aid commitment.[37] It is difficult to measure the proportion of the British decline in exports to India resulting from the rapid growth of external aid as a measure of financing Indian foreign trade, as the aid-trade relationship is bounded by many assumptions (see pp. 117–18). However, it is likely to have been significant.

(iii) BRITISH EXPORT COMPETITIVENESS AND INDIAN IMPORTS

Although many studies (see p. 38) blame Britain's relatively poor export performance on the declining price competitiveness of British exports, this may have less weight in the Indian context. If one removes Indian imports under double-tied aid and barter trade agreements, and also those which Britain cannot supply, there remains only a relatively limited area where price competition could be important. This area covers mainly manufactured goods, which in India may respond less to differentials in prices than in the world market as a whole.[38] In so far as price competition is important in the Indian market for manufactures, who are Britain's major competitors in this area, and how have British prices moved in comparison with theirs?

They are the USA, the USSR and other East European Countries, West Germany, France, Switzerland, Italy, and increasingly Japan. As most of the Soviet-bloc manufactures are part of trade agreements with prices fixed long beforehand, current price competition with British exports is small.[39] Against other major competitors, the British performance was bad (table 3.8), for over 1960–70 the dollar prices of British manufactured exports rose much faster than those of major competitors, while the volume of manufactured goods exported from Britain rose very much more slowly than that of competitors. Table 3.8 once again (if crudely) confirms the existence of a positive price elasticity for manufactured exports in the world market. This is important, for, as the British share in world trade falls, 'the demand for her exports is likely to get more elastic and the price of her exports relative to those of her competitors is likely to become of increasing importance'.[40]

Slightly more detailed analysis has been done on the effect of price competitiveness on British exports to the overseas sterling area (OSA), of which India has been an important member. In 1959/60—1965/6 L. B. Krause maintains that 72 per cent of the decline in the share of Britain in OSA imports is attributable to price differentials;[41] though his figures are dependent on assumed price elasticities, the result does emphasize price as an important determinant of export attractiveness. However, there is only a limited area of Indian imports where price could be important for Britain: those bought from the small pool of free foreign exchange left over after double-tied aid, barter trade agreements, and other commitments have been removed. An official British study has put this pool at 49 per cent of total Indian imports in 1961–3 and 35 per cent in 1965–7.[42] In this period, the share of British exports in purchases from the total competitive pool (100 per cent) fell from 31 to 21 per cent; the Japanese share held steady at 10 per cent, while the share of the USA and 'others' (not separated in the study) rose considerably, from 42 to 51 per cent. No evidence was offered on the causes of Britain's loss of Indian imports from the pool; price competition is hinted at, but why then did Japan do so much worse than the USA and 'others'? Is aid being used even to twist the arm of the lifeguard at the 'free' pool?

The only really satisfactory analysis of the effect of price on British exports to India would be to compare the prices of contracts for manufactured goods put out to tender by the Indian government. However, there can be no doubt that at least some of the fall in Britain's share of the free foreign-exchange pool was due to price factors. If the Krause figure for the OSA is taken for India, then £37mn of the decline in British exports that occurred between 1961–3 and 1965–7 was attributable to the declining price competitiveness of British exports.[43] But as this is equal to the *total* decline as registered by *Commonwealth Trade* over the same period, we strongly suspect that, for India, neither Krause's statistical assumptions nor those of the ODA held.

Certainly British export prices rose rapidly over 1960–70 (table 3.8); and devaluation in November 1967 seemed to have only temporarily checked the rise. As early as 1964, Indian commentators were noting that . . . 'many items of . . . [British capital goods] . . . no longer enjoy a price advantage over similar goods produced in Europe or Japan.'[44] A similar trend has been diagnosed in East Africa [45] and there are numerous commodity inquiries (ominously persisting after the sterling devaluations of 1967) which demonstrate similar results; for example the National Economic Development Committee on the Mechanical Engineering Industry has stated that export price competitiveness with Germany, France, and the USA is declining, mainly because productivity gains have not matched increases in unit costs.[46] The relationship between internal and export prices is complex, but there is a little evidence that sharp changes in the trend of the wholesale price index for home sales of British engineering goods is followed several months later by sharp changes in the export unit value index for machinery and transport equipment.[47]

Within the small pool of free foreign exchange available to the Indians, after aid repayments and other external commitments are allowed for, export prices matter; but other things matter too, especially with machinery and engineering goods.

(iv) NON-PRICE FACTORS AFFECTING BRITISH EXPORTS

Lack of officially guaranteed medium-to-long-term credits for British exports has certainly lost some potential orders. The refusal of the Export Credit Guarantee Department to underwrite credits for more than five years' duration, whereas Italy and Japan are quite prepared to underwrite credits for up to fifteen years, suggests an unfavourable view of India's ability to repay debt *to Britain*, although India has so far met all external liabilities. Some private financing of exports has gone on, but a change in official financing terms would help British exports to compete, especially with the Japanese, in the Asian markets.[48]

There have also been complaints about the delivery dates quoted by some British firms: sometimes years rather than months. Often this has reflected high British home demand, pushing export orders back in the queue; and the closing of the Suez Canal in June 1967 has increased the delivery time for some items. Transport rates have also risen considerably during the 1960s, and as the sea-haul from Britain via the Cape is considerably longer than that from Japan, British goods also suffer from some straight geographical disadvantage, especially as Japan rapidly expanded her merchant fleet, which grew from 5·8mn gross tons in 1959 to nearly 19mn gross tons in 1968, nearly as large as the British fleet.[49]

Another factor mentioned to us is the poorer British sales effort compared with competitors. In the Indian context there has probably been a willingness to leave selling within India in the hands of Indian managing agencies rather than putting in the effort and sales promotion expenditure directly, as the Japanese and West Germans have been doing.[50]

There is also the question as to how much British investment in India has affected British exports to India, by replacing exports with indigenous Indian production (ch. 6). Many of the new British capital projects in India during the 1960s led to the restructuring of exports rather than their cessation. Raw materials, components, and consumer goods used by British firms in India probably went far towards replacing exports lost through new indigenous production. For every £100 increase in net operating assets in India of British companies, an initial effect of about £20 of export orders from Britain, and a continuing annual effect of £3.50, was achieved.[51] If these figures, based on the 1955–64 period, held over the whole of the 1960s, new British investment in India on the whole contributed to total British exports to India.

6. The overall view of decline

It is difficult to unravel the factors in the decline in British exports to India since 1958, when the ability of the Indian holdings of sterling balances to prop up the British share of Indian imports began to fail. The large-scale Soviet-bloc incursion in the Indian market, with tightly-tied aid and balanced trade agreements (reinforced by willingness to help India in other fields, especially defence, when western countries declined); the growing power of Indian import substitution; the relatively minor share of Britain in the Indian aid programme; the less effective tying of British aid; the declining competitiveness of British goods with respect to price, credit, and delivery—have all contributed to the decline. It is virtually impossible to assign to each of the above factors specific proportions of responsibility. Many are inter-related; measurement of others would require heroic assumptions.

7. The future

The experience of British exports to India during the 1960s was dismal. Some of the displacement from the Indian market was unavoidable, but much was seemingly lost by default. Will the future be better, as the dramatic recovery of the early 1970s seems to suggest?[52]

On the Indian side, much depends upon the growth of the Indian economy in general. Even in the projections of imports for the period up to 1980/1 given in 1969 in the draft Fourth Five-Year Plan, total imports were expected to rise only by 36 per cent in value terms over the period 1967/8 to 1980/1.[53] If the UK sets herself the target of regaining the 1967 share of Indian imports—not impossible given the likely increase in real British aid to India and the decline of the American share of imports as food aid ends—then the 1980/1 import target represents an opportunity for Britain to raise its exports to India to £150mn, a level last achieved in 1961. By 1972 UK exports to India had almost doubled in two years, and stood at £141·2mn. Even allowing for inflation, this was well on the way to the 1980–1 target suggested as possible. Part of this sudden improvement was due to short-term factors, but despite the impact of EEC some of it could well persist during the next decade.

However, in the sectors of major potential for Britain (machinery, transport equipment, and metal manufactures), the going will not be easy. There will be a change of emphasis away from the relatively simple and unsophisticated plant that has formed much of Britain's export to India in the past towards more sophisticated equipment that India will require in the future and will not be able to manufacture internally. As Professor E.A.G. Robinson has pointed out, Britain's ability to design, develop, and export competitively such new equipment will largely determine whether she can improve her share of Indian imports.[54] When India, with almost one-sixth of the world's population, begins to accelerate her development, will Britain still want to send her barely one-hundredth of total exports?

Apart from design factors and marketing determination, much depends on British trade policy generally. The Duncan Report, though not officially adopted, has a pessimistic message for British exporters to India: one of its major recommendations implied that British export-promotion efforts should be shifted towards areas like North America and Europe, which were seen as growth markets.[55] Trade opportunities in countries in the 'Outer Area' like India are assumed to be less worth cultivating. Yet the medium-term gains from balanced expansion of Indo-EEC trade, to the economic efficiency and political range of choice of all parties, could far outweigh the gains from continued concentration on exchanges of similar goods among similar countries. Britain's diplomats and commercial counsellors in India recognize the size and the importance of their task, and understand that 'it is very definitely in our long-term commerical interest that the Indian development effort should succeed'.[56] It will certainly be in somebody's interest.

4 INDIAN EXPORTS TO BRITAIN

> The basic index of self-reliance is the strength of the exports of the country. If exports are high and rising, the currency as well as the country will become strong and self-reliant. The expansion of exports must at least keep pace with the expansion of the national product.
> JITENDRA DHOLAKIA, 'Is economic self-reliance attainable?', *Southern Economist*, 15 Aug. 1972.

While the flow of goods from India to Britain (unlike the reverse flow discussed in the previous chapter) has declined little in absolute value during the 1960s, the *share* of India in British imports has been in steady decline, as has the share of total Indian exports destined for Britain. This contraction has been caused partly by economic factors largely outside the control of either country; partly by poor economic management, especially within India; partly by policy measures adopted by both countries; and partly by policy decisions in third countries. Analysis is made easier by the fact that over half the value of British imports from India is accounted for by only six commodities,[1] one of which, tea, constitutes over one-third of the total. This permits a more detailed commodity-level analysis, and thus a fuller understanding of the causes of decline, than for British exports to India.

1. British policy

In imports as in exports, Britain from the 1960s increasingly oriented herself towards other developed countries, especially those outside the Commonwealth. In 1960, 31·6 per cent of the total value of British imports came from l.d.c.s; ten years later, only 24·3 per cent. A parallel reorientation of British trade has also taken place with the Commonwealth, for whereas in 1960, 32·3 per cent of British imports had Commonwealth origins, by 1970 this had fallen to only 23·1 per cent (table 4.1). Of the latter decline, over half was due to contractions in the shares of the less developed members, and over one-fifth to the fall in the share of India alone. The trade lost with the above-mentioned areas has been gained mainly by the developed countries of Western Europe and the USA, which increased their combined share of British imports from 37·0 per cent in 1960 to 46·3 per cent in 1970. Thus by the end of the 1960s about half of British imports came from thirteen countries.

This switch away from the Commonwealth and the l.d.c.s towards the developed countries of the northern hemisphere is partly due to changes in the commodity composition of British imports resulting from the normal process of economic growth (pp. 44–5). Most of it, however, can be attributed either to price factors or to specific British import policies by either government or business.

Although no comprehensive British import policy on the lines of the Indian import substitution drive has existed, ad hoc liberalizations or restrictions[2] have been applied, sometimes, to specific commodity groups or groups of nations. Britain's last attempt at an overall import policy that is relevant to the present analysis was the Commonwealth Preferences (CPs), which were a continuation of the Imperial Preferences that emerged from the Ottawa Agreement of 1932.

Following the repeal of the Corn Laws in 1846, free trade formed a basic tenet of British economic policy until the First World War. By the end of the nineteenth century foreign competition had already begun to affect British markets, both at home and overseas, and as much of the competition was launched from countries with protective tariff barriers, the demands for reciprocal British and Empire measures grew. The movement for tariff reform, launched in 1903 by Joseph Chamberlain, proved to be the first step towards the eventual adoption of Imperial Preferences. These, it was believed, would achieve 'Imperial solidarity, defensive strength, domestic social reform paid for by the foreign competitor rather than out of higher indirect and direct taxation, [and] steadier employment at home based on expanding empire markets'.[3] Though the revival of the British economy between 1900 and 1914 greatly reduced the demands for tariff reform, the war impelled the restriction of luxury consumption and of British merchant naval activities. This led to the introduction of import duties in 1915, which marked the beginning of the end of free trade. Under both the 1915 McKenna Budget and the measures which succeeded it,[4] Empire countries were granted a measure of preferential treatment. The first proposals to institute a comprehensive system of preferences were made at the Imperial Conference of 1923, though not until the Ottawa Conference of 1932 was an actual agreement between Britain and other members of her Empire was finally reached and Imperial Preference introduced.

Since 1945 the effect of these preferences has been much reduced, for both Britain and the Commonwealth trading partners, by the gradual change in the commodity structure of British imports away from the types of goods supplied by the other Commonwealth members. By the end of the 1950s, moreover, CPs amounted to an average preferential margin of only 4 per cent on all imports from the Commonwealth. Subsequently the effects of British concessions to Efta and the impact of the Dillon and Kennedy Rounds reduced the margin even further. From 1957 to 1967/8, the share of all UK imports affected by Commonwealth preferences (CPs) fell from one-fifth to one-seventh. Britain's entry to EEC means that they will be gradually reduced, and will disappear altogether by 1977–8 (though this is not the main way in which, by replacing advantages by disadvantages in the British market, the enlargement of EEC seems likely to harm India).[5] Indeed, for India, the value of any remaining CPs on most of her major exports to Britain has been further reduced, because most of her main competitors are also Commonwealth members.[6] The major exceptions are tobacco and some of the newer manufactured goods.

Moreover, the advantages of CPs have been reduced by the UK's quantitative restrictions in two major Indian export areas: cotton textiles and jute manufactures. The existence of a number of marginal constituencies in the cotton towns of the north of England had led both parties to edge towards protectionism. Britain still imports one-third of her textiles (as against below a tenth in EEC) mostly from l.d.c.s; and the workforce in cotton spinning and weaving has been falling sharply. Nevertheless the imposition and renegotiation of 'voluntary' quotas on India placed high-cost textile production in Lancashire above the right of British families to clothe themselves with cheaper imported products. The government's acceptance of the 1969 report of the Textile Council implied a further shift against Indian imports. Entry to EEC is involving Britain in the gradual imposition of severe new restrictions, for the preferential access to EEC for a small quota of Indian cotton textiles under EEC's generalized-preference scheme (as revised in 1974) does very little to compensate for the loss of the British quota, restricted though it was.

The EEC is also continuing, not reversing, the British retreat from liberal trading in the matter of jute products. The mechanism of jute control was designed to protect the industry in Dundee and Angus. Yet contraction of the British cotton and jute industries has been fairly rapid. Better British regional policies could speed up such a process; protectionism prolongs it. Cheap imports of textiles into Britain from poor countries help both the cause of development and the welfare of the British housewife. In the long run they make British industry more prosperous too, by freeing domestic resources for the things it does best.

But can workers and employers overcome the short-term disruption? Recent experience is mixed. The men and women who lost their jobs in cotton spinning and weaving have mostly found better jobs in electronics and similar light industries. However, several of the firms that were induced to locate around Dundee to replace the declining jute industry announced major redundancies in 1971. Clearly, free trade cannot be popular unless governments seek out the communities bearing its temporary costs and act intelligently to bring them lasting employment opportunities. This might well imply a re-examination of current British regional development policies (in so far as independent regional policies remain possible within EEC) and certainly a much more imaginative use of the European Social Fund.

2. The structure of British imports and Indian exports

(i) BRITISH IMPORT STRUCTURE

If India had still enjoyed in 1970 the same share of the British market in each major SITC commodity group as she had in 1960, then she would have supplied 2·9 per cent of British imports. In reality, her market share dropped from 3·3 per cent in 1960 to 1·2 per cent in 1970 (table 4.5). Therefore the *maximum* part of India's loss of the British market can be attributed to an initial structure ill matched to meet the growth of the various commodity groups is 17·1 per cent (i.e. 3·28–2·92 as a percentage of 3·28–1·17).

Over 1960–70 there were marked changes in the commodity composition of British imports. The share of the three primary product SITC classes—0 (food), 1 (beverages and tobacco), and 2 (inedible crude materials)—fell from 56·4 to 36·4 per cent of total imports, whilst the share of the four SITC classes of manufactures—5 (chemicals), 6 (manufactured goods classified by material), 7 (machinery and transport equipment), and 8 (other manufactures)—rose from 31·2 to 50·4 per cent of total imports (table 4.2). In other words, British imports were getting more like goods already produced in Britain; imports of some items in which India loomed large were losing ground. India's loss in the value share of the UK market cannot be blamed on sluggish prices, as compared with other UK imports. It was the *volume* of UK imports that rose so fast in SITC categories 5–8, and also in category 3, mineral oils (table 4.3).

These tables show that Britain's economic growth caused her import structure to reflect more and more the goods required by affluent consumers—not the goods produced by India. The consumption of tea and tobacco rises very slowly as income grows; purchases of sophisticated machinery, and inputs (including oil) for its use, outpace income. India's exports to Britain in 1960 largely comprised goods with low income-elasticities of demand. Thus perhaps one-seventh of the decline of India's share of the British market in the 1960s can be attributed to changes in the structure of UK import demand resulting from UK economic growth changes that Indian export supply could not conceivably meet by adaptation.

Not all this growth-induced change in British import demand reflects changed requirements from the final consumer. Another structural factor is the tendency for 'an inventive and advancing technology to produce substitutes for natural industrial materials hitherto imported'.[7] Rayon and nylon replace cotton and linen; plastic bags and paper containers replace jute sacks. All this switches trade towards the developed countries which produce the artificial substitutes, and nations like India lose. If *they* try to switch to artificial substitutes for export, they are fored to accept high protective barriers around these new 'infant industries' of the rich world, as the 1973 GATT negotiations towards a long-term agreement for *all* textiles remoreselessly showed.

(ii) INDIAN EXPORT STRUCTURE

In 1960–1 India sent Britain about 26·8 per cent of her total exports; by 1969–70 this had fallen to some 11·6 per cent.[8] If Indian exporters, in each main SITC commodity group, had maintained the share of goods sold to Britain over this period, Britain in 1969–70 would have taken about 25·7 per cent of Indian exports.[9] Therefore, of the decline in this share between 1960–1 and 1969–70, at most 6·6 per cent (26·85–25·68 as a percentage of 26·85–11·68) can be blamed on an initial commodity group structure of Indian sales to Britain ill matched to the 'growth sectors' in Indian export supply.

(iii) CHANGES IN THE STRUCTURE OF TRADE

Since total Indian supply was sluggish, the prospects of a rapid change in structure (to adapt to changing demand in Britain or elsewhere) were poor. But *why* was the supply sluggish? Table 4.4 shows that 80–90 per cent of the value of Indian exports is in three SITC commodity groups: 0 (food—mainly tea), 2 (crude materials—mainly oilcakes and metal ores) and 6 (manufactured goods—mainly cotton textiles, leather, and jute manufactures). Apart from metal ores, which are not analysed here, all these exports depend on the success of the agricultural sector. At least until the mid-1960s, this fact was not fully appreciated by the Indian planners.[10]

Such structural changes as took place during the 1960s in Indian exports did parallel the changes in British import demand, though to a very much smaller degree: a switch from food and raw materials towards manufactured goods and machinery. This reflects the growing diversification of Indian manufacturing, but also the poor export performance of the agricultural sector. Has this parallel switching of UK import and Indian export structures further weakened the structural explanation of decline in Indo-British trade?

Since 1960 India has lost well over 60 per cent of her initial 3·2 per cent share in British imports (table 4.5). The major losses have occurred in SITC categories 0 and 6, which comprise some 80 per cent of Indian exports to Britain, being groups where India has a fairly large share of the British market. The losses here far outweigh the changes in the Indian share of other British imports, indicating a deterioration in India's competitive position in specific commodities in these groups. The facts at commodity level amply bear this out (pp. 49–63). The only major recoupment from items outside groups 0 and 6 comes from tobacco (group 1); here India has seized the chance provided by the British embargo on Rhodesian tobacco. The erosion of Rhodesian sanctions, rather than any lasting response to the health hazards of smoking, is the main short-run threat to these sales.

We have seen that in the 1960s the initial structure of British exports to India was ill-suited to follow the 'growth sectors' both in British supply and in Indian demand (pp. 31–3). Similarly, the 'growth sectors' of Indian supply and British demand were both mismatched to the initial structure of Indian exports to Britain. In no case however can a *major* part of the blame be placed on structural factors. In all cases our analysis in terms of crude commodity-group structures leaves out the particular developments in specific markets. For British exports to India there are too many individual items involved to go into detail; for Indian exports to Britain a commodity analysis is presented below. First, a brief discussion of overall Indian export policy is required.

3. Indian export policies

Under the first two Five-Year Plans, export promotion was generally neglected, and attention was focused on industrialization for import substitution, although initially this meant importing capital equipment. The strong external sterling holdings allowed such imports without a major export effort. The crisis of 1956–8, although the effect of following such a policy, still did not result in major efforts being diverted towards export promotion but rather encouraged India to use the rising import level as a lever to attract external assistance.[11]

The Third Plan, which began in 1961, still understressed exports and concentrated on import substitution, although the first steps were made with export-promotion measures, mainly aimed at the traditional exports such as tea, cotton textiles, and jute manufactures. Hence India had to seek ever larger amounts of foreign aid as food and other imports rose and exports trailed behind. The export-promotion schemes of the 1960s were overshadowed by the continued overvaluation of the rupee.[12] In June 1966 the rupee was devalued, but most of the advantage for exports was eroded by the replacement of export subsidies by export duties on twelve of India's major foreign-exchange-earning goods. As so often in Britain, so in India: the view that key exports are unresponsive to changes in price (or in profitability) turned out to be myopic and crude (see p. 55). In India it confused the *fact* that (for example) total sales of tea by *all* exporters do not respond much to price, and the *fallacy* that the same is true of India's share of the world tea market. Since 1966 the export-promotion policies of the Indian government have been strengthened in several ways,[13] and in February 1970 the Central Budget made a large step forward by removing the export duties on tea and jute manufactures.[14]

India's export policies have lacked co-ordination. Exports were seen as a planning residual, and came very low in developmental priorities. The balance-of-payments crisis of 1956–8, the poor export performance of the Third Plan, and worsening aid prospects slowly produced a realization that better export earnings are critical for development. Consequently 'a sustained increase of exports by about 7 per cent a year is (together with an increased mobilization of internal resources) an essential element of strategy in the Fourth Plan'.[15] Hitherto, in the conflict between export promotion and revenue-raising, the former had lost out, leading to taxes that reduced the competitiveness of exports, or (in the case of jute and tea) their profitability.[16] Some people also argue that the state has played too great a role in foreign trade, and that exports would have done better left to the price mechanism.[17]

This state role has developed rapidly, especially since the inception of the State Trading Corporation of India Ltd in 1956, with its intention of broadening the scope of India's exports. Its main activities so far have been in products other than those traditional exports which loom large in Indo-British trade. It is perhaps significant that the Corporation, which maintains offices around the world to keep in constant touch with the changing trends of trade in world markets, does not have an establishment in London, where trade is dealt with by the High Commission. The continued recent expansion of state trading has culminated in a suggestion for a public-sector corporation to promote exports of packaged tea.[18]

What major problems have faced exports? First, most Indian exports depend on agriculture, and thus not only on internal policies to improve the supply and quality of raw materials but also upon the weather and the relative profitability of food and non-food crops. Secondly, rising urban incomes—together with restrictions on imports—have turned domestic demand towards potential exports such as cotton cloth and tea; together with Indian population growth, this has made the internal market easier and more profitable relative to exports. Thirdly, Indian exports of traditional items have faced increasing competition from new producers in the Third World, principally Hong Kong and Taiwan in cotton textiles, East Pakistan (now Bangladesh) in jute manufactures, and East Africa in tea; from synthetics; and from innovations in packing and handling. Fourthly, throughout the 1950s and 1960s exports of many Indian goods have been hit by tariffs and turnover taxes (tea) and quotas (cotton textiles, jute manufactures) in the importing countries.

How successful has Indian export policy been in the face of the above problems? India's export performance, both in value and volume terms, has been below average for the l.d.c.s (table 2.7) and substantially below world averages. Exports as a percentage of imports (table 4.6) have dropped substantially since 1948 (recovering slightly since 1968). Thus heavier reliance has been placed on foreign aid. The new belief in 'self-reliance' and the worsening aid prospects have compelled revision of this strategy; the 1966 devaluation made revision possible. It would be quite wrong to extrapolate India's poor performance into the 1970s, either in Britain or elsewhere.

There were considerable variations between different commodity groups (table 4.7), but the *volume* of all India's main commodity exports remained sluggish, with cotton and jute textiles, tea, and tobacco all below or little above their 1958 level. Only machinery (from a very low 1958 base), leather goods, and oilcakes achieved satisfactory volume export rises. For the traditional exports, the increases in the value of exports registered over the 1960s were largely due to rising unit values: cotton fabrics being up 71 per cent, jute fabrics 164 per cent, leather 83 per cent, and oilseed cake 108 per cent on their 1958 export prices. However, rising export prices are desirable only if world demand is growing and the exporting country is in a secure trading situation.[19] As we shall see, this was far from the case with India's main export commodities.

4. A commodity analysis of Indian exports to Britain

In undertaking a more detailed analysis of Indo-British trade than of the reverse flow, we are aided by the concentration of Indian exports to Britain. Seven major commodities—tea, tobacco, cotton fabrics, jute manufactures, cashew kernels, oilcakes, and sugar—contribute over 60 per cent of the total value of Indian exports to Britain. This concentration declined over the 1960s, from 71·9 per cent in 1960–61 to 58·0 per cent in 1969–70.[20]

As we shall see, the major influences on changing Indo-British sales are changes in income, prices, and tastes; but 'prices' in particular are proxies for a complex of relationships. How important is India as a supplier of a particular commodity to Britain; is the British market a significant part of the world market; is India a monopolistic, oligopolistic, or marginal trader in the world market; what factors are affecting world and British demand, and Indian supply?

(i) TEA

The export of black tea has long been one of India's major earners of foreign exchange, dominating Indian exports to Britain. The British addiction to tea as a major beverage really dates from the eighteenth century, during which imports for domestic consumption rose from some 26,000 lb (11 metric tons) per annum over 1701–5 to 16·4mn lb (7,400 metric tons) by 1796–1800,[21] with much of the tea coming from the Indian subcontinent. Under British rule, India developed into the world's largest producer and exporter of tea, and naturally Britain became her major market. In 1872 some 17mn lb of tea (worth £1·4 mn) were exported from India, and of this 98 per cent (by weight) was destined for Britain.[22] Although the market for Indian tea widened, Britain remained the major importer with over 80 per cent of Indian exports until the Second World War.[23] Since independence, tea exports have constituted the major trade flow between India and Britain, in 1960–70 averaging over £53mn a year.[24] well above combined British net aid and net private investment flow to India.

The trade situation in black tea would be described by an economist as effective monopsony encountering oligopoly. The UK dominates the world tea trade, importing around 40 per cent of the total; India and Ceylon supply 70 per cent of world exports. Hence the important variables for India are the growth of demand within Britain for tea, and the relative price-output movements and policies of India and Ceylon. Sluggish British demand for tea, East African erosion of the decreasingly competitive Indian product, Britain's dominance of world tea imports (and indeed of the supply in India), and the contraction of India's market in Britain have left the bargaining relation between buyers and sellers—which is what counts in this sort of market—unfavourable to India and favourable to Britain. It is telling that tea was one of the few important commodities almost left out of the explosion in commodity prices in 1972–4.

After 1945 the demand for tea in Britain was suppressed by rationing, but with its removal in 1952 consumption and therefore imports rose. However, once prewar levels of tea-drinking (per mouth) were restored—by the late 1950s—expansion of the market relied on further rises in the intake of tea per person and on population growth. In the event (table 4.10) the 1960s saw a 15 per cent decline in the per caput consumption of tea ,[25]and as population in the UK grew by only 6·2 per cent over the same period total consumption and imports declined considerably over the 1960s (table 4.9).

There are two reasons for this decline in consumption. First, tea has acquired a traditional, middle-aged, canteen image; many young Britons have switched to coffee, with its overtones of affluence: from teashops to coffee bars. Whereas

5·4 cups of tea were drunk for every cup of coffee in 1956–60, by 1971–2 this had dropped to 1·8. The UK Tea Council's efforts to change tea's image with its 'Join the Tea Set' campaign probably helped to slow down the decline in tea drinking during the latter 1960s. In 1970 differences of opinion between Indian, Ceylon, and East African tea producers and domestic UK manufacturers (who jointly finance and promote the campaign) resulted in a cut in the advertising budget to £500,000—just when marketing men believed tea could hold its own with coffee.[26]

The second factor which has reduced consumption, and which bodies ill for the future, is the development of the tea-bag, a typical phenomenon of the 1960s. The more economical use of tea that tea-bags allow—with 350 cups of tea per lb, against 225 per lb of loose tea—results in a 35 per cent reduction in the amount of tea per cup. As tea bags' share of the total UK tea market (in 1970 around 10 per cent) is rising at 40 per cent annually (i.e. to around 14 per cent in 1971, etc.), the prospects for major suppliers like India are grim.[27]

Even in this declining market, despite the fading-out of Indonesian competition, India was unable to maintain its share (table 4.11); it fell from 54·9 per cent over 1958–60 to 40.3 per cent by 1968–70. This loss has been mainly towards East African producers, who compete with India in the common teas market (India and Ceylon compete for the quality market). India's declining share could be due to a number of factors. Total exports could have fallen; exports could have been switched to other importers; or India could have been left with unsold tea, owing to unfavourable prices compared with other producers.

Indian tea production has risen slowly since 1950, although (probably due in large part to deficient incentives) the quality of management of many plantations has left much to be desired, with large areas needing replanting, especially amongst foreign (mainly British) owned plantations.[28] The percentage of tea output exported has fallen steadily; indeed over the 1960s it declined by well over 10 per cent (table 4.12) to around 50 per cent, due to the rise in internal consumption per caput over the last twenty years (table 4.10) and to population growth.[29] Hence in volume terms India has become the second largest tea consumer, after Britain. This growth of internal demand has hit exports, with the result that Ceylon recently replaced India as the world's largest tea exporter.

As well as a decline in Indian tea exports, there has been some redirection (table 4.13). In East European countries tea has featured prominently in barter agreements with India. Africa has recently enjoyed marked rises in tea consumption per person, and in population, notably in Egypt and the Sudan. This redirection has reduced the British share of Indian exports by around one-third over the 1960s.

The importance of relative prices is harder to determine. The market is divided into a number of different quality groups,[30] and it is price differentials within such groups that matter. For 1952–62 Cohen[31] and da Costa[32] found a significant relationship between the relative export prices of tea from India and Ceylon and their share of total UK imports. With the large-scale entry of East

African producers into the UK market in the 1960s the situation becomes more complex. Table 4.14 shows that Indian tea prices for both high and low-grown varieties have been above those of their main competitors for much of the 1960s.[33] However, in both cases the differential has been reversed over the last few years, because of the 1966 devaluation and the removal of the export duty in 1970, with the result that Indian teas were substantially cheaper in both markets. Though part of the differentials may well represent quality differences, they also indicate relative production costs in the three major producing areas. Certainly Indian wage-rates outpaced those of Ceylon and Kenya in 1959–66,[34] continuing a trend of declining competitiveness through wage costs found by Singh for Indian tea exports in the 1950s.[35] By the end of the 1960s internal production costs were a key variable in determining India's share of a glutted world tea market.

Apart from cost problems, Indian producers have also had to face domestic policies unhelpful to exports. Internal cesses and excise duties remained high during much of the 1960s, and the poor state of many of the gardens has been blamed on the high level of internal taxation. Export duties, imposed following the June 1966 devaluation and removed in February 1970,[36] were also thought to harm exports; certainly the combination of export and excise duties tipped the balance of profitability for Indian growers towards sales at home, while Ceylon and East Africa stood ready to fill any consequent gaps in Indian export supplies.

It is hard to see a bright future for Indian tea exports to Britain. In view of the threatened world tea glut, caused by new East African producers and the new high-yielding VP (vegetatively propagated) teas, India and Ceylon in 1970, after a great deal of effort, achieved a short-run international tea agreement. However, the attempts by the FAO to persuade Kenya and Uganda to make this long-term have so far failed. Consumption in Britain will continue to fall as people switch to coffee and to tea-bags. India's ability to maintain her share of the contracting British market will depend on serious efforts being made to hold Indian prices and internal costs in line with her competitors.[37] The value of the tea trade may be maintained by joint efforts with Ceylon and East Africa,[38] but increasingly the future of Indian tea exports seems to lie outside Britain, especially in l.d.c.s and Comecon.[39] The Indian government recognizes that to maintain the trade with Britain greater emphasis must be placed on quality, especially in the face of the future competition from East Africa with its younger and therefore better-quality tea bushes. Replanting subsidies are to be maintained and the Indian government has announced the formation of a Tea Corporation to manage and control the production and marketing of tea in all its forms (black, green, instant, and packet), including 'where necessary' the establishment of blending and packaging units in foreign countries.[40] However with the domestic consumption expected to rise at 3 per cent during the 1970s,[41] tea production will have to grow at 3 per cent just to maintain the current level of exports. As this is substantially above the rate achieved during the 1960s (2·1 per cent—table 4.12), and as the need to replant substantial areas to VP tea involves losing their production for six to eight years, the future for exports and especially of halting the decline in the share of the British market does not look promising, at least until VP areas come into bearing on a large scale (which will not help prices).

(ii) TOBACCO

In 1968/9 unmanufactured tobacco overtook cotton textiles as India's second export to Britain, having risen from 6.3 per cent of the total in 1960/1 to 9·6 per cent in 1969/70.[42] Though this may look promising for India, the future is not so bright.

India is second only to China in her area under tobacco, but low yields keep her production well below that of the USA.[43] Nevertheless, Indian production has risen steadily (table 4.15), and exports have followed suit. India is the fifth largest exporter of unmanufactured tobacco, and has maintained her share of world exports, although she has lost some of the gains of the early 1960s. Britain is the major importer of unmanufactured tobacco, and in fact is India's major market, taking over the 1960s about 37 per cent of Indian export volume.[44] In turn, India is a major source of supply for Britain, providing 12 to 15 per cent of British imports (table 4.16), at a cost of £10–12mn per annum. India has done relatively well in the British market, having steadily increased her share of total British imports since independence, lately helped by the ending of the British tobacco trade with Rhodesia following the imposition of economic sanctions on the latter in 1966. Unfortunately there are four passing clouds on the horizon.

First, British consumption of tobacco has declined from the record levels reached in the early 1960s (table 4.16), and figures for 1969 put the consumption for that year at only 243mn lb,[45] barely above the early 1950s. The main reason for this decline has been the large-scale switch to filter-tips, which by 1969 accounted for 75 per cent of all cigarettes sold in Britain. As filter tips often contain as much as 20 per cent less tobacco, the effect on total consumption has been marked.[46] This switch to filter-tips was encouraged by various increases in tobacco duty, which make it relatively more profitable for manufacturers to produce filter-tips so that their higher-duty tobacco goes further.

Second, following British entry into EEC, India's advantages in the UK tobacco market are being replaced by disadvantages. The special benefits to EEC growers mean little, since EEC imports about 80 per cent of requirements from outside the Community. Nor do the Yaoundé associates supply much of this. Turkey (and, as her special arrangements are restored, Greece), however, is another matter. And, apart from these countries with special access to the EEC, Indian tobacco sales will also face competition (from US and other sources) while enjoying a steadily declining Commonwealth preferential margin in the UK.

Third, India's success comes mostly from replacing Rhodesian tobacco, following sanctions. As several other countries ignore these sanctions with impunity, while Rhodesian Africans have not offered the minority regime serious difficulties, the British government's expectations that sanctions would soften or destroy the illegal regime appear less and less plausible. If, as might happen as a result of mounting pressures, sanctions were lifted, the big stocks of Rhodesian tobacco would drive down world prices, and erode and perhaps wipe out the Indian gains in the British market.

The final, long-term, threat to Indian tobacco exports is the continuing swing of medical opinion against cigarette smoking. It is true that, after each newly-publicized round of medical evidence, cigarette consumption per head dips and then recovers to the previous level; but the rounds are more frequent, the dips deeper and more prolonged,[47] and the recoveries towards milder, more filtered, shorter, and hence less tobacco-using cigarettes—perhaps because of cumulative impact, perhaps because of government action. This, despite the apparent loss of revenue,[48] has already begun with a ban on TV advertising and the introduction of health warnings in other advertisements and on packets. Tobacco in the 1990s could be a useless product, save for a small cigar and pipe-tobacco market where India has little scope. The recent British development of a promising artificial tobacco substitute, offering the potential of substantial import savings and some reduction in the health hazards, could be the final confirmation that Indian prospects in tobacco exports to the UK are extremely limited.

(iii) COTTON TEXTILES

Indian cotton-textile exports to Britain generated more bitterness than any other economic relationship between the two countries during the 1960s, and have threatened to remain a source of friction in the 1970s. Thus it is worthwhile to examine this particular trade flow in some detail.

The production of cotton yarn and textiles dates far back into India's past, and it was said that between B.C. 1500 and 1500 A.D. India practically had a monopoly in the manufacture of cotton goods. In the sixteenth century one early European traveller in Asia remarked that 'Everyone from the Cape of Good Hope to China, man and women, is clothed from head to foot in the product of Indian Looms'.[49] The East India Company recognized the excellent quality of Indian textiles and fostered the establishment of factories to weave cotton (and silk) goods for export to England. By 1677 some £150,000 of Indian cotton goods were being imported by the Company, and British woollen weavers were already complaining bitterly of the ruin which such imports were causing, for they were evidently being used to replace the heavier and harder-to-wash woollen products.

The pressure exerted by British woollen manufacturers was such that in 1701 an Act was passed (11 & 12 Will. III, c.10) which prohibited the wearing of cotton and silk goods and allowed the import of such goods only for the purpose of re-export. English consumers evidently evaded this law for in 1721 a further Act was passed (7 Geo. I, c.7) which prohibited the wearing of calicoes under the penalty of a £5 fine. Although the advent of the power loom enabled British manufacturers to become competitive with certain types of textiles (i.e. yarn), the importation of Indian dyed and printed goods was banned until well into the nineteenth century, and extremely heavy tariffs (66 per cent on calicoes, 27 per cent on muslins) were imposed on those Indian goods allowed in.[50] In 1835 Indian goods still paid $17\frac{1}{2}$ per cent duty, but by 1852 machine production of cotton goods in Britain had become sufficiently well established for the tariff on cloth to be reduced to 5 per cent. By 1858 such protective measures had reduced India to the position of being an exporter of raw cotton and an importer of British cotton goods.[51] With hindsight, it could be said that 'The English goods also supplanted Indian goods in other markets and thus the once great Indian cotton manfacturing industry was almost reduced to the supply of cloth for purely domestic needs.'[52]

Although the first Indian power mill had been established near Calcutta in 1817, the large-scale adaptation of power to manufacture cotton textiles only really got under way in the second half of the nineteenth century. Even so, the recovery of the Indian industry was minimal, and by 1913–14 Britain still supplied over 70 per cent of India's total domestic consumption of cotton goods.[53] During and immediately after the First World War the Indian cotton mills expanded their production considerably, and with the postwar conversion of the British government to a less negative view of Indian industrialization, a degree of protection to the Indian cotton textile industry was granted from 1930 onwards. Nevertheless, Imperial Preference remained under the new tariff system, allowing Britain to keep her competitive advantage over non-Empire (largely Japanese) producers in the Indian market. These preferences were raised during the 1930s to counter Japanese competition, and by the time of the 1935 Indo-British trade treaty, the tariffs had become more a means of enabling British textiles to compete in the Indian market than of encouraging the development of the domestic Indian textile industry.[54] It was not until the removal of Japanese and British competition by the Second World War that the Indian industry was encouraged to develop, and it was only with independence that the export of cotton textiles again became a major source of foreign exchange for India.

However, in the 1939 Indo-British trade agreement, Britain renounced the right to impose restrictions on imports of Indian cotton textiles, a decision which in retrospect was justified by the fairly painless readjustment after 1945 as the British textile industry slipped into decline. Low rates of investment in new mills and growing imports from l.d.c.s produced a sense of crisis in parts of northern England, but rather spuriously, since new industries frequently offered better wages and conditions than old ones (p. 249 n. 58). But in 1959 the resulting clamour for protection led to British government pressure, forcing India, Pakistan, and Hong Kong to impose 'voluntary' quotas on their exports of cotton textiles to the UK.

Thus trade in cotton textiles in the 1960s did not take place in a free market, but (a) with severe restrictions upon non-Commonwealth producers, and (b) for major exporters within the 'voluntary' quotas imposed on India and other countries in 1959. Bearing this in mind, we shall now look at the demand side; the supply situation; and, finally, the various agreements and related developments that took place over the 1960s.

As with many Indian exports to Britain, rapid postwar technical change affected the market, in this instance through the development of artificial fibres. In Britain, cloth and thread are increasingly being made from synthetic fibres as opposed to cotton, with the change over the 1960s being very marked (table 4.17). From 1959–61 to 1969–71 the share of cotton in the UK mill intake of various fibres fell by a quarter; marked relative price movements of the various fibres over the same period encouraged the switch. The rise in labour costs and hence laundering prices also helped synthetics, which are easily washed at home. Although more cloth is still produced in Britain from cotton than from synthetic fibres, the gap has been narrowing rapidly (table 4.18). Hence despite the change in Britain's overall textile position—from a major net exporter of cotton and man-made fibres in 1953, to a major net importer today—India, as a seller of grey and unbleached cotton fabrics, has not benefited. In fact the volume of such cotton fabrics imported into Britain declined.[55] Indeed, by 1970 British imports of woven cotton fabrics were at some 368mn square yards, 32 per cent less than the average over 1959–61. This is one reason why we cannot analyse Indo-British textile dealings in terms of a free-trading India. Threatened Indian manufacturers sought protection, both against man-made fibres and against cheaper and more sophisticated rivals from Hong Kong (and more recently Taiwan and South Korea), in the British market almost as avidly as did British manufacturers themselves.

In a contracting market, buyers have been able to impose more rigorous quality and price and delivery standards. In volume terms India's share of the British market declined in category 652.1 (well over 80 per cent of Indian cotton textile exports), and fell off sharply in category 652.2 (table 4.19). In category 652.1 (table 4.20) India has lost mainly to Pakistan, Hong Kong, and Portugal. The connection between each country's change in share and her relative rise in price, together with India's occasional non-fulfilment of her quota, suggests that prices even in this hamstrung market are important, although qualitative differences make precise statistical analysis dificult. Certainly, cotton-textile export promotion has been poor, and little attention has been paid to the quality of exports, or to improving the Indian cotton textile industry's competitiveness.[56] India's failure to hold its share of British imports, however, does not suffice to prove *overall* uncompetitiveness: she may be switching to other markets, or driven to consume more at home.

India has indeed been exporting less of her production than previously (table 4.21). Exports are a residual 5 per cent of total production after domestic demand is met. But the switch from the UK to other markets (table 4.22) was unimportant throughout the 1960s. Thus the failure in the British market is serious. It is market share that counts; the value of exports of cotton goods to Britain actually rose until 1967–8, but mainly because of the very increases in prices that have eroded India's share; moreover India had in some years been unable to sell or to supply even the restricted quotas allowed into Britain. This was ominous, as it indicated India's failure to sell her textiles hard enough to get Britain 'hooked' before she retired behind EEC protective walls.

The alternative outlets for Indian textiles are unpromising. Much higher exports to other l.d.c.s seem impossible while so many of them persist in seeking an expanded domestic cotton textile industry as a sine qua non for development planning. Comecon countries will switch increasingly to synthetics, although they are oil-intensive (this group will be a net oil exporter until the early 1980s at least). Moreover the new US protectionism, in textiles at least, seems firmly set. Hence the British market remains critical for Indian cotton textiles.

Britain takes a much larger share of her textile consumption as imports from l.d.c.s than other rich countries—over a third in 1968 as against 7 per cent in EEC. Therefore Gatt has let Britain inch her quotas upwards by only 1 per cent yearly, as against 5 per cent required of other rich importers. Renegotiation of the 1959 agreement also produced little change in the size of India's quota in the UK. Within that quota India has suffered from the gradual shift from yarn to made-up and finished cotton goods.

These 'voluntary' quotas have made little difference to the problems of the British cotton-textile industry; imports have formed a rising share of total British consumption of cotton textiles. Thus the high-cost British industry has been gradually displaced by lower-cost imports; between 1959 and 1969 the average number of looms running on cotton and man-made fibres fell from 172,100 to 74,900.[57] The protection provided by the quotas was not enough to prevent an inexorable drift towards efficiency.

After much pressure, the British government in 1969 accepted the recommendations of the Council, to replace all quotas and tariffs by a uniform 15 per cent tariff on cotton textile imports from 1 January 1972 (to which date the quotas were extended), together with certain measures designed to help the domestic cotton mills to re-equip and modernize to face external competition. The Council's proposals were intended to rationalize the method of protection, and, by providing a uniform tariff instead of arbitrary quotas, to decrease, not to increase, its severity; the share of imports in the UK domestic consumption would stay about the same. Defenders of imports into Britain from l.d.c.s have always argued that, by purchasing cotton goods cheaply, Britain gained because the scarce resources could be redirected from textiles to sectors where she was more efficient. This argument gained support from the Council's evidence that l.d.c.s achieved production costs 20–25 per cent below Britain's, and that redeployment in the past had proved surprisingly fast and painless in the British industry.[58] But the argument certainly suggests that, if Britain is to buy a given volume of cotton textiles from l.d.c.s as a whole, they should be bought in the cheapest markets. That implies, as the Textile Council proposed, a global uniform tariff: not, within the Commonwealth, arbitrary discrimination among sellers (which in the 1960s undoubtedly protected India from the growing relative efficiency of other countries, especially Hong Kong, and thus reduced the pressures for better allocation of Indian resources) nor, between the Commonwealth and other l.d.c.s, discrimination against the latter by making increasingly efficient producers like South Korea and Taiwan leap over both a tariff and a quota.

There remained, however, several objections from an Indian viewpoint to the Council's proposals. First, and most basically, the logic of the Council's argument implied not a uniform 15 per cent tariff but a uniform zero tariff. In para. 638 they argued:

'We expect the industry to be internationally competitive by the mid-1970s. *At that point we expect it to be viable, subject only to protection against goods imported at prices unrelated to costs* . . . [and to] the UK participating in any international schemes . . . for the regulation of international trade in textile goods. *We therefore envisage* a dismantling of the quota arrangements and their replacement by *a duty against imports from the Commonwealth.*'

The statements we have italicized contradict each other. If the British industry is to be viable by the mid-1970s—and nobody has shown why Britain, or an EEC including Britain, should indefinitely protect such a high-cost, easily-redeployed sector—then it will need *no* duty against fair competition. (Much Pakistani competition, supported as it is by 30 per cent export bonuses, is a different matter.)

Second, the Council convinced neither India nor many others that it was proposing a fair balance between Asian and European producers. The latter, favoured by Efta advantages (which were not substantially eroded by British entry into EEC), have been taking a fast-growing share of the British market at the cost of India and other l.d.c.s; this trend has little to do with relative competitive efficiency. Indeed, Britain's entry to EEC meant that the Council's proposals have been passed through a highly protectionist filter. Their structure was even further from EEC protection than the 'voluntary' quotas they replaced. The fact that Britain will during the 1970s probably have to revert to quotas lower than before, and with a smaller share for India, owes much to the precedent of the interim tariff period. The drawing up by the EEC of a list under the Unctad's Generalized Scheme of Preferences (GSP) and its application to a very small and fixed amount of cotton textiles is scant compensation for these changes.

Finally, Indians were naturally perturbed that they were not consulted before the UK's decision to introduce tariffs, though there were subsequent discussions. India accepted that the change might not reduce total textile sales by l.d.c.s to Britain, but depite Mr Crosland's 1969 proposal of 'higher' aid as compensation for any lost Indian trade (higher than what?), Indians were upset by this failure to consult. After all, India had twice voluntarily released Britain from trade agreements for Britain's benefit.[59] The 1969 decision was hard to justify on economic grounds: the resources needed to make British cotton textiles competitive behind a 15 per cent tariff wall could, with no such wall, be spent with better effect on both output and the balance of payments in Britain, However, even with freer trade, India's short-run prospects in the British market would not be good. Although rising oil prices may, after 1973, stem any further switch to synthetics, on the recent record not many Indian mills could meet even 'fair' competition from other l.d.c.s, at least unless tempted by the chance of really dramatic and lasting improvements in market access abroad.

For such reasons Indian pressure on Britain took a surprising turn. When India refused to allow Britain to impose the 15 per cent Textile Council tariff unilaterally, Britain gave the statutory six months' notice of her decision to abrogate the Indo-British trade agreement, so as to introduce the textile tariff, with effect from 1 January 1972. One might now have expected India to press Britain for a less protectionist solution; but when the treaty was rescued, one week before expiry, by India's grant of a waiver, a very different picture emerged. Not only did Britain impose the 15 per cent duty on Commonwealth textile imports; she retained quotas as well, and quite clearly Indian pressures as well as British manufacturing interests had been instrumental. India feared the effects on her sales of a 15 per cent tariff, making British manufacturers artificially more competitive, far less than the effects of quota abolition, which would have exposed India to the severe natural competitiveness of cheaper producers in other poor countries.

Thus the main fear of free-trade critics of the Council report—that the least efficient British textile manufacturers would be kept in, and the most efficient Commonwealth producers out, by the proposed 15 per cent tariff *as well as* quotas and not *instead*—was realized. But the method of achievement, paradoxically, involved as much pressure from Indian officials as from British producers. This has two implications for the conventional, and often correct, view that all forms of freer trade eventually help all who engage in it (by permitting them to export what they make cheaply and well, in exchange for other items). First, if a very poor country suffers temporary hardship from a particular method of freeing trade, the costs of adjustment towards more efficient lines of production—while capital is scarce and present needs great—can prove, or at least seem, prohibitive; some forms of freer trade in textiles could conceivably damage India, and the costs to the world of damage to the very poor can be offset only by much larger benefits to the less poor. Second, we live in a 'second-best' world; many poor countries are protected by one or other trading bloc (the EEC Associates, the free-trade areas in Latin America and the Caribbean, etc.) and others evade free trade (e.g. with big export subsidies on textiles, as in Pakistan); in such a world some specific moves toward partially freer trade—and the Textile Council's proposals were such a move (p. 57)—can have perverse effects. All this does not invalidate the basic free-trade lesson. India's order of preference was, and is, (1) quotas and no tariff, (2) tariff and quotas, (3) no quotas or tariff, (4) tariff and no quotas. Britain's was probably (4), (2), (1), (3) for the government, but (2), (1), (4), (3) for the less efficient (and more vociferous) manufacturers. Yet from a world viewpoint the preference was (3), (4), (1), (2), and the worst solution, (2), was eventually adopted.

This was perhaps of short-term benefit to India, but it cannot do India any long-term good to have a protected market in Britain, keeping her South Indian mills struggling along at low levels of efficiency. As the EEC quota restrictions take effect—especially where supplemented by tariffs—the tendency to prefer more to less efficient l.d.c. textile producers (for the small amount that is imported at all) will probably reassert itself. Moreover, on a wider scene, India must surely be trying to open export markets for poor countries, not to close them. As for Britain, she is certainly damaged by raising her protection against labour-intensive exports, especially since the chronic labour shortage of 1942–70, not the temporary unemployment of 1971 and 1974, is the likelier scenario for the *late* 1970s.

For poor countries as a whole, the picture of Britain becoming even more protectionist in textiles—still the manufactured export of most interest to them—even before entry in to EEC was a sad one; that it was painted with obvious Indian collusion seems bound to lead to resentment. It can hardly be kept from other poor countries that 'it was not possible for India to *publicly* complain about [the abolition of] quotas', or that the Foreign Trade Minister 'had impressed on the British Government (in May 1971) that the Indian and British industries had a common interest in persevering with quotas', while 'the British side replied that the abolition of quotas was the kind of trade liberalization measure that developing nations had been waiting for a long time'.[60]

(iv) JUTE MANUFACTURES

Since 1946 jute manufactures (namely jute yarn, woven jute fabric—used for backing floor coverings—and jute bags) have formed a decreasing share of Indian exports to Britain: 2·3 per cent by value in 1969/70, as against 4·7 per cent in 1960/1. The British market for jute goods has declined considerably (table 4.23), because of the introduction of synthetics (plastic floor coverings, artificial rubber backings for carpets, polythene and paper sacks) and the development of bulk storage and transportation of goods such as fertilizer and grain formerly carried in jute sacks. India's share of the declining British market also fell, again pointing to competitive factors (table 4.23).

Although India remains the major world producer of jute manufactures, her position was challenged during the 1960s by Pakistani industry, aided by a large investment programme in new mills and an export subsidy (table 4.24). As with tea and cotton, less of India's production of jute manufactures is being exported as higher domestic demand erodes exports, although the figure for 1966–70 in table 4.24 is affected by the raw jute supply decline caused by the droughts of the mid-1960s.

Britain is only a minor market for Indian jute manufactures (table 4.25) which go mainly to the USA, and to Eastern Europe under barter trade agreements. The decline of the British market has therefore made only a marginal difference to the development of the total Indian trade in jute manufactures, although the impact was worsened by the world-wide decline caused by India's loss of share to Pakistan.

India's major problem has been the lack of a reliable and sufficient supply of raw jute, but her many outdated jute mills have also hindered the expansion of exports. Indian producers also complained bitterly of having to face export duties while Pakistani producers enjoy a 30 per cent export bonus on jute goods. At the end of the 1960s the government of India began to take steps to overcome these problems. A state Jute Corporation was planned to undertake raw jute purchases and aid growers as well as running the jute mills, for which modernization aid was promised. In early 1973 improved relations with the main jute producer (now independent Bangladesh) permitted the establishment of a joint Jute Research Institute.

The Union Budget of 1969–70 provided for the inclusion of jute textiles in the list of priority industries, thus making it eligible for 35 per cent development rebates, and the Budget of 1970–1 finally removed export duties from jute manufacturers.[61] The hostilities during 1971, which substantially disrupted exports of processed jute, helped India to achieve some recovery in her world market share; by mid-1972 the Calcutta jute mills were working at unprecedented loads of capacity utilization, but those of Bangladesh were severely underutilized. In the 1970s the supply situation will be dominated by three factors: the capacity of India, Bangladesh, and perhaps Thailand to agree on a pricing policy that undercuts synthetics by *just* enough; the specialization in growing jute in Bangladesh, and in processing in India, likely to follow the effective opening of the frontier; and the development of high-yielding jute varieties, in a race with the attempts to cut synthetics costs fast enough to outweigh the impact of oil price rises. Indeed, despite the spiralling prices of oil and petrochemicals, the long-run outlook for jute, like tea one of the very few commodities to 'miss out' on the 1972–4 'commodity boom', remains poor.

Britain has her own domestic jute-manufactures industry, and until 1963 it was largely protected from Indian and Pakistani competition by a system of state trading administered by the Jute Control, a survival of the war. This protection was gradually reduced in the 1960s; in mid-1963 some imports were returned to private trade, while other mark-ups were reduced.[62] In November 1968 the British government announced an end to the Jute Control, and from May 1969 all jute goods imports reverted to private trade, but some imports remained under licence and others were subject to quota limitations.[63] Britain's rapidly declining jute industry, which is centered on Dundee and employs only some 14,000 in the area,[64] thus remained protected. Nor do the concessions on tariff levels offered by EEC in 1973 amount to much; given the severe quota restrictions India is unlikely to achieve any greater degree of liberalization of jute exports to Britain. India might gain at the expense of Bangladesh, but in a market that is likely to decline. Furthermore, since early 1973, high rice prices have induced some growers to shift out of jute; if raw-materials shortages again induce the short and delayed deliveries that have bedevilled the trade in the 1960s, buyers' reactions will be sharp.

(v) OILCAKES

The market for 'oilcakes'[65] in Britain is related to the number of farm and other animals in Britain, and to developments in methods of compounding their feedstuffs. Over the 1960s there has been a switch away from imported protein sources, of which groundnut and cottonseed cake and meal are major components, towards home-grown cereals and protein sources.

In a situation where British import substitution in the 1960s produced a declining market, India again failed to retain her share of the market, both in volume and in value terms. This can be seen in the big decline in the Indian share of British imports of groundnut cake and meal over the 1960s (table 4.26).

Indian exports of oilcakes depend on the production of oilseeds within India, and neither groundnut nor cottonseed production has shown a steady rise over the 1960s. Oilseed development was hit by bad harvests in the mid-1960s, low priority both for and within the farm sector, and hence a persistent lack of groundnuts. Export volume rose in the early 1960s, but then fluctuated around the 1962/3 peak (table 4.27), though prices, and thus the overall value of oilcake exports, have risen substantially. An increasing share goes to the East European countries, and Britain declined from being the major market in 1960/1 to equality with several other countries in 1969/70. It is hard to attribute the decline to demand or supply factors without more detailed analysis, but India's loss of the British import market to (mainly) West African producers, together with the switch of Indian exports to Eastern Europe, suggest two causes: trade agreements that—while they last—provide foodstuffs for East European animals, and British importers who naturally turn to cheaper sources of supply. In an export market tied to booming world demand for meat and dairy products—and given that diversion of Indian oilseeds towards domestic feedstuffs would help only the relatively rich consumers of top-grade animal protein—this is an unhappy story.

(vi) SUGAR AND CASHEW KERNELS

Together these accounted for only 2·3 per cent of Indian exports to Britain in 1969/70; therefore detailed analysis will not be resorted to. Consumption of sugar in Britain was static over the 1960s, and imports of raw sugar did not rise. Nevertheless India, finding herself with some sugar available, began exporting to Britain around 1963, and in 1970–72 sold around £2–£3mn annually. India still has a very minor share of the British sugar market, and it is unlikely that her exports, at least to Britain, will rise much during the 1970s, although India is seeking an increase in her quota for exports elsewhere from the International Sugar Organization.[66] India will benefit from the assurances on Commonwealth sugar given to Britain in 1971 (and reiterated, but with growing French opposition, in 1973)—but not much. (The 1974 price surge is short-lived.)

India is the major producer of processed cashew kernels, an increasingly popular 'party food'. Until recently India bought the cashews raw from East Africa, but is now expanding her domestic production, mainly because East African producers intend to undertake the processing themselves in future. Britain is a minor market, for most Indian exports go to the USA and USSR, but British imports have risen; provided India can improve the quality and packaging of the product, there would seem to be good prospects for this income-elastic product.

(vii) NON-TEXTILE MANUFACTURED GOODS

It is here that the hope of major expansion in Indian sales to Britain must lie. Yet such sales totalled less than £20mn even by 1970 (tables 4.2, 4.8). Apart from leather goods, they largely comprised unsophisticated items such as steel billets, rough castings, nails, and hinges. However, by the end of the 1960s Britain was importing increasing amounts of telegraphic and telephonic equipment, railway equipment, scientific instruments, and certain consumer durables from India, as well as some basic chemicals. A small but dynamic sector, India's exports of engineering products rose sharply over the 1960s, mostly directed towards the developed countries, where imports of manufactured goods were rising fastest (table 4.28). Such trade could grow substantially over the next decade, if British firms are willing to consider trading with India—and if Indian firms put more effort into marketing and export promotion.

The Engineering Export Council of India in London tries to expand Indo-British trade in engineering goods. It describes its aims in somewhat simplistic terms: to urge British firms to consider Indian producers when thinking of buying components which have a high labour content (where India undoubtedly has much to offer)—but the advantage to buyers is not made clear;[67] or where there is a need for a good which cannot be produced in Britain because the market is too small—but Britain's GNP is about 2·6 times that of India; or in new areas where India could provide samples cheaply but of requisite quality[68] —but, again, would the comparative advantage of a poor country lie in product innovation? Certainly some joint production schemes could be expanded into joint exports, with India making the high-labour-value components and Britain completing the manufacturing;[69] however, the transport costs involved in suplying the British market could act as a barrier to such schemes.[70] Further, the domestic supply of steel will also have to be expanded considerably if Indian engineering exports are to meet their Fifth Plan targets, for shortage of steel has been a major constraint on exports in recent years, and still is (despite reports that 73,400 tons of steel had been allocated to priority industries in the export sector in the first three months of 1971, the *actual* allocation was only

9,400 tons.)[71] Other problems include the provision of competitive export credit terms and the development of international spares and servicing facilities.

5. The future of Indo-British trade

One cannot be optimistic about Indian exports to Britain over the next decade or so, unless major new steps are taken. Indian trade reorientation towards the USSR—especially since the Indo-Soviet treaty of August 1971 and Britain's entry into the EEC—supplement the continuing trends in the main commodities: goods that respond little, if at all, to rising income of buyers; that face increasing competition from synthetics; that lose when purchasers find 'improved' methods of utilization (such as tea-bags). Yet India often seems unable to keep up with her rivals, who have equally good excuses. It is a pity that advocates of free markets within Britain do not turn their attention to the proposed British—cum —EEC structures of protection against the Third World. Cheaper cotton fabrics would allow British housewives to spend more on goods made in Britain; increased export earnings would allow India to purchase more manufactured goods. The problem from the British point of view is that such trade restrictions as do exist are unlikely to be removed during a period of recession or 'stagflation', for the political consequences of wiping out much of the Lancashire cotton industry or the Dundee jute industry during a period of non-full-employment are intolerable. (So perhaps are the human consequences, given governments mistrustful of direct state action against *regional* unemployment.) This particular 'hidden cost' of fiscal and monetary deflation—its penalizing effect on policies that free trade—should not be overlooked.

However, the major problem facing Indo-British trade is the impact, until 1977, of Britain's gradual removal of preferential Commonwealth tariffs and quotas, and its adoption of freer intra-EEC trade, together with the imposition of a Common External Tariff (and for many 'sensitive' products of quotas) on imports from outside EEC. It is hard to estimate the effect on Indian exports. India will certainly lose some of her current tariff advantages in the British market, although the extent of the loss will depend upon how willing the EEC is to accept demands from l.d.c.s for trade liberalization. Unfortunately, the EEC's response to the Unctad proposal for a generalized scheme of preferences for l.d.c.s' manufactured exports has been ungenerous, rigid and arbitrary,[72] even by comparison with the far-from-generous UK list (which was superseded by the EEC list when Britain entered the Community).

This Unctad proposal was accepted in principle—blessed words!—by rich and poor alike at the second Unctad Conference in Delhi in February 1968. But EEC's version cannot help India much. Textiles receive severely limited GSP access (much too little to compensate for new 'EEC' restrictions in the UK market), and processed foods are excluded. Yet India, from the first, seemed reconciled to Britain's entry in to Europe, and did little to publicize her case to the British (far less than Mauritius or New Zealand). In 1971–2 India expanded the size of the embassy in Brussels (bringing back a distinguished former ambassador to EEC, Mr K. B. Lall, and improving its very thin capacity in European languages)—yet, at this crucial moment for the India-Britain-EEC triangle, India also cut down on her High Commission in London. India's exports to the EEC have remained about 8 per cent of her total exports through-out the 1960s, and until late 1973 the Commission gave little priority to India's request for an agreement, and detailed negotiations on tariff reductions on specific commodities met with limited success.[73] In 1966 Dharma Kumar estimated that if Britain joined the EEC, Indian exports to Britain might fall by 10 per cent in the short term, but rise in the long term, if British economic growth were stimulated.[74] Subsequently British interest in securing EEC concessions for Indian exports lessened, whilst EEC terms hardened. However, the continued decline of the British share in total Indian exports, together with the changes in textile policy and the introduction of the Community's GSP, will mean that any further fall in the British share of Indian exports to the developed west will be less important, being a smaller share of a smaller total.[75] The December 1973, bilateral agreement between India and the EEC (while far short of full Associate status) is at least a *framework* for trade expansion, but the Community has shown little interest in an Indian suggestion made in 1970 of a broad commercial cooperation agreement that would cover not only trade but also aid and technical assistance.[76] On the whole we fear that India's losses in the British market are very unlikely to be balanced by gains in the rest of the EEC.

There was a noticeable change in the emphasis placed on safeguarding the interests of the developing countries of the Commonwealth between the British application for membership of the Community in the early 1960s and that of the early 1970s.[77] The later British attitude was not easy to understand. Britain seemed willing in advance to forego CPs (although accepting the EEC preferences towards exports from the French Community), and to accept the Community's common external tariff and quota proposals on textiles. Under such conditions, India's enthusiasm for expanding Indo-British trade was surprisingly well sustained (though badly publicized). Politically and economically the EEC has much to gain from liberal trading arrangements with South Asia, especially following the vacuum created by the progressive withdrawal of the USA from Asian development.

The EEC Commission was aware of the brief gap between the date of UK entry (1 January 1973) and the start of negotiations for the term of the third, post-1965, Yaoudé Convention of Association of 1 July 1973. The Comission at one time seemed ready to 'freeze' the proposed phase-out Commonwealth preferences until the Yaoundé renegotiations,[78] at least for potential Associates in the Commonwealth. It was thus perhaps unfortunate that India ruled out the associateship option *ab initio*, and accepted the EEC's own classification of Commonwealth Asia as 'non-associable'. But the concentration of the EEC's economic and political concern for l.d.c.s on African countries remains an unhealthy, and fragile, historical relic. With the right sort of boldness in Brussels and Delhi—aiming, say, at a *balanced* tripling of Indo-EEC trade by 1985 or so, with appropriate ancillary aid and adjustment assistance—it could well be the allegedly 'inward-looking' EEC that saves Indo-British relations from succuming to 'outward-looking' Britain's narrow vision. The 'framework pact' agreed between India and EEC, and under consideration by a joint working group early in 1974, could make this possible.

5 INVISIBLES

> The influx of Indian treasure [into eighteenth-century Britain], by adding consider-
> ably to the nation's cash capital, not only increased its stock of energy, but added
> much to its flexibility and the rapidity of its movement. Very soon after Plassey,
> the Bengal plunder began to arrive in London, and the effect appears to have been
> instantaneous; for all authorities agree that the 'industrial revolution' began with
> the year 1770. . . . Possibly since the world began, no investment has ever yielded
> the profit reaped from the Indian plunder.
> BROOK ADAMS, *The Law of Civilization and Decay* (1928).[1]

What should be included in that part of the current balance-of-payments
accounts called 'invisibles'? Should we include military aid and official development grants (both normally left out, and put on the capital account), or restrict
ourselves to the usual invisibles: shipping, air-freight, travel, interest, profits,
dividends, insurance, and banking?[2] If we include private transfers, as the official
balance-of-payments accounts do, can we justify excluding governmental
transfers? Here we exclude military aid, official government development
grants, and aid loans and repayments, as these are dealt with elswhere,[3] and we
include all the other standard transactions.[4]

It is surprisingly hard to find data for invisibles. The British data are obscure.
Transactions in invisibles between Britain and individual foreign countries are
often either not recorded or not made available.[5] Much of what follows is a
guide to recent developments in this relationship between Britain and India
rather than an exact record of their transactions.

1. Britain's invisibles account

Britain, throughout the 1960s, was the second largest world trader in invisibles
after the USA (table 5.1), earning in 1970 some $2,000mn, well ahead of Japan
and Germany. The British invisibles surplus was well below that of the USA,
which dominated world air transport and thus earned much from tourism as
well as from its growing role in international banking. Britain's share of world
invisibles credits fell from 17·7 per cent in 1952[6] to an estimated 10·8 per cent in
1970. However, from 1962 to 1972 British earnings from gross invisible exports
rose by 152 per cent (from £2,375mn to £5,993mn), while visible exports rose by
129 per cent (from £3,993mn to £9,134mn).[7] The role of the City in the British
economy was growing while its role in the world economy was declining.

In the period of British imperial expansion prior to 1914, invisible 'earnings'
could be relied on to provide a handsome surplus to offset the visible trade
deficit. Most of the 'earnings' comprised the returns to the large British capital
investment overseas, which in 1913 were enough to cover around 30 per cent of

Britain's imports of goods and services. This situation did not last. Large amounts of British assets were sold or lost during the two world wars, and by 1950 the invisible surplus financed only a relatively small proportion of visible imports. The decline in Britain's net earnings from shipping (despite growing world trade) and the increase in net government expenditure overseas held down the growth of invisible earnings, while Britain also became a substantial net importer on the travel account as affluence led Britons to travel increasingly abroad, both on business and for pleasure.[8] During the second half of the 1960s the picture improved (table 5.2), and although government expenditure overseas had more than doubled over 1959–69, the earnings from overseas investment, the specialized services, and civil aviation had all risen as fast if not faster, and a surplus had appeared on the travel account.[9] The result was an annual net surplus of invisibles for Britain of £665mn over 1969–71.

2. The Overseas Sterling Area and India

Britain's major trading partners on the invisibles account remain the countries of the OSA[10] (table 5.3), who in 1959–69 contributed some £2,779mn to the British balance of payments. The dominance of Britain in the invisibles account of the OSA countries declined sharply over the 1960s; Britain's share of their net outflow on invisibles (table 5.3, line 3) fell from 42·8 per cent in 1959–61 to 17·7 per cent in 1967–9. Worrying for the poor countries in the OSA was the rapid deterioration of their overall invisibles position: from an unfavourable annual balance averaging £229mn in 1959–61 to one averaging £1,037mn over 1967 9. This was the counterpart of the US and British gains from rising investment incomes and shipping costs. Between 1965 and 1969 major OSA members turned in a wide range of performances (table 5.4). India, Pakistan, and Bangladesh, which neither attract major new private investment nor produce gold, and which have few reserves, could finance their deficits on visible and invisible accounts only by massive injections of official developmental capital. India's net deficit on invisibles in 1965–9 averaged £75 mn (table 5.4)—nearly a quarter of official aid.

Over the 1960s India's invisibles account was dominated by large deficits on investment income as the interest, profits, and dividends on the substantial foreign capital in India left the country. Britain still holds well over one-third of this foreign capital (ch. 6), and thus plays a major role in India's invisibles account. The substantial and growing deficit on the investment income section of India's invisible account (table 5.5) was just outweighed for much of the 1960s by steadily rising net receipts on freight and insurance on merchandise, large-scale private transfers of capital, and net credits on government account, keeping the overall invisibles position in surplus (though a deficit appeared in 1965, the first for some time, and again in 1971). Over 1960–8 India had a net invisibles surplus of £88mn, mainly because the inflow of private transfers averaged over £38mn a year. From the viewpoint of invisible *services* alone, India ran a debit of some £348mn over 1960–9—£34·8mn per year[11] (table 5.6). The big private transfer during 1966, which suddenly boosted the overall invisibles position, was due mainly to the inflow of 'private aid' (Care, Oxfam, etc.) during the crisis caused by the successive monsoon failures of 1965–6 and 1966–7, to the effects of Indian devaluation (p. 78), and perhaps to patriotic remittances in response to the hostilities in Kashmir in 1965.

Over the 1960s the direction of India's relationships with other countries on the invisibles account changed markedly. The major change was the increased influence of the dollar area (mainly the USA) at the expense of the sterling area (mainly Britain).[12] In 1961–5 dollar-area nations dominated India's earnings on the services account (table 5.7), while the sterling area received more of India's payments for services. By 1966–71, these were also veering towards the dollar area, though the sterling area had held its share in India's earnings on the services account. The British role as a provider of services for India was evidently eroded, chiefly by the USA. When one considers the primacy of the USA in India's aid and trade programmes, such a diversion was to be expected, as many of the services or the invisibles account (such as banking, insurance, and transportation charges) are closely linked with major movements in aid and trade.

A similar switch was also evident in the net figures, for whereas the dollar area provided Rs353mn in 1964 for the Indian services account, by 1969 this had turned into an Indian deficit of Rs743mn—a substantial turnround in four years. There was also a deterioration in India's services relationship with Britain, with the net deficit of Rs287mn in 1964 rising to Rs427mn in 1969 (though the figures in table 5.7 suggest a near-static position, as they do not allow for India's relative devaluation).

The addition of private transfers to the services account produces a different picture of India's invisibles account. The 1969 services deficit with the dollar area is changed into a net credit on the full invisibles account, and the 1969 deficit with Britain on services is reduced by 30 per cent by the inflow of private transfers. Obviously such private transfers have been of great importance to India during the 1960s and need examining further.

3. The invisibles relationship between Britain and India

Before independence invisibles accounts as we know them were not available. India must have been in deficit on the services account, for Britain dominated Indian transport requirements (p. 71) and large remittances of interest, profits, and dividends returned to the UK. There seems little doubt that India ran a substantial annual invisibles deficit with Britain for much of the nineteenth century. As one Indian economist noted earlier this century:

In the time of the East India Company, and while its trading monopoly lasted, there was no nonsense about 'Invisible Imports'. . . for the balance [between total Indian exports and imports] represented the [return on the] Company's investment plainly and simply.[13]

The deficit that India ran during the Raj was not so much with Britain as with Britain-in-India, represented initially by the East India Company and later by the Raj. The notorious Home Charges (see pp. 22–3) were just such an invisibles deficit with Britain in accounting terms; but of the invisibles relationship in modern terms (table 5.8) little is known as yet. In 1930 it was suggested that 'the proportion of the vital trading, banking, and shipping business of Britain directly dependent upon our connection with India is 20 per cent'.[14] Kate L. Mitchell remarked that, at the end of the 1930s 'the value of the annual payments transferred from India to Britain in one form or another is estimated at between £130mn and £150mn',[15] but she does not distinguish between invisibles and visibles balances. Certainly during the 1930s India must have been paying heavy service charges to Britain if, as has been suggested, the total value of British capital in British India was over £1,000mn. Pramenath Banerjea suggests that much of the outflow of Rs3,000mn of gold between 1931 and 1937 was to cover invisible payments to Britain.[16]

One has to wait until independence to get any clear idea of invisibles transactions between Britain and India, and until the 1950s before sufficiently disaggregated data are available. India achieved invisibles balance with Britain in 1951, presumably due to British expenses in India connected with the Korean war.[17] In the 1960s India ran a net deficit on the services account with Britain of some £14·6mn annually (table 5.8)—more than the average net aid flow from Britain over the same period. As for total invisibles, the growing flow of private remittances to India, from British citizens of Indian origin, reduced India's overall deficit substantially (see p. 78).

The services deficit—invisibles account excluding private transfers—is entirely due to remittances of interest, profits, and dividends ('investment income') from British capital in India: £196mn in 1960–9. Apart from travel, all the other subsections of the services account registered small net credits for India, although in many cases the mutual gross flows were substantial, and (where British ownership was important) even net credits flowed out of India again as investment income. Major credit earners for India were 'other services' (banking, insurance, etc.) and 'transportation'. That 'other services'[18] should be in credit to India is surprising given the importance of Britain in this sphere although there remains some doubt about the exact size and flows of such services because of the way in which IMF data on India are aggregated.[19] Part of the explanation of the large Indian earnings on this services subsection may well lie in charges made by Indian-owned managing agencies for their services in representing British firms in India (p. 88).[20]

A closer look at the individual categories within invisibles provides some insights into the total figures and flows shown above.

(i) GOVERNMENT SERVICES

Apart from military aid (pp. 182–4), this category comprises mainly embassy and consular expenditures, plus some miscellaneous expenditures by the Indian central and state governments. Little is known about the expenditures of the Indian High Commission in Britain, but as it employs many hundreds of staff and owns substantial property, an annual expenditure of over £3mn would seem plausible (see p. 175). During the 1960s the Indian Government made several attempts to reduce both the local and Indian-based staff employed in Britain.

In 1960/1–1968/9 expenditure on salaries and office expenses of British diplomats in India, plus British Council expenditure and, until 1964/5, Board of Trade expenditure on export-promotion staff attached to the British High Commissions, totalled over £8·8mn.[21] There was also some expenditure by the Ministry of Defence, large-scale investment in a new High Commission building in New Delhi (which cost considerably more than was originally estimated), and salaries for the 600 or so Indian staff employed by the above organizations.[22]

The other major component of the government category, namely military aid and related expenditure, is covered elsewhere, but over 1960–9 India received some £25mn of military aid from Britain. Therefore in the whole 'government services' category a total net flow from Britain to India during 1960–9 of £8·5mn seems reasonable, though there is no way of disaggregating many of the items included, especially in the defence area.[23]

(ii) FREIGHT AND INSURANCE ON MERCHANDISE

On this account India has run a net credit of £17·9mn over 1960–9. Her credits include receipts for reimbursement of freight paid in advance by Indian exporters, and about this little is known. The position is complicated by the inclusion of other freight charges under the 'c.i.f.' of each country's import account and in the general transportation account. Also included are insurance payments by UK importers to Indian insurance firms for goods purchased from India. Many of these credits to India from British importers found their way back to Britain through the investment income account, as Britain had a sizeable stake in the Indian insurance business (reduced since the nationalization measures of May 1971). India's debits cover her payments on freight exports to Britain and also payments for such imports into India as are valued f.o.b. in the trade accounts. Insurance payments do not enter into the debit side. Although no breakdown between UK freight and insurance credits to India is available, for Indian invisibles as a whole such credits (IMF subsection 3) are split about 8:1 between freight and insurance.

(iii) TRANSPORTATION[24]

(a) *Shipping*. The shipping account is Britain's largest invisibles sector, though not its most profitable one. However, before and immediately after the war, British shipping used to produce a substantial surplus for the balance of payments, averaging £57mn over 1952–5.[25] Because the British fleet grew more slowly than world trade or the total world fleet, Britain became a net importer of shipping services from the mid-1950s to 1967,[26] since when the account has been in net surplus again.

India, at independence, had virtually no merchant fleet[27] and thus relied heavily for her shipping on other countries, especially Britain—which had dominated Indian shipping needs up to 1947. Since then India has steadily built up the size of her merchant fleet (table 5.9), whilst the size of the British fleet has risen only very slowly, except for a spurt after 1968.

Before 1939 British ships carried most of India's sea-borne trade, both for international and coastal trading, and thus earned large sums of money. However, Britain's share of the shipping entering and clearing Indian ports (of which a very large proportion carried Indian coastal cargoes) fell by 1960–1 to less than half of its 1938–9 level (table 5.10). Over the next ten years the British share again fell, by 47 per cent; almost half this loss was replaced by India's own ships. The familiar pattern of import substitution combined with diversification from privileged colonial positions is thus not confined to trade (cf. pp. 19–23). The purchase by the Shipping Corporation of India of three 75,000-deadweight-ton bulk carriers from the Scott-Lithgow Group on the Lower Clyde will eventually reinforce this trend.[28]

Other general trade factors are also echoed on shipping account. First, an increasing amount of Indian foreign trade was being tied to foreign aid, and 'ship tying'—notably for PL480 food aid from the USA after 1966—increasingly pushed Indian imports into US and Soviet ships. Secondly, a growing proportion of Indian imports were of oil and petroleum products and much of this was carried in Indian tankers, which increased from less than 3 per cent of the Indian fleet in 1960 to 12 per cent by 1970.[29] Thirdly, the British general cargo tramp ship, wandering around the world and seldom returning empty, was rapidly being replaced by more specialized forms of shipping (tankers, bulk carriers, and container ships) on restricted high-volume routes. Finally, there is some evidence that for general cargo—and at least until the 1967 devaluation—British freight and charter rates had outstripped some major competitors during the 1960s.[30]

It is noteworthy that India, as a relatively industrialized poor country in shipping deficit, is deeply dissatisfied with the post-colonial shipping dispensation. Cartels, she feels, fix prices with scant regard to her interests. A quite astonishing proportion of time at the second (Delhi) Unctad Conference in 1968 was devoted to shipping issues, in large part at India's prompting.

(b) *Civil aviation.* One major reason for a loss of revenue to the British shipping account has been the move from sea to air travel, which accelerated in the 1960s. At the start of the 1960s 70 per cent of passengers travelling between India and Britain went by air; by 1969 it was 99 per cent. As Britain had a major share of the sea-passenger trade between Europe and the Far East, she had earned substantial sums for the invisibles account; but with the switch to air travel Britain faced increasing competition, both from third countries—notably the cartel-busting cut-price flights by Middle Eastern air companies—and from Air India, one of the few 'Third World' airlines normally showing a profit. Air India was strengthened by the immigration flow to Britain (pp. 162–3), by the

Indian official insistence that it be used by Indians travelling abroad, and by an imaginative charter policy. Without more detailed information it is impossible to determine the civil-aviation share of the transportation account or to estimate the balance between Britain and India in this area of invisibles, but during the 1960s an average of 90,000 people per year travelled between Britain and the Indian subcontinent (India, Pakistan, and Ceylon) each year.[31] The earnings for both BOAC and Air India must therefore have been considerable.

(iv) TRAVEL

India has run a sizeable travel deficit with Britain over 1960–9 of around £14mn, mostly due to the large number of Indians studying in the UK (ch. 9).[32] However, although British tourists have flocked to Europe and North America during the past decade, a surprising number of visits is still made to India (table 5.11) —far more than in the immediate post-independence period. Table 5.11 includes a large number of visits made by non-tourists. The average number of visits made by Britons to India was about 20,000 yearly in the 1960s, and the average expenditure per visit in 1965–9, for British visitors to all areas, was about £38 per head[33]—surely more in India, limited to a richer clientele by the cost of air fares, and with her great internal distances. A rough estimate of British travel expenditure in India is £1mn per year—substantially above the figures in table 5.8. A good deal of travel expenditure must be hidden in the 'other services' group, as the IMF sources suggest.

As for India's debits, Britain earned £2·2mn yearly from the travel of Indians. The question is why the figure is not higher, for the IMF category 'travel' includes the educational expenses of Indians abroad. Over the 1960s the Indian government had released up to £600 of foreign exchange per student per year for Europe, including the UK.[34] Even if only 1,500 of the Indian students at all levels in the UK contributed £600 each to the British balance of payments per year, this covers some £900,000 out of the IMF average Indian debit to the UK of £2·2mn. If all of this was borne by India, then the drain on Indian holdings of foreign exchange was quite considerable. Admittedly the long-term benefits of such training probably outweigh the short-term cost, but it does cast doubts on the British decision to raise fees for overseas students in 1966 (pp. 142)–3.

Most of India's remaining debit to Britain comes from Indian visitors. Over 1966–8 some 17,000 Indian visitors arrived in Britain each year,[35] though the true visiting status of a few of them may be open to doubt. If their average expenditure per visit was only *half* the average for visitors from the OSA (excluding Eire, Australia, New Zealand, and South Africa),[36] there was still an annual expenditure here of over £800,000. This is a considerable drain on Indian foreign exchange, and in 1967 Mrs Gandhi requested that foreign travel be kept to a minimum to prevent a heavy drain on the already depleted Indian foreign-exchange reserves.[37] However, the easing of India's foreign-exchange position, in response to the four good harvest years 1967–70 and the delayed effects of devaluation in 1966, permitted a considerable easing of control on foreign travel. From 1970 Indians were permitted to travel abroad once every three years, spending up to £300. It is unlikely that the 20 per cent tax on rupee purchases of international tickets, imposed in the Union Budget for 1971–2 in May 1971, will greatly affect long-distance flows, and the freer travel arrangements could create an excellent opportunity for Britain. Most of India's 'travelling elite' speak English, and the USA is far away. But if Britain is to seize such an opportunity there will have to be a relaxation of the irritating and sometimes hostile entry formalities—especially at Heathrow (p. 171).

(v) INVESTMENT INCOME

This category dominates the Indo-British invisibles relationship, being responsible for a sum well above the overall Indian deficit. Hence it is worth examining in some detail.

(a) *Indian credit entries*. These include the income from the investments of the Reserve Bank of India (RBI) and of the government of India. Little is known about the composition of Indian holdings of capital in Britain, but—apart from insurance interests (pp. 76–7)—they must almost all be portfolio holdings of UK government and local-authority stock. The RBI's holdings of foreign securities are thought to be largely in the UK, but a nation-by-nation breakdown is not available.[38]

(b) *Indian debits*. Much more is known about the composition of the debit side of the Indian account. Over 1961–71 Britain earned £223mn *net* on this account (table 5.8)—far more than the official aid transfer to India (net of capital and interest repayments).

Over the 1960s global net earnings from British overseas capital exceeded new British investment abroad (table 5.12), mainly because the capital built up over past decades is still returning profits, whilst Britain's new investment overseas has been a much smaller proportion of national income than before 1914, or even between the wars. The *crude* net inflow to Britain's balance of payments— i.e. remitted earnings from overseas capital less new investment abroad— therefore rose from an average of £44mn per annum over 1961–2 to £145mn by 1969, though it later fell back somewhat.

For India the global position is, superficially, much more serious. Michael Kidron's careful investigation (table 5.13) revealed that over 1948–61 the outflow of repatriated dividends, interest and profit from India exceeded the new inflow of foreign private investment by some Rs4,713mn,[39] or approximately £353·5mn; 'foreign investors as a whole have taken out of the general currency reserve nearly three times as much as they contributed directly'.[40] However, 'directly' needs triple underlining, especially in view of the concentration of foreign investments in India in sectors producing exports—and delivering tax revenues, thus surrendering incomes that might otherwise be spent on private imports. Nevertheless so big a crude net outflow is unlikely to be turned into an inflow by these considerations.

This situation is repeated with *British* private investment in India. Between 1960 and 1971 some £136mn of net British investment[41] flowed into India, while Britain's earnings from her capital in India amounted to £236·8mn. The *direct* effect was therefore a flow of foreign exchange from India to Britain of some £100mn in eleven years (table 5·14). The rate of return has been only about 8 per cent on new manufacturing investment by Britain in India (p. 93), but with the relatively high security, and in 1967–71 the improving prospects of market expansion, British governments seem anxious to encourage further British private capital flow to India.

There is a further beneficial indirect effect for Britain. British private investment in India has increasingly been in manufacturing industry rather than the traditional plantation and service sectors of the Indian economy, leading to an increase in Indian imports of intermediate goods, components, and machinery from Britain. Britain's readiness to give 'Kipping loans' (p. 108), and the request by the Indian government for foreign companies to export more so as to cover their foreign-exchange remittances,[42] suggest that British and other private investment in India represents both a net benefit to the investing country's balance of payments, and a net cost to the Indian balance.[43]

The composition of Britain's net earnings from her private investments in India is shown in table 5.15 for 1969–71. Very little of the earnings comprise interest charges—about £300,000 per year. Most are profits (including dividends) remitted by Indian branches, subsidiaries, and associates of British firms.

Profit remittances to Britain are not a true indication of the profitability of Indian branches and subsidiaries of British firms, mainly because of the growth of unremitted profits as a source of further British investment in India. For British overseas capital as a whole, unremitted profits rose from 33 per cent of new investment (net of disinvestment) in 1961 to 77 per cent in 1968; on the crude financial flows, therefore, the short-term balance-of-payments burden on Britain has declined. For UK investment in India in 1967, 54 per cent of the total net investment of £10·6mn came from the unremitted profits of subsidiaries.[44] All but £0·2mn of the £18·3mn total net earnings of UK capital in India came from profits and dividends. Thus the crude return on British private capital in India at the end of 1967 came to 54 per cent of £10·6 plus £18·1mn or £23·8mn on a total *book*-value UK investment of £261·9mn,[45] or about 9 per cent (p. 93); but our concern here is the level of remitted profits in the Indo-British invisibles account. Unfortunately, although reliable accounts are available for British and other foreign companies' branches in India, they seldom indicate how much of the profits made by such branches were remitted to Britain.[46]

However, if we compare *dividend* remittances by subsidiaries of British companies and total net earnings from *all* UK capital in India, for 1960/1–1965/6, we find that about 40 per cent of annual remittances to Britain comprised dividends (table 5.16), leaving most of the rest to remittances of profits. Dividend remittances rose fairly steadily, but the total figure fluctuated somewhat as profit levels responded to different economic climates from year to year; clearly it is undistributed profit that 'takes the strain' of Indian trading fluctuations. There are several reasons. Directors are reluctant to allow share values to fall much below asset values (by dividend reductions) for fear of takeover; the dividend policy of multinational companies is unlikely to respond to relatively small impulses from India; and, quite possibly, financial managers of Indian subsidiaries fear that reduced dividend remittances could endanger their own jobs. In any case, it looks as if foreign private reinvestment (out of undistributed profits) may be a destabilizing element in India's economy.

The devaluation of the rupee meant that foreign investment in India had, from June 1966, to earn 50 per cent more in rupees in order to produce as much foreign exchange as before devaluation. Only those few overseas investors producing manufactured exports on a large scale can have benefited; British firms making fertilizers for domestic sale in India, or exporting items unresponsive to price cuts but using items imported into India, suffered. Hence net earnings from British investment in India fell from £25·3mn in 1965 to £21·0mn in 1969; and the rise over the 1960s fell far short of world price increases (table 5.14), although there was a recovery from the low levels reached in the rupee devaluation year of 1966, and the sterling devaluation in 1967 eased the situation greatly. As for dividend remittances, in 1963–4, of total UK capital in Indian subsidiaries and associates of some Rs1,283mn, about Rs116·4mn were remitted, or 9·1 per cent.[47] None of these indicators of return suggests that the Indian government has left UK companies with much 'fat'.

(vi) OTHER SERVICES

The gross flows in either direction on this account were fairly substantial, averaging £14–15mn over the 1960s, but on balance India maintained a small annual net credit of some £900,000 (table 5.8). As yet little is known about the composition of the gross flows (indeed, this seems a profitable area for future research). However, some indications of the nature of the transactions can be seen by looking at some of the main components separately.

(a) *Banking*. Britain has profitably provided banking services for India for well over a century. In the period up to independence, a frequent target for nationalist attacks was British domination of Indian banking, and through it of India's finance, commerce, and industry. Though this domination had been effectively diminished by 1947,[48] a number of British banks remained in operation in India, and British banking skills still financed much of India's foreign trade. By the mid-1950s some 65–75 per cent of the financing of Indian foreign trade was still being channelled through foreign banks[49] and this must have led to a substantial deficit on this account for India.

British commercial banks were still sizeable during the 1960s. The Allahabad Bank, though 92·1 per cent owned by the Chartered Bank, is nominally not a 'foreign bank' and thus was nationalized in 1970. National & Grindlays remains the seventh largest bank in India, with 53 branches and deposits in 1969 of around £100mn, although all the foreign banks together account for only 10 per cent of Indian bank deposits as a whole.[50] Little is known about the amounts or types of earnings by British banks in India.[51] *Total* British net earnings from overseas banking services rose from £22mn in 1966 to £46mn in 1969, but most of the rise was due to the increased volume of London-based banking business in Europe, especially in Eurodollars.[52] One of the few indications of the British position in *Indian* banking is the British share in the total foreign assets held by the Indian banking sector (table 5.17), averaging over 30 per cent in the 1960s.

(b) *Insurance*. British involvement in Indian general (non-life) insurance was sharply terminated by nationalization of the whole sector in May 1971. Despite the banking precedent, foreign interests were not exempt this time.

The British involvement in Indian insurance dates from the early days of the Raj. In 1790 the four insurance companies of Calcutta were under British control,[53] and even at independence 47 per cent of the non-life insurance business written direct in the country was by foreign companies[54] with Britain dominant.

In Britain's *total* invisibles balances, insurance is the most important service, with earnings in 1969 of some £150mn on the financial services account, and £243mn for the total invisibles account.[55] For India, the RBI's statements of India's balance of payments show insurance separately, though the figures presented understate India's insurance payments. Britain insures much of India's foreign trade (Lloyds earns substantial sums on business with India), yet from the RBI accounts India appears to earn more from its business with Britain than vice versa. This is because much insurance on trade enters into the Indian trade accounts rather than invisibles,[56] so that much of the Indian debit in table 5.18 must be non-trade insurance—offset, especially before the nationalization of non-life insurance in 1971, by dividend remissions, for within India British insurance companies still dominated foreign-run non-life business (table 5.19) in the 1960s.[57] The overall premium income on non-life policies effected in India attributed to British companies went up from 64·7 per cent of the total for non-Indian companies in 1939 to 69·9 per cent in 1965. With a total premium income of some £6·2mn from non-life business in India in 1965, Britain must have earned sizeable dividends on the insurance account.

Astonishingly, India's insurance stake in Britain is much greater than vice versa. In 1966, of 175 foreign-owned insurance companies registered in Britain, 11 were Indian-owned—more than any country except the USA, Switzerland, and Australia. Of the 11, 8 were writing non-life insurance, and these earned £17·4mn in non-life general business premium income—far above the corresponding (1965) figure of £6·2mn for UK companies in India.[58] Presumably, even by 1966, these 8 were benefiting from Indian immigrants, who wished to continue policies taken out in India; certainly the companies employed staff who spoke Indian languages.

Indian-owned insurance in Britain helps explain India's large insurance credit with the sterling area on invisibles account; in 1964 and 1967 India's insurance account with the sterling area actually showed a *net* surplus. However, India's insurance deficit had reached Rs31mn by 1969.[59] This might partly explain India's nationalization of UK non-life insurance companies in India. With the removal of such UK earnings from Indian insurance, India will soon return to an expanding net credit with the sterling area, as Britain's population of Indian origin rises and its insurance needs expand.

(c) *Royalties and technical fees*. Clearly Britain is in surplus, by the very nature of the developmental situations of the two nations.

World-wide net British earnings on royalties rose from some £7·2mn in 1964 to £11·7mn by 1969, with British credits rising to £111·8mn in 1969, the bulk of the earnings being technological royalties. In India Britain earned Rs206·7mn in 1960/1–1966/7 from royalty payments, technical fees, and collaboration agreements: 37 per cent of total remittances made by companies covered in the RBI survey (table 5.20). Without the 1966/7 figures, which are complicated by devaluation, British earnings of royalties and technical fees averaged £1·8mn per year, plus £0·5mn yearly in technical-collaboration agreements. By 1970 Indian payments to Britain for royalties had risen to £2·97mn (3·5 per cent of total British royalties receipts)[60] with £1·66mn, or 56 per cent of the total, from Indian subsidiaries of British firms, a somewhat smaller proportion than in the early 1960s (table 5.21). The drain of foreign-exchange reserves involved in such agreements led to the setting up in February 1966 of the Mudaliar Committee on Foreign Collaboration to examine how far, 'at our present stage of economic development, import of technical knowhow from abroad can be dispensed with'.[61] The committee came out against major governmental restraints upon collaboration and technical agreements, but some movement towards the purchase of patents and licences by the Indian government for distribution to Indian industry was mooted, much to the concern of the CBI and the British government.[62]

(d) *Other services*. These include British export houses, merchanting activities (London tea and commodity markets), brokerage undertakings, telecommunications and postal services, construction, film sales, and advertising. There is also a long tradition of British-based consultancy firms that operate in India; however, the Indian government's desire to use local technical resources, and its reluctance to provide foreign exchange either to engage British firms or to meet sterling costs of British firms established in India, means that future consultancy earnings will probably have to be covered by British aid.[63]

(vii) PRIVATE TRANSFERS

It is these that keep the Indian invisibles deficit with Britain below £20mn per year. They cover personal and institutional remittances (including private aid—see pp. 114–15), migrants' transfers, and pensions. In the IMF accounts, only net figures are given; annual Indian deficits with Britain up to 1963 are replaced thereafter by net credits, which had risen to almost £10mn by 1969–71 (table 5.8). Most of these Indian credits were, and are, due to the remittances of persons born in India—but living and working in Britain—to their relatives remaining in India.

There are no published figures on the gross flows which comprise the private transfers account, and the size of the remittances to India from Indians living and working in Britain is uncertain.

Nevertheless, with the Indian population in the UK growing and becoming more important in the UK economy, the size of such remittances could form a substantial drain on the UK invisibles account. In 1970 it was suggested that a rough estimate would be 'of remittances running through official channels of about £10 million a year';[64] the guesswork involved in this figure is revealed by the suggestion that remittances from the UK by Pakistani nationals were then running at £40–50mn per annum,[65] for the Indian community in Britain is substantially larger than the Pakistani (ch. 10). The increase in remittances from Pakistani nationals in Britain was large enough to cover half the excess of Pakistan's actual over planned export earnings during her Second Five-Year-Plan,[66] and as Pakistan ran a £30mn credit balance with Britain on the Private Transfers account during 1969,[67] such private remittances could well have been at least £20mn. This and other evidence suggests that remittances to India by Indian-born persons resident in Britain are far greater than the £10mn referred to above; we must consider these private gifts in more detail in the overall aid context (pp. 114–15).

The large IMF figure for transfers in 1966—a sudden jump to £17mn, from £2mn in 1963—is thought to be due to increased private donations from Indian nationals and others in Britain in response to the bad harvests of 1965–6 and the war with Pakistan in 1965; a sudden accelerated inflow to take advantage of the higher rates following the rupee devaluation was also noted.

Pensions are also included in 'private transfers'. A small sum is paid by Britain to retired members of the ICS and the armed services who have elected to remain in India after retirement, though other Britons who stayed on in the Indian armed services after independence receive their pensions from the Indian government.[68] If Indian-born Britons decide to retire to their birthplaces in large numbers, pension payments will rise sharply.[69]

It is surprising how little is known about the invisibles flow between Britain and India, although from 1960 to 1969 it cost India about £107mn, excluding government transfers. Much of the information is simply not collected; other parts are collected but not made available; yet other parts are available but hidden in little-known publications. When one considers that, for instance, foreign trade and private investment between Britain and India are related to and in some ways dependent upon activities within the invisibles sphere, such lack of information and consequent reliance on guesswork seems strange indeed.

6 PRIVATE INVESTMENT[1]

> The long-term aim . . . [of] my group of companies . . . is to bring the individual companies overseas up to self-government. For instance, you start off by infusing capital and management expertise and skill that you already know. You may take them overseas. We frequently take Indians, for instance, to Canada and that sort of thing. And once they know their jobs then they get promoted within the organisation. And I hope one day, so far as we are concerned, that in every country we shall have a local man at the top. This is real Aid in the true sense because we give them a feeling of partnership from the word go.
> VAL DUNCAN, 'The role of private investment', in A. Shonfield, ed., *Second Thoughts on Aid* (1965).
>
> Facts bear testimony to British monopolies continuing to draw rich profits from India. A substantial portion of these is transferred, which restricts the prospects of broadened reproduction on a national basis in India and is highly detrimental to the independent economic development of the country.
> SOFIA MELMAN, *Foreign Monopoly Capital in the Indian Economy* (New Delhi: 1963).

In 1948 Britons probably owned some 5 per cent of Indian private capital excluding land, dwellings, livestock, and inventories; and they overwhelmingly dominated the foreign investment scene, such as it was. By 1970 the proportion had fallen to 3 per cent or so, and 55 per cent of India's foreign private capital was non-British. Since independence, some 5–7 per cent of all new Indian private investment has come from abroad: Britain has provided only about a quarter, and by 1965 had been replaced by the USA as the main supplier. During the 1960s the share of UK private overseas investment going to India fell from about 6 per cent to just over 2 per cent. Once more, natural post-colonial diversification and British Eurocentricity have marched together. No doubt the exiguous inflow of *new* foreign (especially British) private capital, of the sorts India wanted, has been an effect, and not only a cause, of the gradual tightening of restrictions on *existing* foreign capital, up to the legislation of December 1973; but one wonders how far such natural responses to British unconcern have been considered, in industry or in policy-making, in Britain.

1. The historical background

To understand this major component of British-Indian relations, some quantitative scene-setting is necessary upon three stages: historical; recent British policy and performance on private capital outflow; and recent Indian policy and performance on private capital inflow. Historically, Britain has been an extremely large exporter of capital. Between 1815 and 1913 the UK invested £3,980mn abroad, mostly via the private sector.[2] The outflow of private capital has continued in this century (table 6.1), although for a time in the 1930s, during the flight of funds from Europe, the relative safety of London induced a net inflow. After

1945 net British investment overseas—the balance of long-term capital account—failed to reach pre-1914 levels (despite a record gross outflow) only because foreign investment in Britain rose fast (table 6.2). Between 1952 and 1971, Britain invested a *gross* sum of £7,446mn overseas[3]—a faster real annual rate than ever before.

Little is known about the geographical distribution of British private investment before 1939. Certainly a large share went to the Indian subcontinent. In 1911 Sir George Paish estimated British capital in India[4] at £365mn,[5] and this is plausibly close to an estimate for a substantially overlapping item: £378mn for publicly issued securities in India and Ceylon in December 1913.[6] India, on this basis, contained 10 per cent of total British overseas capital, as against 13·7 per cent in Canada and Newfoundland and 11·1 per cent in Australia and New Zealand.[7]

Very little is known about British private investment in India during the earlier days of the Raj. Shah quotes an annual investment figure for the late eighteenth century of 'about a million and a half sterling per annum', though no definition of investment is given.[8] By the second half of the nineteenth century the British government was actively encouraging private investment in India: for instance, by guaranteeing 5 per cent interest on all private capital invested in Indian railways. This gave India (or rather Britain-in-India) an extensive communications system, but did little to ensure adequate management of such capital.[9] The protective tariffs introduced to encourage Indian industries after 1917 attracted further British capital, so that annual British investment in India rose from £15mn in 1908–10 (9 per cent of total UK capital exports) to £29mn in 1921 and £36mn in 1922. The post-1918 boom in India, when dividends of the cotton and jute mills reached 120–40 per cent, collapsed by 1922, and British investment in India fell to a trickle: £2·6mn (1924), £1mn (1927).[10] This setback did not lead to any large-scale withdrawal of British capital, which by 1930 was about £458mn: 79 per cent of total external capital in India, or 14 per cent of total British long-term overseas capital. Most British capital in India at this time comprised portfolio holdings of central, state, and municipal bonds, though there was a steady switch towards direct investment.[11] In 1930 £200–250mn of total foreign capital in India was in the private sector; a British share of 80 per cent would give assets of £160–200mn.

By 1948 the book value of British private capital in independent India was around £154·5mn or Rs2,060mn.[12] The corresponding true value (at current replacement cost) was about Rs2,370mn (£177·8mn).[13] India's total private capital stock in 1948 (excluding livestock and other inventories, land and dwellings, sectors where foreign ownership was relatively very small) was about Rs49,400mn (£3,700mn).[14] Hence British capital in 1948 was already under 5 per cent of total Indian capital of the relevant types. As British capital in the private sector in *British* India in 1930 was £160–200mn, this figure of £154·5mn in *independent* India in 1948 shows that there cannot have been much total net repatriation of capital between 1930 and 1948, either during the war or before (or immediately after) independence—even allowing for inflation.[15] What of the *composition* of British capital?

Before 1914 British investment in India's manufacturing industry was effectively discouraged, owing to Whitehall's fear that it might damage the large market in India for British manufacturers. Hence in 1911 only 1·3 per cent of British capital in the private sector in India was in industry and commerce, against over 90 per cent in railways, plantations, and utilities (table 6.3). But the development of rival, non-British suppliers to India convinced London that India's industrial backwardness damaged British interests, and led the British government to encourage private investment in India.[16] By 1930 over half British capital in India was invested in industry. At independence, British capital appeared to be slightly more oriented towards agriculture than in 1930, owing to the location of a more than proportionate amount of British industrial investment in Pakistan. Perhaps, too, disinvestment from industry during the Second World War had balanced reinvestment of profits in agricultural plantations. Britain remained, however, the dominant overseas investor in all sectors.

2. British overseas private investment

(i) POLICY

In the immediate postwar period, Britain enforced stringent controls on the export of capital, and allowed it only to countries in the sterling area. Later relaxations in controls, together with developments in the UK tax system, radically altered the situation; by the mid-1960s the tax system encouraged savers to invest abroad, even though the real yield to the UK was often higher at home. The recurrent balance-of-payments crises in the 1960s caused the control on overseas investment to be reapplied and tightened up.[17] Projects were judged on the basis of their ability to repay the capital quickly and to stimulate British exports, and preferential treatment was given to applications to invest to the poorer countries of the Commonwealth.[18] These three policy objectives determined British overseas investment policy in the 1960s. After the 1970 election the new Conservative government re-emphasized the virtues of private investment overseas, proposed an insurance scheme for such investments,[19] and appeared to argue that such investment could fulfil the functions of aid.[20]

(ii) PERFORMANCE

Between 1959 and 1969 the annual rate of private British investment abroad more than doubled; most of this was direct investment (table 6.4). The major source of new direct investment has consistently been unremitted profits,[21] far exceeding the next source—net purchase of new loan and share capital, the classical form of investment. Between 1959 and 1971 Britain invested some £5,860mn overseas, some £450mn annually, of which £4,229mn (72 per cent) was direct.

Did the geographical distribution of this investment really favour the poorer Commonwealth countries? Evidence is available not only from the annual flow, but also from the stock in areas at the beginning and end of the period. Though the figures are far from exactly comparable,[22] they are disturbing from the point of view of the above policy objective.

The stock figures illustrate two major trends (table 6.5). First, both in 1958 and 1971 UK direct capital was concentrated in the developed sterling area (Australia, New Zealand, South Africa, and Eire), the EEC, and North America. Second, it is there that the UK capital stake grew fastest between 1958 and 1971.[23] The slowest-growing area was Asia, and especially India. The proportion of British capital invested in the Third World has fallen steadily since 1962 (table 6.5). It will probably fall still further.

The flow figures (table 6.6) confirm the stock data.[24] The developed countries, especially South Africa, the USA, and the EEC, have gained an increased share of the annual flow of new UK overseas investment, while the poorer countries' share in, and by 1970 even the absolute level of, annual net British private overseas investment were falling.[25] Within the Third World, the non-sterling-area countries have increased both their absolute flow and their share of the total. India, it will be noted, has not done well.

Perhaps the tendency of British firms to redirect investment away from poor countries is merely symptomatic of general world trends? Hardly; the flow of *direct* British investment to the Third World was markedly more sluggish than that of the USA, Germany and Japan (table 6.7).[26] In 1969 UK total private investment in l.d.c.s was $640mn, far below West Germany ($1,500mn), USA ($1,320), France ($780mn), and even Italy ($710mn). Yet during the 1960s the less developed world grew at a real rate of over 5 per cent yearly, and applied severe protective measures—both factors attractive to private overseas capital. World trends, at least on this admittedly cursory look, do not explain why so little British private investment has gone to the Third World.

Can higher rates of return explain Britain's shift of private investment to the developed countries? The definition of 'rate of return' is difficult, because of differential tax rates, tax agreements, and statistical problems created when profits are reinvested. In some cases, profits on initial capital may have been reinvested to avoid taxation on distributed or repatriated earnings; if such reinvestments carry subnormal rates of return, the effective yield of the *initial* capital is lowered.[27] We *can* compare the addition to net operating assets of British overseas investment in manufacturing in 1955 to 1964 with the average *pre-tax* profitability of British investment, in fifteen countries for which the Reddaway Report has given data; we found no significant correlation between the two sets of variables, and whereas the average pretax profitability over the period for all 15 was 14·1 per cent, it was 21·2 per cent for India, making it the fourth highest after Germany (47·8 per cent), Malaysia (28·7 per cent), and Italy (26·9 per cent).[28] Clearly British firms allocating investment among countries try to predict profitability, but either they fail or else their success is 'drowned' in the aggregate data from the mass of firms with little choice but to reinvest profits in the countries where they are realized. We made other attempts to find a relationship between the changing direction of British investment and profitability, but they proved fruitless, and thus it seems that other factors are at work.

A brief attempt was made to see whether the investment flows were related to other variables, such as British exports, population size of the recipient country, growth in per capita income or other factors—but in none of these cases was there a significant correlation.[29] Nor do vague generalities about varying degrees of risk help much. In a period of enormous expansion of British capital holdings abroad, relatively profitable activities in the Third World undertaken by other rich investing countries, and considerable policy incentives to steer British private capital towards poor countries, its share there fell far and fast. As yet, clearly, the forces that determine the allocation of a rich country's private investment outflows are far from understood. Can the fate of British investment in India be better understood in terms of Indian developments?

3. Foreign investment in India

(i) POLICY

The government of independent India has welcomed private foreign investment, within the overall framework of the development plans and strategies. Many foreign investors were unnerved by the Industrial Policy Resolution of 1948, in which the government allocated certain industrial sectors as state monopolies and designated others where state enterprises would play an important role. Consequently foreign investment to India slowed, but in April 1949 the prime minister made a statement on the role of foreign capital which has remained the basis of policy ever since.

The statement's importance rested on three assurances to foreign investors: that the government's general industrial policy would not discriminate between foreign and Indian undertakings; that, allowing for the foreign-exchange position, reasonable facilities would be given for the remittance of profits and the repatriation of capital; and that nationalization was not immediately likely (in 1949), but if it were ever undertaken, investors would receive fair and equitable compensation.[30] The importance of foreign capital in India's future economic development was stressed[31] and since then three assurances given above have been fully respected. The first indeed was actually relaxed in favour of foreign, notably British, investors when Mrs Gandhi exempted overseas banks from the Bank Nationalization Act of 1970, thereby imperilling that Act's constitutionality.

However, during the 1960s the government of India narrowed the boundaries within which new investment is allowed, without introducing any comprehensive framework to assess investment proposals. Each proposal required government approval, and each was judged on its own merits. Briefly the Indian government was most likely to approve investments which would be import-saving and/or export-generating; which would remove bottlenecks to development; which had an Indian majority of the issued equity capital (a sticking point for both parties in dealings between the Indian government and at least one major British investor, ICI); and which would result in the introduction of new technical knowhow and capability.

In 1968 the government of India streamlined the procedures for foreign investment by establishing a Foreign Investment Board, empowered to deal with all foreign investment and collaboration matters where the equity capital involved is less than Rs20mn and where foreign ownership is less than 40 per cent of equity. (Otherwise clearance from a cabinet committee is still required.) At the same time the government established three lists of industries on which to judge future investment proposals, the contents of which will be revised periodically in light of the prevailing conditions. The 1968 measures largely formalize the framework in which foreign investment has been judged during the 1960s, but in 1970 new foreign investment was confined to 17 'core industries' (apart from 'heavy investment' sectors). In 1973, even in this 'core', the path was opened to preferential treatment for Indian firms (there is some reason to believe that existing monopolies legislation had already been used for this purpose in the case of Cadbury-Fry.) Every foreign company, seeking to maintain 'a foreign holding of more than 40 per cent will have to get reserve bank permission'. Outside the 'core sector' 'most will have to dilute foreign holdings to 40 per cent within a specified period'. Even within it a 74 per cent holding will be the limit unless over 60 per cent of output is exported.[32] These great reserve powers will deter new private capital, and are in part a reaction to India's loss of export prospects in the British market, but are unlikely to impede the operation of most *existing* British capital in India—though they will complicate it.

(ii) PERFORMANCE

India has been fairly successful in attracting foreign private investment since independence. The fact that profit repatriations greatly exceeded new inflow is not here relevant: given the liberal policy on remittances, the net outflow would have been even greater without the gross inflow. The rupee value of outstanding long-term foreign business investments in the Indian private sector has risen almost tenfold: from Rs2,646mn in 1948, to Rs15,428mn in 1968 (table 6.9), to an estimated Rs24,000mn by 1971. Thus the 1958–68 annual inflow of Rs980mn was substantially above the 1948–57 rate of Rs297mn, partly due to the big 1958–68 flows of official portofolio investment. Total foreign private investment was 5 per cent of total Indian private investment during the Second Plan and 7·7 during the Third Plan, with almost a quarter of this coming from the UK.[33]

As for composition, table 6.9 shows private overseas capital in 1948 biased towards the service sector (railways, transportation, banking, insurance, and managing agencies) with manufacturing and plantations well behind. By 1968 foreign manufacturing capital was more than double that in the service sector. The flow into manufacturing speeded up in the second decade of independence (Rs607mn per annum against Rs144mn), as it did in the service sector, where, for the first decade it hardly rose at all. Thus foreign investment in India has been mainly into the private manufacturing sector, especially in the 1960s. Within manufacturing, chemicals accounted for 27 per cent of capital that was outstanding in 1967, metal and metal products 21 per cent, transport equipment 10 per cent, and textiles 9.6 per cent.[34]

Another important aspect of the composition of private foreign investment in India has been the shift from direct to portofolio form. In 1960 private direct holdings accounted for 78 per cent of the total foreign capital stock in the private sector, but by 1968 this had fallen to 59 per cent (table 6.10), due to the rapid growth of private and especially official portofolio holdings.

In 1958 Britain remained the largest single owner of foreign private capital in India, but her share fell from 68·2 per cent to 52·9 per cent over 1960–8, and although her portfolio holdings grew faster than her direct capital (and faster than most other countries' portfolio) by 1968 they still comprised less than half of Britain's total Indian capital stake. The USA's total stake in India's private sector nearly tripled over the same period, due largely to the growth in its official portfolio holdings to Rs2,247mn; over half of total US private investment in India by 1968.[35] British aid has never involved portfolio loans to India's private sector, but the rapid growth in US portfolio funds made little difference to the direct involvement of the UK in the Indian private sector, for in 1968 72·9 per cent of private direct investment in India remained British; and this direct British holding in turn represented nearly 39 per cent of all foreign investment, both direct and portfolio, but the post 1970 nationalizations will almost certainly have further eroded the UK share.

Around March 1961, while the current value of India's capital assets had roughly doubled since 1950,[36] long-term private foreign business capital had at least kept pace, doubling in current value between 1948 and 1958 (table 6.9); and between 1958 and 1968 the foreign share in total Indian private capital stock probably rose. Especially during the latter period, Britain was losing out; we would estimate *very roughly* that, as against Britain's share in Indian private fixed investment (excluding land, dwellings, livestock, and inventories) of about 5 per cent in 1948—and a total foreign share of 6 per cent—the respective shares were 4 and 7 per cent in 1957, and perhaps 3 and 8 per cent in 1971. Despite some concentration, this foreign stake is spread over several sectors and thus does not represent anything like the threat of foreign domination, economic or political, so familiar in many smaller countries of the Third World.

Little is known about whether recent foreign *investment* flow has gone to branches of foreign companies, to subsidiary companies, or to Indian companies with minority holdings of foreign capital. In 1965, of the Rs6,133mn of direct foreign *capital* stock in India, Rs2,686mn (43·7 per cent) was in branches or subsidiaries of overseas companies, and Rs3,447mn (56·3 per cent) was in rupee companies.[37] As we shall see below, most of the British investment in India has been in subsidiaries and branches.

4. British investment in India since 1947

(i) SIZE, SHARE, TRENDS

British private investment in India has been mainly direct, thus most of the rest of this chapter will be concerned with direct investment. British capital naturally dominated India's private foreign sector in 1947, and although the Indian government was determined from the start to switch development increasingly towards the public sector, it nevertheless welcomed continued British partici-pation in Indian development.[38] British companies found such participation profitable and by the end of the 1950s British private capital in India was well above the 1948 level. However, measurement of British capital in India is complicated by two factors: the valuation of assets, and the different aggregations used by the British and Indian statistical authorities (see Appendix, pp. 96).

The estimates of the stock of British private capital in India are given in table 6.11. As can be seen, the estimates vary widely, with the Indian official estimate being on average a third higher. Because of the effects of rupee devaluation in 1966, both sets of figures stood only a little above their levels in 1958; if we exclude these effects, the Indian official figures put British capital in India at £312·1mn in 1968 (still apparently the latest date for which figures are available), but this (table 6.11) is clearly a freak low, due to the method of allowing for the devaluations. The normal difference between the UK and Indian figures, around £100mn. may well reflect the British exclusion of oil, banking, and insurance. However one interprets the figures, the market value of British private capital in India in 1971 must have been around £500mn.

The British share of the total foreign capital in India fell quite substantially over the 1960s (table 6.10). In 1948, this share had stood at 80·5 per cent. The causes of this decline included growing US official portfolio investment; the special British problem of having no double tax agreement with India; the effects of decolonization and hence the opening of the Indian market for non-British investors; and the fact that the British, as the biggest overseas investors (and the ones who had come first and taken many 'easy' opportunities), were especially hard hit by the growth of the indigenous Indian entrepreneur, who has in particular sought out investments once undertaken by British companies in collaboration with Indian firms.[39] Other potential UK investment op-portunities were diverted to the state sector under the Industrial Policy Resolu-tions of 1948 and 1956. Finally, there *may* have been some instances when potential investors have been warned off by covertly discriminatory practices. (There are rather many instances of British investment proposals rejected for reasons of quality, or because they involved majority holdings of British capital when the government wished otherwise, or because of royalty agreements which were not considered justified.)[40] Above all the fact that in the colonial period the British government in India reserved many investment opportunities for British firms had kept the British share up; as with trade, the removal of such enforced favouritism explains much of the decline in the British share since independence.

(ii) SECTORAL STRUCTURE

As for the sectoral distribution of British private capital within India during the 1960s (table 6.12), British and Indian data for the end of 1966 were roughly similar.[41] Manufacturing comprises the major share of British private capital holdings in India, and indeed most of the giants of the British economy—ICI, Dunlop, Levers, British Leyland, and GEC Ltd.—are major investors in India, dominating their particular product groups.[42] ICI, for instance, which had a few small factories in India before the war, now heads several Indian subsidiaries such as Indian Explosives, Alkali & Chemical Corporation of India, Chemicals & Fibres of India, and Atic Industries Ltd., worth in all perhaps £50mn in asset value and *remitting* probably over £1mn in profits (net of Indian taxes) annually. The power of ICI in the Indian fertilizer industry was further strengthened when it opened its factory at Kanpur in December 1969.[43]

Much private effort has been helped by British public aid to support India's public investment. Durgapur steel plant in West Bengal was designed and built by a consortium of British firms, and although the history of the plant has been pretty disastrous and expensive since the completion of the first two stages, the blame probably cannot be attached to the British consultants and firms concerned.[44] The collaboration of Messrs Portal in the establishment of the Hashangabad Security Papermill and of British Leyland in the Ashok-Leyland Truck plant are typical examples of more successful joint ventures, albeit with India's private manufacturing sector.

Full understanding of the role of Britain in the Indian manufacturing sector requires far more analysis, but there are two distinguishing features. First, the overwhelming bulk of such investment is by major British firms. Secondly, much of the new investment in the 1960s has been financed by the reinvestment of profits earned in India. In 1967, for instance, out of the total net British investment flow to India of £10·6mn, £5·8mn were unremitted profits of subsidiaries, as against £1·9mn from the net acquisition of share and loan capital and £4·8mn from a change in indebtedness of branches to group parents.

After manufacturing, plantations remain the most important British stake in India. Though the tea plantations are best known, Britain has also had important holdings in coffee and rubber. In the mid-1950s well over 80 per cent of the acreage under tea in India was British-dominated,[45] but since then there has been some drift of ownership to Indian companies, although the process of Indianization, of both management and ownership, is proving slow.

Some state governments have decided to move ahead on their own. At the end of 1969 the Kerala state government had set up a commission to report on the financial aspects of nationalization of the foreign-owned estates.[46] The intentions were obviously in earnest, for in June 1970 it was announced that the state government intended to nationalize *all* foreign-owned plantations, with adequate compensation, and as a first step it took over 76,000 acres of land belonging to the British-owned Kannan Devan Hill Produce Company for distribution to landless farmers. In January 1971 President Giri gave his approval to the nationalization as not contravening the article of the constitution which provides that no property can be compulsorily acquired unless specified compensation was given.[47] In June 1971 the Assam government followed Kerala's example and announced the formation of a tea corporation for the purchase, control, development, and management of the tea industry in the state, though in this case the motivation came from from the concern of the state government over the sales of tea gardens in Assam that seemed to be inspired by an interest 'in making quick money by selling land and forest products from the reserves of the gardens'.[48] Such moves could be only the start of a large-scale removal of British firms from the tea industry in India. British holdings in other plantation industries such as rubber are now very small, and likely to decline further.[49]

In services the British influence remains powerful. The famous managing agencies, under whose guidance much of the British wealth and influence in India was controlled, are still important, though an increasing number of famous names now conceal Indian participation or even outright control. Their problems are compounded by their concentration on declining industries such as coal, jute, and cotton textiles, and they have never really recovered from suffering deep government mistrust during the early 1950s.

In banking Britain remains important, and the specialized business provided by the major British banks, such as National & Grindlays with its 53 branches and deposits of around £100mn (making it the seventh largest in the country), was considered important enough for the government to exclude the foreign banks from the nationalization of private banks carried out in July 1970.[50] Shipping also used to be a British preserve, but Indianization of Indian cargoes is slowly making progress as the size of the Indian fleet grows. In some cases this has been achieved by nationalization, as was the case in 1965 with the Joint Steamer Company, one of the oldest British firms in East India and the main cargo carrier between Calcutta and Assam, which had run at a loss for several years.[51]

Bad feeling between the Indian and British governments arose over another nationalization proposal, for the Calcutta Tramways Company, by the West Bengal government in 1968. The affair was seen at the time by the UK government as having a potentially serious effect on the efforts by both governments to create a favourable climate for increasing British investment in India. By early 1971 terms had still not been agreed,[52] and meanwhile (in 1968) the British High Commission had caused ill-feeling in Delhi by approaching the government of West Bengal directly instead of via the central government.[53]

Much of the general (non-life) insurance business done in India was, until May 1971, also under British control, with 38 of the 106 general insurance companies in India being British-owned—although, of the total gross premia written, the share of all foreign companies was only some 17 per cent (Rs230mn) in 1969, of which seven-tenths were written by British companies.[54] The nationalization measures set out in the General Insurance (Emergency Provisions) Ordinance, 1971, differ from those applied to the commercial banks in that assets were to be immediately taken over along with the acquisition of management, in order that compensation could be accurately and fairly determined after the accounts for 1970 were published and examined.[55] The intention was that, when compensation was finally determined, it should cover all assets as well as compensation for loss of business.[56] Though the establishment of the Life Insurance Corporation of India in 1956 has ended British involvement in life insurance, some reinsurance is still carried out in London. The branches of British banks (not nationalized in 1970) and the British-controlled managing agencies ensured that the British influence in the Indian commercial and financial sectors remained fairly strong throughout the 1960s.

In petroleum and mining, the British presence is also still strong, although much less so than at independence. In mining there was a sizeable withdrawal throughout the 1950s and 1960s, although the largest coal producers in the private sector are still controlled by British managing agencies and British interests are still important in the production of copper, lead, and zinc. In the production and distribution of oil, petroleum, and their derivatives, major British firms like Burmah and Shell control much of the Indian market along with other foreign firms, and both are now working in conjunction with the central government in expanding the domestic production of oil. Oil India Ltd, incorporated in Assam in 1959, and in which the government of India and the Glasgow-based Burmah Oil Company have equal shares, is one major force for the exploration and production of petroleum, crude oil, and natural gas in India. It is currently undertaking a substantial expansion programme,[57] and in 1969 Burmah had offered to finance the foreign-exchange costs of Oil India's exploration activities in the NEFA.[58] Burmah is also a partner with Shell in the petroleum refinery set up at Trombay in 1955. In 1971 both Burmah and Shell, along with other major oil companies operating in India such as Caltex, Esso, Phillips, and Amoco, were much criticized for charging high crude prices and making exorbitant profits,[59] and this may well lead to a move by these companies to protect themselves from outright nationalization by offering the Indian government majority partnerships in all their Indian operations.[60] The purchase of a 74 per cent share by the GOI in Esso (Exxon)—now renamed Hindustan Petroleum—in mid-1974 has been followed by discussions with Burmah, Shell, and Caltex.

(iii) COMPANY STRUCTURE

British companies still play some role in Indian economic development. Much of the more tangible evidence, such as the presence of large numbers of British personnel (pp. 156f.), disappeared during the 1960s, but was replaced by more discreet forms of participation, such as technical and licensing collaboration agreements, and minority holdings in new Indian enterprises. The details of this change are hard to chart, for no figures are published, but some idea of the organizational structure of the British presence in India can be seen in tables 6.14 and 6.15.[61]

The proportion of British companies operating as subsidiaries is below the world average for British overseas companies; the proportion operating as branches and associates, well above. The great role of associates reflects the Indian government's desire to encourage joint ventures with foreign enterprises, with, where possible, a majority of the joint equity held by Indian companies. The high number of branches probably reflects some British companies' wish to avoid operating as subsidiaries or associates, both of which are now open to more or less mandatory Indian involvement.

If we compare company structures within British private capital in India in 1968 (table 6.14), a fuller picture emerges. First, branches and subsidiaries dominated the scene, with 87·8 per cent of direct British capital in only 46 per cent of the British companies. Associate companies, though numerous, contributed only 6·4 per cent of the total investment; but their contribution was mainly in joint ventures with Indian companies. (Assuming 50 per cent shares, British associates were involved in total investment in India of more than £35mn.)

The question of subsidiaries and associate companies was investigated in 1963–4[62] and two points emerged. First, British subsidiaries comprised 70·5 per cent of the value of all foreign-held equity in subsidiaries in India, and British company involvement in these subsidiaries was high, with only 18·7 per cent of shares held by Indians. Second, in minority capital ventures, British partners also dominated the field, again both in respect of frequency and because the non-Indian share of capital was higher than the world average, i.e. 35·2 per cent (table 6.15).

Another indication of British interest in investing in India is the annual number of collaboration agreements signed by British firms (table 6.16). The number of new annual agreements at the end of the decade was well below the levels of the early 1960s, but this is partly a reflection of a slowing-down of new collaboration agreements in general. The British share in total agreements has held up quite well, given that a large number of countries commenced investing and collaborating in India during the 1960s, so that Britain's share was bound to fall.[63] Although in 1968 both the Americans and the West Germans entered more agreements than Britain, over 1958–68 Britain's 759 agreements far exceeded those of any other country. These imply continued returns from royalties for many years and a strengthening of Britain's continued position as the major investor in India.[64] British private investors in India in the 1960s have— perhaps unlike British traders—tried seriously and successfully to maintain and strengthen British interests in ways acceptable to the Indian authorities.

(iv) BENEFITS, REACTIONS, ATTITUDES

What benefits accrued to India from British involvement? In strict financial terms, the remitted return on British capital in India in the 1960s was about 8 per cent, the growth-rate only some 3 per cent. However, the balance of 5 per cent of book values, or by 1970 perhaps — £20–25mn yearly, is not even a provisional estimate of the effects on India's overseas payments. British-owned plantations export tea; British-owned chemical factories replace imports; both effects would of course continue after nationalization, but new foreign investment to expand them would not, and India's sparse domestic savings could barely replace this flow. Conversely, British and other foreign firms create imports, both as industrial inputs and through the purchases made out of the high salaries of managers and sometimes workers. The picture is complex; and in any case India seeks other goals than just a better foreign balance.

The technical knowhow, management training, and technical education that the British companies have brought to India carry important long-term benefits. The Indian official view was, and is, that the activities of many foreign companies have been beneficial to India, but should be confined to 'core' sectors, increase their export share, and raise Indian participation.

Such worries are increasingly affecting policy. In 1969 the government asked— did not compel—foreign-owned companies to make an increased exporting effort, pressuring them with the reminder that India places no restrictions on the remittances of foreign companies.[65] The Indian government now also restricts the activities of some foreign companies that purchase the entire production of other manufacturers and market it as their own. Such activity will not be allowed unless the companies involved agree to introduce 51 per cent Indian participation within five years[66]—in 1973 the share was raised to 60 per cent outside the 'core' sector. Curbs have also been placed on the sale of foreign-owned companies to Indians at 'inflated' prices, by requiring the companies involved to seek the approval of the RBI.[67] In 1970, India's minister of industrial development warned that all large foreign firms wanting to expand their production would have to ensure that the number of shares belonging to Indian citizens was increased, a warning translated into policy in 1973.[68] Despite this tightening of conditions for foreign companies in India, the safeguards given in 1948 have been respected; one major British company manager remarked that India's record on the remittance of dividends is absolutely impeccable,[69] and the Indian government also seems happy about the record.

However, some changes are likely in the structure of British capital invested in India, especially amongst the plantation and mining companies, following the passing of the Companies (Amendment) Act, 1969, which abolished the system of management of companies by managing agents and secretaries and treasurers,[70] and thus brought to an end the main and most typical form of British economic involvement with India during the days of the Raj. How the 1969 legislation will affect British investment is still not clear, though during the 1950s and 1960s the amount of British capital channelled through these agencies constituted a minor and rapidly diminishing share of the total.

How do British companies view their experience in India? Though British press reports sometimes criticize the conditions facing foreign companies in India, these conditions have not been examined in any great detail in *published* material. However, in 1967–8 Messrs Sinha and Castree of the Department of Political Economy at Glasgow University, conducted a small-scale survey into the attitudes and problems of British investors in India[71] and much of the following relies on the findings of this survey. (We do not believe that the '1973 measures' will *in practice* change things much, though any decline in India's market access to, and from, Britain (e.g. resulting from EEC policy) would obviously lower the potential costs to India of much more overt action against British capital there.)

Its conclusion was that most British entrepreneurs find India an attractive opening for investment, showing an awareness of India's problems and a willingness to assist, where profitable, in the process of development. Most respondents had no fears about collaboration with Indian counterparts, and were seemingly not deterred by operating in an environment where the accepted political philosophy was 'socialist' and where the public sector predominated. The firms felt that the private sector had enjoyed 'reasonably adequate facilities' for its development, although there were complaints regarding government interference, both in the operation of business and in the insulation of the Indian from the world economy (though the latter protects business, including private foreign business, from overseas competition and is indeed sometimes sought for this reason). Only a few smaller firms showed alarm at the rhetoric (or self-affrighting ignorance of the content) of Indian politics; one expressed fears that India was 'going communist, like Ceylon'—this during the period when Ceylon was governed by the conservative UNP under the leadership of Dudley Senanayake.

General statements that India had been an attractive country for investment were followed by numerous complaints against Indian government policies in the 1960s. First, there was much predictable criticism of the role of the public sector, mainly on the grounds that the largest and most profitable projects had been reserved for it, leaving only small or, at best, medium-sized developments for the private sector. The role of Indian state production in providing subsidized inputs for private producers was not criticized! The licensing system came in for criticism; most respondents felt that the recommendations of the Swaminathan Committee (then in session) would improve the situation, although these could scarcely have included an improvement in 'the willingness on the part of civil servants to take the necessary decisions'. Other direct controls, such as those limiting the number of foreign nationals employed and price controls, were accepted minor irritants.

Much more serious were the criticisms of the Indian fiscal system, especially the high corporation tax and the tax on withholding dividends. All firms, even those submitting generally favourable replies, felt the Indian tax rates compared very unfavourably with other countries,[72] despite the lower rates offered in 'priority sectors'.[73]

There was also concern over the relatively high tax rates levied on the pay of foreign nationals. Unlike West Germany and the USA, Britain has no double tax agreement with India, so that British companies have to pay especially high gross salaries if non-Indians are to receive internationally competitive net salaries. This situation has not been improved by the decision of the Indian Government to place administrative ceilings on *gross* (instead of post-tax) managerial remuneration in public limited companies,[74] and from May 1971 this control had been extended to all salaries in the private sector.[75] The final two complaints concerned the cumulative nature of taxation on goods (in some cases ad valorem taxes levied on successive stages of production result in a very high effective tax rate—firms did not mention that similar arrangements for tariffs also gave them very high effective protection), and the 'anomalies' in the tariff structure whereby tariffs on component parts often added up to more than on the completed article.

The views of British companies on collaboration, and on the Indian government's desire for a majority holding by an Indian collaborating company, are on the whole favourable, although some had reservations, preferring an Indian share issue rather than collaboration, or a foreign majority holding, or a minority holding with powers to attach representatives to the company. In summary, as Sinha and Castree put it, 'the general opinion seems to be that the British firms have maintained and enlarged their investments in India in spite of, rather than because of, the general policies of the [Indian] government, the main reasons for investment being defence of existing interests and the huge potential market presented by the Indian sub-continent'.

Profitability has been mentioned above; how have British firms fared in India during the 1960s? Reddaway found that over 1955–64 British manufacturers in India had 55·3 per cent of their profits taken by taxation as against an average of 46·1 per cent for all British investment overseas, although Indian pre-tax profitability at 18·3 per cent was above the average of 16·3 per cent. Post-tax profitability at 8·2 per cent was slightly below the average of 8·8 per cent. In terms of direct tax revenue per £100 of capital assets employed, the Indian government got £10·1 as against the average of £7·5.[76]

These high tax rates—though clearly there is a limit—may make sense from the Indian (or at least the Indian governmental) point of view. Uncertainty about future tax policy makes many overseas investors look at pre-tax, not post-tax, profits; the shifting pattern of British overseas investment shows little relation to post-tax returns (p. 82); and to permit high profits and tax them helps the government raise revenue at low cost from big companies with full published accounts, while the benefits of a lower-profit, lower-tax situation would accrue elsewhere, out of control, in the private sector. The relatively high rate of taxation at 55·3 per cent partly reflects the age composition of UK investments in India; the investments in the static plantation, jute, and mining sectors have not until recently been eligible for development rebates against capital investment on modernization.[77]

More restricted evidence is available on the performance of branches of British companies and of British subsidiaries relative to other foreign and domestic enterprises within India (table 6.17). Because of the relatively brief period for which data are available (1965–6 and 1966–7) and its untypical nature (rupee devaluation and economic recession within India), the comparisons need to be treated with caution.

Branches of British companies operating in India appear to have been slightly less profitable in terms of gross profits on total capital employed than the average foreign branch, and substantially less than the branches of American companies (table 6.17, col. 2). The reasons for this poorer performance are hard to deduce from the published accounts without much more detailed analysis, but the sectoral distribution of UK branches and the charges made by managing agents and secretaries—some of which were also British-owned—for administering such branches (averaging some Rs27mn against just over Rs100,000 for *all* other foreign branches) must be part of the explanation for lower gross profits.

Foreign-controlled rupee companies have superior profit and dividend performances to domestic Indian public and private limited companies. This partly reflects the larger size of foreign firms investing in India and their distribution among the high-yielding manufacturing sectors. Within the foreign companies studied by the Reserve Bank, British-controlled firms have fared tolerably well, outclassing all other foreign and domestic groups in terms of both gross profits on total capital and dividends, though their post-tax profit performance has been slightly lower than average for foreign companies (but better than American companies).

It is of interest that the post-tax profits of British companies for 1965–7, as revealed in the RBI survey, of 11·6 per cent on net assets, were substantially better than the figure of 8·2 per cent quoted by Reddaway for the period 1956–64.[78] How much the difference reflects an improvement in profitability over time, rather than differences in the bases of compiling the figures of net operating assets (and indeed of selecting the sample of companies), is hard to determine.

(v) THE FUTURE

India is not Latin America. Foreign private capital is a minor contribution, and a minor irritant, only. Though the situation facing British investors in India during the mid-1960s was full of problems, subsequent Indian moves made it possible to ease certain of the complaints listed above. The 1969 Budget brought some relief to business, abolishing the 7·5 per cent tax on dividends and reducing the surtax on company profits from 35 to 25 per cent, but in 1971 one incentive for foreign companies was ended when the concessional tax treatment of dividends received by foreign companies from closely-held Indian subsidiaries engaged in priority industries was discontinued, and such dividends were subjected to a 24·5 per cent tax.[79] The fears of British investors about the proposed Indian Patents Bill and the possibility of a centralized agency set up to purchase knowhow for free distribution to Indian firms have been allayed.[80] The threat of nationalization has seemingly faded, at least temporarily; future threats of nationalization may not matter much in view of past compensation terms for British assets in shipping, banking, insurance, mining, plantations, and manufacturing; but vague threats without action create many of the drawbacks of public intervention and none of the advantages. The same applies to such highly ambivalent restatements of policy towards foreign companies as that of March 1973, which can be interpreted as liberalizing or as tightening the rules for foreign firms.[81]

Encouraging is the formation of a joint Indian-British technological group to discuss industrial and technical co-operation and also joint ventures in other l.d.c.s. This group first met in 1970, and could develop into a valuable review body, looking at the problems arising from established British investments in India. Such a body which could have been extremely useful during the 1960s.[82]

But the flow of investment will be mainly determined by the growth and the foreign balances of the Indian and British economies, and neither of these can be predicted with any certainty. Since 1970 the British government has expressed a desire to investigate ways of making overseas investment more attractive,[83] mainly as a means of meeting the British commitment to the UN aid target of 1 per cent of GNP flowing to l.d.c.s by 1975. However, the labelling of private investment as 'private development aid' is an illusion: aid loans are at zero or concessional rates of interest, not at market rates of profit! Private investment can benefit recipient and investor alike; it can also involve the recipient country in a drain of resources greater than the initial investment, as may have been the case with India.[84] In any case it is not entirely honest to cloak a commercial relationship with moral approval by calling it 'aid', for which it cannot substitute in many fields, some of which are highly desirable. Private investors might avoid the Durgapurs, but could never replace the many aid projects whose social returns really are high, though quite irrecoverable for the risk-bearers—most notably the research projects in agriculture and elsewhere.

It is thus with mixed feelings that one reads of ODA provisions 'for capital aid to local investment banks . . . for joint ventures with British private capital . . . for basic infrastructure projects associated with particular British private investment plans . . . [and] to meet part of the cost of pre-investment studies by British private firms'.[85] Desirable or not, there things are hardly 'aid', except perhaps to needy British companies. They conflict with increasing Indian doubt about foreign investment, and, since they can hardly bring public capital to India, may cause India to lose British aid, to the benefit of other and less poor countries more welcoming to private overseas investment. As Britain's membership of the EEC is having the same effect via the European Development Fund (pp. 118–20), one has to ask: who benefits?

APPENDIX: ASSET VALUATION

British valuations of assets use book values, reflecting the historic cost of investments, although some companies complicate the situation by including revalued assets in their returns to the Department of Trade and Industry (formerly Board of Trade). The Reddaway Report estimated that for manufacturing investment market values could exceed book values by up to 36 per cent.[86] Outside manufacturing, valuation problems can be much worse. In 1965, when Indian authorities valued British investment in tea plantations at £77mn, assessment at the current replacement cost (i.e. of planting from scratch) gave values as high as £225mn.[87] Book values, therefore, while they do indicate *relative* assets at a point of time, tell us little about size or growth of real absolute asset value. But replacement cost also seldom reflects market values!

It can be argued, moreover, that to impute market values to the assets would involve a degree of subjective estimation. It is also necessary to have a quotation on the stock exchange of the recipient country, as well as one in the investing country, and even then the market values usually represent those that emerge from *marginal* trading, which would probably not correspond to the market value obtainable if the whole of the stock were traded at once. Other problems involve the influence of expectations about future earnings and the influence of technological change on the value of capital assets.

As for aggregation, British figures of overseas capital stocks usually exclude oil and also banking and insurance investments (though the latter are included in the annual investment flow figures!) The Indian figures seemingly include these, but may not have as full a coverage of other British capital as the British official data.

7 AID TO INDIA

> In a very short time [following the outbreak of the American Civil War] prices of raw cotton in the Liverpool market rose to levels 6 to 8 times above the pre-war rates. Indeed, the scarcity was so intense that many Lancashire mills closed their doors and workers were thrown to the wolves [*sic*]. The sadness of the plight of the poor labourers of Lancashire can well be imagined from the fact that in September 1862 a meeting of Bombay citizens decided to raise a public fund to alleviate their sufferings.
> J. D. MEHTA, *The Cotton Mills of India, 1854–1954* (Bombay: 1954).

1. Introduction

In this chapter we examine first the world aid context; next the British aid programme; third the role of aid in India's development; and finally, and in more detail, British aid to India, with special discussions of the aid-trade link and the prospects for 1975–80. By 'aid' we mean grants, or loans on concessional terms, extended by governments of rich countries to governments of poor ones, either directly or through international organizations.

British aid to India in the 1960s followed a pattern distressingly similar to bilateral trade and private investment, but with one major redeeming feature. The similarity stemmed from Britain's slow growth and severe balance-of-payments problems, which curtailed her share in aid as well as in trade and private investment in poor countries as a whole and in India in particular; from India's apparent incapacity to attract a share of aid, as of trade and private investment, remotely in line with her needs, prospects, or importance, from rich countries as a whole and from Britain in particular; and from the erosion of an Indo-British 'special relationship' (expressed in the case of intergovernmental capital movements by the sterling balances), with no replacement by a mature post-colonial substitute such as real aid of comparable importance. The redeeming feature is that British aid disbursements, Indian aid utilization, and especially British aid to India, despite their small and slowly-growing *quantity*, have achieved a high and rising *quality*: a quality expressed in the composition, type, terms, and management of aid flows. Britain seemed in the late 1960s to be providing barely 6 per cent of gross aid to India; but qualitative factors raised the true share to some 13 per cent (pp. 104–5). Indeed, if we include private aid in the full sense (of course excluding investment, but including gifts by private Indian-born persons in Britain to their relatives at home), Britain originated about 40 per cent of current aid to India.

In 1948–58 much of India's investment was financed by British releases of sterling balances that India had run up during the Second World War (p. 22). During the First Indian Five-year Plan (1951–6), foreign aid played a minor

97

role, and British aid to India comprised only Rs4mn, an insignificant proportion of total official aid authorized (Rs3,817mn).[1] India's poor export performance in the 1950s, the import-intensive industrialization strategy of the Second Plan (1956–61), and the growing impact of the still largely unsuspected population explosion on food imports produced the foreign-exchange crisis of 1957–8. This almost exhausted the sterling balances, and suggested that much more aid was needed if Indian development was to continue. In 1958 the USA, Britain, West Germany, Canada, and Japan formed the India Consortium, with a chairman from the World Bank, to co-ordinate and increase aid flows; and the involvement of Britain's aid in Indian development really began.

2. The World Aid Context 1960-70

(i) TOTAL FLOWS

The flow of capital from rich to poor countries is nothing new. Until the Cold War period, however, such investments were aimed at private profit or power only. Private charity across borders is old too; so is famine relief assistance by governments. But official development assistance, aimed partly at advancing the donor's own interests but also at helping poor countries to finance their own development, is a feature of the late 1950s and the 1960s; of the post-colonial struggle for political and economic influence, and the post-colonial awakening in rich countries to their own interest in the long-run prosperity of poor ones.

The annual flow of official resources (net of *capital* repayments) from rich countries rose from around $3,300mn in the mid-1950s to almost $6,800mn in 1970, some 90 per cent of this being net official development assistance,[2] which by 1972 had risen to $8,600mn. Interest repayments, however, ate up almost a quarter of this, and thus the real *transfer* of official resources (net of capital and interest repayments) to poor countries was less than in 1965, if we allow for rising prices. The total gross flow of funds from rich to poor countries in the 1960s was around $104bn (table 7.1), well over 90 per cent from the 16 member nations of the Development Assistance Committee (DAC) of the OECD.[3] Around 60 per cent was official development assistance; the rest was direct and portfolio private investment and export credits (p. 39). Of the official development assistance, two-thirds comprised grants, the remainder being loans (table 7.2).

(ii) BRITAIN IN THE WORLD CONTEXT

The absolute size—though not the quality—of Britain's aid over the 1960s has been disappointing in this context. Whereas total net official DAC development assistance rose by 44 per cent from 1960 to 1970 the British flow rose by only 9·8 per cent; thus the British share in DAC net aid fell from 8·6 to 6·5 per cent[4] (though by 1972 there had been a recovery to 7·0 per cent, mainly because of a declining US effort), and its real value declined substantially. Not only was

British GNP growing much more slowly than that of other donors; the share Britain devoted to aid was falling slightly faster.[5] In the 1960s the declining British, French and US share in total aid was matched by the growing importance of West Germany, Japan, and Canada. Yet Britain remained the third largest source of aid during the 1960s, transferring some $4,900mn to poor countries. Moreover British aid to some extent made up in quality for what it lacked in quantity. The *grant element* of aid from the UK since 1969, as a percentage of GNP, has been above the average for western donors, and improving, and tying, notably to India, was less restrictive.[6]

(iii) INDIA IN THE WORLD CONTEXT

The distribution of DAC aid appears in table 7.4. It can be seen that aid patterns change only slowly, and reflect former colonial involvement; thus over 80 per cent of British aid goes to Commonwealth countries, and nearly 90 per cent of French aid goes to the Franc Zone.[7] Second, Britain in no way dominates Commonwealth aid receipts; in 1960–4 and 1965–8 the USA provided respectively 2·8 and 3·8 times as much aid to the Commonwealth countries as did Britain. Third, the Indian subcontinent received over one-fifth of total bilateral and multilateral aid (though since 1969 the share has fallen sharply); the share rose during the 1960s, accounting for over 70 per cent of total Commonwealth aid receipts. Fourth, the size of Indian and Pakistani requirements has resulted in their dominating the aid efforts of other nations than Britain; Canada, West Germany, and Japan contributed 31 per cent of their aid disbursements in 1960–8 to the Indian subcontinent. So it might seem that India and Pakistan were receiving more than their fair share of aid.

However, the net official aid receipts *per person* present a very different picture (table 7.5). In a typical year in 1966–8, the average Indian benefited from only some $2·3; India ranked equal 69th in per caput aid receipts, along with Nigeria. Though Pakistan did substantially better with $4·00 per caput, it too came well down the per caput league table, along with other populous poor economies, Brazil and Indonesia.[8] The disproportion is worse if the harder terms of Indian aid are considered; the 'grant equivalent' of world gross aid hovers around 80 per cent, but to India around 65 per cent only (p. 110). But even crude net aid receipts per person are lower in more populous poor countries; this is known as the 'small country effect'. Recipient countries seem to receive a minimum amount of aid regardless of size, plus a further amount related to their population size.[9] This is due partly to the fact that much aid is given to promote exports from the donor—big countries like India offer less scope for this, since they supply a wide variety of their own needs and thus have fewer (and more diversified) imports per person; partly to the fact that diplomatic influence in general and UN votes in particular 'cost' less aid if 'bought' in small nations; partly to the prevalence of 'French aid to France' in paying subservient francophone (and often French) civil servants in African mini-states; and partly to the large amounts of aid given to Israel, Jordan, South Vietnam, Malta, Laos, the Dominican Republic, and Panama, following military rather than developmental interests. So India gets little aid per head, but she ranks higher in terms of aid as a percentage of imports of goods and services. The fact that aid covered an average of 43·8 per cent of Indian imports in 1966–8 is however no cause for congratulation; it reflects both the poor performance of Indian export earnings and an extremely restrictive import policy by India.

(iv) AID AND DEBT

As *loan* aid has loomed so large, but has seldom sufficed to help the recipients earn much foreign exchange, many of them have found themselves facing crippling amortization and interest repayments. At the end of 1971 India owed nearly $10,000mn to other governments and multilateral institutions (table 7.6) —more than any other poor country, though far less *per person* than Pakistan, Indonesia, Brazil, or many other major poor countries. Debt service payments rose for most countries over the second half of the 1960s, as the grace periods on earlier loans expired; future service payments will continue to rise for this reason, and also because of the increase during the 1960s in both total aid and the proportion in loan form. Further, though grace periods have lengthened somewhat, in other respects major donors such as the USA and Japan have hardened their terms.

For India, service payments rose from 15·4 per cent of her total exports of goods and services in 1965 to 23·5 per cent in 1971 (higher still in the bad export years of 1966–7). Aid receipts were covering over 40 per cent of India's import bill in the late 1960s, so that their erosion by debt servicing is extremely serious. India is one of the few poor countries whose debt-service problem is created mainly by aid loans rather than profit remissions and interest on foreign-trade credits.

(v) ATTITUDES TO AID

The early 1960s saw a rapid rise in aid, but by 1970 some disillusionment had set in. Support for aid in the big donors weakened,[10] and the levels of aid rose only very slowly. The reasons for the disenchantment are many. Expectations of instant development through minimal aid had been doubly unrealistic. There was a growing revulsion at corrupt use of aid in certain countries, and by certain donors too. When recipients said 'To hell with your aid' and demanded instant virtue from the wicked neo-colonial donors, the latter began to wonder if virtue might mean niggardliness. The major donors also ran into severe monetary and payments crises in the late 1960s, and aid cutbacks were demanded to relieve domestic inflation and balance-of-payments problems; the USA in August 1971, cut aid by one-tenth in her 'balance-of-payments package', a step hardly noticed in the subsequent furore, nor rectified when currencies were realigned and the US import surcharge was removed four months later. Moreover, progress by major donors towards the 1965 DAC recommendation on aid terms,[11] or indeed the goals of the Pearson Report,[12] was far from encouraging for the poor countries; it was the minor donors who showed most determination in trying to comply with the recommendations,[13] whereas the USA moved from bad to worse; since Latin America was exempted from Nixon's 1971 aid cuts, the damage to really poor countries such as India was greater. Finally the steep rise in oil prices in 1973 seems likely to reduce real aid; certainly it increases the need for it in most poor countries, including those, like India, that have made independence from aid a target of planning.

3. The British aid programme

Financial assistance by Britain to poor countries dates back to the Colonial Development and Welfare Act (1940) with its annual expenditure of £5mn. Since then the British effort has grown; by 1971 it comprised £270mn of gross aid. The programme (table 7.4) is still overwhelmingly oriented towards the Commonwealth.

Disbursements of gross British aid ('gross' of repayments of aid loans and interest) rose slowly from £172·6mn in 1961 to £218·8mn in 1970—a compound growth-rate of only 2·6 per cent per annum, or an absolute rise of around £5·1mn annually; given devaluation and inflation, this implies a fall in real terms. Virtually all this 'growth' occured in the first half of the 1960s (table 7.7), though there was some improvement in 1970–73. Between 1966 and 1969 gross British disbursements declined even in money terms, and very sharply in real terms. The trend of 'net aid transfers'—gross aid minus capital and interest repaid—was even worse; the 1969 net transfer was below the 1961 level even in money terms, due to the growing return flow of capital repayments and interest charges as grace and moratorium periods lapsed, though 1970 and 1971 saw a marked improvement. Net aid transfer, as a percentage of gross aid disbursements, fell by 14·2 per cent over the 1960s. Clearly the tortoise-like growth of *new* British aid, relatively to most other donors, made the dead weight of past debts overwhelmingly heavy.

The 1960s saw a steady decline in the percentage of Britain's GNP devoted to official aid (table 7.8); by 1970 it stood at a miserable 0·37 per cent, though there was a slight recovery to 0·40 per cent by 1972. Had she achieved the Pearson target of 0·7 per cent, the gross aid flow in 1970 would have been over £413·9mn, as against the actual level of £218·8mn. The British Conservative government, however, at no time accepted the Pearson target of 0·7 per cent of GNP for official development assistance, but instead was concentrating on the Unctad-Pearson target (1 per cent for 'financial resource transfers' to poor countries by 1975)—which Britain already meets—and on expanding private investment (pp. 81, 95). Though the latter target may well be met, it is not the same as Pearson's *aid* target. Net private investment, unlike public aid, is not under government control. Even if the 1 per cent target is reached, the major gain will be to the British invisibles account in remitted profits and dividends, not to poor countries; private firms are not charities! (Labour accepted the 0·7 per cent target in opposition, but by late 1974 had not announced any change of policy when in government).

Most British aid is bilateral (table 7.9), though the 'multilateral' proportion has risen since 1965–6 at the expense of bilateral grants, which declined from 44·6 per cent of gross total assistance in 1965–6 to 37·1 per cent in 1970, while loans have kept their share of the total. Unfortunately there is little point in discussing grants in detail here; virtually all official UK aid to India consists of loans. The small annual UK grants to India cover technical-assistance payments (ch. 8).

In the early 1960s most British development loans were made through the Export Credit Guarantee Department, typically at 6 per cent for 15 years—market rates or slightly below. Since 1965, however, Britain has taken a lead among the major aid donors by substantially easing the terms of new loans; by 1970, over 90 per cent of new loan commitments were interest-free, with 20–25 years for repayment and 7-year grace periods. These terms have applied since 1965 to all new British loans to India.[14] However Britain still does not quite meet the DAC 1965 recommendations on terms with respect to the overall aid programme (table 7.10).

African Commonwealth nations receive around 60 per cent of Britain's total aid flow (table 7.11), although the largest single recipient remains India. India's and Pakistan's shares rose considerably over the 1960s, but of the 22 countries receiving over £1mn in annual gross aid from Britain, only the Sudan gets less per head than India (table 7.12), and even the Sudan gets more *net* aid per head. The 'small country effect' operates among Commonwealth nations too; Malta tops the list, with net aid flow per person 449 times greater than India's! If India had enjoyed the same British aid per person as the average of countries listed in table 7.12, then since 1965 she would have been receiving £80·5mn of gross aid per year (or £58·1mn of net aid) from Britain, far above the actual levels.

Little is known about the distribution of UK official aid by purpose before 1966. Figures for some years are available, but as the rate of disbursement varies, the analysis of commitments in a single year by function is not helpful. For the second half of the 1960s more information is available (table 7.13); just over half UK official aid over 1966–70 was disbursed for identifiable projects; most went to investment in economic infrastructure. Of the non-project aid, over 60 per cent went to finance current imports, suggesting that the relationship between British aid and British exports to aid recipients is an important one (see p. 116). Much of Britain's aid to India has gone two large projects, Durgapur Steelworks and the Bhopal Heavy Electrical Plant, although non-project support for current imports has also been substantial, especially through the so-called Kipping loans (p. 108).

Little was said officially about the aims of the British aid programme until the establishment of the Ministry of Overseas Development (ODM) in 1964.

The primary purpose is now stated to be the economic and social development of poor countries, in the belief that this promotes stability. It is also claimed that aid promotes trade and that Britain stands to gain by the higher levels of commercial activity which come with the increased prosperity of development (pp. 115–16). A further theme is that the British aid programme should be so arranged as to encourage other donors to co-operate in world development; yet even by the late 1960s the multilateral share of Britain's aid had risen only to 11 per cent, the same as the DAC average, though there was a dramatic improvement in 1969–72.[15]

The ODM was intended to co-ordinate British aid, to clarify objectives, to undertake long-range planning, and to maintain close and continous contacts with all those departments and ministries involved in the administration and execution of development projects. Unfortunately ODM attempted these massive tasks while Britain's economic problems were being seen by the government as good reasons to restrict (alone of all major public outlays) the growth of *aid*. Fixed cash ceilings on total aid—while prices rose and sterling was devalued—made it impossible to cut the *share* of any recipient or project in UK aid without cutting its *cash flow*, so that the defenders of inertia in aid (p. 121) became especially determined and ODM's arguments for redirection remained theoretical.

The cash constraint brought general political weakness. The ODM was hardly consulted on such issues as the renewed Common Market application in 1967; even at the second Unctad Conference at Delhi in 1968, ODM clearly played second fiddle to a rather restrictionist Board of Trade. The ministry lost its Cabinet rank in 1966, and its independence with the merger into the Foreign and Commonwealth Office in 1970.[16] ODM has experienced friction with the Board of Trade over aid untying, with FCO desks about aid to doubtful recipients, and with the Treasury over aid ceilings.[17] Many aid supporters saw the merging in 1970 of ODM into the FCO (as 'ODA', or the division of Overseas Development Administration) as ominous, although the government clearly respected its assurances that the reorganization would not affect the flow of aid (p. 109), or the administrative and executive powers of ODM-ODA.

4. Foreign aid in Indian economic development[18]

(i) AMOUNTS AND SOURCES

Back in 1951, at the start of the first Indian Five-Year Plan, the planners looked forward to 1967, when the economy would achieve 'take-off' into self-sustaining economic growth, with the external sector in balance and no future aid requirements. When 1967 arrived, it was obvious that take-off still lay far down the runway. India, still critically dependent upon aid, was also carrying enormous external debts; and the Indian planners, in drawing up the first draft of the Fourth Plan, required $14,000mn of aid for debt servicing. In the 1970s too, the Fifth Plan outline aimed at ending net aid; but (as of late 1973) oil bills and debt servicing appear likely, between them, to eat up by 1980 about three-quarters of export earnings. Without aid, can there be much development? Furthermore, even paths towards 'self-reliance' (zero net aid) require more *gross* aid—primarily to service debts on earlier aid—than donors will readily supply. Hence even the Fifth Plan (1974–9) in its final version requires almost $600mn of gross aid a year, and the target date for 'zero net aid' or self-reliance has been pushed forward to 1986.

The development strategy of the first two Five-Year Plans, anyway, emphasized substitution for imports, which were to tail off towards the end of the Second Plan. Instead imports soared, exports lagged, and a serious foreign-exchange crisis in 1957–8 compelled the reduction of the Second Plan to a hastily-constructed 'core' heavily reliant on external sources of finance. With the foundation of the Aid India Consortium in 1958, aid began to play a major role in both the Indian economy and Indian politics. Dependence on aid grew rapidly: 5·9 per cent of total investments in the First Plan, 13·2 per cent in the Second, 16·9 per cent in the Third.[19] The public sector's dependence has of course been heavier (table 7.14), and by the annual plans of the late 1960s nearly 36 per cent of public-sector outlays were financed by aid. The Indian planners proposed a much reduced dependence on foreign aid for the revised Fourth Plan (1969–74), although the amounts required were still sizeable:[20] $5,500mn over the five years, but only 45 per cent of it ($2,500mn) net aid available after repayment of past debts.[21]

Between the advent of the First Plan in April 1951 and the end of March 1971, India received Rs92,613mn of external assistance (table 7.15), out of total aid authorizations of Rs102,222mn. The USA supplied over half of total utilized aid, followed by Britain (who contributed bilaterally some Rs6,829mn), the Soviet Union, and West Germany.[22] Britain's relatively small share is partly due to the fact that aid from Britain really started only with the ending of the disbursements of sterling balances in the late 1950s, and partly to the fact that the huge amount of aid required by India dwarfs the British figure, which appears relatively large when seen in the context of the total British aid programme.

(ii) BRITAIN'S ROLE

Britain's real contribution has been larger than the figure quoted in table 7.15, for five reasons. First, some of the aid disbursed to India from multilateral institutions is also of British origin. Second, British aid is useful more quickly; from 1951 to 1970 (p. 110) 92 per cent of British loans authorized for India were utilized, as against 63 per cent of the larger Russian commitment, and 89 per cent of American loans.[23] Third, in 1965–70 most British aid to India was untied in fact if not in form, raising its true value by perhaps 20 per cent compared with other aid (pp. 116–17) though by 1970–1 the new Conservative government had taken measures to see that an increasing proportion of project aid to India was tied to the purchase of British goods.[24]

Fourth, the very generous terms of UK loans *since 1965* have raised the true value of her bilateral gross aid, as measured by the 'grant element', to a level well above its apparent share (7·1 per cent of cash value, for aid received by India as a whole (p. 110)). Finally, from April 1965 to September 1968, some 30·6 per cent of aid utilized by India comprised commodity assistance,[25] the effect of which is reduced because (by lowering prices to domestic suppliers) it induces cuts in domestic production,[26] none of this sort of aid came from Britain. The total effect is that the UK supplied not 7 per cent of utilized aid to India in 1951–71, as table 7.15 suggests, but nearer 13 per cent by true value, at least over 1965–9 when British terms eased. Moreover, the partial re-tying of British aid to India after 1970 was more than offset by a rapid increase in its volume.

(iii) COMPOSITION OF INDIA'S AID

(a) *Project and non-project aid.* The structure of aid to India in the 1960s falls into three distinct periods. Until 1965 aid was directed mainly towards big projects (British aid for Durgapur Steelworks was a typical example), intended to develop an import-saving industrial infrastucture. From mid-1965 to early 1968, while Indian industry (via inadequate supplies from agriculture, inadequate rural demand and diversion of foreign exchange from raw materials to food imports) suffered the aftermath of bad harvests and droughts, many donors switched from project to non-project aid, mainly to finance the flow of imports of components and raw materials; food aid also rose. In 1968–71 the Indian economy picked up, and so did the demand for project aid; but the need for maintenance imports still required that aid be partly directed to the financing of raw materials and components, to raise the shockingly low levels of capacity utilization in large-scale Indian industry; and donors were less willing to meet that requirement.

Future Indian aid needs are likely to be increasingly for non-project, untied aid (which with donors becoming increasingly trade conscious will be even harder to obtain). The structure of requirements by type of goods also poses problems. India is producing more and more of her own machines and processed goods. Her future import needs will be for raw materials and components. Most donor countries are reluctant to supply these under aid agreements, because even where such aid is nominally tied to donor exports it is likely to replace commercial sales. It is very doubtful whether the reinstatement (in November 1973) of India's previously unsatisfactory policy-short-term Soviet loans, to aid new urban and heavy-industrial *projects*—can make up for these gaps.

(b) *Net aid and 'repayment aid'.* Aid may be divided into two parts: net contribution to the recipient's funds for investment, and financing of repayment (of capital and interest) on past aid loans. The steady fall in the former's share (table 7.16) shows that the debt problem associated with foreign aid has become a major burden for India. By the end of the 1960s new aid, amounting to one-quarter of India's export earnings, was required to finance the amortization and interest payments on her past loans. Such repayments—running at some $417·5mn (£173mn) per annum—ate up over 30 per cent of gross aid receipts.

Some of India's individual bilateral aid relationships—notably those involving mainly short-term loans—present an even worse picture. By 1970–1, for example, India was paying back to the USSR some Rs210mn (£11·7mn) *more* than the Rs490mn she received as aid. The position was similar with respect to loans received from Czechoslovakia, Yugoslavia, and Poland, and also Japan—a member of the Consortium—which got Rs33·7mn more in repayments than the Rs150mn it 'gave' in 1970–1. Indeed only the US, Britain, Canada, and the World Bank were substantial net aid donors.[27] One Indian finance minister, Y. B. Chavan when faced with substantial criticism over such negative aid relationships, defended them on the ground that such debt-service payments to Eastern Europe and Japan are made in rupees and not in scarce free foreign exchange, as in the case of western countries.[28]

(iv) INDIAN ATTITUDES TO AID

India, like other recipients (and donors), has her over-general theorists— arguing that all aid creates dependence, or comprises resources for self-reliance, or helps the elite crush the masses, or helps the state destroy private enterprise— and their emotive rumblings are as tedious in India as elsewhere, if mercifully rarer owing to India's experience and sophistication. More interesting are attitudes to specific aid issues. Immediately after independence, there was naturally suspicion of foreign interference in the Indian economy, grounded in past experience of economic exploitation and political domination, which had 'a way of projecting itself into attitudes towards foreign aid'.[29] Such suspicions softened during the foreign-exchange crisis of the Second Plan, when western nations together with the World Bank met in an atmosphere of obvious concern to plan long-term external assistance, and when the East European nations also began a large scale aid programme. Foreign aid was now largely accepted as necessary for Indian development, though there were still many critics of the types of aid accepted and the uses to which it was put. But at least the earlier feeling that the acceptance of aid was equivalent to losing one's self-respect had by 1960 largely vanished.[30] What was widely felt as improper pressure (by the World Bank) towards an ill-fated policy (devaluation in mid-1966, just before an appalling harvest severely tightened the supply constraints on Indian exports) revived suspicions; yet the Indian arguments of the 1970s show little trace of this. They are about the *time-path* along which aid should lead to self-reliant development, not about the dignity or ideology of accepting aid at all.

Indeed, by the end of the 1960s urban middle-class opinion in India largely favoured foreign aid (table 7.17), though nearly half those questioned expressed some reservations about the terms of aid, and opinion was divided as to whether aid had made any difference to the standard of living. From the viewpoint of this study the most interesting feature of the Indian Institute of Public Opinion

(IIPO) surveys was the fall in awareness of Britain as an aid donor. This may damage the image of Britain held by literate Indians, amongst whom the surveys were conducted (pp. 195–6).

During the 1960s India's relations with the various aid donors fluctuated from friendliness to disdain and the attitude towards foreign aid altered in accordance. Donors have used aid as a political weapon, most strikingly the US in 1971 (p. 186), but notably in the 1960s also, with the temporary suspension of much western aid during the Indo-Pakistani war in 1965. Ideological overtones to aid had also crept into some donors' negotiations with India;[31] the monstrous debt burdens from old aid (p. 100) began to discredit new aid; and the 'turnkey' nature of some aid projects, Russian as well as western, was resented. Hence by the late 1960s many Indian commentators were again calling for future development policies to be less dependent upon aid.[32]

Yet at the level of the aid *negotiators* there had developed—at least until autumn 1971—a new and healthier relationship between the donor countries and India. Both agreed that types of aid can be so *selected* as to help self-reliance (e.g. food aid to build up reserves to permit profitable, but otherwise risky or inflationary, policies—not to glut the wheat markets). Recipients realize that they must stand on their own feet as soon as possible, and donors that they will achieve little by sermonizing. Indian planners feel that a reduced dependence on aid is essential even though the domestic rate of saving is low, for to try permanently to meet the gap between investment needs and savings through aid 'would lead to other psychological, political and economic problems which will undetermine the national will to surge forward on its way'.[33] However, the measured warning by India's leading aid negotiator of the 1960s, I. G. Patel, against arrogant and self-righteous attempts to impose 'performance criteria'— especially for small dribbles of hard, tied aid—while promoting visible and ideological exports is worthy of note.[34]

5. British aid to India: 1960–70

In evidence to the Select Committee on Overseas Aid, the purpose of British aid to India was defined as 'to help speed the day when India no longer needs aid from Britain or from any other source but has reached the stage of self-sustaining growth'. Within the aid total, provision is so made as to 'produce a truly cost-effective result; in other words to make every pound tell by wherever possible [looking] for a multiplier effect'.[35] In fact aid, at the end of the 1960s was becoming more costly to Britain (via cheapening and—until 1970—untying of loans) and hence more effective in India. Probably effectiveness was rising faster than cost; certainly some key areas of the Indian economy, where aid would yield high multiplier effects, had been recognized.

Throughout most of the past decade, while British *public* opinion has been lukewarm about aid (though, as shown on p. 115, not as hostile as perfunctory opinion-polling has suggested), *informed* opinion has overwhelmingly supported aid to Indian economic development, with a few notable exceptions.[36] The

Chinese attack of 1962 stirred large-scale sympathy for India in Britain, and for many people refocused British attention on Indian development needs and on the fact that India remained a democracy in an increasingly undemocratic Third World.[37] Britain's accumulated 'experience' in the Third World made politicians and bureaucrats feel specially able to help, or specially guilty, or both, not least about India; though African commitments, to states less poor than India yet somehow conceived of as more in need of British aid, prevented cash flows from matching attitudes (p. 102).

Amongst those most directly concerned with aid, there were some fears over the way British aid was being used in India, especially in major projects such as Durgapur, which began to run into trouble in the mid-1960s. So did the British balance of payments; the willingness to help India was constrained mostly by that consideration, although the commitment remained firm.[38] The visits of Sir Norman Kipping of the CBI to India in 1966 to investigate her economic crisis produced, in response to his report, general-purpose 'Kipping aid' to free raw-materials bottlenecks. The Kipping Report, the terrible harvests of 1965 and 1966, and the need for foreign exchange to meet the near-famine in Bihar in 1966–7—together with a determined pressure-group in London—induced the British government to respond in 1966–7 and 1967–8 by providing India with £7·5mn of food aid and £20mn of debt refinancing (see below, pp. 113–14). This precedent was stressed by Deputy Prime Minister Desai: 'By the liberal terms of its lending and provision of debt refinancing, the UK has set an example to other aid-givers to India.'[39] The ODM worked hard to increase the net aid flow and to alleviate the growing problem of India's external debt, although the stagnant aid total, plus inertia (p. 102), prevented any major reorientation of aid towards India from richer, better-aided, or worse-administered recipients.[40]

The Indian reaction to British aid has been largely favourable. Britain has been among the more efficient aid administrators, has progressively softened the terms of her loans to India, and was one of the first to provide refinancing facilities for Indian external debt. Occasionally there have been disagreements, but for most of the 1960s the aid relationship between Britain and India remained cordial: possibly to the point of complacency, given the dwindling real value of the net aid flows.

(i) QUANTUM

Disbursements of British aid to India rose very little in the 1960s (table 7.18). Gross aid given in 1970 was only slightly above the level of 1966. If we allow for increasing prices of Indian imports, the value of British aid to India was much less in 1970 than a decade earlier. Moreover, because of the growing capital-repayment and interest charges on *past* British loans to India, the net aid transfer to India by British development assistance in the 1960s was less than half the gross flow; terms softened after 1965, but this had no effect until 1972 (p. 110) and will be outweighed for some time after by the growing deadweight of dues upon old loans. Indeed, the net resource transfer (aid *minus* repayments of capital and interest) has been very low, and in 1969 fell to only £12·2mn. Only in the 1970s was there a dramatic recovery: net transfers rose to £29·2mn in 1970, and £42·5mn in 1971, but fell back to £33·9mn in 1972.

Britain has also contributed aid to India via multilateral institutions, mainly the World Bank and International Development Association (IDA). Using Britain's share of subscriptions as a proxy for her share of disbursements, we arrive at £71·3mn of British aid invested 'multilaterally' in India up to June 1970[41] (table 7.19). Further, Britain has also assisted some twenty-eight Indian companies in the private sector through the Commonwealth Development Finance Corporation (CDFC), granting them loans of some £10mn and purchasing equity in around a dozen, for a total of £1·2mn. These CDFC loans have so far been for buying capital equipment, but proposals have been made for CDFC loans to be used by Indian firms to purchase imports of raw materials and components à la Kipping.[42]

If one takes all bilateral and multilateral aid given to India mentioned above, then the gross flow of official assistance to India from Britain in 1950–72 was over £500mn.[43] From tables 7.15 and 7.19, we see that about 12·4 of the resources of international aid-giving bodies comes from the UK and that 13·1 per cent of Indian aid came from multilateral institutions. Thus Britain indirectly supplied 1·6 per cent (i.e. 12·4 per cent of 13·1 per cent) of India's aid inflows in this way.

(ii) TERMS OF AID

Almost all UK gross aid to India in the 1960s consisted of loans. This compares with about half total UK gross aid (table 7.9). Half of all world gross aid, too, comprised 'grants and grant-like contributions';[44] but of gross aid utilized by India over 1961/2–1969/70 from all sources, about 70·2 per cent was loans, only 5·1 per cent grants, and the rest US commodity aid, which lies between the two categories.[45] Thus UK aid to India is prima facie much 'harder' than total UK aid, a pattern also applying to world aid to India, but to a lesser extent. At least one Indian minister visiting Britain has actually approved this, on the 'self-reliance' theme that aid to India should amply cover its costs; but does it make sense? India may be more 'developed' than the African states who absorb most grant-aid (sometimes as thinly-disguised bribery),[46] but she is also poorer, shorter of foreign exchange, receiving far less aid per person, and hence less able to repay. For India herself further to reduce both the real value of her aid and her ability to repay, by opting for a loan-oriented aid programme, does not seem very sensible.[47]

It does, however, make the *terms* of aid loans very important. In the early 1960s the British record here was undistinguished. The 'grant element' in new British aid loans authorized for use during the Third Plan (April 1961–Mar 1966) was 63·2 per cent, as against a world average of 63·7 per cent for new loans authorized to India. Britain's relative performance on 'grant element of total aid' was of course worse (63·2 per cent as against 65·8 per cent for world aid to India) because loans were even more important, and grants less, in the British than in the world programme.

After 1965, however, Britain responded to the problem of India's debt burden (p. 113) and all subsequent British aid to India has been on terms even better than the DAC recommendation (p. 261), viz., interest-free, seven years' grace, and twenty-five years to maturity. Since the grace period on almost all earlier aid had also been seven years, the reduction of UK interest rates in 1965 (from 4·43 per cent in 1960–5) could not benefit India until 1972. However, the grant element in gross British aid clearly registered a sharp rise. An interest-free loan on the post-1965 terms has a grant element of 75·2 per cent, not so much lower than 'soft loans' from IDA. UK aid still consists overwhelmingly of loans, but this grant element is higher than the average for all *bilateral* donors to India, which has probably declined in the late 1960s from the Third Plan figure of 65·8 per cent owing to hardening US terms (and which is overstated in the official data because food aid is counted as a pure grant).

In 1966/7–1969/70, the UK's share in gross bilateral aid authorized to India was 7·9 per cent. Allowance for different rates of utilization raises the share to 8·2 per cent (table 7.15). To allow for the UK's higher grant element—75·2 per cent as against (at best) a world bilateral average of 65·8 per cent—raises the UK share to 9·3 per cent. The UK role in multilateral aid to India (p. 109) adds another 1·6 per cent to her share, and this has a grant element of at least 80 per cent since almost all new multilateral aid to India has been on the ultra-soft IDA terms; so this 1·6 per cent has to be scaled up by at least 80/65·8, to 2·0 per cent. Thus the grant-equivalent share of the UK gross aid flows utilized by India in the late 1960s was at least 11·3 per cent. But the true contribution was even more.[48]

(iii) TYING OF AID

'Tying' of aid may be to specific projects, to procurement of donor exports, or both ('double tying'). Only double tying is usually effective in raising donor exports—and in reducing the real value of aid to the recipient—because procurement-tied aid may be used to buy imports that would otherwise have been bought with 'non-aid' (or 'free') foreign exchange.

The development of British policy on tying of bilateral aid during the 1960s was complex, for there was often little difference between formally and informally tied aid. Thus while in 1963 it was stated that more than half of the bilateral aid was not formally tied, it was also noted that Britain had recently taken steps to ensure that such untied aid was not used 'to finance imports from industrialized nations other than Britain . . . except where British industry cannot supply the goods or services required on reasonably competitive terms'.[49]

The true position was accurately summed up by Sir Andrew Cohen in evidence to the Select Committee on Overseas Aid in 1968:

We do in fact tie, formally or informally, a very large proportion of our aid programme. As far as our bilateral aid is concerned, the general policy is to tie unless there is some special reason to the contrary. It would be better if all aid were untied . . . but since we have been unable to persuade others, particularly the United States, not to tie, we have been obliged, because of our own economic situation, to adopt this policy.[50]

By 1969 43 per cent of UK bilateral aid was formally tied (excluding technical assistance, aid for compensation and pensions, refinancing and other compensatory payments) and this had risen to 48 per cent by 1970. In addition to this fully tied aid, further procurement in the UK arises from the bilateral UK aid tied to UK or local goods and services in proportions not always laid down in advance; it has been estimated that such procurement, at 11 per cent in 1969 and 16 per cent in 1970, raised the estimated total of effectively tied UK aid to 54 per cent in 1969 and 64 per cent in 1970.[51]

However, this is spurious precision. The possibility of 'switching' by the recipient—spending procurement-tied but not double-tied aid on imports required anyway—means that *much aid which seems procurement-tied is not*. From 1965 to 1969 almost all British aid to India (while linked to procurement in the UK) was not tied to specific projects, except at India's request. Hence India was free to use it to purchase any British goods (including some she would have bought in any case) and was thus not forced to buy any overpriced or unwanted UK exports by the 'tie'. Moreover, *much aid that seems non-procurement-tied is;* the variety of practices is enormous, ranging from highly specific commodity lists through insistence on shipping in donor vessels to the questionable use of donor companies or connections or advance knowledge.[52] The estimate that 83 per cent of aid in the Third Plan was source-tied is probably too high, given the possibilities of 'switching' and the fact that some tying was due to Indian policy on import licensing.[53] Clearly the proportion of tied aid was rising until 1965. Hence the UK decision to give a large proportion of her aid from 1965 on a non-project basis had special importance.

However, by the end of the 1960s the continued refusal of other donors to untie aid had induced the British government to take measures to raise the proportion of aid tied to the purchase of British goods. By 1970–1 all the £18mn project aid to India was tied: 'Whereas the idea 18 months ago was to keep much of it untied, this is a policy which runs counter to the patterns developing in international aid to India'.[54] The competitiveness of British exports after the 1967 devaluation doubtless explained the reluctance of other donors to respond to this promising initiative. Certainly untied aid is best, both for donor efficiency and for recipient choice; but tied aid is better than no aid, which (since it is firms in donor countries that provide much of the remaining political muscle for aid) may be the real alternative.[55]

What is the effect of tying on the value of aid? A study for Pakistan,[56] mainly on industrial components, suggests that double-tied aid involves the recipient in paying at least 20 per cent above market rates for the commodities in question. The exact cost and extent of effective tying for India cannot be ascertained.

Certainly if the 'ultra-tied' US commodity aid were sold on the free market, wheat and cotton prices received by the US would fall sharply. If we say that 70 per cent of non-British aid (and almost no British aid) was effectively double-tied between 1965 and 1970 and that double-tied aid is worth 20 per cent less to the recipient than its apparent grant-equivalent value, we shall certainly be erring on the conservative side. But even these estimates raise the real value of grant-equivalent bilateral and multilateral gross UK aid to India in the late 1960s from 11·3 per cent (p. 110) to 12·8 per cent of the total.[57]

(iv) PROJECT AND NON-PROJECT AID

Project tying delays utilization and reduces the value of aid in two ways: by cutting flexibility (governments must use aid for new steelworks while old ones remain underutilized for want of component imports) and by making procurement-tying more effective by reducing prospects for switching. The sketchy data (table 7.20) show a large switch from project aid in the early 1960s to non-project aid by the mid-1960s, reversed from 1969 as the need for general-purpose aid declined with the ending of the Indian recession in 1968–9,[58] and as the decline in British exports to India continued (see p. 23). British aid has been devoted to over thirty projects, apart from the more notable ones at Bhopal and Durgapur, on which by 1968 over £100mn of British aid had been spent.[59]

Apart from project aid, Britain has assisted the Indian private sector through the Kipping loans (p. 108). As Kipping put it, this aid was mainly directed to breaking import bottlenecks at points where 'a lakh of expenditure at once will create a crore of production', mostly in British-owned or British-oriented firms. Although difficult to administer,[60] Kipping loans proved popular and effective in providing the Indian private sector with essential components. More recently they have become integrated into general UK non-project aid, and the Kipping label may well soon disappear; there are few advantages in keeping it separate. The switch from general purpose aid, given in the mid-1960s, to the more recent category of maintenance aid is aimed at reducing switching, which has probably lost Britain a good deal of trade;[61] if it succeeds, as is unlikely, the untied nature of UK aid, with its attendant advantages to India (p. 112), would vanish.

The other type of loan given by Britain was the food loan of 1966, made available to meet the emergency caused by the poor harvest. Since then Britain has given further food aid, principally a loan of £1·2mn for Indian purchases of foodgrains, mainly from Argentina.[62]

(v) STRUCTURE OF AID

Britain has large *private* investments in India outside manufacturing (pp. 88–9), but most British *aid* has been to projects and for purposes in the manufacturing sector (table 7.21).[63] Much UK aid has gone to specific projects, notably Durgapur Steelworks, Bhopal Heavy Electricals Plant, and the Nahorkatiya Oil

Pipe. So far—partly because the Indian authorities, with aid as with imports, reject things they *could* make themselves even if they do not—very little aid has been devoted to such key areas as crop storage, where multiplier effects would be high.

Only 7·0 per cent of utilized British aid from 1956 to 1970 went *identifiably* to the private sector in India, but the real share is much higher. General-purpose mixed public-private sector loans comprise 42·0 per cent of utilized aid. Further, the British private sector has supported some loans to the Indian public sector, presumably at rates made possible only by British government guarantees, and hence with an aid component. Such 'aid' has been limited to a loan from Lazard Brothers in 1957 of £11·5mn for Durgpaur Steelworks (repaid fully by 1964), a credit of Rs530mn (now worth only 460mn because of sterling devaluation) made by Barclays Bank to the public sector in 1966–7 but unutilized by March 1971,[64] and a loan of over £13mn by the Burmah Oil Co. to Oil India Ltd, disbursed over 1962–8.[65]

(vi) DEBT BURDEN

As noted earlier, the terms of all British loans to India since 1965 have been 'soft' when compared with those offered by some other bilateral and multi-lateral donors,[66] especially by those who untie aid by permitting repayment in rupees (see p. 106 above) but charge high interest rates and allow only a brief repayment period. Britain took a lead in the AIC in trying to obtain some collective action on debt refinancing and rescheduling. A Consortium report in 1968 proposed rescheduling $300mn of Indian debt-service payments due over 1968–71; the British share of this was $54mn. The Consortium agreed to this programme after much haggling, and largely through pressure from Britain, applied despite her running balance-of-payments crisis.[67] She had earlier taken the lead in debt rescheduling by giving $23mn of relief in 1966–7, another $28mn in 1967–8, and $18mn of refinancing in 1968–9.[68] By 1969–70 the UK had become the major source of debt-relief assistance, providing some $36mn of utilized relief out of a total of $107mn.[69]

Britain may be keener than other donors to provide debt relief and encourage others to do likewise because it is felt that British exports will benefit, even though debt relief supplements free foreign exchange rather than tied aid. British administrators in India, however, realize that the problem of debt servicing is more serious in the long run, for already the net aid transfer is below 60 per cent of the gross flow (p. 106) and in the British case lower still, owing to the hardness of past aid terms to India (p. 109).

The situation could arise where net aid becomes negative—when further aid does not suffice even to cover past aid debts (see p. 104). If these circumstances arise before India can finance her own desired investment rates, then the temptation to default—and, especially perhaps as ties with the USSR strengthen, to act against the (still largely British) foreign holdings of private capital—will mount. In so far as creditors dislike defaults, it pays Britain to review carefully Indian debt to her (table 7.22). By 1975 Indian debt-servicing charges to Britain are expected to be almost £25mn yearly and they will rise subsequently, although after 1990 they will fall as the interest-free post-1965 loans begin to predominate. There is a case for writing off the interest charges on past loans as one way of increasing the net aid flow, even though this suggestion would be opposed by some Indian advocates of self-reliance as well as by the UK Treasury.[70] Voluntary relief from creditors is not the same as breach of contract by debtors; it may indeed be the only way to prevent such a breach.

(vii) PRIVATE AID

This chapter has been primarily concerned with the flow of official resources from Britain to India (and vice versa), but recent evidence suggests that the contributions to Indian development made by individual Indians in Britain are more important than the official aid flow. Voluntary agencies, too, produce a quite considerable sum.

As yet little is known about the content, magnitude, and direction of British private aid to l.d.c.s. Only at the end of the 1960s did the OECD-DAC's sub-committee on statistical problems turn its attention to the many problems associated with charting the flows of the voluntary agencies (i.e. the development and welfare activities of the missionary societies and the charitable foundations such as Oxfam, Freedom from Hunger, and War on Want)—and these flows are minor, compared to the other component of private aid (personal remittances). First estimates put the total voluntary-agency flows from developed countries to l.d.c.s at around $840mn (£350 mn) in1970, and the UK's total flow at $42·3mn (£20mn).[71]

How much of this private aid goes to India is unknown, for detailed break-downs have not as yet been made available. However, there are indications that, as with official aid, proportionately more goes to Africa (resulting from the more recent colonial presence) even though major voluntary agencies have emphasized the importance of judging aid needs on a per-head basis, so as to avoid discrimination against countries with large populations.[72]

All the major British voluntary agencies make contributions to India, providing both technical assistance personnel (pp. 127f.) and equipment, mostly administered directly at the local level, and thus probably 'better' than much official aid in terms of development impact. Examples of the many local private aid schemes of this type are the Scottish War on Want projects in Alipur in central India, where Church of Scotland missionaries are demonstrating the efficient use of fertilizers, irrigation, and insecticides; providing farmers with loans to buy equipment, seeds, and fertilizers; and running a workshop to train local apprentices in metal-work. In Jalna in Western India, the same group helps to run a project where wells are being dug and hand pumps manufactured.[73]

A further important type of private aid to India is medical aid. Many of the hospitals in India are staffed by British medical missionaries and nurses (see p. 268) and in parts of the UK the unwanted free drug samples that pour on to doctors' doormats are collected and sent (after careful screening, one hopes) to India.[74] A more personal and dramatic instance of such aid is the restoration of the sight of Indian children by grafting corneas donated in Britain.[75]

During the discussion of 'invisible' flows between Britain and India (p. 77) we suggested that the remittances made by Indians in Britain to their relatives and associates in India were grossly underestimated in official data; in fact, there is reason to believe that they had reached over £40mn per annum by the end of the 1960s. Though remittances are not conventionally included in private voluntary aid, such resources effectively function as development aid within India. The effect of this private resource flow, which is certainly greater than the annual official net British aid to India, can often be both dramatic and productive, especially in the home villages of the immigrants, where such remittances have enabled housing, irrigation systems and water pumps, tractors and farm machinery to be provided, together with increased investment in land, livestock, and agricultural inputs such as fertilizer and improved seeds.[76]

Some of these remittances pay for extra consumption (though this is also true, indirectly and to some extent, of aid).[77] However, as these private resources flow directly to the villages and are spent on local needs, one could argue that their development impact was more immediate as well as more durable than official assistance; on the other hand, there is no direct contribution to the government's capacity to plan or finance overall development.

Clearly these private gifts, if added to public aid, raise Britain's share in the external finance of Indian economic development, arguably from 13 per cent (p. 112) to something around 40 per cent—a staggering result. However, to the extent that the gifts flow from immigrants educated in India and contributing to Britain as a result, the relevant education costs (p. 136) should be deducted from these personal aid flows, with appropriate forward discounting (p. 135).

6. Aid, trade, and the British balance of payments

(i) AID AND TRADE

We have attributed (pp. 36–7) much of the fall in Britain's share of total Indian imports to the increased role of tied, non-British, public aid in financing Indian imports since the exhaustion of India's sterling balances in 1958. This will be examined in more detail here. However, it should also be borne in mind that the share of India's total import trade *open* to Britain contracted during the 1960s with the success of Indian import-substitution policies and with the expansion of barter-trade agreements with East European countries. Given these factors and the slow growth of Indian export earnings it was inevitable that foreign assistance would play a larger role in residual Indian imports. Further, as most aid donors strove through procurement tying to minimize the losses to their balances of payments from aid, the area of Indian imports open to competition by suppliers was smaller still. In such a situation, the amount of aid given and the effectiveness of its tying are important determinants of trade shares.

As can be seen from table 7.23, the aid given to India by most major donors became increasingly related to imports from these donors. The most dramatic rise in the aid-trade ratio[78] is that of Britain; by 1969–70 only some 19 per cent of British exports to India were outside the total UK aid disbursed in India. The sub-periods, 1960–6 and 1966–70, demonstrate different explanations for the rising aid-trade ratio.

(a) *1960–6*. At the start of the 1960s many Indian importers were still linked by tradition to British suppliers and thus the British share of Indian imports of manufactures was little changed from the post-independence levels. Britain, as has been the case throughout the 1960s, was only a minor aid donor to India, giving around 8·5 per cent of total utilized aid during the Second Five-Year Plan.[79] British aid was largely directed at big projects and was pretty effectively tied to imports of British capital goods. By 1966 this had changed substantially.

In 1968 the ODM analysed Indo-British aid-trade relationships in 1961–7, to determine the reasons for the decline in the British share of total Indian imports.[80] The examination suggested that, apart from an element of natural post-colonial decline, the trade contraction and consequent rise in the aid-trade ratio could be explained by the factors listed in table 7.24. The main cause of Britain's falling sales to India was the rising share of total Indian imports tied to bilateral aid— around 27 per cent by 1965–7[81].

It is of interest that, by 1966, Britain was softening the terms of her aid to India and also giving the majority of the aid in non-project form, which is almost by definition more difficult to tie effectively. Further, Indian producers were beginning to switch to other suppliers for imports bought from the competitive pool, as British competitiveness waned in the mid-1960s (p. 38).

(b) *1966–70*. Between 1965–6 and 1967–8 almost all British aid was given in budgetary support (general purpose) form, to help India over an acute shortage of foreign exchange for maintaining existing industry. Such general-purpose aid made switching easy and certain, as

disbursements from general-purpose loans were authorised if the Government of India presented evidence that purchases had been made from Britain up to the amount claimed, without having to demonstrate that purchases had been made against licences specifying Britain as the supplier from which the importer was authorised to purchase. Thus with the general-purpose loans the Government of India had no need to direct importers to purchase from Britain in order to utilise our aid.[82]

It seems that, under such aid arrangements, British aid was rapidly switched, reserving the free foreign-exchange pool for other essential imports, and raising the British aid-trade ratio.

Since early 1969 all non-project aid has been contained within annual maintenance loans (except for Kipping loans and debt relief) and a single-country licensing system has been adopted. Under this system, the Indian government issues licences for use on British goods and thereby commits free foreign exchange to pay for them. Once payments have been made to British exporters, proof of payment and a certificate of origin are sent to ODM (in 1970–3, ODA) which then reimburses the GOI.[83] This procedure minimizes switching, and also brings British goods to the notice of would-be importers, by including British aid along with tied aid from other donors on the lists issued by the central import licensing authority and the state import controllers. The method does not involve any greater degree of formal tying, only more effective anti-switching administration.

However, the British aid-trade ratio had risen by 1969–70 to 81 per cent; Britain's performance in competing for Indian imports from the pool of free foreign exchange had deteriorated further from the position shown by ODM for 1965–7. The dramatic recovery of British exports to India since 1970 seems to be related to the larger volume of British aid to India, to the recovery of the share of project aid in total British aid, and to the growth of overt retying of both project and 'maintenance' aid, as well as to a revival in Britain's competitive position and to once-for-all arms sales.

No detailed study has emerged of export orders resulting from official British aid, or of the problems encountered by British firms exporting under the official aid system. Further, no regular or easily available list of such exports is produced, save for the press releases of ODA; thus no comprehensive analysis of such export orders is possible. However, we have assembled a six-month sample of export orders resulting from ODA loans to India from November 1970 to April 1971 (table 7.26).

(ii) AID AND THE BALANCE OF PAYMENTS

The simple aid-trade ratio gives us little indication of the effect of aid disbursements on the donor's balance of payments. It neglects the complex interactions of switching and reflection effects, and indeed says nothing about the effects of foreign assistance on the domestic economy of the donor.

Andrzei Krassowski estimated in 1965 that the net cost to the UK balance of payments, after allowing for switching and assuming that tied aid will not put inflationary pressure on the UK economy, was around 44 per cent of net British bilateral assistance in 1963 (48 per cent if one includes multilateral aid) though no breakdown by individual aid recipients was attempted.[84] Richard Cooper later suggested that every £100mn of British foreign aid imposed balance-of-payments costs of £62mn, though the assumptions underlying this estimate are not entirely clear.[85] The most detailed analysis of the effect of the British aid on the balance-of-payments was that of Bryan Hopkin, who estimated for 1964–6 that of every £100 of bilateral aid (capital and technical assistance) some £62·70 returned to the UK after allowing for switching and reflection effects (table 7.27).[86] Hopkin's analysis is valuable in the context of British-Indian relations in that he provides estimates of the balance-of-payments cost to Britain of individual bilateral aid relationships. As can be seen in table 7.27

and in more detail in table 7.28, the net cost of UK bilateral aid to India over 1964–6 was some £42·40 for every £100 given: somewhat less favourable than for British bilateral aid as a whole, though this is probably outweighed by the beneficial effects of interest repayments owing to the 'harder' structure of British aid to India.

Hopkin's estimate of the cost to the UK external balance of payments of aid to India is specific to 1964–6, and not applicable for the whole of the 1960s.[87] First, as we saw above, between 1966 and 1968 very little project aid was given, and instead assistance was largely in non-project general-purpose form which was highly susceptible to switching, though the increased cost to the British external balance that this implies would have been reduced by the end of the 1960s when UK aid tying tightened up. Further, Britain was a major supplier of multilateral aid to India (p. 109); though there are indications that Britain does extremely well in regard to obtaining export orders from such aid, it must be less tied (formally or informally) than bilateral aid. Any estimate of the total external cost to Britain of aid to India over 1960–70 would (like the ODM's) be highly responsive to the many assumptions required (tying, disbursement rates, aid types, etc.) so we have refrained from such an attempt.[88] Any such figure would not be applicable in the future, when aid terms and types will almost certainly be different. Further, in the UK of the mid-1970s, which will probably be running at higher levels of spare capacity in the domestic economy, the 'capacity effect' will be less, and thus the real drain on UK resources lower.[89]

7. The future

Given India's exceptional poverty, below-average aid per head, and seriously administered efforts to develop in a democratic framework, she has struck most observers as especially well qualified for aid,[90] yet she does far worse than she could justifiably expect. In such a context, and assuming Indian development (and pluralism) to be in the British interest (pp. 226f.), what can Britain do in the aid relationship in the 1970s and beyond to help India achieve her development goals? Certainly trade (including EEC trade), and in particular market access, means more to India's development prospects than aid; but aid will count for much. Even a path towards 'self-reliance' will require substantial aid to meet past debts (p. 100). Britain's aid depends upon the likely future development of the British economy. *If* it can grow at, say, 3 per cent or more without severe new balance-of-payments troubles, the aid budget will certainly expand again, and India should stand a good chance of claiming a large share of any increments. The political reaction in Britain against black Africa is a contributory factor here, however unfortunate in itself.

Now Britain is in the EEC, she must contribute to the European Development Fund and the European Investment Bank (EDF and EIB), which are at present confined to EEC associates and hence give nothing to India. (A British attempt in November 1973 to insert, as a 'thin end of the wedge', a $10mn yearly EDF contribution to non-associates, won general Commission approval, but was shelved under French pressure, based on the argument that Britain, alone in EEC, did not recognize the UN target for intergovernmental aid—no doubt a bad thing, but really irrelevant if Britain is to be a fully contributing member of EDF.) This may well divert British aid from India, and indeed the limited British 'assurances'—that *money* aid to India will not *fall*, as prices and British aid totals rise!—are more ominous than re-assuring. Probably Britain with an overall aid ceiling predetermined by quinquennial public-expenditure plans, themselves in 1973–4 under severe downward pressures—will have to enlarge her aid flow into these organizations by about as much as the French or German contributions. This would have meant in 1968 a net public commitment by Britain of about $45mn, or 10·5 per cent of her total net aid disbursed in that year:[91] but for three reasons this understates the likely burden on Britain's aid programme.

First, EDF-EIB aid seems likely to grow rather faster than UK aid in the 1970s.[92] Second, Britain's *gross* commitments to EIB loans, and to the loan component in EDF (about 10 per cent of it in the 1970s), will be larger relative to *net* commitments than for EEC members, who are already receiving repayments from earlier loans through these institutions. Third, 90 per cent of EDF commitments (which are to be $900mn in 1970–5, as against $100mn of EIB loans) is in grant form, as against under half the UK programme. By 1977 the true burden of EDF-EIB commitments (as a proportion of either the net or the grant-equivalent-gross UK aid programme) is unlikely to be less than 15 per cent, even if Britain adheres to the total aid targets laid down in November 1969 and accepted by successive governments.

With EDF-EIB in their present form, this must surely damage UK net aid to India. Its dramatic recovery in 1971–2 (p. 109)—partly due to the softening of aid terms in 1965 (pp. 110–12)—cannot be simply extrapolated. India is the biggest single recipient of UK aid and hence a natural target if room has to be made for EDF-EIB under the aid ceiling. Currently 'all grants and loans from EDF (and EIB) go to the states, countries and territories associated with EEC . . . and to the French Overseas Departments';[93] indeed these institutions were created to persuade France to enter EEC in 1957.[94] Possibly the few remaining British colonial relics could benefit from EDF-EIB under present arrangements. Much more important, all Commonwealth countries in Africa and the Caribbean are 'associable'; the more of them that associate, the greater (in theory) is the British aid burden transferred to other European shoulders. But this will do very little to offset the extra cost of aiding French Africa via EDF; all eight members of EEC, except Britain, will wish to reduce *their* commitments to EDF, and will thus insist that Britain's contribution to the Fund rises with the number of Commonwealth countries choosing to associate.

Need this mean that British aid to India is affected? The classification of India as 'non-associable' is taken for granted. Yet more ambitious arrangements—even associateship and membership in EDF for India, if she were interested—could be on the political agenda. Nobody, except France, much likes the present allocation of EDF aid funds, or the restrictionist and geographically arbitrary associateship arrangements. Renegotiation is always possible once Britain is in EEC (although in law the interests of the original associates in EDF-EIB are probably vested). It has to be admitted that, once 'Yaoundé III' begins in 1975, India's arrangements with the EEC will be hard to alter basically until it ends in 1980. Yet, with or without association, a closer Indo-EEC link (much more ambitious and comprehensive than the trade agreement of 16 December 1973) would enormously benefit not merely EEC's trade prospects, but its entire political and economic posture vis-à-vis the Third World.

During the 1973–5 negotiations for the third quinquennium of the Yaoundé arrangements, Britain might well press for radical changes in EDF and EIB. At present they steer massive European aid as 'budgetary support' to help France buy trade, capital, and political allegiance in countries, many of which are (or were until recently) corrupt and minuscule francophone timocracies, and which grow costlier as they become increasingly restive. Within the EEC Germany, in 1970–71 giving more gross aid than Britain to India, would certainly support any effort to redirect EDF-EIB aid towards South Asia; she has sound commercial and political reasons for such a line, and so probably has Italy. Under such circumstances the tactical ruse reported on p. 119 is unlikely to freeze EDF in its present anti-Asian posture for very long.

Nevertheless, the present EDF-EIB set-up presents a prima facie threat to UK aid to India and to Indo-British relations in general. Since a sound Indo-EEC relationship is perhaps *the* most important 'hidden' world issue of the 1970s, this is very serious. The early 1960s, when it was reasonable to see British entry to the EEC enhancing her aid relationship with India,[95] seem far distant today; but with imagination, with a refusal to see EEC as being mainly about butter prices, much is possible.

If Britain wishes to raise her net aid to India, how should it be done? It would help to forego interest payments on some past loans, and to shift future aid towards grants. The effectiveness of aid might be improved by working with the Indian government to select, for British aid, sectors and projects (a) where British expertise has something to offer; (b) with high rates of return; and (c) offering the best prospects for helping India to sustain *herself* the levels of growth, minimum income-per-head, employment, and exports she wants. In the Indian economy, these sectors almost certainly include minor irrigation; research into levels of the water-table and the costs and benefits of raising it; on-farm cereal storage, especially in anticipation of suddenly rising rice output; research into improved millets and pulses; training of female para-medical personnel for rural family-planning work; technical and adult education; and agro-industry. These priorities have been recognized partly by the Pearson Report, and substantially by the British aid administrators.[96] There may be a chance of reorienting the British aid programme and of focusing it much more sharply on a few of the key sectors mentioned.

Non-project aid is clearly needed to help flexibility (p. 112); the Indian economy, faced by oil price explosions and mounting debt burdens, will be chronically short of foreign exchange for maintenance imports. Indeed, to present aid as 'debt relief' not only relieves Indian worries about self-reliance; it also prevents older aid projects from standing half-idle for want of spares or inputs. Yet a similar goal can be achieved by foreign-exchange support for programmes with chiefly local costs. Probably an annual British outlay of, say, £15mn on family-planning programmes in India could achieve more towards advancing Indian self-sufficiency, in job creation as well as in savings-for-growth, than the same amount of general-purpose or maintenance aid. However, in this particular sector, the extra income-per-person generated (being in millions of households enabled to 'prevent' the birth of extra mouths) is not such as to generate direct repayment. Hence the relevant projects (e.g. para-medical personnel, nurses, and equipment)—with their widely-diffused, albeit enormous, benefits—would probably require grant rather than loan aid. Residual Indian sensitivity on the matter would be reduced if Britain at the same time recognized her own environmental interest in zero population growth; a truely joint Indo-British family-planning exercise would not be beyond the range of political vision.

An alternative strategy might be to concentrate aid spatially within India, perhaps on the problems of Calcutta and its rural hinterland—although this would involve a deliberate subsidization of a selected group of people which, in the Indian political climate, might well be unacceptable. But the central point is that an expanding total British aid programme is needed to overcome inertia, whether to steer a higher share of aid to India or a higher share of India's receipts to certain sorts of target. If totals stagnate, shares stagnate too; it is desperately hard to impose a cut.

8 TECHNICAL ASSISTANCE

> Transferring skills is a more difficult task than the relatively simple financial trans-actions needed to transfer capital . . . [for] . . . new skills involve new ways of thought, new habits, new aims in life, new philosophies. Technical Assistance, you could say, is virtually the art of persuading people to change the way they live and the way they think.
> ADRIAN MOYES, in A. Shonfield, ed., *Second Thoughts on Aid* (1965).

India is a net donor of technical assistance (TA) to Britain. We have chosen the assumptions most unfavourable to this surprising hypothesis; but the value to Britain of Indian training for skilled persons, mostly doctors, who later serve in Britain (net of the flow of training services in the opposite direction and of UK payment for skilled personnel and educational equipment in India) was at least £5·2mn per year, about 23 per cent of average net British public capital aid to India, in the 1960s.

The true relative value of TA flows in both directions is understated by these figures, for three reasons. First, accounting conventions overstate the value of capital aid, compared to 'manpower aid'. If Britain lends India £3mn at con-cessional rates to build a factory, the entire sum counts as aid. If Britain 'lends' India technicians for three years, paying their salaries at £1mn per year and getting £3mn back when they finish their work, this counts as exactly the same—£3mn. Yet the capital 'value' of those technicians—the cost of training them so that their services are worth £1mn per year—is closer to £8mn.

Secondly, much TA consists of free training. Britain trains lawyers for India. Willy-nilly, India trains doctors for Britain. A major component of training costs, the capital costs of universities or training institutions, is largely excluded in TA estimates, which mainly cover such items as teaching and maintenance charges.

Thirdly, while British capital loans to India are on soft terms, they are not nearly as soft as British or Indian TA. This is given free (involuntarily by India, though not of course by the personnel themselves, in the major case of doctors trained in India who work in Britain). Allowing for all three factors in a rough-and-ready way, we estimate that Indo-British net flows of technical assistance reduce by about 30 per cent the true value of net British public capital aid to India. That is roughly the true cost to India of, inter alia, saving the British National Health Service from collapse.

TA covers the free or concessional supply to l.d.c.s of advisers and operational personnel, usually to maintain public services ('manpower aid'); of technical training for certain types of equipment (usually educational); and of policy-oriented surveys and research.[1] Expenditure on TA is normally included with aid disbursements; there is in fact a continuum between capital aid and TA,

122

which ranges from free or subsidized commercial consultancy services[2] to outright grants for equipment. A purist would doubtless exclude some such items from TA, but they will all be included here.

1. The growth of technical assistance

A striking feature of international aid in the 1960s was the large increase in TA, despite the very small rise in total official aid flows (table 8.1). By 1969 TA accounted for 24 per cent of total net official aid given by DAC nations[3] (which contribute over 95 per cent of total bilateral aid flows) and multilateral institutions, and amounted to $1,763·9mn.[4]

Several factors underlie this switch in aid disbursements towards TA. Most clearly, balance-of-payments problems have induced several donors to seek forms of aid certain to involve their own personnel or goods (pp. 110–11), and TA qualifies par excellence. Second, TA salaries increase much faster than the price of capital goods exported under aid contracts, because such salaries, to attract personnel of a given standard, must reflect not only inflation but also the real growth in levels of living in the developed country. Third, and apparently more positively, donors have come to realize that TA plays a crucial role in the efficient functioning and utilization of capital aid, especially with the rapid development of increasingly sophisticated equipment and techniques in donor countries, and hence the increased technical-training needs at all operational levels; but even here a sceptic might argue that capital aid geared to the recipient's level of technical skills, rather than to the curing of spare capacity among the more vociferous sectors of heavy industry in donor countries, would be preferable to TA to remedy, ex post, the scarcity and inappropriateness of capital aid, Finally, the growth of TA reflects the near-universal expansion of educational and health programmes in l.d.c.s. This rapid growth has happened despite the fall in compensation payments on TA budgets (p. 124); it was helped along by another accounting item, the transfer of expatriate personnel from colonial administrations and budgets to TA grants.

Of the DAC nations the USA was until recently by far the largest donor of TA, and although her share fell during the 1960s it still remained at nearly 50 per cent by 1968–9.[5] This figure fell sharply in 1970 to around 36 per cent, and the stagnation of US TA, while that of other DAC countries grew, had by 1972 slashed the proportion to 29·6 per cent—overtaken by France (32·2 per cent).[6] Britain comes fourth after Germany as a source of TA (table 8.1), and both France and Germany spent far more per head of their domestic populations than the UK. Further, over the 1960s Britain's share of DAC TA fell, and her TA growth-rate of 10·2 per cent per annum over the 1962–9 was substantially below the DAC average of 15·1 per cent; even by 1972, Britain's share of DAC TA had recovered only to 8·2 per cent (from a low in 1968 of 6·7 per cent), far below the shares of other countries in DAC with similar residual obligations from the colonial period.[7] Such comparisons are, however, less than fair to Britain; for India and Pakistan, which receive a major proportion of the total

British aid budget, have a small and declining need for TA, in contrast to the African countries with government machinery that relies very heavily on French TA personnel and expenditure.[8]

The increased expenditure on TA during the 1960s has been matched by an expansion in the number of TA personnel, both in donor and recipient countries. Here DAC nations accounted for the great bulk, even on generous assumptions about efforts by communist countries. The provision of training for students and technical trainees was fairly evenly divided between the four major DAC donors (table 8.2), but France and Britain—because of their colonial past—supplied most of the experts and volunteers, though the US had overtaken Britain by 1965. Within the expansion shown in table 8.2, there were important changes in the composition and distribution of TA personnel, and probably a decrease in their quality.[9] For Britain the main change was the expansion of the programme for students and trainees, compared with the growth in the provision of experts and volunteers (although these still formed 59 per cent of British TA personnel in 1970).

The distribution of TA among recipients follows no simple pattern. One can well imagine levels of underdevelopment at which absorptive capacity, at least for complex and thus costly TA, is low; and levels of sophistication where little TA is needed. India's inclusion in the latter camp shows that income per head tells us very little. Relevant factors are the level and structure of educational development; the nature and development relevance of ex-colonial links; and the administrative capacity of the recipient nation. In the 1960s Asian countries have received little TA but almost half of the total aid; Africa has received almost half of total TA expenditure though less than a quarter of total aid flows; and Latin America has received one-sixth of total aid and one-fifth of total TA.[10] India receives very little TA, partly because of her large population but also because of the nature of her economic development in TA areas, sufficiently advanced to make India a major donor of TA to other l.d.c.s.

2. The British TA Programme

While total UK gross financial aid to l.d.c.s rose by 44 per cent between 1960 and 1970 to £213·8mn, TA disbursements rose by 368 per cent to £51·6mn, just under a quarter of the UK gross aid in 1970 (table 8.3). Since this is almost all in grant form, while the grant-equivalent of the whole UK gross aid programme is only about 80 per cent (p. 99), TA made up just over 30 per cent of the UK programme in grant-equivalent terms in 1970; 86 per cent of this TA was bilateral. Contributions towards multilateral TA programmes have grown much more slowly, partly because multilateral institutions were still engaged in formulating programmes and determining priorities for much of the 1960s, and partly because UK TA was dominated by ex-colonial relationships which pre-empted much of the TA expenditures. It should be stressed that cash transfers to l.d.c.s were substantially less than the sums shown in table 8.4, for much TA expenditure is used to pay teachers and administrators in the donor country.[11]

Much British TA—by 1970 one-third—went to supplement the salaries of British experts overseas (table 8.4). The training of l.d.c. personnel and students was the next largest category (16·7 per cent in 1970), though only around 4 per cent of such expenditure was made in l.d.c.s themselves. Other major outlays were on research programmes relating to l.d.c. problems, on consultancies (in both cases the finance being spent mainly in the UK), and on land surveys. The biggest change has been the fall in the compensation payments made to expatriate officers, which between 1965 and 1970 fell from nearly 20 per cent of total UK TA disbursements to just over 1 per cent, reflecting the removal of many colonial ties rather than a true fall-off in TA.

Britain's TA disbursements are heavily concentrated in Commonwealth countries (table 8.5). They receive over 80 per cent of total expenditure, largely in Africa, where Britain had a major post-war colonial presence; by the end of the 1960s Commonwealth African countries were receiving over half of total British TA. The Asian share held up, though within it expenditure was switched to non-Commonwealth nations, largely in war-torn South-East Asia. However, given relative populations, the Asian share was extremely modest. In terms of personnel (table 8.6), Africa's dominance of British TA was even more marked, and indeed increased during the 1960s; even where British colonial administrators and operational personnel in Africa were replaced by expatriate experts, these were often still financed by TA grants to the ex-colonies. The Asian share fell sharply, and by 1970 India was receiving less than 1 per cent of total British TA personnel, though slightly more (1·5 per cent) of expenditure.

3. British TA to India

Though India has received about 20 per cent of gross British bilateral aid, her share of British TA has been small: only some £772,000 annually, or just about 1½ per cent of total UK TA, and only 2 per cent of India's annual aid from Britain (table 8.7).

The major reason for Britain's small TA effort in India lies in the advanced state of Indian expertise in most technical, scientific, economic, and social subjects compared with other l.d.c.s.[12] Except in areas of British or other specialization, Indians are able to provide the necessary technical services themselves. Indeed during the 1960s India had begun to be a major donor of technical assistance to other l.d.c.s, mainly in Asia.[13]

Low British TA in India is thus not worrying; it partly reflects an infrastructure of training and expertise in a wide range of desciplines and occupations and professions, some of it imparted to the Indians by the British during colonial rule.[14] When independence arrived, most of the necessary expertise has already been transferred; India was at the other extreme from the Congo, where the ruling colonial power had made virtually no attempt to train the indigenous population. It is true that no technical training by a colonial power, even one preparing to leave, is ideally suited for independent development; but it is much better than nothing, and can create awareness of its own deficiencies (see pp.

156f). Hence it is not surprising that the proportion of TA in total aid is extremely small.[15]

The role of Britain's gross contribution in India's total TA is hard to determine, as figures for the undoubtedly large Soviet contribution are not available. But Britain supplied 10 per cent of 1968–9 disbursements in India on educational equipment and technical co-operation from major western donors (table 8.8): much less than the UK's share in capital aid proper, though more than her share in food aid. Over 1965–8, Britain's total expenditure on TA to India was nearly $15·5mn, around 13 per cent of the total from major western donors. Between 1950 and 1970 British TA expenditures on India came to around £7·2mn,[16] of which only about £0·8mn was actually spent in India.[17]

The bulk of the UK's total outlay on TA in the 1960s has been devoted to paying the salaries of advisers and experts (table 8.9), but British TA to India has been largely expenditure on students and trainees, though their share of total UK TA to India has fallen slightly during the period. The rise in expenditure on experts for India during the mid–1960s (to just over half the UK's total TA) is largely due to the advisers and operational personnel seconded to help commission major UK capital aid projects in India such as Durgapur and Bhopal, and to the Indian Institute of Technology (IIT) at Delhi. Since then the fall in numbers recruited for such tasks has led to reduced expenditure in this area, though this has been matched by increased expenditure on equipment and other donations. By 1970 just over half British TA expenditure on India went on students and trainees, so it is worth looking briefly at these first (concentrating on the trainees, as the students are discussed on pp. 140–4).

(i) TRAINEES

Here India has perhaps the most developed and comprehensive expertise of all l.d.c.s, and her huge internal education programme (including advanced technological universities—p. 146—and technical training schools) means that relatively few Indians need to go abroad for basic or lower-level specialists training,[18] except in very specialized disciplines that India has not yet developed, or in subjects where a short visit to see how a comparable system or industry operates in a different context is thought to be valuable. Over 12,300 Indians[19] had been trained abroad under the auspices of the Colombo Plan and the American TCA during the first three Five-Year Plans;[20] even by 1963 nearly 1,900 engineers and operatives from the three new public-sector steel plants had been sent abroad for training.[21] Apart from such training of Indians overseas, the USSR has contributed to local training schemes for more than 25,000 specialists, including 10,000 for Bhilai steel plant alone.[22] However measured, such TA input into India's training needs has been substantial.

In 1950–69 Britain provided some 2,600 official training places for Indians in Britain, nearly 30 per cent of total places in the Colombo Plan countries (table 8.10). By 1970 most of the Indian trainees visiting Britain remained for relatively short periods, mostly less than a year (table 8.12). The biggest group came to learn industrial and commercial subjects, both by attachment to individual firms and by attendance (often on sandwich courses) at higher education institutes. Major groups have also come to study trade unionism and labour administration, medicine and health, transport and communications, social sciences, and agriculture.[23] Little is known about the types or levels of Indian trainees within British industry, but they cover such fields as insurance (where students are trained both by private companies and at the Chartered Insurance Institute College at Surbiton) and engineering (where, in relation to her size, India seems to be under-represented—at least in terms of winning CBI scholarships—in table 8.12).

(ii) EXPERTS AND ADVISERS

During the first three Indian Five-Year Plans, some 3,200 experts arrived in India from the major western donors;[24] perhaps 10 per cent were British. This relatively small proportion reflects the big new US role, the fact that much of the relevant British expertise had been transferred before independence, and the concentration of Britain's major effort in this field in the private sector (p. 129).

Over 1951–68, 353 British experts were seconded to India, largely under the auspices of the Colombo Plan organization. In the 1950s, most of the TA personnel were advising on industry, commerce, and communications, whereas by the late 1960s the major British effort was going into education, chiefly into the IIT.[25] No experts have advised on the Indian system of administration, as India has a well-established and experienced administrative service. In the late 1960s British advisers in India included engineers—several at Heavy Electricals (India) Ltd at Bhopal, one at the Security Paper Mill at Hashangabad, and one in pressure die-casting; a field-drainage expert advising the director of the Tea Research Association Experimental Station at Tocklai, Assam; and consultant geologists and mining engineers assisting the National Mineral Development Corporation Ltd diamond mines in Madhya Pradesh.[26] Spiritually if not in the accounts, TA covered the distinguished service of Sir Verrier Elvin to the formulation of tribal policy under Nehru, and—in a more modern genre—the services of Mr H. L. Elvin to India's refreshingly multinational Education Commission in 1964–6.

In higher education, India is as developed, as mis-developed, and as uneven as many a rich country. Most countries, especially open and democratic ones, expect to give and receive 'expert TA' and India adds little that is specifically 'underdeveloped' to such requirements. Hence, with some exceptions in social science research, most Indians welcome foreign experts.[27] Some are less appreciative, especially of the value of visiting economists.[28]

British TA experts and advisers, as a whole, are not too happy with the administration and organization of their periods of secondment, and many faced serious problems, especially in training local personnel.[29] However, as India receives only senior specialists and consultants from Britain, such problems are less likely to have been encountered there.

(iii) EQUIPMENT

Most of the equipment provided has been for educational and research establishments, with a major share going to IIT. Some personnel financed by private charities, in technical support of their capital equipment donations, should really be added to our (official) British TA figures. Thus medical and educational staff have been provided by the various missionary bodies.[30] In support of £40,000 worth of fertilizers donated to India by the UK Freedom from Hunger Campaign over 1966–8, experts from ICI and Fisons have supervised their use in two pilot credit and distribution schemes in the Kanpur-Lucknow area. Most of the major British 'tropical research' institutes have also undertaken projects for India, such as an investigation of pesticide residues in India carried out by the Tropical Pesticides Research Unit. Since the late 1960s there has been an expansion, in Britain, of TA-linked, policy-oriented applied research on India in the social sciences; for example, at the Institute of Development Studies (IDS) at Sussex University, the ODM-ODA have sponsored an interdisciplinary project on the Kosi development area in Bihar,[31] a field study (jointly with the Indian Grain Storage Institute) on the costs and benefits of improved rice storage in Andhra, an analysis of the riskiness of Indian rainfall, and—together with ILO and the UK Social Science Research Council—a study of the methods, and the conclusions regarding migration, employment, and demography, of over 2,500 Third World 'village studies', over half of them Indian.

4. Private-sector training and 'private TA'

Apart from aid by private charities (p. 114), substantial TA is provided—especially in education and health—by private-sector charitable or non-profit organizations, and OECD has estimated that by 1969 the total annual flow in this area alone came to some $300mn.[32] Further private TA[33] often accompanies official bilateral capital aid (e.g. instruction given by private-sector firms on the operation and maintenance of equipment supplied by them), and this may sometimes be included in the official TA accounts. However, it has become popular to define as 'private TA' also the training efforts of firms with investments in l.d.c.s. This is not quite as silly as defining 'aid' to include private investment, because the trainees seldom remain in the training firm for ever, so that there is a genuine TA element of 'external benefit', even though training is primarily geared towards the firm's own needs.[34] Since Britain dominates private foreign investment in India (pp. 86–7) private training from Britain to India is substantial, and its TA component is not negligible, though most trainees are keen to stay with the firm that trained them.

Many respondents to the 1967 Glasgow University survey of British firms operating in India (pp. 92–3) felt that the training of local personnel was one of the key areas where British firms could aid the development of the Indian economy. Most such firms train Indians. The bigger the firm, as a rule, the more advanced and sophisticated is the training of Indian personnel, partly in response to pressure to Indianize the management since independence,[35] partly because of genuine desires by large UK companies to prepare their foreign associates or subsidiaries for self-government where ever possible (it is cheaper), and partly because, in the case of India, the burden of taxation on expatriate personnel encourages companies to train indigenous replacements quickly.[36] The prime example has been the training provided for the engineers and operatives of the Durgapur Steel Plant by the British steel industry, and by the British manufacturers of the plant used at Bhopal, in both cases under the auspices of the Colombo Plan. The Indians seem to have been satisfied with the quality of training provided by Britain for these projects.[37]

Though little more is known about British private-sector training within India, some more detailed evidence is available about such training within the UK. In May 1965 the then Ministry of Labour (now Department of Employment) estimated that 2,700 overseas trainees were studying in 7,000 organizations in British industry.[38] As many courses were short (2–6 months), the Ministry estimated total overseas trainees at 10,000 for 1965 as a whole. Of these, 64 per cent came from l.d.c.s, of whom 64 per cent were on the payrolls of the organizations training them. Most trainees were taken on at the request of a foreign associate or subsidiary company, though a quarter were taken on at their own request and just under a fifth at the request of the government or government agency of the trainee's home country. Nearly one-third of the trainees were technicians on training related to higher and ordinary national certificate or diploma level, and City and Guilds courses, while 38 per cent were listed as being above that level, mainly at postgraduate or senior management level. The main fields of training were electrical, mechanical and production engineering, commerce and, somewhat surprisingly, construction, where a significantly higher proportion of trainees were 'on the payroll' than in other industries.

The 1965 survey noted that, amongst trainees from l.d.c.s, Indians and Nigerians predominated. Separate figures are available from the Department of Education and Science for overseas trainees registered for higher and ordinary national certificate or diploma level, City and Guilds, and other vocational courses at grant-aided further education establishments in England and Wales. For 1965 these show that out of 9,959 overseas students on the courses outlined above, 504 were from India,[39] a level which remained fairly stable throughout the 1960s. A further 150–200 Indians were arriving yearly in Britain for industrial training (under the 1962 and 1968 Immigration Acts—table 8.13), where once again India dominated the scene. If one allows for industrial training of Indians in further education establishments in Scotland and Northern Ireland, and for postgraduates and management trainees not included in the above figures, perhaps 750–800 Indians per annum received technical training under private-sector TA schemes in the UK. Some were on scholarships (table 8.12); others were paid by firms or self-financed. The diverse methods of financing and types of training—and the difficulty in assessing the share of its benefits retained in the firm itself—prohibit any sensible estimate of its value as private TA. Further, not all the costs are borne in Britain, and many trainees are on part-time courses and thus function as employees for part of the time. But the cost, to British companies, of all *activities generating* private TA to India must be considerably more than the cost, to the British programme, of official bilateral TA; these private training activities would certainly repay further investigation. It must be emphasized, however, that from the 'donor's' viewpoint TA training is undertaken voluntarily by, and generates benefits mainly for, the British companies doing it; while from India's viewpoint only the benefits not retained in the companies can really count as TA. Thus, while private training in Britain for India is substantial, its true TA component is much smaller.

5. Future British TA to India

Good TA trains its replacements; it is not likely that British TA to India will increase greatly. Future British TA in India will probably concentrate on preliminary investigations of areas where

. . . we think there is a priority need and . . . where there are problems . . . on which the Indians might be interested to have the views of our specialists . . . and on which we benefit by better identification of areas where future UK TA could be employed from advice given by British experts who are actually involved and engaged in work here.[40]

Because of the rapid development of Indian expertise in most fields, future British experts are likely to be of a 'rather high, very confined specialization . . . the sort of specialization which we need ourselves in Britain . . . These are difficult men to find.'[41]

If they can be found, and if greater effort can be directed to identifying potential areas of technical assistance,[42] then there could be substantial returns for both Britain and India. India, by identifying such problems and formulating policies and programmes for their solution, one would in effect be breaking developmental bottlenecks. Britain, therefore, could without fear of resentment suggest that major consultancy contracts, and *where appropriate* items of capital equipment, were purchased here by India as a result of the initial exploratory work.

A further major area of promise (analogous to Indo-British joint investment ventures in third countries—see p. 95) involves British support to Indian-based institutions for research and training on matters of development importance to several countries. A major endeavour is the Institute for Crop Research in the Semi-Arid Tropics (ICRISAT), which opened at Hyderabad in 1974 under the joint sponsorship of the Indian government, the Canadian and British aid programmes, and the Rockefeller Foundation. Combining social and biological sciences, this new Institute will tackle problems of water conservation and use, farm management and seed breeding directly relevant to the world's poorest and most risk-prone (and under-researched) farmers, in many parts of Asia and Africa. From a TA viewpoint, an Indian-based yet international venture such as ICRISAT is a real path-breaker. It combines Indian experience and research skills (well in advance of most countries in their developmental relevance) and international capital and expertise in a TA project with yields far beyond India's borders.

6. Indian TA to Britain

(i) REVERSE TA

How could India possibly provide TA to Britain? Is this not a function which only developed countries can undertake? The definition of TA (n.l, p. 266) covered 'the provision of scholarships and education for overseas students'. If one's own nationals use their education to work abroad, 'abroad' gets TA; on this basis India does provide considerable TA to Britain, greatly to Britain's benefit, and almost certainly to India's detriment. It is true that, unlike British TA personnel in India, Indian personnel in Britain receive current salaries (and purchase commodities with such salaries) from their country of residence, not from their country of origin. When an Indian doctor works in Britain, India 'saves' the value of food, housing, etc. he would otherwise have consumed in India. However, the salary of a doctor or engineer (and above all the part of it which is consumed) understates his social contribution. That is the reason why he is often trained at the public expense. Britain pays the salaries of her doctors, be they Indian or British. If India pays for their training, and they practise for many years in Britain, then India is giving Britain TA to the extent of Britain's saving in training costs—just as Britain gives India TA by training Indian lawyers who are later paid by India to practise there.

(ii) THE PROFESSIONAL BRAIN GAIN TO BRITAIN

The operation of an international market for highly skilled manpower such as doctors, engineers, scientists, and teachers is a well established fact. The best of them, in search of higher salaries, often move from poor countries to rich ones. Countries like India—producing large numbers of these expensive commodities —have to live with this. The social value of a doctor is greater, but his reward much smaller, if he cures worms in West Bengal rather than neuroses in Northampton. India can ill afford to train costly doctors for Britain; yet to keep them at home she would need to pay them even more, making them costlier and increasing inequality. For steps to *make* them stay in India—or reimburse training costs if they leave—have so far proved either impracticable or unacceptable to the Indian elite.

During the 1960s several factors led to a continuous flow of highly-trained Indian manpower to the UK: initially liberal UK immigration laws; their gradual and well-advertised tightening, which induced potential migrants to act quickly; the continued shortage of highly skilled (especially medical) manpower in the UK; its aggravation by Britain's own brain drain to the USA; the increasingly crowded state of the Indian employment market; the attraction of the educational and research systems to be found in the UK; and the natural desire of the best Indian specialists to compete with and among scientific and medical peer groups in a congenial cultural, intellectual, and physical climate.

Nearly three-quarters of the Indian graduates who chose to register with their Directorate of Scientific and Technical Personnel (DSTP) as being abroad at January 1971 were in the USA or the UK, with slightly more in the former, and another 6.3 per cent in Canada (table 8.14). This partly reflects the low expertise in languages other than English, which remains the major language of instruction in higher education in India. Scientists, engineers, and medical personnel constitute 94 per cent of immigrants.

Emigrants in particular disciplines select particular countries (table 8.14). Almost half the Indian graduates in West Germany are engineers, thus keeping up a long-established tradition (pp. 271); over half of Canada's immigrants from India are scientists; most Indian immigrants to the USA (which dominates every field except medicine) are engineers and scientists. For the UK over 60 per cent of graduate Indians who arrive are doctors, and of the 2,258 Indian doctors overseas in January 1971, 72 per cent were in the UK. There are many reasons for this concentration of Indian doctors in the UK: the reputation of the British medical system and training; the tradition of medical training in Britain that grew up during the latter days of the Raj; and, perhaps, until the late 1960s, the relatively easier entry conditions compared with the USA, where doctors require not only visas but also to pass the exams of the Educational Council for Foreign Medical Graduates in the English language and basic medical knowledge. The Indian figure for doctors (table 8.15) is much lower than statistics gathered in the UK (pp. 269), because registration with the DSTP is not compulsory. However, these Indian data do indicate the trends, show the structure by countries and subjects, and above all provide *minimum* (yet still huge) estimates of the size of this reverse trainee flow from India to the developed nations. These are without doubt net recipients of TA from India.

More detailed Indian estimates of *registered* skilled emigrants are available for 1968 (table 8.15), where the broad trends of table 8.14 are reflected, except that the UK gained larger numbers of engineers in 1968. 660 doctors are shown entering the UK, whereas UK figures give either 768 or 859, depending on the sources used.

The main category in the India-Britain flow, then, is of Indian doctors who arrive in Britain, initially (and often purely nominally) for further postgraduate and specialist training. They usually end up as 'invaluable underpinning for the National Health Service'.[43] Most of the following discussion will be centred on the role of the Indian doctor in the British Health Service, and the cost to India of training such skilled manpower for Britain.

(iii) INDIAN DOCTORS IN BRITAIN

Without foreign doctors, many British hospitals would have to close, and several towns would be almost denuded of GPs.

(a) *Total stock*. Figures for the total number of Indian-born doctors permanently resident in Britain must await the publication of the 1971 Census. These elusive notions of permanency and return matter little; the gain to Britain, and the loss to India, is measured by the number of 'doctor-years' made possible by training in India, but worked in Britain, in any particular year.

If the doctors providing these man years return to India, with technically high but largely irrelevant training and expectations—and with many of their most active years behind them—they are unlikely to be 'worth' more or less than the new Indian doctors who come to Britain in their place. Hence gains or losses on 'human capital-gain account' can be ignored. What count are the *flows* of services, from Indian-trained doctors provided to Britain.

The figure that matters, therefore, in measuring the transfer is that for Indian-born doctors practising in Britain. The number in England and Wales was put at 3,450 at the end of September 1967.[44] Allowing for similar employment in Scotland and Northern Ireland, there must then have been some 4,000 Indian-born doctors in Britain. The net-flow estimates discussed in the next section suggest a rise to 5,000 by the beginning of 1971, but another estimate[45] (6,000 in mid-1969) implies that one in ten British doctors was born in India.

How does this compare with Britain's stock of *all* foreign-born doctors? In 1967 some 10,600 were working in the NHS in England and Wales (15 per cent of the total of 63,000)—8,000 in hospital service, the rest as GPs.[46] These were almost all trained abroad; 'at least two-thirds [in less developed] countries, primarily India and Pakistan'.[47]

(b) *Inflow*. So one in seven British doctors is foreign, and the dependence is growing. Probably the poor Commonwealth countries *alone* bore the main cost of training one in *four* of the new doctors entering service in Britain in 1967[48] (table 8.16)—mostly Indians. From 1947 to 1961 some 4,000 Indian doctors entered Britain,[49] some to take Fellowships at British medical colleges (pp. 143–4) or to receive specialized training; but many did not return, and many more practised for several years in Britain before India received any benefits from the costs incurred in their initial training.

The number of Commonwealth doctors entering the UK under 'B' vouchers of the Commonwealth Immigration Act of 1962 rose until 1968, but seems to have fallen since.[50] It is only with the 1968 Commonwealth Immigration Act that detailed figures become available (table 8.17), which show that Indian doctors remained in the majority, though the total number admitted on 'B' vouchers declined substantially, about which more below. More detailed information for 1965–7 (table 8.18) shows that the stock of Indian doctors in Britain—at least in the mid-1960s—was growing at around 300 per annum, or about 40 per cent of the gross inflow. This roughly replaced the net *loss* of British and Irish-born doctors of around 350 per annum.[51]

Since the mid-1960s the rate of inflow of Indian doctors into the UK has fallen considerably, and in 1970 only 211 entered under the 'B' voucher system.

This decline is almost entirely due to changes in the 'quotas' of various professional immigrants allowed into Britain. In March 1968 stricter entry criteria were introduced for teachers and science and technology graduates—partly as Danegeld to those who dislike non-whites, but partly because of real and growing evidence that such entrants were failing to find satisfactory employment in the UK. These restrictions did not initially affect doctors, who therefore formed a larger percentage of the smaller waiting list and thus received a larger number of vouchers. 'If this had been allowed to continue it would have resulted in doctors being admitted at a rate faster than that at which they could be absorbed into suitable employment in this country'.[52] Therefore on 24 July 1969 the secretary of state for health and social security announced that the number of vouchers for doctors had been limited to 2,000 in any one year, though doctors who come for a recognized postgraduate study course combined with employment are exempted from the voucher scheme. Although this has sharply cut 'B' voucher entry by Indian doctors, it remains possible—especially after the new rules are fully absorbed—that the same number will enter, though many fewer will come with the stated intention of taking up permanent employment and residence.

There are three points to notice here. First, there seems no doubt that the 'skilled persons' work-voucher provisions of the Commonwealth Immigration Act have been used as an instrument for recruiting medical men from poor countries for service in Britain. However, against this, there is little relationship between the number of 'B' vouchers issued to doctors and the prospects of a job in Britain. Declining job prospects in Britain—as our medical training programmes have grown, and the drain to the US has slowed—have meant that since the late 1960s only about half of the 'B' vouchers issued to doctors overseas have been taken up;[53] even so, the number of Indians and other Commonwealth doctors coming to Britain and failing to find a job has risen sharply, especially in pre-registration posts, which are in short enough supply for British graduates.[54] Thirdly, most Indian doctors who come to Britain are usually formally considered as postgraduate students here for advanced training, though 'the line between a foreign post-graduate medical student and an immigrant doctor is not clear'.[55]

(c) *Conditions of work.* The situation facing Indian doctors arriving in Britain, by definition, suffices to attract them; yet it seems far from attractive. First, they have only about half as good a chance as a British doctor of working in a teaching hospital, and therefore of receiving the full-scale postgraduate training they are usually alleged to have come for. Secondly, they must almost certainly work outside London if they seek a higher medical grade, such as Consultant or Senior Registrar. 'The further from London you go, and, the lower down the rating scale is the hospital, the higher is the proportion of immigrant doctors'[56] (tables 8.19, 8.20). Thirdly, Indian and other overseas doctors are mainly concentrated in (or, more important, can get promotions only by learning) specialisms such as geriatrics, ear-nose-and-throat, or traumatic and orthopaedic surgery, which are less attractive to British doctors, or which, to put it harshly, are generally in less modern units—even though they normally have the best promotion opportunities.

At least over the 1960s, then, Indian and other foreign-born doctors have functioned as cheap labour with which to staff unattractive (to British doctors) hospitals and specialisms, rather than as postgraduates receiving a training. The British medical graduates meanwhile filled the more attractive jobs here in Britain, or emigrated to the better-paid medical professions of North America. Meanwhile India's dramatically young population, troubled with TB, dysentery, and worm infestation, must have found the few returning doctors, building on their costly Indian basic training with specialized work in geriatrics or ortho-paedic surgery, a poor advertisement for British TA.

Why do Indian doctors come to Britain, knowing well the conditions they are likely to face? Basic, of course, is the pay; but there is more to it. Some migrant doctors consider that a period spent in Britain would help their career prospects once they return home, especially if they are able to pass one or more of the Fellowship exams. (Yet, lacking supervised postgraduate teaching, few candi-dates for Fellowships pass at the first attempt; most need many attempts.)[57] Others come to Britain because their whole medical education has been western-oreinted, and thus a trip westwards is almost mandatory.[58] Yet others come because training in their particular specialism is lacking, or very scarce, in their home country. Whatever their reasons, Britain welcomes them as the Walrus welcomed the Oysters; though less than in the early 1960s, they remain essential to make up shortages caused by insufficient output of the British medical schools and by continuing emigration of British doctors overseas.

(d) *Value*. What is the value to Britain of her medical TA from India? In the mid-1960s it cost some £3,660 per year, for five years, to produce a British medical graduate.[59] It would have cost Britain at least that amount to train each *extra* British doctor, to replace a foreign doctor employed in Britain. But to avoid any overestimate, let us suppose these would have cost only £3,000 per year each. Then Indian medical TA in the 1960s must have a value, to Britain, equal to the savings of £3,000 per year for five years on training each doctor needed to replace the 300 or so (net) Indian doctors entering Britain yearly (table 8.18 and p. 133). Thus each year India presented Britain with new doctors 'costing' 300 × £3,000 or £900,000, in saved training fees, for each of the past five years. This is worth more than £4·5mn (or 5 × £900,000) when the doctor enters Britain, because the money saved on his training *last year* could have been invested to yield a present value of capital plus interest, at even a modest return of 8 per cent, of (£900,000 × 1·08) or £972,000 by the time the doctor enters Britain; the training fees of £3,000 × 200, or £600,000, saved *two years ago*, would have produced present value (capital plus yield) in an alternative use of at least (£900,000 × 1·08 × 1·08) or £1,050,000 by now; and so on. The sum saved on training over the whole five-year period would have produced a *present* value (at the moment when the doctor arrives, fully trained) of at least £5·7mn.[60] This is the absolute minimum value of gross medical TA, *per year*, from India to Britain on 'doctor account'.

This £5·7mn per year *for the 1960s*—which covers only doctors—is far greater than Britain official TA to India over the same period (table 8.8) But of course not all the 5,000 or more Indian doctors working in Britain at the end of 1970 entered in the 1960s. If we assume the 5,000 level stable, and similarly calculate the saved UK training costs, we arrive at £95mn.[61] This *grant* by India to Britain (for training doctors who almost all migrated since independence) on TA account—and remember it is a conservative estimate of medical-training costs alone—is well over half total bilateral aid from Britain to India since independence, net of capital (but not interest) repayments on the *loans* that dominated such aid.

The real value of this TA may be even higher, as the figures above cover British savings on pre-graduation medical training only. Firstly, such doctors as return to India have often (because of the employment situation in Britain mentioned above) been trained in specialisms which are not the most relevant to India's needs: here re-training costs are often imposed. Secondly, the shift to Britain, which is often at first (at least nominally) for postgraduate training, means that some Indian postgraduate medical places are not being taken up; here wasted capital costs and, if full utilization was expected, wasted costs on professorial contracts are imposed on India.[62] Thirdly, the migrant doctor would 'add more' to human health and thus have a higher social return in India than he will in Britain, where his training was valued at £3,000 yearly for five years.

India, with an incomparably graver health problem than Britain (plus much greater need for doctors-per-person in public health and family planning), nevertheless has a doctor/patient ratio almost six times smaller than Britain's; yet India, unlike Britain, has no free source of trained doctors from a poorer nation. Thus scarce Indian capital is invested in training personnel to be sent overseas to staff another (developed) country's hospitals, where they learn skills not appropriate to Indian needs and are oriented towards an urbanized and sophisticated type of medical service, thus further discouraging most of them from returning to *rural* practice in India, where they are most needed.[63]

Need, of course, is not cash demand! Paradoxically, despite the acute health needs of India's poor, India has an underfinanced public medical sector, and hence many unemployed and underemployed doctors 'competing' for very limited cash demand from private patients. A 'marketeer' could thus argue that India, being able to train doctors 'cheaply', should function as a medical school and charge Britain for its trainees at the going rate. A 'developmentalist' would argue that such trainees should be directed to areas of need within Indian medicine, and paid from general taxation. What cannot be argued is that Indian taxes should support British medicine free of charge. One wonders if British aid administrators fully appreciate that this is the reality behind their claim that Indians provide a 'valuable underpinning of the National Health Service'.

(iv) OTHER INDIAN TA TO BRITAIN: SCALE AND VALUE

There has been an average yearly flow of 50–60 Indian nurses into Britain over the 1960s.[64] Nearly all settle permanently in this country. If one estimates the cost of training a nurse at around £700 (excluding building costs, but including equipment)[65] then—allowing very roughly for interest—the saving to Britain, by employing the Indian-trained nurses reaching Britain in the 1960s, was some £42,000 per year. These nurses, like Indian doctors, also tend to be employed in the less attractive hospitals, and in less attractive specialisms such as geriatrics or mental illness.

The other large group of entrants has comprised teachers, but the problems of identifying the net flow of these throughout the 1960s makes any precise calculation impossible; for example some of the science graduates have entered teaching posts in the UK. Further, there has since 1968 been a restriction on the number of teachers eligible for 'B' vouchers (pp. 146f.). If one takes a minimum estimate of 100 per year (the only detailed figures being 262 in 1968, 14 in 1969, and 6 in 1970), throughout the 1960s and puts the cost to Britain of training a replacement at only £500 per year for three years[66] (though most Indian teachers are graduates), then—discounting at 8 per cent for interest—one arrives at about £175,000. On top of these there are also various other skilled, qualified and professional entrants to Britain from India (tables 8.15 & 8.18); no estimate of the value of their TA to Britain is possible as a detailed breakdown of them is not available.

7. The net balance

On the estimates of net flows and UK training costs India, by training manpower for Britain, becomes a net donor of TA to Britain of some £5·2 mn per year in *grants* (table 8.21)—almost a quarter of British aid to India (mostly *loans*, net of capital but not interest repayments). In the early 1960s and even more in the 1950s, when the outflow from India was higher and aid smaller, this ratio was even larger. The conclusion that India has contributed something like £60mn, gross, of extra trained manpower to Britain over the 1960s is perhaps startling; but in real terms the cost to India is likely to have considerably exceeded this figure.[67]

The policy conclusions of this brief analysis are three. First, Britain must presumably expand the output of her medical schools and train her own manpower from her own financial resources. This has been accepted in Britain, and the Labour government announced in April 1969 that it was expanding the number of medical school places in the UK by 1,000 to a total of 3,700 by 1975. This will be achieved partly by expansion of existing institutions and partly by the formation of new medical schools at Nottingham and Southampton Universities. Following this, it is expected that the annual net gain of overseas doctors needed to maintain the expansion of the NHS is likely to decline gradually over a period in the region of ten years and *even then* [our italics] substantial numbers of arrivals may be needed to replace those who leave.'[68] Thus the expected decline is more apparent than real. To stop the loss of qualified British doctors overseas, which is mainly responsible for the present situation (p. 133), it may well be necessary to alter the structure and salaries, *or regulations*, of the British Health Service to curtail the drain of British medical manpower abroad. Secondly, the real costs to India of the provision of educated manpower for Britain should be recognized when establishing future aid levels and priorities. Thirdly, when Indian medical and other gradulates and skilled personnel come to Britain, they must be provided with the training and conditions of employment that they are led to believe are available and not simply treated as cheap labour to undertake jobs that are unattractive and undesirable for their British counterparts. Finally, it is *not* a necessary consequence of our analysis that Britain should, in paternalistic fashion, restrict the rights of individual Indian brains to be gained; the onus for such restrictions, if they are desirable, must fall mainly on the countries of origin.

9 EDUCATION AND RESEARCH

The very special understanding which Britain and India had of each other because so many Indians had been educated in Britain and learned to love it, and so many Britons loved India and made it their life's work, is disappearing.
M. and T. ZINKIN, *Britain and India* (1964).

It is obviously not worth while to spend £1000 on training a technical scholar, if on his return to India he fails to find industrial employment and takes refuge in the law or teaching profession.
Cd 7160 (1913), para. 3.

1. The education of Indians in Britain

(i) THE COLONIAL IMPACT

The impact of British colonial rule on the Indian elite was at once softened and made more insidious by that elite's exposure to the British educational system, both here and in India. Alongside many Britons, a fortunate few Indians spent their formative years in preparation for leadership, one purpose of which was to ensure the peaceful continuance of India within the British Empire. Neither that education nor the tradition it bequeathed to India was specially suitable for 'development', or for a 'mature relationship' between Britain and post-colonial India.

Colonial India was provided with many schools, colleges, and later universities modelled on the British pattern and largely staffed by British graduates and teachers, providing an education that differed little from its British equivalents.[1] A British education at such establishments, or better still at a school or university in Britain itself, was virtually essential after 1864 for Indians seeking to enter positions of responsibility and seniority in the Indian Civil Service[2] or, indeed, to achieve 'respectability' in trade or commerce. At the top of an ambitious Indian's list of educational aspirations would be a degree from Oxford or Cambridge, or at least being called to the bar via the London Inns of Court.[3] The Indian elite passed through an educational system which produced Indian scholars with capabilities and achievements equal to any of their western counterparts;[4] but scholars so oriented as to satisfy those counterparts, to win promotion from them before 1947, and hence, later, to form the backbone of the educational system in independent India, despite her new and distinctive needs.[5]

(ii) INDIAN STUDENTS IN BRITAIN AFTER 1947

With independence, at least the training of the *future* elite began to change. Financial exigencies encouraged the Indian government to restrict foreign

139

exchange for overseas education. There was also a wish to expand and improve the educational system for all levels in India. Hence increasing numbers of Indians were educated in India. As we shall see, this not only reduced the proportion of Indian education undertaken abroad; it also changed the type of student going overseas.

Little is known of the number of Indian children attending primary, secondary, or college-level education in Britain. Some of the richer Indian families still regard a period at a British public school as an essential part of their children's upbringing, although the numbers coming here are probably not as high— expecially since the 1966 Indian devaluation—as immediately before and after the 1939–45 war. Although detailed figures are not available, British immigration statistics reveal that in the late 1960s only 40–50 Indian schoolchildren were admitted each year.[6]

Turning to further education outside the university sector in Britain, there were in 1970 just over 700 Indians in grant-aided establishments in England and Wales[7] (table 9.1), 28 per cent fewer than in 1962, and fewer than from Cyprus, Malaysia, Iran or Kenya (table 9.2). Most of these Indian students were taking first degrees or equivalent higher qualifications, mainly in technical and applied subjects such as ophthalmology, physiotherapy, printing technology, process chemistry and other subjects seldom available at universities. (There is, however, some need for caution when interpreting these figures, for many polytechnics and higher technical colleges in the further education sector were given university status in the second half of the 1960s, and thus some of the decline in the number of Indians involved in advanced courses can probably be explained by their transference to the university sector.) There is a similar emphasis in less advanced coursework for OND-ONC and the City and Guilds examinations, where the number of Indians involved has changed little over the 1960s. These both provide practical training in radio and telecommunications design and servicing, automobile and transport engineering, and similar crafts and professions. In all these non-university courses Indian students are sent here for training because comparable instruction is not available in India. The rise in the number of Indians taking non-advanced courses can be explained purely by an increase in the number studying for the GCE, probably to satisfy entrance requirements for further education. It seems probable that many of the GCE candidates in the colleges are self-supported and from the less affluent among the families in India that are striving to maintain a tradition of British university education. (Of course such families are almost all in India's 'top 1 per cent' by income-per-head anyway.)

As for Indians coming to study at British universities, changes have occurred since independence. Firstly, despite the large increase in overseas students at UK universities between 1960/1 and 1970/1 (table 9.3), full-time *Indian* students diminished steadily from the peak levels (1,500–1,600) of the late 1950s. Asian students as a whole, however, still make up the largest continental representation among Britain's overseas university students, as the decline in Indians matriculating at British universities has been outweighed by increased numbers from richer Asian countries, especially Malaysia, Hong Kong, and Japan. Students from India still made up the third largest contingent in 1969/70 (after the USA and Canada), but they had fallen from their dominant position of a decade earlier.

There are four reasons for the decline. First, the foreign-exchange constraint has led the Indian government to refuse foreign exchange to anyone who wants to study abroad a subject that 'could as well' be studied in India. Hence, apart from a few rich families, the old favourite degrees of Indian students in Britain—arts, languages, medicine—have virtually disappeared at undergraduate level, though not at postgraduate level.

Secondly, the rapid growth of university education in India[8] has made it unnecessary for most undergraduates to go abroad. Hence emphasis has shifted to certain recent fields like electronics, transportation planning, business management, and operational research (table 9.6). In the arts, medicine, agriculture, and the basic sciences, virtually all undergraduates now study in India.

Thirdly, fewer Indians who do study abroad come to the UK. Before independence, relatively few Indians studied in the USA or indeed (with the exception of some engineers) in Europe.[9] Indians now tend to go to the best university or research institution in their particular field of study, and this increasingly means the USA[10] and the USSR. In 1966, out of 10,941 Indian 'students and trainees' abroad, 7,018 were in the USA, 1,883 in the UK, and 2,040 elsewhere.[11]

Finally, some of the decline during the 1960s in the number (not in the proportion) of students studying in Britain who are Indian-born reflects a change in the definition of 'overseas student' in 1967–8 by the Association of Commonwealth Universities, who collect and publish the statistics. For Indian students, the 1969–70 figures should be raised by around 9 per cent to be comparable with previous years, although Indian students have been marginally less affected by the revision than overseas students as a whole. Hence one has to treat the movement of numbers over the decade with caution, although the estimated proportion of Indian students is much less affected.[12]

While the proportion of Britain's foreign students from India in 1970–1 was 4·7 per cent, less than half as large as ten years ago (table 9.3), an even more marked change has taken place at graduate level. The Indian share in Britain's total overseas graduate students fell from 15·4 per cent in 1960–1 to 6·1 per cent in 1970–1. This, however, means only a slight fall in the absolute numbers of Indian graduates studying at British universities (table 9.4), and India's emphasis on graduate, as against undergraduate, study abroad has become even stronger. In 1960–1, just over half Indian students overseas were graduates, and by 1970–1 this had risen to over three-quarters (table 9.4), which reflects—as for other major nations—the growing domestic university sector. The share of graduates in total Indian students in the UK also varies by subject-group (table 9.6), being complete in agricultural and veterinary sciences; high in other areas of well-developed and recognized Indian competence (physical sciences, medicine, and biology) or where the subject in Britain is mainly taught at postgraduate level (town planning or business studies); and low in areas where undergraduate standards in Britain are still recognized as being superior (engineering, technology, and education). The growing emphasis on graduate study reflects the factors mentioned earlier and also the diversion of those few Indians still coming to Britain for undergraduate training into the growing number of specialized and vocational undergraduate degrees in non-university establishments, such as the polytechnics and colleges of technology.

Besides the Indians engaged in full-time study or research at British universities, there were, throughout the 1960s, some 300 Indians enrolled for part-time study or research. In both 1959–60 and 1969–70 Indians formed the largest single contingent of overseas students in this category, mostly at graduate level. However, there are problems involved in defining 'overseas students', especially in the case of part-time students, where the boundary between 'immigrant' and 'student' is especially imprecise.[13]

There has also been a change in the type and financing of Indian students coming to the UK. An analysis by A. K. Singh showed that around 1959–61 there were two distinct groups of Indian student in the UK.[14] About 38 per cent were westernized upper-class students, schooled in Britain, usually from families with a tradition of being educated here. Of this group, most were single, under 25, undergraduates (74 per cent) and supported by parents or family (92 per cent). The other group—62 per cent of students—were middle-class, mainly over 25, married (usually with a wife in India), postgraduates (84 per cent), and partly financed from prior employment in India (73 per cent). Of these students, only 28 per cent were supported by parents or family, 45 per cent by their savings or by working during the vacations, and 27 per cent by a scholarship or grant.

Although no strictly comparable figures are available for the end of the 1960s, the same division seems to hold. Of the 269 Indian undergraduates at British universities in 1969–70, only 27 per cent held a scholarship or award, which, although higher than Singh's 5 per cent for 1959–61, suggests that many undergraduates support themselves, and thus are probably of upper-class origin. The rise in the number of postgraduates holding awards, to 58·4 per cent of 720 postgraduate Indian students in 1969–70 reflects, not only the intention of the Indian government to reward bright students with scholarships for further study abroad, but also the effect of the UK government's decison in 1966 to raise the fees for foreign students. This has almost certainly cut the number of postgraduate Indians (apart from the very rich) who could hope to study in Britain without an award and/or a vacation job.[15] The rise in fees has thus probably reduced the number of Indians who would have come here, and pushed up the proportion holding awards.

The 1966 decision was in retrospect unfortunate, for it made little difference to the really brilliant or affluent students, but rather hit hard those who by determination, hard work, and financial sacrifice had looked forward to a period of postgraduate study in the UK as a means of improving their position when they return to India. One doubts whether the relatively small sum that was brought into the British exchequer was worth all the bitterness and disappointment, not to mention the loss of educational opportunity, it caused.[16] The Indian government went some way to reducing the impact of the decision by deciding in April 1967 to add fees to the £600 per year of foreign exchange released to students going to the UK and continental Europe, and by raising from four to five years the period over which exchange could be released, where the students desired to take up a Ph.D course in addition to a degree course.[17]

As noted earlier, 536 of the Indian full-time graduate students in the UK in March 1970 held awards or scholarships of various kinds. Of these, 86 (just over 16 per cent) were holders of the prestigious Commonwealth Scholarships; indeed Indians held more in Britain than did any other Commonwealth nation (table 9.7). Their share, however, has fallen slightly over the 1960s: partly because other Commonwealth countries in the Third World began to produce graduate students of scholarship quality, and partly because Indians winning Commonwealth Scholarships began to consider Canadian and Australian universities as suitable, and in some fields preferable, alternatives to a period of study in Britain. This may be a commentary upon the agitation in Britain against non-white minorities rather than on the development of a multipolar Commonwealth. In any case, of the Indians who win Commonwealth Scholarships, 60 per cent still study in Britain (table 9.8). Most of the rest go to Canada, and a few to Australia or New Zealand.

A rather low proportion of Indians hold CBI graduate engineering scholarships (table 8.12). This is probably due to the opening of the Indian Institutes of Technology at Kharagpur, Bombay, Madras, and Kanpur, and the later upgrading of Delhi Polytechnic into a fifth such institute. The institutes, whose standards in comparison with other Indian centres of higher education are extremely high, have, except in a few specialized fields, become the major focus of Indian postgraduate instruction and research in engineering and technology.[18] Consequently there is less need to apply for scholarships abroad, although (table 9.6) engineers and technologists still form the largest number of Indian postgraduates in Britain, mainly in specialized fields not yet well established in India. Despite the quality of the institutes, many of their graduates still go abroad (table 9.9), mainly for advanced graduate study, but of these hardly one in five goes to the UK.[19] Once more, the USA is now the main attraction.

One other aspect of Indian education in Britain will be dealt with here. As we saw in the previous chapter, many Indian doctors still come to sit the fellowship examinations of the various colleges of physicians and surgeons in Britain.[20] They normally do a period of hospital work in the UK, while receiving tutoring for the always difficult Fellowship examinations; to pass these is still considered eminently desirable in Indian medical circles. The numbers of Indian candidates reached a peak in the early 1960s, and have steadily declined since (table 9.10),[21] partly because of the establishment of the All-India Institute of Medical Sciences by the Government in New Delhi in 1956. It provides both undergraduate and graduate training in medicine, and has quickly built up a reputation for graduate medical qualifications rivalling the British Fellowships. Many of the 300 or so graduates who attend the Institute would have otherwise come to Britain but, as noted above, of the medical who do go abroad,[22] an increasing proportion goes to the USA. Further, as fewer Indians do their undergraduate training in Britain, so fewer stay on to take their Fellowship examinations. Among overseas students who do take the Fellowship examinations, of the Royal College of Surgeons of Edinburgh for example (table 9.11), Indians still form the largest single national group, and at least from March 1968 to October 1969 out-numbered even the British candidates.

2. Britain and education within India

(i) BRITISH STUDENTS IN INDIA

Although many Indian students come to the UK for their education, the reverse flow is small, though growing. Most British students who do go abroad are graduates on scholarships who tend to congregate in North America, Europe and the 'white Commonwealth'. This is partly to follow available funds, and to keep down travel costs. A leading British anthropologist was compelled during the 1960s to switch his research and his graduate supervision from India to Europe, largely because he found it so difficult to fund travel costs for his research students.

However, for university students as a whole, India attracted a growing number (table 9.12) from the UK, rising to 120 by 1969–70. These form a very small proportion of the total number of overseas students in India (table 9.13), most of whom come from East Africa, where there is a large Indian population, and South-East Asia, where India is taking a leading role in TA towards university education.

Another indication of India's attractiveness is the number of UK Common-wealth Scholars who prefer study in India to other Commonwealth countries (table 9.14). As expected, most Commonwealth Scholars go to Canada and Australia,[23] although arts scholars have found India attractive. Many of the arts scholars who go to India (table 9.15) have chosen Indian subjects, such as Indian drama, history, philosophy and music, and Sanskrit. As well as Commonwealth Scholars, there were in 1969 six British students in India on Indian government scholarships (all receiving ODM supplementary awards to 'make their modest stipend more realistic') working on social-science research projects in Indian universities.[24]

Further British involvement in education in India has been limited, perhaps because there has been insufficient identification of the areas in which Britain could help most effectively, or of the most efficient ways of providing such help. Within the Indian educational system, the major problem is the acute shortage of qualified teachers, especially in science and mathematics, in technical and vocational training, in the engineering polytechnics and technical faculties of the colleges, and above all in the university agricultural and medical faculties, where student places are being greatly expanded.[25]

(ii) BRITISH EDUCATIONAL AID TO INDIA

During the 1960s the British educational aid programme has developed into a complex and wide-ranging set of activities, covering capital aid given to help the construction of new educational institutions, the supply of books and equipment, the provision of British teachers and educationalists to l.d.c.s and the training within Britain of their counterparts from l.d.c.s.[26] In 1968, bilateral UK aid to education was about £27mn: £7mn to supplement salaries and allowances of British teachers and educationalists in l.d.c.s, £6·5mn to train overseas nationals in the UK (see pp. 140–1), and £8·5mn for capital aid, including books and equipment.[27]

Much of this outlay is for TA, and of this much is spent in Britain. Hence the role of education in British bilateral financial aid is very much smaller (table 9.16), and in 1970 some £4·0mn was made available to l.d.c.s for educational purposes, as against £15·0mn towards transport and communications projects and £10·7mn for industrial development.[28] However, the share of education has grown over the 1960s, supported by a burgeoning (if rather over-fashionable) literature on 'human resource development', and probably by its low balance-of-payments cost to the donor.

For historical reasons, Britain's educational aid programme is concentrated within the Commonwealth. Of British teachers and educationalists in l.d.c.s, in 1970, only 11·4 per cent were in non-Commonwealth nations. Three-quarters were serving in the African Commonwealth—Zambia, Uganda, Kenya, and Nigeria alone employed over half (table 9.17). India had barely one in a hundred. The origin is again historical. As ODM noted in 1970,

though a government dominated by British officials concerned itself from Macaulay's minute onwards with developing an educational system derived in large measure from British models and guided initially by British personnel, the guidance (prior to 1947) was not given from London, nor was there financial help from Britain for a system that was well established long before independence.[29]

Since independence, the Indian educational system has developed rapidly: the areas where British and other foreign educational assistance can really help are few, though important.[30]

British educational aid during the 1960s featured a growing Voluntary Service Overseas (VSO) programme. Nevertheless, by 1970 only 47 qualified graduates and 10 cadet teachers from Britain were working in India. This persists, and seems a missed opportunity, especially given India's difficulty in staffing some key fields with teachers of the requisite quality. The main reason is that such volunteers are usually teachers in secondary schools and teacher-training colleges; in both skills India has educated unemployed.[31] Some volunteer teachers might contribute more to Indian development by teaching not in elite schools but in the villages; indeed, despite the language barrier, the British VSO programme in India has been shifting volunteers from elite schools to agricultural projects.[32] Overall, the smaller effort in India (with its large and since 1947 wholly independent indigenous educational system), as compared to the much larger African commitment, can partly be understood.

Although the £1,050,000[33] of educational aid to India in 1969–70 was a smaller proportion of total aid than in many other British country programmes, Britain has contributed to several major projects, led by the IIT at New Delhi, on which over £1mn has been spent on equipment and nearly as much on staff training. The Delhi Institute, despite the criticisms directed against it and the other institutes,[34] was set up and initially staffed by the British, with equipment donated by the British government and British industry. It has been fairly successful so far, although the rationale for British involvement was none too clear: partly prestige, partly a wish to influence future Indian engineers to buy and use British equipment (unlikely under present or future Indian import policies),[35] and partly a desire to participate in a key area of Indian economic development.

At least two university links have been established: between the Medical Research Council at Hammersmith and the Post-Graduate Institute of Medical Education and Research at Chandigarh, and between Edinburgh and Baroda universities. British financial aid and a few volunteers have also been involved in 18 of the 30 centres of advanced study set up in Indian universities in order to raise standards, especially at postgraduate and research levels.[36] Much of British educational assistance has been steered through the Colombo Plan organization, as with the provision of a Professor of Electronics for Calcutta University, and a top anaesthetist for the King George Medical College, Lucknow, in 1963. However, such links are far fewer than with African countries. Whereas only two British universities have major links with Indian counterparts, four (Glasgow, London, Birmingham, and Durham) have such links in Africa, and several more have departmental links. This contrast is again understandable in terms of India's greater educational infrastructure and Britain's more recent colonial withdrawal from Africa; but it is also due to the refusal by several Indian universities to have specific links with British institutions, on both political and educational grounds. Moreover, relatively little recruitment is done for Indian universities by the Inter-University Council for Higher Education Overseas, partly because, through precedent and accident, the Council has become oriented principally towards the Caribbean and Africa, and partly because Indian universities prefer to do their own recruitment or, more often, to use the services of the British Council.

A better reception has been given to British offers of help in introducing sandwich courses, at both university and other institutions, probably because this type of teaching suits India's current needs. One of the first British institutions to suggest this approach was Bradford University, which expressed a willingness to send teaching staff to selected centres in India to introduce a programme of integrated education which would bring universities into closer contact with industry.[37] Since then, following a visit of the Indian minister of education to Britain, Brunel University sent an expert out to discuss the introduction of such courses, one of the chief aims of which is to prevent Indian students from finding that a long chain of university education ends with employment outside India. The Huddersfield College of Technology is involved in a project in Madras at the Technical Teacher Training Institute, in which technicians are trained as teachers. The British government is keen to extend this valuable scheme to other Indian colleges, in the belief that at this stage of Indian development middle-level technical training in engineering is at least as important a field for aid as high-flying university education. The British Council, perhaps the major educational aid force in India, is also involved in preparing radio broadcasts, mainly of English-language lessons to teachers, both serving and in training, and to schools, and some British volunteers (57 in 1970 excluding missionary personnel) are also teaching in schools throughout India.

As well as personnel, Britain has provided substantial educational resources in the form of teaching equipment and materials; in this area India has received a larger share of Britain's total educational aid. The IIT at Delhi, the Tractor Training and Testing Station at Budai, the Delhi Polytechnic, the IIT at Kharagpur, the National Metallurgical Laboratory at Jamshedpur, and the Haffkine Institute at Bombay have received major donations of equipment, books, and periodicals.

A major role in British educational assistance to India is played by the twelve British Council libraries, with a total stock of nearly half a million volumes and a membership of nearly 50,000. These libraries issue over 3mn books annually, mostly to university students; perhaps their most valuable contribution is the provision of textbooks through the Textbook Loan Centre in Delhi with a stock of over 70,000 volumes.[38] A low-price book scheme is also operated, which makes major British textbooks available to students throughout India at greatly reduced prices.[39] Unfortunately increases in prices of books under this excellent scheme—both absolutely and relatively to comparable US and Soviet schemes—and distributional problems have (especially in social-science books) in the early 1970s reduced the contribution made.

(iii) THE ENGLISH-LANGUAGE QUESTION

A discussion of the British role in assisting the Indian educational effort seems a fitting context in which to examine perhaps the major legacy remaining from the Raj: the English language. Shaw once said that Britain and the US were separated by the barrier of a common language. Nevertheless, the fact that India's elite is still English-speaking is a favourable and important factor in most Indo-British relationships. Yet Britain—partly because of a wise rejection of paternalism, but largely for lack of thought—has never given the diffusion overseas of language or literary culture the attention or the funds that one associates, say, with the Alliance Française. There is no reason whatsoever why 'colonialism', in any of its manifestations, need be associated with some of the features, the reverse of cultural dependence, characterising the indigenous elite of India in the 1880s— men who 'speak English better than most Englishmen, who read Mill, Max Muller and Maine, . . . who edit newspapers in English and correspond on equal terms with the scholars of Europe'.[40]

English remains the common language of most of India's elite: a language beset with problems and threats. The need for scientific and technical communication ensures its importance in India. Could and should Britain do more to ensure its future? To answer sensibly, we should first try to understand its past.

Under British rule, proficiency in English was essential to pass the Union Public Service Commission examination to obtain a worthwhile government job. After independence fourteen Indian languages were recognized, but English was retained to keep the (mainly regional) language groups in communication. From January 1965 Hindi became the official language of the Union, although provision was made for the continued use of English as a joint official language, and its position was if anything, strengthened by the Official Languages Acts of 1963, 1965, and 1967.[41] Although English is now spoken by only 2–3 per cent of India's population, it is this educated elite that runs the government, heads most of the large businesses, and reads the daily papers, of which one copy in four is in English (pp. 200–1). While English does still help language-groups to communicate, problems have emerged in its role in education.

In the first few years following independence, political and social pressures led many universities and other teaching establishments to switch much of their instruction from English to regional or even local languages, despite the absence of textbooks or even instructors in the language concerned.[42] Though in certain areas of scientific teaching English is likely to remain firmly established, in subjects such as engineering its role is less clear-cut. Because of a switch away from English at all levels, encouraged by the Report of the Indian Education Commission in 1966,[43] the consensus in India is that the proficiency of students in English is deteriorating rapidly. Given the reluctance of top scientists to publish (let alone translate) high-level scientific and technological papers in Indian languages, this must damage the quality of overall educational attainment (though it may set up pressures to alleviate the shortage). Further, given the importance of English to industry and commerce, the usefulness of graduates must also be impaired by declining linguistic standards. Hence the rate of return on educational expenditure will be lowered.

Currently, future language policy remains uncertain. Any firm decision is bound to offend many people: Hindi-speakers, or Anglo-Indians, or the large number of regional language speakers who see communication in English, in government and business, as a protection against a real or imagined threat of Hindi-speaking domination. This fear is especially strong in South India. There, Dravidian languages remote from Hindi are used; the Jana Sangh party is locally weak and is seen as a threat from the Hindi-speaking North; and the proportion of English speakers, even some way 'down' the elite, is much larger than elsewhere in India. The Centre's reluctance to take clear decisions, its eagerness to seek refuge in 'three-language formulas', is in this environment understandable and even laudable, given the role of language disputes and riots in violence and communalism in so many nations. But the delay, uncertainty, and confusion of language policy have resulted in a situation where the proficiency in English of entrants to higher education is rapidly declining.

The consequences are already appearing. The failure rates in Indian institutions where English has been retained are rising, and good graduates of Indian universities are sometimes failing to gain Commonwealth scholarships or similar awards solely because of their poor English. Further, the English of some Indian doctors who come to Britain for further study is such as to create barriers of communication between them and their patients, and fellowship examiners have commented on the quaint English spoken and written by some of their candidates.[44] In India students resentfully rely on textbooks in a tongue increasingly unfamiliar to them. Matriculate and even graduate unemployment in India probably owe much to the poor English of applicants for jobs which reduces their value as employees. And the ideal of English as a pan-Indian lingua franca, even for the elite, is mocked by frequent blank incomprehension among the 'half-Englished' from different regions. Is this not an area where British educational assistance could help? The problem is recognized by the British aid authorities, but they have to tread very carefully as it is a 'very sensitive subject', so sensitive that the issue of proficiency tests in English could not even be raised at a Commonwealth educational conference. Given the regional interest groups in India, this caution is probably justified, but some first steps have been taken to halt the decline. In this effort the British Council is playing a major role.

The Indian government, which is well aware of the problem, has established seven English Language Teaching Institutes throughout India; Britain contributes 10 per cent of their total costs. In three of these institutes, with British Council help, English-language radio programmes are transmitted to teachers and to schools. In the Delhi programme alone something like 400 classrooms in the district are involved; there are plans for major expansion of the whole English-language programme, especially to primary schools.[45] Films are also used and the English Language Book Society (p. 147) helps with its subsidized textbooks. The problem has been recognized, and the most effective methods and areas of application seem to have been identified; and yet many feel that in this crucial area the British effort is not big enough. Has the UK government felt that such effort could benefit the USA more than India or Britain? This could profitably become *the* area for the concentration of future British educational aid to India, and there are signs that it will.[46]

3. Teaching and research on India in Britain

When one considers the intimate and lasting involvement of Britain and India, it would seem natural that from such a relationship there would evolve a large body of expertise and a sympathetic understanding of India in Britain. The actual position is far from this. In the schools, teaching and study of modern India hardly exists. For most examination papers in modern history, India ceased to exist after 1947, and Warren Hastings and Clive are more important than Gandhi or Nehru.[47] The situation in the universities is little better. At the end of the 1960s an undergraduate wishing to specialize in some aspect of South Asian studies had a much smaller range of choice, of both courses and institutions, than one interested in pursuing American, Hispanic, or indeed Celtic studies.[48] There are certainly far more courses and specialisms offered in African studies than in Indian studies. 'Following independence, India was very largely dismissed from the British mind—and the British conscience. It had Africa to think about instead.'[49] At undergraduate level, the major centre remains the School of Oreintal and African Studies at the University of London; some progress is being made in teaching South Asian Studies at other universities.

At independence in 1947, Britain was certainly better informed about India than about any other part of the modern world. In some Indian subjects the leading experts were British, not Indian.[50] The two centuries of imperial involvement had produced an accumulated store of knowledge, mostly collected by the administrators, the soldiers, the missionaries, and the businessmen who spent much of their lives in India, and who were immersed in its traditions and culture. Hugh Tinker remarks, 'When a study of India in this country was mooted thirty years ago [for Chatham House], it was possible to look to the mainstream of British public life for support, and to a vigorous tradition of scholarship, rooted in service to the Raj, for active participation.'[51]

Though it would be hard to imagine the same response today, there is nevertheless a dedicated and growing group of academics (and others in industry, government, and commerce) engaged on research into India and its problems. These scholars are (according to taste) more scholarly and non-paternal, or else more arid and remote, than those whose expertise relied mainly on experience in the Indian Civil Service or Army. Nevertheless, in numbers, overseas expertise on India has become increasingly non-British over the past decade or so; more specifically, American.[52]

If we compare British studies of South Asia and of other areas, the change from the 1930s stands out starkly. The African Studies Association, founded in 1964, has around 450 members, while 200 university staff are listed as having interests in Latin American studies. Yet in 1970 only 155 people, not all in universities, were listed as South Asian (not even specifically Indian) scholars.[53] When one considers the relative lack of involvement of Britain in Latin America compared with the large-scale and long-lasting ties with South Asia, these figures seem to indicate lack of interest in a very important part of the world. However, Britain does still appear to have substantially more people interested in India and South Asia than other European countries (table 9.18), though certainly not than the USA, or probably the Soviet Union or even Japan.

Most British 'Asian scholars' are engaged in research in social sciences (especially economics) and history; sampled Latin American scholars' main interests lie in history, geography, and above all language and literature (table 9.19). However, even in developmental social-science research,[54] Africa takes up half the UK research projects identifiable by area (table 9.20). Although Asia comes second with 27 per cent of the projects, barely a third of these are devoted to India: i.e. one-fifth of the projects on independent Africa, for twice the population. Most 'Indian' projects in 1970 were in economics, with a few in geography, and none at all in sociology or social anthropology as such (there were a few interdisciplinary projects).[55] This evidence is confirmed by the Department of Education and Science list of research in British universities and colleges,[56] which shows that Asia (including India) is much less researched in the physical, biological, and social sciences than Africa, though more than Latin America. All the above sources seem to support D. A. Low: compared with Asia, 'the amount of work devoted to Africa in British universities is clearly very much more substantial; and the number of books and journals devoted to Africa is by contrast legion'.[57]

The lack of teaching and research on Asia in Britain was recognized early in the 1960s, when the Hayter Committee of the University Grants Committee recommended the setting up of new centres to pursue research and teaching in this area. This conclusion was accepted by the UGC, and funds were made available for their establishment. The resulting centres, such as the South Asian Centre at Cambridge, have been criticized by some as being *de novo* institutions not founded on a true desire to study and understand Asian problems, but they have at least laid a basis for the expansion and encouragement of Asian, and particularly Indian, studies in British universities. A further important step was the formation in spring 1970 of the British National Committee for Asian Studies, which was designed as a national body to represent to the UGC the need for a continuing expansion of Asian studies in general.[58] Within the National Committee it was agreed that area sections should be formed, with one specifically for South Asia. Again the dominance of African is demonstrated by the establishment of a similar National Committee for African Studies well before the Asian one. However a new British Council scheme to enable 'suitably qualified British scientists, engineers and social scientists to visit India', the Younger Scientists' Exchange Scheme, advertised in 1973, may improve matters.

Indian students and scholars in Britain have one major asset which other area specialists envy: the India Office Library. This is the finest collection of material on India and South Asia in the world. Both India and Pakistan valued its contents so highly as to forget their post-independence enmity to deliver a joint note to Britain in 1960, claiming the right to part of the collection, and requesting the return of their respective shares.[59] In the end the library remained in Britain, and after an unseemly delay was even rehoused in a new building, though it has not yet been officially designated the major national library for contemporary South Asian studies, as its international importance merits.[60] Such a designation, backed up by increased financial provision to allow it to purchase and collect modern Asian materials, would be a major advance for Asian studies in Britain. At least the library did not suffer the fate of the Indian Institute at Oxford, where 'the University commemorated the long and honourable connection of her sons with the ICS by pulling down the Indian Institute, in order to put up an office for clerks'.[61]

The role of the India Office Library in providing current as well as historical material for modern Indian studies is being backed up by other centres, most notably the IDS at the University of Sussex, where the Librarian has produced a detailed source bibliography on modern Indian studies.[62] Also important was the inauguration in January 1965 of the *Union Catalogue of Asian Publications*, formed as a result of recommendations made by the Hayter Committee, and aimed at establishing a central bibliographical record for Asian studies in the UK.[63] Besides this general catalogue, which has five annual supplements, there is a three-volume *South Asian Government Bibliography*, prepared under the aegis of the Centre of South Asian Studies at the University of Cambridge as part of a national programme to record Asian material in UK libraries. The largest volume lists all GOI publications for 1947–68; the information comes from the twelve libraries in the UK with the most comprehensive and pertinent material.[64]

In other areas the picture is less promising. The Indian High Commission in London has closed down its retail bookshop for lack of demand (although the High Commission Library will not suffer), and although Dillon's in London and Blackwell's in Oxford issue comprehensive and regular Indian and Asian book lists, modern Indian publications are not stocked anywhere in quantity, mainly (one is told) for lack of demand.

The future of British teaching and research on India and South Asia may well have looked bleak in the early 1960s,[65] but recent evidence points to some resurgence of interest and effort. At Sussex University, interest in India at undergraduate level (mainly by historians and social scientists working in the School of African and Asian Studies) now seems to be coming to match that given to Africa; young academics (and to a lesser extent graduate students) are beginning to choose India as an area of interest and fieldwork. Research is also becoming more problem-oriented, as with the multidisciplinary work being done by young researchers from the IDS on the Kosi Development Area Project in Bihar, and the constraints upon farmers' plans there.

The India Group (since 1972 the South Asia Group, but still devoted substantially to Indian themes) meets regularly at Chatham House, and experiences growing excess demand for its two dozen or so 'seats' from senior academics, diplomats, journalists and (to a much lesser extent) businessmen and MPs.[66] The Britain-India Forum meets regularly at the High Commission; again, the organizers' problem is accommodating all those with specialized interests who wish to attend. The Nehru Appeal Fund, to institute an annual memorial lecture at Trinity College, Cambridge, and to provide six scholarships for Indian students to study at a British university, soon reached its target, and later the British government donated £50,000.

Though there was clearly a hiatus in British Indian studies during the 1960s, as the older generation of personally involved, historical, and generalist scholars became less active, the increasing growth of organized interest amongst the younger generation of scholars, working in specialized centres and supported by specialized finance, may help to restore Britain's position in this field, to the advantage of both countries. The benefits could spill over into other relationships as well. For this reason it is important that the promising researches begun in the late 1960s be encouraged and furthered. One hopes that the suspicion and irritation sometimes felt in India towards foreign scholars—understandable and often justified as it is—will not too seriously damage Indo-British research links.

It would be splendid if there were a parallel development of research on Britain by Indian scholars. The lack of genuine reciprocity in research is one of the last relics of the old, unhappy paternalism. Such reciprocity seems to us the only clear-cut way to relieve academic research from the suspicion of neo-colonialism. It would greatly improve the reception (and ease of operation) of British scholars in India; there were growing signs in 1972 that some of the unpopularity of the US in India was 'rubbing off' on to young British social-science researchers in some States, notably as regards tax treatment and residence permits, and persistent rumours that all foreign research will in future require *central* clearance (with its attendant delays) have not helped. But research reciprocity is not here proposed as a public-relations gimmick to help British scholars in India! Apart from the value of information and knowledge as such, there are numerous areas of British policy and problems where first-hand field study could help Indians, both in avoiding British mistakes and in deciding which successes were worth following. Naïve analogies must be avoided, but British race policy, Ulster, and 'foreign' private investment—English as well as US—in Scotland suggest themselves as topics, obviously relevant to Indian conditions, where a scholarly Third World view would be of great interest and value to Britain. In practice, most applied research by Indian social-science scholars, on grants in Britain, is applied to the country they have just left—an odd situation. British scholars do not go to India to study Britain!

10 POPULATION EXCHANGES:

BRITONS IN INDIA AND INDIANS IN BRITAIN

> In one way or another, India has touched the lives of most English families in the last two centuries.
> Philip Woodruff, *The Men who Ruled India* (1963).

By choosing to live abroad a man sacrifices many advantages of language, friendship, and physical and cultural acclimatization. He will seldom do this unless he expects big material advantages. These will be offered only if he can sell something fairly scarce and special to an employer in the country to which he moves. There is thus a prima facie assumption that a British transport designer in India, or an Indian transport worker in Britain, adds to both social and private welfare by migration.

There are four main qualifications to this rule. First, the lost skill may be less important, though better paid, in the migrant's country of destination than in his country of origin—especially if the latter is poor, because in poor countries market imperfections and income inequalities impede the mass of the people from turning their needs for doctors or teachers into effective cash demands. Second, even if there is a net gain from migration 'at world level', opponents of gross inequality would argue that a transfer of resources from a poor to a rich country was damaging, though this might be made good by private remissions (pp. 67–9), or by compensation from the employers or government in the country of immigration. Third, a massive influx of foreigners may create cultural or racial hostility from natives. Fourth, income distribution within a poor country can be harmed by the 'brain drain', because (for example) Indian doctors but not Indian dustmen are able to travel towards British salaries, so that within India doctors' wages and overall inequality are 'bid up'. Although all four qualifications apply to Indo-British migration after 1947, the residence in each other's countries of people born in India or in Britain has made some contribution to the social and economic development of both. Unfortunately, the services to Britain of Indian doctors and dustmen have been submerged in 'the migration problem', to the detriment of Indo-British relations.

1. British nationals in India

Following the establishment of the first trading factory at Surat in 1612, the East India Company's operations in India expanded rapidly and soon developed into a large territorial empire. In 1700 there were still only 1,500 English people living in India, including 'wives, children and transient seamen'.[1] 150 years later, in an India shortly to be shaken by the mutiny of sepoys in the Bengal army, the number of Europeans in the service of the East India Company had risen to

39,631, mainly British, and concentrated in the presidencies of Bengal (15,628), Madras (13,335), and Bombay (10,668).[2] In the decades following the mutiny, British troops and administrators, businessmen and clergymen, judges and journalists poured into India. During the state visit to India of King George V and his Queen in 1911, there were 122,860 Britons resident in India.[3]

Although the numbers rose even higher during the First World War, the growing rate of 'Indianization' in the ICS, trade and commerce, and elsewhere resulted in a steady reduction in the numbers of resident British-born. They were not recorded separately in the first post-independence Census (1951), but were then estimated at 28,000.[4] By 1961 the figure had fallen to around 14,000: the third largest group of foreigners, after Nepalese and Pakistanis, but far outnumbering Chinese, Russians, or Americans (table 10.1).[5] By 1969 the British-born in India had fallen to about 6,500,[6] and were now outnumbered by US citizens.[7] British nationals are still to be found in the same areas as British assets (table 10.2); both concentrate in the big commercial centres—Bombay, Calcutta, Madras—and the plantations of Assam, Kerala, and Andhra.

A major change since independence is in the composition of the British in India. For some time after 1947 retired administrative and military officers and their dependants made up a substantial proportion of the total. Time has removed most of these living links with the Raj; they have been replaced by a more transient population of businessmen, technicians, and experts seconded to India for short periods. This change has no doubt contributed to the growing pragmatism of Indo-British relations. Mrs Pandit, when High Commissioner in London, feared 'that our links could grow weaker as those who shared these special common interests pass out of the picture'.[8] Certainly the change requires that links of mutual self-interest replace links of sentiment.

Though the British population has fallen since independence, the fall has been less than was expected in 1947. One reason is that 'Indianization' had in many services been largely completed by August 1947, and consequently most remaining employed Britons were in UK companies or otherwise not replaceable by Indians for some time. In the ICS, Indianization had begun as early as 1864 (p. 271) and by 1939 Britons had fallen to 759 from their 1919 peak of 1,177, while Indians had risen from 78 to 540.[9] By 1942, of 5,500 higher administrators (Commissioners, District Officers, Session Judges, etc.), only 630 were British.[10] Most Britons remaining in the ICS and other major central and state services in 1945 soon left for other colonies or for Britain. At independence, 600 out of 1,150 senior members of the ICS (later renamed the Indian Administrative Service) were British; only 33 remained after August 1947.[11] 'Within a few months the governments in India, State and Central, were run essentially by Indians.'[12] By 1963 only one executive post in the IAS was held by a Briton; and in the Punjab, one remaining British Chief Justice provided a last link with the generations of British lawyers who had founded modern India's legal administration and code.[13]

In the armed forces, post-independence Indianization took rather longer, for there were no suitably trained Indians for certain technical and senior positions;

it had also always been British policy to restrict the ranks to which Indians might rise; in 1947 the highest-ranking Indian officers were three acting Brigadiers. In the army, command soon passed to Indians; in 1955 a few British electrical and mechanical specialists were still at work, but all had left by 1960.[14] The Indian navy had relied more on Britons, and in 1949 120 British naval officers and Admiralty civilians were still employed, though all ships had been under Indian commanders since January 1948. In 1953 only 56 Britons remained in the INS, but despite repeated demands by politicians for complete Indianization, this had to await the appointment of an Indian to the post of Chief of Naval Aviation in 1962.[15] The Indian Air Force, which had employed 63 British officers and civilians in 1953, also took some time to change over, this being completed in 1960.[16] The gradual disappearance during the 1950s of Britons from the Indian services may have led to some weakening of the British influence in India; but nobody has ever shown that British officers after 1947 exercised much influence anyway, and the fate of Glubb Pasha in Jordan (an incomparably more dependent country militarily than India) suggests otherwise. However, in the absence of formal treaties, loss of informal sources of pressure may be important.

Of the other Britons who remained, many were managers and other staff employed in British-owned plantations. In the 1960s, although facing increasingly difficult economic conditions and a steady take-over by Indian companies (p. 88), many Britons still held senior plantation jobs: in 1966 there were over 500 in North-East India alone,[17] and in 1968 over 250 remained in Kerala.[18]

Britons also retain some key positions in industry and commerce. In 1947 6,901 British employees were working for non-Indian (mainly British) enterprises alone; by 1955 this had fallen only slightly to 6,462.[19] Even then, British personnel maintained control of the majority of higher salaried posts in these companies (table 10.3):

In the salary group Rs1,000 (per month) and above, consisting of practically all the key jobs, both technical and managerial, even though the number of Indian personnel has shown a continuous increase, the strength of foreign personnel has remained almost unchanged . . . the increase in Indian personnel in the higher salary groups was effected through the absorption of Indians in newly created employment and not through the replacement of non-Indians . . . British personnel continue to maintain the large majority of salaried posts in the foreign-controlled companies in India.[20]

This 'top-end loading' of expatriate personnel has meant that they—and especially the British—have had more influence than the crude numbers indicate; it is concentrated, because British companies tend to dominate particular sectors of the Indian economy (pp. 87f.). It is, however, safe to assume that this influence has declined somewhat since the mid-1950s, although it remains qualitatively very important.

As with the British population in general, the composition of the commercial group has changed. Before 1939 men fresh from Westminster School or Cambridge, arriving to carve out a career in such traditional firms as Andrew

Yule, Jardine Skinner or Birds, saw their future within India.[21] Now, with many managing agencies Indian-owned (p. 88), the arriving Briton is usually a highly qualified technician or management specialist, seconded to an Indian subsidiary by a multinational company for a specified period. Though he may regard the secondment as a chore that has to be endured in his progress up the company ladder, most of the companies view their Indian appointments as valuable experience for management material, providing a 'good training ground that gives them the chance to show what they can do in unfamiliar surroundings and . . . provides quite soon . . . a feedback of knowledge that you would not have got if you had stuck to your home pitch'.[22] Some multinational companies seek ultimately to bring their branches overseas up to self-government, with Indians, trained by western postings, being eventually promoted to the top in their own country. Others cannot envisage this for some time; they see a long-continuing need for British managerial cadres as local representatives of parent companies.[23] Unfortunately the 1961 Census does not distinguish between Britons in India on short-term secondment and those in the longer-residing managerial cadres, nor indeed does it specify the total number of Britons in Indian industry and commerce, although it was estimated in 1966 to be between 2,000 and 3,000.[24]

Indian government policy here was set out by Nehru in 1949:

In the matter of employment of personnel, Government would not object to the employment of non-Indians in posts requiring technical skill and experience when Indians of requisite qualifications are not available, but they attach vital importance to the training and employment of Indians even for such posts in the quickest possible manner.[25]

Thus the government has evolved a tax structure which discriminates between two groups of expatriate personnel. During the 1960s the short-stay ('secondment type') personnel, such as technicians and others with specialized knowledge and experience in manufacturing operations, power generation, or construction, have been exempt from tax on salary incomes for three years from arrival in India. If they remained longer, the tax on their salary might be paid by their employer for a further five years, without tax liability to himself. Foreign nationals in India for more than eight years, or not in the category of necessary technicians (this category excludes most UK managerial expatriates), were liable to Indian income tax at the same rate as residents, currently 30 per cent of income plus 3 per cent surcharge. This discrimination, understandable from the Indian point of view, has almost certainly been the major cause of the increasing dominance of the foreign-secondment nationals over the residential ones, for it very rarely paid to settle for more than eight years.

There is some evidence that the tax burden on longer residence even deters overseas investment. Almost all British companies claim that the tax burden on senior residential management personnel is higher in India than anywhere else, and have sought tax relief to reduce the huge gross salaries they must pay in India if they are to bring net salaries in line with those in other parts of the world. One British company with large interests in India remarked:

In a new undertaking it is essential in the initial stages to depute expatriates from parent organisations to establish and commission the Indian plant and to train a management team. Few such expatriates are likely to qualify as technicians who may be entitled to a tax-free salary in India. The present controls on managerial remuneration in the context of the present high rates of personal taxation make it virtually impossible to offer terms of employment attractive to the non-technician expatriate executive in the fields of general management, marketing and finance.[26]

The Indian government argues that such discrimination is not serious, and that it is necessary to encourage such companies to train Indians for managerial and technical roles. All non-Indian nationals are also given some relief in that they are allowed deductions from their taxable income for the educational expenses of their children abroad and for leave passages, and are exempted from taxation on the interest accruing from their Indian bank accounts and from the compulsory savings scheme.[27]

The situation is complicated for many British nationals by the lack of an Indo-British double-taxation agreement, though the UK does provide some unilateral tax relief. Negotiations to secure an agreement have been continuing for several years, and at one point in 1970 Indian officials thought they 'had it in the bag', but negotiations came to nothing, apparently because of problems over the Indian government's taxation of British shipping. The signing of such an agreement would probably bring some relief to Britons in India. For the Indians any steps which encouraged British firms to employ a given number of expatriates not as short-stay personnel but as long-stay managerial and technical staff would be economically justifiable, at least in the medium term, in that such people usually take at least five years to become fully conversant with the Indian scene, and thus are currently encouraged to leave just when they are becoming potentially most valuable.[28] In the longer term, however one can understand Indian concern to keep up the pressure on firms to train Indians for senior posts.

British companies are well aware of the personal taxation problem; as one director said:

There is an element of sacrifice in employment overseas. Under present regulations in India (in 1967) it is virtually impossible to obtain Government approval for a salary worth more than £2,750 per annum after tax. This provides no incentive for the right sort of expatriate top management.[29]

We should not forget, however, that income-per-head in India averaged barely £25 per year. Can one pay British executives 'attractive' salaries in this environment? Possibly if firms were to withhold part of the salaries until their return to the UK (to avoid too much demonstration in India of foreign affluence), tax concessions might be possible as a quid pro quo.

The position for Britons in India was worsened by the devaluation of the rupee in June 1966. Most, then as now, were senior men, with wives, paying around Rs9,000 in British and Indian on annual earnings of around Rs36,000. If they had two children being educated in England—and even in state schools this implied a maintenance cost of somewhere around £75 per month—this cost them Rs1,000 before devaluation, leaving a married couple Rs1,250 monthly to live on. Devaluation raised the rupee cost of this £75 to about Rs1,600 per month,[30] leaving the parents barely half their previous rupee income in India, with which to meet a cost of living itself swollen by devaluation. Hence companies had to offer an enormously increased salary (except for the very senior men for whom the employing company might pay the cost of schooling in sterling in the UK), especially as Indian tax-rates rose sharply above Rs36,000.

Many British companies operating in India, already squeezed by Indian company taxation (pp. 92–3), felt unable to offer such increases to their expatriate staff, and many Britons were thus forced to dip into their savings and gratuities at a time of life when such finance was soon to be most needed. Some tea firms encouraged their British employees to resign, waiving normal penalties on premature retirement; others simply dismissed them. Many planters, especially in the north, argued that some tea firms were using the opportunity presented by devaluation to retrieve their precarious economic positions by employing cheaper Indian staff. Overall, it was feared that the loss of foreign nationals, and especially Britons, would have 'wide effects on the whole British commercial and industrial establishment in India' and that 'it will henceforth be almost impossible to make it worth a man's while to work in India'.[31]

Fortunately, within eighteen months, the devaluation of sterling partly restored the position; but for a while many middle-aged British planters and industrial managers, with half a lifetime spent in India, faced a bleak return to the UK, when jobs were not easy to find. The discontent aroused at the time among the British expatriates in India can have done nothing to further UK-Indian relations, especially as it came during a period of bitter Indian feelings towards Britain following the Indo-Pakistan war of 1965.

In addition to economic problems, Britons in India have been subjected to periodic political discomforts. Occasionally, the British community has provided a safety-valve; thus in the Kerala riots of February 1968, the plantation strike over the non-payment of a 9 per cent bonus developed into a crusade against British interests in general. Encouraged by a statement of A. K. Gopalan, secretary of the Communist Party (Marxist) in Kerala, that he wished the present struggle in the Munnar area developed into one against the continuance of British interests in the State',[32] rioters stoned British cars and—in one case reminiscent of the days of the Raj—caused one couple to sit it out in their bungalow for over three weeks. Even this is less extreme than several instances during the early days of independence; then, in West Bengal, four British staff were thrown into a furnace and burned alive.

Relations between Indians and the Britons who reside in India are now for the most part cordial; many Britons are respected members of their local community, playing major roles in Chambers of Commerce,[33] welfare organizations, and recreational activities. Some Britons have incurred the displeasure of the Indian authorities, especially after the 1965 war, when several were detained and later 'requested to leave' for breaches of the security regulations. The government of West Bengal reportedly wished to deport all Britons, but officials in New Delhi were firmly opposed to any blanket deportations without investigation, stressing that they would harm relations with Britain.[34] Britons are welcomed in most parts of India, and have done something to repair damage caused to the relationship by British policies on immigration and other matters. For example, British businessmen have been eagerly received in the village of Khem Karan, twenty-five miles from Amritsar, since the Associated Chambers of Commerce (to which a large number of British firms belong) launched a crash scheme to restore land to cultivation, provided ten tractors, and built a modern shopping centre to repair damage caused by Indo-Pakistan hostilities.[35]

Another legacy of British rule in India are the Anglo-Indians, or descendants of marriages between Britons and Indians. They have a strong association, and have contributed much to India, especially in education and the armed forces,[36] and above all in the management and operation of the railways. Their special position was recognized by two reserved seats in the Lok Sabha (out of 543) and by special facilities allowing free repatriation of capital from India on emigration, which was mainly to Britain or Canada. However, these exceptions to Indian emigration laws were withdrawn in January 1968, although special consideration could be given to those members of the Anglo-Indian community who had entered into definite commitments prior to 1 February 1968 in anticipation of actual emigration.[37]

The relative position of the Anglo-Indians has deteriorated since independence, and although some communities remain which try to preserve their distinctness, intermarriage and emigration seem certain to erode it further.[38]

Tourism has already been discussed (pp. 72–3), but it is worth emphasizing that, since independence, from being a place where Britons went to work, India has become a potential pleasure ground, and mass air travel has made India an accessible as well as a prestigious holiday area. Most glossy British magazines carry enticing advertisements for holidays in India; for the young, the overland 'expedition' to India by Landrover has become big business, following the Comex student tours of India. British visitors to India increased three and a half times between 1951 and 1966; Britons are the second most frequent visitors to India, overtaken since 1957 by Americans (table 5.11).[39]

2. Indians in Britain

The first Indians to settle permanently in Britain probably came as personal servants of retiring East India Company nabobs in the early eighteenth century. By the end of the century Indian servants could be seen in many portraits of the English gentry, sometimes featuring prominently, as in the case of Stubbs's portrait of an Indian servant holding his master's prized leopards in the setting of a classically landscaped garden. Later, more affluent Indians began to settle in Britain, some in the universities, others in commerce and the East India Office.

Very little is known about numbers, for until recently censuses enumerated people by the country of their birth. Hence virtually all of the 62,974 Indian-born people resident in Britain in 1911 were of British parentage, though born in India.[40] By 1900 there were probably several hundred Indians resident in Britain,[41] but one has to wait until 1932 for the first hard estimate (7,128), which may include students (then about 2,000 from British India) as well as Indian nationals settled permanently in Britain.[42] After the Second World War more Indians (from the armed forces) made their homes in Britain.

Between 1946 and 1962 perhaps 150,000 persons from the subcontinent settled in Britain (table 10.4), excluding expatriate Britons leaving in the post-independence period. Most of these new settlers arrived after the mid-1950s (table 10.5), and even between 1955 and 1960 the annual net inflow averaged only some 5,500 (compared to 26,900 for West Indians). Net immigrants of Indian 'ancestry' were somewhat more numerous, as some arrived from countries such as Guyana, Kenya, and Mauritius.

The 1960s saw the birth of a new science in Britain: rhetorical demographic statistics. Feeding heavily on scarce and ambiguous demographic data, this consisted of the manipulation of the exact size, composition and colour—present and future—of the immigrant population of Britain. While we shall endeavour not to indulge in this fashionable and politically volatile activity, we shall briefly examine the evidence available. This reveals, as with so many other relationships covered in this book, a dramatic change in the early 1960s.

In the immediate postwar period, and especially throughout the 1950s, the West Indies were the largest regional source of Commonwealth immigrants arriving in Britain. Nearly one-quarter of the total entrants between 1946 and 1962 came from the Caribbean, and indeed the initial racial clashes and problems were largely focused on areas with many such inhabitants, notably Notting Hill. Between 1963 and 1970 the West Indian share was falling markedly, and the attention switched to Asia, whence came over two-thirds of the net inflow, of which India contributed some 142,000 (table 10.6). Simultaneously the migration flow between Britain and the developed Commonwealth countries went into reverse, resulting in a net outward migration of over 75,000 between 1963 and 1970.

Although fairly detailed annual immigration statistics have been published since 1962 under the auspices of the various Immigration Acts, there are a number of reasons for treating these annual flow statistics with caution. The main problem concerns people who are not nationals of the country from which they enter Britain; this distortion is especially important in the case of Indians who enter Britain from countries with substantial Indian populations, such as Guyana or Kenya (see table 10.8). These may well count as Guyanese or Kenyans in the immigration statistics, and Indians in the decennial censuses. Thus the flow and stock elements in the immigration debate cannot always be reconciled. The evasion of enumeration by the illegal immigrants landing at dawn at Sandwich or at deserted airfields in the Midlands made very little difference to the annual figures (as the aftermath of Mr Jenkins's 1974 amnesty proved). Such immigrants also had to avoid census enumeration, and their numbers were thus unrelated to the apparent discrepancy between the total inflow of 210,000 between January 1962 and December 1970 as shown in the immigration statistics, and the intercensal increase of 156,800 between 1961 and 1971 (table 10.7).

Certainly the progressive tightening of controls has greatly reduced the annual net immigration of Indians. Throughout the 1950s the entry of Indians to Britain had been at a very low rate, and even in 1960 there were only 5,900 arrivals. However, by 1961 the figure had soared to 23,750, and although between 1963 and 1966 it was fairly steady around 17,500, it climbed to 22,638 in 1967 and a peak of 28,340 in 1968: at once anticipating and provoking the 1968 Control of Commonwealth Immigration Act, which in turn was responsible for the decline to 12,338 in 1969 and to only 8,416 in 1970.[43] Further declines seem almost inevitable after the 1971 legislation, which is discussed in greater detail below.

As with the flow figures, so also are there difficulties in estimating the current Indian population resident in Britain. This theoretically should be equal to the net inflow plus the natural increase of the population already present. The main, and indeed overwhelming, complication is that the relevant census classification is based on 'birthplace' rather than on nationality or race. For instance, this classification covers considerable numbers of pinko-grey Britons who were born in India under the Raj, and yet excludes many young 'Indians' who have been born in Britain in the 1960s. This introduces considerable complications for those involved in serious demographic analysis, but gives great opportunities to practitioners of rhetorical statistics. According to the 1961 and 1971 censuses (table 10.7), the largest absolute increase among foreign-born population groups was recorded by 'Indian-born', with a growth of nearly 157,000, although the percentage increase of those born in Pakistan and in the Commonwealth African countries was greater. One presumes that most of the growth of 157,000 is due to immigration in the current sense of the word, although there is a disturbing discrepancy between the 74,430 increase in the British population of persons born in India that occurred between the 1961 and the 1966 sample-survey and the 47,580 persons who in 1966 were enumerated as having had addresses in India in 1961;[44] *part* of the explanation may lie in the entry-from-a-third-country problem mentioned above.

The large increase in the Indian population in Britain, between 1961 and 1971, more than matched the natural increase of British home population, and yet even so, Indian-born persons comprised a mere 0·60 per cent of the total British population in 1971, a proportion far less than that found in other countries where there are major Indian communities. Whatever the exact size of the Indian community in Britain, it is thought to be the seventh largest Indian community overseas, and the largest in any developed nation (table 10.8).[45] At 0·6 per cent, or even 1·0 per cent if we make a major allowance for 'Indian' children born in Britain, only marked spatial concentration could make a problem for the community. What kind of Indians come to Britain; where do they come from; where do they go; and what kind of future faces them when they arrive?

To determine the type of Indian who comes to Britain to settle, we must first separate out the immigrants holding employment vouchers from short-term and long-term visitors and students. Most Indians admitted to Britain are *short-term visitors*—businessmen and tourists who come for three months or less; these more than doubled between 1964 and 1970 (to 29,760—table 10.9); a growing proportion comprises Indians visiting immigrant relatives, especially as air-charter flights have drastically reduced the cost of travel. *Long-term visitors* (for more than three months) form only a small share of Indians admitted, though a few eventually settle permanently. Indian *student*[46] numbers fell from 2,015 in 1964 to 953 by 1970, though the decline in immigration pushed their share of all Indian long-term entrants (except officials) in 1970 to over 11 per cent; again, some drift into permanent residence.[47]

In 1964 nearly a quarter of all Indians admitted (table 10.10) to the UK held employment vouchers. Since then the numbers have fallen under the weight of the 1962 and 1968 Immigration Acts, and whereas 8,300 came in under this category in 1963, by 1970 the annual inflow was down to 791, mostly (pp. 165–6) professional and skilled personnel entering with category 'B' vouchers.[48]

By far the largest group of long-term entrants to the UK from India during the 1960s comprised the dependants of those Indians already settled and working in Britain. By the second half of the decade they contributed over three-quarters of admissions under the 1962 Act (table 10.10), rising to a peak of 18,718 in 1968. Since then the flow was reduced drastically to just over 5,400 by 1970, and the 1968 Act thus lengthened the list of dependants waiting in India.[49] No detailed breakdown of dependants is available, but of those granted entry certificates in Bombay between May and December 1969, 53 per cent were children under 16; 30 per cent wives; 7·7 per cent children over 16; 4·4 per cent fiancé(e)s; and 4·2 per cent other dependent relatives.[50]

The 'dependants' category gives immigration officers, both in the UK and India, some of their greatest headaches, for posing as a dependant offers one way for illegal immigrants to try to avoid immigration controls. The main way of combating this is to trace details in India of the applicant's family tree and then compare it with the UK sponsor's statement of his family circumstances and relationships. However, the bogus sponsors are now supplying family trees to order; 'bogus dependants are so well primed now, for example, that a family tree as presented by a typical bogus dependant is so sparse as to make it difficult to believe that there are indeed 530 million inhabitants of India'![51] However, this problem should be viewed in perspective; the number of bogus dependants seeking admission to the UK from India is small, as the amnesty (pp. 170f.) showed.

Indians who emigrate to Britain are highly concentrated by origin, in the Jullundur, Hoshiapur, and Kapurthala districts of the Punjab, and the Surat, Kaira, Broach, and Baroda districts of Gujarat. A few also originate in Rajasthan, Uttar Pradesh, and Harayana, and a very small number in other areas within India. This concentration is even more marked than at first appears, for within the districts most of the emigrants come from a relatively small number of small towns and villages, perhaps 80 in the three Punjab districts and 50 in Gujarat.[52]

This has two important implications. First, it is likely to lead to geographic concentration within the UK; following domestic patterns, Indian migrants to cities almost always are sponsored by and go to live with relatives or friends from their home village or district. Secondly, this promotes homogeneity amongst each Indian community in Britain, which can continue cultural, communal, and to some extent commercial activities on familiar lines. Thirdly, the remittances from the large Indian population in India, which we earlier estimated at £40mn per year (p. 78), are similarly concentrated within India and thus in these areas there have been substantial and highly visible benefits for the relatives who remain, by way of new housing, improved irrigation systems, school and college extensions, and land and stock purchases.[53] With emigration to Britain providing such tangible benefits, the demand for entry vouchers by those still remaining is strong, and as one visitor remarked,

There seems to be an extraordinary eagerness to go . . . [to the UK]. All over India I was asked by complete strangers in trains and buses how they could get to the UK . . . [and for] . . . the names of firms to whom they could apply for work vouchers or for the names of colleges of further education.[54]

The concentration of places of origins has also been partly responsible for the congregation of Indians within Britain in a small number of areas. Indeed, in a few towns, such as Southall, Smethwick, Bradford, and Leicester, Indians now comprise a substantial proportion of the population. The Indians arriving in Britain under the category 'A' vouchers, to take up a fixed offer of employment, are most likely to be going to areas where their friends and relations are already settled, whereas those entering under category 'B' (doctors, nurses, and other professional people) will be much less likely to congregate. Over the two years in question, nearly two-thirds of 'A' voucher Indians went to London, the South-East, and the West Midlands; another 20 per cent went to the Eastern, Southern, and the Yorkshire and Humberside regions (table 10.11). This concentration is not as great as that of immigrant West Indians or Maltese (who virtually all settle in London and the South-East); and over half the Pakistanis go to the mill towns of the North.

We shall have to wait for further particulars of the 1971 Census results, but a little detail is available from the distribution of immigrant schoolchildren[55] among local authority areas, and among standard British regions (table 10.12). Immigrant pupils are highly concentrated, with just over half in Greater London (one-quarter within the Inner London Education Authority). Of the rest, most are in the County Boroughs, and especially those within the West Midlands, the South-East, and the Yorkshire and Humberside regions. The distribution of *Indian* immigrant pupils, however, is markedly different, with over half being in the County Boroughs, and 38 per cent in the East and West Midlands. There are relatively few in the ILEA, though more in the Outer London Boroughs, and indeed the Greater London region has the largest single share of total Indian pupils.

What of the concentration of Indians *within* immigrant communities? In January 1970 Indian pupils comprised only 19·8 per cent of total immigrant pupils, but in some areas the proportion was much higher (table 10.12): West Midlands, 36·7 per cent; East Midlands, 30·9 per cent; and the Northern region, 26·0 per cent.

This concentration of Indians is self-reinforcing. As well as providing parents (and sponsors—see p. 164), it makes Indian associations and clubs more viable, and provides a large enough local market for Indian commercial enterprises to flourish. In towns such as Southall, perhaps the centre of Britain's Indian communities, Indians are already having a distinct influence on the local culture, not always to the delight of the natives.[56] There are already Indian councillors, a flourishing Indian press is beginning to emerge, and Indian shops, banks, and offices are being set up along many British High Streets.[57]

We saw above that most of the Indians who have come to the UK in the postwar period have come from Gujarat and the Punjab. Rather than Muslims or Hindus,[58] it is the Punjabi Sikhs who have come to dominate the Indian communities. Sikh temples have been established in Southall, Smethwick, Leeds, Birmingham, and other large cities; more are planned. Their secular and religious lives are co-ordinated and their interests represented by the Shiromani Akali Dal, the Supreme Council of the Sikhs of Great Britain. The battles fought by the Sikhs to retain their customs and rights, typified perhaps by the turban versus peak-cap conflicts in bus transport, were in many areas the first steps towards the development of a community consciousness among immigrant groups.[59]

Most Indians who arrive in the UK under employment vouchers now do so under category 'B', as professional or skilled persons (table 10.9), whereas for all immigrants, more enter under 'A' than 'B'. Thus Indian immigrants are nowadays highly skilled professional people (doctors, science and technology graduates, teachers, etc.) whose value to India is probably higher than to Britain, but who are paid less in India. This is because India is a poor country, made poorer and more inegalitarian *not* by their migration on its own, but by its combination with refusal of rich countries to take unskilled Indians, although the economic demand for their labour is often there. (Even in 1972, with about a million unemployed, Britain clearly lacked enough builders' labourers, cleaners or dustmen to meet demand in the South and the Midlands.)

At the 1961 Census there were 81,900 Indians in employment in Great Britain (table 10.14). Many (16·4 per cent) worked in professional and scientific services, while other large concentrations were in engineering and electrical goods (12·5 per cent); transport and communications (10·7 per cent) and the distributive trades (8·6 per cent). The largest group of male Indian workers were in engineering, where the restriction of category 'A' entrants by the 1962 Commonwealth Immigration Act led to some labour shortages in the Midlands.[60] This restriction was reinforced by the 1968 Act and thus over the second half of the 1960s the dominance of category 'B' entrants (table 10.9) has strengthened the position of Indians in the tertiary sector, though we shall have to wait for the full 1971 Census results for accurate knowledge of the distribution of Indians amongst the various sectors of the British economy.

In 1968–70 76 per cent of Indians who arrived in Britain with 'A' vouchers were destined for jobs in manufacturing industry, 6·6 per cent in professional and scientific services, and 5·0 per cent in the distributive trades.[61] However, the figures for manufacturing—a total of 660 Indian entrants over 1968–70—conceal a large number of highly skilled craftsmen, who sometimes should have had 'B' vouchers.[62] All in all, Indian immigrants ever since 1960 have had a higher level of skill than the average Commonwealth immigrant. This is partly reflected in the fact that Indian incomes were higher than those of the other two main immigrant groups in the working population sampled in the Rose-Deakin Report.[63]

It has recently been suggested that the younger Indian immigrants are better educated than their Pakistani or West Indian counterparts, and hence have more confidence and detachment; that their easier adoption of many British customs and norms results in their being 'poised between English and Indian cultures', but 'energetically pulling themselves up by their own bootstraps'.[64] Certainly most Indians in Britain are relatively undefensive in their attitudes, being much less swayed than other immigrant communities by either assimilationism or black (or brown) power. For example, the Indian Workers' Association, based in the Indian heartland in Southall, has developed into a militant and outspoken, but not ranting, body.[65] This is of a piece with the surprisingly cool reporting of British race issues in the elite Indian press (pp. 202–3).

The Indian community in Britain will certainly increase, both because so many Indians in Britain are at or below reproductive age and because of the likely—though after 1971 greatly reduced—continued immigration of dependants; it was estimated by Rose and Deakin that by 1986 Indians in Britain will have risen to 768,000 (based on lower fertility estimates), and will then comprise about 37 per cent of the total coloured population of Britain (estimated at 2mn) as against 26·3 per cent in 1966.[66] The subsequent influx of Ugandan Asians expelled in 1972 will require modification of these estimates.

This is no place to chew over the pros and cons of non-white immigration into Britain,[67] especially as the 1971 Immigration Act has virtually ended it, at least on the scale of the mid-1960s. However, three special points about Indian immigration may be made. First, the Indian community plainly lies between the 'more English than the English' dependence of *older* West Indians and the cultural isolation of many Pakistanis, and may well avoid the possible drawbacks of both extreme attitudes. Second, relatively to other immigrants, the high skill-level and low child/adult ratio of Indians means that (even more than most immigrant groups) they probably contribute more quickly to supply than to demand in Britain, and are more clearly net *contributors* to the financing of the social services[68]—but, by the same token, they are a relatively severe loss to their country of origin. Third, the whole tone of the 'immigration debate'—from the repatriationists and 'Yellow Peril' birth-rate distortionists to the 'liberals' who assure the public that there are really not so many of these people, and that they breed quite slowly—is not only personally, humanly hurtful to the Indian community in Britain; amplified throughout India, however coolly, it is bound to damage Indo-British relations.

There is a less controversial category of Indians who arrive in Britain—those who visit for business and pleasure. Between 1964 and 1970, the numbers of short-term visitors doubled from 14,000 to 30,000 (table 10.9), whilst the much smaller numbers of long-term (i.e. more than three months) visitors declined. These visits only represent some 2 per cent of the total visits by British Commonwealth nationals—understandably, given the relative income levels of India and (say) Australia or Canada. A major limitation has been foreign exchange, especially before the relaxation of 1970; indeed, one Indian paper has complained of excessive visits by Indian ministers and officials to London, and of the resultant heavy drain on already depleted foreign-exchange reserves.[69] Visits to Britain by Indian officials produced yet another bout of Indo-British bitterness during the second-half of the 1960s, as we shall see in the next section.

3. Immigration and Indo-British relations

The immigration of Indians into Britain, and restrictions upon it, have been a major and persistent source of friction between the two countries ever since the 1962 Act. Other Indo-British disputes have flared up and died down; but successive British Acts of Parliament, accusations of evasion, British citizens of Indian origin from Kenya shuttled around airports, incidents involving Indians at Heathrow, and the sheer volume of diplomatic time consumed by applications have ensured that the immigration issue remained a constant irritant to India and Britain alike.

The increasingly vociferous hostility that appeared in the early 1960s (while Commonwealth immigration was unrestricted) towards Indian and Pakistani immigrants in Britain was already beginning to affect Indo-British relations.[70] Nevertheless, the introduction of the 1962 Commonwealth Immigration Act gave the Indians a jolt. The deputy minister of external affairs stated that India would have liked a greater degree of prior consultation, but was faced with a fait accompli. However, he saw some justification:

We ourselves are against illiterate or semi-illiterate Indians going to the United Kingdom or any other country in search of employment . . . (and) . . . have for some years past been exercising fairly severe restrictions against the issue of passports to such persons desiring to proceed to the United Kingdom.[71]

The GOI accepted the Act, although clearly believing that it was based on colour discrimination, partly because Britain's Labour opposition opposed the Act on the grounds of the special damage to Commonwealth citizens and of its racial undertones. In 1964–70 the Labour government were to pass further, much more restrictive, measures; but in 1962 Labour's stand against the Bill convinced the Indian government that in the Labour Party it had a real ally in Britain; hence it confined itself to hints that further restrictions on immigration might impede Britons' rights of free entry to India.[72]

Starting with the 1965 Immigration White Paper, however, and coinciding with a sharp decline in the real value of aid (though of no other major item of public expenditure), the Labour government embarked on a series of highly restrictive measures, nominally 'colour-blind' but actually ignoring Irish immigrants, and felt to be especially hostile by the Indians. The 1962 Act, which Labour had bitterly opposed, was extended and tightened up in August 1965, when category 'C' vouchers were abolished; this particularly affected India and Pakistan, with thousands of applications outstanding under this category at the time of abolition. At the same time an annual limit of 8,500 vouchers had been introduced (1,000 to Malta alone), biased towards countries still under colonial rule.

The 1968 Act, which really upset the Indians and still does so, was originally designed to deal with one particular 'problem'. In 1962 Duncan Sandys, the then colonial secretary, in a guarantee welcomed and endorsed by all parties in the House of Commons, had reminded the Asian minority in Kenya that their British passports represented a prescriptive claim on entry to the UK in the event of discrimination against them. Believing the word of the British government, many did not take out Kenya citizenship and in 1968 the Kenya government deprived them of many of the rights of Kenyan nationals. It now became inconvenient for the land of W. E. Gladstone to honour its pledge to 20,000 Kenyan Asians holding UK passports and fearing persecution in the land of their adoption.

India, besides her outrage at this particular sequence, saw the Act as aimed at all coloured immigrants. The most bitter pill was that it had been a Labour government that had introduced the restrictions, seemingly under racial pressures. Many Indian papers reprinted the judgement of *The Times* describing the Act as 'probably the most shameful measure that Labour members have ever been asked by the Whips to support'.[73]

John Freeman, then British high commissioner in New Delhi, was summoned to the Indian Foreign Office and told that 'the curb would be an act of bad faith, and would destroy what little enthusiasm there is still left [in India] for the Commonwealth concept'. India's major disappointment was over the British attitude to her East African citizens, usually of Indian descent, and (unlike any white holder) finding their passports reinterpreted ex-post by the British government as not guaranteeing admission until that government consented to honour them. As an editorial in the *Hindustan Times* asked: 'What is the British Government's plighted word worth?'[74]

The Indian attitude to the East African Asians since the mid-1960s has been described as hypocrisy, continually expressing sympathy but denying any responsibility; but one might respond, no less tendentiously, that there is no reason why India should honour Britain's dud cheque. Indeed, in February 1968, India announced that Asian holders of British passports would no longer be permitted to enter the country. Having opted for Britain in earlier times, they had—of their own free will—terminated India's responsibility for them. Nevertheless, in July 1968 the UK and Indian governments reached an agreement whereby, for any UK citizen of Asia origin leaving Kenya, if the UK High Commission in Nairobi endorsed his passport with a certificate entitling him to enter the UK from India should he and his family so desire, the Indian authorities would issue them a visa for travel to India with a view to permanent settlement.[75] Thus Britain stamped a broken promise with another, which presumably she proposed to keep.

The Indo-British agreement of July 1968 offered British passport-holders of Indian origin in East Africa one way of avoiding the immigration control that Britain had extended to them under the 1968 Act. Although, to gain the endorsement[76] on their UK passport, they had to declare their intention to settle permanently in India, if they changed their minds after reaching India they were automatically given an entry certificate to the UK. In early 1970 Sir Stanley Tomlinson, deputy under-secretary of state at the FCO, noted that 'we have no evidence of people . . . going to India and trying to come immediately to the UK', yet of the 1,456 endorsements issued between August 1968 and December 1969, 270 had been admitted to the UK by the end of 1969, 18 per cent of endorsements within 18 months,[77] which, if one allows for lags between issuing and travelling, seems to indicate some immediacy; but numbers are small compared with the 6,249 UK passport-holders from East Africa admitted to the UK in 1969.

During the period leading up to the agreement, the GOI's attitude had been partly based on the fear that if India admitted the British citizens concerned, she would somehow reduce Britain's moral or legal responsibility; but a reluctance to admit large numbers of businessmen, from unpopular 'rich' groups in India—many East Africans of Indian origin are Marwaris—played a big part. Much of the emotion behind Indian charges of racial discrimination is based on a disbelief that Britain could ever dishonour British passports, but some is a cover for Indian embarrassment at closing her doors on people whom at other times and in other contexts she proudly includes in the Indian family.[78]

The 1968 agreement over the East African Asians was only a temporary halt in the Indo-British disputes over immigration, for in 1969 the combination of the Immigration Appeals Act of 1969 and the secretary of state's instructions to immigration officers (Cmnd 4051) imposed the complication of entry certificates upon the 1968 Act.[79] These were introduced primarily to end the inconvenience and hardship caused to Commonwealth citizens who, on entering the UK without clear evidence of their entitlement to admission, had often undergone searching examination on arrival, occasionally leading to prolonged detention and increasingly to refusal of admission. Indeed, there had been incidents bordering on harassment of Indians (and others) entering Britain (caused mainly be overworked Immigration Officers struggling with ill-defined instructions) prior to the 1969 Act, but the Act seemed to make matters even worse. Indian journalists, scholars, and officials were accused of attempted illegal immigration for settlement and sometimes refused entry'.[80]

In response, the GOI again warned about visas for Britons visiting India. Even the *Indian Express*, a pro-Commonwealth and especially pro-UK paper, commented on the entry-certificate system by arguing that 'Britain, the mother-country of the Commonwealth, has prided itself on privileges accorded to Commonwealth citizens. But if the mother in her old age becomes neurotic, the children will have to alter their relationship'.[81]

Both the British High Commission (BHC) in India and the GOI began to advise everyone travelling to the UK, *even senior government officicials making short visits*, to have entry certificates: yet still the harassment at Heathrow and other entry points continued. In mid-1970 the GOI was reported to be preparing to introduce a visa scheme for Britons entering India, though it was not introduced, probably for fear of discouraging tourists, who make up an important part of entrants from the UK.[82]

India's conviction that there was a racial base to the British immigration policy was further confirmed by the 1971 Immigration Act: the so-called 'Patrials Act', which 'repealed' (only to strengthen) the 1968 and 1969 Acts and most of the 1962 Act. The chief aim of the Act was to assure the British public that 'there would be no further large-scale immigration'.[83] Its placing of Commonwealth citizens on virtually the same basis as aliens was seen by Indians as hammering yet another nail into the coffin of the Commonwealth concept.[84] The Indian government protested strongly over the Act, pointing out that it was racially biased and violated the 1968 agreement over the British citizens termed 'East African Asians'. This Britain seemed to ignore, although the home secretary announced in May 1971, while the Bill was still going through Parliament, that the annual number of vouchers for 'East African Asians' was to be doubled to 3,000 from 1 June and that there would also be another 1,500 once-and-for-all vouchers for allocation in 1971: a belated recognition of their prior claim, or the price of Indian acquiescence?

The Act was finally passed in October with certain modifications to reduce the risk of unpleasant confrontations between police and non-whites, and to the definition of 'patrial' (at one time it had seemed possible that the definition would allow up to 1mn Anglo-Indians into Britain).[85] This confirmed the end of substantial immigration from India into Britain, especially as it was also announced that the total number of employment voucher holders to be admitted would fall from 4,000 to 2,000 per annum from 1972 onwards, with reductions to occur in both 'A' and 'B' categories.[86]

Immigration in the late 1960s comprised a large part of the Indo-British 'relationship', and immigration control became the single most time-consuming issue for the British High Commissions in India and other Commonwealth countries,[87] thus diverting effort and attention from more positive and long-term issues, such as aid and trade. Commonwealth governments can hardly deny Britain the right to control immigration, since they all exercise that right themselves. However, such Commonwealth links as remain are badly strained by unilateral and overtly racial imposition of that right; and whether or not it is 'fair', the Commonwealth is not yet multipolar enough to prevent members from applying, in such matters, higher standards to Britain than to Uganda (or Australia). Successive British governments have not fully realized that the immigration issue, especially as it affected ex-colonies, requires not merely 'tact' and 'patience' but high standards of humane conduct. In fact an almost cavalier attitude seems to have been the order of the day: 'If any change in immigration policy is impending, it is not our practice to consult Commonwealth Governments directly as a matter of practice'.[88] True, the GOI was visited for consultations over the tightening up of the employment vouchers in 1965 (by Lord Mountbatten), and in 1969 (by Sir Roy Wilson's Committee on Immigration Appeals). However, it seemed to Indians in the 1960s that the steady drift towards respectability of racism in British politics—the absence of a clear non-racial lead—was the real issue. Immigration affects the individual Indian more tangibly than most topics dealt with in this book. 'In many villages in Punjab, . . . there are people who have been deported from Heathrow. . . . Everybody in the village—and indeed in the District—hears about their cases and the feeling grows that others wishing to enter Britain will not get fair treatment'.[89] Two hours of emotion at Heathrow, like two careless sentences in a political speech, can ruin many years of patient work in New Delhi.

It seems to be true, as one Indian remarked, that 'instead of being colour-blind, the Commonwealth has become far too colour-conscious'.[90] If the 1971 Act has any virtue, it is that its apparent finality over immigration might allow Britain and India to concentrate on more concrete and profitable areas in their relationship. In any case the Indians expect no better from the party of Winston Churchill; their hostility to the legislation of 1965–9 stems largely from false expectations raised by the idealistic professions of the party of Kingsley Martin, Harold Laski, and Stafford Cripps.

4. Diplomatic representation

In discussing the interchange of populations, we have left out a small but, for Indo-British relations, a crucial group: the diplomats. Until 1947 the nerve-centre of relations between the subcontinent and Britain was the India Office in London, which not only (under Parliament) has the ultimate authority over the citizens of British India, but was also 'the communications centre of the greatest imperial possession on earth'.[91] With the rapid departure of most of the British members of the ICS, the official connection passed to the diplomatic services of the two countries, which now oversee, co-ordinate, or direct many of the relationships discussed elsewhere in this book.

(i) BRITISH REPRESENTATION IN INDIA

At the end of the 1960s there were about 6,400 UK-based members of the British diplomatic service, about half of them overseas.[92] Their distribution reflected Britain's major overseas interests, with proportionately more in High Commissions and Embassies in Western Europe, North America, and the Middle East than either the number of countries or the populations would indicate (table 10.15). The distribution of officers dealing with aid naturally mirrors the areas in which Britain's aid is concentrated, and similarly commercial manpower in the diplomatic service reflects Britain's trading relationships. Indeed, there seems to be a clear statistical relationship between British diplomatic expenditure in foreign countries and the amount of trade that takes place. However, the apparently impressive statistical fit does not, however, indicate whether diplomatic activity precedes or follows increased trade.[93]

UK representation in India, in any event, is rather more than one would 'predict' on the basis of this statistical fit. The BHC in Delhi and the subordinate consulates at Bombay, Madras, and Calcutta (table 10.16), together make up Britain's seventh costliest diplomatic community,[94] her fourth largest in terms of UK-based staff, and her second largest in terms of total staff. It is also one of the senior posts as measured by the salary given to the Head of Mission. The Duncan Report suggested that the scale of the Indian mission partly reflects its past; as with other Commonwealth countries, it was established at independence, when British involvement in the affairs of India was ubiquitous.[95]

The number of UK-based diplomatic personnel in India seesawed in the 1960s, rising from around 104 at the start of the decade to 145 in 1966/7 before falling steadily to just over 100 in 1969/70.[96] The peaking of the mid-1960s reflects the growing aid relationships of the early 1960s, the large defence aid and sales after the 1962 hostilities with China, and perhaps above all the control requirements of the UK's 1962 and 1965 immigration legislation. The contraction in the second half of the period anticipates some of the recommendations of the Plowden Committee on Overseas Representational Services (Cmnd 2276), but probably has more to do with stagnant aid and falling UK exports than with changes in the efficiency of the administration of the diplomatic services or with any rethinking of the role of Commonwealth missions.

Of the 107 UK-based staff listed in the Indian mission in 1970 (table 10.16) about 70 were in career grades, the remainder being junior clerical and administrative staff, security personnel, etc. In fact the number of career-grade diplomats rose from 52 in 1960 to 70 in 1970,[97] with 39 in the New Delhi High Commission and the rest in the three subordinate DHCs: 14 in Bombay, 11 in Calcutta, and 6 in Madras.

The concentration in these three centres of the old Presidencies of the Raj mirrors the areas where Britain retains important trading and private investment interests. Some specialization developed between the four posts during the 1960s, although New Delhi remains the most important post in all major fields. Since 1965 Bombay has become increasingly involved in immigration-control work, and the May 1969 regulations resulted in a further four UK-based posts being added to the establishment there, including a chief immigration officer from the Home Office for three years or so. The Calcutta post deals with very few immigration inquiries; like Madras it concentrates on British trading and especially private-investment interests, of which around one-third are in West Bengal.[99] (During the negotiations over the proposed take-over of the British-owned Calcutta Tramways by the West Bengal government, the deputy high commissioner in Calcutta created a minor diplomatic incident by presenting an aide-mémoire direct to the state government instead of the central government.)[100] The administration of the British aid programme is mainly a function of the Delhi Commission, where an economic adviser at first secretary level is fulfilling an important function in evaluating potential aid projects.[101] Delhi also houses the British Defence Liaison staff, of which there were five at the end of 1970, under Major-General J. H. Penrose (see ch. 11).

There are in addition some 570 local Indian employees working for the BHC: 250 are in Delhi, 80 in Bombay, and the rest in Calcutta and Madras. There were also about 250 Indians employed on maintenance work by the British Ministry of Public Building and Works (now part of the Department of the Environment) in New Delhi,[102] making a total of some 800 Indians employed by the British government in India.

These employees represent one set of potential immigrants not covered by the British Immigration Acts. Under section 6(1) of the British Nationality Act of 1948, any person employed in a British Embassy or High Commission abroad who serves for more than five years has an *automatic* right to obtain UK citizenship. As the head of Chancery in the BHC in Delhi remarked: 'It seems a slight anomaly, I think, in our legislation'.[103] The locally-engaged Indian staff have availed themselves of this facility; in New Delhi alone, between 1960 and 1968, 90 of the have taken out UK citizenship.[104]

As noted above, the High Commission in India is one of the most important of the British diplomatic posts abroad, and since independence the high commissioners appointed by Britain have been men of outstanding quality[105] and all have been well received by the Indian government. At times—like their US colleagues, notably Messrs Galbraith and Keating—they have suffered from poor liaison, consultation, and support from the home government. Thus in 1962 Duncan Sandys and Averell Harriman tried, laudably enough, to bring about a settlement in Kashmir; but, in the bruised state of Indian sensibilities after the Chinese invasion and withdrawal, this attempt, linked as it was to heavy hints regarding arms supplies, was counter-productive. Perhaps the most damaging of the British government's gaffes was the famous Wilson statement of September 1965, made it now appears on the basis of imperfect information, which accused India of attacking Pakistan. To Indians already prone to believe that the UK was pro-Pakistan, this was final confirmation and the then high commissioner, John Freeman, was left with 'an albatross around his neck' which 'inevitably denied him high popularity with the Indians', and had to spend uncomfortable months wearing down anti-British sentiments.[106] Throughout the 1960s the British high commissioners, much more so than their Indian counterparts in London, have had to bear the brunt of the recurring periods of acrimony and accusation that often seem to characterize Indo-British relations.[107] However, the sheer triviality of some of the issues of diplomatic friction—while militating against a profound diplomatic review of this archetypal 'rich-poor' relationship—seems to confirm the continued existence of some special bond; we seem to be concerned with petty family quarrels rather than serious international disputes.[108] In such a context the strictly *diplomatic* qualities of the UK and Indian high commissioners acquire special significance.

The appointment of John Freeman to New Delhi in 1965 was one of the most important British diplomatic appointments of the 1960s, reflecting a genuine desire by the Labour Party to strengthen the ties with the nation that it had brought to independence eighteen years earlier. It also demonstrated Harold Wilson's estimation of the strategic importance of the Indian subcontinent, not long after he had declared that 'Britain's frontiers were on the Himalayas' (p. 282). The Indians in turn welcomed Freeman not least because of his status as Kingsley Martin's successor at the *New Statesman*, whose persistent pressure for independence had before 1939 earned it immense esteem with India's potential leaders. Despite the 1965 debacle, Freeman worked hard to put Indo-British relations on a 'footing of reality by brushing away the old cobwebs of sentiment'.[109]

The extreme strains of 1965 have not recurred, despite such moments of tension as the 1968 Immigration Act or the 1970 proposals for UK arms sales to South Africa. Indeed, the British position during the 1971 Indo-Pakistan hostilities over Bangladesh bought diplomatic relations to a new level of cordiality, confirmed by the last-minute (if temporary) resolution of the cotton-textiles issue (p. 58), and the revival of aid and trade in 1970–2 (pp. 40, 117). It remains to be seen whether this revival will last, given the realignment of both Britain and India. Britain thought little about India during the 1971–2 EEC negotiations; India little about Britain as she drew closer to Comecon in her trading patterns. In this context, it is small comfort that most British high commissioners enjoyed their time in Delhi; John Freeman found 'Indian officials very exciting to work with. In fact I don't think I've ever worked in such a stimulating atmosphere'.[110]

In view of the evident importance attached to India by Britain, it is surprising that the Duncan Report consigned India to 'the Outer Area'. It is true that India does not offer quite the scope of richer nations for international work at departmental level with the UK—a scope by which the Duncan Committee was understandably excited—though even here something is possible. Nevertheless, excessive downgrading of Indo-British diplomatic links would endanger the very complementarities that could make the UK a useful member of EEC. The report recognized this:

It would . . . not be in Western Europe's long-term interest if Britain's considerable diplomatic expertise derived from long and profound experience of the problems of the Indian Ocean were now simply cast aside, perhaps prompted by a feeling that this rejection would in some sense make Britain more truly 'European'.[111]

It seems as if the relegation of India to the Outer Area has been postponed; self-interest, as indicated by the relationships discussed in this book, suggests that it should be cancelled.

(ii) INDIAN REPRESENTATION IN BRITAIN

As with the British High Commissions in Commonwealth countries, the Indian diplomatic mission in Britain has been inflated by the past colonial link. It remains one of India's top three diplomatic posts in terms of staff and expenditure, along with Washington and Moscow, and well above the Indian mission to EEC, with its regrettable dearth of linguistic expertise.

The influence of the old colonial links upon the size of diplomatic missions can be seen in table 10.17, where four out of the 'top' five London missions are from Commonwealth members. Although the USA dominates the London diplomatic community, the IHC is still the second largest of the diplomatic posts, in both accredited diplomats[112] and total personnel (including dependants) given diplomatic status. It has also the largest number of military attachés (p. 185). The size of the IHC, whose major building dominates London's Aldwych, did not grow during the 1960s, at least in terms of listed diplomats, for 52 were listed in 1958, 48 in 1964, and 54 in 1970.[113] This was, however, not the total number of diplomats in the UK: there are Deputy High Commissions in Birmingham, Liverpool, and Glasgow, each under an assistant commissioner. They probably employ about six diplomatic staff between them.[114]

The IHC employs as well some 850 local personnel, including 350–400 Indian passport holders recruited in London.[115] This makes it by far the most populous diplomatic post in London—over twice as large as the US Embassy. Most of these Indian nationals are long-term residents, and many have been here long enough for their children to have taken their 'A' levels and 'gone on to fill up the vacant science seats at British universities, and, of course, read medicine!'[116] A few are personal and domestic servants, recruited in India and given entry certificates as a matter of course.[117]

Yet the IHC has lost some of the status that it had in the immediate post-independence period, when it was represented by such outstanding high commissioners as Mrs Pandit and Krishna Menon. Since then the focus of Indian diplomatic activity has shifted first to Washington in the late 1950s, as US aid began to play a major role in Indian planning, and more recently to Moscow, which has come to be the dominating influence in Indian trade (and possibly defence planning) and which sealed this with the Indo-Soviet treaty of August 1971. There has, further, been some switch of activity towards the Indian embassies in the EEC countries. The IHC in London was also shrunk by a series of economy cuts, first suggested after a visit by an Indian Foreign Service Inspection team in 1967[118] and epitomized by the closure of the Indian government publications bookshop in 1970 and by a cut in its library purchasing fund.

Yet by the end of the 1960s the IHC had recovered from the low point of November 1967 when it had ' . . . languished for months without a High Commissioner',[119] as three ex-cabinet ministers—all defeated in the February 1967 Indian general election—had turned the London appointment down, fearing that once they left India they would be forgotten as politicians.[120] The post was at last filled by Shanti Swarup Dhawan, described by a serious and pro-Indian newspaper as 'a talented, charming, somewhat elderly gentleman . . . (with) . . . little weight in Delhi.'[121] Nevertheless, under Dhawan and under his really distinguished successor, Apa Pant, its stock rose although (as with BHC in India) it is often plagued by trivia. (The Indian government was in 1968 taken to task in the Lok Sabha for not removing the British Crown over the entrance to India House in London).[122]

Indian diplomatic representation in Britain might either lose or greatly gain importance with Britain in the EEC. It will not rapidly decline to a small size. The growing British population of Indian origin; the recovery in arms shipments and general trade; the recent revival of aid; and perhaps a resurgence of UK private investment: all tend to maintain its importance.

11 DEFENCE AND MILITARY RELATIONS

We [Britain] have command of no sea in the world, except the North Sea at the moment . . . and many times I have been reminded of what happened in the days of the decline of the Roman Empire, when pressure at the heart forced them to call their legions home to Rome . . . So long as we are strong, India is a strength to us, but the moment we are no longer believed to be strong it becomes a source of weakness to us.
BONAR LAW, in the House of Commons, 25 July 1912.

In our imagination the vanishing last vestiges, south and east from the Straits of Gibraltar, of Britain's once vast Indian Empire have transformed themselves into a peacekeeping role on which the sun never sets, whereby under God's good providence and in partnership with the United States, we keep the peace of the world and rush hither and thither containing Communism, putting out brush fires and coping with subversion. It is difficult to describe, without using terms derived from psychiatry, a notion having so few points of contact with reality.
J. ENOCH POWELL, at Hanwell, 25 May 1967, quoted in *Freedom and Reality* (1969).

India has the capacity to maintain her independence. This is not a matter of apprehension for us.
SIR ALEC DOUGLAS-HOME, in New Delhi, 8 Feb. 1972 (*Financial Times*, 9 Feb. 1972).

For nearly 200 years India formed the heart of the British Empire and shaped much of Britain's strategy. The pattern of imperial conquest, not only in the Middle and Far East but also in the Mediterranean and Africa, was largely determined by actual or potential threats to the routes between Britain and India. So were quasi-colonial involvements, such as that with the Suez Canal. As late as 1904 Sir John Brodrick, then secretary of state for war, claimed that the main function of the British Army was the defence of India.[1] The First World War diminished India's importance in Britain's defence strategy, but much of Britain's military forces and expenditures remained tied to the subcontinent, and India's influence still entered into the formulation of British policy towards continental Europe.[2]

After Indian independence in 1947, military and defence relations with Britain naturally began to change, but Britain retained a major interest in Indian defence, and thereby in the Indian Ocean generally, for some years. Indeed, in defence as elsewhere, disengagement lagged behind decolonization by 10–15 years. Possibly because of the persistence of British colonial involvement in Africa, it was not until the 1960s that Britain's gradual realignment of major strategic objectives towards the North Atlantic and European theatres was reflected by a major military withdrawal from the Indian Ocean area, and the process was delayed by the 'confrontation' with Malaysia, declared by Indonesia under Sukarno, until 1966–7. It was only the recurring balance-of-payments crises of the 1960s, with their obvious implications for overseas expenditure, that prompted the Labour government to withdraw Britain's major military presence in Asia—despite an initial commitment to 'frontiers on the Himalayas'.[3] For India at least, the decision of the Conservative government in 1970 to delay the withdrawal from East of Suez did not alter the basic picture. The 'last gasp', the attempt to create an Anglo-American naval presence in Diego Garcia in the 1970s, met with clear Indian disapproval.[4]

In defence, as in other matters, mutual disengagement and diversification reflect Indian as well as British concerns. India, burdened by development expenditures and increasingly interpreting her defence needs in terms of China and (until 1971) Pakistan, has been less and less inclined to share Britain's preoccupations with a Russian naval presence in the Indian Ocean or abortive efforts to form a South Atlantic Treaty Organization. The events of 1962 and 1965 persuaded India to change her stance on neutralism and non-alignment: instead of seeking a world role as leader of a 'third bloc' (to the partial neglect of her own defences), she became determined to acquire an increasingly self-sufficient defence establishment, and (in response to Pakistan's policy of 'bilateralism') good military relations with both the USA and the Soviet Union if possible. But India's geography—and the apparent US alignment with Pakistan in 1971—made the Soviet alliance increasingly important.

Since the Chinese invasion of 1962 Indian defence policy has been dominated by diversification, the quest for independence, and a higher priority for defence spending as such. All these trends were bound to weaken the defence relationship with Britain, but its nature in the 1950s made such weakening even more certain. Before 1962, in the absence of any major apparent threat from her neighbours and with an obvious primary concern with development, India had been content to inherit her defence policies and strategy (as well as her equipment and senior officers) from the British period. Indeed, even today most of her top officers are British-trained. Until April 1954 the chief of air staff was British, and as late as April 1958, so too was the naval chief of staff. Military establishments therefore remain closely linked, although without any formal commitment to mutual defence by treaty.

The Chinese attack of 20 October, 1962, following several months of skirmishing between Indian and Chinese troops in the NEFA, demonstrated to the Indian military establishment the need for rapid and reliable sources of equipment supplies, and for an independent national defence policy. This quest for self-sufficiency extended to equipment after 1965; though Britain, like France and the USA, had sent prompt help to meet the Chinese attack in 1962, military supplies were immediately cut off from both India and Pakistan in 1965 (p. 183). This gave India 'a taste of what it is to depend so much on supplies from abroad, however friendly the source and however close the relationship might be.'[5] For India, the need for self-sufficiency was underlined by what appeared to be British partiality towards Pakistan, although this may have rested upon a slip of the tongue.[6] In any case, all this resulted in a rapid change in the mutual defence attitudes of Britain and India. Britain's influence of the 1950s seemed by 1971 to have largely disappeared. Unlike some of the weakening relationships, this was a matter of events and decisions, not just neglect, nor the winding-up of a misconceived or neo-colonial relationship. Nevertheless, the apparent revival of defence sales in 1970 and 1971 (pp. 23, 117), together with Britain's refusal to follow the US policy of suspending such sales during the 1971 hostilities with Pakistan, may have begun to create the 'mature relationship' for which Michael Stewart called (p. 16). Such relationships frequently rest upon transactions in lethal weapons.

1. Equipment and weapons sales

In 1960 India depended largely upon military equipment manufactured in or designed by Britain. This was especially true of the Indian Navy and Air Force, but the Army also relied on British weapons for its heavy artillery and armoured vehicles. The subsequent switch away from British equipment reflected the desire for self-sufficiency, reinforced by the arms embargo of 1965.[7] By 1969 the growing influence of the USSR as a supplier and India's own developing defence production organization had begun to alter the picture; even so British equipment still had a major role in the INS and IAF (tables 11.1, 11.2), and still more in telecommunications, radar monitoring and repair. Other than the purchase of submarines from France and the USSR from 1967 onwards (mainly in response to Pakistan's earlier acquisition of a submarine), and the recent arrival of the *Petya*-class frigates from the USSR, most ships in the Indian Navy were throughout the 1960s British built or designed (table 11.1), purchased from the Royal Navy during the 1950s, and rapidly becoming obsolete. British dominance was much less marked in the IAF (table 11.2), where since the 1962 war the USSR has been the major supplier of aircraft. This was probably due mainly to the UK's refusal or inability to do business with India rather than to a marked Indian preference for Russian aircraft.[8]

It is virtually impossible to determine in detail the extent of the trade in military equipment to India during the 1960s. Comprehensive accounts are not issued, and India publishes no details, even under broad trade headings.[9] For Britain, at least officially, military exports to India (with the exception of a major loan in 1962, discussed on pp. 183–4 below) have been at full commercial prices:[10] partly because the UK has no wish to be branded as a neo-colonialist and partly because she wants the money. India has not favoured *overt* military aid, mainly because of her neutralist position, but she has been increasingly forced to shop around for the best terms in the light of the foreign-exchange constraint.[11] During the 1960s Indian arms imports switched towards spare parts and equipment for her aircraft, ships, and vehicles; arms of non-Indian manufacture; scarce raw materials such as copper and nickel; and components used by major Indian defence establishments such as Hindustan Aeronautics and Bharat Electronics at Bangalore. Small arms and ammunition, except in a very few cases, are now manufactured internally.

From the scant evidence available, Britain remains—especially after the 1970–1 recovery in sales—a major supplier of defence equipment to India, mainly in the area of spares and components for the British equipment already in service with the Indian armed forces. In sales of new equipment the UK lags far behind the USSR, and probably behind France as well. Certainly India remains an important arms market for the UK. In recorded flows of arms, ammunition, and military stores alone (table 11.3) during the 1960s India bought 5–10 per cent of Britain's arms exports.[12]

India does not publish any details of her military purchases, but some inferences are possible. Presumably expenditure on armaments is included in the national import figure (both to permit the assessment of economic trends in the Finance and Trade Ministries and to avoid large and inexplicable inconsistencies between the balance of payments and monetary movements). Certainly the figures support this assumption. The Indian authorities classify goods entering into foreign trade according to nine major subsections, I–IX, corresponding respectively to the SITC 0–8. Thus SITC category 9 (which includes armaments) would be equivalent to an Indian category X, which unfortunately does not exist. However, the grand total for the Indian classes I through IX, in every year of the 1960s, falls well short of the total of imports as listed by India in the Trade Accounts—in 1962 by as much as 8 per cent of total imports. The pattern of these 'missing' imports over the 1960s closely follows both Indian military activities (table 11.4) and reported defence sales to India by other countries. While SITC 9 includes items unrelated to defence (India merely notes that the grand total includes 'miscellaneous transactions and commodities'), it is almost certain that the bulk of the missing imports are arms and ammunition. We would guess that between 1960 and 1969 India spent around £200mn on armaments, out of a total of £255mn of hidden imports. British arms exports to India (f.o.b.) over 1960–8 were £26·6mn—10–15 per cent of the total.

There is some confirmation under the heading 'Charges in England'[13] in the Indian Defence Estimates (table 11.5), which suggests that in 1963/4–1968/9, around 2½ per cent of India's total defence outlay was spent in the west: some £14 mn annually, compared with a yearly average spent in the UK on arms and ammunition alone of around £3mn. On this alternative but also restricted evidence, the UK supplied about 20 per cent of India's *western* arms purchases. France, Canada, and the USA have all sold arms and equipment to India during the 1960s, but as such sales are not listed in trade accounts in any detail, their respective shares cannot be determined.

The actual value of British sales of military goods to India is undoubtedly far higher than the figures shown in table 11.3, because much of the equipment goes through the British and Indian foreign-trade accounts under 'civilian' headings. If even half of the Indian defence expenditure in table 11.5 under the 'Charges in England' head is actually spent on military equipment and related components and spares in Britain, then perhaps half British defence sales to India go through civilian categories in the trade accounts. If so, then 6–8 per cent of *total* British exports to India have been related to Indian defence needs. However, without more detailed figures of defence sales, which obviously exist in both Whitehall and New Delhi, the true role of Britain in India's defence purchases remains an intriguing mystery.

We shall argue (pp. 188–90) that, in defence sales as elsewhere, experience since 1962 (and especially since 1971) suggests that a Euro-British concern is essential if India is to preserve international, and perhaps even domestic, options. India's need to be on cordial terms with *either* the USSR or China— given the threat potential against her of either unless deterred by the other—is perhaps the only unalterable datum of India's foreign-policy motivations. In this context, and in view of Sino-Indian hostility since 1962, what has been the Soviet response to India's diversifying arms purchases?

Subrahmanyam estimates that, in 1965–6, 11 per cent of defence expenditure was in foreign exchange.[14] This may have fallen since, because of India's drive for self-sufficiency, which seems to have concentrated on cutting western-oriented expenditure. If we assume a 10 per cent foreign-exchange content in India's defence expenditure over the 1960s, it follows from the above evidence that around three-quarters of India's overseas defence expenditure was *not* spent in the west. Certainly the purchases of equipment from the USSR during the 1960s were considerable—a recent speech by Mrs Gandhi suggests as much as £100mn. per year—[15] and this figure may well be realistic. Since the position of arms supplier implies the power to deny spares, this clearly reflects the degree of Soviet influence on India.

British aid advanced to India in response to the Sino-Indian hostilities of 1962 led to a large expansion in arms sales in 1963 and 1964 (table 11.3). Although suspended in 1965 upon the dispute with Pakistan, the supply was quickly resumed and figures for the late 1960s are well up on the start of the decade, although some of the rise is attributable to India's devaluation in 1966. Nevertheless the 1960s saw the *growing* influence of the USSR as a major military supplier to India, for three reasons. First, the USSR did not suspend supplies in 1962 *or 1965*. Second, there is some evidence that British equipment has not always been competitive in price or performance. Third, the Russians have evidently allowed the Indians to pay for some of their defence imports in both rupees and commodities, as against the foreign exchange demanded by other arms suppliers.[16] In 1962 the UK offered India Lightning fighters to strengthen the IAF, but cost, timing, and delivery made them unattractive compared with Soviet offers.[17] Two Canberra bombers were also scheduled to be delivered to India under the 1962 defence aid agreement, though the British arms embargo of 1955 caused the Indians to lose interest in them (see pp. 183, 284).[18] Britain's subsequent resumption of arms sales implied a recognition of the need for better terms; in 1967–8 India apparently purchased a number of refurbished Hawker Hunter F56a's on more favourable credit terms than those agreed between India and the USSR for the Sukhoi SU-7b fighters at the same time.[19]

The reputation of both British-built and British-designed arms in action remains good; the performance of the Centurion tanks against Pakistan's more modern—though smaller—American Pattons has been satisfactory, and the Folland Gnat—turned down by NATO in the 1950s as of little use—performed creditably against Pakistan's Starfighters.

A major change during the 1960s in the British-Indian defence relationship was the switch away from direct sales of equipment to their manufacture under licence in India. Thus since 1956 India has been producing the Folland Gnat at NAL Bangalore, and the Avro 748 transport aircraft has been produced in India since the early 1960s. Since 1970 the Indian Navy has completed the construction of three *Leander*-class frigates at the Mazagon Dock in Bombay, and the Vickers-designed Vyjayanta medium tanks are being produced at Avadi. In these and a few other areas of defence production, the UK gets some return as royalties, unidentifiable but probably small except on the Gnats, though in the 1970s the return on the Vyjayanta could become substantial. It is hard to interpret the Indian Defence Ministry's decision (in April 1973) to discontinue collaboration agreements; in the long run it signals an intensification of the move towards home production, but in the short run the existing arrangements for work-in-progress, and associated payments, seem sure to stay.

2. UK military aid to India

After independence India's leaders had held that the acceptance of military aid was incompatible with a neutralist or non-aligned position. Thus, because British military aid was tied to political ends for much of the 1950s, India received hardly any up to 1960 (if we exclude the sizeable amounts of equipment transferred from the British Indian armed forces in 1947).[20] Such British military aid to India as existed up to 1960 consisted mainly of technical advice and training, the loan for three years from 1953 of three *Hunt*-class destroyers ultimately purchased by India, and at most around £1·9mn of financial aid.[21]

After 1962 India's official position became that military aid was compatible with non-alignment if the strings of a formal treaty or alliance were absent. From 1960 to 1970, almost £90mn—over 40 per cent of UK military aid (table 11.6)—went in outright grants to individual Commonwealth countries, India being the largest single recipient, and with Malaysia and Kenya accounting for the overwhelming proportion of such aid. Between the Chinese attack in 1962 and the Indo-Pakistan hostilities of 1965, she received some £20mn, almost all as grants (table 11.7). India was a bigger recipient than the Federation of South Arabia which, along with other Persian Gulf territories, loomed so large in British defence discussions. It is interesting to note the imbalance between the public debate and the financial (and political) realities of overseas defence outlays (table 11.7).

British aid was thus both offered and desired mainly as a response to the Chinese attack of 1962, which found the Indian armed forces short of both suitable high-altitude equipment and general defence spares and reserves. Within hours of the main attack New Delhi had sent an urgent request for military supplies to London and Washington, receiving an immediate response from both governments. The first consignment of British aid arrived in two RAF Britannias on 29 October with further loads following, though Britain turned down a 'desperate appeal' by Nehru for more direct military assistance in the form of bomber squadrons to attack the rapidly advancing Chinese troops.[22]

In all, the UK committed military aid grants of £31·7mn on arms and defence equipment in 1962, but it is not clear exactly how much was delivered, as hostilities with Pakistan in 1965 caused the revocation by Britain of her military aid agreement, with some £11·5mn remaining unspent. It may have been logical to suspend arms deliveries to the subcontinent in the wake of the 1965 hostilities, but the case for denying military aid, while freely selling arms, is less obvious. In July 1966 the British government, carefully balancing morality and commerce, decided that outstanding deliveries under the *aid* programmes should remain in suspense, but that India should be permitted to *buy* any of the items earlier promised as aid. 'In practice they were given first refusal of some material which hitherto they had hoped [or been promised] they were going to get for nothing.'[23] The goods now offered for sale were none too attractive, for although in some cases the Indians made cash offers, by December 1968 £7mn worth remained unsold. This failure to sell military equipment, some of it specifically designed to meet Indian needs, was an embarrassment for HMG, which in early 1969 was criticized by the Estimates Committee for being laggard in disposing of it.[24]

The balance of £24·7mn (i.e. £31·7mn–£7·0mn) tallies with the known figure of £24·9mn of military aid given to India up to 1968/9. Therefore it would seem that all British military aid to India has been given under the 1962 agreement. On this basis there is no reason to suppose that such aid will be continued in the 1970s, unless another situation similar to that of 1962 develops.

The 1962 aid ran to several hundred items and certainly included armaments, ammunition, and telecommunications, radar and survey equipment, but whether it also included direct cash that could be either spent on UK arms exports (under SITC 951 or other headings) or switched to other external defence purchases is not known. Nor do we know whether the aid figures include items such as the cash the UK is known to have made available for the establishment of a shell-filling factory at Bhandara which began production in 1965, or the technical assistance to the plant to manufacture 30mn aircraft ammunition at Khamaria near Jabalpur in 1964. Some of this may well have gone through under UK Ministry of Defence expenditure.

As well as these grants, Britain also made available a £4·7mn credit in 1964 to cover the external costs of the *Leander*-class frigates currently being constructed. Up to 31 March 1970 £3.6mn of this credit seemed to have been used, partly on modernizing the dockyard itself and partly on the frigates, and further credit over and above the amount agreed in 1964 has evidently been promised. The terms are not known, though interest payments up to 1969 suggest an interest rate of around 5 per cent, with a 1- or 2-year grace period.[25]

Britain also promised India around £1,118,000 of military TA under the 1962 agreement and, despite the 1965 embargo, it was decided that the funds set aside within the military aid programme for the TA and the training courses would remain available for this purpose. By 1965 only £348,000 of the sum originally allocated had been spent;[26] presumably most of the remaining £770,000 was utilized by the end of the 1960s.

3. Joint staff courses and military training

The defence relationship remains active as regards the attendance of officers at staff courses in each other's country, and the training of Indians in certain specialized skills in the UK. Some twenty Indian officers, all senior, from all three services, come to the UK each year to attend specialized courses (table 11.8). Just prior to independence the numbers arriving in the UK for training were much higher, but India soon established her own training establishments; hence the more general training of officers in the UK has ceased. At lower levels of officer training, self-sufficiency dates back even further; the last Indian entry into Sandhurst was in 1932.

There remain only the senior courses: at the Royal College of Defence Studies (until 1971 the Imperial Defence College), the Joint Services Staff College and the individual services' Staff Colleges, and some specialized training in fields like rocket technology and propulsion (Cranwell) and aviation medicine (Farnborough). The numbers of Indians under training rose for a period after the 1962 Chinese attack, when under the military TA agreement technical officers, perhaps thirty in all, arrived in the UK to learn how to operate and service the more specialized equipment included in the new UK military aid given at that time.

The number of Indian service officers coming to the UK may have to be limited, as there are only a few places for many applicants from many (mainly Commonwealth) countries, and in autumn 1971 the Joint Services Staff College at Latimer was renamed the National Defence College and confined to British students. Whether this will affect the attendance of British officers at the Indian equivalent (Wellington) is not yet known. Incidentally, Indian and Pakistani officers attending courses in Britain have got on well, even during the hostilities of 1965 and 1971.

It is yet another indication of Britain's reorientation of her defence interests towards Europe and the North Atlantic that European students have recently begun to attend the Royal College of Defence Studies in London (8 students from 6 European countries in 1970; 10 from 7 countries in 1971). This increase, however, is seen as improving the overall defence input at the College and, as a College spokesman stressed, not only is there 'no intention of sacrificing the interests of India or Pakistan', but it is envisaged that their students will gain from this increased range of contacts.

UK officers also participate in courses in Indian defence establishments (table 11.9). The National Defence College in New Delhi, established in 1960, was modelled on the Royal College of Defence Studies in London and, like the

RCDS, it aims to let officers study the military, scientific, industrial, social, economic, and political factors involved in war, and the advanced direction and strategy of warfare. The British influence is still strong at the National Defence College, as at the Defence Services Staff College at Wellington in South India, the Indian counterpart of Latimer.

4. Other military relations

The Indians have become the recognized experts in certain aspects of warfare —especially in high-altitude warfare and logistics (i.e. above 14,000 feet). Britain has been without a mountain division since 1946, whereas India now has ten, all re-equipped (partly by the USA) and intensively trained to ensure that the 1962 debacle does not recur. In 1969, at the 'Exercise Unison' Commonwealth Defence Seminar in London, the Indian delegation was invited to speak on High Altitude Warfare; India is, as it were, now consultant to the Commonwealth on this topic.

The other main area of contact is the stationing of military attachés in each other's countries. The Indians regard London as an important centre, along with Washington and Moscow, for intelligence, general defence liaison, and the purchase and supply of arms. Hence they retain in the defence account the heading 'Charges in England', covering the purchase of spares, components and new equipment from Britain and some of the European countries, mostly through the Indian Defence Supply offices in London.

India has one of the largest military attaché establishments in London (table 11.10). Though Britain's representation of six attachés places India in her 'top seven', it is more instructive to notice the balance between India's London representation and British representation in India, compared with the equivalent balance for North America, the major EEC countries, and Australia, where the British presence is at least on a par with that of the other countries in Britain. This indicates the orientation of British strategic and commercial military interests. However, Britain still attached importance to the Indian military situation; this was indicated by the promotion of Brigadier Lunt to Major-General and his appointment as defence adviser to the British High Commission in Delhi in 1966.

5. The defence relationship and the future

Though the ties remain, they are weaker than in the early 1960s, when observers noted the pervasive influence of the UK in the Indian military system, especially in the senior officer corps.[27] Equipment is being bought increasingly from non-British (especially Russian) sources; self-sufficiency develops rapidly; problems and policies become steadily dissimilar and unrelated. In the 1970s and beyond, Britain will clearly continue to direct her main defence effort towards Europe, as current joint-defence production agreements with France indicate. The defence and security emphasis in the Conservative government's advocacy in 1971 of

British entry to the EEC indicated that this was not just an economic issue.[28] But what are India's interests?

Even after the removal in 1971 of any *credible* military threat from Pakistan, and even if there is a Sino-Indian rapprochement, the Indo-Soviet defence link represents a permanent Indian interest. Of the two nearby nuclear giants, China and the USSR, India must always seek the alliance—if not the protection—of one, to reduce the threat potential of the other. In any case, the Soviet Union's interest in the Indian Ocean is nothing new. Recent Soviet naval expansion in the area is at least as natural a geopolitical extension of her areas of strength as is the world pattern of US nuclear bases—whether or not we follow the somewhat tortuous view that such expansion forms 'a pattern consistent with the [alleged] secret protocol to the draft 1940 Four-Power pact, in which the Soviet Union declared "that its territorial aspirations centre south of the national territory of the Soviet Union in the direction of the Indian Ocean" '.[29] Throughout the late 1950s and 1960s the Soviet Union steadily expanded her activities in the Indian Ocean area, and became the major supplier of military equipment as well as being an important purchaser of exports from the area. Thus Soviet influence in countries bordering the Indian Ocean, such as the Yemen, South Yemen (Aden), Somalia, Iran, Pakistan, Indonesia, and even Malaysia (where she has become the major purchaser of rubber), has grown. India has been no exception; Soviet help in arming India for the 1971 war with Pakistan was a further episode in the rapid development of a mutually important relationship, formalized in the Indo-Soviet treaty of August 1971, and probably strengthened in the agreements following Mr Brezhnev's Delhi visit in late 1973.

Since the 1971 treaty, it has been claptrap to argue that India remains non-aligned. She has tacitly accepted that the expansion of Soviet power is partly in her own interest, and to this end has granted the Russians bunkering and other limited naval facilities in the Andaman and Nicobar Islands, and has allowed them to use Visakhapatnam as a supply depot where some Russian training of Indian naval personnel will also take place.[30] Indeed, the 1971 treaty, whatever its short-term intentions and motives, reflects a theme as permanent in Indian policy as was the European balance of power in Britain's: that good relations with either the USSR or China must be maintained to deter the other. So far, at least publicly, India has not merely denied the USSR an Indian naval base but also strenuously advocated a 'zone of peace' in the Indian Ocean. Yet strategically, if India were to encourage a Soviet naval presence in the Indian Ocean at the cost of her previous attachments, it would be a reasonable reading of her own national interest. An alliance with the Soviet Union can—on this reading—further increase Indian bargaining power vis-à-vis Pakistan; curb the growing Chinese influence in Africa and Asia; and support India against China directly.

The US alienation from India, following her open support of Pakistan in the 1971 hostilities, removed the main potential countervailing influence. Alone, a distant (and increasingly uninterested) middle power like Britain can help little in the purely military sphere. On the other hand the Soviet Union has a declared interest in the Indian Ocean, backed up by a rapidly expanding naval force containing helicopter carriers, a growing number of shore facilities at appropriate foreign ports, and long-range air transports able to land at sympathetic and strategically sited airports. She has a capacity for effective intervention that she previously lacked. The Arab use in 1973 of the 'oil weapon'—while Comecon is in oil surplus but 'the west' in massive oil deficit—sharpens these issues greatly.

What of Britain's interest in the Indian Ocean? At the start of the 1960s, Britain had a military presence east of Suez, based in a number of colonies or dependent territories and chiefly employed in protecting British trading interests. The Indian Ocean loomed large in Britain's strategic calculations, and following the introduction of the annual defence review in 1964 it had even been suggested that 'Britain might assume a special responsibility for the air control of the Indian Ocean throughout the 1970s'.[31] With the progressive loss of territory in the Persian Gulf on which bases could be sited, the various islands and coral reefs dotted around the Indian Ocean assumed a new importance, reinforced by the growing Russian influence in the area. Air cover from such 'baselets' was seen to be essential if the British navy was to continue its policing role with the oil route from the Gulf round the Cape, and until 1967 through Suez, protected. Thus in 1965 an Order in Council established a new colony, the British Indian Ocean Territory, comprising certain islands (Aldabra, Desroches and Farquhar Group and the Chagos archipelago, just purchased from Mauritius for £3mn). This new colony, perhaps Britain's last, was to form the basis of British Indian Ocean defence capability in the late 1960s and for the 1970s.[32]

By the late 1960s the direction of British defence policy had changed. Europe was now seen to be the focus of attention. Britain no longer wished to protect her trading and investment interests outside of Europe by military means, and lacked the foreign exchange (or the will) to build up the forces and bases such a policy would entail. The withdrawal from east of Suez began, although its pace was slowed down after the Conservative government came to power in 1970.

The visible build-up of the Soviet fleet in the Indian Ocean, together with growing uncertainties about relying on South African naval facilities, led to a renewed British interest in the Indian Ocean during the early 1970s. 'Britain', her foreign secretary announced in Delhi in February 1972, 'had obligations to five powers in South-East Asia and also wanted to protect its trade routes from the Gulf round the Cape of Good Hope, since vital oil supplies were concerned'.[33] He also made plain his determination that no navy should have a monopoly of the region. Britain had already started building up a naval communications base on Diego Garcia jointly with the Americans, and it seemed likely that some British military presence would remain in the Indian Ocean for the rest of the 1970s. The Labour government's defence cuts in November 1974 ensure that the presence will be tiny; the focus is increasingly on Ulster and Germany.

The British government in 1972 expressed no misgivings about the Indo-Soviet Treaty of Peace, Friendship and Co-operation, since 'India has the capacity to maintain her independence'.[34] However, it seems likely that in spite of this capacity India's future options will be reduced by the treaty, and not only in defence. How binding is Mrs Gandhi's alliance, since 1971, with the pro-Moscow Communist Party of India—or her absolute majority in parliament, which has so far reduced her dependence on that alliance? What happens if—or when—the USSR seeks base facilities in India? It is folly to speculate on *how* this will work out—futurology is not a science—but clearly the treaty, and India's growing diplomatic, economic and perhaps logistic dependence on the USSR, as revealed in August 1971, *does* reduce India's options. In the light of this, and the other developments outlined above, what future is there for Indo-British military relations?

The prospects for an open military alliance between Britain and India during the next decade are negligible.[35] Indian Ocean interests differ, and there are few other areas of common military concern. Over the Indian Ocean India has not shown much sympathy to western interests for a decade or more and has recently become increasingly hostile to the presence of any foreign powers in the area. In 1969 the Indian defence minister, Swaran Singh, declared that Indian policy over the Indian Ocean was that no superpower try to occupy the area after the British went, and that it should be left alone.[36] When Britain proposed in January 1971 a Commonwealth Study Group to examine the defence of the Indian Ocean, India at first accepted, and it looked for a time as if a useful dialogue would begin between Britain and India, but India's withdrawal, in protest against the sale of British arms to South Africa, led to the collapse of the Group and renewed Indian anxiety about the British presence in the area. The expansion of the Indian navy, largely with Soviet vessels, could be a growing source of British concern. India will be more dependent upon Soviet naval power and thus less likely to be sympathetic to Britain's interests in the Indian Ocean. Yet, despite reports of disagreement between the Indian prime minister and her chief of naval staff on India's capacity to exercise power in the area,[37] it seems unlikely that, even with Soviet naval assistance (and despite disputes in early 1974 about the US-leased base at Diego Garcia), India will try to force a complete British withdrawal from the Indian Ocean. Such a policy could only still further reduce her options vis-à-vis the Soviet Union and China.

It is plainly a western interest (of democracy rather than of capitalism) that India's options should not be too much reduced by her growing military closeness to, and diplomatic dependence on, the USSR. Yet the so far un-explained behaviour of the USA over the Indo-Pakistan hostilities of August 1971, and her major withdrawal from Asia (in aid terms, as well as militarily) must for some time rule her out as a counterweight. Britain can do little alone, but can perhaps do much in the EEC, whose present relations with the Third World are concentrated, far too heavily for the comfort of most member states, on frankly quasi-colonial mini-states in Africa. The construction of a mutually beneficial, non-neo-colonial link between the large, politically demo-cratic economies of Western Europe and Asia—a link that might well develop defence elements—is perhaps the main 'hidden' international issue of the 1970s. But it is very unlikely to be initiated by Britain alone, or to start with a defence relationship as such.

Perhaps the main prospect for specifically *British*-Indian defence relations during the 1970s lies in India's scarch for modern armaments, hardly any longer to deter Pakistan, but certainly to raise the costs of conflict to China, and (we fear) just possibly for internal policing work. Such modern technology will not be available from domestic sources for some time[38] and as much of the existing Indian equipment is outdated or second-hand the market potential must be considerable. With around 900,000 men under arms, India offers a big market potential, much less morally questionable than most, to British military exports; it can be met if more effort is put into drawing up suitable credit terms, and concentrating on the sale of technical knowhow and licences rather than the actual equipment.

In the short run, judging by past experience, components and spares for the British equipment currently in use with the Indian armed forces will provide a substantial market for Britain.[39] Table 11.5 suggests that new purchases from the west could well rise in the 1970s, especially for army equipment, where Britain has some potentially attractive vehicles and armaments to offer. A further candidate is the Hawker Harrier 'jump-jet', well suited to an area lacking in large airfields.[40] However, the competition will be fierce, especially from Russia, previously a supplier when Britain refused (1965; submarines; frigates) and sharing India's strategic interest in limiting Chinese power.

Might the USSR install troops or (more likely) naval bases in India directly? If this were requested and granted (unlikely, even assuming a coalition in Delhi unable to survive without communist support), the risk of anything approaching the 1967 coup d'état in Czechoslovakia is negligible, given India's size, location, and power. Russia's wish for good relations with Pakistan, and India's for US aid, are further guarantees. The danger is more subtle: a progressive reduction in India's range of military (and thus diplomatic) options.

Although military relations between Britain and India zig-zagged downwards in the 1960s, few senior British defence officials doubt that, were India to be subjected to another sudden Chinese assault of the 1962 variety, Britain would again offer immediate arms aid if requested. If no such incident occurs before 1980, and if (as we judge is likely) no multilateral Commonwealth defence arrangement in the region attracts India, then it would seem logical to expect the military relationship to wither away, unless concerted efforts in fields such as joint-defence production have been made.

But this is questionable. We have suggested that it is a shared Indian and British interest to reduce the extent to which India's pressing strategic priority—to have good military relations with China or Russia—compels her to reduce her options by increasingly favouring one of them (currently the USSR) to the exclusion of third parties.[41] If so, is not that shared interest likely—in an EEC context for Britain, and perhaps in a regional Asian contest for India—to issue sooner or later in some kind of military link? At present British tanks, planes, and ships in Indian service are about as important as Russian ones, but the balance is steadily shifting. Despite the Indian drive towards self-sufficiency,[42] neither aid nor imported parts (such as engines) are ruled out. India has apparently, since early 1972, opted for stability rather than expansion on the subcontinent, and she is thus a market to which 'inoffensive' (to others) sales are possible. Some sales prospects must be open; India can hardly have a comparative advantage in the efficient production of very capital-intensive defence items, although these are probably of interest to India only given assurances that spares and essential supplies will continue during conflicts.

No recent western sales to India match the French sale to Pakistan of 24 Mirage III's in 1967 and 30 Mirage V's in 1970 (for delivery in 1972).[43] One has to admit that regional arms *control* would be a better contribution than arms sales to South Asian stability and development; but arms control in Asia will not, in this day and age, be achieved from any non-Asian capital city, especially since Chinese motivations and preferences remain in doubt. And of India (unlike some other countries) it is just possible to argue, with moral as well as practical respectability, that if someone is to arm her it could as well be the UK in an EEC context.

12 THE MEDIA:

IMAGES AND OPINIONS

> We probably don't think about India as much, or as deeply, as some did in the days when the voyage out took 4 months under sail and you couldn't expect a reply, or find out whose child had died of cholera or who had married which rising ICS man, in less than a year. India to most people seems to mean Oxfam, or the Maharishi, or bus conductors who want to wear turbans, or nothing much.
> ANDREW CAVE, *The Guardian*, 22 July 1968.

> [There is] a curiously complex attitude in Britain towards India, which cannot be described simply as friendly or unfriendly. It is compounded of both emotion and shrewd political calculation; a mixture of admiration and resentment, confidence and distrust, respect and envy.
> K. S. SHELVANKAR, *The Hindu*, 14 January 1962.

Without doubt the most regular and influential contact between the *citizens* of Britain and India has resulted from mutual reporting. Here measurement is far more difficult than in such concrete areas as trade or population movements. However, the images created by the media have had an important influence on mutual relations, often affecting—and affected by—the other relationships.

Most of the time readers in Britain and India have understood that both countries have a free press, whose omissions and biases cannot be blamed on the government or the people. But the mutual images presented by the state-owned media are a different matter; the BBC is more independent of its government than All-India Radio (AIR), but this is not grasped clearly in India. This produces situations where, for example, the showing of a French-made and non-pro-Indian film series by BBC-TV in 1970 led to the closure of the BBC's Delhi office, the temporary imposition of censorship on television crews (p. 196), and a prolonged storm about an Indian image in a British teacup. When real relationships decline, mutual images assume special importance instead.

1. The British media and India

(i) THE PRESS

Before independence, most major British papers and magazines had substantial sales in India. They represented the major means, especially in the pre-radio era, whereby the many expatriates could keep up with events at home. Since independence, sales have naturally fallen considerably. There are fewer expatriates to read English papers: their price has gone up sharply; and news can be obtained more immediately by radio. During the 1950s, when nearly all the British servants of the Raj had departed (see p. 155 above), there still remained some Indians whose education had instilled a preference for British papers. A few, however, stopped reading out of political distaste; more looked on, frostily, as even 'journals of record' found that, while abrasive comment was free, facts were expensive.

As for sales in India, some British papers—such as *The Times*—do not release information; some copies reach India via trade agencies in the UK, or privately in diplomatic bags, or amongst company goods. Probably in 1969 some 570–600 copies of the four British quality dailies were sent to India (table 12.1), plus perhaps another 50 copies of other British national and regional papers. The sales of the three leading weeklies (per copy) are much higher, with the *New Statesman* in the lead. One should add perhaps a few hundred copies of assorted weekly and monthly journals, mainly scientific and academic publications. We were unable to compare the sales of the British press within India with that of other countries; both US and Soviet sales must have risen during the 1960s with the increased presence of advisers and experts in India.

Although British sales are undoubtedly well below the immediate post-independence level, they probably picked up during the 1960s. To judge by incomplete data for three publications (table 12.2) is hazardous, but these sales did rise, apart from a dramatic decline in 1965–7 period. A newspaper spokesman attributed this to cancellations in reaction against Wilson's 'Lahore speech' (p. 173); to British reporting of Indo-Pakistani hostilities; to the imposition of import duties by India on newspapers and journals; and to the rupee devaluation of June, 1966. After 1967 sales picked up again, and by 1969 they were back around the 1963 levels.

Few British papers reveal sales by country, but for *The Economist* (table 12.3) India's share of total overseas sales has fallen quite considerably since the mid-1950s, while Pakistan's has doubled.

Most of the major British papers sell at a loss in India.[1] This is accepted because sales there attract advertisers, especially as British papers are read mainly by members of India's metropolitan elite who can afford expensive imported consumer durables. The continued sales deficit may well be commercially justified.

Only two newspapers, the *Sunday Times* and the *Daily Telegraph*, keep records of sales to various parts of India. Both stated that most copies were sold in Bombay, with New Delhi a fairly distant second. Very few are sold elsewhere.

There are only two newspapers represented by full-time resident British reporters in India: *The Times* and *Daily Telegraph*. Both reporters are expected to cover events elsewhere on the subcontinent, including Pakistan and now Bangladesh; during the 1960s they sought to cover both sides of Indo-Pakistan disputes simultaneously.[2] Most British papers rely on part-time Indian correspondents, but although they may be excellent, their commitment is inevitably not total. In 1969 a Calcutta date-line in one serious British daily was exposed, in the *India Weekly*, as coinciding with a trip to Paris by the part-time correspondent. However, another newspaper acknowledged by informed readers in both Britain and India as providing the best and most regular Indian coverage, the *Financial*

Times, combines an excellent Indian part-timer and an outstanding London foreign desk with frequent visits to India by specialists, and hence produces detailed, well-written articles.[3] Reuters' coverage of Indian events during the 1960s was done by a skilful British man-and-wife team in Delhi, but Reuters' task and tradition excludes interpretation, and its Indian news is spread over many countries apart from Britain.

There are more resident British reporters in Africa than in India, but it is difficult to estimate how this affects the amount of Indian news that appears in British papers. We considered undertaking a content analysis of selected British newspapers on the lines of that undertaken in the 1948 report of the Royal Commission on the Press,[4] but decided that this would be too time-consuming, and that the results could be misleading. There are three major problems involved: first, it is extremely difficult to choose a (typical) year or month; second, the coverage of particular countries varies among newspapers over any period; and third, coverage by any single paper may change because of changes in editorial policy or in correspondents stationed overseas.[5]

We looked at the number of leading articles devoted to various countries and areas by *The Times* in 1950, 1960, and 1970, as listed in its *Index* (table 12.4). Unsatisfactory as the results are, they do seem to show some lessening of interest in India since independence, during the 1950s rather than the 1960s; concern over the United States has risen sharply, as has that over Europe, South Africa, and Arab-Israeli relations over the 1960s, though 1970 was untypical with respect to South Africa as the entries include a large number of leaders relating to the British anti-apartheid lobby's successful campaign to stop the cricket tour.[6]

(ii) RADIO AND TELEVISION

A major reason for the decline in the importance of British newspapers in India was the development of more instant news and comment from radio broadcasts.[7] There are two separate aspects that need examining: the transmission of programmes from the UK to India, their type and content; and the reporting by British radio and television of events in India.

In 1950 the BBC was the world's largest external broadcaster, transmitting nearly 650 programme hours per week. By 1960 its output had actually declined, and it had fallen to fourth place, far behind the USA, the USSR, and mainland China (table 12.5). Although output rose again by nearly a quarter during the 1960s, the BBC had by 1970 slipped to fifth place, overtaken by West Germany, a relative newcomer to external broadcasting. However, as with newspapers, too much attention can be focused on quantity, to the neglect of quality and effectiveness.

The BBC's main problem in planning external broadcasting during the 1960s —finance excluded—was whether to concentrate on English-language or vernacular broadcasts. As the managing director of BBC external broadcasting remarked in 1969:

If somebody could decide definitely whether it is more important to broadcast to the elite of a country than to the masses of the country, perhaps we might have the beginnings of the answer of the relative importance of vernaculars and English, but that in itself is a most unanswerable question in the long term.[8]

Later in 1969, the Duncan Report found little difficulty in answering this 'unanswerable question': 'In the long term advantage lies with broadcasting in the English language, and broadcasting in foreign languages is of lower priority' —implying, perhaps, a questionable theory of the relative role of anglophone elites and of non-anglophone 'masses' in forming opinions.[9] At the suggestion of the Duncan Report, the FCO undertook an urgent review of BBC's foreign-language broadcasting, but its verdict in the spring of 1970 reversed that of Duncan, finding that 'each of the BBC's foreign language services was worthwhile and had a significant audience'.[10]

In fact, over the 1960s the share of English in the BBC's total external output fell slightly, from 30·8 per cent in 1960 to 28·9 per cent in 1970, while the share of European languages also showed a small drop from 38·2 to 36·3 per cent, despite an expansion in broadcasts in Portuguese and Spanish broadcasts to Latin America.[11] This distribution indicates that the BBC, unlike the Duncan Commission, did not interpret the need to provide support for Britain's com-mercial effort—a need it explicitly recognized—as involving retrenchment in areas where British exports did badly in the 1960s.

Overseas broadcasts in non-occidental languages are dominated by trans-missions in Arabic (table 12.6), though they declined during the 1960s. The relatively large output in Arabic and Persian probably reflects British concern over the Middle East and her dependence upon Arabian oil. In such a situation concentration of news effort may well have been justified. What happened to other languages?

By 1970 transmissions in Persian had been overtaken by those in Hindi and the Kuoyu Chinese dialect, and the transmissions in all other languages than Japanese, Malay, and Sinhala had been expanded. However, if we look at transmissions in these languages in relation to the total potential audience in each language (table 12·6), the four Indian languages listed—Bengali, Hindi, Tamil, and Urdu— together with Indonesian and Japanese, do badly.[12] There is no reason why broadcasting time should exactly reflect language-population size, but weekly transmission times of only 1·50 hours in Tamil or 4·00 hours in Bengali do not seem to demonstrate a serious attempt to influence people through information and example. What of the comparison with other major external broadcasting nations?

As for external transmissions in the vernacular languages of the Indian sub-continent (table 12·7), in 1968, of the six nations listed, only West Germany has a smaller total effort than the UK. Indeed, except for West Germany, the BBC was outdistanced by all 'competing' in each language. The BBC did transmit five languages, more than China, Egypt, or the USA; but the USSR transmitted, in twelve languages, total programme hours nearly five times Britain's.

The British effort may, however, still be more *effective* than that of the USSR or the USA in languages—including English—where the countries are in competition; a high quantity of programme output means nothing if the quality is such that no one listens to it. Unfortunately, the evidence of radio listening habits in India is ambiguous and drawn mainly from urban samples (around 80 per cent of India's population lives in rural areas). However, radio listening is practically universal amongst the literate segment of the metropolitan population in India, with an estimated 89 per cent of homes having a radio.[13]

How many Indians listen to the BBC? Despite increased competition from other external broadcasters, the IIPO surveys (based on random samples of adults in 35 cities) suggest that the BBC has held its share of the urban audience, and has recovered the losses of 1959–62.[14] In September 1967 some 12 per cent of those interviewed claimed they were regular listeners to the BBC, with 3 per cent listening daily or nearly every day.[15] By 1969 the number listening 'daily or almost every day' had risen slightly to 4 per cent, with another 4 per cent listening once or twice per week[16] (table 12.8), suggesting some growth in audience. On the basis of the survey, the BBC's audience must be well over 1mn *regular* listeners in the 35 cities alone, as against comparable figures (covering all listeners, urban and rural) for the BBC German service of 800,000, the French service of 500–750,000, and for the service to the Jewish population in Israel of 150,000. Probably the Indian audience is greater than in the USSR, where the BBC unofficially estimates that it has well over a million regular listeners.[17]

The 1969 IIPO Survey shows some peculiar features, which throw some doubt on its representativeness. Although the BBC is shown as doing slightly better than the USA's Voice of America, both are outperformed by the broadcasts of Radio Ceylon, to which 26 per cent said they listened almost every day. Further, no one is listed as tuning to broadcasts of the Soviet Union, China, or Egypt, all of whom were shown earlier (table 12.7) to be major broadcasters in the Indian vernacular languages. As it is unlikely that these countries would broadcast if they knew that no one was listening, the most likely explanation appears to be that the literate urban population, which forms the basis of the IIPO surveys, is unusual within India in that its foreign radio listening is done in non-vernacular languages. This is certainly true for the BBC, for the 1969 urban survey showed that of those who listened to BBC broadcasts, 84 per cent listened to the English-language service and only 2·6 per cent to Bengali and 2·6 per cent to Hindi transmissions.[18] Probably the main audience for vernacular broadcasts lies in rural areas, although no surveys are available to substantiate this.[19] Whatever the rural position, the BBC's urban audience in India appears to warrant further expansion in transmissions in English of news and programmes designed specifically for India.

Unlike most British newspapers, the BBC has always regarded India as a key assignment, requiring a full-time reporter of top quality. In 1970, however, a relatively trivial incident concerned with the transmission by BBC television of a series of films about India by Louis Malle (p. 203) led to the enforced closure of the BBC Delhi Office for two years, and the transfer of its correspondent, Ronald Robson.[20] The Malle affair even affected a team from Thames Television who were filming a report on the political situation in West Bengal for the 'This Week' programme. If the GOI reaction to the BBC was severe, its action against the Thames team was hard to defend: it impounded their equipment, seized some of their exposed film, and presented the team with a set of 'restrictions . . . worse even than those which totalitarian governments sometimes seek to impose'.[21] Consequently, for the first time since independence, British broadcasting media were without permanent representation in India (although AIR's reporters are still at work in Britain).

The closure of the BBC Delhi office has certainly affected the British radio and TV news and current affairs coverage of the Indian subcontinent, as well as the external broadcasts in Hindi. Although there have been discussions between Britain and India over the restoration of the BBC office, it remained firmly closed until spring 1972, and has since functioned on a reduced scale.

(iii) BRITISH REPORTING ON INDIA

Throughout the 1960s the reporting of events in India by the British news media has been frequently questioned by the Indians. The Indian take-over of Goa; the behaviour of India troops in the Congo (and especially the notorious Katanga ambulance incident); the Indo-Pakistan war of 1965; the appointment of high commissioners (see p. 176); the Nagaland rebellion; the death of President Hussain and the appointment of President Giri—British reporting and comment on these and many other occurrences produced strong reactions from Indian commentators. The feeling in India was that, with a few notable exceptions,[22] reporting in the British press was biased towards the disasters, failures, and frailties, the sensational and unpleasant rather than the encouraging, promising, and constructive in Indian society.

There is much truth behind the charges, despite one major exception (general, perhaps excessive, support in the British media for India in her border disputes with China) and one qualification (that reporting in democratic countries concentrates on bad news, domestic and foreign). The problem is not one of deliberate bias but of differences in the way in which reporters in the two countries perceive news, and it has been enhanced because of changes in the character of some of the more influential British dailies.

It is hard to explain to Indian pressmen, who (as we shall see) model themselves on older British traditions, the forces that have led the British press to its apparent coolness not just to India but to very many objects of commentary and report. The symptoms include a prevailing mood of instant abrasiveness, preference for free comment over expensive facts, and a 'good news is no news' attitude. These symptoms spring in part from the economics of the national press, especially as it faces the competition of television. Newspapers have been compelled to cut down on serious (especially foreign) news by the twin pressures of unions seeking higher wages and advertizers seeking high circulations that require price restraint. Probably, too, widespread dissatisfaction with India's performance has induced readers to demand hostile stories, both about domestic politicians and about ungrateful or inefficient foreigners.

Whatever the causes, the results affect British press coverage world-wide, but the Indians feel them keenly. At the level of the journalist and the TV producer, there is the 'cult of personality', where a personal opinion about the desirability of Indian growth counts as news. Moving up, we find the sub-editor who cuts the serious news to make room for the striking but facile headline; and the editor for whom good news, especially from far away, is no news. All this applies fully to several once-serious newspapers and programmes. When a TV journalist inserts a two-minute slot into a BBC news bulletin during a lightning trip to Delhi in 1970, 'explaining' glibly that India remains as unsatisfactory as ever, it is not that India is singled out: the man is doing well just what the licence-holder pays him to do, namely to flit around the world reporting in undemanding fashion upon its follies to largely apathetic British viewers. The Indian reader, seeing an account of this in his newspaper, wrongly concludes that his country is being singled out for this sort of reporting.

The Indian elite understands the Beaverbrook inheritance, and at a more serious level the paternalist, but not hostile, scepticism of the *Daily Telegraph*, but the change in *The Times* is resented.[23] Indians remember the very special position of its correspondent between the wars, when he sometimes sat at the Viceroy's table, but sent London impartial news, expected publication rather than skilful sub-editing, and kept comment separate from facts.

The Indian elite is also not as thin-skinned as often alleged. In 1967 *The Times'* reporter in India, Neville Maxwell, remained quite popular while he seriously informed his British readers that these were probably India's last free elections (and that a 'Man on a White Horse' was nigh), because Maxwell's hard work, sincerity, and scholarship were not in question. Since then, things have changed, though whether this is due to journalists, sub-editors, editor, or proprietorship we cannot say.

To understand why Indians resent British reporting, let us examine two events of the late 1960s: the adjudication of the Rann of Kutch dispute between India and Pakistan in 1968, and the death of President Hussain of India in 1969.

On the Rann of Kutch,[24] the international tribunal to determine the Gujarat-West Pakistan border gave its award on 19 February 1968. On 14 February *The Times* diarist had predicted that a decision against India

could even be the last straw that topples Mrs Gandhi. India, although pledged to accept the tribunal's verdict, has, in fact, got itself into a position where it would have great difficulty in doing so even if it wanted to. Having denied that the Rann is disputed territory and said that it was wholly Indian, it would require a constitutional amendment to cede any portion of it. There is no prospect of the present Government getting the required two-thirds majority to make such an amendment on this issue.

The last two statements were as inaccurate as they are ungrammatical.

On 19 February the award was announced, conceding most of Pakistan's case.

The Times quoted Mrs Gandhi's indication to the Congress parliamentary party executive that the award was an international commitment and the question of not honouring it did not arise. That this report refuted earlier statements in the 'journal of record' was not recorded.

On 24 February *The Times* ran a story under a three-column heading: 'Indian Political Chaos Spreads'. Most of it dealt with the troubles of *one* of India's 17 state governments; the last quarter of the report ran:

In her first formal statement on the Kutch award, Mrs Gandhi told the Lok Sabha, 'India will honour her commitment on the Kutch award . . . it would be a sad day if we fail to meet our international commitments'. It is now apparent in Delhi that the initial rumours suggesting that India and Pakistan might clash again over the results of the award are unfounded.

On 28 February the prime minister reaffirmed in parliament that India would implement the award. Under the headline 'Party Threat to Kutch Findings', *The Times* reported from Delhi that 'the Opposition' in parliament threatened to prevent Mrs Gandhi from implementing the Tribunal's findings by challenging her right to cede Indian territory without amending the constitution. Which party the headline referred to is obscure, as both Swatantra and the Communists had tacitly indicated that they supported the government's pledge.

Also on 28 February Mr Moraji Desai powerfully defended the government's acceptance of the award, reiterating the point made by Mr Shastri when he agreed to submit the dispute to a tribunal: that no cession of territory was involved, only the demarcation of an undecided frontier—obviating constitutional amendments. On 29 February, the Indian Lower House rejected the no-confidence motion brought by a section of the Opposition against the government for its handling of the Kutch dispute by 203 votes to 72. Neither of these further developments was reported in *The Times*. Evan Charlton writes: 'I assume both were cabled from Delhi but crowded out for lack of space. This is the kind of news treatment which Indians, and many other people, will regard as inadequate and unfair'.

The Rann of Kutch dispute illustrates the bias that can consistently appear in *one* newspaper's reporting of a story; but similar bias can often be found permeating the British media when they cover a major Indian story. On May 3 1970 the death of President Hussain was announced in Britain. It was at once clear, apart from his personal distinction, that the succession battle would be a major political event. Yet, although both BBC-TV and ITV carried the news in their bulletins from midday, they put it far down the list, and stressed that he was 'the first Muslim President of a predominantly Hindu India'.[25] Most evening papers ignored the story or hid it away in some quiet corner.

On 4 May one would have expected serious discussion in the quality Sunday papers. The *Sunday Times* managed seven lines on page 9, while *The Observer* rose to seven lines on page 3. The *Sunday Telegraph* alone regarded the story as important, carrying a fairly lengthy and informative piece by David Loshak. (The *Sunday Express* kept up its tradition by heading their brief report ' "Irish-

Rebel" President': a reference to the fact that the acting President, Dr V. V. Giri, had been expelled by Britain from Ireland in 1916 on suspicion of aiding and abetting the Irish independence movement.)

Next day the *Morning Star* carried a Reuter report without comment, while both the *Guardian* and the *Financial Times* speculated about (but did not really analyse) the future challenges to the prime minister and Congress. Peter Hazelhurst, in his dispatch to *The Times*, began with a moving appreciation of Dr Hussain, but then slipped into speculation about a successor, capped by some sub-editor's headline: 'Untouchable could be India's next President.'[26] Even this was nothing compared to the Peterborough column in the *Daily Telegraph*, which celebrated Dr Hussain's death by describing him as 'a quiet yesman', before proceeding to insinuate that he held pro-Nazi sympathies, for instead of going to a British university he had gone 'to that home of liberty, Berlin'.[27]

Solid and generally reliable reporting of Indian events had characterized the British press in the immediate post-independence period. Yet, as revealed above, the situation had severely deteriorated by the end of the 1960s. Indeed, the dismal and repetitive predictions of doom were perhaps in part responsible for Indo-British friction, though probably the major direction of causation was the other way.

In several cases, however, the Indians have alleged that British reporting damaged either their external image or internal Indian political developments. The latter complaint was recently voiced by Surendra Pal Singh, the deputy minister for external affairs, who charged in the Lok Sabha that the *Observer* was aiding the Naga rebels, among other things by printing CIA-inspired articles and by refusing to publish a letter from the IHC in London. Although these charges were refuted, and Singh later apologized for misleading parliament, the affair demonstrated the special touchiness which seems to mark the Indian view of the British press.[28] Yet the *Observer* was by no means blameless. It 'no longer finds India sufficiently interesting to maintain a full-time foreign correspondent',[29] and the excessive concentration on Nagaland (and a one-sided concentration at that) was quite disproportionate. For weeks Nagaland alone on the subcontinent made regular (and tendentious) news. Indeed, the *Observer*, whose coverage of African affairs was exceptionally good, had—through morally laudable editorial concern, uninformed by balanced, or indeed any, on-the-spot permanent coverage—become involved in one-sided propaganda for Naga secessionists, thereby damaging its credibility on all Indian matters, both within India and among serious readers in Britain. As of late 1974, this situation persists.

Although the Indians have complained frequently and bitterly about British press and radio–TV coverage of India, there has been general approval of the BBC external broadcasts to India to which the average Indian is more likely to be exposed. If the serious press (with the exceptions noted earlier) and BBC–ITA television had similarly sought a reputation for reliability—which is not the same as dullness—in their India reportage to Britain in the 1960s, more

Britons would realize that India is the world's biggest working liberal democracy; would be able to follow 'instant crises' through to their tortuous but so far (with the exceptions of the Sino–Indian and Indo–Pakistan wars) peaceful resolution; and would know something of the scope and limits of Indian steel and 'miracle' wheat. India would also think more kindly of Britain if many of the transitory images of the British media were to reflect a little more deeply.

2. The Indian media and Britain

(i) THE PRESS

British journalism has had a deep and lasting influence on the form and content of Indian journals. There is a flourishing English-language press: despite a rapid growth of Hindi and other vernacular papers during the 1960s, at the end of 1968 some 27 per cent of the more than 10,000 registered newspapers and journals published in India were in the English language, including 63 daily papers, 254 weeklies, and 896 monthlies.[30] Although outnumbered by Hindi *publications*, the *circulation*[31] of English-language publications remained by far the largest of any single language, at around 6mn;[32] probably the English-language dailies increased their share of Indian daily newspaper circulation during the 1960s.[33]

The English-language press is essentially an urban phenomenon, although one or two of the leading national dailies have large rural circulations. In Indian cities in mid-1969, about 61 per cent of literate adults read only English-language dailies, 24 per cent only Indian-language dailies, and 11 per cent both.[34] The most important English-language dailies were *The Times of India* (19 per cent of total English-language circulation): the *Hindu* (18 per cent); the *Indian Express* (13 per cent); the *Hindustan Times* (9 per cent); the *Statesman* (9 per cent); and *Amrita Bazar Patrika* (2 per cent), each with distinct regional strongholds.[35] Although 'public opinion . . . [is] . . . not the English-language press'[36] the major national papers listed above either influence or echo India's cosmopolitan, affluent, and urban elite.

Many English-language dailies were once owned, staffed, and edited by Britons, and these, such as the *Statesman* or *The Times of India*, tended to reflect British interests. Although in 1969 there were still two Britons on the staff of the *Statesman*, the departure in 1967 of Evan Charlton from the editor's chair ended a long period of British editorial participation in the Indian news media. The sale of the same paper in 1962–3 by the old-established managing-agency firm of Andrew Yule had also ended direct British ownership of Indian papers.[37]

The English-language press in India is now firmly Indian, in contrast to the days of the Raj, when it existed primarily for the British community in India.[38] Yet the British influence lives on in the layout, content, and editorial style of the major newspapers and journals.[39] The top four daily papers regularly carry London diaries or columns; most serious journals frequently reprint articles from the British press; and crosswords[40] and comic strips are still largely purchased from British papers.

An important feature, partly reflecting the days of the Raj, is the large amount of space devoted to foreign news by the English-language press.[41] The demand for international news is still largely met by the use of British news agency services. The *Hindustan Times*, for instance, relies for much of its foreign news coverage on the *Daily Telegraph* and (since 1959) the *Observer* news services, while the *Hindu* uses the *Guardian* news service.[42] However, the new Indian editor of the *Hindustan Times* (George Verghese, an ex-PRO man for Mrs Gandhi) feels that the newspaper's own correspondents should cover the news, both to preserve independence and to save foreign exchange.[43] Other newspapers will, it is understood, continue to use British news services, just as nearly all will receive most foreign news via Reuters.

Reuters had been much criticized by the Indians during the 1950s and early 1960s for its overemphasis on British events and the British line. This was eventually overcome by establishing a special Indian desk at Reuters in London, staffed by Indians who selected news and comment to be forwarded to the Delhi agencies (PTI, UNI)[44] for circulation to news media within India. Reuters have long employed Indians as correspondents, both within India (although currently their top Indian reporters are British; see p. 193) and elsewhere overseas.[45]

The main reason for the importance of British and other foreign news agencies to the Indian press is that the foreign-exchange cost of keeping Indian correspondents abroad is too high for all but the largest Indian dailies. For the dailies which do have correspondents abroad, London still ranks as one of the principal stations.[46] India has more and probably better reporting on Britain than vice versa: in the mid-1960s the Indian Journalists' Association in London had nearly 50 members.

The style of the major Indian English-language papers remains patterned very largely on the British press. Recently, however, their technical development has lagged behind that of their British counterparts, mainly because foreign-exchange constraints have led to difficulties in obtaining modern printing technology and equipment. This led one British journalist with substantial experience in both countries to remark 'The best Indian papers have the quality of the better British papers of the early 1930s'. This may be a disadvantage technically, but at least the *Hindu* or the *Statesman* are still under the influence of the scholar-journalists rather than the businessman-proprietors. Though there are no multi-coloured, full-page advertisements in even the best Indian papers, one can normally distinguish between news and opinion, opinion and advertising, content and gimmick.

As for sales of Indian papers in Britain, the *Statesman, The Times of India*, the *Hindu*, the *Hindustan Times, Amrita Bazar Patrika*, the *National Herald* and the *Leader* have subscribers, mostly for their weekly editions.[47] Sales have been falling during the 1960s; the declining expatriate readership has not been offset by increased sales to the growing Indian community in Britain. As with British papers in India, most copies are sold at a loss, and with the growth in Britain of 'British' Indian newspapers (both in English, such as *India Weekly* and in vernacular languages) sales of Indian-published papers will decline still further.

(ii) ALL-INDIA RADIO

The external broadcasts of All-India Radio (AIR) concentrate, like those of the BBC, on fact and entertainment rather than comment. However, they concentrate more on Britain than does the BBC on India.

Since independence AIR has developed into one of the world's major external broadcasters (table 12.9) and by 1970 was transmitting around 271 programme-hours per week. This total will obviously rise in the future when the two new 1,000 kw, medium-wave transmitters are introduced.[48] In 1969, about 33 hours of English programmes were broadcast to the west (table 12.9) out of a total weekly output of 68 hours in English, though much of the programme content is shared with non-UK listeners (and India's external broadcasting effort in English has concentrated on the large communities of English-speaking Indians in East Africa and South-East Asia: p. 162).

AIR's overseas emphasis on the UK is certainly greater than the BBC's on India. However, the UK audience for AIR's English-language broadcasts is certainly far below the Indian audience of the BBC. AIR maintains a London office (despite the expulsion of the BBC from India in 1970) and has a link with the BBC via the AIR External Programme Exchange Unit which receives material from overseas radio organizations, in return for Indian items.

(iii) INDIAN REPORTING ON BRITAIN

What of Indian coverage of British events? Evan Charlton, in his paper to the Britain-India Forum, identified two fairly consistent features. First, there is what he terms "echo-reporting", which at its worst consists of cuttings from British papers, sent to Indian papers by their London correspondents together with some comments, as dispatches: British journalism presented as British news.[49] This reached its height during the Indo-Pakistan conflict of 1965, when the Britain view of events took on a quite disproportionate importance in India. Charlton cites the 'echo-copy' sent to the *Hindu* from London between 2 and 17 September 1965. The headlines tell their own story, all being of the variety: 'UK Press Wakes up to Pak Designs'; 'UK Press Caution Pakistan'; 'Pro-Pakistan Attitude of British Press', and 'Indian Victory Vital: British Columnist's View'. Clearly, British views and opinions will feature in reportage to India at such a time; but the best British journalists would not support the implicit assumptions in such dispatches that the British press is well-informed, influential, and representative on India affairs.

Secondly, Indian journalists reporting home from London concentrate understandably but excessively, on items of narrowly Indian interest. Thus in the late 1960s an inordinate amount of attention was paid to Britain's race and immigration problems,[50] to the changes in import controls imposed upon cotton textiles, and to the effect of British entry into the EEC upon India. Although these events were generally reported fairly, the comparative narrowness did not help Indian readers to grasp the really important and fundamental changes in British society. There are also the occasional fatuities, such as the talk by Frank Moraes—one of India's best journalists—that was broadcast by AIR in September 1965, which argued from Harold Wilson's speech of 6 September to a British plot to recolonize the subcontinent!

While the BBC would never parallel this, the *Statesman* or the *Hindu* generally give a fuller and probably a fairer picture of Britain than do *The Times* or the *Daily Telegraph* of India. However, Indian opinions of Britain usually pass unnoticed in Britain. Indeed, few British people could name even one Indian paper.

3. Images and opinions

Does a nation's image, as projected in the media of another nation, form or merely reflect public opinion? This debate may lie (or gnaw) at the root of Indo-British relations since 1960.[51] Many actions of the Indian government and 'media men' indicate a firm belief that ill-disposed British communicators were to blame for India's poor image in Britain. True or false, the belief affected other, more tangible relationships.

India cares deeply and passionately—perhaps too passionately—about what other countries think of her, and especially about the British image of India.[52] This persistent touchiness reached a new peak during the 1960s. In 1964, for instance, members of all sections of the Lok Sabha expressed indignation at reports of exhibitions of photographs throughout Britain by the Freedom from Hunger Campaign which depicted some Indians as starving and naked.[53] The accurate but hyper-sensitive reviews of British reporting of Indian events in *India Weekly* are another indication of India's concern over her British image, a concern not shared by (say) Nigeria or Jamaica, nor indeed by France or the USA.

In 1970 the BBC screened a series of films on India produced by Louis Malle. These had earlier passed without Indian comment when televised in France and Germany. The films, while often beautiful, were characterized by a naïve hatred of modernization; they were antiquarian, but certainly not anti-Indian. India's violent official hostility to their showing on BBC-TV may well have been inspired by other political events (immigration disputes, the Diego Garcia project, cotton-textile import restrictions). Probably, too, BBC-TV paid the price for the carelessness of others (pp. 196–9) in constructing what some Indians misread as an image *designed* to discourage aid. Certainly the reaction was astounding. 'In the Louis Malle film', the deputy minister for external affairs, Surendra Pal Singh, told parliament in New Delhi, 'the whole nation, the whole country has been maligned [by] an unfair and distorted image of India'. He stressed that the government's decision—to expel the BBC—did not indicate any animosity towards the British government or people. 'On the contrary, we value their friend-ship and do not wish such misrepresentations of our life and culture . . . to adversely affect our relations.'[54]

Unfortunately the censorship of TV films, unsuccessfully demanded by the India government in 1970, darkened the very image that it sought to improve. Very rarely has India censored serious British non-fiction, although in 1965 it banned Ronald Segal's *The crisis of India*, a superficial and hostile paperback, on the grounds that it insulted the memory of Shivaji;[55] however, on at least one occasion the Indian government has acted to protect the *British* image.[56]

India has tried in more positive ways to improve her image in Britain, but expenditure on promotion of tourism or scholarships for British students is largely 'preaching to the converted'. A more ambitious project to set up an Indian Centre in London, 'to project the image of India in the world in all its aspects', does not seem to have come to fruition, despite financial backing from the Indian government.[57]

British interest in Britain's image of India was virtually non-existent through-out the 1960s; in fact, serious investigations of earlier British attitudes to India were done elsewhere, principally in the USA.[58] A revealing recent scholarly American investigation is Greenberger's survey of British attitudes to India, as demonstrated in British fiction set in India between 1880 and 1960.[59] Green-berger identifies three successive British views of India and of their role in India, which he labels as The Era of Confidence (1880–1910), The Era of Doubt (1910–35), and The Era of Melancholy (1935–60). The brief review of the press attempted above would seem to justify labelling the post-1960 period as 'The Era of Oblivion', although a cursory examination of books on Indian topics pub-lished in Britain in the 1960s, with the heavy emphasis on the history and develop-ment of the Raj, might produce an alternative title, 'The Era of Nostalgia'—cul-minating in the much-criticized and mass-marketed Indian sections of BBC-TV's 'The British Empire' series in 1971–2.

Educated (and televised-at) to be potentially better informed about world events than ever before, the average Briton does not seem very responsive to the outside world, save when (as often) it caters to his appetite for disasters. This taste was present in the British attitude to India a century ago,[60] but increas-ing parochialism is also revealed in surveys by *The Times* of the opinions of Britain's more influential people as listed in *Who's Who* (table 12·10).[61]

If the British pay so little attention to India's image, why should Indian officials react to its besmirching so much more violently than to real and sub-stantial issues, such as UK policy on Indian textile exports, the EEC regulations, or even immigration? The Indian concern for the half-informed views of distant British commentators surely reflects a misjudgement of priorities. The Indian diplomatic energy (and the British diplomatic goodwill) used up in such com-plaints is no longer available for much more serious economic and political issues. However, if the Indians' inferiority complex is misplaced, the media in Britain have made things worse by an equally misplaced superiority complex.

Their constant Cassandra-like prognoses for India, never proven, never retracted, are bad enough; but worse is the scant attention paid to one-sixth of the people of the world—a neglect interrupted by lightning visits and instant, often inane comment. A decade or more of such treatment has naturally produced an Indian inferiority complex, but one hardening into contempt. We hope that Indians will come to feel that it is what British politicians do, not what British media say, that counts most for them.

What of the Indian view of Britain? We cannot accuse the Indians of lack of interest. British policies, both domestic and foreign, have been well covered by the Indian press, perhaps because (as with immigration or cotton textiles) Indians have been more affected by British decisions, and hence more moved to hold opinions about Britain, than vice versa. Assessment is eased by regular surveys, carried out by the IIPO, into India's images of other major countries.[62] In two of the more recent surveys, sampling literate adults in the four major metropolitan areas of India (Bombay, Calcutta, Delhi, and Madras), a mixed view of Britain emerged (table 12.11). The legacy of the Raj is fast becoming a memory; the most pervasive influence on India was judged to be the USA, with the UK in second place. The British influence was on balance considered beneficial.

The IIPO surveys over the 1960s suggest that the popularity of Britain altered quite dramatically. Before the 1965 Indo-Pakistan war 63 per cent of respondents rated Britain favourably, but already by February 1965 this had fallen to 25 per cent, and the same proportion awarded a negative ranking. By January 1966 some recovery had begun; favourable opinion held steady at 25 per cent, but negative votes fell to 11 per cent. By April 1968 the positive score was back to 36 per cent; by July 1969 the prewar situation had been restored, with 56 per cent favourable.[63] By mid-1970 there had been a slight relapse, to 45 per cent.[64]

These volatile reactions—probably due in part to sampling error—should be placed in context. The USA scored far higher favourable ratings throughout the 1960s, and the USSR also consistently outscored Britain. By 1969 the most popular country was the rising Asian power of Japan, with 85 per cent of respondents favourable.[65]

Although in August 1970 over half of those interviewed felt that India and Britain had common interests, the poor state of the British image is shown by Indian responses when asked to identify the country that could look back over the 1960s with satisfaction for what it had achieved (table 12.11). The USA clearly dominated the responses, with Japan second and—a degree of self-satisfaction—India third. Britain, however, is included among 'Others', who between them polled only 5 per cent.

1969 was not a happy year for Indo-British relations, but the low opinion corresponded to Indian reporting of Britain in the late 1960s. The Indian press, in its preoccupation with echo reporting noted earlier, at times in 1965–71 resorted to studied insults, which had they appeared in British reporting on India would have led to diplomatic protests. A senior Indian journalist 'in a reputable paper [explained] partisan British reporting by "their unchangeable,

incorrigible, and utterly shameful colonial soul'''.[66] Such Indian opinions, and
indeed the opinion-poll findings noted above, usually pass unnoticed in the UK.
Is it felt that it doesn't really matter what the Indians and other foreigners
think about us, as long as our image with the Europeans and North Americans
(and now the Arabs) remains unblemished? British businessmen, in search of
licences to import or invest in India, might not agree.

What of the image of Britain held by those Indians who come into contact
with her in the context of the more important relationships such as trade, private
investment, and defence—senior Indian politicians, administrators, and businessmen? Until about 1960 the special link with Britain remained strong, reflecting
the underlying economic connection (pp. 23–5), partly because Indian leaders,
especially Nehru, had personal links with Britons sympathetic to India. This
was typified by the special friendship that existed between the *New Statesman*
and the Indian Congress. This link, extending after independence, created expectations in India that were not fulfilled by the British press as a whole, and many
influential Indians came to realize that the *New Statesman* was not typical of
British views and attitudes and was thus very much a minority voice, especially
with Conservative governments. Therefore, although Nehru and his contem-
poraries and officials had been well acquainted with this journal, and through
it with leading British socialists (with whom they felt affinity), many of the newer
leaders of the Indian government and Congress, especially where these had come
to power via state Congress Parties in areas where British influence had never
been very high, have never seen it, or at least never read it regularly. To such as
these, the views of *The Times* or the *Guardian* or *Daily Telegraph* come to represent Britain, and to form the basis of their images. *The Times* itself recognized
the demise of the influence of the *New Statesman* when it observed that it
'stands in this context as the symbol of the whole Indian current of political
thinking which until recently was the dominant influence. Already it is foreign
to the mainstream of Indian political thought and it is on the way to being
alien'.[67]

In summary, the 1960s have seen an inevitable conflict of images and attitudes.
The Indian inferiority complex towards their former rulers is matched in the
British press by something of a superiority complex. There would seem little
hope of 'normalizing' relations between the two countries unless each learns to
view the other as an equal. In this the media have an important role to play.
'Behaviour depends on the image . . . The meaning of a message is the change
which it produces in the image.'[68]

13 INDO-BRITISH RELATIONS IN A DIVIDED WORLD, 1960–80

The post-colonial weakening of Indo-British relations did not really get under way until the later 1950s, with a decline in the share of British trade that involved India. By the late 1960s the decline had accelerated, had affected the balance among India's activities as well as Britain's, and encompassed aid, education, and military and diplomatic relations as well as trade. The patterns of decline, and of the tentative recovery of the 1970s, are summarized on pp. 209–10 below.

Was the disengagement in the interests of either or both countries or of their elites?[1] (pp. 210–17.) India could have avoided 'dependence' without so great a reduction in the importance of her links with Britain. Nor did that reduction, in itself, imply Indian rejection of 'partnership' with rich countries. In fact some aspects of the decline damaged India—the loss of aid, of cheap imports, of export markets. Others—the chance to diversify trade and to become more self-reliant in military and other matters—benefited India. On balance, the damage to India outweighed the benefit. As for Britain, the few substantial commercial gainers from Indo-British disengagement spoke louder than the many small losers; but the losses almost certainly outweighed the gains. Moreover, commercial and bureaucratic resistance to expanded economic relations, in Britain and in India, reinforced one another.

Finally, in comparing costs and benefits of Indo-British disengagement, we must consider side-effects also. In Britain, these were political: because of her reduced power and resources and of her impending entry into the EEC, Britain had to choose a few from among her Commonwealth links for special emphasis; that choice, to the extent that it was made consciously, was distorted and delayed. In India, the side-effects were largely economic: her exports to Britain are labour-intensive and her imports from Britain capital-intensive, so the trade decline meant losing mainly jobs and wage incomes, and gaining profit incomes from the domestic production of items using a good deal of heavy equipment. Hence the distribution of income suffered in India, and of political energy in Britain.

It makes little sense to compare the costs and benefits of a sunset. Was the Indo-British disengagement inevitable? While it was the last act in a long, slow process of decolonization, it might surely have been more selective. We briefly examine, as an example of the blanket rejection of 'historical relics', the recent role of India's civil service, and argue that India's strength among poor countries (and Britain's weakness among ex-colonizers) render fears of neo-colonialism misplaced. Neither the past nor reaction against it *compelled* disengagement on the scale of the 1960s (pp. 218–19); nor did the newly-perceived roles assigned their countries by British and Indian elites. India's 'in principle'

principle—the refusal to have done for the country what it might in principle do for itself—need not have 'selected against' Britain as much as it did. Britain's new Europeanism would have gained, not lost, from more attention to the Indian connection (pp. 223–4, 228–9).

Hence, to the extent that the Indo-British disengagement of the 1960s went too far, neither historical nor geographical *compulsions* can be blamed. What of economic *causes* (pp. 223–6). They certainly pushed domestic pressure groups in Britain and India—though not the national interests—towards disengagement. They also created the shortages and strains in which a bogus tough-mindedness can plausibly interpret foreign 'special relationships' indiscriminately as costly liabilities. Above all, countries growing slowly, or suffering adverse balances of payments, tend to reduce their overseas activities and consequently their importance to other countries declines. Where both parties to a relationship are in that condition (as were Britain and India in the 1960s) there is a double squeeze on that relationship. Each country will tend to be replaced, in its relationships with the other, by third countries. Given the reduced 'economic mass' (relative to other countries) of both Britain and India, special efforts would have been required to prevent their mutual 'gravitational attraction'—their relationship—from weakening. These were not forthcoming. However, in 1975–85, the growth performances and foreign balances of both Britain and India seem likely to be better, *relative to other comparable countries*, than in the 1960s. Given political impetus, the means to restore the 'gravitational pull' would then be less scarce than in the past.

This suggests—as does much of the argument of the book—that bilateral relations between geographically distant middle powers—in the absence of obvious territorial or other political disputes—depend substantially on what each has to contribute to the other's general economic progress. That view is open to two objections, of which the Indo-British case is a suitable test. The first objection is that a believer in 'the primacy of politics' in poor countries would assert that the main motivation of their elites is not economic development but the retention of power. The sort of links with Britain, by which the Indian elite might improve its chances of retaining power, are obscure and dubiously acceptable, in Britain or in India. However, Indian experience suggests that an extreme 'primacy of politics' view is unduly cynical; and that, even to retain office, elites in democratic countries have to deliver some economic goods to electorates. Britain can certainly help to relieve the constraints preventing this—especially if British and Indian governments surmount their 'crises of ambition', recognize the need for non-superpowers to select a few from among the many bilateral links they might emphasize, and succeed in improving domestic economic performance. In the 1960s, certainly, economic factors were causes rather than effects of changing Indo-British relations (pp. 223–6).

The second objection is that bilateral alignments last for several years and resist pressures to change in face of economic opportunities. In particular, regional realignments might irreversibly foreclose the options of India and

Britain to strengthen the economic bases of their relationship (pp. 230–3). Certainly the international priorities of the 1970s, with Britain in the EEC and India closer to the USSR and less nervous about Pakistan, differ from those of the 1960s. However, both Britain and India need to diversify their foreign policy 'portfolio', Britain (and the EEC) from exclusive emphasis on relations with other rich states, India from a similarly one-sided Russian alliance. It would not be plausible to argue that a revived Indo-British relationship should, or could, seek to divide India from the USSR, or Britain from EEC. Rather, such a renewal should concentrate in the first place on providing trade alternatives. To give real content to the 1973 Indo-EEC framework is of special importance and could, while avoiding paternalism, benefit both participants.

We believe, then, that the half-conscious erosion of the Indo-British link in the 1960s did more harm than good to both peoples; and that a reconstruction, already under way in economic matters, could be accelerated, to the advantage of both countries, though not of all parties within them. On pp. 1–14 we have examined the relevance of this story for relations between rich and poor countries as a whole. The similarity of Indian and British political procedures (though not cultures) and the complementarity of their economies should have cemented strong bonds between them.

What, then, does the erosion of even this relationship suggest for rich-poor relations: that less favourable cases will fare worse still, that ex-colonizers are likely to have a particularly hard time (p. 1), or even that they more easily preserve some sort of active relationship with balkanized neo colonies than with genuinely independent 'equal partners'?

1. The shape of decline

The trade figures show the sharp acceleration, in the 1960s, of a prolonged though gentle weakening of the Indo-British bond—a weakening starting long before independence. Britain sold 9·1 per cent of her exports to British India in 1879, and 7·1 per cent in 1938; the proportion in 1956 was still 6·1 per cent, and in 1961 5·1 per cent. By 1969 it had fallen to 1·6 per cent. In 1879 British India supplied 11·2 per cent of British imports; in 1938 it was 5·4 per cent and for the corresponding areas in 1956 4·2 per cent, in 1961 3·8 per cent—and in 1969 only 1·7 per cent (table 2·3).

From India's standpoint, too, the basic trading relationship dramatically weakened. In 1960–1 Britain supplied 19·3 per cent of Indian imports; in 1970–1 only 7·8 per cent (table 3·6). Britain was overtaken as an exporter to India, first by the USA, then by the USSR. Even in current prices, British sales to India fell by more than half between 1960 and 1970 (table 3.2).

The other relationships followed the trading trends, usually with some delay and with less severity. In the 1960s, while Britain's invisible transactions roughly doubled on both credit and debit sides (and India's grew, though slowly), Indo-British exchanges showed no uptrend (tables 5.2, 5.7, 5.8). As late as 1959–61 as much as 6·1 per cent of British private foreign investment went to India (about the same as the share of British overseas assets there already); by 1969–71 the proportion had fallen to 1·6 per cent (table 6.6). In the 1950s the sterling balances financed over half India's import surpluses; in the late 1960s the roughly corresponding figure, Britain's contribution to India's aid receipts, was about 6·6 per cent (table 7.15). From 1947 to 1955 the number of Britons in *non-Indian* firms in India fell only from 6,901 to 6,462; by 1966 there were fewer than 3,000 in *all* firms in India (table 10.3; ch. 10, n. 24). In education, India supplied 11·7 per cent of foreign students at British universities in 1947–8, 12·2 per cent in 1960—but only 4·7 per cent by 1970–1 (table 9.3). Britain's immigration laws, India's defence supplies, mutual press representation—all have followed a similar pattern: a fairly high maintained level of Indo-British contact until the late 1950s or early 1960s, a rapid decline for a decade or so, and some signs of recovery in the last few years. British involvement in India, like British exports to India, usually declined sooner and further than the reverse flow.

2. Disengagement in whose interests?

The weakening of the Indo-British links owed much to inattention by decision-makers in both countries (pp. 15–16). However correct as a *reason*, this begs the question as an *explanation*. The decision-makers, and (especially in Britain) the commentators and thinkers who influenced them, were inattentive to the relationship because, in ranking the competing claims on their attention, they accorded it a low priority: because they sensed that the relationship must, or should, weaken. Why? Were they right?

In part, the changing priorities reflected global developments—Britain's decline as a colonial power, India's new links with the USSR, the emergence of China and the EEC. In part, they reflected *changes* in British and Indian interests during the 1960s. But the main cause of the Indo-British drift apart was Indian independence itself. Both our data and the known political facts show a fairly stable relationship between independence in 1947 and the late 1950s; yet clearly independence, once its consequences were grasped, implied new priorities. Hence the question, 'Could and should the decline of the 1960s have been prevented?', largely boils down to another: 'Was it in India's or Britain's interests that their elites (after a ten to fifteen-year lag) responded to Indian independence by permitting, even encouraging, a drift apart—whether towards regionalism or towards autarchy?' Since the enlargement of options resulting from independence, and also the previous constraints on action, were clearly greater for the *Indian* policy-makers, it is their actions that we must mainly examine.

If India was to develop, was it necessary for her connections with the capitalist world, particularly with Britain, to be so severely attenuated? A growing number of marxists, neo-marxists, and 'structuralists' argues that—especially in poor countries—domestic and foreign policies are liable to be determined by the support that domestic ruling groups receive from wealthy foreign concerns. Whether Indian development required an erosion of the British connection in the 1960s, then, may depend on a prior question: do close relations between a rich country and a poor country in general promote dependence or partnership?

It may help to state two polarized points of view. At one extreme, some see 'dependence' on rich countries by a poor country as: (a) resulting inevitably from its acceptance of trade, capital, and other economic and political relationships with them; (b) enriching 'compradors'[2] in the poor country, but (c) retarding its modernization and mass advancement, by fixing it in the production structure of 'hewer of wood and drawer of water'[3] for rich 'dominant' countries. At the other extreme, some see trade and capital-flow 'partnership' between a poor country and the rich world as: (a) carrying limited risks of international exploitation, because the countries and cultures are remote, distinct, independent, and aware of the dangers; (b) a damaging and needed *challenge* to (largely feudal) ruling groups in the poor country; (c) helpful to its growth, modernization, equality (since workers' incomes and employment are increased through specialization in, and export of, labour-intensive goods), and developmental capacity (by aid or private capital for investment).

For the 'partnership' school, underdevelopment is a *state*, with largely domestic causes. Post-colonial contacts with outsiders (including capitalists) can be part of a *cure* for that state, if carefully selected by an independent developing country. The 'dependence' theorist denies that such independence is possible once there is major contact with powerful foreign interests, especially those of a rich capitalist country. He denies, too, that the elite of a poor country will act in the interests of the people rather than of foreign paymasters.[1] Certainly the massive and archetypal decolonization of India by Britain from 1857 to 1970—of the largest colony by the most extensive colonizer—must be incorporated in any successful general theory of rich-poor relations: 'partnership' or 'dependence' or anything else.

At first glance, the Indian evidence lends support to the 'partnership' view.[5] A big, poor, diverse country proved too expensive to colonize, or even to neo-colonize. After independence, India was too complex and powerful to be at risk of 'domination' by any one developed country; she diversified her trade relations, and obtained virtual independence in defence production (pp. 178–9) and investment finance (pp. 84–5). The latter avoidance of 'dependence', indeed, has been ashes in the mouth; India's capacity to pay for the Fifth Plan, and thus to become self-reliant, is seriously threatened by the 'aid famine'.[6] Paradoxically, lack of aid from the rich countries poses a greater threat to India's self-reliance than aid ever did.

At a deeper level, however, the Indo-British relationship invalidates the whole partnership-dependence, neo-liberal-neo-marxist debate. Obviously Mr Nehru and Mrs Gandhi (and their advisers) cannot be described either as dependent compradors or as social-democratized but basically Manchester-style-liberal 'partners'.

Obviously, too, India has picked different sorts of relationships in different fields, here autarchic, there liberal, somewhere else (for example, where a new technology must be acquired through a joint venture) avowedly if temporarily 'dependent'. Both 'partnership' and 'dependence' theorists could easily modify their accounts to fit these facts. However, the real trouble with their ideological debate (a trouble which eats at the root of contemporary international theory) as revealed by the Indo-British relationship is that the characteristics of the *participants* must form the basis of any theory about their *relationships*.

Indeed the Indo-British link makes both 'partnership' and 'dependence' theories look at once unhistorical and ungeographical. How can either theory come to terms with Indo-British history since the opening of the senior ICS to Indian nationals in 1864, through independence in 1947 when barely half the senior ICS was British, to 1963, when there was only one Briton left (p. 155)? This was neither a 'comprador' administration, nor conscious and voluntary partnership in decolonization (ask the Indian National Congress!), but a colonial link that simply became too costly for *both* parties.

Nor can any general theory of partnership or dependence deal with India's proximity to two nuclear powers, compelling close links with one as insurance against the other, and thus inducing links with other powerful countries or groups (such as EEC) likely to diversify, and hence to reduce, Indian 'dependence'. Timeless, placeless, and social-classless theories of relations between 'the' poor and 'the' rich country are bound to fail. The Indo-British link only makes this obvious. Dependence theory can *seem* plausible in Latin America; the initial colonial metropolis, Lisbon or Madrid, is almost irrelevant, and the new and potentially dominant metropolis in the US has no clear rival; but even the governments and firms of Peru and Brazil are not puppets without volition. In India London is still important in many fields, but competes for influence against other countries near and far, socialist and capitalist—and also against major private and public sectors in India.

Rich-poor relations are in fact based on what policy-makers in specific countries want, can do, and are pressed to do by their domestic 'constituencies'. It is just as unfruitful to argue that such relations are *in general* exploitative, and that the weakening of the Indo-British bond in the 1960s was therefore desirable because it reduced India's 'dependence',[7] as to argue *in general* that India and Britain had to be 'partners in development' whose strong links around, say, 1955 helped India to develop. These links owed far too much to colonial history for it to be credible that India would not gain by diversifying them. Nevertheless, the evidence of the previous chapters suggests that, for India as well as for Britain, the erosion of several *aspects* of the relationship went too far in the 1960s; that this could and should have been prevented; that the new regional alignments have diverted energies from the reconstruction of the relationship; but that, as recent events show, its erosion had gone so irrationally far that a natural reaction towards reconstruction has begun and can be consciously extended by policy.

What did India lose from erosion? Most obviously, the real value of her aid from Britain fell by over one-fifth between 1964 and 1970.[8] Such aid was on relatively easy terms (pp. 109–10) and was relatively 'untied', but its contraction had much to do with the fall of over 60 per cent in the real annual value of British goods entering India over the decade (tables 3.2, 3.8). Indian objections to *British* aid, at least, are usually expressed—even on the left—in what would count in Latin America as right-wing terms, advocating self-reliance rather than claiming that more aid means more neo-colonialism. The replacement of Britain by aid-donors who exacted harder terms represented a clear loss to India, even on 'self-reliance' criteria. The expansion since 1971 of British aid to India—though not on quite as easy terms as before—represents a major sign that the relationship is recovering.

A further clear Indian loss was the fall, by over 40 per cent, in the cash value of her exports to Britain over the decade (tables 4.2, 4.5), substantially reducing India's access to convertible currency. Conversely Britain lost most of her sales to India in the 1960s (table 3.1).

Looking at the 'bundle' of trade foregone by both parties, one can make out some sort of a case for the disengagement from India's viewpoint, along the lines of freeing her from 'dependence'. Some of the commodities sold by India to Britain, notably perhaps tea, were good commodities to reduce reliance upon—sluggish in demand, fluctuating in price, and sold in markets dominated by foreign buyers. By curtailing purchases of some commodities in Britain in the 1960s, and making them domestically instead, India has set up some 'infant industries' that may become sturdy adults. But the case is not a strong one. The contraction of trade with Britain—and of the availability of sterling—formed part of the cause of India's increasingly severe trade restrictions. These restrictions damaged agriculture, discouraged exports, and redistributed income towards the rich.[9]

The capacity to trade substantially with Britain, mainly by selling labour-intensive products; the capacity to rely on sterling balances or aid to supplement exports in paying for developing imports—these presumably confer potential benefits on the masses as well as on the elite; they can hardly have reduced 'socialist–capitalist' options in a country with as wide a range of suppliers, domestic and foreign, public and private, as India. If a poor country denies the benefits of its trade and aid relationships to its masses—not that we assert this in India's case—then the blame attaches to the poor country's decision-makers, not to the trade and aid! Only in some non-economic fields, notably educational and military, did growing Indian self-reliance (and diversification of foreign sources) probably require the weakening of British links.

The relative unimportance of private foreign capital, in particular, has reduced the risks to India from 'dependence'. Britain owned most of this in 1947, and still does today, though the dominance is smaller (pp. 84–5); but even in 1947 Indian firms or individuals owned 95 per cent of national capital (p. 80). There was neither scope nor (given the cost) much incentive for Britons or other foreigners to 'dominate' India through her asset structure. Foreign capital in India is really more closely comparable to the occasional western factory in

Eastern Europe than to western companies in Brazil, let alone Liberia or Gabon.

Thus the risks of foreign, and even more of British, 'dominance' in Indian economic development are small; in most fields the gains from trade and aid contacts for India are large; and the Indian elite, possessed of a strong and unsuborned will of its own, and subject to considerable (if conflicting and manipulable) popular pressures, is able to choose. Therefore, the commonsense conclusion that the declines in aid, export prospects, import choices, etc., as the British relationship weakened were losses to India, holds. This does not contradict the fact that the Indian development process *entailed* some damage to British links via import substitution, both literal (textile machinery) and metaphorical (military self-reliance).

Both because Indian independence was the main new factor and because of our earlier quantitative discussions, we consider more briefly the possibility that Indo-British relations declined because such a decline was perceived by the *British* elite as being in their own or in the British national interest. On the whole, the decline was not perceived in Britain at all. One can argue at length about whether the run-down of Britain's Third World connections in the 1960s was imposed by the balance of payments and/or the European priority, or—as we would suggest—was harmful to both. But the decline of India *within* Britain's Third World priorities (tables 3.1, 4.1, 6.6) is surely not defensible as meeting any British interest. The notion that decision-takers in London coolly appraised (for example) relations with Mauritius as more important than with India is obviously absurd. Even on the crudest level, the repatriated profits of British sugar companies from Mauritius are puny compared with those of British firms in India. More basically, the relative importance to Britain of her trading and political links with Mauritius and India is not far out of proportion to their relative populations. Yet the British negotiators with EEC in 1971 fought harder and more successfully for trade concessions to Mauritius than even for serious trade *discussions* with India, and for Mauritian sugar than for Indian cotton textiles. Such priorities clearly do not represent the British interest.

Nor do they reflect the outcome of a conflict in Britain between the interests of the governing and the governed. Neither gain from diverting British resources to producing things supplied more cheaply by India. The main explanation of why Britain's trade and other links with India, and in general with South Asia, have suffered as compared with African links lies largely in the very different impact, on articulate worker and employer groups in Britain, of South Asian and African trade structures.

Most of the non-Asian Third World sells Britain mainly raw materials and non-temperate, unprocessed foods and beverages. To ensure that these enter cheaply and without restriction not only helps British consumers (like almost all freer trade), but presents no threat to any major group of British workers employers. From South Asia, however, Britain buys not only goods for which cheap and easy access keeps down the pressure for wage rises (e.g. tea) or upon input costs (e.g. raw jute), but also more controversial goods, notably cotton textiles. Even here, it is in Britain's interests to admit such goods freely and redeploy her labour and capital to more efficient uses; the total level of employment in Britain is determined largely by the government's decisions on the management of aggregate demand, so that fewer jobs for people making goods inefficiently have to be set against more jobs, in more efficient activities, elsewhere. But it is difficult to put over such a case when unemployment is rising, and it is not surprising that the period 1957–72 in Britain saw both such an uptrend and growing restrictionism against imported cotton textiles (pp. 54–8). The well-organized interests of a few producers usually count for more than the total interests of consumers. That is especially so because the consumer interest in cheaper cloth consists of a small weekly improvement in the family's budget, while firms and workers making cotton textiles stand to lose everything. This underlines the importance of a serious policy of adjustment assistance to damaged firms, workers, and regions in making acceptable, to the minority, the freer trade with poor countries that clearly benefits the majority.

A further aspect of trade structure which helps to explain why British import restrictionism impinged more on South Asia than on other poor areas is that in many such areas—especially in South-East Asia, the Caribbean, and 'anglophone' Africa—British-based firms devote a larger part of their output to exports to Britain than do such firms in South Asia. Hence they are concerned to mobilize in Whitehall pressures against protective measures. (The success of Booker Brothers in spearheading the campaign for favourable terms for Commonwealth sugar in the EEC is an illustration). Precisely because the South Asian markets, though very poor, are relatively to African markets big and industrially sophisticated, British private investment there caters largely for the home market. This is reinforced by the highly protectionist nature of *Indian* import policies, which induces firms like ICI (India) and Hindustan Lever to use their Indian capacity to leap India's own market barriers; such emphasis on intra-Indian sales is bound to reduce the interest of ICI (London), and Lever Brothers is pressing for mutual Indo-British tariff reductions. By contrast, in small countries of Africa and Latin America, big foreign-owned plants are almost forced to be export-oriented, so that their parent company will press for import derestriction to benefit such exports in its country of origin.

Just as India's (and indeed Asia's) higher level of industrialization[10] induces in Britain stronger sectional pressures against 'cheap-labour' exports than are felt in Africa, so it leads to increasing pressure, in India, against imports *from* Britain. Indian manufacturers in the growth sectors are well placed to insist on protection, often informally via foreign-exchange policy. Up to 7 per cent of the fall in Britain's share of Indian imports can be accounted for by a trade structure especially prone to such factors (p. 33). India supports 'industrialization' by numerous devices of foreign-exchange management. As such a policy takes hold, it is bound to create new pressures for selective protection and to strengthen old ones. The likeliest victim is the most obvious presence; the biggest market

share; the supplier relying on what was once a captive market; the exporter of
of products replaceable, in early industrialization, by domestic output of, say,
wool tops or textile machinery. British sales to India in the 1960s—partly because
of India's growing shortage of sterling (pp. 116–17)—suffered. If competitive,
they faced increasing protection, in the interests of Indian producers whose
efficiency was in most cases at best potential. If uncompetitive, British goods
were increasingly replaced by rival suppliers.

The parallel to Indian sales to Britain is striking. Slow growers and fast
inflaters tend to lose shares in each other's markets. If they are being replaced by
lower-cost suppliers, all parties may benefit. But it is another matter if they are
being replaced by high-cost domestic suppliers who are good at lobbying, or by
third-country suppliers (whether Portugal in the case of British textiles, or the
USSR over a wide range of Indian imports) as part of trade treaties that have
little to do with efficiency. Both Indian exports to Britain and British exports
to India were in the 1960s especially vulnerable to these sorts of disruption. In
this sense the dramatic and trade-centred weakening of the relationship was
preventable and undesirable.

Both Britain and India can normally expect to raise *total* output by moving
from autarchy to specialization and efficiency. But what of income distribution?
In India, where there is large-scale unemployment, such extra trade is likely to
benefit very poor people by employing them, because it is goods with a high
labour content whose sales to Britain are easiest for India to expand. In Britain,
where the volume of employment (again the main determinant of income distribution) depends mainly on the management of *aggregate* demand, the level
of trade with India is not likely to affect income distribution much. Thus the
level of consumption in both countries, and its distribution in India, should
improve as a result of freer Indo-British trade. The incapacity of both countries
to compensate the few who lose from freer trade—and their increasing commitment to trade-based regional alliances—stood in the way in the 1960s.

It is not an abuse of metaphor to extend the notion of specialization—and of
the losses to Britain and India from its bilateral abandonment—from trade to
other fields. Movements of capital and labour clearly seek to achieve the results
of trade by other means. In education, communications, and other topics of this
book, the great differences between Britain and India clearly increase the benefits
to both from exchanges between them, though these benefits cannot be quanti-
fied, as 'gains from trade' perhaps can be.

These potential benefits are increased by the recent realignments of both
countries. Especially with India close to Soviet views on world policy, and
Britain to a slowly emerging EEC foreign economic policy, the complementarities of Britain and India—complementarities that are mutually comprehensible
owing to a partially shared history, language, and culture—count for much. The
EEC lacks an economic policy towards Asia, and its vision of the Third World—
and vice versa—is coloured by the relations between France and the African
associates. India needs freedom of action and options in her relationship with

the USSR—alternative sources of trade and capital, and of diplomatic entente, especially to the extent that the US link is largely discredited in Delhi. In this sense India and Britain currently have more to offer one another than in the early 1960s. In so far as new alliances can build upon old ones, the weakening of Indo-British links was preventable and should have been prevented, and is reversible and should be (and to some extent is being) reversed.

3. Decolonization

But is all this too hopeful about the range of human choice? Could disengagement have been implicit in decolonization? Much of the non-formal colonial apparatus had been dismantled long before independence. Until then, some of the most unpleasant realities remained—Britain's capacity to destroy India's hard-won interwar surplus on the balance of payments by imposing arbitrary 'Home Charges' (pp. 22–3), serious restraints on Indian political activity, above all Britain's decision to take India into two world wars without consultation. But many of the underlying relationships had begun to decline long before independence, and the pace did not accelerate for ten or more years afterwards. However, while it would be mistaken to interpret the *fact* of the decline in the 1960s as overdue decolonization, the *pattern* depended partly on which colonial relationships had been retained longest, because they were most vital to British control; and on which relationships it suited powerful Indian groups to retain, or which for other reasons seemed able to generate their own protective inertia.

Nowhere has the latter been more important than in the celebrated 'steel frame': the ICS (after independence the IAS). Half-Indian at independence—contrast the Congo or even Zambia! —and wholly Indian by the mid-1960s, the IAS is often alleged to have remained British in its procedures. Indeed, its critics claim, it showed all the inertia to be expected of a steel frame, or rather of the bone frame of a white elephant. Its more serious critics concede the beast certain bourgeois virtues: reverence for hard work, plodding integrity, neutrality on matters of conventional party politics. But inertia-ridden civil services are also alleged to resemble white elephants in their preference for moving slowly, in a constant direction—and in files.

But when one looks at almost any non-totalitarian poor country, how beyond price do those staid administrative virtues appear! They are not prevalent in most Third World countries that were once British colonies. Especially in Africa, the transfer of power was prepared too little, too late, and too fast. Other European ex-colonists—Belgium, France, Holland, probably now Portugal—left themselves no time at all to prepare: they resisted the 'wind of change' to the last moment, then caved in suddenly. Even in British India, the indigenous civil servant was educated in the administrative virtues for largely the wrong reasons: to reduce cost without carefully assessing benefit; to make the trains run on time rather than to select the right places for new railways; to replicate in India systems of government, and of education, formerly suitable in Britain.

And, while honesty, etc., survived pretty well at the upper levels in India and Ceylon, they did less well in parts of the subcontinent under even severer strains: from high-level political corruption in Pakistan before 1958, from politico-administrative chaos in Burma, or (one fears) from the massive reductions in civil service salaries, and a consequent exodus of the most capable, in Bangladesh since 1972. In India, however, the 'survivals' in the IAS tradition have surely made a big contribution.

In both Britain and India, the civil service is a convenient scapegoat for politicians wishing to claim radicalism without doing many radical things.[11] In both countries, however, outsiders acceptable to the government can be brought in—indeed India has ad hoc bodies, notably the Planning Commission, that institutionalize the process—and drastic changes of direction can be enforced by tough ministers. Both civil services, contrary to the critics' views, have been better at expanding than at economizing, and have been superb at implementing major, and allegedly distasteful, expansions of the public sector (by Mr Attlee and Mrs Gandhi).

Is it fair to allege that Britain—as a status quo power, slowly evolutionary at home and in India not concerned mainly with development[12]—has left behind an IAS system geared to 'keeping things going' but stubbornly resistance to change? Consider two examples of IAS response: to the switches of rural policy in Delhi around the 'community development' theme; and, even more impressive in men few of whom serve in their home state, to the diverse permutations on the formula of 'democratic decentralization' tried out by the different Indian states. Surely that alleged 'white elephant', the IAS, has been notably more flexible than its mahout?

But suppose this is all wrong. Suppose we accept that the IAS is the last refuge of the English gentleman, and (contrary to appearances in Delhi) that this connotes not social graces but disgraceful anti-socialism. Well, if the white elephant is impeding progress, it is not sacred in India; it can be slaughtered. Certainly it gets less and less plausible as time passes to classify the IAS as a Trojan Horse, left by a remote colonial power.

All this is central to our theme. First, it shows how little the post-colonial impact of Britain on India was predictable from, let alone determined by, decolonization. Second, it matters to Indo-British relations if the top Indian bureaucrats read London newspapers, listen to the BBC, and send their sons—their successors?—to Oxford and Cambridge. If all this meant an attempt to impose British patterns, or even worse British political preferences and economic interests, upon India, the consequences for Indo-British relations would be very bad. Yet one has the impression that Indian bureaucrats and politicians recognize the risk and select what *they* want of Britain.[13] The growing relative importance of other influences, cultural and intellectual as well as economic and political, has also been documented in this book. But certainly one feels that the usefulness to Britain of a quite above-board 'influence' in India is often underrated. The perhaps excessive caution with which English-language training has been treated (pp. 147–9) is an illustration. Would it not pay HMG to subsidize British art, theatre, etc. in India even more?

It is exactly because the decolonization of the Indian economy is so complete —and was started so long ago—that the above suggestions are tolerable. Soviet 'influence' in Finland, US 'influence' in Mexico—to propose publicly steps to increase these would not be popular in Finland or Mexico. Genuine influence as opposed to disguised power, among equals and without arm-twisting, is a different matter. Is Britain perhaps made unduly passive in India by guilt about her past colonial role, or about her present conduct to small countries whose arms *can* be twisted?

Anyone in doubt about the prolonged, steady nature of colonial disengagement need only look at figs. 1 and 2 of Chapter 2. The decline in the role of Indo-British trade, from the peaks of the late 1870s and 1880s to the accelerated fall of the 1960s, was steady for India, and interrupted for Britain only by the severe cyclical trade fluctuations of 1919–39.[14] The decline in the role (though not the quantum) of British private foreign investment is documented on pp. 85–6.

Political and economic omens of independence clearly arrived together, and very early. By 1947 India had a big indigenous capitalist class, indigenous trade unions, an indigenous bureaucratic and political elite, many of them committed neither to 'capitalism' nor to Britain—and a diversified structure of trade and investment. The subsequent pattern of neutralism, US aid, and now the Soviet alliance cannot be understood if one persists in seeing colonial or neo-colonial influences, or in general non-Indian agency, behind every tree. India is independent: the blame or credit for her fate is her own. That very fact, together with Britain's independence, rules out at least the extreme interpretations of post-colonial disengagement as an unavoidable continuation of decolonization. And with the moderate interpretation—that *some* of the things 'disengaged' by India in the 1960s were colonial relics—we can warmly agree, while pointing to the IAS as a wholly transformed and Indianised relic, and hence an object-lesson in the dangers of pushing history-based explanations too far.

4. National role and international change

How, then, are we to account for Indo-British disengagements that outran the benefits to either nation? In part, the role perceived by their policy-makers for both India and Britain has adversely affected the relations between them. For India the theme, persistently through neutralism and effective alignment with each superpower in turn, has been self-reliance. This has meant more than the word might suggest to a small, trade-based country like Britain: not 'balancing the books' in trade, but rather doing all one can oneself and minimizing imports;[15] more than steadily reducing aid inflows, but (at least in the 1970s) attempting to rely entirely on capital raised at home; and so on. In aid, in trade, even in education, India's stated policy—hard to interpret at times—has been, not 'let us do what we are good at', but rather 'leave to us all we are in principle able to do'—the 'in principle' principle.

Even Indian exports to Britain have been marked by this approach. Initially, export promotion was neglected in favour of rather high-cost import substitution (pp. 46–8). Later, the tendency of the export promotion councils to multiply, and of these councils and the State Trading Corporation of India to prefer new to traditional exports, ushered in a phase where large numbers of new export lines—all in principle producible, at a cost, in India—were pushed. This led to some neglect of more important lines, notably tea and cotton textiles; and to a considerable dispersion of scarce R. and D. marketing talent. There were some successes, notably in leather products, but the traditional staples of Indian exports to Britain languished, partly because of this flexing of non-traditional muscles. Indeed, but for the fortuitous opportunities offered India in the replacement of Rhodesian tobacco after sanctions were imposed in 1965, the export performance to Britain would have looked terrible. Even in exporting, attempts to do everything can reduce total performance.

The 'in principle' principle operated most rigorously upon Indian imports. Import licences are in general refused for products that *can be* made in India (p. 30). For example, to import any but the very tiniest item of engineering equipment, Indian purchasers must in effect show that there is no domestic supplier. If there is, however tentative or costly or delayed his offer, no import licence is issued (p. 31). Why should British exports suffer particularly from such procedures? British export structure, Indian import structure, British price uncompetitiveness, above all Indian foreign-exchange policies in the presence of untying of British aid relative to other donors: all played a part. However, perhaps the main point (though the hardest to quantify) is that Britain's colonial history must have made her sales to India the 'soft underbelly' of Indian imports: the obvious, big area for import substitution. In any case, India's emphasis on doing things at home—even at high cost—proved especially damaging to exports from Britain.

India's desire for self-sufficiency in defence supplies (p. 179) is understandable given the (also understandable) failure of foreign suppliers to keep spares flowing during the 1965 hostilities. But this has not been a major source of British export contraction, or a lasting one; we believe that a new Indian thrust to diversify arms purchases away from the USSR accounts for much of the recent recovery in British exports to India (pp. 178–80, n. 9, and table 11.4). The quest for self-reliance in India takes some forms less easy to understand than this one.

For example, India's aid receipts (net of capital and interest repayments) fell from Rs8,626mn in 1967–8 to an estimated Rs966mn in 1972–3.[16] Some of this is attributable to non-Indian action, but the regular advocacy of almost instant self-reliance by Indian leaders, even if intended for Indian ears alone, helps to promote such action. The senior bureaucracy still feels constrained to remind the planners publicly of the need for self-reliance when they try to solve the enormous financial problems of the Fourth Plan even by quite minor recourse to aid.[17] And Mr Nixon's package of March 1973, resuming at once the sale of 'non-lethal' arms (*sic*) to the subcontinent—which, given the pattern of sources and supplies, means to Pakistan—and aid to India, was rejected by India's politicians with a vehemence that seems strange given the USA's negligible remaining 'leverage' in India, India's continuing shortage of foreign exchange, and the small amount of aid. Such attitudes affected British aid too (if to a lesser extent). British project offers were sometimes rejected on the grounds that India could 'in principle' undertake the relevant production without aid. It is such *refusals* of aid, and not aid itself, that suggest a gap between elite and mass interests in India.

In technical assistance, private investment, management, education, and research, we have also seen this 'in principle' principle at work in Indo-British relations. The principle is made plausible by the size, diverse capacities, and (by Third World standards) highly 'developed' economic and educational structure of India. There is almost always some person, university, or firm able 'in principle' to deliver the goods, manage the firm's finances or train the engineers. Four points need making, however.

First, some of these operations will be carried out in India at high cost, or at less-than-optimal efficiency at a given cost; such policies cannot be defended by reference to the need for 'learning-by-doing' where they involve, say, the rejection of qualified trainers available under an aid programme. Second, the 'in principle' principle involves a fallacy of composition. When India rejects technical assistance schemes (or imports, or aid projects, or overseas training possibilities) because she could 'in principle' do *each one* herself, the fact that she could not at once do *all* herself is not taken into account. Third, those Indians in charge of public sector approvals of any activity that could be performed by foreigners surely recognize an obligation to encourage it *unless* they expect it to add less to Indian welfare than (by inhibiting new Indian activities or reducing the domestic return upon the existing ones) it deducts. In short, the 'in principle' principle—that Russians or British or Americans may not do a thing desirable for India because one day some Indian might like to—is unlikely to increase welfare in India. The glow of pride in national achievement that comes from applying the principle is genuine and honourable, but it is confined to a few well-off decision-takers; the consequent income losses are spread among many poor Indians.

The fourth point refers to 'self-reliance' in a world context. By comparison with other l.d.c.s, India combines extreme poverty with 'development'—administrative skill, industrial diversity, educational sophistication, and power.[18] Her decision-makers have little need to fear dependence, provided their foreign contacts are diversified. Autarkic procedures in India, such as the 'in principle' principle, could help to fragment the world economy. An increasing opening-up of India, apart from representing the strongest bargaining-counter in Indian efforts to secure opening-up *towards* her by developed countries (especially in trade), could help to pioneer a genuine 'partnership in development'. Of the entire Third World, perhaps only India and China have the strength, diversity, and self-confidence to initiate that. Both are 'developed' enough to be tempted by the siren of autarky; poor enough for the associated losses to matter; and strong and independent enough to render somewhat neurotic any fears that foreign devils might endanger their political virginity.

India's natural development path, of labour-intensive modernization, would have substantially increased contact with Britain (and probably China). This path was partly blocked by Indian interpretations of self-reliance, and partly— especially until the mid-1960s—by over-emphasis on heavy industrialization. Meanwhile, decision-makers in Britain too have been moved away from regarding India as a priority through a new conception of Britain's 'role', and specifically by a growing European pull. In this drift from Asia, too, there has been blanket overreaction to quite specific anachronisms. 'East of Suez' policies involving huge strain on Britain's precarious foreign balance—whether through direct military presence or through tax incentives to private investors overseas—were sensibly abandoned during the 1960s. But we doubt whether Britain was made more attractive to Europe by her surrenders to isolationist forces who, by successfully boarding the Little Europe bandwaggon, advanced their own interests: the protectionists of inefficient natural-fibre processing in Britain; some inward-looking elements in the BBC and the press (pp. 193–5); and those who made immigration policy progressively, or rather retrogressively, more and more colour-conscious.

All these matters are discussed in earlier chapters. We would reiterate only that Britain's appeal to many enlightened Europeans rests precisely in her 'open seas' policy towards the Third World—the elements of free (or freer) trade and contact and understanding rather than the colonial or neo-colonial elements— and in particular in her possession of a strong Asian link, especially to India. Yet when Britain entered the EEC her annual flows of aid and private investment to India had shrunk below West Germany's; and, except for a somewhat vapid commitment to negotiate treaties and protect interests, Britain secured nothing for the Asian Commonwealth in her Treaty of Accession to the EEC.

Nations, like actors, get set in roles they have played for a long time. Sectional interests, like an actor's gesturing hand, find they receive beneficial exercise from roles whose continued adoption may hypostatize the body politic. In Britain, firms and unions involved in making shoes and textiles—as the EEC quotas strengthen their protection—will become increasingly ardent opponents of a more rational Indo-British link. In India, too, powerful beneficiaries, private and bureaucratic, from otherwise rigid and costly barter arrangements with the USSR and Eastern Europe will oppose any diversification that might increase India's range of alternatives to such arrangements. Therefore, as time passes, it becomes increasingly difficult to correct the extreme postures of any particular role. The body tires of it eventually, however, and the total reaction when it comes is the more extreme and unreasonable. Hence the overreactions of Indo-British disengagement in the 1960s; hence, we suspect, the overreactions of mutual rediscovery in the 1990s or thereabouts, unless a relationship with much more real economic content is constructed soon.

Since this is in the general interest of the EEC as a whole as well as of Britain and India, a major effort to build the necessary basis—a really comprehensive, liberal and *reciprocal* trade treaty—seems desirable soon. To let US disapproval obstruct such a treaty, in the interests of a multilateralism that the USA does not herself practise, would be foolish. To let GATT ideals of universality obstruct a treaty—given that without one India will be driven into increasing autarky, regionalism, or bilateral links with the USSR—would be to make the best the enemy of the good.

5. Economic causes of decline

Hence the real (as against the *perceived*) needs of a self-reliant India and a European 'Britain' are not at all inconsistent with strong links between them. Yet, though they might be desirable and in the general interest of consumers and productive efficiency in EEC and India alike, the prospects would seem bleak if there were no more to be said. Fortunately, though the micro-economic pressures for disengagement retain their force, both India and Britain may well be operating in a macro-economic climate less damaging to their relationship than that of the 1960s, at least in the *late* 1970s.

Certainly, however, the micro-economic and short-term signs are not very hopeful. Interests such as British firms hoping for salvation through EEC protective quotas and the Common External Tariff, and Indian firms enabled to delay modernization because of markets secured by barter arrangements with Eastern Europe, will be strengthened by the new inward-looking regionalism, and will be better able to resist liberalization and international diversification. Moreover, majority British reactions against EEC show few signs of being outward-looking. Rather they seem negative and parochial: today, demands for cheaper butter; tomorrow, perhaps, complaints that EEC cars are competing too well in the British market as internal EEC tariffs come down. As for the Community's external policy, Britain's concentration is naturally upon the trade impact of the common agricultural policy (CAP), which (while very damaging both to European consumers and to some poor countries) has little impact on India; and on the need for trade and monetary arrangements reducing the dangers of trade contraction among rich countries, yet acceptable at once to the countries favouring gold (France and Germany) and to those able for a time to create international reserves by printing them (the USA and the UK).

In India too, the *micro*-pressures on foreign economic policy—especially as the implications of the move from aid become clearer—are not turning her towards Britain or the EEC. They will presumably concentrate on increasing the size, and improving the terms, of the barter deals (largely with communist countries) that increasingly determine India's access to imported capital equipment. These rather rigid deals fit naturally into India's growing emphasis on state trading, even if less well into her changing patterns of import requirements.

Hence the short-run pressures for more (and not just, ephemerally, more 'cordial') Indo-British relations are none too strong, especially at the micro-economic, and in particular the trading, base. The weakness is even clearer given the countervailing strength of interests in both countries benefiting from Indo-British protectionism, or from realignment, or both. It is a tautology that, since India and Britain both benefit from freer mutual trade (and more generally from freer mutual contact), the pressures for these general interests *potentially* outweigh the special counter-pressures; but it is not so in reality, largely because consumers are dispersed and producers of specific products concentrated (pp. 55–9), 60–1 but also for two other reasons. First, British consumer interest groups such as the Consumers' Association have not so far seen it as central to their function to press for cheaper and more varied imports; nor have their counterparts elsewhere in the EEC (such as the strong Dutch group) or indeed in the USA. Secondly, India (like other poor countries) has not so far seen it as a major task for diplomats, even in Commercial Sections, to persuade major *industrial* consumers of their exports to work with them for import liberalization. If these things changed—for example, if EEC consumers' groups pressed for an end to trade restrictions that raised the price of carpets, while the commercial representatives of India and Bangladesh combined with EEC's carpet manufacturers to attack restrictions on the import of cheap jute backing—the whole economic base for Indo–EEC relations would be broadened. But it would be unwise to rely on these pressures while concentrated and articulate groups of workers and employers, feeling they stand to lose all, operate, almost unchecked, in the Community's jute-processing industries, in Dundee and elsewhere.

This last example brings out the role of economic policy in providing a sound base for Indo-British relations. Adequate programmes for adjustment assistance —and more generally for high and stable employment levels extending further than such regions as 'Londbirm' and the Ruhr—could well reconcile, to freer trade, enough of the EEC's less efficient producers of carpet-backing (and processed cotton and foodstuffs) to ensure the success of consumer and diplomatic pressures on the lines indicated. But in general, getting the macro-economy right, or less wrong, comes first.

The remediable errors of economic management in Britain and India since the early 1960s have been, for two such different economies, surprisingly similar in type and effect. In both countries, overvalued exchange rates were retained for too long, and when they were adjusted this was seen as a *substitute* for essential structural change. In both, governments allowed powerful pressure groups to secure heavy subsidies for uneconomic ventures, public and private. In both Britain and India, these policies were pursued at the cost of growth and the foreign balance at once. We have supplied evidence (pp. 25–7) of the relatively poor performance of output and exports—for Britain as compared with other rich countries, and for India as compared with other poor countries.

There is a purely arithmetical effect that, under such circumstances, must weaken Indo-British relations. Suppose, as is reasonable, that every country, roughly in proportion to the speed of its overall growth, tends to increase imports and exports; to invest more abroad and to demand more foreign investment; to send and receive more foreign educands; and so on over the whole range of its overseas activities. Then the various countries, including Britain, dealing with India will be expanding their exports to India, imports from India, etc. at rates retarded by India's slow growth, while their dealings with other countries grow relatively more rapidly. India's share in total British dealings—exports, imports, investment, education or whatever—therefore tends to fall. Since Britain is also growing slowly on a world scale, exactly similar tendencies also depress Britain's share in India's various transactions, to the benefit of other nations growing more rapidly than Britain.

As with growth, so with foreign exchange. Countries with current deficits and dwindling reserves, such as Britain, will tend to contract activities overseas, including activities in India, while better-placed third nations expand such activities. Meanwhile India tends to find activities in Britain less attractive by virtue of Britain's reduced capacity to pay for them. The effect also works the other way: India's activities abroad, and Britain's activities in India (as compared to those, say, in Malaysia), are deterred by India's relatively worsening foreign-exchange position and hence capacity to pay.

These pressures—which make themselves felt in the balance-sheets of companies, and even in universities, well in advance of (and indeed sometimes obviating) public action—show how much the weakening of the Indo-British bond in the 1960s stems from the simple rule: if country A gets poorer, or less able to find foreign exchange, relative to country B, then country B in general strengthens its links with other countries C at the expense of country A. If both A and C (India and Britain) get poorer *and* shorter of foreign exchange relative to B (the rest of the world)—as they certainly did in the 1960s, despite A's and C's *absolute* improvement in income per head—there are *four* sets of pressures making A and C less important to each other, and B therefore relatively more important to both.

Thus the chance of an Indo-British relationship strengthened at its economic base (as opposed to ad hoc or euphoric reactions, either to present political events or to past neglects) depends on the *relative* improvement, in the 1970s and 1980s, of Indian and British economic performance. If India and Britain can both grow faster and improve their foreign balances more (i.e. export more, and become more *able to* import), relative to the USA, Japan, EFTA, and the USSR, than in the 1960s—then Indo-British relations in all the fields discussed in this book would be likely to increase. (They may not 'improve'.)

The improvement of relations in 1970–3 owed much to the delayed recovery of both countries' balances of payments after devaluation. India actually recorded a surplus on current account in 1973. Britain in 1969–72 and India in 1967–71, enjoyed slightly faster growth. This is no place to join the many debates about just how and why internal economic management, in both Britain and India, fell short of rival countries in achieved improvement in domestic welfare and external balance. One can only say that a reasonably happy resolution of these domestic debates, both in India and in Britain, would greatly help them to strengthen their links.

It might be thought that the great increase in world oil prices makes less likely a 'macro-economic' recovery in British and Indian growth and foreign-balance performances, and hence in their relationship. But (apart from the major Indo-British joint interest as oil consumers) this is to misunderstand the effect. What influences Britain's links with India from the side of the British macro-economy is its growth and foreign balance *relatively to third countries*. Britain's access to North Sea oil means that she will suffer less than other European countries and Japan (and possibly in the 1980s less than the USA and even the USSR) from high oil prices. Hence oil developments probably increase the *relative* capacity of Britain to 'afford' expanded links with India. A less strong 'oil factor', admittedly, pushes India the other way: she is more industrialized and hence more oil-dependent than most poor countries, so that rising oil prices more seriously reduce her capacity to 'make' foreign policy: in 1972 India spent 1·1 per cent of her national income to import oil, but on reasonable price-assumptions it could well be around $3\frac{1}{2}$ per cent by 1980.

The formulation espoused here—that the strength of a bilateral relationship depends partly on each partner's macro-economic success as compared with third parties—has a symmetry that, if pushed too far, would be aesthetic rather than realistic. Indeed, there is one crucial policy asymmetry. In the short run British aid, if carefully managed, can help India in a way in which no counterpart in India can help Britain. The *cumulative* benefit to Indo-British relations represents a special 'pay-off' for British aid to India, especially in so far as EEC regulations permit Britain to build on the growth and foreign-balance benefits of her new freedom from the sterling shibboleth. Apart from this asymmetry, the macro-economic explanation remains powerful—and somewhat paradoxical. Poor economic performance produced overseas retrenchment; the resulting retreat from specialization and exchange worsened performance. Conversely, it is realistic to expect the future of the relationship to depend largely on the future success of macro-economic policy.

6. Economics, politics, and measurement: a relationship and its future

It has, however, been powerfully argued[20] that scholars fail to understand poor countries because social science, dominated by economists, has failed to recognize 'the primacy of politics'. On this view, the statesmen of poor countries, knowing that domestic and foreign intellectuals (whose articulateness often and whose analysis occasionally proves useful) react favourably to the language of growth, development, and increasingly also employment and equality, use that language. However, especially in poor rural countries—where the income and status gap between power and powerlessness is enormous—politicians are allegedly motivated chiefly by the wish to stay in office, and to obtain its fruits for themselves and their families and clients. Such conduct, and the developmental doubletalk, are (we are told) accepted as quite normal by the masses. Only foreigners, unaware of the alleged need for corruption to lubricate the system, feel, or affect, moral outrage.[21]

If the above account applied to India, one's analyses and predictions of Indo-British relations would be quite different. Yet India would seem ideal for it. *Pace* West Bengal, her politicians normally rely on persuasion—largely through promises of economic advancement—rather than on force to stay in office. The pull of family and patron-client relations is as powerful as anywhere, and the income and status gap between political power and political opposition is extremely wide. If the implications for foreign powers of the above analysis were followed out in India, they would be brutally simple: bribe the political elite, especially by means (military or, via projects geared towards sensitive groups at electorally critical moments, economic) of helping it to stay in power. It is not surprising that those who begin with a belief in 'the primacy of politics' (in the sense of the previous paragraph) end with models of a totally self-seeking elite in poor countries, subservient to foreign paymasters ('comprador') and indifferent to the interests of the mass of its people.[22]

However, not one foreign power has, to our knowledge, attempted to regulate its *high-level* dealings with Indian politicians by the direct political bribery here implied. (Allegations, by Jana Sangh and the CPM,[23] that Congress has accepted political contributions from, respectively, the USSR and the USA are among the self-cancelling hilarities of election propaganda.) For example, aid is certainly intended inter alia to further the donor's foreign-policy interests. All major donors think this is best achieved by, in India, steering aid to projects with high yield for the recipient country; and the policies for achieving this, while probably often misguided and sometimes unduly responsive to pressures (notably from exporters) in the *donor* country, have never been seriously alleged to be affected by concessions to significant regional, caste, or other sectional biases that help the Indian ruling party to retain state or central office. Only two conclusions are possible: either all donors misconceive their interests in regulating their aid relations with India; or else the doctrine of the 'primacy of politics', as least for India, is in need of modification.

The latter is certainly more plausible. But it would be silly to react by treating Indian (or Kenyan or British) statesmen as normally concerned with the national economic interest *above* sectional political advantage. The point is, rather, that the dichotomy is false. The political advantage of the ruling group is, except in the very short term, best achieved by increasing the quantum of deliverable economic goods. *Panis* as well as *circenses* was demanded by even the most gullible of political audiences, which the Indian electorate is certainly not. 'Abolish poverty', *garibi hatao*, was the election slogan that not only returned Congress in 1971 (and may yet defeat it), but underlined the increasing place of national, economic, and non-sectarian issues in Indian politics, at least at the level of central elections. The ruling group—Old Congress, Reform Congress, Mrs Gandhi's group, or whatever—that fails to deliver the goods will be at increasing risk. And *panes* not *circenses*—loaves rather than steel mills?—are increasingly the goods that count.

Hence Britain—or any other country—seeking effective foreign relations with

India must offer trade, aid, investment, educational, even perhaps military links that (preferably at low cost, or even with benefit, to the offering country) help India to develop the capacity to raise mass welfare, *thereby* improving the Indian elite's chances of surviving, and in particular the politicians' chance of a vote of thanks. Retaining office may be the primary motive of politicians, but economics determines their *success* in retaining office. Therefore, we do not feel that the 'primacy of politics' challenge, properly considered, weakens the case for seeing Indo-British relations as standing or falling by measurable economic links, of the type principally analysed in this book.

For both Britain and India in the 1960s, economic constraints have limited the attainment of political goals.[24] The decade 1955–65 in both countries saw a sort of 'crisis of ambition'. In India, the domestic aim of instant industrialization proved industrially inefficient, agriculturally almost disastrous (given population growth), and macro-economically an intolerable foreign-exchange strain; the related policy of non-alignment proved implausible in face of the increasing import surpluses required by Indian industrialization. Thus India's ambitions proved incompatible with the prior, overriding needs to provide the electorate with enough of the fruits of growth and to manage the external accounts in such a way as to preserve some freedom of economic manoeuvre.

With appropriate changes, the above paragraph applies also to Britain in 1955–65. 'Policing', 'frontiers on the Himalayas', even the 'role of sterling'—such notions, in Britain's case, provoked ever sharper clashes between ambition and the requirements of growth and the foreign balance. As in the case of India, Britain could have given continuing priority to her ambition; but both countries were blessed with statesmen who lacked *that* sort of political will.

Unfortunately, both sets of statesmen also failed to appreciate enough, or soon enough, the harshness of the choices forced upon them by the need to trim their international sails. For far too long, both India and Britain retained visions: India of non-alignment, Britain of a global but undefined 'role'. Had Britain *chosen* in 1960 the overseas connections she would most want to maintain as a member of the Community after 1972, it is inconceivable that she would not have emphasized India, even at the cost of Malta. Had India *chosen* in 1960 the de facto alignment with the USSR after 1971 and the consequent estrangement from the USA, she would certainly have sought to strengthen the links with Britain (shortly to join EEC) in order to preserve her international options. But neither Britain nor India, until much too late, faced the fact that a major new alignment, under conditions of resource scarcity, requires harsh choices among *traditional* alignments. Both countries found themselves in a last-minute scramble, during which both Britain and India have made a rushed and curiously arbitrary selection of subsidiary relationships for emphasis (Nepal is perhaps in some ways India's Malta).

The rise in oil prices has cast doubt on India's hopes of facing, in the period after 1975, less harsh economic constraints than in the previous nine years, with their two wars and three exceptional droughts. The poor, too, are increasingly articulate, and the planners, with their goals of guaranteed minimum incomes, are to some degree responding to their demands. This will require very careful foreign-exchange management, if the resulting rise in consumption is not to produce an import explosion that constrains India as severely as before. As for Britain, with a floating exchange rate and the prospect of North Sea oil, the *late* 1970s should see major improvements in both the foreign balance and the growth rate. Yet in Britain, as in India, greater internal economic equality is a key to foreign policy: in Britain, because the trade unions will certainly demand it in return for accepting an effective incomes policy, without which there are few prospects for a foreign balance strong enough to allow much effective choice in foreign policy.

The economic constraints on policy formation, then, will probably leave India and Britain more able after 1976 than they were in the 1960s to take basic decisions about foreign economic policy. Many such decisions on trade, of course, are progressively ruled out for Britain acting alone, as the Treaty of Rome takes effect. Indeed Britain, to nobody's surprise, had not been a member of the EEC for many hours before she initiated action to annul the Indo-British trade treaty,[25] which she had saved, in 'Perils of Pauline' fashion, not many moths previously (pp. 57–8). However, a strong Britain would certainly be able to press for substantial liberalization of EEC policies towards India; West Germany, partly through her aid policy and partly through her interpretation of EEC tariff and quota rules on cotton textiles, has already done something in this direction, and Britain's special knowledge could achieve much more. However, in closing, we should look at two issues. We have already suggested (p. 226f.) that the retention of political office *within* India (and Britain) requires economic success; but has our predilection for measurement pushed us too far towards an economics-based interpretation of Indo-British *relations*? And how do the global political realignments of the early 1970s affect the likely future of those relations?

Inevitably, in the present state of the arts, an emphasis on measurement means a bias towards economics and away from politics. We hope we have avoided preferring quantifiable but wrong hunches to unquantifiable but right ones. Economics has advanced much further, in the use of measurement in explanation, than other social sciences. Sometimes this is because economists avoid crucial questions about power; often it is because economists are fortunate in having Pigou's 'measuring-rod of money' with which to compare, however roughly, incomes and values. We have, however, tried to measure also the 'Indo-British' movements of a few crude non-economic indicators: press coverage, diplomatic representation, educational and research emphasis, and so forth. These indicators do appear to follow, rather than to lead, the economic indicators in time.

Nevertheless, there is some danger of undue emphasis on the policy-maker's view of all this. Our tables illuminate many of the small things that, to ordinary people, do far more than trade *or* diplomacy to make up the texture of a bilateral relationship: tourism, press and television coverage, students abroad. All these show clearly the essential *asymmetry* of a rich-poor relationship, even where the rich country is not a great power and the poor country is large and diversified. Still it is the rich country that can afford to send large numbers of tourists to the poor country, and the poor country which on balance is a major receiver of educational resources—and influences—from the rich country; and London is a major centre of Indian journalism, whereas British press treatment of India seems to us seriously to underrate India's importance both in itself and to Britain (compare, for instance, the disproportionate concern with South Africa).

However, many of these non-economic links are too dependent on particular individuals or events, and in general too secondary to the availability and concentration of resources, to form valid indicators of a bilateral relationship. The use of such links to indicate 'stability' or 'decline' in the Indo-British nexus would, without support from economic or diplomatic data, be impossible to justify. The main challenge to our emphasis on the measurement of smoothly-changing (in the jargon, continuous) economic variables—and the reader will decide for himself whether that emphasis is useful in the context of this book—comes, not from non-economic continuous indicators we have assembled, but from non-continuous, 'yes/no' political facts. Are not such internal changes as the Conservative victory of 1970 or Mrs Gandhi's triumph in 1971, the Indo-Soviet treaty or Britain's signature of the Treaty of Rome, the events that determine the shape of Indo-British relations?

We do not think so, though we will shortly point to a more powerful sort of 'yes/no' fact. Indo-British relations, even very indirectly, are not the stuff of major domestic political conflict in either Britain or India, now that British inter-party disagreement on immigration has been damped down (albeit by tacit agreement upon formulas with some nastily racist implications). India's partial alignment with the USSR, Britain's entry into the EEC, are parts of gradual, trade-based and trade-heralded developments; the treaties, historically interpreted, will seem little more than inevitable but somewhat ritual blips on the graph. (So, if that happened, would be the annulment of the treaties.)

Much more important 'yes/no' facts than treaties—facts certain to affect at least the style and the limits of any future Indo-British relationship—are the *realignments* culminating in the early 1970s. The South Asian realignment is the most certainly irreversible one. Bangladesh is independent. Certainly her gratitude (for Indian intervention against Pakistan in 1971 followed by prompt withdrawal and massive food aid) was already, during her election campaign of February–March 1973, being replaced by the usual big-brother rumblings of suspicion. India will never again have to face, on two fronts, the outcome of feelings over Kashmir largely confined to the Pakistan Punjab. Indeed, there is much to strengthen the economic links between India and Bangladesh, notably the urgency of agreed policies on jute and to a lesser extent on river developments.

Pakistan herself, while she introduced a form of conscription into a 'people's army' in December 1972, is preoccupied with the problems of national unity, which may be under threat both in Sind and from the Pakhtoons of Baluchistan.

Pakistan seems unlikely for many years to present an effective military threat to India; even without a generous (and perhaps desirable) recognition by India of the case for self-determination in Kashmir, the common interests of Pakistan and India in a relaxation of tensions should fairly soon reassert themselves. (This was written before the prisoners-of-war agreement of September 1973—it seems even clearer after it.) If they do, it will be in spite of a US interest, astutely analysed by Robert Jackson,[26] in preventing further Soviet penetration of Indian trade via the opening of land routes that would follow any major Indo-Pakistani rapprochement.

India, then, is more closely aligned to the USSR, and more secure militarily, than ever before. Yet the euphoria of late 1971, when a decisive electoral victory for Mrs Gandhi was followed by the defeat of Pakistan and the creation of Bangladesh, was largely dried up in the drought of 1972 and the simultaneous aid shortage. Indeed, with the reduction of US aid, the relative importance to India of Britain and West Germany have greatly increased. In other fields as well, a search for diversification by India seems likely. Soviet aid is too short-term, and barter trade too tied to unwanted or half-wanted products, to be fully satisfactory in the long term (despite the short-term pressures—see p. 34)—though the existence of European alternatives would enable India to press the USSR for a better deal. The point is that, with India fairly secure on the sub-continent, those alternatives should be overwhelmingly economic. Only against a possible threat from China might India now need military support, though in arms supplies too India would presumably welcome an enlargement of options.[27]

Britain's membership of the EEC, while not as clearly or immediately a new 'alignment' as Bangladesh's independence and friendship with India, is in our view almost as unlikely to be reversible as are the subcontinental realignments. Mr Wilson's pledge to renegotiate, now being implemented by his fourth administration, might bring about a period of 'Gaullist' tensions, with Britain vetoing most Community 'decisions', and culminating in the substantial revision of the CAP; this last is eminently desirable, but the whole process would not constitute British 'withdrawal'. This, while perfectly possible (whatever the lawyers may say) if the House of Commons so legislates, would be disruptive and costly. Mr Wilson has been careful to say that it is the upshot of 'renegotiation' that he will submit to referendum, not membership of the EEC on present terms, nor British policy regarding any impasse during attempted renegotiation. It is hard to envisage an outcome so bitterly fought over, and (presumably) backed as an improvement by all three major parties (though the Conservatives would argue it was not worth the delays and disruptions), being defeated at a referendum. In any event, Labour's conditions for accepting the results of 'renegotiation', while including a rather vague requirement of greater respect for Third World interests, contain little of direct consequence for Commonwealth Asian countries.

With Britain firmly in the EEC, then, her Commonwealth trade preferences will continue in the 1970s to wither away—though probably no faster than they did in the 1960s thanks to EFTA. Special access to the London capital market for Commonwealth countries, not recently of much relevance for India, will cease. The generalized scheme of preferences of EEC—which would be marginally more favourable to India[28] (were it not overwhelmed by restrictive textile quotas)[29] than the British scheme—will probably be applied. Most important by far to India, her exports of textiles *to the UK* will be severely constrained by the EEC quotas. Since India is agreed by all parties (almost a guarantee of error) to be non-associable, the trading base of her relationship with Britain depends mainly on what meat is put onto the 'skeleton' Indo-EEC trade treaty, concluded in December 1973, when Britain's application of EEC tariff and quota rules to India began (all non-members are *fully* affected by 1977). Unfortunately the long delays of the Brussels Commission in even considering the successive sets of Indian proposals, and the failure of Britain to apply much pressure (as against successful French pressures for further delay), augur badly. However, perhaps too much need not be made of this. The European interest in ample supply of labour-intensive imports from India is permanent, the application of EEC entry conditions to the UK market gradual, and an insufficiently liberal Indo-EEC treaty accordingly remediable. If India presses her interests in London and (not least by appointing more European linguists) in Brussels, and if Britain takes a a lead in seeking subsequent liberalization, then the Indo-British relationship could continue to recover despite an initially illiberal Indo-EEC treaty.

Two points should be made about the content of any 'good' treaty. First, for reasons of substance and not of 'tact', it should embody an exchange of substantial and equal advantages—in market access principally—in part to help form a lobby, favourable to the treaty and balancing the textile lobby, among European workers and businessmen exporting to India. Second, the 'double-bind' nature of India's situation should be recognized: the fact that export expansion is in many fields constrained by supply (including marketing) as well as by demand. As India's failures to fill the UK textile quotas show, freer trade *alone* will not do much; but neither, *alone*, will measures to improve India's productive or marketing capacity in export sectors. Both are needed simultaneously, in the context of a trade treaty identifying imports into EEC that are 'non-sensitive'—or, more frequently, that can be made so via industrial restructuring and adjustment assistance—*and* that can be efficiently produced and marketed by India. India's supply capacities and EEC's absorptive tolerances must be built up rapidly, but *simultaneously*, perhaps through imaginative aid linked to the trade treaty.

We have argued that (unlike the short-run economic pressures—see pp. 15–16) the recent changes in British and Indian circumstances and regional environments, perhaps surprisingly, are favourable to the continued recovery of Indo-British relations. From the Indian viewpoint, the strong Soviet link makes diversification obviously desirable, to preserve options; and the new sub-continental balance of power could give India a secure base, from which such realignment could be undertaken with minimum risk. As for Britain and EEC, they should find a major and (as compared with Franco-African links) equal, non-exploitative and mature Asian connection a strong attraction; the disadvantages of illiberal trade policies are cumulative, and the numbers of British and European workers that gain from them anyway declining; and, at least arguably, the economic constraints on 'overseas' policy that plagued Britain before 1968 have been substantially relaxed by the new exchange-rate policies, and can be further relaxed by a (necessarily, and desirably, somewhat egalitarian) incomes policy. But what does the changing *world* environment, caused by the new relations among the superpowers, do to this rather hopeful prognosis (of the possibilities at least)?

It is rather surprising how little effect the Nixon détentes with China and the USSR have had upon the subcontinent. They did little to slow the serious deterioration in Indo-US relations. The role of China and the US as joint military suppliers to Pakistan is unchanged. In Bangladesh, for all the overt—and historically understandable—hostility to the US, it is in 1972–4 US (even more than Indian) foodgrains that prevent mass starvation. The Indo-Soviet Treaty of 1971 was certainly helped along by the increasingly open partisan role of the USA against India over Bangladesh and the refugee issue; but that treaty, we have argued, was just one milestone along a lengthy, and primarily economic, road. After the Nixon détentes the central subcontinental issues remain as before: Sino-Indian border disputes (and *perhaps* ideological ones), Indo-Soviet alignment, in the background the Sino-Soviet rift, and—of decreasing importance—a Pakistan hostile to India and backed by both China and the USA. Certainly US disengagement from India reduces the risk that Indian links with the EEC would make the Indian left suspicious of 'capitalist' infiltration; on the other hand, China's relative warmth towards the Community could be dispelled by, and hence raise the costs to the EEC of, a liberal treaty with India. However, it is not plausible to argue that superpower realignments *substantially* affect the costs and benefits, to India or to Britain, of a stronger link between them.

There is one final issue of the macro-political environment to be considered: the world food situation. Perhaps the most neglected fixed point of world politics is that only the USA has, or is likely soon to have, a surplus of cereals sufficient to make the difference between famine and survival to a country as large as India (or even Indonesia, Pakistan, or Bangladesh). How could that matter, given the alleged 'green revolution', and if that fails India's capacity to buy grain on world markets? And, even if it did matter, what is the relevance for relations between India and other countries, especially Britain? Without the green revolution[30]—the adoption since the mid-1960s of dramatically more fertilizer-responsive varieties (HYVs) of wheat, maize, and (to a much smaller extent) rice and millets—India would today be facing either widespread famine or continued dependence on US food aid. The green revolution has prevented India's food situation from deteriorating, and has restored food output per person to the level attained in 1964–5 (or indeed 1960–1), before the disastrous droughts of the mid-1960s. But it does not follow, first, that India's food output per person has shown any significant uptrend since the mid-1950s, before or after the green revolution began;[31] or, second, that we can confidently expect a continuation of the trends of 1967–71, when increases in output-per-Indian from the 10–15 per cent of cereal lands sown with HYVs slightly outweighed *reductions* in output-per-Indian on the remaining 85–90 per cent.

The new and serious emphasis on planning to help the really poor—a central feature of India's Fifth Plan—implies, if successful, a rapid acceleration of established growth-rates in the demand for food, and it will be some time before a slowing-down in the rate of increase in population significantly relieves the pressure. Future trends in output are likely to confirm the past: extra grain from the green revolution output has comprised overwhelmingly wheat from larger ($7\frac{1}{2}$-acres-plus) farms in Punjab, Western Uttar Pradesh, and to some extent Haryana. These farmers are now continuing their 'progress' largely by mechanization that 'saves' (or unemploys) labour, but does little to raise output further. In the other main wheat area, Madhya Pradesh, water control is too unreliable to favour much spread of the existing HYVs. The rice HYVs show a few patches of dramatic output expansion, notably the Kosi project area of North Bihar, coastal Andhra, and the Tanjore district in Tamil Nadu—but do not at present promise an immediate breakthrough on the scale of the wheat breakthrough in the Punjab, or indeed the rice breakthrough in Taiwan.

The drought of 1972, while minor by the standards of 1965 and 1966, came as a warning of the fragile and perhaps temporary nature of India's approach to self-reliance in food. Her stocks were severely depleted by massive food aid to Bangladesh in early 1972—requests for such aid are almost certain to recur— and the need for relief, especially in Mararashtra, had by early 1973 reduced them to dangerously low levels. So, on the demand side, there is population increasing at about 2·5 per cent per year, and income per head planned to grow at a further 2·5 at least, to the intended benefit mainly of the poor, who will spend extra income mainly on food. On the supply side, there is a wheat revolution probably near its plateau, a rice revolution reluctant to take off,[32] and yet a growing feeling among officials that the agricultural problem is solved and it is time to turn to industry. (In reality, however, even during the 'top-priority' years of 1965–72, agriculture—with 70 per cent of India's workforce and nearly half her GNP—never received even one-quarter of public investment). Under these circumstances India's prospects of avoiding substantial reliance on food imports in the mid-1970s remain touch- and-go, critically dependent on technological good fortune with rice HYVs.

Nor—and here we come to India's foreign relations—is it at all clear where such imports would come from. Not from aid, on present trends (p. 220), which speak for themselves. As for commercial imports, the current-account balance-of-payments surplus of 1972, welcome as it was, had mirage-like attributes: it rested on big 'sales' to Bangladesh, which the latter is unlikely to be able to pay for soon, or in convertible currency; and it would evaporate with any real pick-up in the level of capacity (and hence imported-input) utilization in Indian industry.

Faced with US protectionism, increasing barriers in the British market, and growing difficulties in arranging mutually satisfactory barter with the USSR and Comecon, where is India to find the foreign exchange for industrial and food imports? Certainly, India's political leaders cannot take substantial risks on the food front: '*garibi hatao*' must be tested electorally by 1976, the postwar euphoria is over, and Mrs Gandhi could hardly risk a major breakdown in food supplies.

Apart from the availability of foreign exchange to pay for food, there is the question of where the food would come from. Only the US has supplies on the scale required. As the aftermath of the Russian harvest failure of 1972 underlined, the climatically induced claims on these surpluses—commercial or concessional—from many countries can well coincide. Under such circumstances, with cereal prices high, the US naturally downgrades concessional deliveries, and within them gives priority to relief-and-rehabilitation crises (today Bangladesh, tomorrow . . .), areas of obvious strategic rivalry with the USSR, and countries with less cool bilateral relations with the USA than India's. Whatever their public statements of confidence on the food front, India's leaders are aware of these facts, and most draw the obvious conclusions. Given the alignments of the USA during and since the 1971 Bangladesh crisis, however, there is a limit to the prospects of Indo-US rapprochement.

Well, if the capacity of the poorer country to feed its people is a prime mover in its international relations with a richer country; and if this is at least as likely to apply to Indo-British or Indo-EEC relations as the events of 1972 showed it was to relations between the USSR and the USA; then what should Britain as a member of the Community do about it? Her positive and long-run interest is clear: a prosperous and democratic India, 'dynamically complementary' (in production patterns), as it develops, with a growing European economy, so that both India and Britain can reap, and spread, the gains from efficient but flexible specialization and trade. That sounds nice, but will be frustrated unless Britain also considers her short-run and negative interest in relations with India: to help the Indian government avoid a food crisis that, especially under conditions of great internal inequality, will cause major internal upheavals and/or compel India to align herself very closely with *any* potential supplier of food or foreign exchange.

But how can that interest be safeguarded? The EEC is unlikely in the near future to develop a major exportable surplus of cereals. (Britain, of course, is a major cereal deficit country.) There are, notoriously, EEC farm surpluses, but 'let them eat butter' is not, given transport costs and problems, a very promising solution; however, Britain could well ask the Commission urgently to study the possibility of encouraging European farmers to change the structure of output, so that, where efficient, commodities more useful in food aid programmes were produced.

Much more important, however, could be steps by the EEC to improve, profitably to itself, India's general foreign-exchange position (and hence command over food imports in emergency) via a major bilateral trade expansion between the EEC member states and India. In respect of her increasing reliance on state trading and barter, India is developing many of the trade aspects of East European countries, with whom members of the Community conclude frequent bilateral bilateral barter deals without transgressing the Treaty of Rome; possibly the same policy could be considered in the short run by Britain vis-à-vis India, especially if the 'meat' on the Indo-EEC trade treaty is delayed or illiberal. Alternatively, a major short-run barter package between the Community and India could be considered; competitive bidding by EEC firms would be perfectly compatible with this.

Of course, trade for cash is an enormous advance on barter. For India, too, convertible earnings are a much better safeguard against harvest failure than even the form of EEC or British barter offer best suited to raise Indian farm output—agricultural inputs, or the plant to make them. We suggest barter deals solely because they could be more rapidly practicable on a big scale than other arrangements, given the delays of negotiations and the constraints of both EEC and Indian trade regulations. But in the medium term only a liberal, bilateral Indo-EEC treaty would do.[33] Only such an arrangement could provide the Community with a relationship with India that would be better than a residual 'second best' to its relationship with other major trading partners. India too, has found barter arrangements unsatisfactory when they tie too large a part of the imports of a changing economy to an inflexible list of goods.

While the trade relationship needs attention most—certainly given the present fairly favourable Indo-British *political* climate—the aid relationship is also important, especially given India's food risks. The decline of food aid, and Congressional suspicions of all aid, surely render the contraction of US aid to India, at least in part, permanent. The *net* flow of Soviet aid to India, on account of its short-loan nature, has for some years been negative. Hence British and West German aid have grown in stature because 'rivals' have shrunk, and British aid to India has recently also increased substantially, though its value per £ has been somewhat reduced by more stringent tying (pp. 111–12). France, the largest bilateral donor in EEC, gives almost nothing to India, however, and there are some grounds for fear that British contributions to European Development Fund may be in part at India's expense (p. 119).

Does it matter to Britain—or to the Community—to construct her trade and aid relations in the Third World in such a way as to concentrate on big, poor, democratic, comparatively uncorrupt countries; countries, moreover, where extra foreign exchange could decisively affect, not the Swiss bank accounts of a tiny minority, but the prospects of national independence, democracy, and economic development? We believe that not one of the words in the last sentence is rhetoric. They accurately reflect the contrast between India and *most* of the African countries in receipt, currently, of EEC bilateral and multilateral aid, attention, and advantageous trading arrangements. Can it be in the interests of any country—even France or the USSR—that Indian prospects should not be improved, and choices enlarged, by a relationship with the EEC rooted in the realities of expanding trade and capital flows, and not in lingering colonial sentiment?

UK COMMAND PAPERS, HOUSE OF COMMONS PAPERS, AND PRINCIPAL ABBREVIATIONS

Command papers

C.1373. *Statement of trade of British India with British possessions and foreign countries* . . . 1869/70–1873/4. 1875.

Cd 7160. *Report of Indian Students' Department, July 1912–July 1913.*

Cmd 7317. *Report of the Royal Commission on the Press,* 1948.

Cmnd 1174. *Annual report and accounts of the BBC,* 1959–60.

Cmnd 3779. *Annual report and accounts of the BBC.* 1967–8.

Cmnd 3180. Ministry of Overseas Development, *Overseas development: the work in hand,* 1967. 1967.

Cmnd 3569. *Report of the Royal Commission on Education,* 1965–8. 1968.

Cmnd 4107. *Report of the Review Committee on Overseas Representation,* 1968–9 [Duncan Committee] 1969.

Cmnd 4273. *17th annual report of the Consultative Committee of the Colombo Plan,* 1970.

Cmnd 4620. Home Office, *Control of immigration statistics,* 1970, 1971.

Cmnd 4715. *The United Kingdom and the European Communities.* July 1971.

Cmnd 4824. *Annual report and accounts of the BBC,* 1971.

Cmnd 5111. *Annual reports and accounts of the BBC,* 1971–2.

House of Commons papers

HC 442, sess. 1967–8. *Seventh report from the Estimates Committee* . . . *with part of* . . . *Minutes of Evidence taken before Sub-Committee C* . . . *Overseas aid.*

HC 387, sess. 1968–9. *Third report from the Estimates Committee.*

HC 205—I, sess. 1969–70. Select Committee on Race Relations and Immigration, —vol. I: *Evidence* . . .; HC 205—II, vol. II: *Evidence and appendices, index.*

HC 288, sess. 1969–70. Select Committee on Overseas Aid (Sub–Committee C), *Minutes of evidence* . . . *India/Pakistan.*

HC 203, sess. 1969–70. *Civil appropriation accounts,* 1969–70.

HC 302, sess. 1970–1. *Supply estimates,* 1971–2.

Principal abbreviations

As. R.	*Asian Review*
As. Stud.	*Asian Studies*
Bhagwati/Desai	J. N. Bhagwati & P. Desai, *India: planning for industrialization.* London, 1970.
BHC	British High Commission
BMJ	*British Medical Journal*
BNEC	British National Export Council
BOIES	*Bulletin of the Oxford University Institute of Economics and Statistics*
BOTB	*Board of Trade Bulletin*

237

BTJ	*Board of Trade Journal*
CCE *Statement*	HM Commissioner for Customs & Excise, *Statement of trade of the UK with the Commonwealth and foreign countries*, ii, 1960–9
CEC	Commonwealth Economic Committee
CP	Commonwealth Preference
CSO	Central Statistical Office
Econ. J.	*Economic Journal*
FAO, *Monthly B.*	FAO, *Monthly Bulletin of Agricultural and Economic Statistics*
FBI	Federation of British Industries
FCO	Foreign and Commonwealth Office
FT	*Financial Times*
IBRD	International Bank for Reconstruction & Development
ICICI	Industrial Credit & Investment Corp. of India
IDS	Institute of Development Studies (Sussex Univ.)
IIPO, *Monthly Survey*	Indian Inst. of Public Opinion, *Monthly Public Opinion Survey*
IIT	Indian Inst. of Technology
Ind. Econ. J.	*Indian Economic Journal*
India [year]	GOI, *India: a reference annual* [year]
India, *Pocket Book*	India, *Pocket Book of Economic Information* (annual)
Int. Aff.	*International Affairs* (London)
J. As. Stud.	*Journal of Asian Studies*
l.d.c.s.	Less developed countries
Lipton/Tulloch	M. Lipton & P. Tulloch, 'India and the enlarged EEC', *International Affairs*, Jan. 1974.
ODA	Overseas Development Administration
ODI	Overseas Development Institute
ODM	Ministry of Overseas Development (UK)
OECD/DAC	Organization for European Cooperation & Development, Development Assistance Committee.
OSA	Overseas Sterling Area
Q.J. Econ.	*Quarterly Journal of Economics*
RBI, *Report* . . .	Reserve Bank of India, *Report on currency and finance* (annual)
SBI	State Bank of India
Streeten/Lipton	P. Streeten & M. Lipton, eds. *The crisis of Indian planning*. London, RIIA, 1968.
TA	Technical Assistance

NOTES

Notes to pp. 1–18

Chapter 1. Relations between Britain and India 1960–70

1 This statement survives most sensible interpretations: demographic, cultural, political, economic, or military; whether we see the relationship as one of direct or indirect control, commercial exploitation on even mutual influence; and considering the effects both on Britain and India, or on third parties—notably in Africa and Europe.

2 Other relevant attempts include J. O. N. Perkins, *Britain and Australia; economic relationships in the 1950s* (CUP, 1962); and Univ. of London, Inst. of Commonwealth Studies,

Notes to pp. 19–27

Seminar Papers (Oct. 1967–Mar. 1968), *The changing role of Commonwealth economic connections* (London, 1968).

3 The Supreme Court in effect delayed bank nationalization in 1969 and effectively compelled the Congress government in 1970–1 to obtain a new mandate before it could abolish the princes' rights to Privy Purses.

4 In 1968 the Government broke a promise to honour the passports of British citizens of Asian descent living in Kenya. In Ulster, until the beginning of the 1970s, equal rights in housing, in employment and in voting were largely denied to the Catholic minority; in 1971, while suspects were being interned without trial, some prominent British politicians advocated withdrawing the province's right to continued unity with Britain, denying the majority in the province its right to choose.

5 The importance of the security argument is revealed in the 1971 White Paper: '. . . Her Majesty's Government are convinced that our country will be more secure, our ability to maintain peace and promote development in the world greater, our economy stronger, and our industries and people more prosperous, if we join the European Communities than if we remain outside them' (Cmnd 4715, July 1971).

6 In particular with some influential Labour ministers and some civil servants. It has also, of course, damaged India's chances to mediate in West Asia.

7 Just how small this minority in Britain is can be seen from E. J. B. Rose, ed., *Colour and citizenship; a report on British race relations* (London, 1969), ch. 28: 'The incidence of race prejudice in Britain'. 'Surveys and interviews carried out in 1966/7 showed that only 10% of the population were prejudiced on racial matters, with a further 17% inclined to prejudice (pp. 553f.).

8 R. Cassen, 'Population policy', in Streeten/Lipton.

9 By a country's 'elite', we mean the interlocking groups of people—ministers, senior civil servants, directors of large privately-owned or nationalized concerns, perhaps some leading officials of the ruling political party, and a few key communicators and educators—which among them affect most major decisions on home and foreign policy. It is not implied that a national elite conspires, meets, or even necessarily thinks alike. It is more akin to what C. Wright Mills described in *The power elite* (OUP, 1956), than to that vague, curiously British entity 'the establishment'.

10 For a thorough examination of India's growing links with the Eastern block, see Asha L. Datar, *India's economic relations with the USSR and Eastern Europe, 1953 to 1969* (CUP, 1972).

11 M. Lipton, 'Labour and British economic policy towards Asia', in Fabian Society, *Labour in Asia* (London, 1972).

12 The fact that foreign capital in India is not substantially in mining has admittedly eased the problems.

13 M. Lipton, 'Prospects for Commonwealth cooperation and planning', in P. Streeten & H. Corbet, eds., *Commonwealth policy in a global context* (London, Cass, 1971), pp. 202–3 and n. 11.

14 Data on invisibles and capital are improving, but (as with trade) we are seldom given the basis of conversions when statistical series change, making historical comparison needlessly difficult.

15 Notably by operations on SITC Category 9; see pp. 180–1.

Chapter 2. British–Indian Trading Relations: the Context

1 G. W. Southgate, *The British Empire and Commonwealth* (London, Dent, 1961), pp. 173–4. Though Lancaster was reputedly the first Briton to bring a shipload of Indian goods to the British Isles, it has not been established whether it was achieved through trade or plunder.

2 Jawaharlal Nehru, *The discovery of India* (London, Asia, 1956), p. 297. The result of such measures was that the flourishing Indian textile industry collapsed, and the dismissals of much of the artisan class led to massive unemployment; in 1834, the Governor-General of India, Lord Bentinck, was moved to include in the annual report the statement that 'the misery hardly finds a parallel in the history of commerce. The bones of the cotton weavers are bleaching the plains of India' (ibid., p. 298). As late as 1882, because India was still

seen largely as a market for British goods, she was compelled to impose a 5% duty on imported textile machinery and to retain nil duties on British textile imports. The destruction of the weaving industry is illustrated by the importation in 1872–73 of £14·1mn. of cotton piece goods whilst £10mn of raw cotton was exported that year (C. 1373, 1875).

3 See e.g. Bhagwati/Desai, pp. 281f.

4 S. B. Linder, *An Essay on trade and transformation* (Stockholm, Almqvist, 1962).

5 T. S. Ashton, p. 10 of Introduction to E. B. Schumpeter, *English overseas trade statistics 1697–1808* (Oxford, Clarendon Press, 1960). Schumpeter's figures (tables V & VI), indicate an apparent balance of trade deficit of England and Wales with the East Indies of some £55·3mn over the whole of the period 1701–1800. How much of this enormous deficit was paid to the East Indies by bullion shipments is not clear.

6 They include different inflation rates, devaluations, political boundaries (of India), political constraints on trade (between India and Pakistan), and non-comparable export compositions. Also, after 1947, India had to import from (and export to) Pakistan what formerly counted as trade within British India. If we deduct, from exports of India and Pakistan in 1950–1, the goods they sold each other, the British share in 'India plus Pakistan' exports rises from 22·6 to 25·1%; and similarly in imports from 20·8% to 24·0%. These are really the figures to be compared with pre-1947 data (CEC, *Commonwealth trade 1950–7* (London, 1959), pp. 31–2). After 1952 Indo-Pakistan trade was reduced, and stopped completely after 1965; hence comparison with the pre-independence shares of Britain in exports and imports becomes sensible again, since in neither period did Indo-Pakistan trade figure.

7 The earliest year for which a countrywide breakdown is available for the trade of British India on a basis consistent with later statistical series is 1872–3. Thus caution is needed in interpreting would-be historically consistent trade comparisons of 'British India' with what later became India-plus-Pakistan (table 2.2), or indeed with India alone. Of the 1872–3 trade, about 5·6% featured points of entry or exit in Burma, 42·6% in Bengal (perhaps two-thirds being trade of the area that after 1947 became East Pakistan), and 1·6% in Sind (all of it trade from what was to be West Pakistan)). Thus 'British India' includes much more than modern India, for only trade via Madras (11·6%) and Bombay (39%) overwhelmingly comprised exports from or imports for areas now in independent India. However, 'British India' *may* also exclude too much, in that the trade of the princely states cannot be determined on a comparative basis, though the great bulk of such trade must have used British Indian ports as entrepôts. Further, no allowance is made for price rises: consequently the later value figures overstate the real (volume) growth in trade. Unfortunately, a long-term volume index would be extremely difficult to construct, for the structure of trade (and even the nature of such goods as raw cotton) has changed radically. Finally, it seems unlikely that the earlier data are adjusted to a consistent c.i.f. or f.o.b. basis.

8 These Home Charges included payments due in connection with civil departments in India: India Office expenses (an especially nice touch, with Indians being asked to pay for their own subjection!); both effective and non-effective army and marine charges; civil and military pensions and gratuities; furlough expenses; purchases of government stores; costs of management of all types of debt; and railway and irrigation annuities.

9 K. L. Mitchell, *India; an American view; a 1942 survey* (London, Bodley Head, 1942), pp. 134–5.

10 See chs. 5 & 6 where the situation will be discussed in detail.

11 A. Ghosh, *Indian economy; its nature and problems*, 9th ed. (Calcutta, World Press Private, 1965), p. 549.

12 Commonwealth Secretariat, *Commonwealth trade 1960–1*; 1970.

13 Ibid., *1970*, pp. 65–6, 91–2. Figures were converted into pounds sterling prior to aggregation at rates of £1 = Rs18·0 for India and £1 = Rs11·188 for Pakistan. For India alone the proportions were slightly higher, the shares of total India exports going to the USA and USSR being 30·5% and 7·7% respectively. In 1969–72, the Soviet share of subcontinental trade continued to grow sharply, but the US share declined somewhat (IMF, *Direction of trade annual 1968–72* (Washington, 1973), pp. 256–8, 266–7).

14 Most Indo–Soviet trade agreements involve barter exchanges of goods, with the value of trade in both directions being equal. Aid repayments, as well as aid loans, are tied to goods. (See also p. 243n.26 and Datar, *India's economic relations with the USSR ...*, ch. 4.

15. The bilateral surplus with the UK helps to cover not only other bilateral deficits, but also

invisibles debts, and certain military expenditure which does not go through trade accounts (chs. 5 & 11). This eroded the developmental imports allowed by the bilateral visible surplus.

16 *Commonwealth trade 1970.* In this subsection and the rest of this chapter, 'India' means independent India. For the dramatic recovery, see IMF, *Direction of trade annual 1968–72,* p. 104.

17 CSO, *Monthly digest of statistics,* no. 192, p. 145; no. 264, p. 139; & no. 308, p. 123. This is £72·9 × 100/123·6—the apparent value (in £mn) of British sales to India in 1970 at 1957 export prices—as a proportion of 1957 British exports to India. However, this figure needs qualification as it is based on both export prices and volume index for *total* British exports, and as we shall see in ch. 3, these have a slightly different composition from the UK trade with India.

18 IMF, *International financial statistics,* Jan. 1961, Jan. 1965, Jan. 1968, & July 1971.

19 For methods of calculation, see n. 17.

20 CSO, *Ann. abstract of statistics,* nos. 106 & 107 (1969, 1970). It is hard to estimate the real balance available, as the figures given measure imports as c.i.f., exports f.o.b., and do not take into account the relative changes in the sterling–rupee rate in 1966 and 1967.

21 Like all inter-country comparisons, table 2.6 must be treated with caution. The sizes of the links depicted vary, the distance between country pairs varies, there were different dates of independence and differing degrees of imperial control, and, finally, there were greatly differing trade structures and internal economic needs and stages of development. For an alternative approach, see G. Myrdal, *Asian drama; an inquiry into the poverty of nations,* 1 (Harmondsworth, 1968), table 13–4, pp. 592–3.

22 Some export complementarity is the result of colonial rule, not natural advantages. Had India not been colonized, she might have been exporting many more manufactured goods and fewer raw materials. Had Britain not colonized countries in the Third World, she would have developed techniques using fewer of their complementary raw-material inputs.

23 These figures have been based on the dollar value of exports to reduce exchange-rate problems, though in the new world of shifting and floating dollar rates we do not envy anyone trying to update this analysis.

24 For instance, over the period 1959–69 India's general wholesale price index rose by 81%, compared with 37% for a sample of 10 other LDCs competing with India. Meanwhile, the wholesale price of finished goods in Britain rose by 29%, compared with 22% for a sample of 10 developed countries (UN, *Statist. Yb., 1969* (1970), table 174; *Monthly B. Statist.,* Sept. 1971, pp. 148–59).

25 T. Wilson & others, 'The income terms of trade of developed and developing countries', *Econ. J.,* Dec. 1969, p. 826. Income terms of trade are defined: I (income term of trade for a country) $= (Px/Pm) \cdot Qx$ where $Px =$ export prices; $Pm =$ import prices; and $Qx =$ quantity (volume) of imports.

26 Thus in 1970 the *FT,* in a number of dispatches from its Latin American correspondent, uncovered valuable export orders which had not been dealt with in Britain, even after expensive telex reminders, because of the alleged ineptitude of some (especially medium-sized) British companies. Did rivals do better? Would greater efficiency be worth the substantial cost?

27 For details of these arguments see M. Lipton, *Assessing economic performance* (London, Staples Press, 1968), pp. 164 f.

28 R. E. Caves & others, *Britain's economic prospects* (London, Allen & Unwin, 1968), pp. 209–14. An earlier study had established that British export unit values were a significant variable explaining British export performance, though not in every market (H. B. Junz & R. R. Rhomberg, 'Prices and export performance of industrial countries 1953–63', IMF *Staff Papers,* July 1965. See also 'International comparison of costs and prices', *Economic Trends,* no. 163, May 1967; and Lipton, pp. 170 f.)

29 G. C. de Costa, 'Elasticities of demand for Indian exports—an empirical investigation', *Ind. Econ. J.,* July–Sept. 1965, pp. 43, 53. He means that the world demand for commodities of which India is a major producer, such as jute manufactures, cotton textiles, and tea, is inelastic with respect to export prices; but that over a long period, such as 1953–62, the relative export prices of a similar commodity produced by two countries will help to determine trade shares. In such a situation, a lower export price of country A for commodity x against country B's export price of commodity x, if sustained over a period, will lead to a loss of market share from B to A, although the total demand for x will not be

increased by any sizeable amount. Put like this, the contradiction vanishes. The above situation has some relevance for India.

30 B. J. Cohen, 'The stagnation of Indian exports 1951–61'. *Q.J. Econ.*, Nov. 1964, pp. 604–20.
31 See da Costa, *Ind. Econ. J.*, July–Sept. 1965, pp. 62 f.
32 Among these are, for Britain: R. J. Ball & others, 'The relations between United Kingdom export performance in manufactures and the internal pressure of demand', *Econ. J.*, Sept. 1966, pp. 501–18; L. Krause, 'British trade performance', in Caves & others, pp. 198–228; Lipton, pp. 162–74; J. R. Parkinson, 'The progress of United Kingdom exports', *Scot. J. Polit. Econ.*, Feb. 1966, pp. 5–26; J. O. N. Perkins, *The sterling area, the Commonwealth and world economic growth* (CUP, 1967); G. F. Ray, 'The competitiveness of British industrial products: a round-up', *Woolwich Econ. Papers*, no. 10, Oct. 1966; S. J. Wells, *British export performance; a comparative study* (CUP, 1964). For India: Cohen, *Q.J. Econ.*, Nov. 1964; da Costa, *Ind. Econ. J.*, July–Sept. 1965; S. J. Patel, 'Export prospects and economic growth—India', *Econ. J.*, Sept. 1959, pp. 490–506; M. Singh, *India's export trends and the prospects for self-sustained growth* (Oxford, Clarendon Press, 1964); S. J. Wells, 'Foreign trade: a commodity study', in Streeten/Lipton; J. A. Rosario, *Productivity in Indian export industries* (Bombay UP for Ind. Econ. Ass., 1964).

Notes to pp. 28–41

Chapter 3. British Exports to India

1 *Commonwealth trade 1960–1; 1970.* The figures quoted exclude S. Africa; if one includes S. Africa, the developed countries received 52·3% of total British exports to the '1958 Commonwealth' in 1958, 54·4% in 1968, and 64·6% in 1970.
2 *FT*, 15 Apr. 1965.
3 Textile Council, *Cotton and allied textiles*, vol. i (Manchester, 1969), pp. 128–9.
4 *FT*, 18 Oct. 1971, quoting the president of the Oldham & Dist. Textile Employers' Ass.
5 Cmnd 4107, p. 88: 'Commercial work is the most urgent task of our overseas representatives', yet 'We also recommend that the shift of Britain's export promotion resources to [advanced industrial countries] shall continue'. While India is presumably envisaged for a comprehensive mission within the 'Outer Area' (p. 52), she is presumably also included in the proposal that 'Outer Area' representation 'should be organized in a way that will facilitate a wide range of successive retrenchment decisions in the future as well as an occasional move in the opposite direction' (p. 47).
6 *Guardian*, 30 Jan. 1964.
7 *FT*, 7 Aug. 1970. As BNEC stated: 'This steep decline in exports (£128·8 million in 1964 to £65 million in 1969) to this huge country has been causing BNEC Asia concern for some time.' The Chairman of BNEC Asia said: 'Everyone to whom I speak advises me that our poor export performance to India is a direct reflection of India's economic position [but] in my view this is too simple an approach. . . . Our international competitors have not failed as badly as ourselves and we must understand the reason for this.' The BNEC's later examination of the cost-effectiveness of its promotional work is also relevant (ibid., 21 Oct. 1970, p. 6).
8 The above can be deduced from Sir Michael Parsons, 'New patterns of trade in the Indian sub-continent', *Trade & Industry*, 29 Mar. 1973, pp. 670–2. As a dynamic alternative in the area, the BOTB decided to 'establish contact with the India, Pakistan and Bangladesh Association as a means of obtaining advice on policy' (p. 672)!
9 Imports were liberalized in 59 groups of products which were selected for their contribution to exports, but other import controls were not relaxed; nor were tariffs lowered. Some steps were taken to try to prevent higher import prices working through into export prices.
10 See RBI, *Report . . . 1969–70*, for detailed import policy situation as at March 1970.
11 In some cases, the availability was theoretical; in others, it took no account of quality or the performance of the indigenous products, compared with foreign equivalents. At the beginning of 1971, similarly, Pakistan banned a variety of consumer-goods imports, initially for six months. The period of import liberalization in South Asia has been at least interrupted, perhaps halted; are US and European import and aid restrictions partly to blame?
12. *FT*, 26 Mar. 1971, p.6. Since then, the state control of India's imports has increased substantially (see 'Import policy for 1972–3', SBI *Monthly R.*, May 1972, pp. 192–8.

13 See pp. 116–17. In 1965 Britain ended the practice of double-tying her aid, with the consequence that India could buy what she liked in Britain with the aid-granted exchange. If this aid exchange was used to buy goods that would have been bought anyway in Britain, then the foreign exchange previously used to buy such goods was freed to purchase other goods from Britain—or elsewhere. Most other countries still double-tie their aid. (See also Datar, *India's economic relations with the USSR* . . ., ch. 4.)

14 India, Min. Information & Broadcasting, *India 1968; a reference manual* (1968), pp. 345–6.

15 L. B. Pearson & others, *Partners in development* (London, 1969), p. 297. See also I. M. D. Little & others, *Industry and trade in some developing countries* (Paris, OECD, 1970).

16 Indian figure from questionnaire answer to Glasgow Univ. study of British investment in India (see ch. 6); British figure deduced from the provisional input–output table in *Economic Trends*, no. 178, Aug. 1968.

17 C.1373 (1875).

18 Board of Trade, *Overseas trade statistics of the United Kingdom, Dec. 1970* (1971), p. V25. This figure would be even larger if one could allocate the large 1970 export of goods in category 9 (almost certainly arms and ammunition).

19 Throughout this chapter, and in others, the trade group numbers used in the SITC will be avoided wherever possible and titles used instead.

20 These figures do suggest the real trends; and both 1960 and 1970 are fairly 'typical' years.

21 See, e.g., Statement 3, 'Net domestic product by industry & origin at 1960–61 prices', in RBI, *Report* . . . *1968–9*, p. S11.

22 Initially we have discussed the UK's exports to India on a *value* basis, and have thus neglected the effect of price changes. Volume indices of British trade with India by commodity group are not available. They could not greatly affect our conclusion that the 1960 structure of UK exports to India has little to do with their subsequent decline; since their structure differs little from that of total UK exports, their overall price change cannot differ much either.

23 By 1968 the unit values of the major classes of UK exports had risen as follows: (1961 = 100): non-manufactures (SITC 0–4), 106; manufactures (SITC 5–8), 126; chemicals (SITC 5), 113; metals (SITC 6), 130; machinery & transport equipment (SITC 7), 128; and other manufactures (SITC 8), 128 (*Monthly Digest of Statistics*, Dec. 1969, p. 143, table 171).

24 The contents of table 3.4 are constructed from two sources, UK and Indian trade statistics, in the absence of a detailed commodity breakdown by countries for Indian imports. There are some problems involving the c.i.f./f.o.b. calculation, and the fact that the Indian figures are for financial years and the British for calendar years, but the indications of the loss of British share nevertheless hold. See also table 3.10.

25 The figures for SITC groups 0 and 1 are unimportant: for group 0 (food and animals) because the share of this group has always been low for the UK; for group 1 because Indian imports of this category comprise only 0·05% of total imports, and the large British share is due almost entirely to imports of Scotch whisky.

26 In one example of a Soviet-Indian trade agreement, that signed on 20 December 1968, the imports from the USSR are mainly manufactured goods such as machine tools and metal-working machinery, cranes, ball-bearings, tractors, dredgers, newsprint, helicopters, etc.), whereas the exports from India are chiefly of agricultural products (tea, coffee, cashew kernels, spices, etc.), some jute goods, leather shoes, woollen knitwear, and railway wagons (RBI, *Report* . . . 1968–9, p. 223. See also Datar, esp. ch. 4; and M. Kidron, *Pakistan's trade with Eastern bloc countries*, (New York, 1972, pp. 29–41).

27 Donors and recipients agree on the need to phase out food aid as rapidly as possible, but there is little sign that the US Congress is prepared to replace it by other sorts of official development assistance. The exemption of Latin America from the 10% aid cut in the 'Nixon package' of August 1971 implied a further reduction in the share of US aid going to other l.d.c.s, including—and perhaps principally—India. Moreover India seems likely to be the main sufferer from the bizarre alliance (of outright opponents of aid with those who saw it as necessary and sufficient for 'neo-colonialism') that produced the nominal rejection of the Foreign Aid Bill by the US Senate in October 1971.

28 Indian representatives pointed out that the purchases for the Allied armies were at controlled prices which were much lower than prevailing market prices (Ghosh, *Indian economy*, pp. 549 f.). See also D. E. Moggridge, 'From war to peace—the sterling balances', *The*

Banker, Aug. 1972, pp. 1032–5, for a concise analysis of the problems facing the UK, and also the role played by Keynes.

29 The indicator of sterling balances used in Fig. 3.1 is foreign-exchange holdings held by the RBI, which were and are mainly of sterling and long-term sterling securities.

30 Though 1957–8 may seem to be an exception, it should be noted that the subsequent falls in actual imports from the UK are greater than the fall in the percentage of Indian imports coming from the UK. The 1957–8 fall is partly attributable to the Indian government's decision to cut private-sector imports by 38% over that and the following year as part of the measures to counteract the foreign-exchange crisis. As much of the British trade at that time was with the private sector, this had a noticeable effect on export levels, especially over 1958–9.

31 Ghosh, p. 77.

32 See ch. 7, where the relationship between trade and aid is discussed in greater detail.

33 RBI, *Report 1969–70*, Statement 97, pp. S152–3. See also table 7.14.

34 Single-tied aid is tied to purchases from a specific country but not to specific commodities, and double-tied aid is tied both to a specific country and to specific commodities exported from that aid donor. See ch. 7.

35 During the period 1964–6, around 63·4% of total British aid to India was 'switched' to purchases outside the British aid agreements. Of the aid, 15·5% (or approx. a quarter of the switched aid) was spent on other British goods. A further 4·5% of total British aid was spent in the UK by other exporters to India who had been paid by some of the switched aid (the so-called 'reflection' effect) (B. Hopkin & others, 'Aid and the balance of payments', *Econ. J.*, Mar. 1970, p. 13, table IV).

36 For example, British exports to India are heavily concentrated in SITC groups 5–8. SITC groups 0–4 only comprise 3·5% of British exports to India, but 38·5% of total Indian imports (see tables 3.2 and 3.3).

37 HC 442, sess. 1967–8, p. 14, question 5. Conversely it can be argued that Indian licensing practices effectively raise the share of double-tied aid (see Bhagwati/Desai, pp. 197–201).

38 Among the reasons are the following: (1) An l.d.c.'s industrial imports are partly determined by previous imports—'British' steel mills in India generate further import demands for specific British equipment to be used in conjunction with them. (2) Some potential capital-goods imports may *seem* similar but differ technically; then price may not be crucial, especially given the specific knowledge possessed by scarce *experienced* engineers and mechanics in India. (3) British concerns in the Indian private sector prefer British goods (perhaps made by another branch of the same concern), even though alternative sources may be slightly cheaper. (4) India is a battleground for various nations' export-credit schemes, and there is some evidence (see pp. 39; 102) that British credit terms are insufficiently competitive to overcome unfavourable price differentials. (5) Because of the large Indian government stake in the Indian foreign-trade sector, not all import decisions are made on purely market criteria. Although some of the above factors apply in other British markets, in hardly any are they so powerful.

39 There is also room to doubt how far the prices put on particular Soviet-bloc manufactures, especially in the context of barter deals including many items, reflect their real market prices. (See Kidron, op. cit., pp. 47–54.)

40 Parkinson, *Scot. J. Pol. Econ.*, Feb. 1966, p. 21.

41 'British trade performance', in Caves, *Britain's economic prospects*, p. 217, table 5.9.

42 ODM, *An analysis of aid/trade relationships in India* (mimeo., 1969). The size of the pool depends on assumptions about aid tying, export credit terms, etc.: '[The UK] share of the pool, as well as the total size of the pool, is very sensitive to the statistical assumptions we have made about the degree of effective tying of others donors' aid' (p. 29).

43 The figure is from ODM, table 8, p, 25, and Krause, in Caves.

44 *Hindu*, 9 Oct. 1964.

45 *FT*, 4 Dec. 1970.

46 Ibid., 7 Dec. 1970.

47 M. C. Fessey, 'Short-term forecasting of United Kingdom exports', *Economic Trends*, May 1967.

48 Krause (in Caves, p. 221) has a more favourable view of British export finance.

49 Chbr. of Shipping of the UK, *Ann. rep. 1970*, p. 19.

50 *The Economist*, 27 Jan. 1968, pointed out, for instance, that while the West German firm

Siemens had 147 sales engineers in Britain at one period in 1967, a comparable British firm, English Electric, had only 4 in Germany (p. 43). Nicholas Stacey also indicated the lack of effort put into exporting by British firms when he estimated that during 1960, expenditure on overseas marketing research and advertising came to only 0·52% of the value of manufactured exports ('Problems of export marketing', *Planning*, 19 July 1962). It is not, of course, proven that higher outlays are profitable in such markets to British firms, or even that they would be *net* earners of foreign exchange.

51 W. B. Reddaway, *Effects of UK direct investment overseas; final report* (CUP, 1968), p. 216, table xvi.1.

52 In 1970, for the first time in many years, the value of British exports to India rose, by about 12%, from £61·3mn to £72·9mn. In 1971 there was a truly dramatic jump—93% in dollar terms—with a further 5% rise in 1972 (IMF, *Direction of trade annual 1968–72*, p. 112). However, this seems in part to be a once-and-for-all effect due to (a) the delayed effects of Britain's 1967 devaluation (India's share in total British exports changed little); (b) the re-tying of some British aid; (c) India's partly recovered capacity to import (though Britain's share in total Indian imports also leapt, from 6·6% in 1970 to 15·0% in 1972); and—perhaps most importantly—(d) sales of armaments, since much of the rise in British exports to India seems to have occurred in SITC category 9, which covers (classified) items such as arms and ammunition. See ch. 11 for a fuller discussion of this rather interesting section of the International Trade Accounts.

53 The projections in table 3.9 are, of course, at 1967–8 prices. As the Indian economy got under way after the setbacks of the mid-1960s, imports ran above the plan projections, and given the current aid shortage new balance-of-payments strains appeared.

54 'Economic progress in India', *Three Banks R.*, Mar. 1970, p. 20.

55 For instance, it was specifically advised that the UK delegation to the EEC should be strengthened and a cadre of officers with a special knowledge of European economic affairs built up. The orientation towards the developed countries was also seen in the recommendation that 'the careers of commercial officials should concentrate on either the area where new export opportunities are to be won by active effort in *advanced industrial countries*, or in areas where this effort depends more on the traditional inter-governmental diplomatic activity and also on responsive work to the needs of exporters. We also recommend that the shift of Britain's export promotion resources *to the former area* should continue' (our italics). See Cmd 4107, July 1969, p. 88.

56 HC 288, sess. 1969–70, para. C63, p. 30.

Notes to pp. 42–65

Chapter 4. Indian Exports to Britain

1 Tea, cotton textiles, jute manufactures, tobacco, oilcakes, and cashew kernels accounted for 71·9% of Indian exports to Britain in 1960/1 and 56·7% in 1969/70. Although some diversification has occurred, this still represents a very concentrated import structure (RBI, *Report 1969–70*, pp. S.137–41, S.148).

2 These sometimes provoke specific responses. For example, in response to the import deposit scheme of November 1968 (which required UK importers to place six-month interest-free deposits with Customs to the value of 50%—later reduced—of the value of their imports) the RBI, to enable Indian exporters to grant the necessary credit facilities to UK buyers of commodities covered by the scheme, allowed Indian firms eight months from the date of shipment for realizing 50% of the proceeds of such exports, while the other 50% had to be ingathered within the normal six months allowed (RBI, *Report . . . 1968–9*, p. 205). Britain ended the import deposit scheme in 1970.

3 D. Winch, *Economics and policy; a historical study* (London, Hodder, 1969), p. 59.

4 Measures involving some degree of imperial preference began with the selective tariffs in the 1915 budget, and continued with the Safeguarding of Industries Act, 1921, and with the 1925 budget and Import Duties Act of 1932 (R. Fay, *Great Britain from Adam Smith to the present day*, 4th ed. (London, Longman, 1937), p. 86).

5 794 HC Deb., 193, 22 Jan. 1970; see also FBI, *The British Commonwealth, Commonwealth preferences and the sterling area* (London, 1958), pp. 15–16, M. Lipton & P. Tulloch, 'India and the enlarged EEC', *Int. Aff.*, Jan. 1974.

6 For a CP to be potentially valuable to an exporter such as India, the commodity concerned must (a) be a major export (i.e. tea, cotton or jute textiles, cashew nut kernels, tobacco, or oilcakes); and (b) exposed to potential competition from non-CP exports in the Commonwealth markets. A crude test of (b) is a large share of non-CP exports in world trade. Thus in tea CPs cannot have helped India much, because typically only around 21% of world tea exports come from non-Commonwealth sources (Int. Tea Cttee, *Ann. B. Statist. 1971* (London, 1971), table C1, p. 11). In jute textiles, India and Pakistan accounted for most exports (83·5% of world total—see p. 59) and thus CPs meant little. In cotton textiles growing non-Commonwealth competition might have made CPs important, but the 1959 Indo-British trade agreement introduced a quota system, which (though protecting India against the growing relative efficiency of Hong Kong and later Pakistan) removed most of the potential gains from CPs (see M. & T. Zinkin, *Britain and India; requiem for empire* (London, Chatto, 1964), p. 161, and pp. 43–4 below).

7 Parkinson, in *Scot. J. Pol. Econ.*, Feb. 1966, p. 31. As we shall see later in the commodity analysis, this particular feature of progress has also affected Indian exports to Britain.

8 RBI, *Report . . . 1969–70*, Statement 93, pp. S.146, S.148.

9 Total Indian rupee exports in calendar 1960 f.o.b. by SITC group have been obtained from the (last published) monthly figures given in the Composition of Exports tables in the RBI *Bull.*, May 1961–Apr. 1962 inclusive. UK (1960) imports from India, sterling and c.i.f., in each SITC group are from table 4.2, and they were converted to rupees at the IMF sterling selling rate for 1960 (£1 = 13·3854 Rs). These UK imports were then adjusted to remove the f.o.b.–c.i.f. discrepancy by applying, to each SITC group, the ratio of *total* Indian-recorded exports to the UK to *total* UK-recorded imports from India converted to rupees, both totals being for calendar 1960. (On this basis transport and insurance costs come to some 14·7% of the value of exports c.i.f.). The share of India-to-Britain exports f.o.b. in total Indian exports f.o.b. was now calculated for each commodity group for 1960. Then for each commodity group of total Indian exports in 1969/70 (RBI, *Report . . . 1969–70*, Statement 91, pp. S.142–3) the 1960 share was applied, and the products added and finally expressed as a percentage of total Indian exports in 1969–70. The result was 25·68%.

10 See below, pp. 47f. The Fourth Five-Year Plan, and the annual plans for 1967–8 and 1968–9, both placed—at least verbally—'top priority' on improving the agricultural sector and the inputs for it.

11 S. J. Wells, 'Foreign trade: a commodity study', in Streeten/Lipton, pp. 293 f.

12 During late 1965 and early 1966 the black-market rate for the rupee increasingly reflected the unreality of the official market rate, Rs13·3 = £1. By early June 1966 the black-market rate had risen to Rs30 = £1. Speculators, at least, believed that devaluation was inevitable.

13 They have included the activities of the Export Credit and Guarantee Corporation (such as the provision of export guarantees and insurance cover for Indian exporters); fiscal incentives to help exporters plough back profits to develop markets; grants-in-aid to export houses to promote marketing efficiency and overseas market research; the establishment of the Kandla free-trade zone; schemes for supplying exporters with raw materials at international prices (as in polythene and PVC resins); replantation subsidies for tea estates; loan assistance to the jute industry, etc. For details see the RBI *Reports . . .* (appendices on Export Promotion Announcements).

14 *FT*, 2 Mar. 1970.

15 RBI, *Report . . . 1968–9*, app. 10, 'Fourth Five-Year Plan: a draft', p. 225.

16 B. I. Cohen, 'The stagnation of Indian exports', *Q.J. Econ.*, Nov. 1964.

17 B. R. Shenoy, *Indian planning and economic development* (Bombay, Asia, 1966), pp. 30 f. However, most of the countries normally cited in support of such a view required substantial state action to encourage exports in the first place.

18 *FT*, 12 Aug. 1970. Other state corporations have been set up recently to deal with trade in raw cotton and raw jute, with the intention of boosting exports of manufactured cotton and jute goods by providing a stable and better-quality supply of the raw material, and in March 1971 a Trade Development Authority was established to boost India's export trade (ibid., 16 Mar. 1971).

19 Singh, *India's export trends*, pp. 16 f., has an excellent outline of the relative importance of external and internal factors affecting export performance.

20 RBI, *Report . . . 1969–70*, Statements 84–90.

21 Schumpeter, *English overseas trade statistics*, table XVIII, pp. 60–2.
22 C.1373 (1875). In 1872, however, tea comprised only 2·7% of exports from British India (raw cotton 18%; raw jute 6%; rice 4%; indigo 3%).
23 In 1934–5, for instance, Indian exports of tea were Rs200 mn, of which 86% went to Britain (Pramathanath Banerjea, *A study of Indian economics* (London, Macmillan, 1944), pp. 148–9). Much of this was, and still is, re-exported from Britain.
24 CCE *Statement*, ii, 1960–9.
25 From 9·8 lb. in 1956–60 to 8·4 lb. in 1969 (*FT*, 30 July 1970). Though consumption rose again slightly in 1970, there were signs that the decline was continuing, for by 1972 per caput consumption was down to only 8·0 lb. per annum, nearly one-fifth down on the level at the start of the 1960s (*Trade & Industry*, 22 Mar. 1973, p. 656).
26 *FT*, 17 July 1970.
27 Ibid. Tea-bags are not, however, 35% cheaper, as the difference in volume of tea needed per cup is made up by more costly packaging and the current level of advertising. Even if the economy in the volume of tea used allowed some future reduction in tea prices, it seems unlikely, given the low price-elasticity of demand for tea in Britain, that much expansion of sales would follow. Richard Stone (*Measurement of consumers' expenditure and behaviour in the UK during 1920–38* (CUP, 1954, vol. i) suggests an income-elasticity of demand of 0·04, and a price elasticity of 0·3, in 1920–38. Rising incomes have since lowered the first figure, while growing acceptance of coffee as a possible alternative has raised the second.
28 Singh, pp. 71–2. See p. 88 below for a discussion of the British involvement in tea plantations in India.
29 Indian exports of tea in 1969 (table 4.12) are not comparable with previous years as tea shipments were severely hampered by continued labour disputes in the Calcutta docks and warehouses and in many of the tea-growing areas.
30 Even within groups such as 'high grown' teas, teas from different districts and even different gardens in one district tend to be differentiated, at the highest level on the lines of the various wine chateaux. Thus they do not form a perfect market with perfect substitution.
31 Cohen, *Q.J. Econ.*, Nov. 1964, p. 610.
32 da Costa, *Ind. Econ. J.*, July–Sept. 1965, pp. 49 f.
33 Indian tea production is split roughly 60:40 between common or low-grown teas competing mainly with East African teas, and high-grown or quality teas which compete mainly with Ceylon. One cannot, however, assume a 60:40 split in Indian exports, as more low-grown teas are consumed internally than exported, and most high-grown teas are exported.
34 A rough idea of relative increases in wage costs can be gained from the following:

	1959	1966	% increase 1959–66
Ceylon			
Earnings in tea plantations, day (Rs)	Rs2·65	Rs2·84	7·02
India			
Earnings per day of agric. workers (Rs)	Rs1·15	Rs2·20	91·31
East Africa–Kenya			
Earnings per months of agric. workers (EA/-)	69/-	110/-	59·42

(*Source:* ILO, *Bulletin*, Oct. 1969, p. 638.)

In 1966 the average daily basic wage for Assam Valley male tea plantation workers was fixed at around Rs2·22 per day, plus dearness and foodstuffs allowances. This is close to the figure of Rs2·20 above (*Indian Labour Yearbook 1966* (1968), pp. 52–3).
35 Singh, p. 65.
36 Export duties had been levied on Indian teas earlier, but were reduced in 1962 and abolished in 1963. Export quotas were removed in 1961.
37 In September 1968 a replantation subsidy was announced by the Indian government for tea bushes over 50 years old.
38 India and Ceylon have an international agreement on joint tea marketing which came into force in June 1968. This provides for joint action in the fields of promotion, marketing,

and research to improve the economic viability of the respective tea industries, including joint blends. The major aim on the export side is to obtain a better price (RBI *Report . . . 1968–9*, p. 205). However, Ceylon denied in late 1970 that one way of achieving this goal would be for India to buy Ceylon's entire tea exports in order to control supplies (*FT*, 6 Oct. 1970). Joint action did have some success in raising world tea prices. The Mauritius conference of tea exporters in 1969 agreed to cut tea shipments by 90 mn lb in 1970, pushing prices up from 77d/kg in 1969 to 109d/kg over the first ten months of 1970 (ibid., 1 Dec. 1970). These prices were, however, still well below earlier levels. In April 1973 the Tea Council was able to resume its advertising campaign in Britain, aiming at the 13–24 age group, with the slogan 'Tea goes pop' (*FT*, 26 Apr. 1973, p. 31).

39 In 1971 the Indian foreign trade minister said that although India had lost 12% of her tea trade with Britain because of competition from Ceylon and African countries, this had been made good by export to other countries (ibid., 10 June 1971). He mentioned the USSR and USA as particularly promising markets, though this neglects the potential competition from Chinese tea in the latter market.

40 *FT*, 30 Apr. 1971.

41 SBI, *Monthly R.*, July 1971, p. 251.

42 RBI, *Report . . . 1968–9*, p. S136 f.

43 In 1970 India's tobacco *yield* at 0·78 metric tons per ha. was substantially less than those of other major producers, namely USA (2·37), Mainland China (1·17), and Brazil (1·00) (FAO, *Monthly B.*, 26/6, p.22).

44 Commonwealth Secretariat, *Plantation crops* (London, 1964–9), gives (in mn lb):—

	1960–2	1965–7
Indian exports to UK—annual average	44·6	39·8
Total Indian exports—annual average	112·7	112·5
UK share	39·5%	35·3%

Other major buyers were Egypt, EEC, and the USSR.

45 *FT*, 20 Feb. 1970.

46 The number of cigarettes smoked in Britain rose from 113·4 bn (10^9) in 1960 to 124 bn in 1969, a 9·7% increase. The change to filters and its effect can be seen from the reduction in the weight of tobacco used in cigarettes in Britain compared to the number of cigarettes produced.

	1968	1969
No. of cigarettes produced (bn)	121·8	124·0
Weight of tobacco used in cigarettes (mn lb)	220·2	216·5
No. of cigarettes/lb tobacco	553	572

(*FT*, 20 Feb. 1970, quoting figures from Tobacco Advisory Council.)

Britain is also importing more of its tobacco in 'stripped' form, and thus with waste products removed the weight of tobacco imported will fall, even though the amount of utilizable tobacco remains constant.

47 Ibid., 17 Jan. 1972. The identification of genetic factors, exposing perhaps 55% of persons to specially magnified cancer risk from cigarettes, may at last produce a permanent reduction in the habit (*Sunday Times*, 2 Dec. 1973).

48 'Apparent' because some money would be diverted from tobacco to dutiable goods. To this would also have to be added the decline in health costs, etc.

49 F. Pyrard, *The voyage of François Pyrard of Laval to the East Indies* (Paris, 1697), ii, 245, quoted (as a 'picturesque exaggeration' of an Indian cotton-weaving industry, nevertheless 'one of the great feats of the industrial world of the year 1600'), in W. H. Moreland, *India at the death of Akbar* (London, Macmillan, 1920); A. S. Pearse, *The cotton industry of India* (Manchester, Inst. Fed. of Master Cotton Spinners' & Manufacturers' Ass., 1930), p. 15.

50 Pearse, pp. 19–20.

51 In 1958 British India exported £4·3mn of raw cotton and only £0·8mn of manufactured goods, whilst importing English (*sic*) cotton goods to the value of £5·6mn (ibid., p. 21).

52 Ibid. At least one historian has suggested that in the absence of such duties, tariffs and prohibitions, '. . . the mills of Paisley and Manchester would have been stopped at the outset and could scarcely have been set in motion even by power of steam' (W. Wilson, *History of India* (London, 1840), i, 385).

53 Pearse, p. 191. India represented over 40% of the market for British cotton textile exports.

54 Mitchell, *India; an American view*, p. 134. The conflict of interests and purpose between Indian and British textile manufacturers produced by the Indian tariffs and the Ottawa Agreement, led to both the 1935 and the 1939 Indo-British trade agreements being defeated in the Indian central legislature. In both cases, the votes were overruled by the GOI and the agreements were ratified in the face of strong opposition from Indian textile manufacturers.

55 Most of the trade in cotton textiles between the two countries is in goods in SITC categories 652·1 (grey, unbleached, unmercerized fabrics) and 652·2 (bleached, dyed, mercerized, printed, and otherwise finished). The former category predominates in the share of total Indian cotton textile imports to Britain. From the 1962–3 average to the 1969–70 average, however, the former fell from 95·6 to 87·4% by volume, and from 88·2 to 84·6% by value.

56 The problems facing the industry are legion. Raw cotton is in short supply, and consequently its price was, historically speaking, a high share of production costs since 1960. Cotton mills are old, and in the 1950s automation, and in general big urban mills, were not encouraged as they would interfere with the programmes to create small-scale rural loom employment. Wage costs have risen rapidly, and mills are running at low levels of utilization. The Indian government has recognized the danger of the situation, and among measures designed to help the industry are the establishment of a National Textile Corporation, the introduction of export-promotion schemes, the establishment of a Cotton Trade Corporation, and investment allowances to encourage automation.

57 CSO, *Ann. abstract of statistics 1970*, p. 177.

58 Textile Council, *Cotton . . .* 1, 37, shows total yarn costs for 205 yarn (including winding) in pence per lb for 1968 of 48·6 (20·25 new pence) in the UK, 39·2 (16·33) in India, 38·8 (16·16) in Hong Kong, and 37·7 (15·70) in Pakistan. Evidence of redeployment is on p. 28 (table 3) and pp. 86–8, where the juxtaposition of table 1 and para. 416 is of special interest.

59 In 1959, when India imposed pseudo-voluntary quotas on cotton-textile exports to Britain; and in 1960, when India released Britain from the 1939 agreement to let Britain enter Efta, provided India would not suffer from Efta competition, a proviso violated by Portugal's textile sales to Britain, The import surcharge of 15% in 1964 and the 1969 import deposit scheme (p. 57), however, set precedents for unilateral, non-consulting violation by Britain of her trade treaties with India (and others).

60 This embarrassing frankness is cited in *India Weekly*, 13 Jan. 1972.

61 RBI, *Report . . . 1968–9*, p. 206; *FT* 20 Nov. 1970.

62 *FT*, 2 Apr. 1970.

63 Annual quota levels will now be fixed. These will only be increased if the UK market for such jute goods increases, and if an increase in imports will not endanger the employment position in the jute industry (Commonwealth Secretariat, *Industrial fibres*, no. 18 (1969), p. 215).

64 Major Dundee jute firms, such as Tay Textiles, have moved out of jute into synthetics such as polypropylene, and as a result redundancies in the jute industry, now facing a recession, have at times run high; 800 in the Dundee area alone between June 1969 and January 1970 (*FT*, 5 Feb. 1970).

65 'Oilcakes' consist mainly of meal and cake from groundnuts, cottonseed, castor, linseed, and rape. Most of India's exports to Britain are of groundnut cake and meal, though some cottonseed cake and meal is also exported.

66 *FT*, 4 Aug. 1970. As Mauritius and the West Indies diversify, Britain (and France) may increasingly find it cheaper to import raw sugar from India rather than to maintain domestic beet production, often at a high cost.

67 However, it has recently been stated that 'a good market potential has also been identified for a few labour-intensive engineering products in the developed countries of the West' (SBI, *Monthly R.*, May 1971, p. 180).

68 *The Times*, 14 Nov. 1966.

69 *FT*, 12 May 1967.

70 High freight rates do seem to constitute a major bottleneck for Indian exports of manufactured goods, even when the markets are geographically close to India. For example, the freight costs of sending bicycles to Mauritius can amount to over 31% of the f.o.b. price of such goods and Latin American markets are said to be out of reach, with freight accounting for 55–80% of the f.o.b. value of Indian exports (SBI, *Monthly R.*, May 1971, p. 182). Unless Indian goods have either distinct production cost advantages or technical merit, such transfer costs will make competition with European and North American producers in the British market difficult.

71 Ibid., p. 181.

72 R. Cooper, 'Tariff issues and the third world', *World Today*, Sept. 1971, pp. 401–10; D. Wall, 'Trade issues for the developing countries', in ODI, *Britain, EEC and the third world* (London, 1971), esp. pp. 41–5.

73 The EEC has reduced its duty on tea in containers to 5% (from 23%) and suspended totally its duty on bulk tea (from 18%), though these concessions have been largely annulled by rising turnover taxes (notably in Germany), and anyway would confer little benefit on LDC tea producers (who face no competition from EEC and hardly any from Associates), especially as tea is not price-elastic. Other concessions are small; EEC has reduced the rate of duty on *unground* pepper from 20 to 17%, on sports goods, and on coffee (not much help to India, as in any case regulated by International Coffee Agreement export quotas).

74 *India and the European Economic Community* (London, Asia, 1966), p. 221. For discussions of recent developments, see P. Tulloch, *The seven outside* (London, ODI, 1973); and Lipton/Tulloch.

75 Dharma Kumar, 'The new Community and the developing Commonwealth', *Round Table*, Oct. 1971, p. 480.

76 *FT*, 24 Sept. 1970, p. 9.

77 Kumar (*Round Table*, Oct. 1971, p. 475) puts the change succinctly: 'In 1962–63 . . . the consequences to other members of the Commonwealth were considered of major importance by all the parties concerned. The negotiators drew up detailed plans to reduce the potential losses of trade to such countries as India. Gaitskell emphasized the damage that would be done nevertheless to India and Pakistan. . . . In 1971 only Commonwealth sugar and a few industrial raw materials were mentioned in the White Paper. Scarcely anyone mentioned the poorer countries of the Commonwealth in the House of Commons debate on the Community. . . . Everyone, from anti-market MPs to the Asian countries themselves, seems to believe that if the Commonwealth rouses feelings in Britain, it is feelings of kinship towards Australia, New Zealand and Canada, not of brotherhood with the multi-coloured poor.'

78 M. Lipton & others, *The effects of an enlarged European Economic Community on less developed countries*; report of a conference at Falmer, July 1970 (Sussex Univ., Centre for Contemporary European Studies, 1971).

Notes to pp. 66–78

Chapter 5. Invisibles

1 The truth of Adams's assertion remains to be proved, for although capital did flow into Britain from India from the 18th century onwards, no one knows whether it went into investment in British manufacturing, into new colonial ventures, or indeed into consumption. The 'nabobs' presumably invested mainly in land and property in England, given their class background: perhaps the surpluses yielded by such investment were later transferred to industry.

2 '*Invisible exports* represent the overseas earnings of banks, insurance companies, merchants, and shippers together with the foreign profits made by the oil companies and the receipts of interest, profits and dividends from investments overseas that generations of British companies and individuals have built up over the years as well as the cash foreign tourists spend in the UK' (*FT*, 14 Apr. 1970, p. 27). There are also invisible *imports*—British payments—in each of the above categories.

3 See chs. 7 & 11.

4 Non-aid intergovernmental transfers; transportation and travel; specialized services (such as insurance, banking, and export-import trading); the remittance of interest, profits, and dividends from overseas investments; and private transfers. These are the IMF's *Balance of payments yearbook* categories 3–9; 3–8 are 'services' and 3–9 are 'invisibles'.

5 'Although collection of figures for the UK has improved and will go on improving, statistics for the various sectors of the world invisibles market—how they are expanding or contracting, how much of a particular market the U.K. accounts for—are still in very short supply. It is a matter of guesswork' (*FT*, 14 Apr. 1970). We ruefully concur.

6 K. Drake, *Britain's exports and the balance of payments* (London, Sphere Books, 1970), p. 69.

7 *Economic Trends*, no. 239, Sept. 1973, p. xxiv.

8 A. E. Holmans, 'Invisible earnings', *Scot. J. Pol. Econ.*, Feb. 1966, pp. 50, 63.

9 There were several causes: sterling devaluation in 1967, the attractiveness of 'swinging Britain', and the restriction on the overseas holiday spending of British travellers resulting from British balance-of-payments considerations.

10 The OSA includes most of the major countries of the Commonwealth, except Canada, together with a number of other countries which rely on sterling as their reserve currency.

11 In 1965–8 the annual debit on invisible services came to £58·4mn (IMF, *Balance of payments yearbook*, vols. 17–22), or £74·2mn (CSO, *Economic Trends*, Sept. 1970). This huge difference, partly due to definitions, highlights the problems of finding comparable invisibles data. However, reliance will be placed mostly on the IMF data, which are roughly consistent with (although more aggregated than) the RBI data included in the *Annual Reports*. The IMF has labelled all the data on Indian invisible as 'preliminary' (1960 excepted), and has not yet issued a set of finalized invisible accounts. For this reason, the RBI figures may be slightly more accurate.

12 The British share of India's dealings with the sterling area in the services account (IMF 3–8) fell slightly between 1964 and 1969: credits from 65·4 to 61·4%, debits from 84·6 to 77·6% (table 5.5).

13 K. T. Shah, *Trade, tariffs and transport in India* (Bombay, National Book Depot, 1923), p. 53. He also quotes (p. 54) a reply by Montgomery Martin to a House of Commons Select Committee in 1840: 'It is a curious calculation to allow, that estimating the sums of money drawn from British India for the last thirty years at three millions per annum, it amounts, at 12 per cent (the Indian rate of interest), compound interest, to £723,997,971.' It is unlikely that British development assistance to India over the next thirty years will be of the magnitude of the above figures expressed in 1970 prices. Compare M. ul-Haq, 'Mr Polarski's dilemma', in B. Ward et al. (eds), *The widening gap* (Columbia, New York, 1971), pp. 278–9.

14 *Daily Mail*, 16 May 1930.

15 See ch. 3 for a discussion of this valuation (Mitchell, *India; an American view*, p. 53).

16 'Up to 1931, there was always a net inflow of specie into India from foreign countries. This inflow of gold served to pay for a portion of the balance of payments, the remaining portion of which was accounted for by "invisible imports". The items consisted of the Home Charges, interest on foreign capital invested in India, and payments for shipping, banking, insurance and other services rendered by foreigners in this country . . . these . . . payments . . . exceeded in value the balance of trade in merchandise only. The difference was made up in exports of gold' (Banerjea, *Study in Indian economics*, p. 150).

17 Between 1930–1 and 1939–40 India ran an average yearly surplus on *visible* trade of some Rs731mn, and had net outflow of gold and silver specie to Britain of Rs2170mn, mostly on private account. Thus there was a yearly net flow of specie towards Britain of around Rs217mn (£16·3mn) (*Statistical abstract for British India* no. 72, C.6441 (1943), tables 254, 256, 261 f.).

18 'All unclassified payments have been entered in this item because it is believed that most of them are for services'. It also includes agency services, motion-picture film rentals, royalties, subscriptions to periodicals, and and technical and professional services (IMF, *Balance of payments yearbook, 1970*, India, p. 3)—all, however, areas where Britain would expect to be in surplus with India. Perhaps a further explanation lies in payments by British firms operating in India for services from Indian banks and government agencies—transactions with hardly any counterpart 'the other way' because Indian investment in Britain is negligible.

19 The IMF *Balance of payments yearbooks* start to disaggregate the data in 1956, when India ran an invisible surplus with Britain of around Rs236mn (£17·7mn). Earlier IMF *Yearbooks* give little detailed information, but if one combines the figures for investment income, other services and government transactions for 1950 and 1951, one achieves the following (Rsmn):—

	1950	1951
Total Indian invisibles balance	−13	−7
Indian invisibles balance with Britain	−17	0

20 One other (Indian) estimate for net Indo-British invisibles exists, and it is consistent with the IMF figures in table 5.8, although on a different basis. These Finance Ministry estimates (India, *Pocket book 1965*, p. 123) are for financial years, and no subcategories are available. However, both series are of the same order of magnitude as IMF data, and move in parallel:

Values in £mn	1960	1962	1963
IMF—calendar years	−7·7	−13·7	−6·1
Pocket book—financial years (e.g. 1960/1)	−10·5	−12·8	−8·2

21 UK Treasury, *Civil estimates, 1960/1* to *1969/70* (published as HC Papers), Votes on Class II/3; Class II/2; and Class IV/1. These estimates do not form a comparable series; definitional changes and reorganization complicate the issue.

22 The total staff employed by the IHC rose from 691 in 1960/1 to 765 in 1968/9 (UK-based staff from 95 to 115), but by 1970/1 total staff had fallen to 597 (108) (HC 302, sess. 1970–1, pp. II–12–13). (See pp. 172–3 for details.)

23 Also included in this category is the expenditure of any other British official and semi-official agencies, such as the Commonwealth War Graves Commission. About £1,000 per annum is spent in maintaining the graves and cemeteries of Britons buried in India; such graves, even at the turn of the century, numbered over 2 mn (Philip Woodruff, *The men who ruled India* (London, Cape, 1963), ii, 202).

24 The RBI's figures for Indian invisible trade are presented on a slightly different basis to those of the IMF (tables 5.5, 5.8). In the RBI accounts, which are available only for major groups of countries such as the Sterling and Dollar Areas, all 'transportation' is combined, and includes the freight charges and payments of IMF categories 3 and 4. Thus this section will review what evidence exists on the whole transportation relationship, and will therefore also cover some data from section (ii) above.

25 Drake, p. 73.

26 Other factors damaging British shipping included the rapid loss of passenger revenue to air travel; the relatively slow growth of sterling-area trade which accounted for most British shipping business, coupled with the faster growth of trade in areas where Britain was not a major provider of shipping services, such as Europe and Japan; and the growth of subsidized, prestige fleets of countries such as the USSR and Eastern Europe, and of 'flags of convenience' (i.e. tax avoidance), such as Liberia and Panama.

27 This does not mean that India was not a maritime nation. In shipbuilding, for example, India has a long, and to Britons perhaps surprising, record. In 1819–20, of the few ships over 1,000 tons trading with India, 9 were built in India, including the largest merchantman, the *Earl of Balcarres*, of 1417 tons GRT, owned by the East India Company and built in 1815 in Bengal. *Lloyds Register of Shipping 1819* also reserved their highest classification for Indian teak-built ships. The first steamship built in India was launched in Bombay in 1829, though later India found it hard to compete with European shipbuilding centres like the Clyde in producing iron and steel ships. Consequently, shipbuilding remained relatively unimportant until the past decade or so. For the view that Britain deliberately destroyed Indian shipbuilding capacity to build up her own, see Nehru, *The discovery of India*, p. 297. See also ch. 9 for a discussion of military shipbuilding.

28 *FT*, 17 Dec. 1970. The first two ships ordered were worth £10mn and were due for delivery in 1973–4.

29 UN, *Statist. Yb.* 1970, pp. 429–30.

30 Between 1960 and 1967 British freight and charter rates (in dollars) for general cargo rose by 20·6%, against a rise of only 8·5% by West Germany and 5% by Norway, and Holland's rates actually fell by 19·3% (ibid., *1968*, p. 431). This is inconclusive: shipping statistics and rates are very complex, covering cross-trading, time-charter freights, and earnings from foreign ships on charter. Further, the structures (by type, distance, and rates) of shipping by major nations have altered in different ways. Yet it does seem that—despite devaluation—British rates for general cargo have deteriorated further relative to West Germany and Norway since 1967 (ibid., *1970*, p. 433). Certainly in the (small but suggestive) *passenger* shipping sector, the UK's share of passengers fell in the late 1960s; from 64 to 53% of shipborne arrivals to the UK and from 62 to 52% of departures, from 1967 to 1969 (excluding intra-European travel): Chbr of Shipping of the UK, *British shipping statistics 1970–1* (London, 1971), p. 57.

31 CSO, *Ann. abstract of statistics 1970*, pp. 239–40.

32 The IMF figures in table 5.8 rely on the Indian exchange record for the credit figures and are not comprehensive, for some unidentified travel expenditure is included in the 'Other Services' category. The debit entries are more accurate, and cover private and official Indian travel (and educational expenses) in Britain.

33 *BTJ*, 23 Sept. 1970, p. 663. Average expenditure per visit—all countries.

34 In April 1967 this was raised to £600 plus fees, and the duration of release from 4 to 5 years to cover Ph.D. courses (RBI, *Report . . . 1967–8*, p. 136).

35 See table 11.10.

36 *BTJ* 23 Sept. 1970, p. 658, table 1. For the 'Other Sterling Area' in 1966–8, annual visitors averaged 218,300; expenditure averaged £21·1mn. (Ave. expenditure per visit: £96.)

37 *Dawn*, 17 Nov. 1967, quoting *Indian Express*. *Dawn* further alleges that the request was in part ignored by the senior Indian ministers and officials who 'come to Britain in droves', and whilst here engage in expensive shopping tours for personal consumer goods. If there is any truth in this, some of the expenditure may well appear under the 'Government' heading in the IMF statistics, whilst other travel debit items are known to be included in 'other services' expenditure.

38 At 31 March 1970 the RBI held some Rs3,314mn of foreign securities (RBI, *Report . . . 1969–70*, statement 27, p. 842). How much of these holdings were of British securities is not known, though it is known that the foreign assets held by the Reserve Bank are 'mainly sterling and include some long-term securities' (IMF, *International Financial Statistics* Dec. 1969, p. 161).

39 M. Kidron, *Foreign investments in India* (London, OUP, 1966), pp. 309 f., esp. table 21, p. 310.

40 Ibid., p. 310. This is no new state of affairs: even in 1931, there was an excess (for British India) of some £25mn annually (RIIA, *The problem of international investment* (London, 1937), p. 223).

41 Net investment is defined as gross investment *minus* gross disinvestment.

42 *FT*, 30 Oct. 1969. The report notes that in 1968 remittances of profits, dividends, and royalties (included in 'Other Services', p. 75) came to £33mn, and were 'a severe strain on the country's limited foreign exchange resources'. Official circles insisted that foreign companies would not be compelled to make such an export effort, but that they were expected to do much more to increase exports so that 'their foreign exchange earnings can at least match their remittances'. Compulsion came later (ibid., 2 Jan. 1975).

44 *BTJ*, 9 May 1969, p. 1302, table 8 and text, and p. 1313.

45 Ibid., 23 Sept. 1970, p. 645. Since book values of capital understate market values, this probably corresponds to the Reddaway estimate of 8% (see also p. 93).

46 RBI, *Bulletin*, June 1970, pp. 936–46; accounts of 184 branches of British firms in India and 223 subsidiaries are examined. No details are given of remittances.

47 RBI, *Foreign collaboration in Indian industry; a survey* (1968), pp. 15, 18, 45, 47, tables 8 & 14 (ch. 2) and 7 & 12 (ch. 3).

48 Even the foundation of the RBI in 1934 was seen by many Indians as a British attempt to maintain control of Indian finances should Indians obtain some voice in the central government. The Imperial Bank was also British-controlled, as were most of the exchange banks operating in India. But the key fact is this: the share of total Indian deposits held by foreign banks had fallen from over 70% in 1914 to 57% in 1937 and finally to only 17% by 1947 (J. J. Pardiwalla, 'Exchange banks in India', *Economic Weekly*, 10 Feb. 1951, p. 154).

49 Kidron, p. 218. Also p. 4, where he notes an RBI Survey in 1951–2 which found that 'more than two-thirds of import and export trade financing (was) by the foreign "exchange" banks'.
50 *The Times*, 22 July 1969; *FT*, 2 Apr. 1970.
51 Only the net receipts of banks from services they provide to 'non-related' customers (arbitrage, net receipts on lending and borrowing in foreign currency, banking charges, and commissions) are included in the 'other services' section of the invisibles account. Other receipts are included under 'interest, profits and dividends' or 'services rendered to or by UK enterprises'.
52 *BTJ*, 23 Sept 1970, p. 642.
53 A. Tripathi, *Trade and finance in the Bengal Presidency, 1793–1833*, p. 11, quoted in Bhagwati/Desai, p. 18.
54 Kidron, pp. 4–5.
55 *BTJ*, 23 Sept. 1970, p. 642. As with banking, part of insurance earnings appears under 'interest, profits and dividends'. In 1969, the total invisible earnings of insurance was made up of earnings of companies, £111mn; earnings of Lloyds, £91mn; and earnings of brokers, £41mn.
56 Imports are recorded c.i.f., and thus they include all but a portion of expenditure or insurance' (RBI, *Report* . . . (all years), notes to Current Account table).
57 Of the 63 non-Indian insurers operating in India at the end of December 1969, 38 were British, 7 from the USA, 4 from Switzerland, and 14 from other countries (SBI, *Monthly R.*, May 1971, p. 166). See also ch. 6.
58 Dept of Trade & Industry (UK), *Business and insurance statistics; Dec. 1966 to Aug. 1968* (1971), pp. 70–73. No Pakistani insurance company operated in the UK.
59 RBI, *Report* . . . *1969–70* (1971), p. S130.
60 *Trade & Industry*, 30 Mar. 1972, p. 576, table 2. There was a slight fall in royalty payments in 1971 (ibid., 12 Apr. 1973, p. 106), to £26mn, just above the 1970 level. It had earlier been suggested that Indian royalty payments to Britain had been running at £5mn yearly (HC 288, sess. 1969–70, p. 30, col. 2, para C64), but this figure is almost certainly an over-estimate in the light of current data.
61 Min. of Industr. Dev. & Company Aff., *Report of the Committee on Foreign Collaboration, May 1967* (1968), p. 1.
62 See *Hindu*, 1 Dec. 1968, for a report of the official statement on the unresolved talks between a British delegation and the Indian government on this issue.
63 HC 442, sess. 1967–8, p. 216, col. 2, para. 960.
64 HC 205–1, sess. 1969–70, p. 249, para. 1023. This figure had been quoted to one of the High Commission staff in New Delhi by an Indian official, but it was noted that ' . . . it did not include people bringing back money in pound notes' (ibid., p. 249).
65 Ibid., p. 174, para. 680. A figure quoted by the High Commissioner to Pakistan.
66 S. R. Lewis, Jr, *Pakistan; industrialization and trade policies* (London, OUP, 1970), p. 125. These remittances were placed into the export bonus scheme which diverted much foreign exchange from black-market to official channels.
67 IMF, *Balance of payments yearbook 1965–9* (1971), June 1971—Pakistan, p.2.
68 Members of the ICS who are British nationals have their pensions paid by Britain under a financial arrangement in 1955 with the Indian government, which had been paying the pensions until then.
69 During the visit of the Select Committee to Pakistan in January 1970, the high commissioner remarked: 'There is going to be a very strong incentive to the Pakistani with his wife to come back to Pakistan and receive the £8 (pension) here because it will buy very much more for him than £8 will . . . (in Britain) . . . You may find that the Zamindars in Pakistan in 20 years time are all old-age pensioners of the UK, which might add very considerably to our present movement of invisibles from Britain to Pakistan' (HC 205–I, sess. 1969–70, p. 175, para. 682).

Notes to pp. 79–96

Chapter 6. Private Investment

1 This chapter deals mainly with UK private investment in India in 1958–69. Official capital flows are examined in ch. 7. The returns to Britain from overseas private capital—interest,

profits, and dividends—are examined with other invisibles in ch. 5. Throughout this chapter, 'private investment' means the direct and portfolio acquisition of capital by British companies and persons in Indian (and other external) branches, subsidiaries, and associates, plus the profits unremitted (i.e. reinvested in India) by such companies, as measured in the long-term capital account of the British balance of payments. For want of information, portfolio investment will not be discussed; also *new* Indian investment in Britain is hardly touched on, primarily because it has been extremely small (see, however, pp. 73–5). For some relevant warnings of the pitfalls likely to be encountered in measuring international private capital flows, especially in the Indo-British context, see Myrdal, *Asian drama*, i, 612–13. We still await the final revised publication of S. Lall & A. Elek, 'Balance-of-payments and income effects of private foreign investment in manufacturing: case studies of India and Iran' (UNCTAD, Committee on Invisibles, TD/B/C 3 Misc., Geneva, 1971, mimeo.)—clearly destined to become the standard treatment of its subject.

2 A. H. Imlah, *Economic elements in the Pax Britannica; studies in British foreign trade in the 19th century* (Cambridge, Mass., Harvard UP, 1958), pp. 70 f.

3 CSO, *The British balance of payments 1972* (1972), p. 26

4 Until 1947, India includes Pakistan and Burma.

5 Quoted in Mitchell, *India; an American view.*

6 RIIA, *Problem of international investment* (London, Cass, 1965), p. 121.

7 Ibid., p. 121. A figure of £379mn of British investment in India 'by 1914', in R. F. Mikesell, ed., *US private and government investment abroad* (Eugene, Oregon, 1962), p. 19. Thus the general magnitude seems about correct.

8 Shah, *Trade, tariffs and transport in India*, p. 53.

9 By 1911, over £140mn had been invested in Indian Railways and Tramways. The first 6,000 miles of railways built before 1872 cost £100mn and, as W. N. Massey, the former Indian finance minister, told the 1872 Parliamentary Enquiry on Indian Finance, 'the contractors had no motive whatever for economy. All the money came from the English capitalist, and so long as he was guaranteed 5% . . . it was immaterial to him whether the funds he lent were thrown into the Hooghly or converted into bricks and mortar' (Mitchell, pp. 98–9).

10 Ibid., pp. 116, 133.

11 RIIA, *Problem of international investment*, pp. 142, 223, 261. The *Manchester Guardian*, in its editorial of 3 January 1930, enormously overstated British capital in India at £1,000mn —Mitchell's 1943 figure!

12 RBI, *Bulletin*, Apr. 1960, p. 477. Book value.

13 2,060 rupees times 1·15, roughly the average ratio of replacement-cost to book values found for March 1950 by M. Mukherjee & N. S. R. Sastry, 'An estimate of the tangible wealth of India', in R. Goldsmith & C. Saunders, eds., *The measurement of national wealth* (Cambridge, Bowes, 1959), p. 374.

14 M. Mukherjee, *National income of India; trends and structure* (Calcutta, SPS Publications, 1969), p. 393, gives Rs52,300mn, for March 1950; this is about one-third of total capital stock. Hence to get back to a 1948 estimate, we deduct about one-third of net domestic capital formation in 1948 and 1949 (ibid., pp. 330, 333).

15 There are, of course, problems with relative prices—less than might appear, because these are book values—and with the definition of private investment in 1930 and 1948. Nevertheless, the relative magnitudes are roughly correct.

16 In November 1915 Lord Hardinge, the then Viceroy, wrote to the secretary of state for India that 'a definite and self-conscious policy of improving the industrial capacity of India will have to be pursued after the war, unless she is to become the dumping ground for the manufactures of foreign nations . . .' (Mitchell, p. 115). Similar sentiments were also expressed by the Montague-Chelmsford Report on Indian Constitutional Reform in August 1918. For an excellent and detailed account of pre-independence investment and investment policy, see A. K. Bagchi, *Private investment in India 1900–39* (CUP, 1972).

17 In spite of the restrictions, the control of British investment overseas is more liberal and flexible than the systems operated in France or Germany. One senior official at the French Ministry of Finance is quoted as wondering whether the present British controls 'are not too intelligent for the country whose balance of payments is as bad as yours' (*Sunday Times*, 1 Feb. 1970).

18 Douglas Jay, when visiting India in 1965 as president of the Board of Trade, stressed

these points when addressing the Federation of the Indian Chambers of Commerce: 'I am greatly in favour of overseas investments, especially in developing countries, and particularly when it is linked with the promotion of British exports'. He added, 'Unfortunately one cannot invest money which one has not got' (*FT*, 24 Apr. 1965).

19 In a parliamentary answer on 1 February 1971, Mr Nicholas Ridley, the under-secretary at the Dept of Trade and Industry, announced that the government was 'studying the feasibility of introducing a National Investment Guarantee Scheme and good progress is being made'. The reasons for the adoption of such a scheme, after years of strong opposition, were said to be firstly a response to indications that some private companies were beginning to run down their investments in underdeveloped countries, and secondly that a guaranteed scheme seemed to offer a financially attractive way for the government to meet its aid promise to the UN (ibid., 15 Feb. 1971, p. 32).

20 Britain had promised the UN that it would 'use its best resources' to reach the UNCTAD target of 1% of GNP for 'financial resource transfers' to LDCs by 1975 (see ch. 7, pp. 101–2). Given the restrictions on expanding public expenditure, the Conservative government evidently considered that encouraging private investment by insurance and guarantee schemes was the cheapest way of reaching the UNCTAD target (ibid., 15 Feb. 1971, p. 32). The Conservative government in 1970 specifically rejected the associated target of 0·7% for public development aid. Labour has not so far confirmed, in government, its commitment to that target while in opposition.

21 Part of this figure can be explained by the existence of tax disincentives and direct restrictions on the remittance of profits in certain countries. In such cases reinvestment is the sole solution.

22 The major problem is that the stock figures are measured in terms of the book value of net assets which seriously (and probably growingly) underestimates the true value in most cases, whereas flow figures mix up book values and current values.

23 Latin America is an exception; the major item must have been manufacturing rather than mineral investments (*BTJ*, 23 Sept. 1970).

24 It was not possible to construct table 3·5 on the same breakdown for all years, so its presentation differs from this one.

25 In 1970, for the first time in five years, the net flow of British private investment to the (non-oil) l.d.c.s fell, from £147mn in 1969 to an estimated £131mn in 1970, although this was still more than double the 1967 level of £63m (Answer by Under-Secretary, Trade & Industry, 12 July 1971, 820 HC Deb., Written Answer 76).

26 OECD/DAC, *1970 Review*, pp. 176–7; for trends, see p. 173. There are serious problems of comparability here, and it would seem the OECD definition of new direct investment covers only the net acquisition of new share and loan capital, and not the other factors noted in table 6.4. Oil and petroleum have been excluded where possible in table 6.8, as this is really a separate category of investment.

27 This question is dealt with further in ch. 5.

28 Reddaway, *Final report*, p. 358. Post-tax profitability was the same in l.d.c.s and developed countries at 8·7% with India slightly worse at 7·7%, but tax rates are so unpredictable that it can be strongly argued that the pre-tax rates count for more, especially in view of the problem of tax-defensive reinvestment noted above (see also n. 78).

29 The only relationship significant at even 10% (but not 5%) was between total UK private investment flows (1961–67) and the share of UK exports (1960–67), for 19 countries. This (mildly) suggests that investment did not take place to avoid protective barriers.

30 Constituent Assembly of India (Leg.) Deb., IV, 1, 2385–6.

31 Ibid., 2385: 'Indian capital needs to be supplemented by foreign capital not only because our national saving will not be enough for the rapid development of the country on the scale we wish, but also because, in many cases, scientific, technical and industrial knowledge and capital equipment can best be secured along with foreign capital'. This, of course, was in the days before aid.

32 RBI, *Report . . . 1968–9*, p. 40; K. K. Sharma, *FT*, 21 Mar. 1973, 26 Sep. 1973, & 27 Dec. 1973. The Foreign Investment Board is a by-product of the Mudaliar Committee's *Report on Foreign Collaboration* (Ch. 5, n. 61), which examined the whole question of permissible foreign investment. For the impact, see K. Rafferty, *FT*, 2 Jan. 1975.

33 RBI, *Bulletin*, Aug. 1969, p. 1150; Streeten/Lipton, 391; *Times of India Yearbook & Directory*, 1972, p. 309. The figures for 1968 in tables 3.10–3.12 allow for revaluation changes conse-

quent to devaluation. They may overstate the importance of such capital in India; in manufacturing, average sales of firms with big private foreign involvement in 1961 were only 1·9 times as large as the average for all Indian public limited companies, though capital value was 2·5 times as high (Lall & Elek, pp. 109, 113).

34 India, *Pocket Book*, 1970, p. 47; see also Lall & Elek, p. 94.

35 Most of these official US portfolio holdings were from loans granted by the US AID and the Eximbank to companies in the Indian manufacturing sector. Over the 1960s as a whole, the growth of portfolio investments, mainly in the form of suppliers' credits, has been an important factor in the development of the Indian private manufacturing sector, as it has allowed enterprises to import raw materials, components and capital equipment, produce the goods, and then pay for the imports by repaying the suppliers' credit.

36 Mukherjee, p. 392.

37 Of the 224 subsidiaries of foreign companies examined, over half (mainly those established before 1947) were wholly foreign-owned. However, over two-thirds of the subsidiaries incorporated between 1956 and 1964 had less than 74% foreign participation, in consonance with giving an increased say to Indian partners (RBI, *Foreign collaboration in Indian industry*). Of subsidiaries registered in the 1960s, most have an even greater share of Indian participation, with foreign investment tending to be increasingly in collaboration agreements rather than direct capital holdings.

38 'Although it is the policy of the Government of India to encourage the growth of Indian industry and commerce . . . to the best of their ability, there is and will be considerable scope for the investment of British capital in India' (*Const. Ass. of India* (*Leg.*) *Deb.* IV, I. 2386 (1949)).

39 The great expansion of Indian entrepreneurs in industries other than the staples of cotton textiles, jute and coal-mines is a post-independence phenomenon (M. & T. Zinkin, pp. 155 f.).

40 K. M. Kurian, *Impact of foreign capital on Indian economy* (New Delhi, People's Publishing House, 1966), p. 300 f. Kurian also states that there is 'no co-ordinated or systematic procedure' for screening foreign investments, but this changed when the Foreign Investment Board was set up in 1969.

41 The only British figures available at time of writing are those for the end of 1968, and these exclude oil and most of the banking and insurance sector. The Indian estimates for a roughly comparable period, March 1967, are still 21 months earlier than British ones, but if we subtract from British data the net flows into the various sectors in 1967 and 1968, then we arrive at a rough sectoral breakdown for the end of 1966, i.e. only 3 months out. But this figure may well be £10mn or more out, as it is impossible to build in the full influence of rupee devaluation in 1966. Yet on the two sets of figures the shares of major sectors are roughly the same, though the Indian total, which includes insurance, banking, and oil, is probably nearer the mark.

42 For a full and lucid account of the penetration and persistence of British companies in India, see esp. Kidron, *Foreign investments . . .*, ch. 5, pp. 188–221. When spelt out in detail, as by Kidron, the range of British interests is astonishing.

43 *FT*, 8 Dec. 1969.

44 See ch. 7, pp. 112–13, and also HC 442, sess. 1967–8, pp. 432–3, App. 9, 'Durgapur Steelworks'.

45 Plantation Enquiry Commission, *Report* (New Delhi, GOI, 1956), pp. 17–22.

46 *FT*, 30 Dec. 1969.

47 *Scotsman*, 16 Jan. 1971, p. 9.

48 *FT*, 8 June 1971, p. 4.

49 In 1968 sterling companies owned only 6·7 of the 407,000 acres under rubber (*Hindu*, 6 Mar. 1968). Deputy-Minister of Commerce and Industry Mohammed Safi, speaking in the Lok Sabka, also revealed that sterling companies held 360,000 acres of tea estates, while 482,000 acres were under the control of Indian companies, many of which, however, are still under British control via managing agencies. See also pp. 50–2 on Indian exports, where the problems of tea plantations are discussed further.

50 However, among the 14 banks nationalized under the Act of 1970 was the Allahabad Bank which was 92% owned by the (British) Chartered Bank. Chartered was reported as saying that although they were disappointed by the 'breaking up of the family', the compensation terms for the 130-branch, £500mn deposit bank were 'unobjectionable'. This

suggests that India is more than keeping her promise made in 1948 to provide fair compensation when nationalisation was desirable (*The Times*, 22 July 1969).

51 *Daily Telegraph*, 30 Jan. 1965.

52 Under the 1951 Calcutta Tramways Act, the Indian government had until 1971 to buy the company from Britain at a price agreed in 1957 of £3·75mn, payable in sterling. In 1968 the company offered to adjust this to allow part of the purchase to be made in rupees, and the sterling portion payable by instalments spread over 5 years (*Sunday Telegraph*, 24 Mar. 1968). In November 1970, the company—making little progress in its negotiations with the West Bengal government—offered to sell its installations for £2mn (*FT*, 27 Nov. 1970), but the state's negotiating committee set up by the state government to advise on the amount that 'might be justifiably offered for the purchase of the company' recommended that the purchase price should not exceed £500,000 (ibid., 12 Mar. 1971). At the time of writing the issue remains deadlocked, although the West Bengal legislature, as early as July 1967, had passed a Bill (Calcutta Tramsways Co. (Taking over of Management) Bill) providing for a limited take-over in the public interest (*Hindu*, 14 July 1967).

53 *Sunday Telegraph*, 24 Mar. 1968.

54 SBI, *Monthly R.*, May 1971, pp. 167–8. From figures published in this source, it would seem that British companies wrote some £6,420mn of net premium income in India during 1969. How much of this found its way to Britain under the invisibles account is not known.

55 Ibid., pp. 165–6. Compensation is monthly: average monthly profit in 1967–9 or 0·25% of 1969 premium income, whichever is higher. If all companies chose the latter, the cost would be £15,600 per month.

56 *FT*, 17 May 1971, p. 6.

57 Ibid., 19 May 1971, p. 8. By 1971 Oil India had produced some 21mn tons out of its estimated reserves of 40mn tons, and thus the search is one to discover and prove new reserves.

58 Ibid., 28 July 1970. See also ibid., 3 Jan. 1975 (letter from Mr M. M. Malhatra).

59 Ibid., 8 July 1971, p. 8. The petroleum and chemicals minister, P. C. Sethi, told parliament in July 1971 that proposals for either equity participation or nationalization were being considered, though either of these measures depended upon overcoming the legal problems involved in the refinery agreements with foreign firms which gave them the right to import crude from sources of their own choice for 25 years. There were also the problems of large foreign-exchange payments consequent on nationalization, and of whether India could find alternative (and cheaper) sources of crude.

60 By 1970 the major foreign oil companies had already offered to participate in the public sector (*Hindu*, 13 Feb. 1969; *FT*, 26 Nov. 1970).

61 352 companies were involved in the Board of Trade survey which forms the basis of the table, compared with an Indian figure of 363 British companies at work in India on 31 March 1968. But as the Indian definition of foreign companies is of 'joint stock companies incorporated outside India but having a place of business within India', it probably excludes some associate companies or minority holdings in Indian companies. (From the viewpoint of registered as distinct from operating companies, the number of British-based companies with Indian interests is probably far greater, as a glance through *Who Owns Whom* will reveal.) (*India, 1969*, p. 198.)

62 RBI, *Foreign collaboration* . . .

63 The reasons for the decline are threefold: first, India is increasingly relying on internal skills; secondly, the strain on the foreign-exchange reserves of the royalties and technical fees involved in collaboration agreements could become intolerable if agreements were continued at the former level; and finally, to avoid the foreign-exchange problem, potential agreements are now vetted by the government much more rigorously than formerly.

64 Though no complete figures for later than 1968 are available at time of writing, Britain headed the list of countries whose companies have been permitted foreign-collaboration arrangements with Indian counterparts to set up manufacturing units in the last quarter of 1970, with 10 agreements out of 49. Now ventures which will be started by British companies include the manufacture of chemicals (ICI); golf balls (Dunlop); air rifles (Webley and Scott); soot-blower equipment (Diamon Power Speciality Corp.); paper-mill machinery (Greenson & Waite); electrical furnaces (Wild Barfield), and diaphragm valves (Saunders Valve Co.) (*FT*, 1 Jan. 1971, p. 7).

65 Ibid., 30 Oct. 1969. It could well be replied that the Indian Government, by reducing

domestic protection, could at a stroke render Indian sales less profitable relative to exports for all firms, including British and other foreign investors; in so far as such investors press for this protection themselves, however, the force of this reply is weakened. Lall & Elek (p. 322) clearly indicate that the more protection is applied to a sector in India, the greater is the risk that private foreign investment will do overall harm to the Indian balance of payments. The thrust of their evidence and analyses, however, is that the net balance-of-payments effect of *new* private foreign investment in India is likely to be very small.

66 *FT*, 5 Feb. 1970 & 27 Dec. 1973.
67 Ibid., 22 Feb. 1970.
68 Ibid., 19 Aug. 1970.
69 *Sunday Times*, 12 June 1966.
70 RBI, *Report . . . 1969–70*, p. 147. See also Blair King, 'The origin of the managing agency system', *J. As. Stud.*, Nov. 1966, pp. 37–48; S. K. Basu, *The managing agency system; in prospect and retrospect* (Calcutta, World Press, 1958); and Ghosh, *Indian economy*, pp. 274–86.
71 R. P. Sinha & J. R. Castree, *The attitudes of British companies with investments in India* (Univ. of Glasgow, 1968, mimeo.). The survey was based on a questionnaire distributed to a sample of Britain's major industrial companies who were known to have large interests in India, and also to some Indian industrialists, whose views in the main supported those expressed by the British firms. We are grateful to Dr Sinha and Mr Castree for permission to quote at length from their findings.
72 The Chairman of British Oxygen, which has substantial investments in India and through-out the world, rated India along with Ceylon as the worst investment areas. 'With high taxation, about 70%, you are then expected to bring the profits back, pay British income tax and have something for the shareholders' dividends' (*FT*, 2 Feb. 1970). The relatively high rate of taxation (actually 55·3%) on profits of British companies in India is partly due to the age-composition of UK capital; see below.
73 Until the 1971–2 Union Budget, priority industries were allowed tax exemption on 8% of their profits. This has now been reduced to 5% and the number of priority industries reduced (SBI, *Monthly R.*, May 1971, p. 173).
74 *FT*, 20 Nov. 1969.
75 SBI, *Monthly R.*, p. 173. The extension was made with a view to discouraging payment of high salaries and remunerations, 'which go ill with the norms of egalitarian society' (p. 173). The allowable overall ceiling on remuneration and perquisites now stands at Rs6,000 per month.
76 Reddaway, *Final report*, p. 219, table XVI.2.
77 Ajit Mazoomdar, *Overseas investment and Indian taxation*, paper presented to Conference on Private Investment and the Developing Countries by the Society for International Development, London, Sept. 1969, p. 15.
78 Reddaway, *Final report*, p. 219, Table XVI.2. Reddaway presents several distinct post-tax profitability figures for British investment in India: 8·2% (p. 219, table XVI.2); 9·0% (p. 221, table XVI.4); 8·6% remitted to UK (p. 326, table XXV.8) and 7·7% (p. 358, table IV.5), depending on how one wishes to define terms.
79 SBI, *Monthly R.*, May 1971, p. 173.
80 *FT*, 10 June 1969.
81 Ibid., 21 Mar. 1973. The 'core' sector (where foreign capital is largely welcomed) of the 1970 policy statement is actually enlarged to include two more industries (paper and cement), making 19 in all (the others are metals; boilers; prime movers; electrical equipment; transportation; industrial, earth-moving and agricultural machinery; machine tools; industrial and scientific instruments, fertilizers, chemicals, drugs, paper, tyres, plate glass, ceramics, and cement). But, in these sectors too, 'small and medium entrepreneurs' are to be given preference if competent', which, it is implied, is seldom!
82 After the first meeting of this group it is reported that the Indian members feel that 'while British industrialists are willing to start such collaboration in fields where they face competition from other countries, they are not so anxious to release markets where Britain has a stranglehold because of historical reasons . . . [and] . . . therefore . . . there is a basic conflict in the British desire for collaboration for mutual benefit . . . and her traditional role as a trading country' (ibid., 22 Oct. 1970, p. 9). Meanwhile, the Indian Ministry of Industrial Development has *recommended* that companies importing foreign technology should com-

pulsorily prescribe minimum expenditure on R & D at least equal to the cost of the imported knowhow during the period of collaborating (ibid., 11 May 1971, p. 9, our italics).

83 Ibid., 11 Nov. 1970.

84 Kidron, p. 310, showed that over 1948–61 profit remissions and royalty fees from India—mainly to the UK—were Rs5,773mn (£433mn) against an inflow of new investment in cash and kind of Rs2,471mn (£185mn), resulting in a net deficit to India of some Rs3,302mn (£248mn). On top of this, a further Rs1,411mn of capital was repatriated, giving a total debit balance of Rs4,713mn (£353mn) on the foreign capital sector's balance of external payments. Earlier, we had noted a similar situation for British investments in India over the 1960–71 period (table 5.14, p. 74), with an Indian debit balance of some £90mn. Such figures do not exhaust the true resource flows on the balance of payments since they ignore export promotion, import substitution, and free 'imported' training; to base a condemnation on such data alone is to mistakenly assume that a curtailment of private foreign investment would have curtailed profit remissions too. There is much more to such investment than (possibly) harmful balance-of-payments effects, most notably extra savings resources. For all that, the crude flow data given above are impressive.

85 FT, 21 Sept. 1972.

Footnotes to Appendix

86 Reddaway, *Effects of UK direct investment overseas; interim report* (CUP, 1967), pp. 56–7.

87 *The Economist*, 11 Sept. 1965, p. 1021. See also: Reddaway, *Final report*, pp. 376 f. For a different view of tea plantations, see above, pp. 87–8.

Notes to pp. 97–121

Chapter 7. Aid to India

1 RBI, *Report . . . 1964–5* Statement 85, p. S139. Against this, Britain also released some £252mn of sterling balances in the period up to 1958, most of which went to India. This, however, does not represent aid, but simply drawing on funds earned by right.

2 IRBD/IDA, *Ann. rep. 1970* (Washington, 1970), p. 46; ibid., *1973*, pp. 86, 92; for prices, see UN, *Monthly B. Statist.*, Sept. 1973, pp. xi–xv. 'Net flow' means 'net of repayments of capital but not interest'; if interest repayments are also deducted the remaining item is 'net transfer', which in 1968 fell short of net flow by over 11%, and in 1971 by over 25%. A further deduction might be made for concealed military aid and support. The 'grant equivalent' of gross aid flows is about 80%; the value of net transfers must also be reduced by about 10–15% to allow for tying. Population growth in recipient countries and export price inflation in donor countries have reduced real aid per recipient person by over 4% per year since 1964.

3 The DAC members are Australia, Austria, Belgium, Canada, Denmark, France, Germany, Italy, Japan, Netherlands, Norway, Portugal, Sweden, Switzerland, the UK, and the USA.

4 OECD/DAC, *1970 review*, p. 171; *1973 review*, p. 181. The fall was only partly due to the fact that all aid is calculated in dollars, in terms of which the UK devalued in 1967.

5 Ibid., p. 181. Aid (net of capital repayments) from all DAC countries stood at 0·52% of GNP in 1960 and in 1962, and 0·34% both in 1970 and in 1972; the UK figures were 0·56% and 0·37% (see table 7, OECD, Press Release of 28 June, 1971, and OECD/DAC, *1973 review*, p. 189).

6 OECD/DAC, *1970 review*, p. 150; *1973 review*, pp. 173–4 'Grant element' in aid comprises total new grants, *plus* the present value of interest forgone on new loans (gross of repayments of capital on past loans). See pp.109–10. The apparently high US grant element is substantially overstated because of the prominence of food aid.

7 The OECD/DAC has calculated that during the period 1960–8 the 'inertial element' in aid flows (measured by the correlation coefficient between the aid given by a particular donor to a particular recipient in different years) has for no pair of successive years been lower than 0·92; if anything, it increased in the second half of the 1960s (*1969 review*, p.178).

8 Over 1967–9 India received an annual average of $1·76 bilateral and $0·27 multilateral net official aid per caput. Against this total of $2·03 per caput, all Commonwealth countries received $4·23 (OECD/DAC, *1970 review*, pp. 202–3). Further, while per caput official

net aid to all developed countries rose from $3·89 over 1960-6 to $4·23 over 1967-9, per caput official aid to India fell slightly, from $2·10 to $2·03.

9 The DAC has investigated the size of this effect and found that, over the period 1960-7, the annual average flow of total net bilateral aid was distributed in such a way that each of the 102 developing countries included in the analysis received $21·3mn, plus $2·00 per caput of its 1965 population. The 'minimum amount per country irrespective of size' hypothesis appears to explain 42% of the flow, with the rest being explained by population size, with a correlation coefficient of 0·88 (OECD/DAC *1969 review*, pp. 178–9).

10 We refer to elite rather than popular attitudes here. Elite support for aid has been eroded from both right and left; see the papers by P. Bauer & K. Griffin, respectively, in T. Byres, ed., *Foreign resources and economic development* (London, Cass, 1972). Popular opinion is on the whole favourable to aid, especially to promote self-help. It is the worst-informed (and least interested) in Britain who like aid the least, and factual information (such as ODA descriptive pamphlets) increases support for aid. See I. Rauta, *Aid and development* (Govt. Social Survey, London, HMSO, 1971).

11 The recommendation of 1965 called for donor countries to give 70% or more of their aid in grant form, or to fulfil three alternative provisions relating to loans and grants, namely:—
   1. At least 81% of official commitments as grants or loans at 3% interest charges or less.
   2. At least 82% of total commitments as grants or loans with a maturity of 25 years or more.
   3. A weighted average grace period of 7 years or more.
In 1969 a DAC supplement to the 1965 recommendation established new objectives leading to softer terms which would substantially reduce debt service payments of poor countries. For details of the new recommendations, see OECD/DAC, *1969 review*, pp. 223 f. These have not yet had time to take effect, whereas one can measure the progress of Britain's acceptance of the 1965 DAC terms (see below, p. 110).

12 The Pearson recommendations were briefly as follows—1. Donors to increase resource transfer to a minimum of 1% of GNP as soon as possible and certainly by 1975; 2. Official assistance to be 0·7% of GNP by 1975 or at least 1980; 3. Terms of aid loans to be: interest below 2%, maturity 25–40 years, grace period 7–10 years (Pearson, pp. 152, 167). Apart from these specific recommendations on terms, from which one member of the Commission dissented, there were other suggestions on debt rescheduling, technical assistance, untying of aid, project aid, etc. The second and main recommendation contrasts with an uninterrupted decline from 0·52% in 1961 to 0·34% in 1970.

13 Britain's performance in the light of the 1965 and 1969 recommendations will briefly be discussed below (p. 110).

14 'We are at the moment in a position to give pretty soft terms in cases which merit it. We would not regard a further easing of loan terms by the United Kingdom as a matter of high priority' (HC 442, sess. 1967–8, Min. of Overseas Development, evidence of Sub-Committee C, para. 1556). The question of aid-tying will be discussed on pp. 110–12.

15 OECD, *Resources for the developing world 1962–8* (Paris, 1970), p. 265. From 1967 to 1972, UK multilateral contributions rose from 10·9% to 21.0% of official aid—as against a rise from 11·3% to 21·9% for DAC aid as a whole (OECD/DAC, *1973 review*, p. 140).

16 D. Seers & P. Streeten, 'Overseas development policies', in Wilfred Beckerman, ed., *The Labour government's economic record, 1964–70* (London, Duckworth, 1972).

17 Ibid.; see also the evidence from both the Treasury and the Min. of Overseas Development to Sub-Committee C of the Estimates Committee in 1968 (HC 442, sess. 1967–8).

18 For an excellent discussion in detail, see Bhagwati/Desai, ch. 10.

19 Pearson, p. 298.

20 'Dependence on foreign aid will be greatly reduced in the course of the Fourth Plan' (p. 225). The aid requirement totals Rs25,140mn (p. 229, table 4); total requirements of foreign exchange are Rs100, 500mn (Rs96,300mn for imports, Rs1,400mn for net outgoings on invisibles and Rs2,800mn for repayment to IMF. In addition, Rs22,800mn will be required for debt service payments (p. 228) (RBI, *Report . . . 1968–9*, App. x).

21 *FT*, 22 May 1970, p.9. Amortization and interest on past aid, as proportions of gross aid utilized, were 12·1% in the First Plan, 13·5% in the Second, 27·0% in the Third, and 38·6% by 1967–69 (Bhagwati & Desai, p. 179). The average for all poor countries in 1968 was 36·1%, very close to the Indian figure (IBRD/IDA, *Ann. rep. 1970*, p. 46).

22 For details of other donors, see source for table 7.15. The fact that in some cases utilized aid may be greater than authorized aid is explained by the various changes in the par values of the currencies, notably the rupee devaluation of 1966.

23 'Official spokesmen of the Government of India have expressed, both in public and in private . . . their appreciation of the speed with which we take decisions and carry our aid decisions into effect. At times they have drawn some very favourable comparisons with the practices followed by other aid donors' (HC 288, sess, 1969–70, p. 5 para. C12). For an excellent discussion on the lag problem, see Bhagwati/Desai, pp. 187–97.

24 *FT*, 22 Apr. 1971, p. 6. See also p. 111.

25 Bhagwati/Desai, pp. 172–3.

26 J. S. Mann ('The impact of PL 480 imports on Indian economic development', *J. Farm Econ.*, Feb. 1967, 49/1, pt. 1), estimates that the total effect on Indian domestic wheat output of a sustained import of 1 ton of PL480 'free' wheat is a cut of about $\frac{1}{3}$ ton. Clearly some of the land and labour is diverted to make other products. We assume, probably too conservatively, that one-sixth of commodity aid is cancelled out by losses of domestic output caused by price-disincentive effects due to glutting.

27 *FT*, 9 July 1971, p. 9.

28 The fact that the USSR and East European countries accepted repayment in Indian goods probably helped little; there is no evidence that they regularly accept goods that India could supply at low opportunity cost, e.g. out of spare capacity.

29 V. K. R. V. Rao & Dharm Narain, *Foreign aid and India's economic development* (Bombay, Asia, 1963), p. 69. 'The old fears of interference influence and strings accompanying aid still lingered in respect of inter-governmental aid and led to vociferous demands for guarantees of various kinds to govern aid from foreign governments' (ibid., p. 71).

30 'We didn't know how to ask for aid, and we were afraid it would hurt our newly won independence . . . There was also at the base of it all the traditional idea which likened aid to eating someone's salt, thus courting personal slavery' ('Change of philosophy of aid at both ends', *Times of India*, 30 Jan. 1960).

31 In 1966–7 negotiations over US aid for the construction of fertilizer plants (of 2mn tons per annum capacity) collapsed when the USA withdrew her offer to provide an inter-governmental loan of $150mn to cover the estimated foreign-exchange costs of the project, and suggested instead that negotiations be carried on with private US firms. This rankled in India, especially as the poor performance of the private sector had been largely to blame for fertilizer shortfalls at the end of the Third Plan. Suspicions of donor pressure, too, darkened (and on balance probably postponed) the 1966 devaluation.

32 Such arguments have been partly the cause of the drive to reduce dependence on foreign aid in future development plans. In fact the World Bank felt that the planners are cutting aid requirements by too great a margin in the Fourth Plan, and that realistically India needs at least double the latest plan estimates.

33 *FT*, 17 July 1970, p. 9.

34 I. G. Patel, 'Aid targets for the 1970s' in B. Ward & others, *The widening gap* (Columbia, 1971).

35 HC 288, sess. 1969–70, p. 1.

36 On the Right, Prof. Bauer opposes aid because it strengthens 'the State' and subverts that sturdy private initiative which has so notably developed India and Africa in the past two millennia. On the Left, aid is attacked for supporting (by permitting them to raise their consumption and avoid basic reforms) reactionary elites, who in the past two millennia have done so notably badly without it (P. Bauer & B. Jackson, *Two views on aid* (London, 1966); K. Griffin (*BOIES*, May 1971, pp. 156–61). For analysis of public opinion as a whole, see Rauta, *Aid and development*.

37 'We are convinced that . . . it is a prime interest of Britain and the West to increase rather than diminish non-military aid to India. India is a vital growth point in the developing world. With the continuance of economic aid she has the capacity to make herself viable in the course of time. On her success may well depend the future of democracy in Asia and perhaps far beyond' (letter from John Strachey, Douglas Jay, and George Thomson, *The Times*, 21 May 1963).

38 'Although Britain is going through balance-of-payments difficulties it will contintue to aid India' (Douglas Jay, president of the Board of Trade (in India), *Hindu*, 25 Apr. 1965).

39 Ibid., 17 Dec. 1967.

40 'In the context of international politics it is a vain hope to think that the subcontinent will have its share of the aid funds increased from less than 15% to the 30% or 40% [of total international aid flows] it deserves' (*The Economist*, 7 June 1969, p. 72).

41 Theoretically, IFC investments in India really do not come into the category of aid, but are included here, as they are not really private investment either, being made multi-laterally by an international organization. Incidentally, it can plausibly be argued that, since IBRD (though not IDA) aid relies on private capital inflows, supplemented or guaranteed by governments, share of subscriptions is a *bad* proxy for share of disbursements. There is no practicable alternative, however; and as the role of IDA grew in India in the 1960s relative to that of other IBRD aid, so the approximation improved.

42 *Hindu*, 2 Apr. 1969. CDFC loans are comparable to project aid, although on slightly harder terms because CDFC has to borrow on the London and continental markets to make its loans.

43 Bhagwati/Desai, pp. 172–3, supplemented by ODA, *British aid statistics*, passim, as for all other data in this section not attributed elsewhere.

44 IBRD/IDA, *Report* 1970, pp. 46, 71

45 When US commodities are given, the US authorities accumulate rupee 'counterpart funds' roughly equal to the rupee takings expected when the Indian government sells such commodities on the market. In the 1960s, about 9% of such funds were used for US official purposes in India; 20% were given to the GOI; and the rest were loaned, all but 5% so the public sector. Since such loans are to be repaid in the distant future at no interest and in inflated and devalued rupees, and since US official uses are making a declining percentage claim on counterpart funds, many of these loans are really grants too. One might treat arbitrarily half as grants and the rest as interest-free loans for 25 years. Conversely, the 9% of funds used by the US in India, mostly for diplomatic expenses, should be deducted from the stated value of commodity aid altogether. So should about one-sixth of the value of food, to allow for the depressant effects on Indian agricultural output (n. 26 above). See Bhagwhati/Desai, p. 210.

46 See, for instance, *New York Herald Tribune* (Int. Ed.), 16 Feb. 1971. Another aspect is revealed by the World Bank's unusual step of explaining why an aid request was refused, in the case of Gabon in June 1971; the Bank felt that the yield, while adequate, would materialize mainly in France.

47 India already uses about 40% of new gross aid to repay capital and interest on past aid loans—far above most poor countries and expected to rise (see p. 105 and n. 20). In 1967–9 the grant element of OECD–DAC countries' aid to India was 79%—bilateral aid about 76%—both figures being over-statements because US food aid is counted as a pure grant. OECD–DAC *world* aid had an 85% grant element by 1969 (OECD/DAC, *1971 review*, pp. 62, 158).

48 Maturity, interest rates, and grace periods from Bhagwati & Desai, p. 184, applied to loans from ibid., p. 172, col. 9, at an assumed commercial discount rate of 10%. For example, the 'grant element' (i.e. the present value) of a 3-year loan of £100 at 2% with one year's grace followed by equal yearly repayments of £50 (plus interest on the sum outstanding at the moment before repayment) is £18·6, comprising:—

(a) 10% on 100, the interest 'saved' at the end of the year 1, discounted once by 10% to the time of loan, i.e. £10 × (1/1·1) or £9·1; plus

(b) 10%, minus 2% paid on £100, 'saved', i.e. £8 × (1/(1·1²)) or £6·5; plus

(c) 10%, minus 2% on the outstanding £50, 'saved' at the end of the year 3 when the loan matures; thrice discounted at 10%, i.e. £4 × (1/(1·1³)) or £3·0.

The 'grant element' on total aid was estimated by adding to the grant element of loans authorized the full value of grants authorized, plus 67% of the value of newly authorized commodity aid—deducting 9% for US government uses of counterpart funds, 16% for Indian food production losses and 8% for the non-grant element of the remainder (half of the remaining 75% being a true loan, with a grant element of about 80%, leaving 20% of (half of 75%), or 8%, as a non-grant element).

49 HM Treasury, *Aid to developing countries; session 1963–4*, pp. 12–13, para. 35. 'Reasonably competitive terms' covered delivery dates, after-sales service, and other relevant factors as well as price.

50 HC 442, sess. 1968–9, pp. 14–15, paras 4 & 5, 50.

51 FCO/ODA, *An account of the British aid programme* (1971), pp. 13–14, para. 55. Note

also para. 56: 'Budgetary Aid, of which the UK provides £10mn in 1970, by its nature cannot be tied formally to overseas procurement. However, the arrangements with the recipient countries are that they will procure in the UK from expenditure supported by this budgetary aid except where it would be clearly uneconomic to do so.'

52 OECD/DAC, *1970 review*, pp. 52–57: 'Untying will only work well if member countries are determined . . . to remove all informal tying practices' (p. 57); ho, hum. See also Bhagwati & Desai, pp. 198–212, and note the similarity to bogus 'liberalization' of tariff—but not informal—barriers against exports from poor countries.

53 Bhagwati & Desai, p. 201 & p. 197.

54 *FT*, 22 Apr. 1971, p. 6.

55 T. Balogh, 'Bilateral aid', in R. Robinson, ed. *Developing the third world; the experience of the 1960s* (CUP, 1971).

56 M. ul-Haq, 'Tied credits: a quantitative analysis', in J. Adler & S. Kuznets, eds, *Capital movements and economic growth* (London, Macmillan, 1968).

57 Of every 100 units of gross aid to India, valued at grant-equivalent to allow for differences in terms and to reassess the value of commodity aid (p. 105), 11·3 units came from the UK, and were de facto untied and hence 'worth' the full 11·3. Of the other 88·7 units, at least 70% (or 62·0 units) were effectively procurement-tied and hence 'worth' 20% (or 12·4 units) less, so that non-UK aid was really worth 76·3. Hence the UK's 11·3 units represented 11·3 ÷ (76·3 + 11·3) or 12·8 of true value.

58 '. . . we now have a pretty finely balances programme in respect of our financial aid, recognizing that one should, perhaps, no longer talk simply in terms of project and non-project aid, but rather in terms of a spectrum . . . all the way from projects at one end to debt relief, which is free foreign exchange, at the other, and including between these capital investment aid, aid to development banks for capital investment, Kipping aid and maintenance aid' (HC 288, sess. 1969–70, p. 15, para. C31). There had recently been some problems in getting project aid flowing again (ibid., p. 27).

59 HC 442, sess. 1967–8, pp. 432–4. There have been severe problems at both plants, especially Durgapur, and both are still far from functioning at full capacity or at a profit.

60 For a discussion of utilization lags on Kipping aid, see P. Streeten & R. Hill, 'Aid to India', in Streeten/Lipton, esp. p. 325.

61 For a discussion of this problem see para. 72 of HC 288, sess. 1969–70. There it appears that switching took place under general-purpose aid, though it is later claimed for maintenance aid that 'there is no greater degree of tying whatsoever. All that is different is the method of claiming against the loan that the Government of India has to follow' (ibid., para 73). Methods of compelling aid recipients to buy British, where they would not choose to do so, amount to support for inefficient 'lame ducks' in the British export sector.

62 *FT*, 12 Feb. 1970.

63 From independence to the end of the Third Plan, 13·5% of world loans and credits utilized by India had supported iron and steel, 57·5% other industries 12·8% railways, 4·1% transport and ports, 3·9% wheat stockbuilding (aid *against* agriculture) and only 1·0% agricultural development. (The proportion authorized, at 1·7%—2·7% in the Third Plan, was rather higher, but for 70% of the population making 45% of GNP . . .!) (Bhagwati/Desai, p. 186).

64 RBI, *Report* . . . *1970–1*, Statement 102, p. 5173.

65 IMF, *Balance of payments yearbooks*, vols. 19 & 22, India—Tables A.

66 For instance, an IBRD loan to ICICI in India in 1970 was made at a 7% interest rate, a three-year grace period, and a 14-year repayment period; terms much harder than Britain's (IBRD, *Ann. rep. 1970*, p. 94). IDA credits are much softer, at ¾% with a ten-year moratorium and 39–40-year repayment periods (ibid., p. 106).

67 HC 288, sess. 1969–70, para. 45.

68 RBI, *Report* . . . *1968–9*, p. 44.

69 Ibid., *1969–70*, p. 49, table 29.

70 HC 442, sess. 1967–8, p. 343, para. 1443, Treasury evidence: 'As regards the terms of loans that have been given and accepted in the past, we believe that there is a sanctity of contract and that it is important that all countries, however poor they are, should be determined to honour their obligations'. It is hard to see how a remission of aid debt, proposed by Britain, could interfere with 'sanctity of contract'. However, although India is recognized

as an exceptional case for 'a number of reasons', the nearest approach to contract-breaking (or rather mutual alteration) acceptable to the Treasury was the Consortium rescheduling.

71 The OECD notes that the amounts 'are presumed to understate—rather than overstate—the real flow of resources involved; in particular, the activities of the small agencies may not be fully reflected' (OECD/DAC, 'Development assistance 1970 and recent trends', Press release of 28 June 1971, p. 38). In 1970 the largest donors of private aid (with such flows as a percentage of respective GNPs in brackets) were West Germany, $77·8mn (0·04); Canada $47·9mn (0·06); UK $42·3mn $42·3mn (0·03); and Sweden $25·2mn (0·08) (ibid,, p. 39).

72 See HC 442, sess. 1967–8, pp. 276 f., esp. Q1178, p. 281.

73 The War on Want schemes are of especial interest in that emphasis is being placed upon the reproducibility of aid, with loans being preferred to grants on the grounds that loans encourage recipients to invest the resources productively so that the loans can be repaid and then loaned out again as a new round of seedbed capital.

74 *The Times*, 28 Oct. 1969.

75 *Daily Telegraph*, 22 Nov. 1969.

76 'It may be true that, in comparison with India's problem as a whole, emigration to Britain has made little impact. But in specific areas, the homes of many people now in Britain, the aid that it has brought has been hard-earned and has made self-improvement possible for many people living in comparative poverty' (*The Times*, 12 Nov. 1971).

77 See the papers by E. Eshag & F. Stewart in *BOIES*, Aug. 1971.

78 Caution is needed in accepting the simple aid-trade ratio at face value, for it has risen partly because of the *fall* in total Indian imports and partly because of the *rise* in aid receipts, which are not necessarily related. The decline in the USA's ratio during the annual plans reflects the changing composition of US aid, with declining PL 480/665 imports; trade agreements which make it unnecessary to tie East European aid in the same way as western countries; and the Canadian decline is due to the fast growth of Canadian exports to India from very low levels at the start of the 1960s coupled with static aid donations (largely in grant form).

79 RBI, *Report . . . 1964–5*, Statement 85, pp. S134–139.

80 ODM, *An analysis of aid-trade relationships in India* (unpubl. memo., 1968).

81 The conclusions of the ODM memorandum are highly sensitive to changes in the assumptions—especially with regard to the degree of tying (table 7.25). More analysis is needed to criticise the memorandum in detail, but we agree with the main conclusions.

82 HC 288, sess. 1969–70, pp. 34–5: 'We [the British High Commission in Delhi] felt that the new trade was going elsewhere and the general-purposes aid was being used to finance imports that would have taken place anyway' 'Under the general-purposes loan procedure importers applying to the import controller for licences were told that there was no allocation against free foreign exchange reserves, which were not favoured by the Indian authorities unless they were satisfied that all the aid available had been utilized first.'

83 Ibid., p. 35.

84 Andrzej Krassowski, 'Aid and the British balance of payments', *Moorgate & Wall Street R.*, Spring, 1965, p. 32. The assumptions about tying would certainly not hold today.

85 In Caves, *Britain's economic prospects*, pp. 180, 196.

86 Bryan Hopkin & others, 'Aid and the balance of payments', *Econ. J.*, Mar. 1970, p. 11, table III. Hopkin's detailed and thorough analysis indicates that if multilateral aid is included the net return rises to £67 per £100 of total aid (p. 118), though this is reduced to £53·5 with the inclusion of the so-called capacity effect—i.e. the effect on normal commercial exports if displaced by aid-financed exports. In 'stagflation' conditions, the 'capacity effect' will be greatly reduced. See also M. S. Levitt, 'Aid and the balance of payments', *Manchester School of Econ. & Soc. Stud.*, Sept. 1970, pp. 247–57, who estimates an external cost of around 55% (p. 251).

87 Moreover, we have doubts about Hopkin's classification of UK capital aid to India as 100% tied during 1964–6, even if informal tying is included.

88 Hopkin is also concerned with the short-run cost to the UK, and neglects the long-term capital and interest repayments on the loans given, though he acknowledges this to be important (*Econ. J.*, Mar. 1970, p. 2 (d)).

89 See e.g. F. D. Holzman, 'The real economic costs of granting foreign aid', *J. Dev. Stud.*, Apr. 1971, pp. 245–55, who argues that on the basis of 1963 figures the addition of primary

employment and multiplier effects results in capitalist nations netting a small gain from giving aid and 'converts aid from a burden to a large blessing with most nations gaining more from aid as a percentage of GNP than they would appear to lose when unadjusted gross aid is measured as a percentage of GNP'.

90 See e.g. Streeten & Hill, in Streeten/Lipton, p. 332; *The Economist*, 7 June 1969, p. 74; and Pearson, esp. p. 298: 'It may well be that the larger amount [of aid to India if India received as much per caput as Chile] could not be effectively used, but the debate rarely reaches that question because of usually unspoken assumptions that it is somehow unseemly that any one country, no matter how large, should receive much more than the present flow to India. This is one of the least defensible aspects of current aid policy' (see above, p. 99.

91 OECD, *Resources for the developing world*, pp. 254–5, 263. UK gross commitments and gross disbursements get out of line in particular years, but the differences are usually small and not biased either way, so this ratio (EEC potential net commitments to UK actual net disbursements) is quite realistic.

92 Ibid., p. 225, shows EDF and EIB commitments scheduled to rise from $800mn in 1964–9 to $1,000mn in 1970–5. The UK gross aid ceiling was $625mn in 1966–7 and was to reach $732mn by 1973–4 (ibid., p. 178–97).

93 Ibid., p. 233. A valuable reassessment is D. Jones, *Europe's chosen few* (ODI, 1973).

94 M. Lipton & others, *An enlarged European Community and the LDCs*, p. 25.

95 Dharma Kumar, *Britain, India and the European Economic Community* (London, Asia, 1966), p. 220. She does also suggest that if the EEC were to become closely linked to Africa (as it became in aiding the francophone elites) British aid might continue 'to be concentrated there' after entry. More recently she notes: 'If Britain's balance of payments deteriorates, it will largely be because other members of the community have gained, and they should be pressed to increase their aid programme, at least to the extent to which the British cut theirs'. Also she argues that there must be similar adjustments on the recipient side. 'If France gains at UK expense it should not lead to diversion of aid from Asia to Africa'. Further, the argument that increased aid will be a substitute for potential losses of trade by l.d.c.s when the EEC expands must be countered, for 'any such compensation is likely to be short-term' ('The new community and the developing Commonwealth: problems of aid and trade', *Round Table*, Oct. 1971, p. 482).

96 HC442, sess. 1967–8, paras 963–4. 'Something like a year ago [1967] we started trying to concentrate our efforts on agriculture'. During the evidence given in May 1968 in New Delhi, no mention was made of population policy, but the Population Bureau at ODA, set up in 1969 under the direction of Dr David Wolfers, is short of good projects, but certainly not of either drive or the money to back it.

Notes to pp. 122–38.

Chapter 8. Technical Assistance

1 Also included are the education of overseas students; the provision of scholarships and other types of financial assistance for such students; the release of teachers and other educational personnel for service overseas; and the supply of educational equipment and teaching material. Though the *financial* flows relating to this educational TA are covered in the present chapter, the impact of the programmes and personnel is dealt with in the following chapter. Technical training and the accompanying scholarships are covered in this chapter. The volunteer movement, counted as part of TA, will be examined briefly in ch. 10.

2 Commercial consultancy services and in-firm training abroad provided for an l.d.c. are not TA *from the donor's viewpoint*, except in so far as they are financed by the donor government or other external bodies; otherwise they merely add to the 'donor' nation's earnings on the invisibles account. *From the recipient's viewpoint*, the 'external benefit' of in-firm training abroad makes it, de facto, part of the aid relationship. See pp. 128–30 and n. 34 below.

3 Little is known about TA from communist countries; in view of Soviet and (increasingly) Chinese involvement in l.d.c.s, it must be considerable. At the beginning of 1966 about

16,500 Soviet experts and technicians were employed in l.d.c.s (about the same as total UK TA personnel), while about 28,000 l.d.c. technicians and specialists have been trained (V. Vassilev, *Policy in the Soviet bloc on aid to developing countries*, Paris, 1969, p. 84). Soviet TA to India has been substantial; the USSR 'has contributed to local training schemes far more than 25,000 specialists, including 10,000 for the Bhilai complex and 10,000 for the oil industry' (ibid., p. 80).

4 OECD/DAC, *1970 review*, p. 60 (table iv–i), p. 66 (table iv–7), & p. 172.

5 OECD/DAC, *1973 review*, p. 196.

6 OECD/DAC, *1970 review*, p. 60; *1973 review*, p. 196.

7 OECD/DAC, *1973 review*, p. 196.

8 Teresa Hayter, *French aid* (London, ODI, 1966), pointed out that half of total French aid was TA, and that half of that was spent on salaries of French personnel; one-quarter of French aid was thus spent on salaries of French personnel; one-quarter of French aid was thus spent on paying French civil servants, many of whom still provide the administrative and operational personnel in ex-French colonies in Africa.

9 For recent developments, see OECD/DAC, *1970 review*, ch. 4, and Anthony Hurrell, 'An introduction to manpower aid', IDS *Bull.*, Jan. 1971, pp. 4–15. See also Pearson, pp. 179–85, and OECD/DAC, *Technical assistance and the needs of developing countries* (Paris, 1968).

10 Pearson, p. 180.

11 In 1964–8, when total UK bilateral TA disbursements averaged £29·3mn per year, 31·7% was spent by the British government in the UK (Hopkin & others, *Econ. J.* Mar. 1970, p. 11, table 3). Further, the ultimate return of UK TA was put at 95·2% of total disbursements; thus TA involves very little drain on the UK balance of payments. Nor is the resource cost always large. During periods of slack domestic demand for technicians, expanded programmes for British TA personnel overseas form a useful non-inflationary way to employ members of this highly articulate group. This does not imply zero benefit to l.d.c.s, but it does suggest strongly decreasing returns to them, at least from rapid expansion of TA.

12 As one recent British high commissioner put it, 'The basic difference between Indians and most other Asian countries is that they have really now got a technological infrastructure of their own which is pretty formidable' (HC 442, sess, 1967–8, p. 219).

13 From the inception of the Colombo Plan to June 1969, India had spent, on TA to other Colombo Plan countries: trainees Rs29·1mn; experts, Rs4·5mn; equipment & supplies Rs3·6mn; total Rs37·2mn. 4,161 training places had been provided and 151 Indian experts sent to member countries, mainly Nepal, Bhutan, Ceylon, Malaysia, Afghanistan, and Thailand (Cmd 4273, 1970, p. 348).

14 As far back as 1912, there were 26 Indian technical scholars receiving education in Britain in fields as diverse as mechanical and electrical engineering, geological chemistry, sugar engineering, flour milling, and architecture, plus a large number of non-scholarship students reading engineering, chemistry, zoology, agriculture, forestry, etc. at British universities and colleges (Cd 7160, 1913). Further, some British educational institutions specialized in providing technical education and training for India. The Dept of Forestry at Edinburgh University was founded by Britons with experience in Indian forestry. Teaching was largely based on Indian experience and most of its (British) graduates entered the Indian Forest Service. Later, when recruitment to the IFS was restricted to Indians, large numbers of Indians—especially immediately prior to independence—passed through the Department (C. J. Taylor, 'Forestry at Edinburgh', *Univ. of Edinburgh J.*, Autumn 1970, pp. 262–8).

15 Totals are not available, but this is suggested by evidence from four major donors, Australia, Canada, Britain, and the USA (Cmnd 4273, pp. 332, 344, 394–5).

16 See table 8.9 (1950–68) & Table 8.8 (1969–70); 1950–68 figure converted at US $2·80 = £1·00.

17 Hopkin estimated that £0·67mn of the £0·75mn annual average UK TA to India over 1964–6 was spent in the UK (89·3%). Thus £7·2mn − (7·2 × 0·893) = £0·8mn. He also estimated direct and indirect purchases in the UK from TA to India at 98·7% of the amount disbursed (*Econ. J.*, Mar. 1970, p. 12, table 4).

18 'The scale of such assistance [to India] has not had to be large because India's educational facilities have reduced the need to absorb large amounts of technical assistance from abroad . . . [except within heavy industry where there has been] significant reliance on

technical assistance programmes designed to provide the immediate personnel and also to train Indian nationals in unfamiliar technical jobs' (Bhagwati/Desai, p. 213).

19 These estimates are made vulnerable—unavoidably—by the large number of sources of TA training help to India: UK and other Colombo-Plan-sponsored schemes; other Western European nations, principally France and West Germany; Soviet bloc countries; multilateral institutions such as the various UN organizations; and private charities, notably the Rockefeller and Ford Foundations. Further, some TA is provided by private firms (pp. 128f.) and also under normal bilateral project and disbursements.

20 Bhagwati/Desai, p. 213. They also reveal that, between 1950 and 1961, 1,421 Indian nationals received scholarships from multilateral institutions for foreign training.

21 Rao & Narain. *Foreign aid and India's economic development*, p. 51. Because of the expansion programmes of India private-sector steel plants, all of the 2,000 engineers and operatives required for the three public-sector plants had to be trained abroad, By 1963, of the 1,976 sent abroad, 755 had gone to the USSR; 580 to the USA; 353 to Britain; 131 to West Germany; 76 to Australia, and 1 to Canada (ibid., p. 51).

22 V. Vassilev, *op.* cit., p. 30.

23 In 1967 and 1968, of the 362 training places provided for Indians in Britain, 86 were in engineering, 54 in administration, 42 in industry and commerce, 26 in transport and communications, 20 in social science, and 15 in agriculture, forestry, and fishing (Cmnd 4273, pp. 317, 385).

24 Bhagwati/Desai, p. 213, table 10.13.

25 See ch. 9, pp. 146–7, for a more detailed discussion of British involvement with this Institute.

26 Cmnd 4273, pp. 317–85.

27 'A mere listing of the number of experts who have visited India . . . does not go far in indicating the contribution of such assistance' (Rao & Narain, p. 47).

28 'The "experts" may be no more than successful bankers, publicists, businessmen, or administrators in their respective countries and may not themselves claim any mastery over the intricacies and subtleties of economics, much less over India's prevailing economic predicament, which during the past two decades has acquired a unique complexity; or they may be professional economists, philosophers, or historians carrying with them the "authority" of venerable Harvard or Oxford, in which case their views may receive special attention' (Shenoy, *Indian planning and economic development*, pp. 44–5). The former point is well taken; but Professor Shenoy's major criticism of the latter group seems to be that it comprised 'statist' or left-wing or neo-Keynesian economists; for his writings elsewhere suggest that he welcomes the equally remote and dubious 'authority' of venerable Chicago for his own *marketismus*.

29 A. MacBean & Kathryn Morton, 'A note on factors affecting the effectiveness of technical assistance', IDS *Bull.*, Jan. 1971, pp. 35–9, and P. Selwyn, 'Conflict in technical assistance', ibid., Aug. 1971, pp. 44–7.

30 Of the beds in Indian hospitals, 25% are provided by Christian hospitals, usually run by medical missionaries. These hospitals are often situated in areas commercially and socially unattractive to most Indian medical staff; nevertheless, the Indian government is actively reducing expatriate missionary staff—mainly to provide more employment opportunities for indigenous doctors (I. R. Lawson, 'Comparative clinical management in Punjab and the north-east', Scot. Home & Health Dept's *Health Bull.*, 27/4, pp. 65–8).

31 See ch. 9, p. 152.

32 OECD/DAC, *1970 review*, p. 67.

33 See OECD, *Pilot survey on technical assistance extended by private enterprise* (Paris, 1967), and works listed in its bibliography.

34 In effect, unless the indigenous employees who receive such training are bound by contract to remain with the firm that trained them, such training provides external economies for for the host nation as trained employees move out into local firms. There is no evidence that foreign firms are troubled by this.

35 Kidron, *Foreign investments in India*, pp. 294 f.

36 See ch. 10, pp. 157–9.

37 Rao & Narain, p. 51.

38 ODM & Min. of Labour, *Survey of industrial training of overseas nationals* (London, 1967).

39 See ch. 9, table 9.1.

40 HC 288, sess. 1969–70, p. 43. This type of approach could be called, as one British administrator put it, 'technical assistance to produce technical assistance', namely financing work of an investigatory character from London, usually via ODA.

41 Ibid., p. 44.

42 One of the major criticisms of TA made in the Pearson Report (pp. 180–1) was that there had not been enough TA in project selection.

43 HC 288, sess. 1969–70, p. 8.

44 775 HC Deb., 261, written answer, 16 Dec. 1968. (At the same date there were 670 Pakistani doctors in similar employment.) In view of the known pressures on foreign doctors to go to less 'popular' areas (p. 134), a disproportionate number must have been working in Scotland and Northern Ireland; we make the most conservative plausible assumption.

45 Oscar Gish, private communication.

46 Gish, 'The Royal Commission and the immigrant doctor', *The Lancet*, 29 June 1968, p. 1423. Much of what follows is drawn from Gish's valuable research into international migration of medical personnel. Gish's work also exposes the lack of sound statistics of medical migration.

47 Ibid.

48 Derived from Gish's work once again; we assume that doctors from Australia, Canada, and New Zealand arrive as working holiday-makers (Gish, 'Britain and the immigrant doctor', *Inst. Race Relations Briefing Paper*, 1969, p. 2).

49 Gish, private communication.

50 There are several estimates of the inflow of Indian doctors into the UK in 1965–70, with 1968 being an especially rich year for confusion:—

	1965	1966	1967	1968	1969	1970
A	—	—	—	782	735	211
B	~870~	~960~		—	—	—
C	—	—	702	859	—	—
D	—	—	—	660	—	—

Sources; A See table 8.17 for B voucher holders admitted
 B See table 8.18 figures are from Oct. to Sept.
 C HC Deb., quoted in *BMJ*, 6 Dec. 1969, p. 630
 D See table 8.15 (DSTP)

In 1968 only 660 of the Indian doctors going to the UK registered with DTSP; the 77 difference between the two British figures may be due to Indian doctors entering for UK-recognized post-graduate courses, denying any wish for employment after gaining their fellowships etc., and thus not needing vouchers. But the statistical situation is somewhat confused.

51 797 HC Deb., 343–4, written answer, 11 Mar. 1970.

52 HC 205–II, sess, 1969–70, memo. by Dept of Employment & Productivity, pp. 462–3, para. 9.

53 787 HC Deb., 438–9, written answer, 24 July 1969.

54 See Dr Alan Gilmour, 'Overseas doctors—confusion and hardship', *BMA News*, Oct. 1969, p. 4: 'Doctors regard their vouchers as being issued because doctors are needed here, and assume that there are jobs waiting for them. This assumption is in fact wrong. It is nothing short of folly that so many entry permits should have been issued to overseas doctors who were eligible only for provisional registration.'

55 Gish, *The Lancet*, 29 June 1968, p. 1424. 'The profession considers junior hospital grades to be training posts, yet the doctors who occupy a significant proportion of them require Commonwealth Immigrants Act work vouchers to enter Britain, and are considered, by the government, to be immigrants.'

56 Gish & A. Robertson, 'Britain's medical "brain gain"', *New Statesman*, 14 Mar. 1969, p. 353.

57 See ch. 10, p. 143, and Gish, 'Training of Surgeons' (letter), *BMJ*, 4 June. 1969, p. 54.

58 See e.g. D. Naidoo, 'The brain drain and medical education' (letter), *The Lancet*, 2 (1967), pp. 670–1.

59 Cmnd 3569 (1968). The £18,300 quoted ignores the hidden cost of forgoing the contribution the student might have been making to GNP, but does include an allowance for the capital cost of buildings; since this is average not marginal cost, it substantially understates the cost of training extra doctors.

60 It is irrelevant that medical training costs less per year than £15,000 in India; here we are measuring British TA to India, 'net' of the cost *Britain* would have to bear if she decided to produce doctors internally, instead of importing India's free. 8% is the real rate of return the Treasury expects of capital in UK (and Indian) nationalized industries. It is below the social rate of return on technical education—the likeliest alternative use of such saved resources—in either India or Britain. Nor can we sensibly deduct remissions to India by Indian doctors working in Britain—unless we wish to deduct remission home by British personnel abroad from Britain's TA!

61 This figure, taking into account higher past rates of Indo-British medical TA, is also tenable, as it represents the cost to Britain if the 5,000 or so Indian doctors in Britain were to be replaced by British medical graduates.

62 There are places for 6,000 medical postgraduates yearly in India. Only 7,500 people qualified each year to fill them; yet nearly 900 have been going to Britain each year and as many again to North America and Western Europe (see Commonwealth Secretariat, Second Commonwealth Medical Conference, *Report* (Kampala, 1968), i.37.

63 Patients per doctor in developed countries vary from about 670 to 1,000, with the UK at 870 (1966), USA 670 (1965), and Switzerland 680 (1966). India's ratio is 1/4830 (1966) and Pakistan's 1/5980 (1966) (UN, *Statist. Yb. 1968*, pp. 702–4, table 206).

64 According to a statement by the Secretary of State for Social Services made in a written reply to a question in the Commons on 25 November 1969, the number of qualified nurses entering Britain was as follows:

	1967	1968	1969 (Jan. Sept.)
India	97	57	56
Pakistan	12	9	8
West Indies	12	6	7

Quoted in *BMJ*, 6 Dec. 1969, p. 630. As can be seen from table 8.18, we have chosen a low estimate.

65 Figure supplied by the Nursing Superintendent of the Edinburgh Royal Infirmary for total cost of training a nurse entering at age 18, of which some £200 is for equipment (personal communication). The figure is approximate and guide only.

66 This is the average cost of training a non-graduate teacher in Britain. (Figure supplied by Scottish Council for Research in Education, Edinburgh, personal communication.) The figure is approximate and a guide only.

67 Throughout the preparation of the estimates, the lowest figure has been taken in every instance where a range of figures are available, and often further downward estimates have been made in order that the argument will not be spoilt by overstatement. If one had taken the top range of estimates, the figure for technical assistance from India to Britain may well have lain around £10mn per annum for 1961–70.

68 HC 205–II, sess. 1969–70, p. 517, para. 15. The last remark is ominous; if overseas doctors such as Indians are presumed to be staying only for relatively short periods in the UK—a situation implied by the passage—then it follows that they will still be used to fill up the less desirable jobs and specialisms in less desirable hospitals pp. 134–5 above), leaving the better jobs to Britons.

Notes to pp. 139–53

Chapter 9. Education and Research

1 In Britain, some schools were founded specifically for, and others relied for a large share of their pupils on, the sons (much more seldom the daughters) of those engaged in the administrative and commercial life of India. Yet in such establishments, and to a lesser extent even in the universities, such students learned little of India. Usually, the study of *European* classical languages and history was considered of greater value to an aspiring

entrant to the ICS than Indian history or culture, though in some specialized schools and colleges there were examinations in major Indian languages.

2 In 1864 Rabindranath Tagore's elder brother, Satyendranath, became the first Indian to enter the ICS (Michael Edwardes, 'Signs of progress, images of change', *Folio*, Oct.–Dec. 1971, p. 16).

3 'Before 1939, if one wanted to do well as a lawyer in India, it was helpful to become a British barrister. If one wanted a post in the Civil Service or one of the great merchant houses, one stood a much better chance if one had a degree from Oxford or Cambridge. If one had money and merely worked to be acceptable in society, to have spent a period in Britain, preferably at a university, was of great assistance' (T. & M. Zinkin, *Britain & India*, p. 154). Indeed, for at least part of the pre-independence period, a degree from a British university and English bar qualifications were a prerequisite for any Indian wishing to practice before the High Courts of Allahabad, Bombay, and Calcutta.

4 These, however, included many of the leaders of the independence movement, notably Gandhi and Nehru, 'The products of this expansion of Western-style education [among lower-middle-class Indians] resented the entrenched position of the upper-middle class and their association with the source of real power, the British. They found themselves without an outlet for their newly acquired education, for there was only a limited number of appointments in government service and even fewer in the world of commerce. . . . The dissatisfaction of the deprived Indian middle class was to lead to political activism, to a demand for Western democracy, and ultimately to Indian independence' (Edwardes, pp. 16–17).

5 For a description of a similar process of recruitment of 'nationalist' elites in 'francophone' (i.e. elite francophone) Africa, see Franz Fanon, *The wretched of the earth* (Harmondsworth, Penguin, 1969), ch. 4. Fanon concentrates on the power of such recruitment to impede or warp the formation of a 'national culture'; in India this is not a problem, given the age and strength of local culture, but the effect on elite attitudes and educational systems have been very serious.

6 We must distinguish between true visiting pupils and what the official statistics term 'Indian pupils' (including both immigrants and British-born children). The latter will not be discussed further here, as they are covered in ch. 10, pp. 164–5, except to note that in January 1969—the latest year for which statistics are available—there were 48,539 'Indian' pupils at primary and secondary grant-aided schools in England and Wales (the Scottish Education Department does not publish statistics on this subject), out of a total of 249,664 'Immigrant pupils' (again following the official terminology, under which immigration is hereditary for one generation!). 'Indian' children number less than half the 'West Indian' children at school here (106,126) (Dept of Education and Science, *Statistics of education: 1969* (1971), i (Schools), and table 38, p. 71; and p. xiv, para. 30). The numbers of visiting Indian schoolchildren admitted under the Commonwealth Immigration Act, 1962, in the mid-1960s were: 1966, 52; 1967, 37; 1968, 45. This may well be an underestimate, and it may represent only *new* arrivals. At high levels of education it is often hard to distinguish visiting students and immigrants, for many start their education in Britain in the first category, but end it in the second, especially with science and medical students (pp. 161–3).

7 There are very few in Scotland or Northern Ireland, although there lack of published statistics on overseas students at grant-aided further education establishments has compelled the authors to rely on personal communications.

8 Whereas in 1950 there were 27 universities (4 of which—Allahabad, Bombay, Calcutta and Madras—date back to the 19th century), by 1967 there were 70, with others planned. Indian students in Britain represent a tiny proportion of total Indians receiving university education.

9 'It was not merely because of the British rule in India that the Indian scientists and engineers used to go to England. Britain's advancement was unsurpassed in science and technology in those days. The emphasis somewhat shifted to Germany about the First World War when many of the Indian scientists and technologists went to Germany for study and research. Since World War Two, the USA has attracted most of our students and researchers' (K. Ray, *Scientific and technical personnel*, Monograph No. 1, Census of India 1961 (1966), p. 75.

10 'To have been to MIT, or the Havard Business School, is today even more fashionable than to have been to Oxford or Cambridge' (M. & T. Zinkin, p. 155).

11 'Elsewhere' is mainly Canada, where Indian student members have risen from 152 in 1958–9 to 1,273 in 1968–9 (*Statesman's Yearbook*, *1969–70*, p. 333). (No source is given, or a definition of 'students and trainees'.) Among Commonwealth countries in 1968–9 there were 1,273 Indians at Canadian universities out of a total of 17,423 foreign students; in New Zealand, 12 Indians out of 1,566; and in Pakistan, 1 out of 1,012. On this basis there are more Indians at Canadian universities than at British ones (Assoc. of Commonwealth Universities (ACU), *Commonwealth Universities Yearbook* 1970 (London, 1970)).

12 See note to table 9.3.

13 The 1967–8 ACU change in definition of an overseas student particularly affected the 'part-time' category. Under the old definition India provided 345 part-time students; under the new definition it fell to 231. The differences between the two definitions suggest that the missing 114 were really 'immigrants' and thus included with British students in other statistics.

14 A. K. Singh, 'Indian university students in Britain', *Planning*, 13 Nov. 1961, pp. 283–313.

15 Indeed, a vacation job may now be technically illegal, for a student 'seeking an extension of stay has to satisfy the Home Office of his continuing ability to support himself *without working*' (our italics) (HC 205—I, sess, 1969–70, i.438, para. 6). Even before this restriction, one Indian who had undertaken postgraduate study in the UK remarked to us: 'The ones to be hit by the UK decision will be a large group of mainly middle-class students who have no chance of a scholarship, but who had hoped to work in their vacations to earn their fees. Prior to the decision, if they earned £300–£400 in vacations, they were able to live on £25 a month and pay the fees of £60–£70. The decision rules this out completely now.' In the early 1960s, of those students who did go abroad from India to study, 6% supported themselves by their own money, 24% had foreign assistance, and 10% had Indian scholarships (K. Ray, p. 77, table 13.4).

16 Furthermore, as fees rise and admission standards stay the same, the number of foreign students will probably be lower than it would have been without the fee rise. Hence UK balance-of-payments inflows, and the total UK Treasury revenue, will increase by a smaller proportion than the fee (and might in principle, though not so far in practice, actually decrease). However, since even at the increased fee overseas students enjoy a subsidy, each student 'frightened off' by the fee increase means a *net* gain to the UK Treasury (through reduced education costs), whatever happens to nominal fee revenue. In practice, it is hard to see the effect of the increased fees, chiefly because of the ACU's redefinition of 'overseas student' in 1967–8.

17 RBI, *Report . . . 1967–8*, ch. VI, p. 136. Note that the Indian government is prepared to back promising students for up to 5 years, instead of merely for a first degree. The 5 years, however, allowing for a normal 3-year Ph.D., often covers a 2-year M.Sc. or M.A. graduate qualification first, rather than a first degree. On this basis the Indian regulation seems aimed mainly at graduate students, presumably mainly in science and technology.

18 S. K. Bose, 'Technological institutes: a new dimension in education in India', *Impact of science on society*, 15/3 (1965), pp. 187 f. However, even the institutes have high wastage rates and show a sharp deterioration in the English spoken by the entrants; yet English is retained as the medium of instruction. For British participation in these institutes, see pp. 146–7 below.

19 K. Ray, p. 75.

20 There are 6 colleges, 3 of surgeons (including ones at Edinburgh and London), 3 of physicians (including one at Edinburgh), and a mixed Fellowship of Physicians and Surgeons in Glasgow. The membership trends of each are broadly similar, and thus the findings for the two Edinburgh colleges can be taken as representative.

21 The figure are for Asian candidates (Indian, Pakistani, and Ceylonese), but Indians make up the overwhelming majority of the group.

22 Fewer Indians go overseas for their first medical degree, for under the Indian Plans the admission capacity of the medical and dental colleges has been raised from 3,660 in 1955 to 11,500 in April 1969 (*India 1969*, p. 101). During the Fourth Plan, a further 10 new medical colleges are to be added to 93 colleges presently in operation (see also ch. 8).

23 In science, for example, scholars wish to go to centres of established or specialized interest with good facilities. As these lie overwhelmingly in Australia, Canada, and New Zealand, and as (despite the phenomenon of US groups agitating for 'black physics') there are no specific regional 'areas' within the framework of physical science, very few choose to go

to India. Hence, over 1960–9, only 3 science scholars went to India as against 24 arts scholars and 8 social science scholars (table 9.15)
24 HC 288, sess, 1969–70, p. 44, col. 2.
25 For a critical review of the Indian educational system and its problems see David Ovens, 'Investment in human capital', in Streeten/Lipton, pp. 187–249.
26 For a review of British educational assistance to l.d.c.s see Cmnd 3180 (1967), pp. 57–64, and ODM, *Education in developing countries; a review of current problems and of British aid* (1970).
27 ODM, *Education in developing countries*, p. 9.
28 Sources: as for table 9.16.
29 ODM, *Education in developing countries*, p. 8.
30 Recent British discussions of the development of the education sector in India and its problems include Ovens, in Streeten/Lipton, pp. 187–249; Mark Blaug, 'Education, economic situation and prospects of India, 1971', IDS *Bull.*, June 1971, pp. 4–14; and Blaug & others, *The causes of graduate unemployment in India* (London, 1969). The recent Indian locus classicus is, of course, the *Report of the Education Commission 1965–6* (Delhi, Min. of Education, 1966).
31 In 1967 there were 121,500 unemployed graduates in India, and the number has risen greatly since then. Surpluses in certain educated categories coexist with shortages in others. In some Indian states university teachers and trained mathematics and science teachers for higher secondary schools are very scarce (B. B. Pawar, 'The problem of unemployment— its dimensions', SBI, *Monthly R.*, Apr. 1971, p. 114. See also Blaug & others, esp. pp. 82–7).
32 HC 288, sess. 1969–70, p. 12. See also p. 44: nearly half of the British volunteers are in development projects (in India) rather than in straight education.
33 Ibid., p. 16. This includes the budget of the British Council and money spent through the CEC and the Colombo Plan. There have been criticisms of the administrative effectiveness of this tripartite educational assistance programme, especially as CEC was not designed to find projects for educational aid, whereas British Council funds are, at least in part. Further, education is only marginally involved in the Colombo Plan, which was devised before the recent work on the developmental importance of education (ibid., p. 37, col. 1).
34 The major criticism, especially within India, is that the training provided by the institutes could have been carried out more cheaply by the Indian government itself. Instead, it is argued, the institutes have become prestige projects to attract foreign aid. Besides the British, the Germans, Russians, and Americans each run one. The net result is allegedly duplication of expensive facilities and one-upmanship in the quality and sophistication of building and equipment.
35 'It may be supposed that students who have been at IIT, Delhi, have been using, to some extent, British equipment, have been taught by British professors, and have certainly been getting the mainstream of their academic influence from British sources, and hence will be predisposed to Britain therafter.' John Freeman, British high commissioner to India, in evidence to Sub-committee C of the Estimates Committee, 15 May 1968 (HC 442, sess. 1967–8, pp. 225–6, para. 1002).
36 Apart from help with finance and equipment, there are also a few British volunteers working in these centres, which are intended to be focal points for advanced research from which other universities' standards will be raised by the interchange of staff and students.
37 *Hindu*, 20 Aug. 1968. The IIT at New Delhi is already anxious to introduce sandwich courses for her institution, as this encourages students to see the practicality of what they are doing rather than to overstress an academic qualification.
38 These British Council libraries also help to alert potential Indian buyers of British books. There have been suggestions recently that it could be made part of the function of these libraries to offer information and hold reference stocks for book-buying institutions. The British Council's libraries are more numerous in India than anywhere else, and its expenditure in India (£485,000 in 1969–70) is greater than in any other single country, though per caput it is far less than in Pakistan (£394,400 in 1969–70) (British Council, *Ann. rep. 1968–9*; HC 288, sess. 1969–70, pp. 12, 39).
39 This scheme is run by the English Language Book Society, and produces, with British government aid, subsidized textbooks. So far, something like 6mn of these books have been sold in India at roughly one-third of the standard British price, mainly to university students.

40 Sir Henry Cotton, cited in Woodruff, ii: *The guardians* (London, 1963), p. 173. Cotton argues that the educated Indian 'thought and talked like an Englishman and claimed to be judged by English standards'; but note that 'Mill, Max Muller, and Maine' were contributors to *Indian* scholarship. Even in the 1880s the English-educated elite were not 'cultural renegades'—consider the Tagore family!

41 Under the 1963 Act, the right to use English in the central parliament was guaranteed; under the 1967 Act English was to be used for purposes of communication between the Union and states which have not adopted Hindi as their official language, and between Hindi-speaking and non-Hindi speaking states.

42 For a comprehensive discussion of the whole English language problem see S. S. Harrison, *India; the most dangerous decades* (Princeton UP, 1960), pp. 55 f.

43 Ind. Education Commission 1964–6, *Report* (1967). The Commission recommended the abolition of English teaching in early grades of primary schools, and suggested starting its teaching at the fifth grade, with the bulk reserved for secondary school. As 55% of Indian children never get beyond primary school this would seriously reduce the effective amount of English-language teaching. (The current plan to expand broadcasting in English for primary schools (p. 149) suggests that this recommendation has been rejected.) The other major recommendation was that the universities should replace English with regional languages in some functions within ten years, again a move which would do much to reduce the role of English in India.

44 See ch. 8, p. 132.

45 HC 288, sess. 1969–70, p. 39. A major problem is evidently the lack of a simple, robust language laboratory suited to Indian conditions. The institutes already set up are concerned with teacher-training, revision of curricula, examinations, the use of mass media, and the preparation of teaching material, though under the Ministry of Education, the British Council, and All-India Radio both play active roles.

46 'All the indications are that the need, and demand, for assistance to English-language teaching in Commonwealth and non-Commonwealth countries will remain an important growth point in UK aid. The volume of our educational aid resources being put into ELT . . . amounts probably to at least £2mn per annum. It is likely to need to expand substantially in the next 10 years' (ODM, *Education in developing countries*, p. 30). The review goes on to note: 'The overall requirement is too great for the UK alone, and for this reason the Ministry and the British Council (who have primary responsibility for the task of promoting the English language abroad on behalf of HMG) will need to go on seeking for patterns of multi-donor co-operation with the US and Commonwealth countries to define needs and patterns of aid' (p. 31). See also FCO, *An account of the British aid programme*, p. 21, para. 94 for a discussion of the mechanism of British aid in ELT.

47 For a critical examination of the position of South Asian studies in British schools, see J. B. Harrison, 'South Asian studies: the weak link in the schools', *As. Stud.*, Jan. 1969, pp. 94–104.

48 An examination of the UCCA's *How to apply for admission to university*, (annl.) or the Cornmarket Press's *Which university?* will confirm this point.

49 D. A. Low, 'South Asian studies: finding the next generation', *As. Stud.*, Jan. 1969, p. 91.

50 For just one example of the expertise developed under the aegis of the British Raj, see J. A. Voelcker, *Report on the improvement of Indian agriculture* (London: Eyre & Spottiswoode, 1893). Voelcker (who was the consultant chemist to the Royal Agricultural Society of England) produced a report which, in some technical issues and general insights, may be still unsurpassed in its field, but which has been forgotten and lies neglected (if present) in most libraries. Similar examples can be found in virtually every discipline.

51 Hugh Tinker, 'The rediscovery of India', *Int. Aff.*, Jan. 1969, p. 94.

52 One has only to compare the number of Ph.D. theses on British-Indian relations (defined in the widest sense) done in British universities and listed in Aslib's *Index to higher theses in GB and Northern Ireland* with those done in American universities and listed in *Dissertation abstracts international* to appreciate this. Among 1970 American Ph.D.'s listed in the latter, one can find work on 'British attitudes towards India: a selection of documents' (D. K. Cody, Columbia); 'The economic impact of decolonization: the Britain-India case' (T. Mukerjee, Colorado); and 'Marginal man in transition: a study of the Anglo-Indian community in India (R. D. Wright, Columbia). Not one 'British-Indian' doctorate was awarded in the UK in 1970.

53 African scholars: Low, *As. Stud.*, Jan. 1969, p. 89; Latin American scholars: London Univ., Inst. LA Studies, *Latin American studies in the universities of the UK 1968–9* (1969); S. Asian scholars: Cambridge Univ., Centre for S. Asian Studies, *List of scholars resident in Europe 1970* (1970).

54 IDS, *Register of social science research projects in the field of development studies being carried out in the UK* (mimeo., Sept. 1970).

55 The fuller IDS Register for 1971 reveals much the same picture, with 32% of the 384 research projects listed being devoted to Africa, and 21% to Asia. IDS, 'Cross-tabulation analysis of 384 projects listed in the 1971 development studies research register' (mimeo., 1971), table 1.

56 Dept. of Education & Science, *Scientific research in British universities and colleges, 1969–70*, 3 vols (1970). The index gives a fairly good idea of relative regional interest. Thers are few biological science area projects listed, but in the physical sciences major entries per area are as follows:—
    Africa 70, Asia & Middle East 19 (Indian 4), Americas 39, Europe 129, Oceania 11, Others (i.e. Arctic, Antarctic &c.) 23.
In the social sciences the annual *IDS Register* is probably a better source, but in the DES list, whereas Indian research was sufficiently sparse to appear under one index heading, African research had to be divided into a number of sub-areas.

57 Low, *As. Stud.*, Jan. 1969, p. 91.

58 The initial meeting of the South Asian section of the National Committee agreed to bring to the UCG's attention the need for paid leave and financial provision for alternative teaching; the video-taping of lectures; and the compilation of union catalogues to aid the more economical use of library resources. The expansion of undergraduate and research recruitment to Asian Studies will, of course, need more than this.

59 *Hindu*, 29 Mar. 1960.

60 The importance of the library was stressed by S. Ansari, the documentation librarian at the Indian School of Int. Studies, Delhi, when he pointed out that from a perusal of Aslib's *Index to higher theses in Great Britain and Northern Ireland* over the years 1950–1 to 1962–3, 91 out of 124 theses in the subject group 'Language, Literature and History' were completed by scholars from the Indian subcontinent, all of whom had made use of the library. Ansari went on to argue that, in spite of the Indian and Pakistani demands for its return, the library was so important that it should be retained in one place (*The Times*, 11 Dec. 1965). See also J. C. Lancaster, 'The India Office records', *Archives*, June 1970, pp. 130–41.

61 Hugh Tinker, *Experiment with freedom; India and Pakistan* (London, RIIA/OUP, 1967), p. 164. This is splendid and true in spirit, but the building is physically *in situ*, and the library well-housed at the top of the New Bodleian.

62 M. H. Rogers, 'Some aspects of the provision of materials for Modern Indian Studies', *Education Libraries Bull.*, Autumn 1968.

63 The *Union Catalogue*, compiled and edited in the SOAS Library at the University of London, is an author catalogue giving systematic coverage to some 25 British libraries with sizeable oriental collections and partial coverage to another 39 libraries not specializing in Asian studies. It lists most books from Asia bought by British librarians since January 1965. Accessions are currently reported at around 1,400 per month. In the context of national library resources the catalogue—though expensive—is invaluable for Asian specialists, as it will help to indicate duplication, and also to pinpoint areas and languages at present inadequately covered.

64 Rajeshwari Datta, *Union catalogue of the central government of India publications held by libraries in London, Oxford and Cambridge* (London, Mansell, 1970).

65 For instance, M. & T. Zinkin, p. 160: 'In another ten or fifteen years, India will no longer be a place all of whose problems are fully understood by somebody in London, but a place about which people in Britain know very little more than they do about Southern Italy.' Or even more recently, Tinker's extreme pessimism: 'I believe that the study of India in Britain has already been seriously eroded: and in thirty years' time the situation is likely to be very bleak indeed' (*Int. Aff.*, Jan. 1969, p. 94).

66 A conference organized by this group in 1967 led to a book published in 1968 (Streeten/Lipton). This present book is a further outgrowth of the work of Chatham House. In autumn 1972 the group marked the impact on India of British entry into EEC with a

conference on the subject; the findings were reported, and in part endorsed, in Lipton/Tulloch.

Notes to pp. 154–76

Chapter 10. Population Exchanges: Britons in India and Indians in Britain

1 W. S. Churchill, *A history of the English-speaking People*, iii: *The age of revolution* (London, Cassell, 1962), p. 175.

2 *Census of Great Britain 1851* (1854), Population Tables, vol. i, p. cccli. India was still a man's world for the Europeans; in 1851 men outnumbered women by 28,526 to 11,105 (ibid.).

3 *Census of England and Wales 1911* (1915), Summary Tables, table 99, p. 423. However, on the same basis (i.e. and enumeration of 'Natives of the UK' living overseas), there were 781,000 Britons in Canada; 590,000 in Australia; 191,000 in Africa—considerably more than in India; and no less than 1,294,602 in the USA.

4 We are grateful to the British High Commission, New Delhi, for this information. All the figures exclude diplomats and their families; in 1960, there were just over 100 UK-based diplomats in India (see pp. 172–3), and perhaps a further 150–200 dependants.

5 *Census of India 1961*, as in table 10.1, gives 14,387 British residents; but the BHC estimates that about 30% were not British-born—mainly East African Asians with British citizenship. The frequent assertion that India contains as many Britons 'now' as at independence (see 'The British in India today', *As. R.*, 5 Apr. 1964) is certainly quite mistaken.

6 BHC figures, for 30 June 1969; there were about the same number of East African Asians with British citizenship resident in India.

7 Chester Bowles (*Eastern Economist*, 1 Sept. 1967, p. 404), estimated over 8,000, but unlike the British figure including US diplomats and their families—numbering around 1,900, a far higher proportion than for British residents.

8 *Guardian*, 19 Nov. 1960.

9 Woodruff, *The men who ruled India*, ii. 363–6.

10 Edwin Haward, quoted in F. Yeats-Brown, *Indian pageant* (London, Eyre & Spottiswoode, 1942), p. 151. British membership of other services was: Police, 6,000 of 187,000; Medical Service, 200 doctors of 6,000; Forest Service, 240 of 16,000; Public Works Dept, 500 of 7,500.

11 C. P. Bhambhri, 'The Indian administrative service', *J. Admin. Overseas*, Oct. 1970, p. 263. 'One of the most important legacies from the British to India is the Indian Administrative Service modelled, as Philip Woodruff and others have shown, on the pattern of the Administrative class in Britain.'

12 M. & T. Zinkin, *Britain and India*, p. 154.

13 *As. R.*, 5 Apr. 1964.

14 L. J. Kavic, *India's quest for security; defence policies, 1947–65* (Berkeley, Calif. UP, 1967 p. 92).

15 Ibid., p. 122.

16 Ibid., p. 103.

17 *The Times*, 3 Oct. 1966.

18 *Hindu*, 4 Feb. 1968.

19 Kurian, *Impact of foreign capital*, p. 251.

20 Ibid., pp. 251–2.

21 Many of these entrants retired as rich and prosperous merchants. For instance, when Sir David Yule died in 1929, he was reputed to be worth over £20mn, all earned trading in India (Gordon Donaldson, *The Scots overseas* (London, Hale, 1966), p. 203).

22 R. D. Young, deputy chairman of Alfred Herbert, in A. Shonfield, *Second thoughts on aid*, p. 73.

23 One position of importance in overseas subsidiaries is that of Finance Director. Some British companies prefer to have a local man holding this post as it allays fears about profit and dividend remittances to the investing country. Other British companies insist that this position above all must be held by Britons—even though the Managing Director and all other directors are local—because of the importance of remittances and the skill needed to actually get them remitted!

24 *The Times*, 10 Aug. 1966.

25 Lok Sabha Deb., 6 Apr. 1949, quoted in India, *Pocket Book 1965*, p. 244.

26 Sinha & Castree, *Attitides of British companies*, and MS. replies to questionnaire.

27 Mozoomdar, *Overseas investment and Indian taxation*. See also ch. 5, pp. 72–3.

28 The taxation problem also affects official government aid to India. 'If H.E.I.L. wished to recruit an engineer and to recruit him they had to give him a net salary of £5,000, they would have to pay in fact a very much larger salary, perhaps two or three times the amount, in order that he should have that sum left after paying tax in India. When we provide men under the Colombo Plan we pay the salaries ourselves and they pay tax on the salary in Britain depending on their individual tax position, depending on whether he became, for tax purposes, an ordinary resident or not . . . In India he is free from tax. But depending on the date he left England in a particular year he might find he had to pay tax. But the advantage to H.E.I.L. financially is that it has under the Colombo Plan a man who receives a salary appropriate to the post without having to pay additional large sums of Indian income tax' (HC 442, sess. 1967–8, p. 222: Evidence to the Committee from Mr J. D. Rimington, BHC, New Delhi).

29 Sinha & Castree.

30 Why a rise from Rs1,000 to 1,600, when Indian devaluation was only 35%? Because this is calculated on the basis of the *new* sterling rate, not the old one. Before devaluation of the rupee in June 1966, the official rate for the £ was Rs13·33; afterwards it became Rs21·00. Now 21 minus 13·33, or 7·66, is indeed 35% of the new rate of 21·00, but it is 56% of the old rate of 13·33. Therefore British residents in India had to pay 56% more for their sterling, and since a spread of rates between buying and selling was introduced with devaluation the real increase was closer to 60%. Hence a rise of 60% on Rs1,000 to Rs1,600.

31 *The Times*, 10 Aug. 1966.

32 *Hindu*, 6 Feb. 1968.

33 In 1967 there were seven British Chambers of Commerce in India. The first of these voluntary bodies had been established in Calcutta in 1833, when the East India Company opted out of trading. Further Chambers were established soon afterwards at Madras (1834) and Bombay (1836), and down to the 1880s all the Chambers established were purely British. By the end of the Second World War, 11 out of the 38 Chambers in India were British, but since then there has been a growth of Indian Chambers and also the establishment of an Indo-German one. The British Chambers in India tend to have high incomes because their members are large concerns and because 'several of them are located in ports and enjoy a considerable income from weighment fees . . . [They also] . . . provide a larger range of consultancy and information services than most Indian Chambers' (M. V. Namjoshi & B. R. Sabade, *Chambers of Commerce in India* (Poona, Gokhale Inst. of Politics & Economics, 1967), p. 21).

34 *Dawn*, 3 Aug. 1966. However, this report from Karachi is perhaps open to doubt, coming as it did in the aftermath of the Indo-Pakistan conflict.

35 *Daily Telegraph*, 13 Feb. 1967.

36 The Anglo-Indian Keeler Bros. were for instance, two of India's most successful pilots in the 1965 Indo-Pakistan war.

37 RBI, *Report . . . 1967–8*, ch. 6, pp. 136–7. Under the new restricted emigration procedures, an annual ceiling of R1smn was instituted for total remittances by emigrant Indian nationals (mainly Anglo-Indians). 'Applications for grant of emigration facilities within this ceiling are considered by the [Reserve] Bank provided the applicant has compelling reason for leaving the country and settling abroad, and where the denial of the facility is likely to cause undue hardship.'

38 See V. R. Gaikwad, *The Anglo-Indians; a study in the problems and processes involved in emotional and cultural integration* (London, Asia, 1967), and R. D. Wright, *Marginal men in transition; a study of the Anglo-Indian community in India* (Ph.D. thesis, Univ. of Missouri, Columbia, 1970, summarized in *Dissertation abstracts international*, Nov. 1970, p. 2530A).

39 Indian data do not separate business and other visits. Nor do British figures; many so-called 'business trips' are in part excuses for a holiday, and many 'holidays', even on package tours, include an element of business. The figures presented are indicators, rather than detailed explanatory evidence. However, in 1969 66% of British residents going abroad gave 'holiday' as the purpose of their visit, and only 15% business. On this evidence, about 3,000 of the 1966 British trips to India were business trips. This looks about right, considering the size of British interests in India (*BTJ*, 23 Sept. 1970, p. 656. See ch. 5 where tourism is discussed.)

40 *Census of England & Wales 1911* (1915), Summary Tables, table 80, p. 390. Of these 62,974, three-quarters were from the provinces of British India, and the rest from the princely states and agencies under British 'protection'.

41 For instance, the Indian Students' Dept. in London was staffed by Indians recruited in Britain.

42 C. Kondapi, *Indians overseas* (New Delhi, OUP for Indian Council of World Affairs, 1951), App. I, p. 528. He also estimates that there were 2,405 Indians in the USA in 1947.

43 Cmnd 4620 (1971).

44 General Register Office, London, and General Register Office, Edinburgh, Sample Census 1966, Great Britain, Commonwealth Immigration Tables (London, 1969), table 2, p. 18. As the introduction to this volume cryptically remarks (p. vii): ' . . . in [these] volumes a person's birthplace has no bearing on whether or not he or she is classed as an "immigrant"'. See also Kondapi.

45 There are a number of doubts about this table. Some of the countries have unreliable population statistics, and we can seldom tell whether the figures cover settled residents only, or all Indians (including students, visitors, etc). A US estimate for 1967, for instance, gives the number of Indians as over 50,000 (versus the 32,000 of the table), of whom about 7,500 are temporary-resident students. Of the rest, 'many are American citizens or intend to become so', including a sizeable Sikh farming community in California, and several thousand Indian faculty members at US Universities and colleges (Bowles, *Eastern Economist*, 1 Sept. 1967, p. 404).

46 The figures in table 10.9 seem to square with those in tables 9.1 and 9.4. In 1968, for example, there were 1,660 full- and part-time Indian students at British universities, and around 1,000 at other further education institutes, say 2,600 in all; while 985 students arrived that year. As not all Indian students are taking 3-year post-graduate or undergraduate degrees—many are doing two-year post-graduate courses or even one-year courses at technical colleges—the figure of 2·6 years (2,600 ÷ 985) seems a fair indication of the average stay of Indian students in Britain.

47 A sample survey of Commonwealth students, undertaken in September 1969 to determine the extent of evasion of immigration control, found that $7\frac{1}{4}$% had stayed without permission after the expiry of their permitted stay, i.e. had neither embarked nor applied for an extension of stay, and had not had their conditions waived. 'Experience indicates that some of the $7\frac{1}{4}$% will in fact have embarked without record; that some will be eligible for revocation of conditions; and that some will have good grounds for an extension of stay but will have failed to apply out of negligence or inattention. Of the remainder, some will prove to be genuine students who have found themselves unable to meet the required standard, or whose source of funds has dried up, and the residue will have come here with the intention of evasion' (HC 205—I, sess. 1969–70; i.438–9, memo. by Home Office. See also pp. 241–3).

48 See also ch. 8 for a discussion of doctors admitted under Category B.

49 There is no way to estimate dependants remaining in India, for although voucher-holders record the number of dependent relatives that they may wish to call to Britain at a later date, there are no figures for the dependants of the numerous Indians who went to Britain before the introduction of the voucher system. This led the British High Commission in New Delhi to express doubts as to whether they 'could produce any figures on the basis of the statements made by voucher holders which would be very useful in estimating the potential numbers of dependent relatives left behind in India' (HC 205—I, i.251). The Committee quotes Eversley and Sukdeo, *The dependants of the colonial and Commonwealth population of England and Wales* (London, Inst. Race Relations, 1969) as stating that for the whole Commonwealth there were some 236,000 dependants overseas at 31 December 1967.

50 HC 205—I, i.260.

51 Ibid. p. 223. Dependants and sponsors are also questioned about the family house, their neighbours, their land-holdings, and crops and animals owned in order to detect the bogus. Such interviews are carried out with great care for 'a lot of our applicants are illiterate, a lot of them are from a rural background, a lot of them may not ever have seen a British official before, a lot of them may not ever have sat in an office before, a lot of them may naturally fear authority' (ibid., p. 234).

52 Ibid., pp. 342, 344. In the Punjab, 'there is visible evidence of emigration as houses are

empty and locked . . . It is estimated that 500 people have already emigrated from the village of Moranrali in Hoshiapur . . .' (ibid., p. 342). In Gujarat, it is estimated that 75,000 had gone from the Kaira district to Britain, and from 'one place, Sojitra . . . [with] . . . a population of 15,000 to 18,000, about a thousand were now in Britain' (*The Times*, 12 Nov. 1971).

53 HC 205–1; also ch. 5 & 7.
54 Ibid., p. 342.
55 The Dept of Education and Science define 'Immigrant pupils' as including both (a) children born outside Britain who have come to this country with, or to join, parents and guardians whose countries of origin were abroad, and (b) children born in the UK to parents whose countries of origin were abroad and who came to the UK on or after 1 January 1960. They exclude children from Eire and children of mixed (i.e. immigrant and non-immigrant) parentage (*Statistics of Education 1970* (1971), Schools, note 34, p. XIV).
56 For instance in Southall Indians owned two of the town's three cinemas by 1970, and were negotiating for the third; had they succeeded, Southall residents would have been forced to travel to Hounslow or Ealing to see English-language films! (*Daily Telegraph*, 4 Jan. 1971, p. 13).
57 Even in the early 1960s Elspeth Huxley could write of Indian women in Southall that 'Most of their own food they buy from Indian grocers, who fill a social function as well as a commercial one. Wholesalers in London import spices, pulses, rice, oils and all the mysterious ingredients of curries, and the Indian grocer takes them round by van; he's probably a kinsman, and not only a purveyor but a courier, newspaper, antenna, employment agent and advisor as well. He's part of the closed circuit of Indian life . . .' (*Back street, new worlds; a look at immigrants in Britain* (London, Chatto, 1964), p. 96.
58 Most Gujaratis who have settled in Britain have been Hindus. Many belong to societies in Britain that remit money to India for projects such as that reported in Sojitra, Gujarat, for a building where 'remains could be cremated in Hindu style and under shelter in the rainy season' (*The Times*, 12 Nov. 1971).
59 A notable battle concerned the funeral customs of some of the Sikhs. They wished to scatter ashes on the Thames, but this was liable to a fine under anti-litter ordinances. It was resolved in the end by the Community Relations Commission and the Port of London Authority; ashes can now be taken by boat and scattered far down the Thames Estuary (ibid., 28 June 1971).
60 The 1962 Act dried up the major source of labour for the iron and brass foundries of Smethwick. Ironically, the foundries affected found it cheaper and easier to buy in rough castings from India for finishing (ibid., 14 Dec. 1966).
61 Home Office, *Control of immigration statistics, 1968, 1969, 1970.*
62 The actual trades of Indians who collected their 'A' vouchers from the Bombay High Commission in 1969 were given in the evidence to the Select Committee on Race Relations and Immigration. The 102 voucher-holders include an accountant, an analyst, a diamond cutter, a dress designer, 2 engineers, 19 machine operators, a manager, a screen technician, a sub-editor and a welder. It also includes 10 nurses, 7 physiotherapists—all of whom one would have expected to have had 'B' vouchers—and a priest (HC 205—I, i.285).
63 E. J. Rose & others, *Colour and citizenship*, quoted in *The Times*, 10 July 1969.
64 *The Times*, 25 Feb. 1971: Peter Evans, 'A survey of race relations in Britain, part 3'. The article, which was based on a survey, started rather directly: 'If a direct comparison could be made between West Indians, Pakistanis, and Indians, the Indians would come off best.'
65 See e.g. its evidence to the Select Committee on Race Relations and Immigration, HC 205—I, vol. xi, pp. 597–602.
66 Rose & others, p. 635, table 30.2.
67 The best discussion remains that of Rose & others, plus the evidence given to the various sessions of the Select Committee on Race Relations and Immigration.
68 Rose & others, pp. 647–9, and K. Jones, 'Immigrants and the social services', *Nat. Inst. Econ. & Soc. Research R.* Aug. 1967. The conclusion of L. Needleman & E. Mishan ('Immigration: long-run economic effects', *Lloyds Bank Review*, Jan. 1968, pp. 15–25), that the initial capital requirements of immigrants are such that for eleven years they boost demand more than supply, is too pessimistic given the lower housing standards of most immigrants (mostly 'delayed scrapping'). The figure would anyway be smaller for Indians because of

lower dependency ratio, and bigger for a typical English school-leaver, starting a family and work between 15 and 18 years of age. For three other brief discussions of the economics of immigration see the memos. by Prof. M. Peston, K. Jones, and Prof. E. J. Mishan in HC205—II, pp. 872–7.

69 *Indian Express*, cited in *Dawn*, 17 Nov. 1967. During 1967, an average of 30 Indian ministers and senior government officials came to London each month, excluding those invited as guests of the FCO (ibid.).

70 *Daily Telegraph*, 26 Sept. 1961.

71 Shrimati Lakshmi Menon, in debate in Lok Sabha, 4 Dec. 1961, quoted in N. Mansergh, ed., *Documents and speeches on Commonwealth affairs, 1952–62* (London, OUP/RIIA, 1963), p. 738.

72 She said: '. . . no restrictions exist at present on British passport holders entering India freely, staying here indefinitely and obtaining employment. The Government of India might have to reconsider the present arrangement . . . in the light of the new system that might be enforced by the British Government' (ibid.).

73 *The Times*, 27 Feb. 1968.

74 Cited in *The Economist*, 2 Mar. 1968, p. 20.

75 Between August 1968 and December 1969 1,456 such endorsements were issued to heads of Indian families in East Africa; many such families are known to have travelled to India with Indian entry visas (HC 205—I, p. 442).

76 The endorsement said 'This is to certify that the holder of this passport is a citizen of the United Kingdom and Colonies who is entitled to an entry certificate to travel to the United Kingdom and he will be issued with such an entry certificate on application to the nearest British Government representative.' See, however, British Passport, inside front cover.

77 HC 205—I, p. 449. The 270 are included in the 'others' category in the Commonwealth Immigration Statistics and are not separately identifiable.

78 The *Times of India*'s table of Indians Abroad, on which table 10.8 is based, is an example of this 'greater India' concept. That India takes the world Indian community seriously can be seen for instance in the endowment by the Indian government of a Chair in Indian Studies at the University of the West Indies in Trinidad, with an Indian professor as occupant (*India 1968*, p. 530).

79 Although Commonwealth citizens had been able to apply to British posts overseas for an entry certificate to cover their journey to the UK, for any purpose, since 1962, the 1969 Act redefined 'entry certificate' as 'a certificate . . . which is to be taken as evidence of eligibility for admission into the United Kingdom'. Under section 20(1) of the 1969 Act, all dependants were required to have valid entry certificates, whereas they had until then had free and automatic entry under the provisions of the 1962 Act.

80 In July 1969 a prominent Indian businessman visiting Britain was detained at Heathrow for 24 hours and refused entry because the Home Office was not satisfied that he was a genuine visitor (*India Weekly*, 10 July 1969). The working of the 1969 Act on dependants was even more unsatisfactory. In one case, a Mrs M. Singh, along with her children, was put on a plane back to India very quickly and methodically when her husband, delayed by a breakdown on the M1, failed to reach the airport in time (HC 205—II, p. 601).

81 Cited in *India Weekly*, 10 July 1969.

82 *FT*, 14 July 1970.

83 *The Times* 25 July 1971.

84 'It is completely turning racial discrimination on its head to say that it is wrong for any country to accord to those with a family relationship a special position in the law of that country', said the Home Secretary, moving the second reading of the Bill (ibid., 9 Mar. 1971).

85 Ibid., 26 Mar. 1971.

86 Ibid., 27 May 1971. Although no more category 'A' vouchers for unskilled or semi-skilled employees would be issued—a restriction less likely to affect India, which supplies mainly skilled employees (p. 165)—an exception was to be made for Malta, also the Commonwealth nation receiving the highest net aid per person (p. 162).

87 Personal discussions in Islamabad, Pakistan, in 1970. When, as British high commissioner in India, Sir Morris James addressed the Indian Council of World Affairs in Bombay in November 1970 on 'India and Britain', he devoted 42% of his time to the immigration

issue (24% to education, 14% to aid, 14% to private investment and 6% to trade) (*Foreign affairs report*, Dec. 1970).

88 Sir Stanley Tomlinson, deputy under-secretary of state, FCO, in evidence to the Select Committee on Race Relations and Immigration (HC 105—I, p. 55): 'Of course, it is relevant I think to point out that at the Commonwealth Prime Ministers' meeting in January [1969] the subject of immigration was raised and all those governments who wished to state a view were given an opportunity to do so . . .'.

89 Ibid., p. 338, memo. by Joint Council for the Welfare of Immigrants.

90 Anirudha Gupta, 'Requiem for the Commonwealth', *Economic & Political Weekly*, 20 Sept. 1969, p. 1511.

91 Tinker, *Experiment with freedom*, p. 146.

92 Cmnd 4107, p. 21.

93 The Duncan Committee seems to imply the former (ibid., pp. 10, 62–7), but one would have to repeat the statistical analysis for, say, a twenty-year period, combining both cross-sectional and time-series approaches, to gain some insight into the true nature of the relationship. Our discovery of an excellent fit (cross-sectional, between logarithms of the variables) is only a first step.

94 Bilateral diplomatic expenditure is affected by distance (travel costs), local cost-of-living differences, and the type of work which predominates within any one country. See also chap. 5, pp. 169–70.

95 Cmnd 4107, p. 41: 'It has not always been easy to see when the first post-independence phase is passed and a smaller establishment therefore possible.'

96 UK Treasury, *Civil Estimates*, HC 104, sess. (1960/1); 118 (1961/2); 93 (1965/6); 336 (1966/7); and *Supply Estimates*, HC 174 (1969/70), Votes on Class II (2, 3) and, until 1964/5 Class IV. These sources, although listing both UK-based and local employees, do not indicate whether the numbers include, for example, those on leave, or those who were formerly listed under other headings, although those in India under the Trade Commissioner Service are included in the figures quoted.

97 CRO *List 1960* and FCO, *Diplomatic Service list 1970*.

98 HC 205—I, p. 263.

99 *FT*, 29 Feb. 1972, p. 6.

100 *Hindu*, 27 July 1967.

101 There is also a First Secretary in charge of the TA Programme, and another who oversees general economic questions (*Diplomatic Service List 1970*).

102 HC 205—I, p. 244.

103 Ibid.

104 Ibid.

105 Since independence the holders of the office have been: Lt-Gen. Sir Archibald Nye (1948–52); Sir Alexander Clutterbuck (1952–5); Malcolm MacDonald (1955–60); Sir Paul Gore-Booth (1960–5); Rt Hon. John Freeman (1965–8); Rt Hon. Sir Morris James (1968–71); Sir Terence Garvey (1971–3); and Sir Michael Walker (1973–).

106 *The Times*, 9 Mar 1968, which adds that Freeman 'was not what (the Indians) expected—reserved, more diplomat than editor, more statesman that *New Statesman*'. For Mr Wilson's version, which blames the then CRO for bad advice, see H. Wilson, *The Labour government 1964–70; a personal record* (London, Weidenfeld, 1971), pp. 133–4.

107 Sir Paul Gore-Booth was driven to complain to the Indian Ministry of External Affairs that Britain was always singled out for abuse because she was an easy target and wouldn't hit back! (*Hindu*, 27 Sept. 1961).

108 For instance, when President Radhakrishnan visited London he requested two pictures of the Queen for his residence. The Indian government later forbade the BHC to hand over the two pictures at a public ceremony, though after angry protests from the BHC it relented provided there was 'no publicity'. This was agreed to; the pictures were handed over and 'formally inspected' by the President and the high commissioner (*Daily Express*, 23 Apr. 1964).

109 *The Times*, 29 June 1968. Freeman was succeeded by an outstanding 'career diplomat', perhaps because another 'political appointment would almost certainly create the impression with the Indian Government that the High Commission was something of a "hot line" to Whitehall—a likely source of further confusion in present circumstances' (ibid., 30 May 1968).

110 *Sunday Times*, 24 July 1966.
111 Cmnd 4107, p. 14.
112 FCO, *London diplomatic list, December 1971*.
113 Ibid.
114 Personal communication. These DHCs are concerned mainly with passports, seaman's welfare, and general welfare work among Indian communities in Britain. They are not on the scale of the British DHCs in India, (reflecting, in a small way, India's federal as against Britain's unitary structure). The Glasgow DHC, which is responsible for Scotland and the North of England, has a staff of two, including the Assistant Commissioner.
115 Personal communication. It is incorrect, however, that 'India has just under 1,000 diplomatic representatives in the UK' (Letter, *FT*, 26 Oct. 1970).
116 High Commission spokesman to authors.
117 HC 205—I, p. 247. Although such personal servants thereby partly bypass immigration control regulations because of their connection with the High Commission in London, they can like normal immigrants apply for British citizenship after 5 years residence in the UK, though since the 1971 Act this is at the discretion of the Home Secretary.
118 *Hindu*, 6 Dec. 1967.
119 *Guardian*, 1 Nov. 1967.
120 *The Times*, 2 Nov. 1967. The three who turned the post down were Sachindra Chaudhuri—who was actually appointed, but then turned it down after he was not given cabinet rank; Tarlok Singh, formerly of the Planning Commission; and Manubhai Shah.
121 *Guardian*, 1 Nov. 1967. Dhawan's subsequent long stint in the 'hot seat' as Governor of West Bengal—if not his rather undynamic term of office in London—belies this somewhat patronizing reference; but he got a rough press in Britain. He was charged with being anti-British, mainly because in January 1966 he had written an article in the left-wing weekly *Blitz* in which he had said that he '. . . saw no future for Indo-British friendship because reluctantly I have come to the conclusion that Britain does not regard the existence of a strong India in her interests and she will shed no tears if India is disrupted' (*Daily Telegraph*, 28 Nov. 1967).
122 *Hindu*, 5 Dec. 1968.

Notes to pp. 177–90

Chapter 11. Defence and Military Relations

1 M. & T. Zinkin, *Britain and India*, p. 33.
2 In 1962 Sir Alec Douglas-Home (then Lord Home) defended Chamberlain's 1938 appeasement policy on the grounds that had the policy been successful it would have detached Hitler from Mussolini and thereby secured the routes to India and beyond (*Observer*, 16 Sept. 1962).
3 Harold Wilson, opening the Nehru Memorial Exhibition in June 1965, declared that: 'Britain's frontiers are on the Himalayas' and that the British government would use all necessary means to maintain India's 'political and geographical integrity' (*Guardian*, 11 June 1965).
4 The then Foreign Minister, Swaran Singh, issued a statement on 15 January 1971 at the Singapore Commonwealth Prime Ministers' Meeting, arguing in it that the decision to create a base on Diego Garcia 'will affect not only our own security but that of other littoral states' and it was based on an 'obsolescent philosophy' as it would not promote stability but merely escalation of power conflict within the area (*Foreign Affairs Report*, Mar. 1971).
5 S. S. Khera, *India's defence problem* (New Delhi, Orient Longmans, 1968), pp. 259–60.
6 See ch 10, pp. 173–4.
7 In 1965, 71% of the effective combat planes of the IAF were British (220 jet fighters, 68 jet bombers), and the armoured divisions of the army were built around a division equipped with Centurion tanks (George Thayer, *The war business; the international trade in arms* (London, Paladin, 1970), p. 230).
8 Defence Minister Menon in the early 1960s had a strong preference for British aviation equipment (Kavic, *India's quest for security*, p. 198). Clearly the Indians, after their experience of 1965 (see pp. 182–3), are also apprehensive about finding themselves in the

position of having their military capability constrained by the refusal of an arms supplier to supply spares. British arms manufacturers are aware of this and they believe that the only way to recapture arms markets—including India—is to guarantee the delivery and spares under all circumstances—if necessary to both sides in a conflict. One aircraft manufacturer remarked '. . . certainly the Pakistanis and Indians won't buy from us in the future unless we guarantee that we won't hold up spares' (Thayer, p. 226).

9 In the case of the UK, the major problem in arriving at a reasonable figure for arms sales is that much goes through under civilian trade headings as opposed to the Firearms and Weapons of War heading (SITC 951) of trade accounts. To reach a true total, an item-by-item examination of the trade accounts would be needed. India's high security-consciousness is reflected by the complete exclusion of details of defence purchases from the trade account; all go through on special forms, which are not forwarded to be aggregated into trade totals. The only hard evidence available is for the 'Charges in England' (pp. 180–1), although some—we hope—intelligent guesses can be made by manipulating the trade accounts (table 11.4).

10 During Mr Michael Stewart's tour of the Far East as foreign secretary, he stressed—in reply to a loaded question about British aid to India being diverted to an arms build-up—that '. . . we sell strictly on a commercial basis, [and] we do not regard military expenditure as a suitable subject for aid' (*Dawn*, 19 Nov. 1968). See, however, pp. 182–3 for evidence that this was not so in 1962–5.

11 Except for 'aid' (see below), military equipment must be purchased with free foreign exchange, which in India's case is extremely scarce. The small amount available each year is allocated according to a strict set of priorities—namely: (1) debt servicing; (2) dividend remittances; (3) the remainder is rationed between (a) raw material and maintenance imports and (b) defence imports. This major external constraint on arms purchases is yet another incentive for increasing the domestic production of major defence equipment, although Gulzarilal Nanda in a letter to colleagues in the Indian Cabinet and to the Planning Commission, warned against building up a massive home defence industry on the grounds that the components, plant, and TA necessary to do so might involve even heavier foreign-exchange costs than the continued direct import of arms, especially with smaller items of equipment (*Statesman*, 21 Aug. 1965). This echoes Latin American experiences, and not in defence alone; there too import substitution often cost more foreign exchange than it saved (see D. Felix, in G. Papanek, ed., *Development policy; theory and practice* (Harvard, 1968); I. M. D. Little & others, *Industry and trade in some developing countries*, pp. 59–64).

12 The share was much higher in 1963 following the emergency aid in response to the 1962 war, since at least part of these sales were covered by UK military aid (see pp. 182–4). In 1967 the major purchases of arms under SITC 951 from the UK were West Germany, £5·3mn; Israel £2·5mn; and India £2·3mn; For 1968 the ranking was Israel £4·3mn; West Germany £4·0mn; Nigeria £3·6mn; Libya £3·2mn; Netherlands £2·9mn; and India £2·5mn (UN *Trade Statistics*, series D, vols xvii (pp. 6851–2) & xviii (p. 7777)).

13 The retention of the heading 'Charges in England' as one of the major subheadings of the Indian Defence Accounts is in itself interesting, though it seems that nowadays this heading covers most if not all imports from western nations. The 1968–9 figure of £13·3mn, according to the Indian Inst. of Defence Studies and Analysis, 'was apparently the expenditure required for the maintenance of the Western equipment still in service in the three services', i.e. spares. The Institute also notes that the sudden rise of expenditure in 1969–70 and 1970–1 would seem to indicate some new purchases of western equipment for the army and the navy (*India in the world strategic environment; annual review 1969–70* (New Delhi, 1970), p. 322). An Indian spokesman added that even the figures given under 'Charges in England' are not complete, as other purchases are made under other heads and direct from India.

14 K. Subrahmanyam, 'Planning and defence', in Streeten/Lipton, p. 374.

15 From 1965 to 12 August 1973, she gave a figure of $1,800mn, pointing out that 'we pay for all our arms from the Soviet Union' (*FT*, 14 Aug. 1973). Major purchases have been 100 MiG 21 FIFLS (apart from those now being produced under licence); 100 Su7Bs; a £15mn of SA-2 missile complex; 2 squadrons of AN-12s; various helicopters; 4 'F'-class submarines; some *Petya*-class frigates; large numbers of tanks and personnel carriers; telecommunications equipment; and other weapons. It is hard to value such goods, but the dominance of purchases from the USSR in India's overseas defence expenditure seems clear.

16 Georgetown Research Project, *The Soviet military aid program as a reflection of Soviet objectives* (Washington, Atlantic Research Corp., 1965), pp. 61–5.

17 *Hindu*, 27 June 1962.

18 The fact that the Indians lost interest in the two Canberras is ominous for British defence salesmen, for they had been 'modified specially [thereby] rendering them unattractive to other potential customers' (HC 88, sess, 1968–9, p. 168). To provide a description of these modifications would make a good *New Statesman* competition.

19 *Dawn*, 13 Apr. 1968.

20 For a description of the arms and equipment transferred from the British Indian armed forces to independent India, see Kavic, p. 241, and Edgar O'Ballance, 'The Strength of India', *Military R.*, Jan. 1962, pp. 28 f.

21 This figure is arrived at by subtracting the aid given between 1960–1 and 1964–5—£14·7mn (table 9.6)—from a figure of £16·6mn cited in a parliamentary reply as the total value of military aid to India between 1950 and March 1965 (710 HC Deb., 249, written answer, 15 Apr. 1965, by the Commonwealth relations secretary).

22 Michael Edwardes, 'Illusion and reality in India's foreign policy', *Int. Aff.*, Jan. 1965, p. 52.

23 HC 88, sess, 1968–9, Winter Supplementary Estimates, Q110, pp, 24, 168. The 1966 decision to sell equipment to India previously promised as aid followed the appointment of Raymond Brown as Britain's first official 'Head of Defence Sales' in January 1966.

24 It is slightly surprising that in February 1967, when the Indians were considering the purchase of some of the 1962 military aid, a request was made to the British government for further information on some of the equipment. This suggests that the Indians were not fully aware of what they had been promised under the 1962 agreement (ibid., p. 19). Sales of equipment—whether to India is not stated—were still being made in 1969, when £513,851 was realized (HC 203, sess. 1969–70, p. II.23).

25 Up to 31 March 1969, £106,128 of interest on a loan of £1,944,407 had been paid. British firms involved include Vickers, Yarrow, and Sir Bruce White, Wolfe Barry & Partners.

26 HC 88, sess. 1968–9, p. 19.

27 'The officers generally reflect their British training, having adopted British military customs, mode of life, organization and uniform almost completely. English is the official language, they keep in close touch with British military developments, and show a keen interest in them . . .' (O'Ballance, pp. 25–35). Many Indian observers saw the situation somewhat differently: for example, 'The navy and air force are a complete mimic of the Royal Navy and Royal Air Force. . . . Whether in regard to foreign policy or defence arrangements, political-legal ideas and trade relations . . . British influence continues to be very potent. This is all the more pronounced in respect of our defence services. As weapons recurringly need servicing and maintenance components, it would not be wrong to conclude that today the operational capacity of the Indian military machine is deeply conditioned by British support' (H. M. Patel, 'Realities of the situation', *Seminar*, June 1962, pp. 20–31).

28 See Cmnd 4715, July 1971, esp. paras 1, 2, 5, & 7.

29 US Dept of State, *Nazi-Soviet Relations 1939–41* (1948), p. 257.

30 See A. M. Rendel, 'Russia's power in the Indian ocean', *The Times*, 15 Sept. 1970. The *Neue Zürcher Zeitung*, 15 Dec. 1968, had earlier reported that India has also offered Russia the use of facilities at Bombay, Cochin, Mormugao (Goa), and elsewhere.

31 Neville Brown, *Arms without empire; British defence role in the modern world* (Harmondsworth, Penguin 1967), p. 51. It is interesting to look back to Brown's analysis of Britain's role in the Indian Ocean (pp. 51–7) made in 1967, and especially to the large emphasis placed on the ill-fated F111 aircraft.

32 The real importance of all this may be assessed from the defeat of plans to make Aldabra into a major base, not by Indian protests about British influence in the Indian Ocean, but by British conservationists, worried about the effect of the base on the island's bird life.

33 *FT*, 9 Feb. 1972.

34 Ibid.

35 However, Mrs. Gandhi during her visit to Britain in the autumn of 1971 evidently offered to sign a treaty similar to the Indo-Soviet one with the UK (A. Pant, Indian High Commissioner to Britain, in a talk at Glasgow University, 16 Nov. 1971). The British response to this offer was negative.

36 *Guardian*, 9 May 1969. Indian spokesmen also registered concern at the presence of 'foreign

naval vessels' in the Indian Ocean in December 1969, but refrained from identifying the Russians as being involved (*The Times*, 20 Dec. 1969).

37 T. B. Millar, *The Indian and Pacific oceans; some strategic considerations*, Adelphi Paper No. 57 (London, 1969), p. 5.

38 This deficiency in internal military research and development is mainly the fault of the UK, who considered it unnecessary in the days before partition for the Indian defence forces to have a scientific organization of their own, as they could always draw upon results and advances achieved in the UK. India therefore had to set up her own Military Science Research and Development Organization from scratch, with help from Britain (see H. M. Patel, *The defence of India* (London, Asia, for Gokhale Inst. Pol. & Econ., 1963)). A similar deficiency also existed with the organization of the intelligence services in the Indian military establishment until 1962.

39 In 1957–63 the spares purchased for India's Hawker Hunter jet fighters had exceeded by 160% the initial cost of the aircraft, many of which had been grounded because the foreign exchange constraint had prevented spares being obtained (*Christian Science Monitor*, 24 Sept. 1963).

40 The Indian Navy was long reported to have shown an interest in this particular plane as a possible replacement for the Seahawks on INS *Vibrant*, although this was vetoed by the Ministry of Defence (*The Economist*, 24 May 1969, p. 79).

41 In 1966 Harold Wilson raised this same issue in a speech to the Parliamentary Labour Party. He suggested that Britain should 'be ready to provide India with an alternative to being forced to rely either on the super-powers for nuclear guarantees or going nuclear herself' (Brown, p. 56).

42 The most recent major indication was perhaps Mr C. Subramaniam's report to the GOI in May 1969 advising the development over the next ten years of an advanced, *Indian-made* ground attack fighter at an estimated development cost of Rs300–400mn. However, the choice between an indigenous and an imported engine was then left open, and foreign aid for guided-weapon development—if 'obtained judiciously'—commended (*India in the world strategic environment; annual review 1969–70*, p. 300). The GOI's decision on these recommendations has still not been made public.

43 *FT*, 17 Sept. 1970. There are indications that UK arms sales to India began to rise again in 1970–1, to perhaps £6mn, but we cannot be sure, because SITC 9 is, since 1968, no longer disaggregated by sales of sub-items (such as SITC 951, armaments) to individual countries. However, it is hard to see how the other miscellaneous items—live animals, postal packets, and exports of less than £50—could cause the sharp rise discerned for category 9 in 1970. See also table 11.5, where purchases from England were scheduled to rise over 1969–70 and 1970–1.

Notes to pp. 191–206

Chapter 12. The Media: Images and Opinions

1 In 1969 the foreign-sales manager of one British daily told the authors that it had lost over £1,000 on selling papers to India during 1968—roughly 2·9 p per copy, but that they con-considered this 'a small price to pay to give their advertisers entry to the huge Indian market'.

2 We are greatly indebted to Evan Charlton for much of the information in this chapter.

3 Kevin Rafferty's excellent reporting for the *FT* during the hostilities of 1971 was an important example of this solid and respectable coverage.

4 Cmd 7317 (1948).

5 'The space allotted to coverage of a country, and indeed the tone of it, has in the past been very much a function of the particular correspondent concerned, both on *The Times* and the *Guardian*. When I was in Tokyo, for instance, *The Times* carried an average of 4,000 to 5,000 words a week from Japan, and this dropped sharply in the week after I had resigned to an average of less than 500 words a week. Since the cause was my resignation, this could hardly have been the result even of a covert policy decision on the part of the paper' (John White, personal communication).

6 An attempt was also made to tabulate all entries under 'India' and the countries shown in table 12.4 in *The Times Index*, but the task proved herculean, and was complicated by the

fact that the method of indexing entries appears to have changed over the years. For India alone, however, the number of entries, around 30–40 per month, does not seem to have altered much since independence.

7 As yet, television in India is insignificant: there were only 6,300 sets in operation in 1968, all within 30 km of New Delhi. The Fourth Plan envisaged the spread of television to Bombay, Madras, Calcutta, Kanpur-Lucknow, and Srinagar, and in 1974 NASA was to loan India its ATS–F satellite for a year to beam programmes of purely Indian origin to a selection of 5,000 villages, which will be the first in the world to receive programmes direct from a satellite (A. K. Agarwal, 'Is India ready for satellite TV?', *New Scientist*, 4 May 1972, p. 280). Britain's reputation and expertise in the TV field could perhaps find a profitable outlet assisting this proposed future Indian development, superficially elitist, yet potentially a very powerful tool of agricultural extension.

8 HC 387, sess. 1968–9, Report on the BBC, question and answer 275.

9 Cmnd 4107 (1969), p. 103: 'We have the impression that a broadcast in the vernacular makes the educated listener, with whom we are dealing here, feel that it is being especially slanted to him and that he is therefore [*sic*] likely to be that much less receptive. Moreover, foreign-language broadcasts are less likely to attract the influential few—i.e. those whom we must rely on to see that Britain's political and commercial case does not go by default.'

10 Cmnd 4824 (1971), p. 69.

11 Cmnd 1174 (1960), and *1970–71*, pp. 224–5.

12 This is a less crude indicator of actual listeners than might appear at first sight. There are far fewer radios per person in, for instance, India than France; on the other hand, the typical audience in India is bigger (in an extended family or even around a communal set in the evening at the village school), and listens longer because, especially in rural areas, alternative entertainment is scarcer.

13 IIPO, *Monthly . . . Survey*, Sept. 1969, p. 6. 'The radio remains primarily an instrument for the dissemination of news and entertainment' (ibid., p. 1).

14 Cmnd 3779 (1968), p. 66.

15 Ibid., p. 66.

16 IIPO, *Monthly . . . Survey*, Sept. 1969, p. 17.

17 Cmnd 3779, p. 66.

18 IIPO, *Monthly . . . Survey*, Sept. 1969, p. 17.

19 However, if this were so, it would parallel the situation in East Africa, where surveys in 1970 showed that in urban Kenya, Tanzania, and Uganda the BBC had a clear lead over the other main external broadcasters in English, although it did less well in its share of those listening to external broadcasts in Swahili (Cmd 4824, p. 77).

20 Indian officials were at pains to point out that the GOI, in closing down the BBC's office, had nothing against Mr Robson, and had not issued him with a personal expulsion order (*The Scotsman*, 28 Aug. 1970).

21 Jeremy Isaacs, Thames Controller of Features, quoted ibid., 2 Sept. 1970. The conditions that the Indians laid down are so remarkable as to be worth quoting: 'We [the Thames team] agree to accept the guidance of the [Indian] High Commission (in London) in respect of any material which is considered objectionable.' Thames accepted this, and then an appendix agreeing that all their exposed film would be taken from Calcutta by an External Affairs Ministry official for immediate shipment to the High Commission in London! 'It will then be processed at the risk and cost of Thames Television and seen and examined by the High Commission, who can delete any material considered objectionable.' Thames eventually gave up, claiming that they had agreed to guidance but not to veto (ibid., 4 Sept. 1970).

22 We should at once name the honourable exceptions with regard to Indian coverage during the 1960s: *FT*, *The Economist*, BBC radio, and the *Scotsman* (one of the few British papers to make sensible use in Indian matters of Agency services). One might add, though as a mark of their goodwill rather than of their coverage, *the Guardian*, *New Statesman* and BBC 2 television. Many other national and provincial papers and weeklies do not misreport Indian news, because they scarcely report it at all.

23 The changing position of *The Times* has also been noted within Britain: 'One used to talk, it will be remembered, *The Times* says this, *The Times* says that. *The Times* in those days was anonymous and accepted responsibility for everything printed; and all its writers down even to its critics accepted *The Times* style and its attitudes and wrote as a collective.

Whether the change is for good or bad, it certainly does mean a certain loss of authority'
(T. C. Worsley, 'Reporting is reporting is . . .', *FT*, 3 May 1972).

24 We rely heavily here upon Evan Charlton's account of British reporting made in his unpublished paper 'Indian and Britain: reflections in a paper mirror', delivered to the Britain-India Forum at India House, London, in mid-1968.

25 'No old India hand was put on to pay homage to a man who was not only distinguished in his own right, but the Head of State of the biggest country in the Commonwealth. The death of a local "pop" singer would almost certainly have been given greater prominence' (*India Weekly*, 8 May 1969, p. 8).

26 A reference to the fact that *one* Congress MP had *suggested* that Mr Jagjivan Ram, the Minister of Food and Agriculture, could be a *possible* successor to Dr Hussain!

27 Peterborough neglected to point out that Hussain had gone to pre-Nazi Berlin. Indeed, as we saw earlier (p. 141), many Indian scholars, especially in science and engineering, had gone to Germany just before and just after the First World War.

28 *The Observer*, 11 Aug. 1968. However, one cannot seriously deny that the enormous and regular coverage given by this paper during 1968–9 to one side only of the Nagaland dispute —as against its virtual neglect of the more important issues of Indian politics, economics, agriculture, and social development—was disproportionate. (It still is.)

29 Charlton.

30 *India 1969*, p. 141.

31 In India, as in most countries, circulation figures are misleading. 'Sometimes, in a remote village, a single copy of a newspaper—which may have reached the village as the wrapping around a parcel brought home from the nearest market town—may be read by every literate villager. Carefully pressed flat, it is shared by all. Many eyes strain at it, many forefingers follow its lines. Those who are literate read aloud to those who are not. Heads nod. It makes no difference if the paper is several weeks old' (B. P. Lamb, *India; a world in transition* (New York, Praeger, 1963), p. 219).

32 *India 1969*, p. 142.

33 Lamb, p. 219, gives the English-language dailies 22·8% of total daily circulation in 1960; by the end of 1968 (*India 1969*, p. 142, table 52) the share had risen to 26·7%. However, as the vernacular press is relatively stronger in rural areas (see n. 31 above), the share of *readership* may be much smaller.

34 IIPO, *Monthly . . . Survey*, Sept. 1969, p. 34. '[Many households] . . . take, in addition to the English newspaper, another paper in an Indian language, mainly for the [ladies]' (*Report of the Press Commission* (New Delhi, 1954), Part 1, p. 22)).

35 IIPO, *Monthly . . . Survey*, Sept. 1969, p. 34. The regional element can be seen in the fact that in Bombay 68% of English-language readers took *The Times of India*; in Madras, 71% the *Hindu*; in Delhi, 37% the *Hindustan Times* and in Calcutta, 30% *The Statesman*.

36 Ronald Segal, *The crisis of India* (Harmondsworth, Penguin, 1965), p. 291. One observer predicted in 1960: 'The English-language press will [in the future] address the well-to-do in cosmopolitan centres, while the regional language papers . . . will bid for the widening mass market in the hinterlands' (Harrison, *India*, p. 85).

37 However, Andrew Yule retained a 13% interest in *The Statesman* as part of the new owning syndicate of 13 major business firms.

38 'I remember that when I was a boy the British-owned newspapers in India were full of official news and utterances; of service news, transfers and promotions; of the doings of English society, of polo, races, dances and amateur theatricals. There was hardly a word about the people of India, about their political, cultural, social or economic life. Reading them one would hardly suspect that they existed' (Nehru, *Discovery of India*, p. 292).

39 In 1959 one American wrote: 'The Indian Press is a product of British journalism with an overlay of US journalism introduced since India's independence' (J. C. Merill, *A handbook of the foreign press* (Baton Rouge, Louisiana UP, 1959), p. 235). Frankly, we see little evidence of the 'overlay', then or now, except perhaps in the *Time*-style format of the left-wing weekly *Link*.

40 Some top Indian dailies have tried to produce their own crosswords, but have found it difficult to achieve a satisfactory compromise between complexity and simplicity. Crosswords are therefore bought from British papers, with those of *The Times* and *Daily Telegraph* being most popular. Hence Indians are faced with such clues as 'Book Dr Finlay for breaking the partnership? (9)', or 'A wartime conference has its place in the History

of the Royal Tank Regiment (5)', or such solutions as 'Carmarthenshire' or 'Elm' or 'Auld Reekie'. (Clues and answers from *The Statesman*'s reprinted *Times* crosswords.)

41 'In the English-language newspapers . . . the proportion of space devoted to foreign news is high. The British, who founded many of these papers, were quite naturally interested in events in the West. The stress on foreign coverage which they initiated has been continued' (Lamb, p. 220). Merrill (p. 235), estimated that 25% of the English-language press was related to foreign news stories, against 15% in the vernacular press. This confirms the earlier findings of the Indian Press Commission which noted that the vernacular (and thus regional) press downgraded not only international but also national (Indian) news, thus producing an 'inordinate parochialism of editorial standards' (Harrison, p. 86).

42 On the similarity between the *Hindu* and *The Guardian*, see e.g. Francis Williams, in *New Statesman*, 16 Aug. 1958, p. 187.

43 *The Hindustan Times* also used the *Daily Express* news service from 1949 to 1955, when its £1,000 annual charge was judged excessive, and its persistent anti-Nehru tone offensive.

44 UNI—United News of India—was started because of fear that the Press Trust of India, the oldest and largest of Indian news agencies, would fall under government control and thus be prevented from handling Reuters. More recently, a further and independent, multilingual agency, Samacher Bharati, has been set up in New Delhi to provide copy for Indian paper.

45 For instance, some of the best reporting of the Italian campaign during the Second World War was by an Indian correspondent working for Reuters.

46 'Only the larger [Indian] dailies have foreign correspondents; most of these are in London, a few in the Middle East (usually in Cairo), and most of the others in nations adjacent to India' (Merrill, p. 235).

47 Many of the Indian papers have ceased to publish weekly reviews, although *the Overseas Hindustan Times Weekly* news magazine still flourishes. *The Statesman*'s circulation in the UK never exceeded 2,000 per week; the other three major papers performed similarly.

48 Cmnd 4824, p. 83. These two new big power stations are to be built at Calcutta and Rajkot, and two 250 kw short-wave transmitters, for external broadcasting, are planned for Aligarh.

49 'Echo-reporting' can, however, also reveal weakness in the original copy and content of British papers. A distinguished Bengali who visited the UK in mid-1969 remarked: 'If the Indian press gives large-scale coverage to the 'invasion' of 144 Piccadilly by the Hippies, would this be surprising? *The Times*, after all, has given great prominence to so small an incident.'

50 Much of the coverage of these British problems is far from radical; one leading Indian cricket correspondent came out strongly *for* the 1970 South African cricket tour of England.

51 'Of late there have been bad feelings in India over what is regarded as a consistently hostile approach in British newspapers and television to the affairs of India . . . any comment on the State of India today might well find the root of misunderstanding between Britain and India in a difference of view over each other's national identity' (Richard Harris, 'India: a supplement', *The Times*, 30 Nov. 1970).

52 Indian observers do not agree that 'What the British government or people thought about the subcontinent no longer had any effect' (Tinker, *Experiment with Freedom*). By not agreeing, they make it untrue!

53 *Hindu*, 26 Feb. 1964. Members wanted to know whether it was true that the Indian government had provided facilities for a team of British journalists and cameramen to tour India to provide the basis of the exhibition. The government denied any connection. The PSP leader, H. V. Kamath, asked the government to tell the UK that hunger and poverty in India were the result of 150 years of British rule.

54 *Scotsman*, 28 Aug. 1970.

55 Segal. The book is certainly shallow and unsympathetic, given to reprinting tales of corruption and economic mismanagement (which certainly exist), and rather glib and facile in the style of its onslaughts upon the founders and leaders of independent India.

56 Shortly before the visit to India by the British royal family in 1960, the Indian Ministry of Culture bought up most of the copies of a book by a pro-Chinese author, Pundit Sunder Lal. The book, *The British Raj in India*, had been circulated to schools and colleges as an authentic history of the Raj, and concentrated on such aspects of British rule as torture, rape, and treehangings (*Daily Express*, 16 Sept. 1960).

57 The centre, sponsored by the Lokmanva Tilak Memorial Trust, was to be set up jointly

as an Indo-British venture at a cost of some £285,000. It was to have a theatre, library, exhibition hall, discussion rooms, club rooms, publication section and accommodation for visiting scholars. The Indian government provided a grant of £23,000, and British sponsors included Lord Mountbatten, the Archbishop of Canterbury, and Lord Russell (*Hindu*, 7 Apr. 1968).

58 Recent examples of American research into British attitudes towards India are Van Aalst, *The British view of India 1750–85* (Ph.D. thesis, Pennsylvania Univ., 1970); Cody, *British Attitudes towards India; a selection of documents* (Ph.D. thesis, Columbia Univ. 1970); and O'Keefe, *British attitudes towards India and the dependent empire, 1857–74* (Ph.D. thesis, Notre Dame Univ., 1968). Van Aalst notes: 'The British view of India in 1750 was an unprejudiced curiosity about an unknown and strange culture, [but] the growing trader's enclaves fostered attitudes of aloofness and suspicion towards Indian society', and increasing contact produced increasingly negative impressions of India and the Indians. Cody found that British attitudes changed dramatically with each succeeding generation throughout the late 18th and early 19th centuries, while O'Keefe found that in the period following the Sepoy mutiny British attitudes displayed 'a pattern of general apathy broken by periods of intense excitement, usually occasioned by a crisis to some possession'.

59 A. J. Greenberger, *The British image of India; a study in the literature of imperialism 1880–1960* (London, OUP, 1969).

60 O'Keefe.

61 '. . . . the world has changed. The last frontier has gone. The last new country is discovered and suburbanized. The oyster has closed. We are all Little Englanders now, at least, until we enter Europe, and alas some of us have little, closed minds' (L. Heren, 'The defence of the British empire', *The Times*, 6 Apr. 1972).

62 There must be reservations about such opinion surveys. In many cases, especially in the examples quoted, most of those questioned are not in possession of enough facts to form a useful opinion. Nevertheless, the images suggested by such surveys are interesting.

63 IIPO, *Monthly . . . Surveys*, No. 165–6, p. 17.

64 Ibid., No. 179, p. 18.

65 Ibid., p. 18. IIPO suggests that this popularity was due to Asian pride in Japan's economic success, coupled with disenchantment with the west. Further, Japan was a non-colonial, non-military power with no difference of opinion with India.

66 Stephen Hugh-Jones, *Guardian*, 5 Jan. 1962. Hugh-Jones added: 'One realises the *Daily Express* has its [Indian] equivalents'.

67 *The Times*, 11 Jan. 1965.

68 Kenneth Boulding, *The image; knowledge in life and society* (Ann Arbor, Michigan UP, 1956), pp. 6–7.

Notes to pp. 207–36.

Chapter 13. Indo-British Relations in a Divided World 1960–80

1 For a definition of 'elite' as used in this book see above, p. 239, n. 9.

2 The term 'comprador' originally denoted the agents of foreign firms in Chinese treaty ports (from the Portugese *compradores*) (E. Wolf, *Peasant wars of the twentieth century* (London, 1973), p. 125); by extension, initially to Latin America, but later to other poor countries, the term has come to denote any group of domestic businessmen or politicians with principal, or substantial, loyalties to foreign firms or to foreign governments representing the interests of such firms.

3 P. Okigbo, *Africa and the Common Market* (London, Longmans, 1967) is a convincing account of *one* such set of relationships. See also review in *Times Literary Supplement*, 6 March 1968.

4 The standard sources are, for 'partnership', *Partners in development*, and for 'dependence', *Capitalism and underdevelopment in Latin America*, by A. Gunder Frank (New York, Monthly Review Press, 1969). A discussion of some of the aid issues appears in T. Byres, ed., *Foreign resources and economic development* (London, Cass, 1972).

5 For a brilliant, if one-sided, interpretation of the British impact on India as 'development of underdevelopment' via the destruction of indigenous industry, see Nehru's *Discovery of India*.

6 See 'Indian officials divided over foreign aid', *FT*, 18 Oct. 1972, p. 8.

7 One wonders, incidentally, how this school of thought would account for the fact that India's largely British-trained and Westernized elite of the early 1960s was insufficiently 'comprador' to sustain the British connection.

8 M. Lipton, 'Labour and British economic policy towards Asia', in C. Jackson, ed., *Labour and Asia* (London, Fabian Society, 1973), p. 12.

9 I. M. D. Little & others, *Industry and trade in some developing countries*, pp. 6–7, 177–83.

10 Despite *lower* levels of income-per-person: South Asia's higher man/land ratio has both sharpened poverty and impelled industrialization.

11 Most recently at the January 1973 Congress Party Conference in Calcutta.

12 A good summary of the evidence is Bagchi, *Private investment in India*, pp. 3–5.

13 The reader may feel this sounds complacent or trite, but it is not therefore false.

14 More precisely, the big fluctuations in Britain's *total* exports and imports, plus the slowness of the decline in her dealings with India, meant that the latter transactions, as a share of the former, showed more marked fluctuations than down-trend between the wars.

15 Self-reliance in this latter sense of self-*sufficiency*, often—probably usually—is an impediment to self-reliance in the former sense of self-*financing*. Setting up inefficient import-replacing industries (a) often requires more imports of equipment and raw materials than it saves; (b) in general, diverts domestic resources from efficient export-oriented activities where they could earn more foreign exchange (see ch. 11, n. 11).

16 *Sunday Standard* (Calcutta), 31 Dec. 1972, p. 4. This enormous fall was made up of a decline (mostly US) in gross aid from Rs11,956mn to an estimated Rs6,000mn, and a rise in debt-servicing (capital and interest) from Rs3,300mn to Rs5,034mn.

17 See footnote 6 of this chapter.

18 This means that a particular adoption of the 'in principle' principle, at a given cost per head in misallocation of domestic resources, is (a) easier to adopt, (b) a larger sacrifice as a proportion of income-per-head, in India as compared with less poor but also less 'underdeveloped' countries in the Third World.

19 The fear that this gives them 'something for nothing' is misplaced. If they print more than the market will take, they will suffer via forced devaluation (and hence dearer imports and cheaper exports) sooner or later.

20 C. T. Leys, 'Political perspectives', in D. Seers & L. Joy, eds., *Development in a divided world* (Pelican, 1971).

21 Leys, 'What is the problem about corruption?' *J. Mod. African Stud.*, 3/2 (1965).

22 Leys, 'Interpreting African development: reflections on the ILO report on employment, incomes and equality in Kenya', mimeo., Univ. of London Seminar, 1973 (adapted from part of a draft for a wider study on Kenya).

23 Communist Party of India—Marxist.

24 For instance, even if Britain had sought to improve relations with India by (say) accepting higher cotton-textile quotas, Indian response was limited—she failed to meet even existing quotas fully in some years. More generally, if inattention to the needs of the relationship (pp. 15–16) had been remedied, economic constraints would still, for both parties, have put limits on its reconstruction.

25 'UK wants 1939 Trade Pact with India Terminated', *Statesman* (Calcutta), 3 Jan. 1973.

26 'Western policy in the sub-continent', *Round Table*, July 1972.

27 The facts that India now makes perhaps 90% of its arms needs (p. 178) and is indeed pushing arms *sales* in Asia ('India to push arms sales in Asia', *FT*, 2 Nov. 1972) in no way reduce the dangers of reliance for some *critical* arms on a single source—a lesson bitterly learned by India in 1965.

28 P. Tulloch, *The seven outside*, is a very useful summary of the facts.

29 R. N. Cooper, 'The European Community's system of generalized tariff preferences: a critique', *J. Dev. Stud.*, July 1972.

30 A useful critical summary of the literature on India's 'green revolution' is T. Byres, 'The dialectic of India's green revolution', *S. As. R.*, Jan. 1972.

31 FAO, *Monthly Bulletin of Agricultural Economics & Statistics*, passim.

32 The hybrid millets, rightly bred for robustness on the drought-prone soil of Western India, normally raise yields by 'only' 25–30%. Even if introduced to as much as 10% of millet land every year, this most desirable innovation could make a merely marginal contribution to *aggregate* grain output.

33 For possible contents of such a treaty see Lipton/Tulloch.

STATISTICAL APPENDIX

I Sources and Notes

A. General

1. 'British India' refers to the pre-independent India of the British raj and the princely states; it is thus broadly equivalent to present-day India, Pakistan, and Bangladesh combined, although until 1930s Burma was frequently included in many statistical series (see notes 6–7 to ch. 2). 'Pakistan', unless otherwise stated, refers to pre-1972 Pakistan (and thus includes Bangladesh). Figures for 'The Commonwealth' refer to those countries which were members at the relevant period, except that South Africa has been excluded from some Commonwealth figures in order to improve comparability over the 1950–70 period.

2. Calendar year information has been distinguished from that which is based on other periods by the usual conventions. Thus, data based on the Indian fiscal year (1 Apr.–31 Mar.), is signified by (e.g.) 1950/1 or 1969/70, and a series of such years by (e.g.) 1960/1 to 1970/1 or 1960/1–1970/1, against 1960 to 1970 or 1960–70, denoting calendar years. Unusual time-periods, such as educational years, are explained in the notes to the tables.

3. Unless otherwise stated, all volume figures have been expressed in metric units, using the standard conversions, namely:

$$1 \text{ ton} \quad = 1 \cdot 0160 \text{ tonnes}$$
$$1 \text{ yard} \quad = 0 \cdot 9144 \text{ metre}$$
$$1 \text{ sq. yard} = 0 \cdot 8361 \text{ sq. metre or } m^2$$

All values have been converted into new pence where appropriate. Other special conversions are explained in the notes to the tables.

4. Where exchange-rate conversions have been necessary they have been based on the relevant dollar-rates given in *International Financial Statistics*. For the period covered by this book, the main conversion rates have been as follows:

	19 Sept. 1949– 6 June 1966	6 June 1966– 18 Nov. 1967	18 Nov. 1967– 31 Dec. 1970	Ave. for 1971
US$ per £1.000	2·800	2·800	2·400	2·432
US$ per Rs1·000	0·210	0·133	0·133	0·133
Rs per £1·000	13·333	21·000	18·000	18·000

5. Details of sources have been telescoped to save space. Further particulars of the construction of the tables are obtainable from the authors.

B. Key to recurrent sources

Note: For list of House of Commons (HC) and Command (C., Cd, Cmd, Cmnd) papers excluded from this list, see above, p. 237.

AAS	Annual abstract of statistics (UK)
AR	Annual report
ASTUK	Annual statement of trade of the United Kingdom with Commonwealth and foreign countries (HM Customs & Excise)
BAS	British aid statistics (1964–9: UK Ministry of Overseas Development—ODM; from 1970: FCO, division of Overseas Development Administration—ODA)
BOPY	Balance of payments yearbook (IMF, Washington)
BTJ	Board of Trade Journal (UK)
CPO	Colombo Plan Organization (London)
CSO	Central Statistical Office (UK/India)
CT	Commonwealth trade (Commonwealth Secretariat, London)
CUYB	Commonwealth Universities Yearbook
DA	Development assistance [year] review (OECD/DAC, Paris)
DC	Development cooperation [year] review (OECD/DAC, Paris)
DT	Direction of trade (IMF, New York)
EJ	Economic Journal (London)
ET	Economic Trends (UK, CSO)
FT	Financial Times
IBRD/IDA	International Bank for Reconstruction and Development/International Development Agency
IFS	International financial statistics (IMF, New York)
IISS	International Institute for Strategic Studies
ITC, ABS	International Tea Committee, Annual bulletin of statistics (London)
JDS	Journal of Development Studies
MBS	Monthly Bulletin of Statistics (UN)
MDS	Monthly Digest of Statistics (UK, CSO)
MPOS	Monthly Public Opinion Surveys (Indian Inst. of Public Opinion)
OTAUK	Overseas trade accounts of the United Kingdom (UK, Dept of Trade & Industry)
OTSUK	Overseas trade statistics of the United Kingdom (name of above changed in 1971).
PBEI	Pocket book of economic information (Government of India)
PC	Plantation crops (Commonwealth Secretariat, London)
RBI, Report...	Reserve Bank of India, Report on currency and finance (Bombay, annual).
RBIB	Reserve Bank of India Bulletin (Bombay)
SABI	Statistical abstract for British India (Calcutta)
SAUK	Statistical abstract of the United Kingdom
SBIMR	State Bank of India, Monthly Review
TIYD	Times of India yearbook and directory (New Delhi)
UKBP	United Kingdom balance of payments (CSO)
UNSY	UN Statistical yearbook
UNYITS	UN Yearbook of international trade statistics

C. Sources and notes to tables

2.1 *SAUK*, 1868–82, C. 3662 (1883).

2.2 *Statement of the trade of British India with British possessions and foreign countries*
. . . 1869–70 to 1873/4, C.1372 (1875).

2.3 *SAUK*, Nos. 23, 41, 51, 60, 68, 75, 82 (1876–1939); *AAS*, Nos 86, 94, 104, 110
(1949–73). *SABI*, C.2673, 5210, 9519, Cd 5345, 8157, Cmd 3882, 6333 (1880–1942);
UNYITS, 1952–73. Notes: (1) All in current prices. (2) There are no reliable figures
for British India's trade with the UK for the 1939–41 period. (3) The early figures
for British India's trade give only an indication of the trading links, for not all trade
passed through the accounts and there are problems concerning the inclusion of
government stores and, in some cases, re-exports. (4) Figures for British India,
except for 1899–1901 & 1909–11, converted from rupees at the following rates:
1869–91, Rs1·00–1/3d (6·25p); 1919–21, Rs1·00–2/2d (10·83p); 1929–31, Rs1·00–1/6
(7.50p). (5) The differences in the two sets of mutual balance of trade figures are
caused by a number of factors: c.i.f./f.o.b. problems; calendar v. financial years;
different exchange rates for exports and imports; different transportation methods
and routes (and hence freight charges), and varying inclusion of items such as
government stores and military supplies.

2.4 *DT*, 1951–73. Notes: (1) Figures in this table are indicative rather than wholly
comparable because of problems inherent in aggregating data for India and Pakistan
(e.g. differential construction of trade statistics; different exchange rates and the real
representative nature of such rates; and the question of whether Indo–Pakistan trade
is fully reported). (2) All figures converted from dollar bases at rate specified above.

2.5 *AAS*, 95–9 (1958–72); *RBIB*, Jan. 1950–Feb. 1972; RBI, *Reports* . . . 1965–6,
1969–70, 1971–2. Notes: (1) The 'annual change in share' is the percentage change
p.a. over the periods as determined by a simple least squares trend line of the form
$Y_n = a - b_n$, and is equal to the b-coefficient. The 'average share' is the simple
average for the period. (2) The Indian data are on a fiscal-year base (UK statistics
on a calendar-year base) and thus run from 1950/1 to 1970/1.

2.6 *UNYITS*, 1951–63 & *DT*, 1968–72. Notes: dates of independence of colonies from
their metropolitan countries are: Philippines 1946; India & Pakistan 1947; Indonesia
1949; S. Vietnam 1955; Tunisia 1956; Ghana & Malaysia 1957; Zaïre (Belgian
Congo) 1960; Algeria 1962; Singapore 1963.

2.7 *IFS*, vols 18–26; *MBS*, vols 6–27. Notes: (1) 'World' excludes communist countries and thus in 1972 equals approx. 86% of a true global total. (2) 'Developed
nations' are equivalent to UN class 1 nations. (3) LDCs are equivalent to UN
class 2 nations. (4) Incl. petroleum exporters. (5) Excl. petroleum exporters.

3.1 *CT*, 1950–7, 1963, & 1970; *UNYITS*, 1952–3. Notes: (1) Developed Commonwealth = Australia, Canada, & New Zealand; Developing Commonwealth = total
Commonwealth minus developed Commonwealth. (2) EEC, though not yet in
existence in 1950, is defined in terms of the six (pre-1973) founder members.
(3) EFTA is defined as being equivalent to the pre-1973 membership minus Iceland.

3.2 *ASTUK*, vol. 1, 1961 & 1965; *OTSUK*, Dec. 1970.

3.3 RBI, *Report* . . . 1971–2. Note 1: 'Miscellaneous' is a residual category derived
by subtracting the total value of Indian imports in SITC groups 1–8 from the figure
for total imports (see esp. ch. 11 for a discussion of this).

3.4 *OTAUK*, 1960, 1965; *OTSUK*, 1970; RBI, *Report* . . . 1971–2. Note: Figures have
been adjusted on to a comparable fiscal-year base.

3.5 RBI, *Report* . . . 1968–9, 1971–2. Note: indices have been converted from an original 1958–100 base.

3.6 RBI, *Report* . . . 1971–2.

3.7 Cols 1 & 2: trade figures, *CT*, 1957 & 1961; aid figures, RBI, *Report* . . . 1967–8. Col. 3: ibid., 1969–70.

3.8 *MBS*, Dec. 1971, p. xvi; Dec. 1972, p. xviii. Countries listed were responsible for about three-quarters of total world exports of manufactured goods in 1970, or about 85% of world exports excl. communist nations.

4.1 *CT*, 1950–7, 1963, 1970; *UNYITS*, 1952–3. See notes to 3.1.

4.2 *ASTUK* for the years 1960, 1965 and 1970. Note: Figures for 1960 were converted from the old A–E classification to the current SITC-based 0–9 classification.

4.3 *MDS*, nos. 180–336 (1960–73). Note: Volume index converted from an original base of 1961—100.

4.4 RBI, *Report* . . . 1971–2. See notes to 3.3.

4.5 *ASTUK* for years 1960 and 1970. See note to 4.2.

4.6 *IFS*, vols. 9–24.

4.7 RBI, *Report* . . . 1968–9 & 1971–2. Note: indices converted from an original 1958—100 base.

4.8 Source as for 4.7.

4.9 ITC, *ABS*, 1965 & 1973.

4.10 *PC*, 10–14; *TI*, 10/12. Note: Figures for coffee incl. coffee extracts and essences, but these have been converted into 'bean equivalents'. All figures converted from an original lb/capita basis.

4.11 *PC*, 10–14. Note: Figures refer to 'gross imports' and are thus unadjusted to take account of subsequent re-exports. Unfortunately a change in the method of collecting UK trade statistics in 1970 ended a long series of 'net imports by origin' that had been published in the ITC, *ABS*.

4.12 *PC*, 10–14. Note: The East African group of tea producers comprises Kenya, Malawi, Mozambique, Uganda, and Tanzania. Prior to 1965 Rhodesia had also exported small amounts of tea and had been included in the above grouping, but it has been excluded from the figures in this and other tables.

4.13 Source as for 4.12.

4.14 ITC, *ABS*, 1967–73 (1967–73). Note: as explained in the text, there are problems involved in such a comparison of auction prices in that each garden's tea is a highly individualistic product and thus there is some lack of homogeneity in the above groups. It is however, accepted that the comparisons above are the correct ones to use.

4.15 & 4.16 Source as for 4.12.

4.17 *AAS*, 100–9 (1963–72); CS, *Industrial fibres: a review*, 16–20 (1966–73).

4.18 *AAS*, Aug. 1971 & passim.

4.19 *OTAUK*, 1959–61, 1964–6, 1969–71; *OTSUK*, 1971; *ASTUK*, 1959–61, 1964–6, 1969–71 vols. (1961–3, 1966–7, 1970–2). Note: figures for 1959–61 are converted from the old A–E trade classification, and figures for 1964 are derived from sub-totals.

4.20 Source as for 4.19. Note: average unit values are in new pence per square metre. As they are based on aggregative data they obviously ignore the important qualitative differences and the composition of the overall imports of woven cotton cloth, which includes everything from terry-towelling to dyed cotton curtains. Thus the average prices are only an indication.

4.21 & 4.22 RBI, *Report* . . . 1968–9, 1971–2.

4.23 CS, *Industrial fibres* . . ., 16–20 (1966–73).

4.24 Source as for 4.23. Note: in future tables published 'Pakistan' will be replaced by 'Bangladesh', as virtually all jute good production is concentrated in the former Eastern Province of Pakistan.

4.25 RBI, *Report* . . . 1968–9, 1971–2; *SBIMR*, 11/12.

4.26 *AAS*, Nos. 100–9 (1963–72); *ASTUK*; FAO, *Trade yearbooks*, vols 16–25 (Rome, 1963–72).

4.27 RBI, *Report* . . . 1968–9, 1971–2; FAO, *Production yearbooks*, vols 20–6 (Rome, 1963–72).

4.28 RBI, *Report* . . . 1968–9, 1971–2; *SBIMR*, 10/5.

5.1 *BOPY*, vols 12–23 (1961–72). Notes: (1) figures excl. transactions of the centrally planned economies. (2) There are a number of problems involved in constructing a table such as this, which is based on an aggregation of the invisible accounts of individual countries as published in the *BOPY*. Perhaps the main obstacle is the absence of accounts for countries which became independent after 1960, such as Chad, Gabon, Kenya, and Algeria. A fairly simple allocation technique has been applied to correct for this, and as the developed countries and the large LDCs dominate the overall accounts, any error caused by this cannot make a large impact on the overall results. The 1970 figures are thus the more accurate of the two.

5.2 *UKBP*, 1967 & 1972.

5.3 & 5.4 *ET*, Sept. 1970.

5.5 *BOPY*, vols 12–23. Note: (1) Travel credits for 1965–7 are estimates based on figures in RBI, *Report* . . . 1966–7 & 1967–8. For details of construction of Indian services and invisibles accounts and their accuracy see notes to the Indian pages in each *BOPY*.

5.6 *BOPY*, vols 14, 17, 23. Note: 1960–5 figures converted from Rs; 1966–9 from dollars at prevailing rates.

5.7 *BOPY*, vols 12–23. Notes: (1) figures for 1961–5 & 1966–71 relate to the services account only. (2) Invisibles figures for 1961–71 are equal to the 'services account' plus 'private transfers'.

5.8 Source as for 5.7. Note: (1) both 1961 and 1971 totals are derived from aggregating annual figures, with the £ sterling figures converted from US$ on an annual base and at the dollar-sterling rate for each year.

5.9 Chamber of Shipping of the UK, *British shipping statistics* 1970–1 (London, 1971).

5.10 *SABI*, no. 72 (1953); *RBIB*, Dec. 1972. Note: (1) tonnage—average of 'tonnage entered' and 'tonnage cleared'. (2) Figures for Indian shipping include native craft.

5.11 India, CSO, *Statist. abstract of the Indian Union*, nos 10–15 (New Delhi, 1961–7); *UNSY*, 1972 (1973). Notes: (1) figures cover those visiting for more than 24 hours but less than 6 months. (2) 1971 figures are on a slightly different basis from those given for earlier years but are broadly comparable.

5.12 *TI*, 7 Apr. 1971 & 29 Mar. 1973. Note: Figures excl. investment by and earnings from oil companies; before 1963 insurance companies were also excluded from the coverage.

5.13 M. Kidron, *Foreign investments in India* (London, 1965), p. 310, table 21.

5.14 Source as for 5.1. Note: (1) figures incl. estimates for 1960.

5.15 UK, Dept of Trade & Industry, *Business monitor M4: overseas transactions* (London, 1970–3).

5.16 RBI, *Foreign collaboration in Indian industry: a survey* (Bombay, 1968), tables 12 & 14. Notes: (1) figures for 1964/5 & 1965/6 are estimates; (2) UK figures are for calendar years; those for India are for fiscal years.

5.17 *RBIB*, Aug. 1969, p. 1151. Notes: (1) assets comprise holdings to foreign currency balances; foreign securities and shares plus fixed assets held abroad; and rupee overdrafts extended to foreign banks. (2) Liabilities cover overdrafts in foreign currencies, rupee deposits of non-resident official institutions, banks, and individuals; holdings of shares, etc. by non-residents in joint-stock banking companies (including their share of retained earnings); and profit and loss account balances and fixed assets of branches of foreign banks. (3) The total for 1967 includes a rise of Rs137mn in assets and Rs47mn in liabilities due to valuation changes resulting from the June 1966 rupee devaluation.

5.18 RBI, *Report* . . . 1964–5, pp. S112, S114; 1967–8, pp. S119, S121; 1964–70, pp. S128, S130.

5.19 *SABI*, No. 72; India, CSO, *Statist. abstract of the India Union*, 1970; *SBIMR*, 10/5.

5.20 & 5.21 Source as for 5.16, tables 21 & 24.

6.1 P. Deane & W. Cole, *British economic growth* 1688–1959 (Cambridge, 1969); *UKBP*, 1972.

6.2 *UKBP*, 1965, 1972. Note: 'Net government' incl. intergovernmental loans, UK subscriptions to multilateral organizations, etc.

6.3 K. L. Mitchell, *India: an American view* (London, 1943); RIIA, *The problem of international investment* (London, 1937); *RBIB*, Apr. 1960. Notes: (1) Tea only. (2) Petroleum excluded from 1911 & 1930 figures.

6.4 *UKBP*, 1970, 1972.

6.5 R. S. May, *JDS*, 4/3; *TI*, 23 Sept. 1970, 7 Apr. 1971 & 29 Mar. 1973. Note: values quoted represent the book values of net assets at the end of each year.

6.6 *TI* (dates as in 6.5).

6.7 L. B. Pearson, *Partners in development* (London, 1969); *DA*, 1971.

6.8 *TI*, 9 May 1969; *UNSY* 1968. Notes: (1) ave. population—1963 pop.—1967 pop./2. (2) Ann. ave. net investment 1963–7. (3) (2)÷(1).

6.9 *RBIB*, Aug. 1970. Note: the 1968 figures allow for valuation changes consequent on the 1966 rupee devaluation.

6.10 *PBEI*, 1965; *TIYD*, 1968; *RBIB*, Aug. 1970. Note: figures for net capital inflow exclude the period Jan.–Mar. 1963, which has been omitted because of a change in coverage from calendar to fiscal years in the published sources.

6.11 British estimates: May, *JDS*, 4/3; *BTJ*, 23 Sept. 1970. Indian estimates: *RBIB*, Apr. 1960, Aug. 1969; *PBEI*, 1965; *TIYD*, 1968. Notes: (1) allowance for portfolio holdings is based on the ratio of direct to portfolio capital in India (80:20) as given in *RBIB*, Aug. 1969, p. 1129. (2) In the published sources, it is stated that 'allowance has been made for the devaluation of June 1966', but there is no explanation of how this allowance was constructed. N.B.: British data and Indian data for 1958 & 1960 are for calendar years. For 1962–6 Indian figures refer to March of the following year (i.e. British figures for Dec. 1962, Indian figures for Mar. 1963). Although this is inappropriate, it does at least reduce the comparability gap from 9 to 3 months.

6.12 *PBEI*, 1965; *RBIB*, 19 Aug. 1970; *TI*, 15 Nov. 1973. Notes: (1) Est. (2) 1971 figures are converted from £ sterling for comparability.

6.13 *TIYD*, 1972; *Who owns whom*, 1971–2 (London, 1972). Notes: (1) Shell Transport & Trading is 40% British-controlled: this is allowed for in calculations. (2) In the case of associated companies, British participation has been taken to be equal to the value of British-held shares in the companies concerned.

6.14 & 6.15 *BTJ*, 23 Sept. 1970; *TI*, 15 Nov. 1973, pp. 370–1, table 2.

6.16 Source as for 5.16, ch. 2, p. 15, table 7. Notes: (1) Ordinary shares in subsidiaries or minority ventures held overseas in country stated. (2) Col. 1 figures as % of column total. (3) These figures are of share held abroad as a % of total issued share capital of companies in India, i.e. a UK subsidiary in India, i.e. a UK subsidiary in India will, on average, have 81·3% of its shares held by the British parent company and 18·7% by Indian shareholders.

6.17 *Eastern Economist*, 15 Aug. 1969, p. xvi.

6.18 *RBIB*, June 1970, pp. 936–46, Notes: (1) incl. 187 foreign-controlled rupee companies. (2) Incl. 71 foreign-controlled rupee companies.

7.1 IBRD, *Trends in developing countries*, 1973 (Washington, 1973); *DC*, 1972. Notes: (1) Excl. grants by private voluntary agencies. (2) Deflated by LDC import price index: 1961–100.

7.2 *DA*, 1970; *DC*, 1972.

7.3 Source as for 7.2. Note: (1) at current prices.

7.4 *DA*, 1969; *DC*, 1972. Note: Total sterling area = India and Pakistan + Other Commonwealth + Other sterling area.

7.5 *UNSY*, 1968; *DA*, 1969. Note: 80 nations were included in the original DAC table.

7.6 IBRD/IDA, *AR*, 1973; *World Bank Atlas*, 1973.

7.7 776 HC Deb., 315; *BAS, 1965 to 1969* (1970) & *1966 to 1970* (1971); *IFS*, vols 19–25 (1966–72); *MDS*, Nos 216–336 (1967–73). Notes: (1) Deflated by export price index for manufactured goods. (2) Deflated by general import price index. (3) Deflated value of net official assistance, 1961–70.

7.8 776 HC Deb., 315; *BAS* (as for 7.7); DA, 1969 & 1970.

7.9 *AAS*, no. 105 (1968); HC 302, sess. 1970–1, notes on classes 5 & 6.

7.10 *DA*, 1969 & 1970; ODA, *An account of the British aid programme* (1970). Notes: (1) Full compliance with the 1965 DAC recommendations meant that either the percentage of total commitments in grant form was greater than 70% or that the following provisions were fulfilled: (a) 81% or more of total commitments as grants or loans at less than 3%; (b) 82% or more of total commitments as grants and loans with maturities of over 25 years; (c) a weighted average grace period of 7 years or greater. (2) The 1970 figures excluded Commonwealth Development Corporation investments, as their terms were not available at publication.

7.11 *BAS* (as for 7.7).

7.12 *UNSY*, 1968; *BAS, 1965 to 1969* (1970).

7.13 ODA, *An account of the British aid programme* (1971).

7.14 RBI, *Report* . . . 1971–2. Notes: (1) Estimates for 4th Plan period are from the *Mid-term appraisal*. (2) Figures for 1966–7 onwards are at new foreign-exchange rates.

7.15 RBI, *Report* . . . 1964–5, 1968–9, & 1971–2. Notes: (1) Figures are unadjusted for the June 1966 devaluation, although this makes little difference to the 1966/7 figures. (2) Refers to first two years of the 4th Plan only. (3) Other assistance is mainly from the USA, covering PL480 & PL665 and third country currency assistance.

7.16 J. N. Bhagwati & P. Desai, *India: planning for industrialization* (London, 1970); RBI, *Report* . . . 1968–9; 1971–2. Notes: (1) Incl. some aid utilized prior to Apr. 1951. (2) Exc. debt rescheduling and postponement of interest agreements.

7.17 *MPOS*, vol. 14, June–July & Sept. 1969; vol. 15, Dec. 1969 & Aug. 1970.

7.18 *BAS* (as for 7.7). Notes: (1) Figures up to 1964 relate to financial years; the rest to calendar years. (2) Comprehensive repayment figure prior to 1965 do not seem to be available on a comparable basis. The amortization data are translated from the information given in vol. 19 of the *BOPY*.

7.19 IBRD/IDA, *AR*, 1970; IBRD/IFC, *AR*, 1970. Notes: (1) UK held 12·93% of original IDA subscriptions, but 14·1% if supplementary subscriptions were included. In the above calculations, 13% chosen as UK share, as being a fair balance between these two figures. (2) We chose an exchange-rate of US$2·70 = £1·00 to allow for the 1967 devaluation. If one used different exchange-rates, the overall UK amount would differ, ranging from £68·7mn at US$2·80 = £1·00 to £80·2mn at US$2·40 = £1·00.

7.20 HC 242, sess. 1967–8, para. 23; CPO, *AR*, 1966–8 (1967–9); HC 288, sess. 1969–70, p. 2; *FL*, 22 Apr. 1971. Notes: (1) Figures may not add exactly as they are compiled from a wide range of sources; there is no complete set of published figures covering UK project and non-project aid to India.

7.21 RBI, *Report* . . . 1965–6, 1968–9, 1971–2. Notes: (1) First 2 years of 4th Plan only. (2) The lack of coincidence in the totals and between authorization and utilization totals is due to the effect of both the Indian and UK devaluations.

7.22 *BAS, 1966 to 1970* (1971).

7.23 RBI, *Report* . . . 1967–8 & 1971–2; *CT*, 1950–7 & 1960 (1960, 1961). Notes: (1) Both aid and trade figures exclude the short pre-devaluation period in 1966–7 (i.e. Apr. 1966–5 June 1966). (2) Fall in USSR figure is due to increased importance of barter-trade agreements, plus slow disbursements of Soviet aid.

7.24 ODM, 'An analysis of aid-trade relationships in India' (unpubl. memo., 1968), table 9.

7.25 Source as for 7.24, table 3.

7.26 *FT*, 6 Nov. & 11 Dec. 1970; 8 Jan., 5 Feb., 5 & 25 Mar., & 8 Apr. 1971.

7.27 & 7.28 B. Hopkin et al., 'Aid and the balance of payments', *EJ*, Mar. 1970, tables III & IV.

8.1 *DA*, 1970; *DC*, 1972; IBRD, *Trends in the developing countries*, 1973.

8.2 *DA*, 1968; *DC*, 1972. Notes: (1) Figures for 1962 are not strictly comparable with those for 1965 and 1970 as the reporting basis for both above categories was changed in 1965. (2) Estimate.

8.3 ODM, *Overseas development: the work in hand*, Cmnd 3180 (1967); *BAS, 1965 to 1969 & 1966 to 1970*. Note: Prior to 1964/5, figures were only available on a financial-year basis.

8.4 *BAS* (as for 8.3). Note: IUC = Inter-University Council for Higher Education Overseas; TETOC = Council for Technical Education and Training for Overseas Countries.

8.5 *BAS* (as for 8.3).

8.6 *Aid to developing countries*, Cmnd 2147 (1963); *BAS 1966 to 1970*, table 22.

8.7 *BAS, 1965 to 1959 & 1966 to 1970*.

8.8 CPO, 16th–18th *AR* (1969–71).

8.9 *BAS* (as for 8.7); CPO, 9th–14th *AR* (1962–7). Note: Figures for 1959–60 refer to financial years, as do those for India for 1964–65. The UK figures for the columns headed 1964–5 actually refer to 1965–6.

8.10 CPO, 17th–18th *AR* (1970, 1971).

8.11 *BAS, 1966 to 1970.*

8.12 Chartered Insurance Inst., *Annual surveys on overseas students training in insurance in the UK* (London, mimeo., 1964–70); *Yearbook of the Commonwealth* (1969), p. 638.

8.13 HC 205–II, sess. 1969–70, Annex 9 (memo. by Dept of Employment & Productivity). Note: The West Indies includes all listed Caribbean Commonwealth countries, plus Guyana and the Atlantic territories.

8.14 *TIYD*, 1968, 1971. Notes: (1) DSTP = Directorate of Scientific & Technical Personnel. (2) Above figures are of scientific and technical personnel who have been abroad after 1 Jan. 1957 for higher studies, training or employment, who were still abroad at the end of Mar. 1967 and Jan. 1971 respectively, and who had registered with the Indians Abroad Section of the National Register of Scientific and Technical Personnel maintained by the DSTP.

8.15 Indian Inst. of Applied Manpower Research, *Fact book on manpower*, 2nd edn New Delhi, 1970), Pt 3, 'Scientific and Technical Personnel'. Notes: (1) Numbers are of those registered with the Indians Abroad section of the DSTP, and who have not returned. (2) Incl. agricultural engineers.

8.16 O. Gish, 'Medical education and the brain drain', *British Journal of Medical Education*, 4/3 (1969).

8.17 Home Office, *Control of immigration statistics under the Commonwealth Immigration Acts of 1962, 1968*, Cmnds 4029, 4327, 4620 (1969–71). Note: (1) Entries under 'Category B' vouchers.

8.18 775 HC Deb., 261.

8.19 HC 205–II, sess. 1969–70, p. 215 (memo. by Dept. of Health & Social Security). Note: (1) Figures for total medical staff are derived from published tables by multiplying up from percentage figures, so may not be fully representative of actual figures in post at that time.

8.20 O. Gish & A. Robertson, 'Britain's medical "brain gain" ', *New Statesman*, 14 Mar. 1969, p. 353.

8.21 Sources are outlined in text & in 8.15–8.20 above. Notes: (1) All Indian 'flows' to UK of TA over 1960–70 are estimated on the basis of saved training costs of new medical and other personnel entering Britain. In each case, minimum estimates are employed (see text).

9.1 Dept. of Ed. & Science, *Statistics of education*, vol. 2, 1962, 1965, 1970 (1963, 1966, 1972).

9.2 Source as for 9.1, and *World Bank Atlas*, 1973. Note: (1) Excl. Singapore; incl. Sabah & Sarawak.

9.3 *CUYB*, 1949, 1962, 1972, Appendices on Overseas Students at British Universities. Notes: (1) In 9.3–9.6 figures for 1970–1 may not be exactly comparable with those for earlier years, because in 1967–8, the Ass. of Commonwealth Universities changed their definition of 'Overseas Student'. An indication of the difference can be seen in that 1967–8 the number of full-time Indian students at British universities under the two definitions were:

old definition: 1568   new definition: 1429.

Thus the decline between 1960–1 and 1970–1 may be somewhat overstated; but allowing for the change in definition, the shares of the individual countries is relatively unaffected. For an explanation of the change see Assoc. of Commonwealth Universities, *Students from other countries in universities in Britain, 1967–8* (1968), p.2.

9.4 *CUYB*, 1962, 1972; IBRD, *World Bank Atlas*, 1973. Note: (1) As % of all students from each country.

9.5 & 9.6 *CUYB*, 1962, 1972.

9.7 & 9.8 *CUYB*, 1971.

9.9 Indian Inst. of Applied Manpower Research, *Report No. 2, Graduates of Indian Institutes of Technology in India and abroad* (New Delhi, 1967).

9.10 & 9.11 Communications from Secretary, Royal College of Physicians of Edinburgh, Mar. 1970 and of Royal College of Surgeons, Edinburgh, Apr. 1970.

9.12 *CUYB*, 1970–2. Note: These are the only countries for which data are available.

9.13 *CUYB*, 1963, 1966, 1972.

9.14 & 9.15 UK Commonwealth Scholarship Commission, *AR*, 1961–71.

9.16 *BAS, 1965 to 1969 & 1966 to 1970.*

9.17 *BAS, 1966 to 1970.*

9.18 Cambridge Univ., Centre of S. Asian Studies, *List of scholars resident in Europe 1970* (1970). Note: (1) Figures in the table give only an indication of the relative strength of South Asian studies in each of the European nations, as many scholars have not yet been contacted for inclusion in the list, and many others have strong South Asian interests, although not primarily concerned with the area.

9.19 Sources as for 9.18 & Univ. of London, Inst. of Latin American Studies, *Latin American studies in the universities of the UK 1968–9* (1969).

9.20 Sussex Univ., IDS, *Register of social science research projects in the field of development studies* (Brighton, 1970). Note (1): It must be borne in mind that the figures quoted in this table are based purely on projects actually listed in the 1970 Register. The Institute estimates that these may well be only about half of development studies projects in progress in the UK in 1970.

10.1 *Census of India, 1961* (New Delhi, 1965), vol. 1, pt. II, Migration Tables. Note: (1) Figures exclude diplomatic personnel.

10.2 Source as for 10.1 & *TIYD*, 1972. Note: The States named in the table are those existing in 1961. Since then, a number of changes have taken place. Madras has been renamed Tamil Nadu (1968); parts of Assam have been split off to form the new state of Meghalaya (1970) and a new Union Territory of Arunachal Pradesh (1972); the Punjab was split in 1966 into the states of Punjab and Harayana, and a new Union Territory of Chandigarh was set up to be their joint capital.

10.3 M. Kurian, *Impact of foreign capital on the Indian economy* (New Delhi, 1966). Note: Because of inflation, the salary scales obviously mean very different things in 1947 and 1965, but we have not attempted to adjust the figures on to a constant price basis mainly because a large number of the non-Indian nations had important non-monetary incomes in the form of company-sponsored travel and housing services. However, the reversal in the relative proportions of Britons and Indians in a mere 8 years is of interest.

10.4 Elspeth Huxley, *Back streets, new worlds: a look at immigrants in Britain* (London, 1964), App. A.

10.5 Source as for 10.4, App. B. Note: The period covered in the table relates to Jan. 1955–July 1963.

10.6 Source as for 8.17, Cmnds 2658, 3258, 4029 & 4620. Notes: (1) + = net immigration; − = net emigration.

10.7 London, Census 1961, England & Wales, Birthplace & Nationality Tables (London, 1964); Census 1961, Scotland, Birthplace & Nationality Tables (Edinburgh, 1966); Office of Population Census & Surveys and General Register Office, Edinburgh, Census 1971, Great Britain, *Advance Analysis* (London, 1972). Notes: (1) The old Commonwealth comprises Australia, Canada, & New Zealand. South Africa has been excluded from the Commonwealth figures in 1961 to ensure comparability. (2) The total includes those with no stated birthplace.

10.8 *TIYD*, 1970; *UNSY*, 1970. Note: Figures for Indians overseas cover both those who are Indian born, and those of Indian descent born in the country involved.

10.9 Source as for 10.6. Notes: (1) Discrepancies between the admissions under employment vouchers in tables 3, 7, & 9 of the 1968 and 1970 statistics given in the White Papers listed arise because tables 7 & 9 are based on 'used and surrendered vouchers' which are not fully accurate, whilst table 3 figures are based on the actual number of Commonwealth citizens admitted as voucher-holders, and these should thus be taken as a more accurate return of the numbers arriving. (2) All percentages relate to rows 2–6 only.

10.10 Source as for 10.6.

10.11 HC 205–II, sess. 1969–70, evidence of Dept of Employment & Productivity, Annexes 3 & 4.

10.12 Dept of Education & Science, *Statistics of education 1970* (1971), Vol. 1, Schools, tables 36 & 37.

10.13 Source as for 10.12, table 36. Note: (1) Immigrant pupils are defined as including: (a) children born outside Britain who have come to this country with, or to join, parents or guardians whose countries of origin were abroad; and (b) children born in the UK to parents whose countries of origin were abroad and who came to the UK on or after 1 Jan. 1960, but excluding children from Eire and children of mixed immigrant-nonimmigrant parentage. (See source, p. xiv, note 34.)

10.14 London, Census, 1961, England & Wales, Industrial Tables, Pt 1; Census 1961, Scotland, Industrial Tables, Pt 2. Note: The above figures are based on a 10% sample.

10.15 Cmnd 4107 (1969), Annex E. Notes: (1) 'Other' incl. Heads of Posts; Information: Consular Officials/Visas; Registry; Typing; Administration; Security Guards; etc. (2) Total excl. 232 members of the Communications Service of the Diplomatic Service.

10.16 HC 174, sess. 1969–70, vol. 2.

10.17 FCO, *London Diplomatic List*, 1971.

11.1 & 11.2 L. J. Kavic, *India's quest for security* (Berkeley, 1967): G. Thayer, *The war business* (London, 1970), *Jane's Fighting Ships 1968–9* (1968); IISS, *The military balance, 1970–1* (London, 1970); various press reports.

11.3 *ASTUK*, 1959–65, vol. 4; UN, *Commodity trade statistics: series D, 1966–8* (New York, 1967–9). Notes: (1) Figures for 1966–8 converted from dollar values at following rates: 1966, US$2·80 = £1·00; 1967, US$2·752 = £1·00; 1968, US$2·40 = £1·00. (2) The British and UN categories involved are not 100 % identical in coverage, viz: H.M. Customs & Excise list 'Arms, Ammunition and Military Stores'; UN list 'Firearms, Weapons of War and Ammunition'. However, in the period 1963–5 the two sets of figures are virtually identical, with roughly 3·7% differences, and these may be partly due to exchange-rate conversion figures.

11.4 RBI, *Report* . . . 1967–8, 1971–2. Notes: (1) Equal to 'Grant Total' in the Indian Foreign Trade, Accounts listed in the above sources, including 'Miscellaneous Transactions and Commodities' which almost certainly includes armaments and defence supplies. (2) Probably comprises postal packets, unspecified imports and armaments, as in UK trade statistics. (3) Converted at following rates: to May 1966, Rs13·33 = £1·00; May 1966—Nov. 1967, Rs21·0 = £1·00; Nov. 1967 onwards, Rs18·00 = £1·00. Flows of imports are assumed to be evenly distributed over the years; thus small errors could be possible.

11.5 Indian Inst. for Defence Studies & Analysis, New Delhi, *India in the world strategic environment*; *AR 1969–70*.

11.6 *UK, Civil appropriation accounts: 1960/1 to 1971/2*, publ. annually as House of Commons papers (1961–72); HC 302, sess. 1970–1; and *Defence Accounts*, publ. annually as House of Commons papers under various titles. Notes: (1) Incl. subscriptions to e.g. NATO, CENTO, SEATO, and UN peacekeeping forces. (2) Incl. para-military expenditure, civil police units, bomb clearance, civil defence overseas, etc. (3) The main votes of relevance in the Civil Appropriation Accounts are Clauses 2 & 10.

11.7 Sources for 11.6. Notes: (1) Balance due on the building of a frigate, which strictly speaking had been supplied outwith normal defence aid. (2) Balance due on purchase of destroyers, which again had been supplied outwith normal defence aid.

11.8 Ministry of Defence (private communication), Sept. 1969 from the Head of Defence Liaison, India; Min. Defence, *Report for 1968–9*.

11.9 Ministry of Defence (as for 11.8).

11.10 UK *Diplomatic Service List*, 1969; FCO, *London Diplomatic List*, 1969. Note: (1) Incl. defence supply and liaison officers.

12.1 Figures supplied by the Circulation Offices of the papers and magazines concerned. The actual number of papers reaching India is probably much greater than suggested by the figures, for some are probably sent privately; others are sent by companies; some arrive, e.g., with airline passengers; others are supplied via Indian wholesalers for sale on newstands. Thus, instead of the 577 copies of the daily papers listed, the true figure may be upwards of 800–900 copies. However, the number involved is still very small compared with the circulation of Indian-produced English-language newspapers, which in 1968 came to about 5·6mn (India, *India: a reference annual*, 1969, p. 140).

12.2 Circulation Offices of the publications concerned, Sep. 1969.

12.3 Circulation Office of *The Economist*, Sept. 1969.

12.4 *The Times Index*, 1950, 1960, 1970. Note: (1) The adjusted figures allow for the change in the average number of leading articles per issue.

12.5 Cmnd 4824 (1971). Notes: (1) Other major external broadcasters excluded are Netherlands (1970 total, 335 hours per week); Cuba (320); Portugal (295); and Japan (259). (2) The list given covers only about a quarter of the countries that produce regular external broadcasts.

12.6 Cmnds 1174 & 4824.

12.7 *India: a reference annual*, 1969, HC 387, sess. 1968–9, Report on the BBC. Notes: (1) The languages listed are spoken by about 83% of the population of India. Major languages not covered incl. Bihari (16·8mn); Oriya (15·7mn); Rajas-

thani (14·9mn); and Santali (3·2mn). (2) VoA = Voice of America. (3) The figures
for Sanskrit are actual estimated total number of speakers, i.e., 25,000.

12.8 *MPOS*, vol. 14, Sept 1969.

12.9 *Overseas Hindustan Times*, 16 Aug. 1969.

12.10 *The Times*, 1 Oct. 1971.

12.11 *MPOS*, vol. 14, June–July 1969; vol. 15, Dec. 1969.

TABLES

2.1 Major British Trading Partners, 1870

	EXPORTS		IMPORTS		BALANCE OF TRADE
	Value (£mn)	% of Total	Value (£mn)	% of Total	(£mn)
USA	31.3	12.8	49.8	16.4	-18.5
France	21.9	8.9	37.6	12.4	-15.7
British India	20.0	8.1	25.0	8.2	-5.0
Germany	28.0	11.4	15.4	5.1	+12.6
Holland	17.3	7.0	14.3	4.7	+3.0
Russia	10.0	4.1	20.5	6.7	-10.5
Australia	10.7	4.3	14.0	4.6	-3.3
Egypt	8.8	3.6	14.1	4.6	-5.3
Belgium	8.9	3.6	11.2	3.6	-2.3
North American colonies	7.5	3.0	8.5	2.8	-1.0
Total British possessions	55.3	22.6	64.8	21.3	-9.5
Total foreign countries	188.6	77.4	238.4	78.7	-49.8
Total - all countries	244.0	100.0	303.2	100.0	-59.2

2.2 Major Bilateral Trade Relations of 'British India', 1872/3

	Exports of British India		Imports of British India		Balance of trade
	Value	%	Value	%	Value
Britain	28.6	50.6	27.4	78.2	+ 1.2
China	12.2	21.6	2.3	5.5	+ 9.9
Persian Gulf	1.3	2.3	0.8	2.3	+ 0.5
Ceylon	2.3	4.1	0.9	2.6	+ 1.4
Straits Settlements	2.0	3.5	0.7	2.0	+ 1.3
Germany	1.9	3.3	0.04	-	+ 1.86
France	2.6	4.6	0.3	0.8	+ 2.3
USA	2.0	3.5	0.06	-	+ 1.94
Total	56.5	100.0	35.0	100.0	+21.5

2.3 British Trade with 'British India', 1869-71 to 1969-71

BRITAIN'S TRADE WITH BRITISH INDIA	British India's % share of Total British exports	British India's % share of Total British imports	Total British balance of trade (£mn)	Balance of trade with British India (£mn)	Britain's % share of Total British Indian exports	Britain's % share of Total British Indian imports	Total British Indian balance of trade (£mn)	Balance of trade with Britain (£mn)	BRITISH INDIA'S TRADE WITH BRITAIN
1869-71 ave.	7.5	9.6	- 55.0	-10.5	52.7	71.5	+ 9.8	+ 0.2	1865/70-1871/2
1879-81	10.3	7.5	-113.3	- 0.6	41.6	74.0	+ 11.5	- 5.6	1879/80-1881/2
1889-91	10.5	7.9	-110.3	- 0.3	34.4	71.0	+ 12.9	- 15.1	1889/90-1891/2
1899-1901	9.5	6.2	-100.7	+ 5.4	27.9	65.7	+ 22.8	- 12.8	1899/00-1901/2
1909-11	9.1	6.2	-140.8	+ 6.1	25.7	62.0	+ 50.4	- 18.1	1909/10-1911/12
1919-21	11.0	5.3	-437.7	+39.6	24.7	50.6	-136.7	-288.9	1919/20-1921/2
1929-31	8.5	4.8	-391.5	+ 5.4	23.5	39.3	+116.4	- 31.3	1929/30-1931/2
1939-41	7.8	5.6	-655.5	-28.0	na	na	na	na	1939/40-1941/2
1949-51	6.8	4.9	-749.2	+12.4	22.3	22.4	- 81.9	- 18.9	1949/50-1951/2
1959-61	5.4	4.0	-807.3	+27.4	24.4	19.7	-294.6	- 28.8	1959/60-1961/2
1969-71	1.7	1.6	-863.7	- 0.7	11.0	9.3	-258.8	- 4.3	1969/70-1971/2

2.4 British Trade with 'British India', 1949-51 to 1969-71 [1]

	1949-51 ave.	1954-6 ave.	1959-61 ave.	1964-6 ave.	1969-71 ave.
British Trade with 'British India'					
1. Exports. British exports to 'British India': £mn [2]	168.3	175.8	198.8	164.3	143.8
As % of total British exports:	6.82	6.02	5.43	3.35	1.75
2. Imports. British imports from 'British India': £mn	155.9	175.0	171.4	158.6	144.5
As % of total British imports:	4.90	4.71	3.97	2.73	1.59
'British India's' Trade with Britain					
1. Exports. 'British Indian' exports to Britain: £mn	140.6	152.6	149.8	208.3	122.2
As % of total 'British Indian' exports:	22.28	27.30	24.44	18.73	11.05
2. Imports. 'British Indian' imports from Britain: £mn	159.5	161.7	178.6	212.7	126.5
As % of total 'British Indian' imports:	22.37	25.19	19.68	11.71	9.27

2.5 Changes in Mutual Trade Shares between Britain and India, 1950-60, 1960-70, & 1950-70

	1950-60		1960-70		1950-70	
	Ave. share %	Ann. change in share	Ave. share %	Ann. change in share	Ave. share %	Ann. change in share
British exports to India as % of total exports	4.65	+0.046	2.37	-0.353	3.48	-0.207
British imports from India as % of total imports	3.69	-0.039	2.27	-0.216	2.97	-0.137
Indian exports to Britain as % of total exports	26.91	+0.396	19.33	-1.508	22.91	-0.700
Indian imports from Britain as % of total imports	21.78	-0.066	11.90	-1.436	16.72	-0.921

2.6 Bilateral Trade between Metropolitan Countries & their Former Colonies, 1950, 1960, & 1970

	EXPORTS						IMPORTS					
	Bilateral exports as % of total exports			Changes in shares			Bilateral imports as % of total imports			Changes in shares		
	1950 (1)	1960 (2)	1970 (3)	$\frac{(2)}{(1)} \times 100$	$\frac{(3)}{(2)} \times 100$	$\frac{(3)}{(1)} \times 100$	1950 (4)	1960 (5)	1970 (6)	$\frac{(5)}{(4)} \times 100$	$\frac{(6)}{(5)} \times 100$	$\frac{(6)}{(4)} \times 100$
1. British trade with India	4.46	4.11	0.90	92.1	21.9	20.2	3.76	3.26	1.17	86.7	35.9	31.1
2. Pakistan	1.86	1.08	0.61	58.0	56.5	32.8	1.00	0.64	0.39	64.0	60.9	39.0
3. Malaysia & Singapore	1.10	2.08	1.52	189.0	73.1	138.2	1.41	1.54	0.88	109.2	57.1	62.4
4. Ghana	1.10	1.24	0.47	112.7	37.9	42.7	0.72	0.48	0.42	66.6	87.5	58.3
5. French trade with Algeria	11.29	15.92	3.10	141.0	19.5	27.5	8.60	8.17	3.33	95.0	40.8	38.7
6. South Vietnam	1.01	0.68	0.17	67.3	25.0	16.8	0.32	0.55	0.03	171.9	5.5	9.4
7. Tunisia	3.39	1.81	0.59	53.3	32.6	17.4	1.95	1.10	0.22	56.4	20.0	11.3
8. Belgian trade with Zaire	3.77	1.56	0.97	41.3	62.2	25.7	7.53	6.67	4.06	88.5	60.9	53.9
9. Netherlands trade with Indonesia	5.65	0.65	0.40	11.5	61.5	7.1	6.56	1.36	0.36	20.7	26.5	5.5
10. USA's trade with Philippines	2.30	1.44	0.86	62.6	59.7	37.4	2.69	2.04	1.19	75.8	58.3	44.2
1. Indian trade with Britain	22.68	27.99	11.58	123.4	41.4	51.0	20.82	19.37	6.60	93.0	34.1	31.7
2. Pakistani trade with Britain	12.55	17.30	10.36	137.8	59.9	82.5	26.29	17.50	10.41	66.5	59.5	39.6
3. Malaysian trade with Britain	13.82	13.02	6.69	94.2	51.4	48.4	17.50	16.34	9.68	93.3	59.2	55.3
4. Ghanaian trade with Britain	33.83	23.81	24.77	70.3	104.0	73.2	56.29	36.93	23.64	65.6	64.0	42.0
5. Algerian trade with France	73.02	80.79	53.54	110.6	66.3	73.3	76.52	79.86	42.40	104.3	53.1	55.4
6. South Vietnamese trade with France	31.37	35.75	48.20	113.9	134.8	153.6	50.51	21.18	6.29	41.9	29.7	12.5
7. Tunisian trade with France	48.98	52.25	24.40	106.6	46.7	49.8	78.53	59.49	34.63	75.7	58.2	44.1
8. Zairean trade with Belgium	58.73	30.16	57.31	51.3	190.0	97.6	39.22	29.98	23.39	76.4	78.0	59.6
9. Indonesian trade with Netherlands	24.05	0.28	4.15	1.1	1482.1	17.3	17.40	3.08	5.10	17.7	165.6	29.3
10. Philippine trade with USA	72.99	50.71	40.81	69.4	80.5	55.9	74.70	42.28	29.32	56.5	69.3	39.2

2.7 Export Performances of Britain and India in the World Context, 1950-72

		WORLD (1)		DEVELOPED COUNTRIES (2)		UNITED KINGDOM		LESS DEVELOPED COUNTRIES (3)		INDIA	
		Value (US $mn)	Share (%)	Value (US $mn)	Share (%)	Value (US $mn)	Share (%)	Value (US $mn)	Share (%)	Value (US $mn)	Share (%)
1. VALUE OF EXPORTS											
f.o.b. current prices	1950	56,100	100.0	37,760	67.31	6,356	11.33	18,300	32.69	1,146	2.04
	1960	112,300	100.0	86,210	76.77	10,349	9.22	26,100	23.23	1,331	1.18
	1970	277,500	100.0	224,000	80.72	19,347	6.97	53,500	19.28	2,026	0.73
	1972	366,000	100.0	297,100	81.17	24.344	6.65	68,900	18.83	2,415	0.66
2. VOLUME OF EXPORTS								(4)	(5)		
1960 = 100	1950	53		51		80		70	na	96	
	1960	100		100		100		100	100	100	
	1970	217		225		158		187	162	124	
	1972	252		262		181		189	203	156	
3. UNIT PRICE OF EXPORTS								(4)	(5)		
1960 = 100	1950	88		85		76		98	na	90	
	1960	100		100		100		100	100	100	
	1970	113		116		136		106	114	158	
	1972	128		130		146		120	119	176	

3.1 Direction of British Exports, 1950, 1960, & 1970

	1950		1960		1970		CHANGES IN PERCENTAGES		
	Value (£mn)	% A	Value (£mn)	% B	Value (£mn)	% C	B as % A	C as % A	C as % B
World	2,174	100.0	3,696	100.0	8,063	100.0	100.0	100.0	100.0
Commonwealth (excl. S. Africa)	924	42.5	1,334	36.0	1,638	20.3	84.7	47.7	56.3
Developed Commonwealth [1]	468	21.5	605	16.3	763	9.4	75.8	43.7	57.6
Developing Commonwealth [1]	456	20.9	729	19.7	875	10.8	94.2	51.7	54.8
India	97	4.4	152	4.1	73	0.9	93.2	20.5	21.9
EEC [2]	243	11.1	567	15.3	1,754	21.7	137.8	195.5	141.8
EFTA (Continental) [3]	266	12.2	394	10.6	1,145	14.2	86.8	116.4	133.9
USA	114	5.2	342	9.2	943	11.6	176.9	223.0	126.0
South Africa	121	5.5	157	4.2	333	4.1	76.3	74.6	97.6

3.2 Value (£mn) & Commodity Composition of Total British Exports and of British Exports to India, 1960–1970

SITC	Commodity groups	1960(1)				1965				1970			
		WORLD		INDIA		WORLD		INDIA		WORLD		INDIA	
		Value	%	Value	%	Value	%	Value	%	Value	%	Value	%
0	Food, animals	107.9	3.0	0.6	0.4	154.7	3.2	0.1	0.1	249.3	3.0	0.1	0.2
1	Beverages, tobacco	94.0	2.6	0.4	0.2	143.1	3.0	0.4	0.4	265.0	3.2	0.6	0.8
2	Crude materials	120.9	3.4	4.5	3.0	144.2	3.0	1.3	1.2	263.5	3.2	1.2	1.6
3	Mineral fuels	132.5	3.7	3.9	2.6	133.4	2.8	1.4	1.2	206.8	2.5	0.3	0.5
4	Oils & fats	6.4	0.0	0.0	0.0	6.6	0.1	0.0	0.0	9.2	0.1	0.0	0.0
5	Chemicals	318.9	8.9	14.0	9.3	441.6	9.3	8.7	7.6	786.1	9.7	6.1	8.4
6	Manufactured goods	895.6	25.1	32.1	21.3	1,210.8	25.6	21.1	18.5	1,989.8	24.6	19.3	26.5
7	Machinery, etc	1,533.6	43.1	88.1	58.5	1,987.1	42.0	71.7	62.9	3,301.2	40.9	34.1	46.7
8	Other manufactures	218.4	6.1	5.1	3.4	357.8	7.5	5.1	4.4	730.8	9.0	2.8	3.9
9	Miscellaneous	126.6	3.5	1.3	0.8	3.8	0.0	3.8	3.3	260.7	3.2	7.9	10.9
5–8	Manufactures	2,966.5	83.2	139.3	92.5	3,997.3	84.4	96.6	93.4	6,807.9	84.4	62.3	85.5
TOTAL	SITCS 0–9	3,555.3	100.0	150.4	100.0	4,727.9	100.0	114.0	100.0	8,062.7	100.0	72.9	100.0

3.3 Value (Rsmn) & Commodity Composition of Indian Imports, 1960/1, 1965/6, & 1970/1

Trade classifications		Commodity group	1960-1		1965-6		1970-1	
UN	Indian		Value	%	Value	%	Value	%
0	1	Food, live animals	2,140.6	19.0	3,540.8	25.1	2,717.7	16.8
1	2	Beverages, tobacco	7.9	-	5.6	-	3.1	-
2	3	Crude materials	1,553.6	13.8	1,230.9	8.7	2,003.2	12.3
3	4	Mineral fuels	695.2	6.2	684.2	4.8	1,360.1	8.4
4	5	Animal, vegetable oils, & fats	46.0	0.4	136.2	0.9	385.0	2.4
5	6	Chemicals	857.0	7.6	1,049.8	7.4	1,922.7	11.8
6	7	Manufactured goods	2,341.6	20.8	2,163.3	15.3	3,448.2	21.2
7	8	Machinery, transport equipment	3,329.8	29.6	4,921.4	34.9	3,845.0	23.7
8	9	Other manufactures	174.0	1.5	186.9	1.3	324.3	2.0
9	-	Miscellaneous[1]	785.7	7.0	166.2	1.1	229.8	1.4
0-9	1-9+	All imports	11,216.2	100.0	14,085.3	100.0	16,239.1	100.0
5-8	6-9	Manufactured goods	6,702.4	59.7	8,321.4	59.0	9,540.2	58.7

3.4 The British Share of Total Indian Imports by
major commodity groups, 1960/1 to 1970/1

SITC	Commodity group	Imports from Britain as % of total Indian imports			
		1960/1	1965/6	1970/1	Change 1960/1-1970/1 %
0	Food, live animals	0.42	0.05	0.12	- 71.4
1	Beverages, tobacco	74.50	97.00	97.00	+ 30.2
2	Crude materials	3.89	1.50	1.09	- 71.9
3	Mineral fuels	7.58	2.76	0.49	- 93.5
4	Animal, vegetable oils, & fats	1.97	0.55	0.17	- 91.4
5	Chemicals	21.89	11.09	5.77	- 73.6
6	Manufactured goods	18.29	13.04	10.12	- 44.7
7	Machinery, transport equipment	35.30	19.44	16.00	- 54.7
8	Other manufactures	39.46	36.39	15.99	- 59.5
9	Miscellaneous	24.72	30.63	62.69	+153.6
0-9	All imports	17.88	10.86	8.10	- 54.7
5-8	Manufactured goods	27.92	17.10	11.81	- 57.7

3.5 Volume Index of Indian Imports by major commodity classes, 1960/1 to 1970/1 (1960/1 = 100)

SITC			1963/4	1965/6	1967/8	1969/70	1970/1
0		Food, live animals	100	195	199	112	96
1		Beverages, tobacco	105	75	105	80	22
2		Crude materials	75	58	68	66	74
3		Mineral fuels	179	126	104	177	168
4		Animal, vegetable oils, & fats	116	291	543	473	546
5		Chemicals	169	178	338	271	327
6		Manufactured goods	87	92	65	52	71
	6.7	Iron & steel	76	83	50	37	59
	6.8	Non-ferrous metals	114	96	102	45	76
	6.9	Metal manufactures	65	70	39	16	22
7		Machinery & transport equipment	99	109	90	60	44
	7.1	Non-electrical machinery	107	120	107	61	42
	7.2	Electrical machinery	72	101	76	25	56
	7.3	Transport equipment	80	77	54	49	55
8		Miscellaneous manufactures	202	88	340	108	120
General import volume index			105	120	130	100	99

3.6 Geographical Distribution of Indian Imports, 1960/1 to 1970/1

	1960/1		1965/6		1970/1		Changes 1960/1 to 1970/1	
	Value (Rsmn)	%	Value (Rsmn)	%	Value (Rsmn)	%	Value (Rsmn)	%
ECAFE (incl. China)	1,793.5	15.9	2,194.0	15.5	2,642.5	16.3	+ 849.0	+ 0.4
– Japan	607.8	5.4	793.3	5.6	833.0	5.1	+ 225.2	– 0.3
Eastern Europe	443.1	3.9	1,566.8	11.1	2,258.2	13.9	+1,815.1	+10.0
– Czechoslovakia	87.6	0.7	211.5	1.4	202.0	1.2	+ 114.4	+ 0.5
– USSR	158.7	1.4	831.7	5.9	1,046.8	6.4	+ 887.1	+ 5.0
EEC	1,958.9	17.4	2,063.9	14.6	1,876.8	11.6	– 82.1	– 5.8
– Western Germany	1,225.2	10.9	1,371.5	9.7	1,068.8	6.6	– 156.4	– 4.3
EFTA	2,475.0	22.0	1,825.9	12.9	1,551.0	9.5	– 924.0	–12.5
– UK	2,171.5	19.3	1,500.9	10.6	1,260.3	7.8	– 911.2	–11.5
Africa	706.8	6.3	558.2	3.9	1,698.2	10.5	+ 991.4	+ 4.2
North America	3,474.1	30.9	5,656.0	40.1	5,634.9	34.7	+2,160.8	+ 3.8
– Canada	198.6	1.7	305.2	2.1	1,173.1	7.2	+ 974.5	+ 5.5
– USA	3,275.6	29.2	5,350.8	37.9	4,461.7	27.5	+1,186.1	– 1.7
Latin America	17.5	0.1	33.5	0.2	142.8	0.9	+ 125.3	+ 0.8
Total	11,216.2	100.0	14,085.3	100.0	16,239.1	100.0	+5,022.9	–

3.7 Utilized Aid as a Percentage of Total
Imports by major aid donors, 2nd Plan;
3rd Plan; 1967/8 to 1969/70

	2nd 5-year plan 1956/7-1960/1	3rd 5-year plan 1961/2-1965/6	Ann. Plans[1] 1967/8-1969/70
USA	71	80	72
Canada	15	56	68
UK	11	19	57
West Germany	22	39	55
Japan	6	25	43
USSR	81	64	20
Eastern Europe (exc. USSR)	na	11	13
Total (above plus others)	21	46	53

3.8 Volumes & Prices of Manufactured Exports
of Major Developed Countries, 1970
(1960 = 100)

Exporter	Manufactured goods exports	
	(Volume)	(Unit value)
Japan	488	103
Italy	386	106
Canada	333	116
Netherlands	290	109
Belgium-Lux	275	112
West Germany	243	114
Sweden	207	128
Switzerland	184	127
France	167	114
United Kingdom	143	121

4.1 Origins of British Imports, 1950, 1960, & 1970

	1950		1960		1970		CHANGES IN PERCENTAGES		
	Value (£mn)	% A	Value (£mn)	% B	Value (£mn)	% C	B as % A	C as % A	C as % B
World	2,609	100.0	4,541	100.0	9,051	100.0	100.0	100.0	100.0
Commonwealth (excl. S. Africa)	1,048	40.1	1,468	32.3	2,094	23.1	80.5	57.6	71.5
Developed Commonwealth[1]	535	20.5	755	16.6	1,147	12.6	81.0	61.4	75.9
Developing Commonwealth[1]	513	19.6	713	15.7	947	10.4	80.1	53.1	66.3
India	98	3.7	148	3.2	106	1.1	86.5	29.7	34.4
EEC[2]	332	12.7	662	14.5	1,822	20.1	114.1	158.2	138.6
EFTA[3] (Continental)	264	10.1	460	10.1	1,209	13.3	100.0	131.6	131.6
USA	212	8.1	566	12.4	1,174	12.9	153.0	159.2	104.0
South Africa	48	1.8	105	2.3	258	2.8	127.7	155.5	121.7

4.2 Value (£mn) & Percentage Composition of Total British Imports and of British Imports from India, 1960, 1965, & 1970 (by commodity groups)

SITC	Commodity groups	1960(1)				1965				1970			
		WORLD		INDIA		WORLD		INDIA		WORLD		INDIA	
		Value	%	Value	%	Value	%	Value	%	Value	%	Value	%
0	Food, animals	1,402	30.7	76.1	50.8	1,571	27.3	71.6	55.8	1,862	20.5	52.3	49.3
1	Beverages, tobacco	145	3.2	9.2	6.1	136	2.3	8.5	6.6	189	2.0	10.5	9.9
2	Crude materials	1,028	22.5	15.0	10.0	1,044	18.1	10.1	7.8	1,263	13.9	8.2	7.7
3	Mineral fuels	482	10.6	0.3	0.2	609	10.5	0.9	0.7	945	10.4	0.4	0.3
4	Oils & fats	53	1.1	3.0	2.0	64	1.1	-	-	100	1.1	0.1	-
5	Chemicals	176	3.8	1.2	0.8	283	4.9	1.2	0.9	542	5.9	0.9	0.8
6	Manufactured goods	734	16.1	41.8	28.0	1,087	18.9	32.2	24.9	1,966	21.7	27.3	25.7
7	Machinery, etc	346	7.6	2.1	1.4	606	10.5	1.3	1.0	1,496	16.5	2.4	2.2
8	Other manufactures	170	3.7	0.3	0.2	276	4.8	1.2	0.9	573	6.3	2.9	2.7
9	Miscellaneous	15	0.3	0.2	0.1	71	1.2	0.7	0.5	109	1.2	0.7	0.6
Total	All commodities	4,558	100.0	149.2	100.0	5,751	100.0	128.3	100.0	9,051	100.0	106.0	100.0

4.3 Volume Indices of British Imports by major commodity groups

SITC		1955	1960	1965	1970
0, 1	Food, beverages, tobacco	88.0	100.0	102.0	104.0
2, 4	Basic materials	95.3	100.0	100.0	102.7
3	Fuels	78.1	100.0	145.7	211.3
5-8	Manufactured goods	61.1	100.0	137.0	223.0
0-9	Total	80.4	100.0	118.8	155.4

4.4 Commodity Structure of Indian Exports, 1960/1, 1965/6, & 1970/1

Trade classifications UN	Indian	Commodity group	1960/1 Value (Rsmn)	%	1965/6 Value (Rsmn)	%	1970/1 Value (Rsmn)	%
0	1	Food, live animals	1,980.5	30.8	2,407.4	29.8	4,126.8	26.8
1	2	Beverages, tobacco	157.7	2.4	216.9	2.6	325.7	2.1
2	3	Crude materials	1,120.6	17.4	1,350.4	16.7	2,516.6	16.4
3	4	Mineral fuels	74.1	1.1	93.1	1.1	125.8	0.9
4	5	Animal, vegetable oils, & fats	98.0	1.5	45.5	0.5	71.2	0.5
5	6	Chemicals	71.9	1.1	111.0	1.3	363.7	2.4
6	7	Manufactured goods	2,633.4	40.9	3,432.6	42.6	6,159.6	40.1
7	8	Machinery, transport equipment	71.9	1.1	111.9	1.3	832.9	5.4
8	9	Other manufactures }						
9	-	Miscellaneous }	215.0	3.3	287.6	3.5	827.5	5.4
0-9	1-9+	All exports	6,423.2	100.0	8,056.4	100.0	15,351.6	100.0

4.5 India's Share of Total UK Imports by commodity class, 1960, 1970

SITC		1960 Value (£mn)	1960 % of total imports in class	1970 Actual Value (£mn)	1970 Actual % of total imports in class	1970 with 1960 shares Value (£mn)	1970 with 1960 shares % of total imports in class
0	Food, animals	76.1	5.42	52.3	2.80	100.9	5.42
1	Beverages, tobacco	9.2	6.24	10.5	5.55	11.7	6.24
2	Crude materials	15.0	1.45	8.2	0.64	18.3	1.45
3	Mineral fuels	0.3	0.07	0.4	0.04	0.6	0.07
4	Oils & fats	3.0	5.60	0.1	0.10	5.6	5.60
5	Chemicals	1.2	0.68	0.9	0.16	3.6	0.68
6	Manufactured goods	41.8	5.69	27.3	1.38	111.8	5.69
7	Machinery, transport equipment	2.1	0.61	2.4	0.16	9.1	0.61
8	Other manufactures	0.3	0.21	2.9	0.50	1.2	0.21
9	Miscellaneous	0.2	1.59	0.7	0.64	1.7	1.59
Total	Total - all commodities	149.2	3.28	106.0	1.17	264.5	2.92

4.6 Indian Trade Performance 1950-70 (six-year annual averages, Rsmn)

	1950-5	1955-60	1960-5	1965-70
Exports (fob)	6,051.8	6,203.0	7,291.0	11,941.3
Imports (cif)	6,802.5	9,157.8	12,108.8	17,242.0
Balance of trade	-750.7	-2,954.8	-4,817.8	-5,300.7
Exports as % imports	88.9	67.7	60.2	69.2

4.7 Volume & Unit Value of Indian Exports by major commodity group, 1960/1 to 1970/1 (1960/1 = 100)

SITC		EXPORT VOLUME					UNIT VALUE OF EXPORTS				
		1963/4	1965/6	1967/8	1969/70	1970/1	1963/4	1965/6	1967/8	1969/70	1970/1
0	Food, live animals	125	116	115	115	123	100	104	158	151	162
	Tea & mate	104	99	102	95	93	86	94	143	105	121
	Oilseed cake	216	188	166	150	194	113	128	189	191	198
1	Beverages, tobacco	143	140	124	115	106	95	98	181	182	195
2	Crude materials	134	141	141	162	179	86	84	121	126	124
3	Mineral fuels	117	117	80	74	67	89	107	155	173	256
4	Animal, vegetable oils, & fats	219	32	20	30	30	95	143	211	174	240
5	Chemicals	100	182	155	262	359	91	88	142	161	141
6	Manufactured goods	118	119	115	137	136	96	109	168	174	171
	Leather, leather goods	112	119	162	215	218	94	95	132	151	132
	Cotton fabrics	88	122	98	101	108	97	89	140	148	156
	Jute fabrics	134	124	125	111	93	106	118	177	203	190
	Jute bags, sacks	97	104	67	36	54	85	113	158	162	176
7	Machinery & transport equipment	149	353	582	1,324	1,682	99	80	89	113	121
8	Miscellaneous manufactures	133	148	173	285	295	114	125	179	130	220
	General export index	126	124	122	143	153	95	103	153	155	157

4.8 India's Major Commodity Exports to Britain, 1960/1–1961/2, & 1969/70–1970/1

Commodity	1960/1 & 1961/2 Value (Rsmn)	%	1969/70 & 1970/1 Value (Rsmn)	%
Black tea	754.4	45.3	556.6	33.2
Leather & leather goods	141.1	8.5	163.9	9.8
Tobacco	103.6	6.2	162.4	9.7
Cotton piecegoods	133.4	8.0	138.0	8.2
Oilcakes	115.2	6.9	96.7	5.8
Jute goods	75.7	4.5	28.9	1.7
Cashew kernels	13.0	0.8	14.1	0.8
Sugar	0.1	-	21.9[1]	1.3
Total 8 commodities	1,336.8	80.2	1,182.5	70.5
Total Indian exports to UK	1,667.0	100.0	1,677.5	100.0

4.9 British & World Imports of Tea, 1959–61 to 1969–71 (annual averages; volumes in 000 metric tonnes; adjusted for re-exports)

	1959-61 Volume	%	1964-6 Volume	%	1969-71 Volume	%
Europe (inc. USSR)	292.9	54.8	277.4	47.5	266.2	42.3
UK	226.7	42.2	224.6	38.4	208.9	33.2
EEC	19.1	3.6	23.0	3.9	23.7	3.7
N. America, West Indies	71.0	13.3	80.3	13.7	89.3	14.2
Canada	20.0	3.7	19.6	3.3	20.0	3.8
USA	50.1	9.4	59.6	10.2	68.2	10.8
Latin America	6.2	1.2	7.3	1.2	10.4	1.8
Asia	56.7	10.6	64.5	11.0	84.1	13.4
Africa	73.2	13.7	88.4	15.1	104.0	16.5
Oceania	35.9	6.7	37.2	6.3	35.3	5.6
Major producing countries	2.0	0.4	4.5	0.7	14.8	2.3
Grand total	534.5	100.0	584.4	100.0	628.9	100.0

4.10 Apparent Consumption of Tea in Britain & India, and of Coffee in Britain, 1951-72 (annual averages)

	1951-5	1956-60	1961-5	1966-70	1971-2
Consumption of tea per capita : kg					
UK	4.08	4.44	4.26	3.96	3.67
India	0.22	0.27	0.27	0.38	na
Consumption of coffee per capita : kg					
UK	0.63	0.81	1.13	1.61	2.06
UK: tea : coffee ratio	6.4 : 1	5.4 : 1	3.7 : 1	2.4 : 1	1.8 : 1

4.11 Origin of UK Gross Imports of Tea, 1951-71 (annual averages; volumes in 000 tonnes)

	1951-5 Volume	%	1956-60 Volume	%	1961-5 Volume	%	1966-71 Volume	%
India	136.1	60.2	137.5	55.4	122.6	48.8	94.2	38.8
Ceylon	54.4	24.0	64.7	26.0	77.2	30.7	71.9	29.6
East Africa	6.8	3.0	23.2	9.3	29.3	11.7	51.4	21.2
Others	29.0	12.8	23.2	9.3	22.2	8.8	25.4	10.4
Total	226.3	100.0	248.6	100.0	251.3	100.0	242.9	100.0

4.12 Production & Exports of Tea in India, Ceylon, & East Africa, 1951-70 (annual averages)

	1951-5	1956-60	1961-5	1966-70
1. Production of tea: 000 metric tonnes				
India	288.9	318.4	357.2	396.2
Ceylon	156.9	184.6	217.0	220.0
East Africa	22.2	34.9	52.1	85.3
2. Exports of tea: 000 metric tonnes				
India	197.7	215.5	209.4	194.0
Ceylon	152.4	174.2	207.1	206.9
East Africa	18.6	30.8	47.0	78.9
3. Exports as % of production				
India	68.4	67.7	58.6	48.9
Ceylon	97.1	94.4	95.4	94.0
East Africa	83.8	88.2	90.2	92.5
4. Share of world exports: %				
India	32.5	40.0	36.4	31.6
Ceylon	25.0	32.4	36.0	33.7
East Africa	3.0	5.7	8.2	12.9

4.13 Distribution of Indian Exports of Tea, 1960-1 to 1970-1 (annual averages; volumes in 000 tonnes)

Destination	1960-1 Volume	1960-1 %	1965-6 Volume	1965-6 %	1970-1 Volume	1970-1 %	Change in share 1960/1 to 1970/1
UK	122.1	61.1	95.7	50.7	77.1	39.4	-21.7
USSR	11.0	5.5	21.6	11.4	35.0	17.9	+12.4
USA	9.7	4.9	7.6	4.0	7.8	3.9	- 1.0
Canada	6.7	3.3	4.4	2.3	3.5	1.8	- 1.5
Sudan	5.3	2.6	5.0	2.7	12.3	6.3	+ 3.7
UAR	14.4	7.2	18.4	9.7	10.1	5.2	- 2.0
Afghanistan	3.0	1.5	5.2	2.7	12.8	6.5	+ 5.0
West Germany	1.6	0.8	1.6	0.8	3.3	1.7	+ 0.9
Eire	6.4	3.2	5.7	3.0	5.2	2.7	- 0.5
Others	19.8	9.9	24.0	12.7	28.7	14.6	+ 4.7
Total	200.0	100.0	189.2	100.0	195.8	100.0	--

4.14 London Auction Prices of Tea, 1959-61 to 1969-71 (annual averages; new pence per kg.)

	1959-61	1964-6	1969-71
High grown teas			
North India	52.90	48.66	43.43
Ceylon	53.66	47.70	45.56
Difference (India base)	-0.76	+0.96	-2.13
Low grown teas			
South India	42.03	40.30	37.30
East Africa	40.06	39.33	40.10
Difference (India base)	+1.97	+0.97	-2.80

4.15 Indian Production & Exports of Unmanufactured Tobacco, 1960-1 to 1970-1 (annual averages)

		1960-1	1965-6	1970-1
1. Indian production of tobacco	10^3 tonnes	301.8	321.6	349.5
2. Indian exports of unmanufactured tobacco	10^3 tonnes	44.9	48.7	51.7
3. Exports as % of production		14.8	15.2	14.8
4. Distribution of exports				
- UK	10^3 tonnes	21.3	15.8	18.5
- USSR	10^3 tonnes	4.6	15.2	12.0
- EEC	10^3 tonnes	5.0	3.6	2.9
5. UK's share of total	%	47.4	32.4	35.8
6. Value of Indian exports of tobacco	Rsmn	157.5	191.4	359.1

4.16 British Imports of Unmanufactured Tobacco, 1951-70 (annual averages; 000 tonnes)

		1951-5	1956-60	1961-5	1966-70
1. Total British imports of unmanufactured tobacco		140.6	146.5	140.1	131.9
2. Origin of imports:	USA	71.6	73.4	56.2	62.1
	Rhodesia + Malawi	32.2	39.0	45.8	8.3
	India	16.7	18.1	17.6	20.1
	Canada	13.1	11.7	16.3	21.2
3. Indian share of total UK imports		11.8	12.3	12.5	15.2
4. UK consumption of tobacco		107.5	118.3	121.6	114.4

		1955	1960	1965	1970
5. UK Consumer expenditure on tobacco (£mn., 1963 prices)		1,135	1,275	1,225	1,248
6. UK Consumption of tipped cigarettes (% total)		4.0	13.6	14.8	74.1

4.17 Consumption, Prices, & Usage of Fibres in UK, 1959-61, 1964-6, & 1969-71 (annual averages)

	Unit	1959-61	1964-6	1969-71
1. UK consumption of yarn in weaving	kg mn	292.5	254.7	193.3
2. Share of yarns in total UK yarn consumption				
a. Cotton	%	55.9	48.3	42.9
b. Man-made fibres	%	33.2	40.6	47.0
i Spun	%	11.7	9.8	8.7
ii Continuous filament	%	21.5	30.8	38.3
c. Other	%	10.9	11.1	10.1
3. Prices of major fibres in UK				
a. Cotton	Index	100.0	100.63	120.51
b. Rayon	Index	100.0	100.61	113.61
c. Nylon	Index	100.0	84.42	71.02
4. UK production of woven cloth	metres mn	1731.5	1458.6	1108.2
5. Share of fibres in total UK woven cloth production				
a. Cotton	%	68.1	61.6	55.2
b. Man-made fibres	%	27.5	33.9	36.5
c. Cotton/man-made fibres mixture	%	4.4	4.5	8.3
6. UK imports of woven cotton fabrics	mn sq. metres	553.5	537.9	464.3

4.18 Production of Woven Cotton Cloth, and of
Cloth Made of Man-made Fibres & Man-made
Fibre-Cotton Mixtures, 1959-61, 1963-5 &
1968-70 (annual averages)

	1959-61	1963-5	1968-70
UK production of woven cloth: weekly ave.			
10^6 lin. yards - cotton	24.8	19.5	13.6
- man-made fibres; mixtures	11.6	11.4	10.6
UK imports of woven cotton fabrics:[1] Monthly ave.			
10^6 sq. yards	45.4	42.9	37.1

4.19 Commodity Breakdown of UK Imports of
Woven Cotton Fabrics into the UK, 1959-61,
1964-6, & 1969-71 (annual averages)

Commodity categories	Unit	1959-61	1964-6	1969-71
SITC 652.1. 'Grey, unbleached, not mercerised fabrics'				
1. Total UK imports	mn sq.m	455.3	421.4	349.2
2. UK imports from India	mn sq.m	162.9	140.9	80.8
3. Indian share of the total $(\frac{2}{1}\cdot 100)$	%	35.8	33.4	23.1
SITC 652.2 'Bleached, dyed, mercerised and finished'				
4. Total UK imports	mn sq.m	93.9	117.8	103.7
5. UK imports from India	mn sq.m	20.2	12.3	8.5
6. Indian share of total $(\frac{5}{4}\cdot 100)$	%	21.5	10.4	8.2
SITC 652.1 + 652.2				
7. Total UK imports	mn sq.m	549.2	539.2	452.9
8. UK imports from India	mn sq.m	183.1	153.2	89.3
9. Indian share of the total $(\frac{8}{7}\cdot 100)$	%	33.3	28.4	19.7
10. SITC 652.1 as % (652.1 + 652.2)	%	82.9	78.1	77.1

4.20 UK Imports of Woven Cotton Fabrics
(SITC 652.1) by major countries of origin,
1959-61, 1964-6, & 1969-71 (annual averages)

Country of Origin	1959-61			1964-6			1969-71			% change 1959-61 to 1969-71	
	% share of total imports		Ave. unit value[1]	% share of total imports		Ave. unit value[1]	% share of total imports		Ave. unit value[1]	Volume imports	Unit value
	Volume (a)	Value	p/m² (c)	Volume	Value	p/m²	Volume (b)	Value	p/m² (d)	(b-a) %	($\frac{d}{c} \cdot 100$) %
India	35.8	31.5	6.35	33.4	31.4	6.89	23.1	21.3	8.99	-12.7	+41.5
Hong Kong	19.7	23.7	8.67	19.5	24.3	9.32	24.4	29.7	11.76	+ 4.7	+35.6
Japan	9.4	8.7	6.64	3.8	3.9	7.61	0.8	1.2	13.01	- 8.6	+95.9
Pakistan	5.6	4.7	5.98	8.9	7.2	5.92	20.5	15.5	7.31	+14.9	+22.2
China	4.5	4.3	6.99	8.9	7.1	5.79	7.9	5.9	7.21	+ 3.4	+ 3.1
Portugal	2.2	2.6	8.69	3.5	3.4	7.06	3.6	3.9	10.40	+ 1.4	+19.7
Total	100.0	100.0	7.22	100.0	100.0	7.39	100.0	100.0	9.69	--	+34.2

4.21 Production & Export of Cotton Cloth from India,
1961-3, 1965-7, & 1969-71 (annual averages)

	1961-3	1965-7	1969-71
1. Indian production of raw cotton (ooo tonnes)	912.2	911.3	939.4
2. Indian production of cotton cloth (mn metres)	7,115	7,420	7,638
3. Indian exports of cotton cloth (mn metres)	522	482	430
4. Exports as % of production ($\frac{3}{2}$.100)	7.33	6.49	5.62

4.22 Destination of Indian Exports of Cotton
Piecegoods, 1960/1-1962/3 to 1968/9-1970/1
(annual averages; Rsmn)

Destination	1960/1 to 1962/3		1964/5 to 1966/7		1968/9 to 1970/1	
	Value	%	Value	%	Value	%
UK	125.7	24.8	136.6	24.3	153.9	21.1
France, Netherlands, West Germany	7.1	1.4	9.9	1.8	34.1	4.7
USA & Canada	46.3	9.1	90.6	16.1	97.3	13.3
USSR	0.8	1.5	29.0	5.2	75.4	10.3
Sudan	33.1	6.5	21.3	3.8	74.8	10.2
Australia & New Zealand	46.7	9.2	35.5	6.3	35.7	4.9
Total exports	506.0	100.0	562.1	100.0	729.7	100.0

4.23 UK Imports of Jute Manufactures, 1951-5
to 1966-70 (annual averages; 000 tonnes)

	SITC	1951-5 ave.	1956-60 ave.	1961-5 ave.	1966-70 ave.
Jute piecegoods	65332	52.3	41.5	36.7	40.6
New jute sacks	65601	21.6	18.7	11.8	6.5
Other	65089)				
	65475)	5.7	4.3	5.6	2.4
	65757)				
Total		79.6	64.5	54.1	49.5
Indian share %		87.7	85.1	76.2	41.6

4.24 Production & Exports of Jute Manufactures, 1951-5 to 1966-70 (annual averages)

		1951-5	1956-60	1961-5	1966-70
Production	(ooo tonnes)	1,979	2,440	2,958	2,989
India		1,013	1,099	1,248	1,053
Pakistan		55	205	320	506
Other		911	1,136	1,390	1,430
India as % of total		51.1	45.0	42.2	35.2
Exports	(ooo tonnes)	945	1,097	1,258	1,214
India		809	859	905	661
Pakistan		13	124	238	434
Other		123	114	115	119
India as % of total		85.6	78.3	71.9	54.4
Exports as % of production					
India	%	79.8	78.1	72.5	62.7
Pakistan	%	23.6	60.5	74.3	85.7

4.25 Distribution of Indian Exports of Jute Goods, 1960/1-1962/3 to 1968/9-1970/1 (annual averages; Rsmn)

Destination	1960/1 to 1962/3		1963/4 to 1965/6		1968/9 to 1970/1	
	Value	%	Value	%	Value	%
USA	520.7	36.9	678.7	41.5	1,024.4	51.5
USSR	49.5	3.5	183.5	11.2	278.0	14.0
UAR	35.4	2.5	71.0	4.3	63.8	3.2
Canada	80.0	5.6	92.6	5.6	133.8	6.7
Australia	98.2	6.9	87.6	5.3	90.4	4.5
Sudan	24.5	1.7	22.7	1.4	47.7	2.4
UK	73.7	5.2	69.4	4.2	33.0	1.6
Others	529.7	37.7	430.6	26.3	317.1	16.1
Total	1,411.7	100.0	1,636.1	100.0	1,988.2	100.0

4.27 Indian Production & Exports of Oilseeds, and Groundnut Cake & Meal, 1960-2 to 1968-70 (annual averages; Rsmn)

	Unit	1960-2	1964-6	1968-70
1. Indian production of oilseeds	000 tonnes	8,992	8,923	9,226
2. Indian production of groundnuts (in shell)	000 tonnes	4,957	4,854	5,239
3. Groundnuts share of total oilseeds ($\frac{2}{1}\cdot100$)	%	55.1	54.4	56.8
4. Indian exports of oilseed cake & meal	000 tonnes	556.6	888.4	811.5
5. Indian exports of groundnut cake & meal	000 tonnes	480.4	743.8	631.5
6. World exports of groundnut cake & meal	000 tonnes	1,088.7	1,554.0	1,424.8
7. Indian share of world exports ($\frac{5}{6}\cdot100$)	%	44.1	47.9	44.3
8. Indian exports of oilseed cake & meal: value	Rsmn	211.3	404.3	487.9
a. to Eastern Europe	Rsmn	60.7	222.7	368.9
b. to UK	Rsmn	129.6	138.1	88.2
9. UK share of total Indian exports ($\frac{8^b}{8}\cdot100$)	%	61.3	34.1	18.1

4.26 Disposals & Imports of Oilseed and Groundnut Cake & Meal,
1959-61 to 1969-71 (annual averages)

	Unit	1959-61	1964-6	1969-71
1. Disposals of oilcake animal feedingstuffs in the UK	000 tonnes	1,845	1,586	1,296
2. UK imports of oilseed cake & meal	000 tonnes	1,229	1,073	938
3. UK imports of groundnut cake & meal	000 tonnes	559	451	341
4. Share of groundnut cake and meal imports as % total $(\frac{3}{2}\cdot 100)$	%	45.5	42.0	36.3
5. UK imports of groundnut cake & meal from India	000 tonnes	320	232	133
6. Indian share of total UK imports of groundnut cake & meal $(\frac{5}{3}\cdot 100)$	%	57.2	51.4	39.0

4.28 Indian Exports of Engineering Goods,
1960-1, 1965-6, & 1969-70 (Rsmn)

	1960-1		1965-6		1969-70	
	Value	%	Value	%	Value	%
1. Indian exports of engineering goods	1,354.9	100.0	2,976.7	100.0	10,636.6	100.0
2. Direction of Indian exports of engineering goods						
a. Africa	200.6	19.0	575.7	19.4	2,947.8	27.7
b. Asia : South East	443.7	42.1	982.3	33.0	2,471.6	23.3
: West	288.6	27.4	720.5	24.2	2,347.9	22.1
c. Europe : East	1.1	0.1	223.4	7.5	1,066.8	10.0
: West	60.7	5.7	292.4	9.8	913.5	8.6
d. North and Central America	25.0	2.4	96.0	3.2	525.4	4.9
e. Other	35.2	3.3	86.4	2.9	363.6	3.4
3. Total Indian exports	6,423.2	-	8,056.4	-	14,132.8	-
4. Exports of engineering goods as % total $(\frac{1}{3}\cdot 100)$	16.4	-	36.9	-	75.26	-
5. Volume index of Indian exports & machinery & transport equipment: 1960-1 = 100	100.0	-	353.5	-	1,325.5	-

5.1 Invisibles Transactions of Developed
and less Developed Countries, 1960 & 1970 ($mn)

	1960				1970				Net balance	
	Credits		Debits		Credits		Debits		1960	1970
	Value	%	Value	%	Value	%	Value	%	Value	Value
1. Developed countries	+31,576	83.4	−29,168	75.6	+87,313	84.1	−81,551	77.3	+2,408	+5,762
a. USA	+ 9,021	23.8	− 8,562	22.2	+23,808	22.9	−19,725	18.7	+ 459	+4,083
b. UK	+ 5,793	15.3	− 5,221	13.5	+11,225	10.8	− 9,174	8.7	+ 572	+2,051
c. West Germany	+ 2,879	7.6	− 2,963	7.7	+ 7,925	7.6	−10,586	10.0	− 84	−2,661
d. France	+ 1,967	5.2	− 1,374	3.6	+ 6,341	6.1	− 6,024	5.7	+ 593	+ 317
e. Japan	+ 945	2.5	− 1,048	2.7	+ 4,009	3.9	− 5,794	5.5	− 103	−1,785
2. Less Developed countries	+ 6,266	16.6	− 9,386	24.4	+16,535	15.9	−23,942	22.7	−3,120	−7,407
a. Mexico	+ 576	1.5	− 481	1.2	+ 1,640	1.6	− 1,680	1.6	+ 95	− 40
b. Brazil	+ 193	0.5	− 691	1.8	+ 378	0.4	− 1,192	1.1	− 498	− 814
c. India	+ 357	0.9	− 294	0.8	+ 378	0.4	− 643	0.4	+ 63	− 265
d. Malaysia	+ 121	0.3	− 225	0.6	+ 183	0.2	− 387	0.4	− 104	− 204
e. Pakistan	+ 101	0.3	− 150	0.4	+ 133	0.1	− 381	0.4	− 49	− 248
3. Total (1 + 2)	+37,842	100.0	−38,554	100.0	+103,848	100.0	−105,493	100.0	− 712	−1,645

5.2 The Invisibles Sector of the British
Balance of Payments, 1961-3 to 1969-71
(annual averages; £mn)

	1961-3 Ave.			1965-7 Ave.			1969-71 Ave.			% distribution of credits		
	Credits	Debits	Net	Credits	Debits	Net	Credits	Debits	Net	1961-3	1965-7	1969-71
Government (nie)	42	400	-358	41	501	-460	51	545	-494	1.7	1.4	1.1
Transport	768	769	- 1	980	955	+ 25	1,659	1,667	- 8	32.4	32.4	37.5
a. Shipping	649	674	- 25	799	803	- 4	1,340	1,389	- 49	27.3	26.4	30.3
b. Civil aviation	119	95	+ 24	181	152	+ 29	319	278	+ 41	5.1	6.0	7.2
Travel	182	217	- 35	215	287	- 71	428	382	+ 46	7.7	7.2	9.7
Other services	513	259	+254	669	343	+326	1,173	506	+667	21.6	22.1	26.5
Interest, profits, & dividends	757	429	+328	977	577	+400	1,374	887	+487	31.9	32.3	20.8
Private transfers	111	104	+ 7	138	162	- 24	193	226	- 33	4.7	4.6	4.4
Total invisibles	2,373	2,178	+195	3,021	2,825	+196	4,878	4,213	+665	100.0	100.0	100.0

5.3 Britain's Invisibles Balance with the Overseas Sterling Area, 1959-61 to 1967-9 (annual averages; £mn)

	1959-61	1963-5	1967-9
1. Britain's invisibles balance with OSA	+240.7	+254.0	+ 288.7
2. Invisibles balance of OSA	-568.0	-888.0	-1,646.0
a. Developed OSA	-339.0	-410.0	- 608.6
b. LDCs in OSA	-229.0	-478.0	-1,037.4
3. 1 as % 2	42.4	28.6	27.8

5.4 Invisibles Balances of Major Sterling Area Countries, Annual Averages, 1965-9 (£mn)

Country	Ann. visibles balance	Ann. invisibles balance	Ann. visibles & invisibles balance		Ann. visibles balance	Ann. invisibles balance	Ann. visibles & invisibles balance
Developed:							
Eire	⊤122.8	+ 96.0	- 28.6	Kenya	- 19.8	+ 9.4	- 10.4
Iceland	- 8.0	+ 0.4	- 7.6	Sierra Leone	- 0.6	- 7.0	- 7.6
New Zealand	+ 71.8	-104.4	- 32.6	Tanzania	+ 9.7	- 11.7	- 2.0
South Africa[1]	-325.8	-153.0	-478.8	Ceylon	- 10.0	- 14.0	- 24.0
Australia	- 21.8	-383.0	-361.2	Trinidad	+ 18.0	- 30.8	- 12.8
Developing:				Zambia	+ 65.2	- 53.4	+ 11.8
Hong Kong	- 74.8	+ 95.6	+ 20.8	Malaysia	+ 94.0	- 70.4	+ 23.6
Singapore	-124.4	+ 83.8	- 41.0	India	-237.2	- 75.0	-312.2
Jordan	- 45.0	+ 48.8	+ 3.8	Nigeria	+ 52.8	-132.4	- 79.5
Malta	- 30.4	+ 32.0	+ 1.6	Libya	+368.4	-504.4	-136.0
Cyprus	- 25.2	+ 25.2	-				
Pakistan	-154.2	+ 17.4	-136.8				

5.5 The Invisibles Sector of the Indian Balance of Payments, 1961-3 to 1969-71 (annual averages; $mn)

	1961-3			1965-7			1969-71		
	Credits	Debits	Net	Credits	Debits	Net	Credits	Debits	Net
1. Government (nie)	+101	- 27	+ 74	+139	- 32	+107	+ 42	- 31	+ 11
2. Other transportation	+ 48	- 52	- 4	+ 54	- 56	- 2	+ 65	- 79	- 14
3. Travel	+ 33	- 23	+ 10	+ 34[1]	- 21	+ 13	+ 37	- 23	+ 14
4. Freight & merchandise insurance	+ 65	- 7	+ 58	+ 72	- 9	+ 63	+ 84	- 17	+ 67
5. Other services	+ 81	- 97	- 16	+ 76	-110	- 34	+ 79	-120	- 41
6. Investment income	+ 24	-189	-165	+ 25	-288	-263	+ 50	-347	-297
7. Private transfers	+112	- 34	+ 78	+165	- 31	+134	+195	- 18	+177
Total services (1 to 6)	+352	-395	- 43	+400	-516	-116	+357	-617	-260
Total invisibles (1 to 7)	+464	-429	+ 35	+565	-547	+ 18	+552	-635	- 83

5.6 Overall Indian Invisibles Balance of Payments, 1960-9 (£mn unadjusted, IMF basis)

	1960	1961	1962	1963	1964	1965	1966	1967	1968	1969	Total 1960-9
Total services /3-87	+22.65	-14.40	-19.28	- 2.47	-11.47	-59.29	-27.85	-61.80	-73.21	-101.25	-348.37
Total invisibles /3-97	+51.00	+11.63	+ 6.07	+26.86	+17.18	-28.94	+35.72	-11.34	- 6.55	-27.92	+ 73.71

5.7 Services & Invisibles Flows between India and Major Countries & Groupings, 1961-71 ($mn)

	1961-5[1] ave.					1966-71[1] ave.					1961-71 overall net balance on	
	Credits		Debits		Net Amt	Credits		Debits		Net Amt	services	invisibles[2]
	Amt	%	Amt	%		Amt	%	Amt	%			
USA & Canada	+134.9	37.6	-106.2	25.3	+28.7	+126.5	34.5	-194.5	33.9	- 68.0	- 264.5	+398.9
UK	+101.5	28.2	-145.3	34.7	-43.8	+ 85.7	23.4	-133.0	23.2	- 47.3	- 483.0	-375.6
Other sterling area countries	+ 44.4	12.4	- 21.4	5.1	+23.0	+ 38.0	10.3	- 18.8	3.3	+ 19.2	+ 230.2	+530.0
Other OECD countries	+ 21.3	5.9	- 59.5	14.2	-38.2	+ 30.5	8.3	- 89.0	15.6	- 58.5	- 542.0	-522.4
Soviet countries and mainland China	+ 27.4	7.6	- 24.1	5.8	+ 3.3	+ 41.3	11.3	- 42.0	7.3	- 0.7	- 20.7	- 18.9
Other countries; unallocated	+ 3.3	0.9	- 35.2	8.4	-31.9	+ 2.2	0.6	- 47.3	8.3	- 45.1	- 430.1	-430.1
International institutions	+ 26.5	7.4	- 27.1	6.5	- 0.6	+ 42.5	11.6	- 47.8	8.4	- 5.3	- 34.8	- 5.3
Total	+359.3	100.0	-418.8	100.0	-59.5	+366.7	100.0	-572.4	100.0	-205.7	-1,544.9	-423.4

5.8 Services & Invisibles Flows between India & Britain, 1961-71 (annual averages; £mm, Indian positions)

	1961-3 ave.			1965-7 ave.			1969-71 ave.			1961-71 total (1)	
	Credits	Debits	Net	Credits	Debits	Net	Credits	Debits	Net	$mm	£mm
1. Government (nie)	+ 15	- 10	+ 5	+ 9	- 9	-	+ 7	- 6	+ 1	+ 23	+ 9
2. Other transportation	+ 24	- 16	+ 8	+ 24	- 13	+ 11	+ 23	- 16	+ 7	+ 91	+ 34
3. Travel	+ 1	- 7	- 6	+ 1	- 5	- 4	+ 6	- 4	+ 2	- 37	- 13
4. Freight & merchandise insurance	+ 8	- 1	+ 7	+ 6	- 1	+ 5	+ 4	- 3	+ 1	+ 44	+ 16
5. Other services	+ 46	- 40	+ 6	+ 45	- 42	+ 3	+ 23	- 36	- 13	- 13	- 6
6. Investment income	+ 14	- 66	-52	+ 11	- 72	-61	+ 16	- 63	- 47	591	-223
7. Private transfers	na	na	+ 4	na	na	+ 6	na	na	+ 23	+ 172	+ 66
8. Total services flows with UK (1-6)	+108	-140	-32	+ 96	-142	- 46	+ 79	-128	- 49	- 483	-183
9. Total invisibles flows with UK (1-7)	na	na	-28	na	na	- 40	na	na	- 26	311	-117
10. Total services (Table 5.5)	+352	-395	-43	+400	-516	-116	+357	-617	-260	-1,545	-610
11. UK share of total services $(\frac{8}{10} \cdot 100)\%$	30.7	35.4	74.41	24.00	27.51	39.65	22.12	20.74	18.84	31.26	30.00

5.9 World Tonnage of Shipping (all ships) & Tonnage under Various National Flags (000 gross tons)

	1939		1960		1965		1970	
	Tonnage 10^3 GRT	%	Tonnage 10^3 GRT	%	Tonnage 10^3 GRT	%	Tonnage 10^3 GRT	%
National flags								
Japan	5,427	8.8	6,486	5.2	11,250	7.3	24,142	11.5
UK	16,892	27.4	20,202	16.3	20,382	13.2	24,061	11.5
Norway	4,686	7.6	10,754	8.7	15,589	10.1	18,606	8.9
USA	8,722	14.1	23,754	19.2	19,931	12.9	15,547	7.4
USSR	1,154	1.8	3,266	2.6	7,455	4.8	10,624	5.1
West Germany	4,185*	6.8	4,318	3.5	5,333	3.4	7,555	3.6
India	_(1)	-	847	0.6	1,536	0.9	2,428	1.2
Convenience Flags								
Liberia	-	-	10,618	8.6	19,332	12.5	33,804	16.1
Panama	722	1.1	4,080	3.3	4,688	3.0	6,060	2.9
World total	61,426	100.0	123,296	100.0	153,964	100.0	209,966	100.0

5.10 British Share of Shipping Entering & Clearing Indian Ports, 1938-9 & 1960-1 to 1970-1

Amounts = 000 tons	1938-9 Tonnage[1]	%	1960-1 Tonnage[1]	%	1965-6 Tonnage[1]	%	1970-1 Tonnage[1]	%	Change, 1960-1 to 1970-1,as % 1960-1
British	7,328.4	66.6	4,104.0	31.2	2,915.9	20.4	2,184.1	12.5	- 46.8
Indian[2]	428.5	3.8	1,467.0	11.2	1,690.7	11.8	4,316.5	24.6	+194.2
Foreign	3,259.7	29.6	7,576.0	57.6	9,617.8	67.8	11,028.5	62.9	+ 45.6
Total	11,016.6	100.0	13,147.0	100.0	14,224.4	100.0	17,529.1	100.0	+ 33.3

5.11 Origin of Visitors to India, 1951-71

Origin of visitors[1]	1951 No.	%	1956 No.	%	1961 No.	%	1966 No.	%	1971[2] No.	%
Britain	5,984	35.5	13,322	20.2	22,191	15.8	21,723	13.6	40.005	13.3
USA	3,500	20.8	12,595	19.1	31,345	22.4	41,459	25.9	54,982	18.3
West Germany	206	1.2	2,141	3.2	4,835	3.4	7,677	4.8	17,867	5.9
Total	16,829	100.0	65,887	100.0	139,804	100.0	159,603	100.0	300,995	100.0

5.12 Net British Overseas Direct Investment & net Earnings from Direct Investment, 1961-71 (annual averages; £mn)

	1961-3	1965-7	1969-71	1961-71 Total
1. Net direct investment by UK overseas	-223.7	-288.3	-570.3	-3,920
2. Net direct overseas investment in UK	+175.3	+187.3	+362.0	+2,610
3. Net flow to UK (1-2)	- 48.4	-101.0	-208.3	-1,310
4. Net earnings from UK overseas direct investment	+284.3	+422.3	+675.7	+5,085
5. Net earnings from overseas direct investment in UK	-143.3	-230.3	-342.3	-2,680
6. Net flow to UK (4-5)	+141.0	+192.0	+333.4	+2,405
7. Total overall net flow to UK (3+6)	+ 92.6	+ 91.0	+125.1	+1,095
8. Net flow from UK overseas direct investment (4-1)	+ 60.6	+134.0	+105.4	+1,165
9. Percentage cover: net earnings from UK direct investment as % net UK direct investment overseas $(\frac{4}{1} \cdot 100)$	127.0	146.5	118.5	129.7

5.13 The Balance of Payments of the Indian Foreign Capital Sector, 1948-61 (Rsmn)

Foreign exchange losses:		
- Repatriation of capital	-1,411	
- Profits remitted abroad	-3,810	
- Royalties, fees, etc	-1,963	
Total		-7,184
Foreign exchange gains:		
- Gross investment in cash	+ 602	
- Gross investment in kind	+1,869	
Total		+2,471
Net balance		-4,713

5.14 Net British Private Investment in India & Earnings from UK Investments in India, 1960-3 to 1968-71 (annual averages; £mn)

	1960-3[1]	1964-7	1968-71
1. Net flow of UK private investment to India	-14.00	-10.75	- 9.25
2. Net earnings from UK investment in India	+21.20	+20.50	+22.50
3. Net flow to UK (2-1)	+ 7.20	+ 9.75	+13,25
4. 1 as % 2	66.0	52.4	41.1
5. Net earnings as % of previous year's book value of UK investment in India %	na	7.62	8.01

5.15 Components of Net Earnings from UK Private Overseas Investment, 1969-71 average (£mn)

	India		Less developed countries		All countries	
	Value	%	Value	%	Value	%
1. Profits & interest	+25.2	3.47	+222.3	30.55	+727.5	100.0
2. Losses	- 2.0	3.77	- 16.3	30.75	- 53.0	100.0
3. Total net earnings (1-2)	+23.2	100.00	+206.0	100.00	+674.5	100.00
a. Net profits of branches	+ 6.2	26.73	+ 65.5	31.80	+125.5	18.60
b. Net profits of subsidiaries	+16.7	71.98	+137.9	66.94	+533.9	79.17
c. Interest charges	+ 0.3	1.29	+ 2.6	1.26	+ 15.1	2.23

5.16 Dividend Remittances of British Private Investment in India, 1960/1 to 1965/6

	1960/1	1961/2	1962/3	1963/4	1964/5	1965/6
a. Dividend remittances: Rsmn	84.0	102.5	132.4	116.0	145.0[1]	145.2[1]
- Subsidiaries with majority UK capital	75.7	92.1	115.4	93.7	112.4[1]	111.0[1]
- Companies with minority capital participation	8.3	10.4	16.9	22.3	32.6[1]	34.2[1]
b. Dividend remittances: £mn	6.3	7.6	9.9	8.7	10.8	10.8
c. Total UK net earnings in India: £mn[2]	19.3	21.4	23.1	21.0	21.5	25.3
d. b as % c	32.6	35.6	42.9	41.5	50.3	42.7

5.17 National Distribution of Foreign Assets & Liabilities of the Indian Banking Sector, 1963, 1965, & 1967 (Rsmn)

	1963			1965			1967		
	Assets[1]	Liabilities[2]	Net	Assets	Liabilities	Net	Assets	Liabilities	Net
UK	119	318	-199	146	220	- 74	394	286	+108
USA	25	70	- 45	27	94	- 67	61	134	- 73
Pakistan	39	18	+ 21	21	26	- 5	29	17	+ 12
Malaysia	15	67	- 52	44	30	+ 14	10	24	- 14
Others	41	365	-324	72	380	-308	56	387	-331
Total[3]	239	838	-599	310	750	-440	550	-848	-298
UK share	49.8	37.9	19.8	47.1	29.3	16.8	71.6	33.7	36.2

5.18 Sterling Area Share of Indian Transactions
in Insurance, 1964, 1967 & 1969 (Rsmn)

	1964			1967			1969		
	Credits	Debits	Net	Credits	Debits	Net	Credits	Debits	Net
All nations & institutions	75	51	+24	125	61	+64	129	125	+ 4
Sterling area	43	38	+ 5	65	35	+30	53	84	-31
British earnings on insurance of	-	81	-	-	79	-	-	50	-
British exports to India (5%)(1)	-	(1964-5)	-	-	(1967-8)	-	-	(1969-7C)	-

5.19 Non-life Insurance Transacted by Overseas
& Domestic Companies in India 1939 & 1969

Country of company constitution	Year	No. of companies	Gross premium income under policies effected in India		Distribution of gross premium income by types of policy (%)			Total assets in India
			Rsmn	%	Fire	Marine	Misc.	Rsmn
UK	1939	44	15.2	-	48.7	21.7	29.6	28.7
	1969	38	107.3	11.9	43.5	23.0	33.5	188.7
USA	1939	5	1.6	-	50.0	50.0	-	1.2
	1969	7	19.6	2.2	49.5	30.1	20.4	29.7
Australia & New Zealand	1939	4	4.6	-	30.4	56.5	13.1	4.8
	1969	5	19.4	2.1	38.6	34.6	26.8	31.5
Other	1939	16	1.8	-	44.4	50.0	5.6	3.8
	1969	13	20.7	2.3	53.1	21.7	25.2	38.1
Total foreign companies	1939	69	23.2	-	44.8	32.8	22.4	38.5
	1969	63	167.0	18.5	44.0	25.0	30.1	288.0
Total Indian companies	1969	72	731.2	81.5	35.0	18.4	46.6	731.2
Total all companies	1969	135	898.2	100.0	36.8	19.7	43.5	1,019.2
Foreign as % total	1969	46.7	18.6	-	22.6	23.6	12.9	28.3

5.20 Countrywide Remittances of Royalties & Technical Fees: Total, 1960/1 to 1966/7 (Rsmn)

Recipient nation	Subsidiaries	Minority foreign capital	Collaboration agreements	TOTAL Amt	%
UK	94.2	63.0	49.5	206.7	37.1
USA	57.4	67.4	59.2	184.0	33.1
West Germany	7.4	34.1	12.2	53.7	9.6
Other	42.1	32.3	37.2	111.6	20.8
Total	201.1	196.8	158.1	556.0	100.0
UK share %	46.8	32.0	31.3	37.1	—

5.21 Remittances of Royalties & Technical Fees to Britain: 1960/1 to 1965/6, (Rsmn & £mn)

	1960/1	1961/2	1963/3	1963/4	1964/5	1965/6	Total 1960/1-1965/6
Royalty remittances: Rsmn	4.1	5.0	6.3	8.1	12.8	17.7	54.0
- UK subsidiaries	2.3	3.0	4.0	3.4	5.5	7.9	26.1
- UK minority capital	1.8	2.0	2.3	4.7	7.3	9.8	27.9
Technical fee remittances: Rsmn	8.7	9.3	9.7	8.5	15.2	14.5	65.9
- UK subsidiaries	6.8	7.1	7.2	4.7	10.9	11.1	47.8
- UK minority capital	1.9	2.2	2.5	3.8	4.3	3.4	18.1
Total remittances Rsmn	12.8	14.3	16.0	16.6	28.0	32.2	119.9
Total remittances £mn	0.96	1.07	1.20	1.24	2.10	2.41	8.98

6.1 Net British Direct Investment Overseas; 1860-9 to 1960-9 (annual averages; £mn)

Period	Value	As % GDP	Period	Value	As % GDP
1860-9	- 29	3.012	1930-9	+ 50	-
1870-9	- 51	3.932	1940-9	+487	-
1880-9	- 68	4.885	1950-9	-150	0.808
1890-9	- 52	3.189	1960-9	- 73	0.239
1900-9	- 85	3.957			
1910-19	na	na	1961-5	- 71	0.259
1920-9	-124	2.426	1966-70	-145	0.387

6.3 Distribution of British Capital in India by sectors, 1911, 1930 (industry only), 1948 (industry only) (£mn)

	1911 (British India) Value	%	1930 (British India) Value	%	1948 (Independent India) Value	%
Commerce & industry	2.5	1.3	112.5	58.8	85.3	44.4
Plantations	24.2	13.3	11.2(1)	5.8	39.1	20.3
Mines	3.5	1.9	11.2	5.8	8.6	4.4
Banks						
Insurance	3.4	1.8	20.0	10.5	5.1	2.6
Railways	135.6	74.6 }				
Trams, public utilities	4.1	2.2 }	29.2	15.2	23.6	12.3
Oil & petroleum(2)	3.2	1.7	na	na	16.7	8.7
Miscellaneous	5.1	2.8	7.0	3.6	13.2	6.8
Total	181.6	100.0	191.1	100.0	191.9	100.0
Government & municipal bonds, etc.	185.2		390.0		na	

6.4 British Investment Overseas by major categories, 1959-61 to 1969-71 (annual averages; £mn)

	1959-61	1964-6	1969-71
1. Direct investment	-224	-282	-531
1. Change in branch indebtedness	- 35	- 11	- 21
2. Unremitted profits of subsidiaries	- 84	-166	-301
3. Net acquisition of new share and loan capital	- 70	- 63	-151
4. Change in inter-company accounts	- 35	- 42	- 58
2. Portfolio investment	+ 23	+ 58	- 67
1. London market loans	- 9	+ 9	+ 7
2. Other loans	+32	+ 49	- 74
3. Oil & miscellaneous	-112	-132	-121
4. Total	-313	-356	-719

6.2 UK Flows on Private Investment Account & on Long-term Capital Account 1952-5 to 1966-70 (annual averages; £mn)

	1952-5	1956-60	1961-5	1966-70
1. Net private investment	-120	-131	- 89	- 63
a. By UK overseas (net of disinvestment)	-180	-298	-328	-584
b. In UK (net of disinvestment)	+ 60	+167	+239	+521
2. Net government(1)	- 40	- 56	- 92	- 85
3. Balance of long-term capital	-160	-187	-181	-148
4. 1 as % 3	75.0	70.0	49.2	42.6

6.5 Values[1] of UK Direct Capital Holdings by Area, 1958–71 (£mn)

	1958		1962		1965		1970		1971		Increase in value 1962–71 %
	Value	%	Value	%	Value	%	Value	%	Value	%	
Developed countries	1,781	65.5	2,131	62.6	2,778	66.0	4,554	71.1	4,807	72.1	+125.6
North America	856	31.5	785	23.0	919	21.8	1,478	23.1	1,466	21.9	+ 86.7
Europe	226	8.3	356	10.4	507	12.0	996	15.5	1,177	17.6	+230.6
EEC	na	–	272	7.9	392	9.3	808	12.6	985	14.8	+262.1
EFTA	na	–	82	2.4	114	2.7	181	2.8	192	2.8	+134.1
Sterling Area	699	25.7	986	28.9	1,335	31.7	2,043	31.9	2,124	31.8	+115.4
Less developed countries	937	34.5	1,273	37.4	1,432	34.0	1,850	28.9	1,860	27.9	+ 46.1
Asia	450	16.5	545	16.0	591	14.0	682	10.6	679	10.2	+ 24.6
India	202	7.4	260	7.6	304	7.2	297	4.6	289	4.3	+ 11.1
Africa	262	9.6	411	12.1	403	9.6	465	7.3	512	7.7	+ 24.6
Latin America & West Indies	192	7.0	276	8.1	359	8.5	521	8.1	488	7.3	+ 76.8
Sterling area	754	27.7	950	27.9	1,061	25.2	1,321	20.6	1,346	20.2	+ 41.7
Total	2,719	100.0	3,405	100.0	4,210	100.0	6,404	100.0	6,667	100.0	+145.2
Commonwealth	na	–	2,049	60.2	2,428	57.6	3,369	52.6	3,365	50.5	+ 64.2

6.6 Net Flows of British Direct Investment,
1959-61 to 1969-71 (annual averages; £mn)

Destination	1959-61 Value	%	1962-4 Value	%	1966-8 Value	%	1969-71 Value	%
Developed countries	131	61.2	174	73.7	259	80.4	464	81.4
Sterling Area	61	28.5	100	42.4	108	33.5	165	28.9
Australia	39	18.2	61	25.8	61	18.9	92	16.1
South Africa	12	5.6	27	11.4	42	13.0	49	8.6
Non-sterling area	70	32.7	74	31.3	151	46.9	299	52.4
USA	17	7.9	17	7.2	59	18.3	102	17.9
EEC	20	9.3	35	14.8	51	15.8	139	24.4
EFTA	5	2.3	13	5.5	7	2.2	13	2.3
Less developed countries	81	37.8	62	26.2	63	19.6	106	18.6
Sterling area	62	28.9	40	16.9	38	11.8	74	13.0
India	13	6.1	14	5.9	7	2.2	9	1.6
Ghana	3	1.4	...	...	3	0.9	4	0.7
Nigeria	6	2.8	-1	-	...	-	22	3.8
Malaysia & Singapore	7	3.2	6	2.5	6	1.8	8	1.4
Non-sterling area	19	8.9	22	9.3	26	8.1	32	5.6
Total	214	100.0	236	100.0	322	100.0	570	100.0

6.7 Direct Investment by DAC Countries in LDCs,
1956-60 to 1966-70 (annual averages; $mn)

Origin	1956-60 Value	%	1961-5 Value	%	1966-70 Value	%
USA	537	33.1	1,307	40.9	1,945	34.9
France	361	22.2	458	14.3	695	12.4
Netherlands	145	8.9	105	3.2	175	3.1
Germany	80	4.9	221	6.9	830	14.8
Japan	26	1.6	116	3.6	376	6.7
Italy	38	2.3	214	6.7	460	8.2
Belgium	53	3.2	85	2.6	122	2.1
Canada	57	3.5	37	1.1	90	1.6
Sweden	16	0.9	32	1.0	69	1.2
Switzerland	40	2.4	166	5.2	131	2.3
Others	3	-	43	1.3	184	3.2
UK	265	16.3	409	12.8	507	9.0
Total	1,621	100.0	3,193	100.0	5,584	100.0

6.8 Net British Private Investment, per caput in Recipient Countries, 1963-7 (annual averages)

Recipient area/country		Average population (mn)[1]	Average inflow of British capital[2] (£mn)	Net investment per capita[3] £
North America:	USA	194.2	31.6	0.16
	Canada	19.6	17.0	0.84
Europe:	EEC	180.7	37.8	0.20
	EFTA	64.7	38.8	0.60
Sterling area:	Australia	11.3	58.6	5.18
	New Zealand	2.6	5.2	2.00
	South Africa	17.8	38.5	2.16
	India	487.4	11.5	0.02
	Pakistan	102.9	1.9	0.018

6.9 Outstanding Long-term Foreign Capital in the Indian Private Sector, 1948, 1958, & 1968 (Rsmn)

Sector	1948 Value	%	1958 Value	%	1968 Value	%	% changes in value 1948-58	1958-68
Plantations	522	19.7	951	16.9	1,225	7.9	+ 82.2	+ 28.8
Mining	115	4.3	118	2.0	96	0.6	+ 2.6	- 18.7
Petroleum	223	8.4	1,184	21.0	1,964	12.7	+430.9	+ 65.9
Manufacturing	707	26.7	2,149	38.2	8,216	53.3	+203.9	+282.3
Services	1,079	40.7	1,223	21.7	3,927	25.5	+ 13.4	+221.1
Total	2,646	100.0	5,625	100.0	15,428	100.0	+112.6	+174.3

6.11 British & Indian Official Estimates of Total British Capital in India, 1958-68 (£mn)

		1958	1960	1962	1964	1966	1968
British estimates							
- Board of Trade - direct only		201.8	227.7	259.7	288.5	207.7[2]	277.2
- allowance for portfolio holdings[1]		40.3	45.5	51.9	57.7	41.5	55.4
- Total	A	242.1	273.2	311.6	346.2	249.2	332.6
Indian estimates							
- RBI	Total	B	299.1	325.4	370.0	404.3	279.5	312.1
Difference:	amount		57.0	52.2	58.4	58.1	30.3	na
	A as % B		80.9	83.9	84.2	85.6	89.1	na

6.10 Capital Stock & Net Flows of Long-term
Foreign Investments in India, 1960, 1968

Country of Origin	Outstanding Capital Dec.1960				Outstanding Capital Mar.1968				Net long-term foreign inflow(1) Jan. 1961 – Mar. 1968				Net inflow as % 1960 stock $\frac{(B)}{(A)} \cdot 100$
	Value (Rsmn) (A)	As % of nation	As % of type	As % of total	Value (Rsmn)	As % of nation	As % of type	As % of total	Value (Rsmn) (B)	As % of nation	As % of type	As % of total	
Private Investment (1)													
UK Total	4,338	100.0		68.2	6,255	100.0		52.9	1917	100.0		35.1	44.2
Direct	4,013	92.5	80.7	63.1	5,051	80.7	72.0	42.7	1038	54.1	50.9	19.0	25.9
Portfolio	325	7.5	23.4	5.1	1,204	19.3	25.0	10.2	879	45.9	25.7	16.1	270.5
USA Total	890	100.0		14.0	1,976	100.0		16.7	1096	100.0		19.9	122.0
Direct	685	76.9	13.7	10.7	1,094	55.4	15.6	9.2	419	37.7	20.0	7.5	59.7
Portfolio	205	23.1	14.7	3.3	882	44.6	18.3	7.5	677	62.3	19.8	12.4	330.2
Other Total	1,133	100.0		17.8	3,594	100.0		30.4	2461	100.0		45.0	217.2
Direct	273	25.0	5.6	4.3	867	24.1	12.4	7.3	594	24.1	29.1	10.9	217.6
Portfolio	860	75.0	61.9	13.5	2,727	75.9	56.7	23.1	1867	75.9	54.5	34.1	217.1
All Total	6,361	100.0		100.0	11,825	100.0		100.0	5464	100.0		100.0	85.9
Direct	4,971	78.1	100.0	78.1	7,012	59.3	100.0	59.3	2041	37.4	100.0	37.4	41.1
Portfolio	1,390	21.9	100.0	21.9	4,813	40.7	100.0	40.7	3423	62.6	100.0	62.6	246.3
Official Investment in Indian Private Sector(2)	na	–	–	–	3,603 (2247 = USA (1356 = Other	–	–	–	3,603	–	–	–	–
Total (1) + (2)	na	–	–	–	15,428	–	–	–	na	–	–	–	–

6.12 Sectoral Distribution of British Long-term
Capital in India, 1961, 1968, & 1971 (Rsmn)

Sector	1961			1968			1971[2]			% change in direct investment 1961-71
	Direct	Portfolio	Total	Direct	Portfolio	Total	Direct	Portfolio	Total	
Plantations	1,005	29	1,034	1,175	35	1,210	1,352			+ 34.5
Mining	108	10	118	39	24	63	na			na
Manufacturing	1,307	146	1,453	2,148	637	2,785	2,976			+127.7
Food, drink, & tobacco							569			
Chemicals, allied inds.							549			
Metal manufacture							328			
Mechanical engineering	na	na	na	na	na	na	188	na	na	na
Electrical engineering							560			
Motor vehicles							120			
Textiles							175			
Other							487			
Petroleum	1,011	3	1,014	892	168	1,060	710[1]			- 29.8
Services	759	98	857	797	340	1,137	682			- 10.2
Transport	–	–	–	–	–	–	49			–
Distribution	na	na	na	na	na	na	239			na
Total incl. petroleum	4,190	286	4,476	5,051	1,204	6,255	5,997	na	na	+ 43.1
Total excl. petroleum	3,179	283	3,462	4,159	1,036	5,195	5,287	na	na	+ 66.3

6.13 British Involvement in the Top 200 Indian
Companies ranked by the value of their assets, 1970-1

Asset	Total assets (Rsmn)	Indian company	Type	British company involved
1	10,266	Hindustan Steel	G	
21	803	Oil India	A	Burmah Oil
24	649	Indian Explosives	S	ICI
31	530	National Organic Chemical Industries	A	Shell Transport & Trading[1]
32	529	India Tobacco	S	British-American Tobacco
39	429	Dunlop India	S	Dunlop Holdings
40	393	Hindustan Lever	S	Unilever
48	368	Binny	A	Inchcape
49	364	Guest Keen Williams	S	Guest, Keen, Nettlefolds
50	364	Gwalior Rayon Silk Mfg (Wrg)	P	
55	298	General Electrical Industries	S	General Electric
60	281	Brooke-Bond India	Pv	Brooke-Bond Liebig
73	247	Ashok Leyland	S	British Leyland
75	237	Metal Box Co. of India	S	The Metal Box
76	235	Burmah-Shell Refineries	A	Burmah Oil
			A	Shell Transport & Trading
78	229	Indian Tube	A	British Steel
81	221	Crompton Greaves	A	Hawker-Siddeley
84	213	Glaxo Laboratories (India	S	Glaxo Holdings
86	212	Madura Mills	A	Coats Patons
95	197	Rallis India	A	Fisons
97	196	ACC-Vickers-Babcock	A	Vickers
			A	Babcock & Wilcox
100	190	Alkali & Chemical Corp. of India	P	
117	156	Indian Oxygen	S	British Oxygen
120	153	National Machinery Manufacturers	A	Stone-Platt Industries
132	142	MacNeill and Barry	A	Inchcape
137	135	Tube Investments of India	S	Tube Investments
145	129	Indian Cable	A	British Insulated Callender's Cables
149	125	Chemicals & Fibres of India	S	ICI
150	125	Atic Industries	A	ICI
156	120	Herdillia Chemicals	A	British Petroleum
166	113	Saraswati Industrial Syndicate	A	Clarke Chapman-John Thompson
183	104	ICI India	Pv	ICI
190	101	Lucas-TVS	S	Joseph Lucas Industries
200	97	Aluminium Corp. of India	P	

					%	
	86,702	Top 200 companies in India ranked by assets in 1970-1			100.00	
	46,913	Government companies	G		54.10	
	38,735	Public companies	P		44.67	
	5,534	British public companies in India			6.38	93.49
	3,876	- Wholly owned subsidiaries	S		4.47	65.48
	1,658	- Associated companies[2]	A		1.91	28.01
	1,054	Private companies	Pv		1.23	
	385	British private companies in India	Pv		0.44	6.51
	5,919	Total British companies			6.82	100.00

6.14 Organizational Structure & Relative Size
of British Companies Investing in India, 1968, 1971

Values in £mn; current prices

		BRITISH COMPANIES IN INDIA (A)					TOTAL BRITISH OVERSEAS COMPANIES (B)					(A) as % (B)		
		No. (1)	%	value (2) £mn	%	(5) value per unit (2)/(1)	No. (3)	%	value (4) £mn	%	(6) value per unit (4)/(3)	No. $\frac{(1)}{(3)}\times\frac{100}{1}$	value $\frac{(2)}{(4)}\times\frac{100}{1}$	value per unit $\frac{(5)}{(6)}\times\frac{100}{1}$
Large companies	1968	246	69.0	261.4	94.3	1.06	4,723	67.7	5,285.7	94.6	1.12	5.21	4.94	94.6
	1971	188	52.7	254.6	87.8	1.35	4,305	54.6	6,127.4	91.9	1.42	4.37	4.15	95.1
- Subsidiaries	1968	89	25.0	131.2	47.3	1.47	2,973	42.6	4,067.9	72.8	1.37	2.90	3.22	107.3
	1971	76	21.3	137.2	47.3	1.80	2,980	37.8	4,959.3	74.4	1.66	2.55	2.77	108.4
- Branches	1968	76	21.0	112.4	40.5	1.47	749	10.7	838.8	15.0	1.12	10.10	13.40	131.2
	1971	49	13.7	97.9	33.8	2.00	559	7.1	639.7	9.6	1.14	8.77	15.30	175.4
- Associates	1968	81	23.0	17.8	6.4	0.22	1,001	14.4	379.0	6.8	0.38	8.10	4.70	57.9
	1971	63	17.7	19.5	6.7	0.31	766	9.7	528.4	7.9	0.69	8.22	3.69	44.9
Small companies	1968	106	31.0	15.8	5.7	0.14	2,251	32.3	299.5	5.4	0.13	4.70	5.27	107.7
	1971	169	47.3	35.2	12.2	0.21	3,582	45.4	539.5	8.1	0.15	4.72	6.52	140.0
Total companies	1968	352	100.0	277.2	100.0	0.78	6,974	100.0	5,585.3	100.0	0.80	5.00	4.96	97.5
	1971	357	100.0	289.8	100.0	0.81	7,887	100.0	6,666.9	100.0	0.84	4.53	4.35	96.4

	SUBSIDIARIES			COMPANIES WITH MINORITY FOREIGN CAPITAL HOLDINGS		
	Value of Ord. shares held (Rsmn) (1)	As % of total shares (2)	% of foreign shares to total (3)	Value of Ord. shares held (Rsmn) (1)	As % of total shares (2)	% of foreign shares to total (3)
UK	900	70.5	81.3	383	56.1	35.2
USA	163	12.7	84.0	138	20.2	18.0
Switzerland	48	3.7	75.0	23	3.3	30.4
Sweden	43	3.3	53.8	-	-	-
Canada	40	3.1	65.6	-	-	-
France	26	2.0	66.7	-	-	-
West Germany	17	1.3	58.6	66	9.6	19.9
Others	40	3.1	76.9	73	10.7	na
Total	1,277	100.0		683	100.0	
Average			78.5			27.9

6.16 Foreign Collaboration Agreements with Indian Industry, 1959-68 (annual averages)

	1959-63		1964-8		1958-68	
	No.	%	No.	%	No.	%
UK	89	29.2	55	23.7	759	27.1
USA	54	17.7	47	20.2	515	18.4
West Germany	45	14.7	39	16.8	433	15.4
Japan	26	8.5	22	9.5	248	8.8
Switzerland	14	4.6	11	4.7	132	4.7
France	11	3.6	10	4.3	109	3.9
Italy	8	2.6	5	2.1	74	2.6
Eastern Europe	12	3.9	15	6.5	141	5.0
- East Germany	5	1.6	7	3.0	62	2.2
Total	305	100.0	232	100.0	2,795	100.0

6.17 Indian Profitability Ratios: Branches of Foreign Companies, Foreign-Controlled Rupee Companies, Indian Public & Private Limited Companies, average 1965-6 to 1966-7

	Gross profits as % of sales net of rebate & discount 1	Gross profits as % of total capital employed 2	Profits after tax as % of net worth 3	Dividends as % of paid-up capital 4	Dividends as % of net worth 5
A 219 Branches of foreign companies	5.05	7.85	-	-	-
(1) 184 Branches of UK companies	5.75	7.80	-	-	-
(2) 24 Branches of US companies	4.25	9.15	-	-	-
(3) 11 Branches of other countries' companies	1.65	5.60	-	-	-
B 365 Foreign-controlled rupee companies	12.60	12.40	12.05	11.65	7.25
(1) 223 Companies with UK control	11.40	12.85	11.60	13.05	8.20
(2) 48 Companies with US control	17.05	11.05	11.10	9.45	5.35
(3) 94 Companies with control elsewhere	13.85	12.50	14.40	9.05	5.95
C 1,501 Public limited companies [1]	9.75	9.45	8.80	9.45	5.55
D 701 Private limited companies [2]	7.75	11.05	11.05	8.20	4.75
E 1,944 Indian-controlled public & private limited companies	8.50	8.85	7.90	8.55	4.80

7.1 Net Flows of Financial Resources to LDCs
by source, 1961-3 to 1969-71 (annual averages;
values in $mn)

	1961-3		1965-7		1969-71		1971 flow as % 1961 flow
	Value	%	Value	%	Value	%	
1. Official	6,281.0	70.7	7,539.0	66.2	8,841.7	56.7	+ 68.9
a. Bilateral official	5,806.7	65.4	6,444.7	56.6	7,265.0	46.6	+ 42.3
i DAC flows	5,501.0	62.0	6,064.0	53.2	6,740.0	43.2	+ 38.0
1. UK	430.8	4.8	491.7	4.3	484.9	3.1	+ 25.4
ii Other	305.7	3.4	380.7	3.4	525.0	3.4	+147.7
b. Multilateral	474.3	5.3	1,094.3	9.6	1,576.7	10.1	+718.3
2. Private : DAC bilateral	2,606.7	29.3	3,856.3	33.8	6,744.7	43.3	+150.7
1. UK	357.1	4.0	423.7	3.7	829.8	5.3	+121.6
3. Total flows to LDCs[1]	8,887.7	100.0	11,395.3	100.0	15,586.4	100.0	+ 96.8
4. UK total flows to LDCs	787.9	8.8	915.4	8.0	1,314.7	8.4	+ 71.6
5. Total flows to LDCs (mn 1961 dollars)[2]	8,268.0	-	8,158.7	-	7,894.5	-	- 9.5

7.3 Flow of Resources under Official Development
Assistance Programmes ($mn; 1960-2 & 1969-71
annual averages, 1960-70 total)

Origin	1960-62		1969-71		1960-70[1]	
	Value	%	Value	%	Value	%
Australia	68.0	1.3	193.1	2.8	1,339	2.1
Canada	57.0	1.1	310.5	4.4	1,560	2.4
France	890.3	17.5	1,004.7	14.2	9,421	14.4
Germany	331.3	6.5	634.5	9.0	4,961	7.6
Italy	72.3	1.4	153.2	2.2	1,051	1.6
Japan	99.3	1.9	468.1	6.6	2,712	4.2
Netherlands	52.0	1.0	185.2	2.6	982	1.5
UK	428.0	8.4	479.6	6.8	4,928	7.6
USA	2,942.0	57.7	3,155.3	44.7	35,608	54.5
Others	161.1	3.2	475.6	6.7	2,715	4.1
Total	5,101.3	100.0	7,059.8	100.0	65,277	100.0

7.2 1960, 1970, & 1960-70 Total and 1970 UK,
Net Flow of Financial Resources ($mm)
from DAC Countries to LDCs & Multilateral
Institutions

Type of flow	1960		1960-70 total		1970 Total		1970 UK		1970 UK share of total
	Amt	%	Amt	%	Amt	%	Amt	%	%
1. Official development assistance	4,703	57.9	65,489	56.3	6,840	45.6	447	35.9	6.53
a. Bilateral grants etc.	3,716	45.7	40,600	34.9	3,323	22.1	205	16.5	6.16
b. Bilateral loans etc.	452	5.5	18,340	15.8	2,393	16.0	195	15.7	8.14
c. Contributions to multilateral instit	535	6.5	6,595	5.6	1,124	7.5	48	3.7	4.27
2. Other official flows	262	3.2	5,383	4.6	1,144	7.6	6	0.5	0.52
a. Bilateral	195	2.4	4,756	4.1	871	5.8	6	0.5	0.68
b. Multilateral	67	0.8	627	0.5	273	1.8	–	–	–
3. Private flows [1]	3,150	38.8	45,362	39.1	7,019	46.8	792	63.5	11.28
a. Direct investment	1,767	21.7	24,457	20.5	3,557	23.7	322	25.9	9.05
b. Bilateral portfolio	633	7.8	7,165	6.1	777	5.2	34	2.7	4.37
c. Multilateral portfolio	204	2.5	2,713	2.3	474	3.2	–	–	–
d. Export credits	546	6.7	11,866	10.2	2,211	14.7	436	35.0	19.71
Total official & private flows	8,115	100.0	116,233	100.0	15,003	100.0	1,245	100.0	8.29
Net grants by voluntary agencies	na	–	na	–	855	–	34	–	3.97
Total net[1] flows	8,115	–	116,233	–	15,858	–	1,279	–	8.06

7.4 Distribution of Net Official Assistance by major currency areas & political grouping ($mn; 1960-71 annual averages)

Donor nations	India & Pakistan		Other Commonwealth		Other sterling area		French franc area		CIAP member nations		Other LDCs		Total LDCs	
	Value	%	Value	%	Value	%	Value	%	Value	%	Value	%	Value	%
Australia	8.4	7.1	4.9	4.2	0.8	0.7	-	-	-	-	102.9	87.9	117.0	100.0
Canada	82.2	58.4	23.9	17.0	0.8	0.5	9.1	6.4	9.2	6.5	15.6	11.1	140.8	100.0
France	4.7	0.6	1.1	0.1	0.3	0.0	717.3	87.5	6.1	0.7	90.6	11.0	820.1	100.0
Germany	96.1	21.6	28.2	6.4	4.3	1.0	31.4	7.1	45.4	10.2	238.5	53.7	443.9	100.0
Italy	4.1	4.3	9.0	9.4	1.5	1.6	8.1	8.5	-2.7	-	72.6	76.2	92.6	100.0
Japan	56.1	23.0	8.3	3.4	16.3	6.7	0.1	0.0	-1.7	-	162.4	66.8	241.5	100.0
Netherlands	8.1	11.4	3.3	4.7	0.0	0.0	0.9	1.3	1.4	2.0	56.9	80.5	70.7	100.0
UK	96.6	23.6	247.1	60.3	12.9	3.1	1.9	0.5	2.0	0.5	49.4	12.1	409.9	100.0
USA	885.2	27.9	123.8	3.9	54.1	1.7	130.6	4.1	520.1	16.4	1,461.0	46.0	3,174.9	100.0
Others	72.7	35.3	-39.0	-	0.5	0.2	3.2	1.6	5.5	2.7	123.8	60.2	165.4	100.0
Total bilateral aid	1,314.1	23.1	410.7	7.2	91.6	1.6	902.8	15.9	585.3	10.3	2,373.8	41.8	5,676.7	100.0
Multilateral aid	87.8	9.6	157.7	17.3	15.9	1.7	127.8	14.0	260.2	28.5	262.7	28.8	912.0	100.0
Total assistance	1,401.8	21.3	568.3	8.6	107.5	1.6	1,030.6	15.6	845.5	12.8	2,636.5	40.0	6,588.8	100.0

7.5   Net Official Aid Receipts: $ per caput, & relative to imports & income, 1966-8

Recipients [1]	1967 Pop. (mn)	Est. income per head 1966 $	Official aid per head		Official aid relative to income per head %	Official aid relative to imports of goods & services	
			$	Rank		%	Rank
India	511.1	77	2.3	69-70	2.9	43.8	9
Indonesia	110.0	91	1.9	73-4	2.0	25.5	22
Pakistan	107.2	108	4.0	52-5	3.7	35.9	11
Brazil	85.6	252	2.4	68	0.9	11.9	43
Nigeria	61.4	68	2.3	69-70	3.3	11.8	44
S. Vietnam	16.9	82(2)	27.5	5	na	54.3	4
Chile	9.1	465	16.3	11	3.5	15.3	37
Tunisia	4.5	169	18.3	10	10.8	32.1	14
Zambia	3.9	200	11.4	15	5.7	7.7	52
Senegal	3.6	182	12.6	14	6.9	29.1	19
Dominican Republic	3.6	222	14.3	12	6.4	24.5	24
Laos	2.7	68	24.4	8	35.8	217.8	1
Israel	2.6	1,159	30.7	3	2.6	6.7	60
Jordan	2.0	214	25.9	7	9.6	30.8	15
Panama	1.3	452	14.2	13	3.1	7.4	54
Liberia	1.1	154(2)	31.6	2	20.5	27.8	20
Congo (Brazza.)	0.8	167(2)	27.7	4	na	29.2	18
Guyana	0.6	262	19.4	9	7.4	10.1	48
Gabon	0.4	266	26.9	6	10.1	19.0	34
Malta	0.3	473	53.8	1	11.3	14.6	39

7.6 Outstanding External Public Debts ($mm), 31 Dec. 1971 & Service Payments as % of Exports, 1965, 1971

Debtor Nation	Debts due to Multilateral Institutions (1)	Official bilateral debt (2)	Other debt (3)	Total external public debt (1)+(2)+(3)	Disbursed debt	Disbursed debt per capita(2)	Service payments as % of exports of goods & services 1965	1971
India(3)	2,165.6	7,319.3	474.2	9,959.1	8,553.5	15.89	15.4	23.5
Brazil	1,295.6	1,846.0	2,094.6	5,236.2	3,653.6	39.38	20.9	17.1
Pakistan	961.4	3,256.9	395.6	4,613.9	3,644.6	28.00	11.8	21.6
Mexico	1,256.2	460.9	2,526.6	4,243.7	3,565.1	70.35	24.8	24.7
Indonesia	276.0	3,629.5	498.5	4,404.0	3,385.9	29.29	10.3	8.6
Argentine	693.2	464.3	1,751.3	2,908.8	2,247.0	96.81	20.2	21.1
Turkey	612.5	2,166.4	202.8	2,981.7	2,191.5	62.20	20.3	19.4
Chile	232.4	1,190.4	1,214.3	2,637.1	2,171.2	222.00	12.2	19.6
Israel	151.6	417.0	2,284.3	2,852.9	1,984.9	682.09	23.7	16.3
Yugoslavia	524.9	972.7	377.3	1,874.9	1,354.6	65.94	14.4	6.5
Total: 80 LDCs	16,142.0	39,080.5	22,995.5	79,218.0	58,345.6	36.48	–	–
India as % of 80	13.41	18.72	2.06	12.57	14.66	43.55	–	–

7.7 Official British Assistance to LDCs, 1961–70, gross, net, & deflated net (£mn)

	1961	1962	1963	1964	1965	1966	1967	1968	1969	1970	Total 1961-70
1. Gross official assistance	172.6	164.7	164.3	194.5	197.3	213.5	208.4	210.6	210.5	218.8	1,955.8
Less 2. Amortization	10.4	10.7	15.6	17.5	24.0	30.3	29.4	32.2	32.0	29.9	232.0
3. Interest charges	11.1	12.3	20.4	23.8	26.2	27.7	28.2	27.7	28.4	29.3	235.1
4. Net official assistance (1−[2+3])	151.1	141.7	128.3	153.2	147.1	155.5	150.9	150.8	150.1	159.7	1,488.8
Net official assistance as % gross	87.5	86.0	78.0	78.7	74.5	72.8	72.4	71.5	71.3	72.9	76.1
Net official assistance: index 1961 = 100	100.0	93.7	84.9	101.4	97.3	102.9	99.8	99.8	99.3	105.7	–
1. Deflated by UK export price index [1] 1961 = 100	100.0	92.9	81.6	95.7	89.1	90.8	88.1	95.1	91.0	90.8	1,383.1 [3]
2. Deflated by LDC import price index [2] 1961 = 100	100.0	94.8	84.9	100.5	95.4	100.8	97.9	98.9	96.0	97.9	1,461.2 [3]

7.8 British & DAC Official Assistance as % of GNP (current prices), 1961–70

	1961	1962	1963	1964	1965	1966	1967	1968	1969	1970
UK	0.59	0.53	0.48	0.53	0.48	0.48	0.45	0.42	0.39	0.37
DAC	0.54	0.53	0.52	0.49	0.45	0.42	0.43	0.38	0.36	0.34

7.9 Official British Assistance by major types, 1957-8, 1960-1, 1965-6, & 1970-1

	1957-8		1960-1		1965-6		1970-1		1970-1 as % 1960-1 value
	£mn	%	£mn	%	£mn	%	£mn	%	
1. Bilateral aid	62.3	95.5	130.3	88.4	185.3	90.6	194.3	88.2	149.1
a. Loans	12.4	19.0	70.4	47.8	93.7	45.8	112.5	51.1	159.8
b. Grants	49.9	76.5	59.9	40.6	91.5	44.6	81.8	37.1	136.5
i. Technical Assistance	3.9	5.9	8.2	5.5	30.0	14.7	14.9	6.7	181.8
2. Multilateral aid	2.9	4.4	17.0	11.5	19.1	9.3	24.7	11.2	145.3
3. Other	na	–	na	–	na	–	1.1	0.5	–
4. Gross aid	65.2	100.0	147.3	100.0	204.4	100.0	220.1	100.0	149.4

7.10 British Performance under 1965 OECD/DAC
Terms of Aid Recommendation, 1964-70

		1964	1965	1966	1967	1968	1969	1970[2]
1. Grants as % of total commitments: (DAC target 70%)	a. UK	54.4	55.2	49.5	57.2	46.0	47.8	54
	b. DAC	60.2	60.9	62.2	56.1	51.4	54.8	na
2. Grants & loans at 3% interest rate or less as % of total commitments: (DAC target 81%)	a. UK	60.8	70.2	93.1	89.8	91.0	91.1	96
	b. DAC	84.1	78.4	85.3	78.2	85.3	75.5	na
3. Grants & loans with maturity of 25 yrs or more as % of total commitments: (DAC target 82%)	a. UK	91.8	84.4	95.3	95.6	95.5	92.5	98
	b. DAC	84.7	76.0	81.2	76.5	77.6	72.9	na
4. Weighted ave. grace period of loan commitments: (DAC target 7 yrs +)	a. UK	5.1	4.8	6.0	5.5	5.6	5.6	6.2
	b. DAC	6.5	4.6	5.8	5.5	6.0	6.7	na

7.11 Geographical Distribution of British
Bilateral Aid, 1965-70 (annual averages; £mn)

		Commonwealth		Foreign		Total	
		Amt	%	Amt	%	Amt	%
Europe & Middle East	1965-6	17.2	9.4	11.0	6.1	28.2	15.5
	1969-70	6.8	3.6	7.2	3.8	14.0	7.5
Africa:	1965-6	64.4	35.4	2.9	1.5	67.3	37.0
	1969-70	59.8	32.0	2.3	1.2	62.1	33.3
East Africa	1965-6	27.5	15.1	1.7	0.9	29.2	16.0
	1969-70	19.4	10.4	1.4	0.7	20.9	11.2
West Africa	1965-6	10.2	5.6	0.2	-	10.4	5.7
	1969-70	15.5	8.3	0.5	0.2	16.0	8.5
Central & Southern Africa	1965-6	24.9	13.7	0.1	-	25.0	13.7
	1969-70	21.4	11.4	0.8	0.4	21.5	11.5
America	1965-6	7.8	4.2	3.6	1.9	11.4	6.2
	1969-70	17.0	9.1	2.7	1.4	19.8	10.6
Asia	1965-6	55.4	30.4	2.9	1.5	58.3	32.0
	1969-70	68.1	36.5	6.3	3.3	74.4	39.9
Oceania	1965-6	3.4	1.8	-	-	3.4	1.8
	1969-70	8.0	4.2	-	-	8.0	4.2
Total	1965-6	159.7	87.8	22.1	12.2	181.8	100.0
	1969-70	164.6	88.3	21.8	11.7	186.4	100.0

7.12 Disbursements of UK Official Aid (gross & net) per head in Recipient Nations, 1965-9 average

	Population 1967 (mn) (1)	Gross UK aid 1965-9 (£mn) (2)	Net UK aid 1965-9 (£mn) (3)	Gross UK aid per caput (2) ÷ (1) £	Net UK aid per caput (3) ÷ (1) £	Per head gross aid rela. to India	Per head net aid rela. to India
India	511.1	36.597	17.109	0.071	0.033	1.0	1.0
Pakistan	107.2	10.662	7.080	0.099	0.066	1.4	2.0
Kenya	9.9	10.555	7.998	1.063	0.805	14.9	24.4
Malawi	4.1	8.197	7.807	1.984	1.890	27.9	57.2
Nigeria	61.4	6.580	3.851	0.107	0.062	1.5	1.8
Malta	0.3	5.623	4.729	17.627	14.825	248.2	449.2
Turkey	32.7	5.621	5.346	0.171	0.163	2.4	4.9
Zambia	3.9	5.025	4.669	1.273	1.183	17.9	35.8
Botswana	0.5	4.796	4.680	8.087	7.893	113.9	239.1
Uganda	7.9	3.996	2.774	0.503	0.349	7.0	10.5
Lesotho	0.8	3.819	3.782	4.315	4.273	60.7	129.5
Ceylon	11.7	3.223	2.754	0.275	0.235	3.8	7.1
Swaziland	0.3	3.179	2.771	8.257	7.197	116.3	218.0
Tanzania	12.1	2.774	2.250	0.227	0.184	3.2	5.5
Jordan	2.0	2.252	2.252	1.104	1.104	15.5	33.4
Solomon Isles	0.1	2.067	2.067	14.158	14.158	199.4	429.0
Guyana	0.6	1.652	.550	2.429	0.808	34.2	24.4
Fiji	0.4	1.608	1.442	3.281	2.942	46.2	89.1
British Honduras	0.1	1.544	1.487	13.633	13.160	192.0	398.7
Laos	2.7	1.445	1.445	0.523	0.523	7.3	15.8
Ave. for above 20 nations	768.9	121.215	86.843	0.157	0.112	2.2	3.4

7.13 Distribution of UK Official Aid by Purpose, 1966-70

Purpose	£mn	% distribution
1. Project aid:	373.0	51.1
Of which: 1. Renewable natural resources, incl. agriculture	44.7	6.1
2. Industry	33.5	4.5
3. Economic infrastructure (power, communications, &c.)	85.8	11.7
4. Social infrastructure (health, education, &c.)	41.0	5.6
2. Non-project aid:	356.0	48.9
Of which: 1. Budgetary aid	60.5	8.2
2. Current imports	224.2	30.7
3. Debt refinancing	39.1	5.3
4. Disaster relief	10.6	1.4
3. Total	729.0	100.0

7.14 Domestic & External Resources used in
Financing of Public Sector Plan Outlays
in India, 1950/1 to 1973/4

Plan period	Date type	Domestic resources		External assistance[2]		Total resources		Ratio of domestic to external resources
		Rsmn	% of total	Rsmn	% of total	Rsmn	% of total	
1st Plan period : 1951/2 to 1955/6	Actual	17,710	90.4	1,890	9.6	19,600	100.0	9.3 : 1
2nd Plan period : 1956/7 to 1960/1	Actual	36,230	77.5	10,490	22.5	46,720	100.0	3.4 : 1
3rd Plan period : 1961/2 to 1965/6	Actual	61,540	71.8	24,230	28.2	85,770	100.0	2.5 : 1
Ann. plans : 1966/7 to 1968/9	Actual	43,300	64.1	24,260	35.9	67,560	100.0	1.8 : 1
4th Plan period : 1969/70 to 1973/4	Est.[1]	133,580	84.0	25,400	16.0	158,980	100.0	5.3 : 1
of which 1969/70	Actual	16,250	73.9	5,740	26.1	21,990	100.0	2.8 : 1
1970/1	Est.	22,460	80.4	5,470	19.6	27,930	100.0	4.1 : 1
1971/2	Est.	25,840	81.8	5,740	18.2	31,580	100.0	4.5 : 1
1972/3	Est.	35,930	90.4	3,800	9.6	39,730	100.0	9.3 : 1

7.15 External Assistance to India by major donors & types, 1951/2 to 1970/1 (Rsm)

	1st Plan 1951/2-1955/6		2nd Plan 1956/7-1960/1		3rd Plan 1961/2-1965/6		Ann. plans[1] 1966/7-1968/9		4th Plan[2] 1969/70-1970/1		Total 1951/2-1970/1		% of total utilized aid 1951/2-1970/1	Utilized aid as % authorized 1951/2-1970/1
	Auth.	Util.	Auth	Util	Auth	Util	Auth	Util	Auth	Util	Auth	Util		
1. Loans	2,268	1,264	12,813	7,247	23,290	19,070	22,396	22,005	12,023	13,902	72,790	63,488	68.6	87.2
a. Repayable in foreign currencies	2,122	1,240	10,509	6,079	22,830	17,514	22,261	21,796	12,020	13,900	69,742	60,529	65.4	86.8
i Multilateral loans	572	338	2,612	2,228	4,116	3,240	3,547	4,249	2,744	1,878	13,591	11,933	12.9	87.8
ii Bilateral loans	1,550	903	7,897	3,851	18,714	14,274	18,714	17,547	9,276	12,022	56,151	48,597	52.5	86.5
1. USA	903	903	1,085	368	7,732	6,389	8,443	7,737	4,150	5,149	22,313	20,546	22.2	92.1
2. West Germany	-	-	-	-	3,080	2,197	1,351	1,873	1,149	1,077	5,580	5,147	5.6	92.2
3. UK	-	-	1,226	1,218	2,420	1,704	1,893	2,237	1,829	1,564	7,368	6,723	7.3	91.2
4. Japan	-	-	268	160	1,380	883	875	1,223	243	482	2,766	2,748	2.9	99.3
5. USSR	647	-	3,190	748	1,005	2,073	2,584	1,365	-	863	7,426	5,049	5.5	68.0
6. Other	-	-	2,128	1,357	3,097	1,028	3,568	3,112	1,905	2,887	10,698	8,384	9.0	78.4
b. Repayable in rupees	146	23	2,304	1,168	460	1,562	135	209	3	2	3,048	2,964	3.2	97.2
2. Grants	1,380	702	1,212	1,603	1,325	1,062	1,661	2,258	923	817	6,501	6,442	6.9	99.1
1. USA	918	443	546	856	218	311	56	106	157	-	1,895	1,716	1.8	90.6
2. UK	4	-	4	4	10	8	53	55	38	39	109	106	0.1	97.2
3. Canada	323	197	571	603	851	544	1,194	1,675	427	487	3,366	3,506	3.8	104.1
4. Others	135	62	91	140	246	199	358	422	301	291	1,131	1,114	1.2	98.5
3. Other assistance[3]	169	51	11,309	5,448	4,506	8,532	6,213	7,194	736	1,452	22,933	22,677	24.5	98.9
4. Total assistance (1+2+3)	3,817	2,017	25,332	14,298	29,121	28,670	30,270	31,457	13,682	16,171	102,222	92,613	100.0	90.6
Utilized as % authorized	-	52.8	-	56.4	-	98.4	-	103.9	-	118.2	-	90.6	-	-
UK as % total	0.10	-	4.85	8.54	8.34	5.97	6.42	7.28	13.64	9.91	7.31	7.37	7.37	-

7.16 Gross & Net Inflow of External Assistance
into India, 1951/2 to 1970/1 ($mn)

	1951/2-1955/6 1st Plan[1]	1956/7-1960/1 2nd Plan	1961/2-1965/6 3rd Plan	1966/7-1968/9 Ann. plans	1969/70-1970/1 4th Plan
1. Gross aid utilized	413	1,860	4,232	4,296	2,156
2. Repayments	50	251	1,141	1,243[2]	1,056
a. Amortization	na	na	643	745	656
b. Interest	na	na	498	498	400
3. Net aid (1-2)	363	1,609	3,091	3,053	1,100
Net aid as % of gross aid	87.8	86.5	73.0	71.1	51.0
Repayments as % exports	0.8	3.9	14.3	25.0	26.9

7.17 Indian Attitudes towards Foreign Aid, 1969-70

			1969	1970
1. Q: 'Do you favour India getting aid from foreign countries?'				
A: (%)	1. Favour strongly		22	22
	2. Favour somewhat		39	39
	3. Oppose somewhat		15	12
	4. Oppose strongly		18	20
	5. Doesn't matter; don't know		6	7
2. Q: 'Are you aware that India is getting aid from ....?'				
A: (% who replied 'yes')	1. USA		96	98
	2. USSR		85	82
	3. UK		67	59
	4. West Germany		64	55
	5. Japan		64	61
3. Q: 'Has too great a price been paid for assistance?'				
A: (%)	1. Too high rates of interest charged			47
	2. Excessive obligations for short-period repayment			43
	3. Don't agree with either criticism 1 or 2			2
	4. Don't know			18
4. Q: 'Do you think that the assistance has improved the standard of living or has it made little difference?'				
A: (%)	1. Improved		51	45
	2. Little difference		43	46
	3. Don't know		6	9

7.18 Disbursements of British Bilateral Aid to India, 1960-70 (£mn)[1]

	1960	1961	1962	1963	1964	1965	1966	1967	1968	1969	1970	1971	1972
1. Gross aid	28.5	17.6	22.8	26.6	30.9	27.7	43.7	37.4	40.1	34.0	44.8	62.1	55.8
2. Repayments:[2]						14.5	20.4	19.4	21.1	21.7	15.6	19.6	21.8
a. Interest						8.3	8.7	8.5	8.2	7.6	7.0	10.3	10.3
b. Amortization	-	-	3.5	5.3	5.0	6.2	11.7	10.9	12.9	14.1	8.6	9.3	11.5
3. Net aid (1-2)						13.1	23.2	17.9	19.0	12.2	29.2	52.8	33.9
4. Net aid as % gross aid						46.9	53.0	47.8	47.4	36.0	65.1	68.4	60.8

7.19 Estimate of 'British' Multilateral Aid Capitalized in India, June 1970

	%	$mn
1. International Development Ass. (IDA):		
1. IDA subscriptions held by UK	approx. 13[1]	
2. IDA and disbursed in India	1,015.3	
3. UK share - 13% of $1,015,284,994		131.9
2. World Bank (IBRD)		
1. IBRD subscriptions held by UK	11.23	
2. IBRD aid disbursed in India	491.3	
3. UK share - 11.23% of $491,315,066		55.1
3. International Finance Corporation (IFC)		
1. IFC subscriptions held by UK	13.46	
2. IFC investments in India	42.3	
3. UK share - 13.46% of $42,332,538		5.6
Total		192.6

7.20 Composition of Gross British Aid Disbursements to India, 1966-70 (£mn)[1]

	1962+63	1966	1967	1968	1969	1970
1. Total gross British aid	50.0	43.7	37.4	40.0	33.9	44.7
2. Project aid	35.0	11.2	7.8	4.3	12.0	18.0
3. Non-project aid	15.0	31.7	28.8	35.7	21.9	26.7
4. Project aid as % total aid	70.0	25.6	20.8	10.7	35.4	40.2

7.21 Sectoral Distribution of British Aid to
India, 1956/7 to 1970/1 (Rsmn)

	Donating UK sector	Authorized aid					Utilized aid					% of total utilized aid	Unutil. aid at 31.3.71 (2)	Utilized aid as % authorized aid(2)
		2nd Plan	3rd Plan	Ann. plans	4th Plan(1)	Total	2nd Plan	3rd Plan	Ann. plans	4th Plan(1)	Total			
1. Industrial development	Mixed	1,226	2,320	1,338	1,559	6,443	1,218	1,704	1,362	1,274	5,558	85.2	885	86.3
a. Public sector	Mixed	353	1,107	276	992	2,728	353	707	629	655	2,344	35.9	384	85.9
i Gen. industrial dev.	Private	-	-	53	-	53	-	-	-	-	-	-	53	-
	Public	-	707	116	936	1,759	-	494	385	578	1,457	22.3	302	82.8
ii Bhopal heavy elect. plant	Public	-	60	105	-	165	-	15	167	34	216	3.3	-	130.9
iii Sindri fertilizer plant	Public	-	-	2	-	2	-	-	-	2	2	-	-	100.0
iv Steel	Mixed	353	340	-	56	749	353	198	77	41	669	10.3	80	89.3
1. Durgapur Steelworks	Public	153	-	-	56	209	153	-	71	41	265	4.0	-	126.8
	Private	200	293	-	-	493	200	-55	-	-	355	5.3	138	72.0
b. Private sector	Public	-	213	218	36	467	-	23	265	167	455	7.0	12	97.4
i Gen. industrial dev.	Public	-	54	-	-	54	-	-	55	23	78	1.2	-	144.4
ii Kipping loans	Public	-	159	200	-	359	-	23	210	141	374	5.8	-	104.2
iii ICICI (1)	Public	-	-	18	36	54	-	-	-	3	3	-	52	5.6
c. Public & private sectors	Public	873	1,000	844	531	3,248	865	974	468	452	2,759	42.3	489	84.9
i Gen. industrial dev.	Public	833	1,000	844	531	3,208	833	966	468	452	2,719	41.7	489	84.7
ii Oil pipeline	Public	40	-	-	-	40	32	8	-	-	40	.6	-	100.0
2. Agric. (1966 food loan)	Public	-	100	-	-	100	-	-	131	11	142	2.2	-	142.0
3. Debt relief & refinancing	Public	-	-	555	270	825	-	-	555	270	825	12.6	-	100.0
TOTAL AID (1+2+3)	Mixed	1,226	2,420	1,893	1,829	7,368	1,218	1,704	2,048	1,555	6,525	100.0	843	88.5
Ann. Ave. British aid	Mixed	245.2	484.0	631.0	914.5	491.2	243.6	340.8	682.6	777.5	435.0	-	-	-

	Total UK aid programme	UK aid to India	India as % Total
1. Amortization & interest charges outstanding as of 31 Dec. 1970	1,398.7	467.4	33.4
1. Amortization	1,016.4	376.1	37.0
2. Interest	382.2	91.3	23.9
2. Amount due 1971-5	310.3	112.7	36.3
1. Amortization	181.4	66.8	36.8
2. Interest	128.9	45.9	34.9

7.23 Utilized Aid as % of Indian Imports from
Major Aid Donors, 1956/7

Donor nation	2nd Plan 1956/7-1960/1	3rd Plan 1961/2-1965/6	Ann. plans 1966/7-1968/9	4th Plan 1969/70-1970/1
USA	71	80	72	72
UK	11	19	50	70
West Germany	22	39	44	62
USSR	81	64	33	31
Japan	6	25	37	32
Canada	15	56	77	68
All countries	21	46	52	50

7.24 Relative Contributions of Various Factors
to Decline in UK Share of Total Indian
Imports, 1961/3 to 1965/7

	Factors causing decline in size of competitive pool (%)	Factors causing decline in UK's 1961-3 share of Ind. imports (%)	% distribution of factors of UK decline
1. UK's share of Indian imports : ave. 1961-3	-	16.3	-
2. Factors causing decline:			
a. Trade agreements with Eastern Europe	3.0	-0.9	11.5
b. Exports directly generated by bilateral aid	12.5	-3.8	48.7
c. Exports directly generated by suppliers' credits	0.5	-0.2	2.5
d. Changes in imports of commercial exports that UK cannot supply	-2.0	+0.6	-
Total decline in competitive pool of free foreign exchange (a-d)	14.0	-4.3	55.1
e. Decline in UK's share of competitive pool (31-21%)		-3.5	44.9
3. Total UK fall in share of Indian imports (a-e)		-7.8	100.0
4. UK's share of Indian imports : ave. 1965-7	-	8.5	-

Programmes of Major Aid Donors, 1961-3, 1965-7 (annual averages)

Country	Type of aid	Degree of tying assumed est. %	Bilateral aid				Directly generated exports			
			ave. 1961-3 $mn	%	ave. 1965-7 $mn	%	ave. 1965-7 $mn	1961-3 5 as % of 1	ave. 1965-7 $mn	1965-7 7 as % of 3
			1	2	3	4	5	6	7	8
USA	PL 480	75	221	45	491	58	165	74.6	368	74.9
	AID	70)								
	Export-Import Bank	90)	249	50	337	40	110	44.1	225	66.7
	Total (incl. grants)		490	100	838	100	275	61.0	593	71.0
UK	Project	90	20	36	19	18	18	90.0	17	89.4
	Non-project	0	35	64	75	70	18	57.1	37	49.3
	General purpose; debt relief	0	0	0	12	12	0	-	0	-
	Total		55	100	106	100	36	65.4	54	50.9
West Germany	Project	90	11	11	30	31	10	90.9	27	90.0
	Non-project	0	48	49	50	51	24	50.0	25	50.0
	Debt rescheduling	0	39	40	18	18	0	-	0	-
	Total		98	100	98	100	34	34.7	52	53.1
Japan	Project	70	na	na	na	na	na	na	na	na
	Non-project	0	na	na	na	na	na	na	na	na
	Total		21	100	53	100	14	70.0	38	70.0
Soviet bloc		100	60	100	94	100	na	na	na	na
Others		75	18	100	97	100	14	80.0	73	75.0
Total		-	682	100	1,224	1,000	373	54.6	810	66.1

7.26 Export Orders Resulting from British Official
Aid to India, 6-month sample, Nov. 1970–April 1971

Date announced	Company	(£000)	Goods involved
5 Nov. 1970	1. Ford (UK)	1,130.0	850 Ford tractors; 256 automatic hitches; tractor spares
	2. Dunlop	500.0	Tyre & tube manufacturing equip.
10 Dec. 1970	1. Railway, Mine & Plantation Equipment	33.8	6 miles of railway track
	2. Inductelec (Sheffield)	22.0	Induction heating equip. plus standard & special accessories
7 Jan. 1971	1. Dunlop (Coventry)	343.0	4000 tons of rims, flange, & lockring steel sections
	2. James Mackie & Sons (Belfast)	173.0	Machinery & spares for processing wool carpet yarns
4 Feb. 1971	1. English Electric (Stafford)	64.3	Weatherbeater switchgear
	2. James Greaves (Manchester)	54.0	Highspeed steel billets
	3. Marconi International Marine (Chelmsford)	63.0	Radio communication equip.
	4. Joseph Lucas (Birmingham)	150.0	Steel, leatheroid, commercial-motor vehicle parts
	5. Watercraft (East Molesey)	21.0	Glassfibre trawler
	6. Giddings & Lewis Fraser (Arbroath)	35.0	Boring, drilling, & milling machine
4 Mar. 1971	1. International Harvester (GB)	900.0	1000 diesel tractors
	2. English Card Clothing (Huddersfield)	35.0	Productive mach. & spares for mfg metallic card clothing, & saw tooth wire
	3. Linotype Machinery (Altringham)	29.0	Offset printing press
	4. Wickham Machine Tools (Coventry)	23.0	Optical profile grinding machines
25 Mar. 1971	1. Scott Lithgow (Greenock)	11,500.0	2 75,000 dwt bulk carriers (Engines by Kincaid (Greenock))
7 Apr. 1971	1. Sim-Chem (Stockport)	870.0	Parts for polyester fibre plant
	2. ICI	175.0	For services & assistance with above polyester fibre plant
	3. Massey-Ferguson (Coventry)	1,300.0	1,000 diesel tractors & accessories
	4. May & Baker	66.0	Chemicals

Recipient nation	% of capital aid tied		Ann. level of disbursed aid 1964-6 £mn			Total return to UK 1964-6 £mn			% return to UK 1964-6 %		
	Fully	Partially	Capital aid	Technical assist.	Total	Capital aid	Technical assist.	Total	Capital aid	Technical assist.	Total
All bilateral aid	44.0	22.4	152.57	29.34	181.61	85.86	27.94	113.80	56.4	95.2	62.7
India	100.0	-	34.74	0.75	35.49	19.70	0.74	20.44	56.7	98.7	57.6
Pakistan	99.8	0.2	9.38	0.89	10.27	4.94	0.86	5.80	52.7	96.6	56.5
Nigeria	84.9	1.5	6.12	1.41	7.53	4.51	1.37	5.88	73.7	97.0	78.1
East Africa	8.9	23.9	19.50	11.51	31.01	14.66	11.36	26.02	75.2	98.7	83.9
Malawi	0.3	27.8	9.07	1.20	10.27	4.63	1.18	5.81	51.0	98.3	56.6
Zambia	-	18.8	2.87	2.04	4.91	2.59	2.01	4.60	90.2	98.5	93.7
Swaziland, Lesotho, Botswana	1.8	26.0	10.86	0.76	11.62	5.13	0.67	5.80	47.2	88.2	49.9
Aden	1.8	18.7	8.15	0.56	8.71	2.48	0.53	3.01	30.4	94.6	34.6
Turkey	100.0	-	5.47	0.35	5.82	0.92	0.32	1.24	16.8	91.4	21.3
Others	21.9	47.8	46.11	9.87	55.98	26.30	8.90	35.20	57.0	90.2	62.9

7.28 Return to UK Balance of Payments of Official
Bilateral Aid to India, 1964-6 (annual averages; £mn)

		Total	Return to UK
1. Capital aid (assumed 100% tied)		34.74	12.71
i Amt. switched		-22.03	
ii Switched but spent in UK		5.40	
iii Reflected UK exports from (i)		1.59	
2. Technical assistance		0.75	0.74
3. Total return to UK			20.44 [1]

8.1 Bilateral & Multilateral Disbursements of
TA, 1962-3, 1966-7, & 1970-1 (annual averages; $mn)

All values are US$mn (current prices)		Bilateral disbursements: DAC					Multilateral disbursements
		USA	France	Germany	UK	Total DAC	
1962-3 annual average							
1. Net flows of official development assistance	US$mn	3,562.0	913.8	450.6	417.7	6,000.1	596.5
2. Disbursements of TA	US$mn	349.6	277.2	61.9	64.3	808.7	111.0
3. Share of DAC TA total	%	43.2	34.2	7.6	7.9	100.0	-
4. TA in total official assistance	%	9.8	30.3	13.7	15.4	13.5	18.6
1966-7 annual average							
5. Net flows of official development assistance	US$mn	3,547.2	804.4	516.3	495.0	6,745.4	1,155.5
6. Disbursements of TA	US$mn	549.5	392.1	110.4	88.5	1,285.3	197.6
7. Share of DAC TA total	%	42.7	30.5	8.6	6.9	100.0	-
8. TA in total official assistance	%	15.5	48.7	21.4	17.9	19.1	17.1
1970-1 annual average							
9. Net flows of official development assistance	US$mn	3,361.0	1,068.5	814.7	513.0	8,490.4	1,686.0
10. Disbursements of TA	US$mn	593.5	463.5	198.3	119.5	1,622.5	317.8
11. Share of DAC TA total	%	36.6	28.6	12.2	7.4	100.0	-
12. TA in total official assistance	%	17.6	43.4	24.3	23.3	19.1	18.8
% increase 1962-3 to 1970-1							
a. Official development assistance : $(\frac{9}{1} \cdot 100)$	%	- 5.65	+16.92	+ 80.80	+22.81	+ 41.50	+182.64
b. TA disbursements : $(\frac{10}{2} \cdot 100)$	%	+69.76	+67.20	+220.35	+85.84	+100.63	+186.30

8.2 Personnel Involved in TA Programmes of
Major DAC Donors, 1962, 1965, & 1970

Donors	1962[1]		1965		1970		Ann. rate of increase	
	No.	%	No.	%	No.	%	1962-5 %	1965-70 %
1. Students & trainees:								
a. USA	9,751	25.7	15,837	25.7	18,272	22.2	+20.7	+ 3.1
b. West Germany	7,846	20.6	10,588	17.1	19,646	23.8	+11.6	+17.1
c. France	10,370	27.3	12,429	20.1	14,191	17.2	+ 6.6	+ 2.8
d. UK	4,039	10.6	8,926	14.4	12,056	14.6	+40.3	+ 7.0
e. Others	5,931	15.8	13,781	22.7	18,264	22.2	+44.1	+ 6.5
Total DAC countries	37,937	100.0	61,561	100.0	82,429	100.0	+20.7	+ 6.8
2. Experts & volunteers								
a. USA	9,689	12.3	17,000[2]	19.6	22,417	22.3	+25.1	+ 6.4
b. West Germany	611	0.7	1,786	2.0	7,399	7.4	+64.1	+62.8
c. France	48,094	61.4	44,194	51.2	38,122	37.9	- 2.7	- 3.2
d. UK	16,092	20.5	16,592	19.2	17,354	17.3	+ 1.0	+ 0.9
e. Others	23,101	5.1	5,730	8.0	15,198	15.1	-23.6	+25.2
Total DAC countries	78,209	100.0	85,302	100.0	100,490	100.0	+ 3.4	+ 3.3

8.3 Flows of Official Gross Financial Aid
& Bilateral & Multilateral TA from the
UK & Proportion of Total UK Gross Official
Financial Aid represented by TA, 1957/8–1970 (£mn)

	1957/8–1959–60	1960/1	1961/2	1962/3	1963/4	1964/5	1965	1966	1967	1968	1969	1970
1. Total gross UK programme	266	147	170	156	173	191	194.8	207.2	200.9	203.0	210.8	213.8
2. Bilateral TA	15	8	20	21	24	28	31.7	30.4	33.5	41.4	43.3	44.8
3. Multilateral TA	3	3	3	3	4	4	4.6	4.9	4.7	5.5	6.4	6.8
4. Total TA	18	11	23	24	28	32	36.3	35.3	38.2	46.9	49.7	51.6
5. TA as % total aid programme ie (4 as % 1)	6.7	7.4	13.5	15.3	16.1	16.7	18.6	17.0	19.0	23.1	23.5	24.1

8.4 UK Disbursements of TA by purpose, 1965, 1970 (£mn)

	1965 Amt (£ooo)	1965 %	1970 Amt (£ooo)	1970 %
1. Bilateral	31,704	87.2	45,572	86.9
.1 Disbursements on students & trainees	4,449	12.2	8,760	16.7
.11 Expenditure on students & trainees in UK	3,424	9.4	6,705	12.7
.12 Contributions to UK bodies receiving students	121	0.3	1,647	3.1
.13 Grants for training in country of origin	904	2.4	408	0.7
.2 Disbursements on experts	23,763	65.4	27,580	52.6
.21 Wholly financed	2,856	7.8	4,665	8.9
.22 Supplements to emoluments of experts	11,119	30.6	17,363	33.1
.23 Compensation to expatriate officers	7,188	19.7	671	1.2
.24 Grants to IUC & TETOC[1]	101	0.2	242	0.4
.25 Grants for volunteers	152	0.4	879	1.6
.26 Research programme	2,268	6.2	3,759	7.1
.3 Other disbursements	3,492	9.6	9,232	17.6
.31 Consultancies	436	1.2	2,081	3.9
.32 Supplies & equipment	1,374	3.7	1,620	3.0
.33 Land surveys	1,480	4.0	1,682	3.2
.34 Geological surveys	150	0.4	108	0.2
.35 General disbursements	52	0.1	3,471	6.6
2. Multilateral	4,624	12.7	6,811	13.0
3. Total TA disbursements	36,329	100.0	52,383	100.0

8.5 UK Disbursements of TA by major geographical areas,
average 1965-6 & 1969-70

	1965-6 £ooo	1965-6 %	1969-70 £ooo	1969-70 %
Europe & Middle East	1,993.5	4.2	2,014.0	3.3
Commonwealth	1,158.5	2.4	563.0	0.9
Non-Commonwealth	835.0	1.7	1,451.0	2.4
Africa	33,469.5	70.9	32,574.1	54.9
Commonwealth	33,005.5	70.0	30,907.5	52.1
Non-Commonwealth	464.0	0.9	1,666.6	2.8
America	2,263.0	4.7	3,870.5	6.5
Commonwealth	1,668.0	3.5	2,645.5	4.4
Non-Commonwealth	595.0	1.2	1,225.0	2.1
Asia	5,051.0	10.7	6,355.5	10.7
Commonwealth	4,182.5	8.8	4,477.0	7.5
Non-Commonwealth	868.5	1.9	1,878.5	3.2
Oceania	1,587.5	3.3	4,891.0	8.2
Commonwealth	1,587.5	3.3	4,891.0	8.2
Non-Commonwealth	-	-	-	-
General	2,783.0	5.9	9,603.5	16.1
Commonwealth	2,663.0	5.6	6,442.0	10.8
Non-Commonwealth	120.0	0.3	3,161.5	5.3
Total	47,148.0	100.0	59,308.6	100.0
Commonwealth	44,265.0	93.8	49,926.0	84.1
Non-Commonwealth	2,883.0	6.2	9,382.6	15.9
India	741.5	1.57	869.0	1.46

8.6 Overseas Appointments made under TA, 1962, 1970, by geographical area

	1962 No.	1962 %	1970 No.	1970 %
Europe & Middle East	154	9.4	139	5.2
Africa	961	58.7	1,922	72.0
East Africa	631	38.5	577	21.6
Central & Southern Africa	167	10.2	994	37.2
West Africa	115	7.0	307	11.5
North Africa	48	2.9	44	1.6
Americas	175	10.6	278	10.4
Central & Caribbean	79	4.8	207	7.7
South America	96	5.8	71	2.6
Asia	287	17.5	173	6.4
India	39	2.3	26	0.9
Pakistan	38	2.2	37	1.3
Oceania	39	2.3	157	5.8
Total	1,637	100.0	2,669	100.0

8.7 UK TA Disbursements, total and to India, 1965-70

	1965	1966	1967	1968	1969	1970	Total 1965-70
1. UK gross bilateral aid disbursements (£mn)	176.2	187.3	181.8	184.3	179.0	193.9	1,102.5
2. UK gross aid to India (£mn)	27.7	43.7	37.4	40.0	33.9	44.7	227.4
3. Aid to India as % total	15.7	23.3	20.5	21.7	18.9	23.0	20.6
4. Total UK bilateral TA disbursements (£mn)	49.3	45.7	47.6	59.4	59.3	59.1	320.4
5. UK TA disbursements to India (£ooo)	689	794	713	698	871	867	4.6
6. TA to India as % total	1.4	1.7	1.5	1.1	1.4	1.4	1.4
7. Total UK bilateral TA as % total gross aid	28.0	24.3	26.2	32.2	28.1	30.4	29.0
8. UK TA to India as % UK gross aid to India	2.5	1.8	1.9	1.7	2.5	1.9	2.0

8.8 TA Disbursements in India by major Colombo Plan donors, 1950-9 & 1968-9 averages

Donor countries	Total TA to India 1950-69 $ooo	Total TA to India 1950-69 %	1968-9 ave. disbursements Technical co-op $ooo	Technical co-op %	equipment $ooo	equipment %	Total $ooo	Total %
Australia	4,178.0	3.0	274.55	2.3	96.05	4.2	370.60	2.6
Canada	6,448.3	4.7	519.45	4.3	3.20	0.1	522.65	3.6
Japan	3,899.4	2.9	622.85	5.2	207.10	9.0	829.95	5.8
New Zealand	663.8	0.5	39.85	0.3	-	-	39.85	0.3
UK	17,213.8	12.5	1,182.00	9.8	262.50	11.5	1,444.50	10.1
USA	104,782.2	76.4	9,395.50	78.1	1,726.00	75.2	11,121.50	77.6
Total (incl. others)	137,196.2	100.0	12,034.55	100.0	2,294.85	100.0	14,329.40	100.0

8.9 Distribution of Total UK TA & of UK TA
to India by purpose, 1959-60, 1965-6,
& 1969-70 (annual averages; £000)

		1959-60[1] ave.		1964-5[1] ave.		1969-70 ave.	
		Value	%	Value	%	Value	%
1. Expenditure on students & trainees:	Total UK TA	na	na	4,566.5	14.7	8,408.5	18.8
	TA to India	206.0	65.3	167.3	30.7	484.0	55.6
2. Expenditure on experts & volunteers:	Total UK TA	na	na	23,040.5	74.1	27,604.5	61.8
	TA to India	93.5	29.6	276.5	50.7	173.0	19.9
3. Expenditure on equipment, surveys, &c.	Total UK TA	na	na	3,451.0	11.1	8,589.0	19.2
	TA to India	16.0	5.0	100.5	18.4	212.5	24.4
Total UK TA expenditure		na	na	31,058.0	100.0	44,602.0	100.0
UK TA expenditure on India		315.5	100.0	544.3	100.0	869.5	100.0

8.10 Training Places provided for Indians by
major Colombo Plan donors, 1950-69; &
Man-months of training in 1969

Places of training	Total training places 1950-69		1969 Man-months of training		
	No.	%	Total	For Indians	Indian share %
Australia	931	9.5	5,425.0	575.0	10.59
Canada	1,145	11.7	2,952.0	546.0	18.49
Japan	491	5.0	3,898.0	252.0	6.46
New Zealand	147	1.5	672.5	53.0	7.88
UK	2,633	27.0	2,180.0	551.0	25.27
USA	4,418	45.5	na	na	na
Total	9,765	100.0	-	-	-

8.11 Indian & Total Trainees in UK at end of
1970 & new arrivals during 1970

	INDIA		COMMONWEALTH		TOTAL	
	Arrivals in 1970	Present end 1970	Arrivals in 1970	Present end 1970	Arrivals in 1970	Present end 1970
Education	22	3	145	10	847	24
Development planning	3	1	17	16	79	19
Public administration	9	2	510	179	650	210
Social services	12	2	167	17	292	25
Works & communications	20	11	259	100	359	158
Industry & commerce	51	25	150	80	436	115
Renewable natural resources	8	2	55	29	193	41
Health	17	8	112	87	466	140
Other	32	3	103	43	243	51
Total	174	57	1,518	561	3,565	783
India as % total	4.8	7.2	42.5	71.6	100.0	100.0

8.12 Overseas Trainees in Insurance in UK,
1961-70, & Holders of CBI Graduate
Engineering Scholarships, 1950-69

Origin	Trainees in insurance: 1961-70		Holders of CBI engineering scholarships: 1950-69	
	No.	%	No.	%
Nigeria	364	16.1	14	3.9
Pakistan	148	6.5	52	14.5
Australia	187	8.2	112	31.3
India	109	4.8	55	15.4
Malaysia	53	2.3	15	4.2
New Zealand	46	2.0	34	9.5
Hong Kong	4	-	22	6.1
Japan	117	5.1	-	-
South Africa	93	4.1	-	-
West Germany	95	4.2	-	-
Switzerland	82	3.6	-	-
France	69	3.0	-	-
Total (incl. others)	2,255	100.0	357	100.0

8.13 Industrial Trainees recommended for
entry into UK under 1962 & 1968
Commonwealth Immigrants Acts, 1968-9
annual average

Country of applicant	No. 1968-9	% of total
1. Developed Commonwealth	187	22.8
Australia	104	12.7
Canada	36	4.4
New Zealand	47	5.7
2. Developing Commonwealth	630	77.2
India	181	22.1
Nigeria	47	5.7
Malaysia	46	5.6
Hong Kong	45	5.5
Pakistan	42	5.1
Ghana	28	3.4
Kenya	28	3.4
Ceylon	26	3.1
Singapore	22	2.6
West Indies[1]	69	8.4
3. Total Commonwealth (incl. others)	817	100.0

8.14 Distribution of Graduate Indians
registered with DSTP, 1967, 1971

	Science 1967	Science 1971	Social sciences 1967	Social sciences 1971	Engineering 1967	Engineering 1971	Technology 1967	Technology 1971	Medicine 1967	Medicine 1971	Total 1967	Total 1971	% of total 1967	% of total 1971
USA	1,106	1,441	23	45	955	936	141	148	244	423	2,469	2,993	38.0	39.9
UK	289	285	19	17	977	665	130	96	801	1,637	2,216	2,700	34.1	36.0
West Germany	118	122	4	3	479	224	103	35	17	17	721	401	11.1	5.3
Canada	227	254	2	8	101	126	11	9	54	78	395	475	6.0	6.3
Other Europe	92	148	6	8	147	134	31	27	21	20	297	337	4.5	4.5
Other	371	268	–	18	158	201	37	10	31	83	397	580	6.3	7.7
Total	2,203	2,518	54	99	2,817	2,286	453	325	1,168	2,258	6,495	7,486	100.0	100.0
% of total	33.9	33.6	0.8	1.3	43.3	30.5	6.9	4.3	17.9	30.1	100.0	100.0		

8.15 Outmigration of Medical Personnel &
Scientists from India, 1968

	USA	UK	W. Germany	Canada	Other European countries	Australia & New Zealand	Other	Total
Registrant engineers	904	1,052	481	104	116	19	127	2,803
Registrant technologists	144	141	105	11	29	14	24	468
Registrant post-graduate scientists	927	273	91	198	93	32	111	1,725
Registrant doctors	214	660	19	47	21	9	21	991
Registrant agric. scientists[1]	112	23	19	29	27	5	17	232
Total	2,301	2,149	715	389	286	79	300	6,219

8.16 Medical Graduates Taking up Employment in Britain in 1967

	No.	% of total
1. Graduates of non-British medical schools	2,053	51.5
a. Commonwealth voucher holders[1]	938	23.5
b. Commonwealth working holiday makers[2]	220	5.5
c. Non-Commonwealth temporary registrants	710	17.8
d. South African graduates	58	1.4
e. Irish graduates	127	3.1
2. Graduates of British medical schools	1,933	48.5
f. Overseas-born	123	3.0
g. British-born	1,810	45.4
3. Grand total	3,986	100.0

8.17 Professions of Indian Immigrants admitted to Britain 1968-70 with Category 'B' Vouchers under 1962 & 1968 Immigration Acts

Professions	1968			1969			1970		
	Total	Indians	Indian %	Total	Indians	Indian %	Total	Indians	Indian %
Teachers	447	262	58.6	96	14	14.6	248	6	2.4
Nurses	116	57	49.1	158	82	51.9	225	79	35.1
Doctors	1,010	782	77.4	996	735	73.8	403	211	52.3
Dentists	23	1	4.3	39	3	7.7	68	1	1.5
Science & technical graduates	440	352	80.0	202	117	57.9	311	92	29.6
Other professions	210	127	60.5	245	115	46.9	289	65	22.5
Total	2,246	1,581	70.4	1,736	1,066	61.4	1,544	454	29.4

8.18 Net Flow of Indian Doctors to Britain, 1965/6 & 1966/7

1965/6

1. Doctors in service at 30 Sept. 1966 but not at 30 Sept. 1965   +870
2. Doctors in service at 30 Sept. 1965 but not at 30 Sept. 1966   -600

Net flow = (1 - 2)   +270

1966/7

1. Doctors in service at 30 Sept. 1967 but not at 30 Sept. 1966   +960
2. Doctors in service at 30 Sept. 1966 but not at 30 Sept. 1967   -630

Net flow = (1 - 2)   +330

8.19 Overseas-Born Doctors in the NHS in England & Wales at 30 Sept. 1969

	Total medical staff[1]		Overseas-born staff		Overseas-born as % total (2) as % (1)
	No. 1	%	No. 2	%	
1. Career grades	10,815	44.8	1,587	19.6	14.6
a. Consultant	9,467	39.3	1,174	14.5	12.4
b. Senior & junior hospital med. officers, med. assistants	1,348	5.5	413	5.1	30.6
2. Training grades	13,270	55.2	6,458	80.4	48.6
c. Senior registrar	1,533	6.3	276	3.4	18.0
d. Registrar	4,531	18.8	2,516	31.2	55.5
e. Senior house officer	4,772	19.8	3,169	39.3	66.4
f. House officer – post-registration	561	2.3	201	2.4	35.8
g. House officer – pre-registration	1,873	7.7	296	3.6	15.8
3. Total	24,085	100.0	8,045	99.5	33.4

8.20   Composition of British & Foreign-born Doctors
in England & Wales, Sept. 1967

	British	Overseas-born
1. % share of doctors by hospital type		
.1 London teaching	89.1	10.9
.2 Provincial teaching	88.0	12.0
.3 London non-teaching	78.9	21.1
.4 Provincial non-teaching	73.8	26.2
2. % share of doctors by grade		
.1 Consultant	87.6	12.4
.2 Senior Registrar	83.3	16.7
.3 Registrar	48.9	51.1
.4 Senior house officer	36.6	63.4

8.21   Estimated Net Balance of TA Flows between
Britain & India, 1960-70 (annual averages)

	£000	£000
1. British TA to India (official, bilateral)	-	751
2. Indian TA to UK[1]		
a. Doctors	5,700	
b. Nurses	42	
c. Teachers	175	
d. Total	5,917	+5,917
3. Net balance in UK's favour (ie 2-1)		+5,166

9.1 Full-time & Sandwich Overseas Students
enrolled at Non-University Grant-Aided
Further Education Establishments in the UK,
1962, 1965, & 1970

Type of education course	1962			1965			1970		
	All students No.	Indian students No.	Indian share %	All students No.	Indian students No.	Indian share %	All students No.	Indian students No.	Indian share %
1. Advanced courses	5,282	642	12.1	6,384	560	8.7	5,396	301	5.6
a. University first degree	2,043	274	13.4	2,035	238	11.6	682	52	7.6
b. CNAA first degree	194	34	17.5	191	21	10.9	1,025	60	5.8
c. HND-HNC awards	563	58	10.3	1,176	106	9.0	1,322	84	6.3
d. Other advanced courses	2,482	276	11.1	2,981	195	6.5	2,367	105	4.4
2. Non-advanced courses	9,812	368	3.7	9,908	396	3.9	10,206	427	4.2
a. OND-ONC awards	727	18	2.4	931	30	3.2	1,522	45	2.9
b. City & guilds	650	24	3.6	548	16	2.9	677	42	6.2
c. GCE	4,607	161	3.4	4,106	193	4.7	5,027	228	4.5
d. Other non-advanced courses	3,828	165	4.3	4,323	157	3.6	2,980	112	3.7
3. Total courses (1+2)	15,094	1,010	6.6	16,292	956	5.8	15,602	728	4.7
4. Advanced courses as % total	35.0	63.6	-	39.2	58.6	-	34.6	41.3	-
5. Non-advanced courses as % total	65.0	36.4	-	60.8	41.4	-	65.4	58.7	-

9.2 Origin of Full-time & Sandwich Overseas Students enrolled at Non-University Grant-Aided Further Education Establishments in the UK, 1962, 1970

Origin	1962			1970			No. per mn 'home' pop. 1970
	No.	% on advanced courses	% of total	No.	% on advanced courses	% of total	
Cyprus	429	24.9	2.8	1,096	15.5	7.0	1,753.6
Malaysia (1)	403	53.3	2.7	1,084	41.1	6.9	99.0
Iran	744	25.1	4.9	863	16.3	5.5	30.1
Kenya	506	35.9	3.3	775	25.7	5.0	68.9
India	1,010	63.6	6.7	728	41.3	4.7	1.3
Ceylon	153	71.2	1.0	694	68.3	4.4	55.5
Nigeria	2,757	38.7	18.3	676	49.3	4.3	12.3
Greece	233	30.0	1.5	641	39.0	4.1	72.1
Pakistan	441	39.0	2.9	631	36.1	4.0	4.8
Uganda	400	37.2	2.6	585	27.9	3.7	59.6
Tanzania	282	35.5	1.9	525	31.6	3.4	39.6
Norway	228	66.7	1.5	297	79.1	1.9	76.6
Jordan	89	38.2	0.6	246	17.5	1.6	106.2
USA	58	25.9	0.4	244	26.6	1.6	1.2
Total	15,094	35.0	100.0	15,602	34.6	100.0	-
Commonwealth	9,320	40.9	61.7	10,067	36.5	64.5	-
Foreign	5,774	25.4	38.3	5,535	31.0	35.5	-

9.3 Full-time Undergraduate & Postgraduate Overseas Students at British Universities, by major areas, 1947-8, 1960-1, & 1970-1

Area of origin	1947-8		1960-1		1970-1	
	No.	%	No.	%	No.	%
Africa	1,582	20.6	3,471	27.9	3,721	20.1
America	1,227	15.9	2,425	19.6	4,569	24.6
Asia	2,055	26.7	4,578	36.9	6,752	36.4
India	900	11.7	1,513	12.2	880	4.7
Australasia	561	7.3	547	4.4	728	3.9
Europe	2,256	29.3	1,383	11.2	2,787	15.0
EEC(6)	na	na	371	3.0	648	1.9
Total	7,681	100.0	12,410	100.0	18,563	100.0
Commonwealth	na	na	7,890	63.6	8,980	48.4

9.4 Full-time Undergraduate & Postgraduate
Overseas Students studying at UK Universities,
major countries, 1960-1 & 1970-1

Country of Origin	1960-1 All students No.	%	Postgraduates (1) No.	%	1970-1 All students No.	%	Postgraduates (1) No.	%	All students 1970-1 as % of 1960-1	No. of students per mm 'home' pop. 1970
India	1,513	12.2	776	51.3	880	4.7	676	76.8	58.2	1.63
USA	1,070	8.6	604	56.4	2,492	13.4	1,243	49.9	232.9	12.16
Nigeria	1,010	8.1	179	17.7	552	2.9	321	57.7	54.6	10.02
Canada	502	4.0	404	80.5	1,052	5.7	928	88.2	209.6	49.13
Pakistan	439	3.5	241	54.9	970	5.2	786	81.0	220.9	7.45
Iraq	428	3.4	150	35.0	488	2.6	404	82.8	114.0	50.41
South Africa	409	3.3	204	49.9	383	2.1	232	60.6	93.6	17.28
Australia	386	3.1	287	74.3	501	2.7	435	86.8	129.8	39.92
Ghana	353	2.8	49	13.9	237	1.3	148	62.4	67.1	27.43
Kenya	351	2.8	42	11.9	483	2.6	77	15.9	137.6	42.93
Egypt	267	2.2	205	76.8	228	1.2	208	91.2	85.4	6.84
Ceylon	248	2.0	147	59.3	460	2.5	339	73.7	185.5	36.77
Commonwealth	7,890	63.6	2,932	37.2	8,980	48.4	5,137	57.2	113.8	-
Foreign	4,520	36.4	2,093	46.3	9,583	51.6	5,890	61.5	212.0	-
Total	12,410	100.0	5,025	40.5	18,563	100.0	11,027	59.4	149.6	-

9.6 Subjects of Overseas & Indian University
Students in Britain, 1970-1

	Indian students				Overseas students				Indian students as % of total	
	Total (1)	(2) as % of total	Post-graduates (2)	(2) as % (1)	Total (3)	(4) as % of total	Post-graduates (4)	(4) as % (3)	Total students	Post-graduates
Education	31	3.5	28	90.3	760	4.1	588	77.4	4.1	4.8
Medicine, dentistry, health	86	9.8	71	82.6	1,757	9.5	860	48.9	4.9	8.3
Engineering & technology	363	41.2	264	72.7	4,588	24.7	2,159	47.0	7.9	12.2
Agriculture, forestry, vet. science	14	1.6	14	100.0	601	3.2	502	83.5	2.3	2.8
Biological & physical sciences	188	21.4	150	79.8	3,315	17.9	2,321	70.0	5.7	6.5
Social admin., business studies	99	11.2	65	65.7	3,849	20.7	2,362	61.4	2.6	2.7
Architecture, planning	11	1.2	8	72.7	407	2.2	266	65.3	2.7	3.0
Languages, lit., area studies	63	7.2	55	87.3	1,618	8.7	988	61.1	3.9	5.6
Non-language arts	25	2.9	21	84.0	1,668	9.0	981	58.8	1.5	2.1
Total	880	100.0	676	76.8	18,563	100.0	11,027	59.4	4.7	6.1

9.5 Distribution of Indian University Students in Britain, 1960-1 & 1970-1

Subject of study	1960-1 No.	%	1970-1 No.	%	Postgraduates as % total 1960-1	1970-1
Arts & social sciences	431	28.5	229	26.0	51.7	77.3
Medicine, dentistry, health	194	12.8	86	9.8	83.5	82.6
Engineering & technology	671	44.3	363	41.2	32.8	72.7
Agriculture, forestry, vet. science	19	1.2	14	1.6	57.9	100.0
Biological & physical sciences	198	13.2	188	21.4	80.8	79.8
Total	1,513	100.0	880	100.0	51.3	76.8

9.7 Distribution of Commonwealth Scholarship Holders studying in UK, 1970

Country of Origin	No.	%
1. Africa	162	29.32
Nigeria	58	10.50
Rhodesia	38	6.88
Ghana	15	2.71
2. Asia	194	35.11
India	86	15.56
Pakistan	57	10.32
Ceylon	20	3.62
3. Americas	70	12.61
Canada	49	8.87
4. Europe	20	3.62
5. Australasia	78	14.11
Australia	59	10.68
New Zealand	19	3.44
6. Other (incl. unidentified)	28	5.06
Total	552	100.0

9.8 Distribution by Country of Indian Holders of Commonwealth Scholarships, 1970

Country of Origin	No.	%
UK	86	60.6
Canada	41	28.9
Australia	8	5.6
New Zealand	2	1.4
Ceylon	1	.7
Nigeria	1	.7
Total	139	100.0

9.9 Distribution of Graduates of the Four Indian Institutes of Technology by country & purpose, 1967

	USA	UK	Canada	West Germany	Others	Total	% of total
Further study	83	18	11	5	3	120	61.2
Employment	6	8	2	2	3	21	10.7
Study & employment	26	5	6	4	1	42	21.4
Other	4	5	-	2	2	13	6.6
Total	119	36	19	13	9	196	100.0
% of total	60.7	18.4	9.7	6.6	4.6	100.0	-

9.10 Asian Candidates for Membership of Royal College of Physicians of Edinburgh, 1955-69 (annual averages)

	1955-7	1958-60	1961-3	1964-6	1967-9
Candidates - no.	294	579	747	644	420
- Index : 1955 = 100	130	257	332	286	186
Accepted for membership	46	81	80	77	54
Success: (%)	15.6	18.4	10.7	11.9	12.9

9.11 Origin of Successful Candidates for Entrance Examination of Royal College of Surgeons, Edinburgh, Mar. 1968-Oct. 1969

Origin of candidates	No.	%
UK	61	25.0
Overseas	183	75.0
India	72	29.4
Australia	28	11.4
Pakistan	17	6.9
Egypt	15	6.1
South Africa	10	4.0
Ceylon	6	2.4
Singapore	4	1.6
Hong Kong	3	1.2
New Zealand	3	1.2
Others	22	8.9
Eire	3	1.2
Total	244	100.0

9.12 Destination of British Students Studying at Overseas Universities, 1968-70

Country	Year	Total overseas students in country	British students in country	British students as % of total
Canada	1969-70	19,921	2,134	10.7
Eire	1968-9	429	159	37.0
New Zealand	1969-70	1,911	39	2.0
Zambia	1969-70	133	63	47.3
Pakistan	1968-9	1,012	2	0.1
Ghana	1969-70	176	22	12.5
Hong Kong	1969-70	144	22	15.2
India	1969-70	8,248	120	1.4

9.13 Origin of Overseas Students at Indian Universities, 1959-60, 1964-5 & 1969-70

Origin	1959-60 No.	1959-60 %	1964-5 No.	1964-5 %	1969-70 No.	1969-70 %
Africa	839	24.9	2,116	46.0	3,852	46.7
Asia	2,323	69.1	2,237	48.7	3,936	47.7
N. &. S.America	50	1.5	56	1.2	80	1.0
Australasia	29	0.9	70	1.5	148	1.8
Europe	13	0.4	65	1.4	196	2.4
UK	6	0.2	24	0.5	120	1.4
Other	107	3.2	54	1.2	36	0.4
Total	3,361	100.0	4,598	100.0	8,248	100.0
Commonwealth	na	na	na	na	5,368	65.1

9.14 Destination of British Holders of Commonwealth Scholarships, 1960-8 & Scholars present, 1970

	Destination, 1960-8 No.	Destination, 1960-8 %	Present 1970
Canada	83	38.3	29
Australia	42	19.2	17
India	31	14.2	8
New Zealand	17	7.8	5
Nigeria	16	7.3	3
Ghana	4	1.8	1
Pakistan	4	1.8	2
Others	21	9.6	4
Total	218	100.0	69

9.15 Subjects studied by UK Commonwealth Scholars in India, 1960-9

Science	3	Arts	24
Exploration geophysics	1	Fine art	9
Chemical Engineering	1	History	5
Chemistry	1	Indian culture	3
Social Science	8	Philosophy	3
Sociology	3	Drama	1
Economics	2	Languages	1
Anthropology	1	Music	1
Geography	1	Sculpture	1
International relations	1	TOTAL	35

9.16 Educational and Other Disbursements of British Bilateral Financial Aid, 1965, 1970 (£mn)

	1965 Grants	Loans	Total	%	1970 Grants	Loans	Total	%
1. Project	29.9	34.2	64.1	44.3	26.6	41.0	67.6	45.6
i Education	2.7	–	2.7	1.8	1.5	2.5	4.0	2.7
ii Other	27.2	34.2	61.4	42.5	25.1	38.5	63.6	42.9
2. Non-project	31.3	49.1	80.4	55.7	13.2	67.7	80.9	54.4
3. Total bilateral financial aid	61.2	83.3	144.5	100.0	39.7	108.6	148.4	100.0

9.17 Distribution by Geographical Area of British Educational Assistance, 1970

	Persons (excl. volunteers) financed bilaterally from public funds overseas on 31.12.70 No.	% of total	Volunteers serving overseas under 1970/1 programme in education posts Graduates No.	Cadets No.	Total British personnel No.	% of total
1. Africa	4,303	87.3	719	83	5,105	80.4
Commonwealth	4,098	83.1	560	70	4,728	74.5
a. Kenya	794	16.1	72	3	869	13.7
b. Nigeria	515	10.4	199	1	715	11.2
c. Uganda	890	18.0	59	7	956	15.0
d. Zambia	1,076	21.8	19	11	1,106	17.4
2. Americas	194	3.9	149	41	384	6.0
Commonwealth	121	2.4	100	36	257	4.0
3. Asia	133	2.7	229	32	394	6.2
Commonwealth	88	1.7	151	18	257	4.0
a. India	16	0.3	47	10	73	1.1
b. Malaya	18	0.3	24	–	42	0.6
c. Pakistan	13	0.2	22	8	43	0.6
4. Europe	119	2.4	10	7	136	2.1
Commonwealth	54	1.0	1	–	55	0.8
5. Oceania	180	3.6	99	44	323	5.0
Commonwealth	180	3.6	99	44	323	5.0
Total	4,929	100.0	1,206	207	6,342	100.0
Commonwealth	4,541	92.1	911	168	5,620	88.6
India	16	0.3	47	10	73	1.1

9.18 National Distribution of European Scholars in South Asian Studies,[1] 1970

UK	155	Czechoslovakia	3
West Germany	24	Austria	2
France	18	Italy	2
Netherlands	10	Yugoslavia	2
Denmark	8	Switzerland	1
Poland	5	GDR	1
USSR	5	Norway	1
Sweden	4	TOTAL	241

9.19 Subject Specialisms of British Scholars in South Asian & Latin American Studies, 1969-70

Discipline	South Asia		Latin America	
	No.	% of total	No.	% of total
Economics	39	27.4	7	8.9
History	32	22.6	19	24.4
Polit. science, public admin.	17	11.9	6	7.7
Sociology, social anthropology	15	10.5	7	8.9
Geography	10	7.0	16	20.5
Literature, languages	8	5.6	20	25.5
Law	6	4.2	0	-
Other	15	10.5	3	3.8
	142	100.0	78	100.0

9.20 Disciplines of Research Team Leaders listed in the IDS 1970 Development Studies Research Register, by major geographical areas[1]

	Economics	Polit. science	Geog.	Sociology & social anthrop.	Demography	Law	Other	Total	% of total
Africa	74	38	24	27	-	4	1	168	50.1
Asia	55	16	11	6	2	1	-	91	27.1
India	16	10	5	-	1	1	-	33	9.8
Latin America	17	6	20	11	-	-	-	54	16.1
Middle East	8	3	5	-	-	1	-	17	5.1
Pacific	2	-	2	1	-	-	-	5	1.5
Total	156	63	62	45	2	6	1	335	100.0
% of total	46.4	18.8	18.7	13.4	-	1.7	-	100.0	-

10.1 Foreign Nationals Resident in India, 1961[1]

Nationality	No.	%
Nepal	133,524	45.1
Pakistan	90,366	30.5
UK	14,387	4.8
Males	8,190	-
Females	6,197	-
China	5,710	1.9
USA	3,650	1.2
Burma	2,912	0.9
Portugal	1,679	0.5
Ceylon	1,477	0.4
Afgahnistan	1,281	0.4
USSR	1,147	0.3
Others	39,941	13.5
Total	295,624	100.0

10.2 Distribution of British Nationals within India, 1961

State or territory	UK nationals No.	%	Total residents No.(ooo)	%	UK nationals per mn total pop.
West Bengal	4,296	29.9	34,926	7.9	123.1
Maharasthra	3,656	25.4	39,554	9.0	92.5
Madras (Tamil Nadu)	1,430	9.9	33,687	7.7	42.4
Assam	787	5.5	12,210	2.8	64.5
Kerala	697	4.8	16,904	3.8	41.2
Gujarat	646	4.5	20,633	4.7	31.3
Delhi	527	3.7	2,659	0.6	202.7
Punjab	459	3.2	18,845	4.3	24.4
Bihar	438	3.0	46,456	10.6	9.4
Andhra Pradesh	418	2.9	35,983	8.2	11.6
Others	1,033	7.2	177,216	40.4	5.8
Total	14,387	100.0	439,073	100.0	32.8

10.3 Employment of Britons & Other Foreign Nationals in Foreign-Controlled Firms, 1947, 1955

	1947 Nos	%	1955 Nos	%
Rs 500-999 per month	3,841	37.7	8,717	44.6
Indian	2,225	21.8	8,169	41.8
Non-Indian	1,616	15.9	548	2.8
Rs 1,000 per month +	6,348	62.3	10,805	55.4
Indian	504	4.9	3,995	20.5
Non-Indian	5,844	57.4	6,810	34.9
All	10,189	100.0	19,522	100.0
Indians	2,729	26.7	12,164	62.3
Britons	6,901	67.7	6,462	33.0

10.4 Estimated Net Total Immigration into UK by Country of Origin, 1946-62 (Commonwealth & Eire only; ooo)

Country of origin	No.	%
1. Developed Commonwealth	122.25	11.4
.1 Australia	80.85	7.5
.2 Canada	18.00	1.7
.3 New Zealand	23.40	2.2
2. Developing Commonwealth	537.00	49.6
.1 West Indies	263.70	24.4
.2 India & Pakistan	150.90	14.0
.3 Cyprus	33.40	3.1
.4 West Africa	20.40	1.9
.5 Malta	16.40	1.5
.6 East Africa	8.90	0.8
.7 Malaya	8.10	0.7
.8 Ceylon	6.30	0.6
.9 Fed. of Rhodesia & Nyasaland	5.60	0.5
.10 Other	23.30	2.1
3. Total Commonwealth (1+2)	659.25	61.0
4. Eire	421.85	39.0
5. Total Commonwealth & Eire	1,081.10	100.0

10.5 Estimated Net Inward Migration of Commonwealth Citizens, 1955-63

Country	No.	%
West Indies	285,540	48.5
India	95,756	16.3
Pakistan	83,678	14.1
West Africa	33,020	5.6
Cyprus	30,748	5.2
East Africa	18,411	3.1
Hong Kong	11,842	2.0
Others	29,775	5.0
Total	588,170	100.0

10.6 Net Migration of Commonwealth Citizens subject to Immigration Control in the UK, 1963-70

Country of origin	No. (1)	% of immigrants
1. Developed Commonwealth	- 75,015	-
Australia	- 4,372	-
Canada	- 55,164	-
New Zealand	- 15,479	-
2. Less developed Commonwealth	+433,125	100.0
Africa	+ 50,365	11.6
Ghana	+ 6,280	1.4
Kenya	+ 6,611	1.5
Nigeria	+ 4,289	0.9
Asia	+291,229	67.2
Hong Kong	+ 13,773	3.1
India	+141,960	32.7
Pakistan	+101,503	23.4
West Indies	+ 63,114	14.5
Barbados	+ 7,556	1.7
Guyana	+ 8,913	2.0
Jamaica	+ 28,291	6.5
Trinidad & Tobago	+ 7,112	1.6
Others	+ 28,417	6.5
Cyprus	+ 11,810	2.7
Malta	+ 5,334	1.2
3. Total Commonwealth	+358,110	-

10.8 Distribution of Indian Populations Overseas, (1) 1969 (000)

Country of residence	No.	% of total	% of host country's total pop.
Ceylon	1,234	25.5	10.5
Malaysia	810	16.7	8.1
Mauritius	520	10.5	65.5
Guyana	342	7.0	50.3
Trinidad & Tobago	302	6.2	29.9
Burma	272	5.5	1.0
UK	270	5.5	0.5
Fiji	241	4.9	49.2
Kenya	172	3.5	1.7
Singapore	125	2.5	6.4
Tanzania	102	2.1	0.9
Surinam	101	2.0	27.8
Uganda	76	1.5	0.9
USA	32	0.6	0.01
Indonesia	27	0.5	0.02
Afghanistan	20	0.4	0.1
Canada	20	0.4	0.1
Other	283	3.7	-
Total	4,829	100.0	-

10.7 Birthplace of Residents of Great Britain, 1961, 1971

Birthplace	1961				1971				1961-71	
	Male	Total	% male	% of total	Male	Total	% male	% of total	Absolute change (mn)	Percentage change %
UK	23,551.3	48,850.1	48.2	95.25	24,433.3	50,514.8	48.4	93.85	+1,664.7	+ 3.4
Eire	335.8	633.9	49.1	1.33	347.2	720.9	48.1	1.34	+ 37.0	+ 5.4
Commonwealth	361.3	651.3	55.5	1.26	702.8	1,302.3	53.9	2.42	+ 651.0	+ 99.9
Old Commonwealth(1)	52.4	110.3	47.5	0.21	67.2	145.2	46.3	0.27	+ 34.9	+ 31.6
New Commonwealth	308.9	541.0	57.1	1.05	635.6	1,157.1	54.9	2.15	+ 616.1	+113.9
India	90.3	165.8	54.5	0.32	175.3	322.6	54.3	0.60	+ 194.6	+ 94.6
Pakistan	26.7	31.8	83.9	0.06	100.2	139.4	71.9	0.26	+ 107.6	+338.4
West Indies	96.6	173.6	55.6	0.33	151.4	302.9	49.9	0.56	+ 129.3	+ 74.5
Cyprus	23.6	42.2	55.9	0.08	39.0	72.6	53.7	0.13	+ 30.4	+ 72.0
Africa	26.7	44.3	60.3	0.08	95.9	176.0	54.5	0.33	+ 131.7	+297.3
Other	45.0	83.3	54.0	0.16	73.7	143.3	51.4	0.27	+ 60.0	+ 72.0
Foreign	411.0	844.3	48.7	1.64	524.5	1,076.9	48.7	2.00	+ 232.6	+ 27.5
Total(2)	25,791.5	51,284.0	50.3	100.00	26,097.4	53,826.3	48.5	100.00	+2,542.3	+ 4.9

10.9 Categories of Indians & of All Commonwealth Citizens admitted to Britain, 1964, 1966, 1968, & 1970

	1964 India No.	%(2)	1964 All No.	%	1966 India No.	%	1966 All No.	%	1968 India No.	%	1968 All No.	%	1970 India No.	%	1970 All No.	%
1. Short-term visitors (< 3 months)	14,267	-	193,950	-	16,000	-	222,477	-	15,498	-	275,830	-	29,757	-	415,366	-
2. Long-term visitors (> 3 months)	696	4.4	20,612	21.3	370	2.0	21,547	25.1	399	1.6	19,056	20.8	373	4.3	20,396	27.6
3. Students	2,015	12.7	20,117	20.8	1,182	6.4	13,831	16.1	985	4.0	13,196	14.4	953	11.2	16,639	22.5
4. Employment voucher holders	3,828	24.2	14,705	15.2	2,433	13.3	5,461	6.3	1,864	7.5	4,691	5.1	791	9.3	4,098	5.5
.1 Category A	-	-	-	-	-	-	-	-	289	1.1	2,141	2.3	339	3.9	2,145	2.9
.2 Category B(1)	-	-	-	-	-	-	-	-	1,581	6.4	2,246	2.4	454	5.3	1,544	2.0
5. Dependants	8,770	55.5	37,460	38.7	13,357	73.1	42,026	48.9	18,718	76.3	48,650	53.2	5,406	63.6	27,407	37.1
6. Others coming to settle	435	2.7	3,735	3.8	918	5.0	2,978	3.4	2,565	10.4	5,771	6.3	961	11.3	5,220	7.0
7. Diplomats & officials	749	-	3,476	-	1,049	-	4,983	-	1,105	-	5,718	-	1,078	-	5,978	-
Breakdown by sex (rows 2-6 only)																
Men	5,931	37.5	34,185	35.3	4,536	24.8	22,913	26.6	4,740	19.3	23,390	25.6	1,922	22.6	23,599	31.9
Women	4,636	29.3	35,048	36.2	5,801	31.7	33,232	38.7	7,737	31.5	33,799	36.9	3,717	43.7	31,364	42.5
Children	5,177	32.8	27,396	28.3	7,923	43.3	29,698	34.5	12,054	49.1	34,175	37.4	2,845	33.5	18,797	25.4
Total (rows 2-6 only)	15,744	100.0	96,629	100.0	18,260	100.0	85,843	100.0	24,531	100.0	91,364	100.0	8,484	100.0	73,760	100.0

10.10 Broad Categories of Indian Citizens arriving in UK, 1964, 1966, 1968, & 1970 (%)

	1964	1966	1968	1970
Long-term visitors & students	17.1	8.4	5.6	15.5
Employment voucher holders	24.2	13.3	7.5	9.3
Dependants & other settlers	58.2	78.1	86.7	74.9

10.11 Distribution of Arrivals under Category 'A',
by UK region and Country of Origin, average over 1968-9

Origin / Region	All sources		India		% new arrivals in region	Pakistan		West Indies		Malta		Hong Kong		Other	
	No.	%	No.	%		No.	%	No.	%	No.	%	No.	%	No.	%
London & south-eastern	1,093	54.1	109	40.6	9.9	74	28.3	360	79.6	234	47.9	56	26.6	260	76.4
Eastern & southern	282	13.9	29	10.8	10.2	21	8.0	28	6.1	140	28.6	33	15.7	31	9.1
Midlands (east & west)	188	9.3	64	23.8	34.0	22	8.4	32	7.0	27	5.5	28	13.3	15	4.4
Yorkshire & Humberside	149	7.3	27	10.0	18.1	66	25.2	19	4.2	18	3.6	15	7.1	4	1.1
North-western	151	7.4	22	8.2	14.5	64	24.5	10	2.2	16	3.2	24	11.4	15	4.4
South-western	80	3.9	8	2.9	10.0	3	1.1	2	0.4	49	10.0	12	5.7	6	1.7
Northern	18	0.8	3	1.1	16.6	3	1.1	-	-	-	-	10	4.8	2	0.5
Scotland	47	2.3	5	1.8	10.6	5	1.9	1	0.2	2	0.4	30	14.4	4	1.1
Wales	11	0.5	1	0.3	9.1	3	1.1	-	-	2	0.4	2	0.9	3	0.8
Total	2,019	100.0	268	100.0	13.2	261	100.0	452	100.0	488	100.0	210	100.0	340	100.0
% of total	100.0		13.2			12.9		22.3		24.1		10.4		16.8	

10.12 Distribution by Major Areas of Indian & of
All Immigrant Pupils in Maintained Primary
& Secondary Schools, Jan. 1970, England &
Wales only

	All immigrant pupils		Indian pupils		
	No.	%	No.	%	As % of total immigrant pupils
1. England & Wales	263,710	100.0	52,361	100.0	19.8
2. By types of authority					
Inner London ed. authority	68,947	26.1	4,233	8.0	6.1
Outer London boroughs	64,531	24.4	13,471	25.7	20.9
English county boroughs	95,947	36.3	27,363	52.2	28.5
English counties	32,854	12.4	7,170	13.6	21.8
Welsh authorities	1,431	0.5	124	0.2	8.7
3. By standard regions					
Northern	1,430	0.5	372	0.7	26.0
Yorkshire & Humberside	17,731	6.7	4,123	7.8	23.3
East Midlands	15,597	5.9	4,821	9.2	30.9
East Anglia	3,370	1.2	192	0.3	5.7
Greater London	133,478	50.6	17,704	33.8	13.3
South-east - excl. Greater London	25,516	9.6	4,963	9.4	19.5
South-west & Wales	6,949	2.6	642	1.2	9.2
West Midlands	42,118	15.9	15,475	29.5	36.7
North-west	17,521	6.6	4,006	7.6	22.8

10.13 Immigrant Pupils in Maintained Primary &
Secondary Schools by Origin in England &
Wales, Jan. 1970

Country of origin[1]	No.	%
West Indies (incl. Guyana)	109,963	41.7
India	52,361	19.8
Pakistan	24,277	9.2
Italy	13,162	5.0
Kenya	11,331	4.3
Other African Commonwealth	9,963	3.8
Cyprus - Greek	9,891	3.8
- Turkish	4,907	1.9
Other Asian Commonwealth	4,956	1.9
Other	22,899	8.6
Total	263,710	100.0

10.14 Indians in Employment in Great Britain, 1961

Industrial group	Males	Females	Total	%
Agric., forestry, fishing	960	170	1,130	1.3
Mining & quarrying	280	30	310	0.1
Food, drink & tobacco	1,200	670	1,870	2.2
Chemicals & allied industries	1,260	530	1,790	2.1
Metal manufacture	2,410	100	2,510	3.0
Engineering & electrical goods	8,350	1,900	10,250	12.5
Shipbuilding, marine engineering	300	10	310	0.1
Vehicles	3,140	260	3,400	4.1
Unspecified metal goods	1,210	350	1,560	1.9
Textiles	1,770	400	2,170	2.6
Leather, leather-goods, fur	140	70	210	0.2
Clothing & footwear	390	670	1,060	1.2
Bricks, pottery, glass, cement	650	110	760	0.9
Timber, furniture	350	120	470	0.5
Paper, printing, publishing	1,310	520	1,830	2.2
Other manufacturing	1,030	380	1,410	1.7
Construction	2,350	300	2,650	3.2
Gas, electricity, water	720	150	870	0.9
Transport & communications	7,630	1,180	8,810	10.7
Distributive trades	4,290	2,790	7,080	8.6
Insurance, banking, finance	1,500	1,020	2,520	3.0
Professional & scientific services	6,760	6,720	13,480	16.4
Mis. services	4,390	3,900	8,290	10.1
Public admin. defence, &c	5,790	1,460	7,256	8.8
Total	58,180	23,810	81,990	100.0

10.15 Distribution of British Diplomats, 1968-9

	Commercial	Aid	Political	Other[1]	Total[2]
Western Europe	92	–	101	612	805
Asia	62	17	62	427	568
Africa	59	28	52	333	472
Middle East	50	3	58	294	405
South & Central America	38	8	34	190	270
North America	39	–	33	149	221
Eastern Europe	17	–	29	168	214
Australia & New Zealand	16	–	10	48	74
Total	392	56	379	2,202	3,029

10.16 British Diplomatic Expenditure & Representation Overseas, 1970-1 (top 20 countries)

| | | Head of mission | | Diplomatic staff | | | Total expend. 1970/1 £000 |
		Salary	Frais de representation	UK-based	Local	Total	
USA	Embassy	9,800	25,989	232	595	827	3,107
West Germany	Embassy	9,800	7,277	185	316	501	1,201
France	Embassy	9,800	26,755	93	212	305	1,019
Canada	HC	9,800	10,336	47	171	218	839
Italy	Embassy	7,100	9,917	55	197	252	690
Pakistan	HC	7,100	4,987	120	325	445	662
India	HC	9,800	6,417	107	573	680	653
Australia	HC	9,800	7,074	50	165	215	564
Nigeria	HC	7,100	5,292	79	169	248	459
South Africa	Embassy	9,800	5,262	56	141	197	418
Japan	Embassy	7,100	7,800	56	104	160	379
Persian Gulf	Embassy	7,100	3,957	57	166	223	365
Kenya	HC	7,100	4,481	46	161	207	351
Spain	Embassy	7,100	7,211	38	163	201	340
USSR	Embassy	9,800	8,557	63	59	122	337
Belgium	Embassy	7,100	11,545	31	91	122	332
Malaysia	HC	7,100	6,078	50	109	159	281
Brazil	Embassy	7,100	12,082	26	118	144	259
Turkey	Embassy	7,100	5,712	43	91	134	250
Singapore	HC	6,125	4,710	33	185	218	248
Total diplomatic representation		-	-	3,265	8,416	11,681	25,833

10.17 Diplomatic Representatives & Dependants Present in Britain, Dec. 1971

Country	Diplomats Total	Of which military	Dependants	Total
USA	76	11	75	151
India	54	14	62	116
Nigeria	52	4	48	100
Australia	49	8	51	100
Canada	49	13	50	99
West Germany	47	7	43	90
UAR	44	3	33	77
Japan	43	1	40	83
USSR	37	9	35	72
France	37	7	38	75
South Africa	34	5	32	66
Saudi Arabia	33	3	21	54
Pakistan	31	7	29	60
Iran	31	8	28	59
Ghana	31	2	26	57
New Zealand	29	4	29	58
Turkey	29	5	24	53
Spain	28	4	29	57
Malaysia	26	4	26	52
Greece	25	2	18	43

11.1 Origins of Major Items of Equipment in
Service with the Indian Navy in 1970

1. Ships
   (i) British-built (all ex-royal navy)

       a. 1 light fleet carrier: Majestic class, INS Vikrant (ex HMS Hercules; purchased 1957, modernized
          and completed at Harland & Wolff, Belfast 1957-61)

       b. 2 light cruisers: 1. INS Delhi (ex HMS Achilles, purchased 1954); 2. INS Mysore (ex HMS Nigeria,
          purchased 1957)

       c. 3 'R' class destroyers: 1. INS Rana (ex HMS Raider); 2. INS Ranjit (ex HMS Redoubt); 3. INS Rajput
          (ex HMS Rotherham). All were initially lent to India and later purchased.

       d. 13 frigates: 1. 3 type-2 Hunt class frigates (purchased 1953); 2. 2 Whitby class anti-submarine
          frigates (1960); 3. 3 Blackwood class anti-submarine frigates (1958-60); 4. 3 Leopard class anti-
          aircraft frigates (1959-61); 5. 2 River class training frigates (1947)

       e. Other: 1. 1 Bangor class fleet minesweeper (1947); 2. 2 Ham class inshore minesweepers (1955);
          3. 4 Ton class coastal minesweepers (1956); 4. various patrol craft and small boats.

   (ii) British-designed

       a. 3 Leander class frigates (building at Mazagon dock under licence; 1970, 1 launched and fitting-out;
          1 launched; 1 building; 3 more projected)

   (iii) Other

       a. 5 frigates: 5 Petya-class frigates (USSR, 1969-70)

       b. 7 submarines: 1. 4 F class submarines (USSR, 1967); 2. 3 Daphne class submarines (France, 1968-9)

       c. Other: 1. 1 submarine depot ship; 2. 2 landing craft (USSR 1969); 3. 1 fleet-replenishment vessel
          (Italy, 1953)

2. Aircraft
   1. British built

      a. 35 Seahawk FGA Mk 6's (24 ex-RN, 1960; 11 ex-Luftwaffe, 1966, on INS Vikrant)

      b. Other: No. of Vampire trainers; 10 Fairy Firefly target tugs (1955)

   2. Other

      a. 12 Breguet 1050 Alize turboprop anti-submarine aircraft, France, 1960;

      b. 10 Alouette Mk 3 helicopters, France 1962

1. British-built aircraft

   (i) Fighters & close-support; 6 squadrons of Hawker Hunter F56a's (160 delivered 1960+; at least 10 others (refurbished ex-RAF) ordered 1968)

   (ii) Reconnaissance: 1 squadron of Canberra PR 57's (delivered 1957+); 2 squadrons of Vampire T55's (late 1950s)

   (iii) Bombers: 3 squadrons of Canberra B1 light bombers (90 delivered 1957-62; rest in late 1963)

   (iv) Others: Some Vampire T55 trainers; Hawker Hunter T66's (22 ordered 1959); 2 Viscount 730's; various small planes

2. British-designed aircraft

   (i) Fighters & close-support: 8 squadrons of Folland Gnats (25 built in UK; 15 delivered in component form 1957-61; remainder built at HAL Bangalore under licence, 1962+)

   (ii) Others: 1 squadron of Hawker-Siddeley 748's, plus another 2 748's not in squadron (first 4 748's built from UK-manufactured components; others delivered from Indian works, 1961+; further 27 ordered by IAF 1968)

3. Other aircraft

   (i) Fighters & close-support; 6 squadrons of MiG 21 F/FL's (USSR, some built in India); 4 squadrons of Sukhoi 7b's (USSR, delivered late 1960's); 1 squadron Mystere IVa's (France, 1956); 2 squadrons of HF 24's ('Marut 1A'; designed and built in India; some powered by British designed Bristol Siddeley Orpheus 6 engines)

   (ii) Reconnaissance: 1 squadron of L1049 (Super Constellation maritime reconnaissance aircraft (USA, 1950s)

   (iii) Other: 2 squadrons of Antonov 12's (USSR, 1960-3); 1 squadron Ilyushin 14's (USSR, 1960; 3 TU -124's (USSR, 1956); some MiG 21 UTI trainers (USSR, 1960); 100 ML-4 helicopters (USSR, 1960); 3 squadrons of C119 G's (USA, 1960-3); 2 squadrons of C47's (USA, 1960); 1 squadron of Caribov's (Canada, 1962-3); 1 squadron of otters (Canada, 1956-62); 120 licence-built Alouette 3 helicopters (French design, 1965+); 36 Harvard trainers (Canada, 1962); some HT-2 trainers (Indian designed and built, 1960s); 12 Bell-47 helicopters (USA, 1960s); 50 SA-2 Guideline surface to air missile launchers; plus other individual aircraft

11.3 British Sales in Category 951 (arms, ammunition, & weapons of war) to India & Overseas Countries, 1959-68 (1)

	1959	1960	1961	1962	1963	1964	1965	1966	1967	1968
Total British sales in SITC 951 (2) (£mn)	27.3	30.4	28.8	22.0	28.2	33.5	33.0	38.1	32.8	42.5
British sales in SITC 951 to India (£000)	1,611.9	2,971.5	1,289.0	1,102.1	6,771.2	3,709.2	2,119.3	2,169.2	2,298.3	2,573.4
Sales to India as % total	5.9	9.7	4.4	4.9	24.3	11.0	6.4	5.7	7.0	6.0

11.4 "Unspecified Imports" in Indian Trade Accounts, 1960/1 to 1970/1

	1960/1	1961/2	1962/3	1963/4	1964/5	1965/6	1966/7	1967/8	1968/9	1969/70	1970/1
Total Indian imports (Rsmn)[1]	11,216.2	10,900.6	11,314.8	12,228.5	13,490.3	14,085.3	19,314.8	20,076.1	19,086.3	15,669.1	16,239.1
Total imports classes 1-IX (Rsmn)	11,145.7	9,934.6	11,244.5	12,161.3	13,396.8	13,919.1	18,848.6	19,394.1	18,192.0	14,971.9	16,009.3
Difference 1-2 (Rsmn)[2]	70.5	966.0	70.3	67.2	93.5	166.2	466.2	682.0	894.3	697.2	229.8
Difference 1-2 (£mn)	5.3	72.5	5.3	5.0	7.0	12.5	24.7	34.4	49.7	38.7	12.7
Military events		Border war with China	UK-USA defence aid			1st Indo-Pakistan war			known large-scale Indian arms purchases		

11.5 Indian Defence Expenditure listed under "Charges in England" & total Defence Outlays,

	Actual expenditure						Budget estimates	
	1963-4	1964-5	1965-6	1966-7	1967-8	1968-9	1969-70	1970-1
1. Charges in England (Rsmn)	202.4	207.1	168.9	298.3	238.2	240.4	292.6	401.5
1. Army	61.9	68.2	56.6	71.4	74.1	95.9	113.8	168.9
2. Navy	28.0	30.5	26.6	45.4	34.4	39.2	48.8	117.5
3. Air force	112.5	108.4	85.7	181.5	129.7	105.3	130.0	115.1
2. Defence outlay (Rsmn)	8,161.2	8,058.0	8,847.6	9,085.9	9,684.3	10,331.9	11,047.4	11,515.1
3. 1 as % 2	2.4	2.5	1.9	3.2	2.4	2.3	2.6	3.4
4. Charges in England (£mn)	15.1	15.5	12.6	16.2	12.1	13.3	–	–
5. British exports SITC 951 to India (£mn)	6.7	3.7	2.1	2.1	2.2	2.5	–	–

11.6 British Expenditure on Military Aid & Related Defence Activities, 1960/1 to 1970/1

Major categories	value (£)	% of total
1. Military aid	172,387,098	79.63
.1 Grants	150,471,999	69.51
a. Multinational[1]	44,829,383	20.70
b. Bilateral	105,642,616	48.81
i. Commonwealth	68,019,317	31.42
ii. Foreign	37,623,299	17.39
.2 Loans	21,915,099	10.12
a. Bilateral	21,915,099	10.12
i. Commonwealth	20,812,912	9.61
ii. Foreign	1,102,187	0.51
2. Assistance with internal security	27,252,732	12.58
3. Expend. on security in Persian Gulf	8,787,503	4.05
4. Other & unspecified[2]	8,039,451	3.74
Total	216,466,784	100.00

11.7 Recipients of UK Bilateral Military Aid & Assistance, 1960/1 to 1970/1 (£000)

Recipient nation	1960/1-1965/6 Value	%	1966/7-1970/1 Value	%	1960/1-1970/1 Value	%	Value of loans outstanding at 31.3.1971
India	20,321.9	31.85	9,483.9	14.18	29,805.8	22.81	4,352.6
- of which grants	20,144.5	31.57	4,961.8	7.42	25,106.3	19.21	-
Malaysia	14,391.8	22.56	10,326.0	15.44	24,717.8	18.91	2,279.5
Kenya	14,746.6	23.11	475.3	0.71	15,221.9	11.65	-
Ghana	208.1	0.32	4,040.1	6.04	4,248.2	3.25	3,782.2[1]
Borneo & Brunei	200.0	0.31	3,458.3	5.17	3,658.3	2.79	-
Singapore	-	-	9,359.5	13.99	9,359.5	7.16	9,584.9
Zambia	-	-	1,190.2	1.77	1,190.2	0.91	-
Tanzania	200.0	0.31	25.0	0.03	225.0	0.17	-
Guyana	-	-	547.0	0.81	547.0	0.41	-
Uganda	250.0	0.39	-	-	250.0	0.19	-
Fed. of South Arabia	10,142.2	15.89	13,490.8	20.17	23,633.0	18.08	-
South Yemen	-	-	8,335.3	12.46	8,335.3	6.37	-
Jordan	1,732.7	2.71	69.3	0.10	1,802.0	1.37	-
Sudan	898.5	1.40	210.7	0.31	1,109.2	0.84	-
Turkey	-	-	1,102.1	1.64	1,102.1	0.84	3,137.5[2]
Greece	-	-	960.4	1.43	960.4	0.73	-
Nepal	361.5	0.56	300.9	0.45	662.4	0.50	-
Libya	293.2	0.45	-	-	293.2	0.22	-
Sonali Republic	46.2	0.07	-	-	46.2	0.03	-
Bahrain	-	-	779.9	1.16	779.9	0.59	-
Anguilla	-	-	2,710.9	4.05	2,710.9	2.07	-
Total	63,792.7	100.0	66,865.6	100.0	130,658.3	100.0	-

11.8 Indian Military Personnel Undergoing
Training & Staff Courses in UK, 1968-9

Institution	Course length	Rank of officers	No. attending
Imperial Defence College London	1 year	Colonels, brigadiers or equivalents - all services (1)	2 per annum - rotated between the three services
Joint Services State College Latimer	6 months - ie 2 courses pa	Majors, lt. colonels or equivalents - all services	2 per course - ie 4 annually rotated
Army Staff College Camberley	1 year	Majors, captains	2 per course
Royal Naval College Greenwich	1 year	Lt. commanders	2 per course
RAF Staff Colleges, Andover, Bracknell	1 year	Squadron-leaders	2 per course

Others: 1968-9:

1 Officer of Indian Army medical corps for specialist training in orthopaedic surgery
1 IAF officer for training in aviation pathology
6 IAF technical specialists for training in rocket technology and propulsion at Cranwell.

11.9 British Military Personnel Undergoing
Training & Staff Courses in India, 1968-9

Institution	Course length	Rank of officers	No. attending
National Defence College, New Delhi	1 year	Colonels, brigadiers or equivalent	2 per course in 1969 - but none in early 1960's. Rotated
Defence Services Staff College, Wellington	1 year	Majors, lt. colonels or equivalent	

11.10 Size of Military Attache Representation:
(a) of other countries in London
(b) of Britain in other countries, 1969

Country	Rep. in London - No. of mil. attaches	Rep. abroad - UK mil. attaches - 1969
India	13	6
Pakistan	7	4(1)
Australia	10	9
Canada	14	11
South Africa	4	4
USA	13	12
USSR	10	9
France	7	8(1)
Germany	6	9(1)
Italy	6	5
Israel	6	3
Jordan	7	3
Iraq	9	nil
Turkey	6	3
Thailand	5	3
South Vietnam	nil	5
Argentina	7	3

12.1 Sales in India of Major British Newspapers & Magazines, 1969

1. Dailies Copies per day

   1. Financial Times: trade   47
      subscription   86   133
   2. Guardian   14
   3. Daily Telegraph   170
   4. The Times (estimate)   250

2. Weeklies & magazines Copies per issue

   1. Sunday Times (estimate)   220
   2. New Statesman   1,400
   3. Economist (1968)   1,297

12.2 Sales of British Newspapers & Magazines in India, 1960-9 (1964 = 100)

	1960	1961	1962	1963	1964	1965	1966	1967	1968	1969
Daily paper 'A'	na	na	na	125	100	116	95	98	103	122
Daily paper 'B'	29	35	59	84	100	119	76	71	77	90
Weekly 'C'	90	na	na	na	100	104	na	91	94	na

12.3 Geographical Distribution of Sales of The Economist, 1955, 1960, 1964 & 1968 (percentages, excluding UK sales)

	1955	1960	1964	1968
Europe	37.2	30.3	30.8	33.4
EEC	20.0	17.0	15.2	16.8
France	6.5	4.8	4.1	4.7
Germany	4.4	3.8	3.9	2.8
Italy	2.7	3.2	2.6	3.8
Other	17.2	13.9	15.6	16.6
North America	23.0	33.0	31.9	29.5
Canada	4.5	5.1	4.9	4.8
USA	18.5	27.9	27.0	24.6
Central & South America	4.8	4.6	4.7	4.2 [1]
Africa	11.3	10.5	11.4	10.1
South Africa	4.2	2.8	2.4	2.5
Nigeria	1.1	1.5	1.6	1.4
Ghana	0.7	1.0	0.8	0.6
Kenya, Tanzania, Uganda	1.3	1.5	1.7	1.8
Asia & Middle East	18.9	17.0	17.1	16.8
India	4.6	4.0	3.9	2.6
Japan	2.6	2.2	2.7	2.2
Malaysia (incl. Singapore)	1.6	1.6	1.7	1.6
Pakistan	0.8	1.1	1.2	1.6
Australasia	4.5	3.6	3.8	5.3
Australia	3.3	2.6	2.7	3.9
Total overseas sales	100.0	100.0	100.0	100.0
Total (1960 = 100)	69.7	100	112.3	157.9
Overseas subscriptions [2] (% total)	na	66.4	68.9	64.2

12.4 Leading Articles in The Times, 1950, 1960, & 1970 (numbers)

	1950		1960		1970		1970 as % 1960 Adjusted %	1970 as % 1950 Adjusted %
	Actual	Adjusted(1)	Actual	Adjusted	Actual	Adjusted		
USA	35	35.0	65	55.3	48	63.9	115.5	182.5
Europe	80	80.0	14	11.9	47	62.6	526.1	78.2
Arab-Israeli relations	-	-	2	1.7	37	49.3	2,900.0	∝
South Africa	3	3.0	21	17.8	31	41.3	232.0	1,376.6
West Germany	36	36.0	25	21.2	18	23.9	112.7	66.3
People's Republic of China	21	21.0	23	19.5	12	15.9	81.5	75.6
India	32	32.0	12	10.2	9	11.9	116.6	37.1
Israel	11	11.0	10	8.5	4	5.3	62.4	48.2
Pakistan	9	9.0	3	2.5	3	3.9	156.0	43.3
Japan	5	5.0	11	9.3	3	3.9	41.9	78.0
Egypt	10	10.0	9	7.6	2	2.6	34.3	26.0
Average no. leaders per day	4.0		4.7		3.0		-	-

12.5 External Broadcasts by Major Nations,
1950-70 (programme hours per week)

Transmitting nation	1950	1960	1965	1970	Increase 1960-70 as % 1960
USSR	533	1,015	1,417	1,908	87.9
USA	497	1,513	1,887	1,907	26.0
Chinese Peoples' Republic	66	687	1,027	1,591	131.5
Warsaw Pact countries (excl. USSR)	386	1,009	1,215	1,264	25.2
W. Germany	-	315	617	779	147.3
UK (BBC)	643	589	667	723	23.7
Egypt	-	301	505	540	79.4
Albania	26	63	154	487	673.0
Australia	181	257	299	350	36.1
India	116	157	175	271	72.5

12.6 BBC External Broadcasts in Non-European
Languages, 1960, 1970

Language	1960 hrs	1970 hrs	1960 as % 1970 %	Prog. hrs/week per mn language speakers 1970 [1]
African languages	10.50	19.25	183.3	-
Hausa	3.50	7.00	200.0	0.233
Somali	3.50	5.25	150.0	2.387
Swahili	3.50	7.00	200.0	0.318
Arabic	84.00	70.00	83.3	0.664
Eastern languages	22.75	41.50	182.4	-
Bengali	1.50	4.00	266.6	0.045
Burmese	1.75	5.25	300.0	0.222
Hindi	5.25	11.75	223.8	0.089
Nepali	-	0.50	-	na
Persian	7.00	8.75	125.0	0.391
Sinhala	1.00	1.00	100.0	0.136
Tamil	1.00	1.50	150.0	0.025
Urdu	5.25	8.75	166.6	0.084
Far Eastern languages	19.25	36.75	190.9	-
Chinese - Cantonese	1.75	3.50	200.0	na
- Kuoyu	3.50	10.50	300.0	na
Indonesian	3.50	5.25	150.0	0.047
Japanese	5.25	5.25	100.0	0.052
Malay	1.75	1.75	100.0	0.350
Thai	-	5.25	-	0.218
Vietnamese	3.50	5.25	150.0	0.138

12.7 Broadcasts in Major Indian Languages by
Main External Broadcasters (programme
hours per week, end-1968)

	Language pop. in India[1]	USSR	China	Egypt	UK (BBC)	USA (VoA)[2]	West Germany
	(mn)						
Assamese	6.8	10.30	-	-	-	-	-
Bengali	33.8	17.30	-	7.00	4.45	7.00	-
Gujarati	20.3	7.00	-	-	-	-	-
Hindi	133.4	24.30	28.00	7.00	5.15	10.30	3.55
Kannada	17.4	7.00	-	-	-	-	-
Malayalam	17.0	7.00	-	-	-	-	-
Marathi	33.2	7.00	-	-	-	-	-
Punjabi	10.9	7.00	-	-	-	-	-
Tamil	30.5	7.00	7.00	-	2.00	3.30	-
Telugu	37.6	7.00	-	-	-	-	-
Urdu	23.3	24.30	7.00	8.45	5.15	7.00	4.05
Total[3]		132.20	42.00	22.45	18.75	27.60	7.70
Total output		1,863.55	1,312.35	598.30	721.30	994.45	721.20
Total English output	184.40	126.00	47.15	255.00	269.45	73.05
S. Asian as % total	7.0	3.2	3.6	2.5	2.7	1.0

12.8 Foreign Radio Listening in India,
August 1969

Frequency	Radio Ceylon	BBC	Voice of America	Radio Pakistan
Almost every day	26	4	4	1
Once or twice per week	6	4	3	2
Once or twice per month	1	3	2	2
Occasionally	13	22	17	9
Once or twice	5	5	5	5
Never	49	62	69	81

12.9 Direction of External Broadcasts by All India Radio, Aug. 1969 (programme hours per week)

	Hrs. per week		Hrs. per week
English	68.25	Gujarati	7.00
To UK & the West	33.25	Indonesian	7.00
Hindi	17.50	Tibetan	7.00
French	14.00	Cantonese	5.25
Tamil	12.25	Kuoyu	5.25
Burmese	11.16	Afghan-Persian	3.50
Arabic	10.50	Sinhala	3.50
Pushto	10.50	Swahili	3.50
Nepali	8.75	Thai	2.33
Persian	8.75	Konkani	1.16
		Total	207.16

12.10 British views on Britain's International Groupings, 1963, 1971

% of people rating the groupings as 'very valuable'

	1963	1971
Commonwealth	69	34
NATO	63	58
US 'special relationship'	53	30
UN	44	31
EEC	42	62
EFTA	22	23

12.11 Indian Public Opinion & Great Britain, 1969-70 (percentages)

	USA	UK	USSR	West Germany
1. Which country has had the most influence on India?				
Very great influence	21	10	5	-
Great influence	31	30	18	-
Total	52	40	23	-
2. Has the influence of the country been beneficial or harmful?				
More beneficial	50	50	40	42
More harmful	29	23	30	17
beneficial:harmful ratio	1.7	2.1	1.3	2.4

3. Which country can look back on 1960-9 with satisfaction for what it has achieved?

USA	41	USSR	5
Japan	15	West Germany	3
India	11	Others	5
China	5	Don't know	15

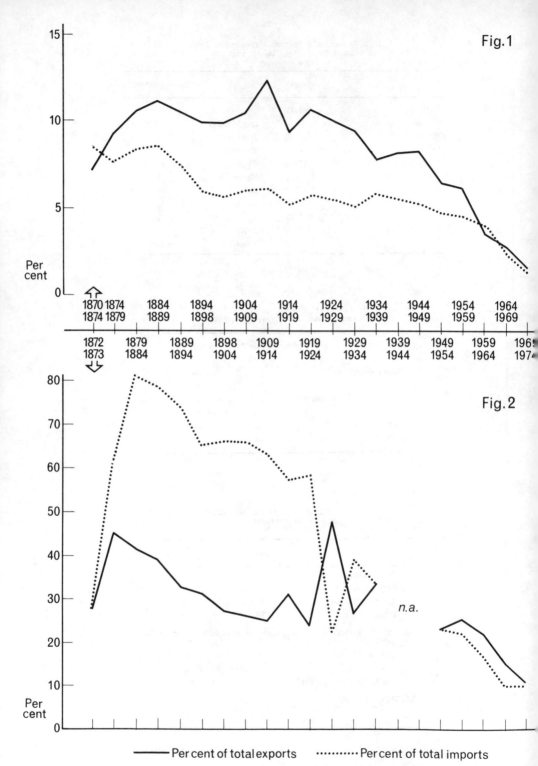

FIG 1: British Trade with British India, 1870–4 to 1964–9, 6-year averages
FIG 2: British Indian Trade with Britain, 1872–3 to 1964–9, 6-year averages

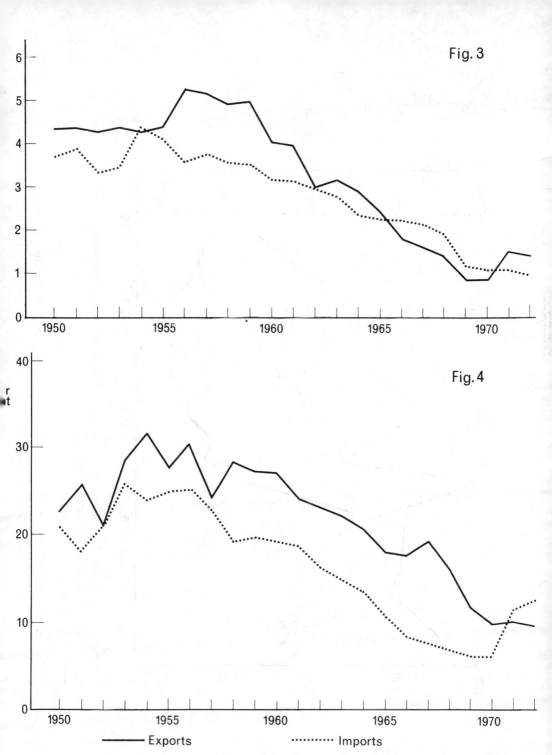

Fig. 3

Fig. 4

Exports .... Imports

Fig 3: Share of Total British Trade held by India, 1950–70
Fig 4: Share of Total Indian Trade held by Britain, 1950–70

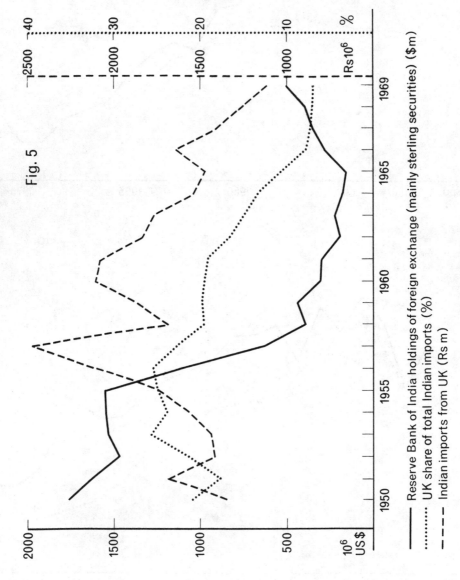

Fig. 5

——— Reserve Bank of India holdings of foreign exchange (mainly sterling securities) ($m)

.... UK share of total Indian imports (%)

– – – Indian imports from UK (Rs m)

FIG 5: Indian holdings of Foreign Exchange & Imports from Britain: 1950–68

Sources:–Trade: *Commonwealth Trade*; foreign exchange: *International Financial Statistics*

INDEX